USSR : A CONCISE HANDBOOK

USSR

A CONCISE HANDBOOK

EDITED BY ERNEST J. SIMMONS

CORNELL UNIVERSITY PRESS

ITHACA, NEW YORK * 1947

Preface

Dᴜʀɪɴɢ the summers of 1943 and 1944, Cornell University, with the support of The Rockefeller Foundation, offered a series of courses known as an Intensive Study of Contemporary Russian Civilization. This program was a unique educational approach to a planned and integrated study of the total civilization of a historical, geographical, and economic area.

At the time the staff felt the urgent need of a survey that would provide students with background information on the many aspects of the civilization of Russia and the Soviet Union that were being studied.

When the various members of the staff and several other scholars, each an expert in a special field, were invited to write the whole section on Russia and the USSR for the *Encyclopedia Americana*, it occurred to some of them that these articles, when brought together, provided the kind of basic, factual survey that was needed for an introduction to the study of the civilization of Russia and the Soviet Union.

Accordingly, with the kind permission of the Americana Corporation, Cornell University Press is now issuing these related articles in book form. Though a serious effort has been made to bring all factual material up to date, recent important events that have taken place in the Soviet Union since these articles were written could not be recorded here. It is the belief of the editor and contributors that this book will serve as a concise introduction for anyone interested in the Soviet Union.

Ernest J. Simmons

October, 1946

Contents

CONTENTS

USSR : A CONCISE HANDBOOK

PART ONE

GEOGRAPHY

CHAPTER I

National and Racial Minorities

By CORLISS LAMONT

Soviet policy toward national and racial minorities has constituted one of the most significant developments in the USSR since the earliest days of the revolution of 1917. The very name of the new state —Union of Soviet Socialist Republics—partially carried the implications of this policy, which is one of *ethnic democracy*. In choosing a name for the new state they were founding, Nikolai Lenin and his colleagues rejected the word "Russia" so that none of the different races and nationalities of the former Russian Empire would any longer feel subordinate to the large Russian majority. The area properly known as Russia became merely one of a number of free and equal republics which together constituted the Soviet Union. By organizing on a federative principle resembling that of the United States of America, the Soviet leaders prepared the way for new republics to join the federation. By 1940 the number of constituent republics had increased from an initial 4 to 16.

In November 15, 1917, little more than a week after it came into power, the Soviet government issued, over the signatures of Lenin as premier and Joseph Stalin as commissar of nationalities, *The Declaration of the Rights of the Peoples of Russia*. This declaration enunciated the main principles of the Soviet minorities policy that have been followed ever since. The new regime pledged itself to uphold (1) the equality and sovereignty of the peoples of the new state; (2) the right of the various peoples to free self-determination, even to the extent of

3

separation and the formation of independent states; (3) the abolition of all national and national-religious privileges and restrictions; and (4) the free development of all national minorities and ethnic groups within the new state.

The Soviet Union, occupying in Europe and Asia a vast territory larger than all of North America, includes more nationalities and ethnic groups than any other nation on the earth except India. An old peasant proverb says, "Russia is not a country; it is a world." In the Soviet world of 1941 there were 174 distinct races, nationalities, or tribes, speaking some 125 languages or dialects and having over 40 different religions. Only 93 of these groups, however, number over 10,000 each; taken together, these constitute all but a fraction of the Soviet population of about 202,000,000 (estimated as of July 1, 1941).[1] A total of 54 separate groups, 44 of them officially mentioned in the 1936 Soviet Constitution, occupy their own autonomous territories. Table I on pages 6–7 gives basic, factual information (subject, of course, to some margin of error) about each of these 54 peoples.

The largest single ethnic division in the USSR is the Slavs, who total over 153,000,000 people—approximately three fourths of the whole population. This group is chiefly of the Greek Orthodox faith. The Slavs consist mainly of (1) the Great Russians, numbering almost 105,-000,000, or over half of all the Soviet people, their huge republic embracing in area over 75 per cent of the Soviet Union; (2) the 37,000,000 Ukrainians, sometimes known as Little Russians, whose republic in the southeast is about as large and populous as France; and (3) the Belorussians, 8,600,000 strong, to the north of the Ukraine. Since Belorussian means "White Russian," these Slavs are often called by the latter name. They should not be confused, however, with the anti-Soviet émigrés, also known as White Russians, who fled abroad during the era of revolution and civil war. The Slav total in the USSR is rounded out by minorities of Poles, Bulgarians, and Czechoslovaks.

---

[1] The usual estimate of a population of 193,000,000 for 1941 is reached by adding to the 1939 census figure of 169,519,127 the estimated populations of the regions subsequently added to the USSR, including Bessarabia, northern Bucovina, eastern Poland, Lithuania, Latvia, and Estonia. The higher and more accurate estimate here given, of 202,000,000 for 1941, has been reached by taking into account the estimated growth in population between 1939 and 1941, computed on the normal rate of increase. No attempt is made to estimate the immense Soviet losses in population during the war period, 1941–1945.

Next to the Slavs the largest ethnic group is the Turco-Tatars, numbering some 21,000,000 and predominantly Mohammedan in religion. The Turco-Tatars, dark-visaged and oblique-eyed, are chiefly descendants of fierce warriors led westward out of Asia in the thirteenth and fourteenth centuries by the mighty conquerors, Genghis Khan and Tamerlane (Timur). They include the highly cultivated Crimean and Kazan Tatars; the Azerbaidzhanians of the Transcaucasus, whose republic contains the great oil-producing center of Baku; and various enterprising peoples of Soviet Central Asia such as the Uzbeks and the Kazaks. This immense, rich land of Central Asia, with its famous, age-old cities like Samarkand and Bokhara, is historically one of the most interesting and picturesque parts of the Soviet Union. Since 1917 the entire region has leaped, in a mere moment of history, from stagnant semifeudalism, characterized by Asiatic tyranny of the most barbarous type, to a progressive, dynamic form of society.

The third largest ethnic group consists of the olive-skinned Japhetic peoples, living chiefly in the mountains and highlands of the Caucasus and Transcaucasus. They number about 7,000,000 and are of mixed religious affiliation. Prominent among the Japhetic peoples are (1) the spirited and colorful Cherkessians, about whom Alexander Pushkin wrote in his celebrated poem *The Caucasian Prisoner;* (2) the Christian Armenians, now free and flourishing in their own republic after a long history of struggle and persecution; (3) the primitive Khevsurs, hemmed in by towering, snow-clad peaks—they are reputedly descended from a lost band of Crusaders and until recently wore medieval helmets, chain armor, and white Frankish crosses; and (4) the gay, wine-drinking Georgians, to whose rugged Mt. Kazbek, legend tells us, Prometheus was chained for having made known to mankind the magic of fire. The most famous native of Soviet Georgia is, of course, Joseph Stalin.

Another major ethnic stock is the 5,000,000 Finno-Ugrians, closely related to the Hungarians and Turks. The Finno-Ugrians in the Soviet Union are the Estonians, Finns, Karelians, and a scattered patchwork of peoples along the middle Volga River. Over 5,000,000 Jews also live in the USSR; and in the Far East there is a special Jewish Autonomous Region, commonly known as Birobidzhan (Birobijan). Scores of other racial and national minorities dwell within the Soviet Union. There are Latvians, Lithuanians, Moldavians, Germans, Iranians, and Mon-

Table I. Soviet Nationalities

Republic, Region, or District	Date of Formation	Population (Estimated as of July 1, 1941)	Predominant Ethnic Strain	National Origins * (In percentage of total as of 1926 census)	Total of Dominant Nationality in All USSR (1941 estimate) †	Area (In sq. miles est. Nov. 1, 1945)	Location	Capital
RUSSIAN SOVIET FEDERATED SOCIALIST REPUBLIC (RSFSR)	1918	114,337,428	Slav	Russian, 73.4%; Ukrainian, 7.8%; Kazak, 3.8%; Tatar, 2.8%	104,833,638	6,612,601	Soviet Europe and Siberia	Moscow
Autonomous Soviet Socialist Republics								
BASHKIR ASSR	1919	3,304,476	Turco-Tatar	Bashkir, 23.5%; Russian, 39.9%	Bashkir 885,747	54,233	Southwest Urals	Ufa
BURYAT-MONGOLIAN ASSR	1923	569,713	Mongol	Buryat, 43.8%; Russian, 52.7%	Buryat 249,534	127,020	Southeastern Siberia	Ulan-Ude
CHECHEN-INGUSH ASSR †	1936	732,838	Japhetic	Chechen, 58%; Ingush, 13%	428,400	6,060	Caucasus	Grozny
CHUVASH ASSR	1925	1,132,350	Turco-Tatar	Chuvash, 80%; Russian, 15.8%	1,437,424	6,909	Middle Volga River	Cheboksary
CRIMEAN ASSR ‡	1921	1,184,070	Turco-Tatar	Tatar, 25.1%; Russian, 42.2%	Tatar 4,518,808	10,036	Black Sea	Simferopol
DAGHESTAN ASSR	1921	977,800	Japhetic	Gortsy, 64.5%; Russian, 12.5%	900,938	13,124	Northeast Caucasus	Makhach-Kala
KABARDINO-BALKARIAN ASSR	1936	377,485	Japhetic	Kabardin, 60%; Balkar, 16.3%	172,442	4,747	Caucasus	Nalchik
KALMYK ASSR ‡	1935	231,935	Mongol	Kalmuck, 75.6%; Russian, 10.7%	141,150	28,641	Lower Volga River	Elista
KOMI ASSR	1936	335,172	Finno-Ugrian	Komi, 92.3%; Russian, 6.1%	429,487	144,711	Northwest Urals	Syktyvkar
MARI ASSR	1936	608,904	Finno-Ugrian	Mari, 51.4%; Russian, 43.6%	505,711	8,993	Middle Volga River	Ioshkar-Ola
MORDOVIAN ASSR	1934	1,248,982	Finno-Ugrian	Mordovian, 37.4%; Russian, 57.3%	Mordov. 1,525,166	9,843	Middle Volga Basin	Saransk
NORTH OSSETIAN ASSR	1936	345,592	Iranian	Ossetian, 84.2%; Ukrainian, 6.8%	372,557	2,393	Caucasus	'Dzaudzhikau
TATAR ASSR	1920	3,067,740	Turco-Tatar	Tatar, 50.4%; Russian, 41.8%	4,518,808	25,900	Middle Volga River	Kazan
UDMURT ASSR	1934	1,281,987	Finno-Ugrian	Udmursk, 52.3%; Russian, 43.3%	636,442	15,015	Middle Volga Basin	Izhevsk
YAKUTIA ASSR	1922	420,892	Turco-Tatar	Yakut, 81.6%; Russian, 10.4%	324,000	1,169,927	Northeast Siberia	Yakutsk
Autonomous Regions								
ADYGEI AR	1922	254,055	Japhetic	Cherkess, 47.8%; Russian, 25.6%; Kabardin, 33.3%; Beskeskabaz, 29.7%;	92,441	1,505	Northwest Caucasus	Maikop
CHERKESS AR	1928	97,233	Japhetic	Nogaitsi, 16.8%; Cherkess, 7.2%	172,442	1,273	Caucasus	Sulimov
JEWISH AR	1934	113,925	Jewish	Jew, 40% (est. 1936)	5,334,824	14,204	Southern Far East	Birobidzhan
KHAKASS AR	1930	284,404	Turkic & Mongol	Khakass, 51.7%; Russian, 48.3%	55,274	19,261	South Central Siberia	Abakan
OIROT AR	1922	169,631	Turco-Tatar	Oirot & Altai, 37.2%; Russian, 52%	Oirot 50,140	35,936	South Central Siberia	Oirot-Tura
TUVA AR	1945	86,400	Mongol	Tuvan, 86%; Russian, 14%	74,304	78,120	South Central Siberia	Kyzyl
National Districts								
AGIN BURYAT MONGOL ND	1937	32,000 §	Mongol	*Figures not available*		10,730	Southeastern Siberia	Aginskoe
CHUKOTSKY ND	1930	14,983 §	Paleo-Asiatic		*Figures not available*	254,991	Bering Strait	Anadyr
EVENKI ND	1930	38,804 §	Mongol			209,057	North Central Siberia	Tura
KOMI-PERMIAK ND	1925	201,000 §	Finno-Ugrian			8,916	Northwest Siberia	Kudymkar
KORIAK ND	1930	12,500 §	Paleo-Asiatic			119,968	North Far East	Palana
NENETS ND	1929	28,125 §	Mongol			82,797	Northeast Soviet Europe	Naryan Mar

National Districts—Continued

	Year	Population	National origin	Figures not available (nationality)		Figures not available (population)	Total Area (Figures available)	Region	Capital
OSTYAGO VOGULSK ND	1930	102,200 §	Finno-Ugrian				293,360	Northwest Siberia	Ostyago Vogulsk
TADYR ND	1930	8,000 §	Mongol				286,643	North Central Siberia	Dudinka
UST ORDIN BURYAT MONGOL ND	1937	110,000 §	Mongol				10,923	Southeastern Siberia	Ust-Orda
YAMAL-NENETSKY ND	1930	12,753 §	Mongol				179,876	Northwest Siberia	Sale Khard
UKRAINIAN SOVIET SOCIALIST REPUBLIC	1919	42,272,943	Slav	Ukrainian, 80%; Russian, 9.2%; Jew, 5.4%		37,043,492	226,792	Southwest Soviet Europe	Kiev
BELORUSSIAN SSR	1919	10,525,511	Slav	Belorussian, 80.6%; Jew, 8.2%		8,595,036	82,131	West Soviet Europe	Minsk
KARELO-FINNISH SSR	1940	512,977	Finno-Ugrian	Karelian and Finn, 43%; Russian, 57%	Karel. Finn	265,431 / 170,341	76,440	Northwest Soviet Europe	Petrozavodsk
ESTONIAN SSR	1940	1,120,000	Finno-Ugrian	Estonian, 87.7%; Russian, 8.2%		1,124,102	18,525	Baltic Sea	Tallinn
LATVIAN SSR	1940	1,950,502	Baltic	Latvian, 75.6%; Russian, 12.3%		1,607,925	25,662	Baltic Sea	Riga
LITHUANIAN SSR	1940	3,134,070	Baltic	Lithuanian, 85%; Russian, 2.5%		2,697,942	24,382	Baltic Sea	Vilnius
MOLDAVIAN SSR	1940	2,321,225	Romanian	Moldavian, 70%		1,624,857	13,143	Southwest Soviet Europe	Kishinev
GEORGIAN SSR ¶	1921	3,722,252	Japhetic	Georgian, 67.7%; Armenian, 11.6%		2,362,801	27,027	Transcaucasus	Tbilisi
ABKHAZIAN ASSR	1921	303,147	Japhetic	Abkhazian, 27.8%; Georgian, 33.5%	Abkhaz.	61,963	3,358	Transcaucasus	Sukhumi
ADZHAR ASSR	1921	179,946	Japhetic	Adzharian, 55.7%; Georgian, 14.5%		91,260	1,080	Transcaucasus	Batumi
SOUTH OSSETIAN AR	1922	111,501	Iranian	Ossetian, 69.1%; Georgian, 26.9%		372,557	1,428	Transcaucasus	Stalinir
ARMENIAN SSR ¶	1920	1,346,709	Japhetic	Armenian, 84.7%; Turkic, 8.2%		2,261,207	11,661	Transcaucasus	Erivan
AZERBAIDZHAN SSR ¶	1920	3,372,794	Turco-Tatar	Turkic, 63.3%; Armenian, 12.4%	Azer.	2,390,374	33,345	Transcaucasus	Baku
NAKHICHEVAN ASSR	1924	133,528	Turco-Tatar	Turkic, 84.5%; Armenian, 10.8%	Azer.	2,390,374	2,277	Transcaucasus	Nakhichevan
NAGORNO-KARABAKH AR	1923	180,063	Japhetic	Armenian, 89.1%; Turkic, 10%		2,261,207	1,659	Transcaucasus	Stepanakert
KAZAK SSR	1936	6,458,175	Turco-Tatar	Kazak, 57.1%; Russian, 19.7%		3,256,193	1,066,533	Central Asia	Alma-Ata
UZBEK SSR	1924	6,601,619	Turco-Tatar	Uzbek, 76%; Russian, 5.6%		5,090,116	160,095	Central Asia	Tashkent
KARA-KALPAK ASSR	1932	436,995	Turco-Tatar	Karakalpak, 39.1%; Kazak, 27%		195,211	79,631	Central Asia	Turtkul
TURKMEN SSR	1924	1,317,693	Turco-Tatar	Turkmen, 72%; Uzbek, 10.5%		853,009	189,033	Central Asia	Ashkhabad
TADZHIK SSR	1929	1,560,540	Iranian	Tadzhik, 78.4%; Uzbek, 17.9%		1,291,399	55,497	Central Asia	Stalinabad
GORNO-BADAKHSHAN AR	1927	41,769	Iranian	Iranian, 87%; Kirghiz, 13%		41,019	25,784	Central Asia	Khorog
KIRGHIZ SSR	1936	1,533,439	Turco-Tatar	Kirghiz, 66.6%; Russian, 11.7%		929,231	78,624	Central Asia	Frunze
TOTAL POPULATION ¶		**202,087,877**					**TOTAL AREA ¶ 8,701,491**		

(est. 1941 for Estonian, Latvian, Lithuanian, Moldavian figures)

* It is to be noted that all the chief peoples of the Soviet Union overflow to some extent the boundaries of the territorial divisions bearing their names. Thus each main division has within it a minority or minorities other than the predominant one. *National origin* does not necessarily coincide with *nationality.*

† This column does not include the totals of the following national groups in the Soviet Union: the Poles, 4,158,250; the Germans, 1,495,854; the Greeks, 300,419; the Bulgarians, 269,242; the Koreans, 189,577; the Gypsies, 100,000; the Kurds, 48,195; the Chinese, 31,124; the Czechoslovaks, 30,006; the Arabs, 22,898; the Assyrians, 21,233; and a number of the smaller peoples.

‡ Dissolved during the Nazi-Soviet war.

¶ The three republics of Georgia, Armenia, and Azerbaidzhan first united in 1922 in the Transcaucasian Soviet Federated Socialist Republic, which then became one of the four original Union republics of the USSR. In 1936 this federation was dissolved and its three constituent members became Union republics in their own right.

¶ Totals of area and population are reached by adding figures for the 16 Union republics, abbreviated as "SSR."

§ Based on 1926 census.

gols in substantial numbers. Numerous small minority groups live in the Caucasus area, including several hundred Negroes; 26 more groups live in the Soviet North, and no less than 80 different ethnic groups live in the Far East. Some of the nomadic Siberian peoples, such as the Oirots and the Chukchis, are evidently of the same ethnic origin as the North American Indian and Eskimo, whose ancestors migrated from Asia ages ago over the Bering Strait, or over some vanished land bridge in that vicinity. Almost all types of skin color, physiognomy, and cultural tradition are represented in the great multinational, multiracial Eurasian federation known as the USSR.

The old Russian Empire, of course, contained all these same peoples; its minorities of Finns and Poles were even larger because its boundaries included all of Finland and most of western Poland. Czarist policy toward national and racial minorities, however, differed radically from Soviet policy and won for prerevolutionary Russia the label "prison of nations." The czarist regime functioned frankly under the twin slogans "One czar, one religion, one language" and "Autocracy, orthodoxy, nationalism." For all the minority groups this meant political oppression, economic exploitation, and enforced (if superficial) Russification. The czarist government made every effort to suppress and destroy the native cultures and languages of non-Russian peoples. Russian became the sole medium of official business, and the use of other languages was severely discouraged or forbidden. This ruthless drive for Russification was relaxed somewhat in Finland, which always maintained a certain degree of autonomy; in the Baltic States, to counteract German influence; and in the Moslem areas, to counteract Turkish influence and also to avoid trouble with the Mohammedan religion.

The dominant class of Great Russians viewed with contempt the subject peoples, who hated them bitterly in return. The relation existing between the imperial government and the Kazaks was quite typical. One czarist official wrote, "There is no other way to manage the Kazaks except through massacres." The Kazaks, on the other hand, had a proverb, "If a Russian travels with you, hold an ax in readiness." The czars followed the well-established imperialist strategy of "divide and rule," stirring up interracial animosities wherever possible: Armenians against Georgians, Poles against Ukrainians, everyone against the Jews. Thousands of Jews were slain and their homes plundered in horrible

8

pogroms that were promoted and protected by both government and the official church. Jews were compelled to live in the Pale of Settlement, and were therefore barred, except under special regulations, from many cities and districts of imperial Russia. They were also excluded from all public administrative posts and from most professions. Many restrictions limited their engaging in agriculture and attending educational institutions. Konstantin P. Pobedonostsev (1829–1907), Cabinet minister under Nicholas II in charge of religious affairs, well expressed church-state policy when he advocated solution of the "Jewish problem" by converting a third of the Jews to Christianity, forcing a third to emigrate, and starving the remaining third. The official anti-Semitism of the czarist regime, which included refusal of passports to American Jewish citizens, aroused intense indignation in the United States at one time and led the American government to let lapse in 1913 a commercial treaty with Russia (the 1832 Treaty of Commerce and Navigation) of 80 years' standing.

The Soviet government completely reversed the czarist policy toward all minorities. Anti-Semitism, which Stalin denounced as "a relic of cannibalism," and all other forms of racial prejudice became a crime against the state. Article 123 of the 1936 Constitution reads as follows: "Equality of rights of citizens of the USSR, irrespective of their nationality or race, in all spheres of economic, state, cultural, social, and political life, is an indefeasible law. Any direct or indirect restriction of the rights of, or conversely any establishment of direct or indirect privileges for, citizens on account of their race or nationality, as well as any advocacy of racial or national exclusiveness or hatred and contempt, is punishable by law." This altogether unique legal statement is the exact antithesis of the hideous racial doctrines promulgated by the Nazis.

The Soviet policy on minorities is a major motif in the country's constitution and in its political organization. The Supreme Soviet of the USSR, the highest legislative body in the nation, consists of two chambers with equal rights. The one is called the Soviet of the Union and has about 670 deputies elected on the numerical basis of one representative for every 300,000 of the population. The other is called the Soviet of Nationalities and has 664 deputies elected on the basis of 25 from each Union republic, 11 from each autonomous republic, 5 from each autonomous region, and 1 from each national district. Thus there

9

is adequate representation in the Soviet Congress for all the main national groups organized in territories of their own. The Armenian Soviet Republic, for example, with a population of about 1,350,000, sends the same number of delegates to the Soviet of Nationalities as the Russian Soviet Republic with a population of more than 114,000,000.

The 19 autonomous republics, 9 autonomous regions, and 10 national districts are set up as subdivisions within the Union republics, 31 out of the total 38 being within the Russian Soviet Federated Socialist Republic. All the various groups maintain and develop their own customs, languages, and institutions, under the Soviet principle that the cultures of the different peoples in the USSR should be "national in form and socialist in content." In general, each group has control over purely local affairs but must conform in all matters to the socialist principles laid down in the Soviet Constitution. Naturally the Union republics possess greater powers than other national divisions. These republics have the constitutional right to secede from the USSR and, under amendments passed in 1944, the right to send their own diplomatic representatives to foreign countries and to maintain their own military formations within the Red Army. The central Soviet government retains the function of over-all direction and co-ordination.

The first Union republics to set up their own commissariats of Foreign Affairs were those of the Ukraine and Belorussia. And at the San Francisco Conference in the spring of 1945 the delegates unanimously voted to invite the Ukrainian and Belorussian republics to attend the conference to be initial members of the General Assembly of the new United Nations organization to preserve world peace. Hence in that organization the Soviet Union as a whole, the Ukrainian Republic, and the Belorussian Republic each has a vote in the Assembly as distinct from the Security Council where the chief and ultimate power lies. V. M. Molotov, Soviet commissar for foreign affairs, stressed the great and direct contribution that the Ukraine and Belorussia had made in the war against Nazi Germany.

One of the most important factors in the flourishing of minority cultures within the USSR since 1917 has been the use and development of the native languages. The constitution provides that all laws passed by the Supreme Soviet be published in the 16 languages of the Union republics. Article 110 is also revealing: "Judicial proceedings are conducted in the language of the Union Republic, Autonomous Republic or Autonomous Region, persons not knowing this language being guaranteed every opportunity of fully acquainting themselves with the material of the case through an interpreter and likewise the right to use their own language in court." Soviet experts have worked out written alphabets and drawn up dictionaries for about 40 of the smaller peoples who possessed only oral languages. More than 30 peoples have substituted simplified alphabets for the complicated Arabic script, or in some cases, Mongol or Chinese script, upon which they previously relied. At least 70 languages are used in schools of the USSR and throughout the country. Books are printed in no less than 110 languages. This encouragement of native tongues has been a great factor in increasing literacy among groups whose illiteracy was formerly very high. As late as 1926 only 3.7 per cent of the Tadzhik Republic in Central Asia was literate; the census of 1939 showed literacy of 70 per cent. After his 1942 trip to the Autonomous Republic of Yakutia in Siberia, Wendell Willkie reported 98 per cent of the Yakuts to be literate as contrasted with 98 per cent *illiterate* before the revolution. Such spectacular advances in literacy are only one aspect of a general educational awakening among Soviet minorities.

Another outstanding feature of this cultural renaissance has been the progress of women. In the empire of the czars women had even less freedom among the subject nationalities, especially in Moslem areas, than among the Russians themselves. Since then women in typically Mohammedan districts, as in the Caucasus, Transcaucasus, and Central Asia, have gone far toward attaining full equality with men. This process has been aided by both education and law. Laws forbid such traditional practices as polygamy, bride purchase, bride abduction, and child marriage. Mass propaganda campaigns and public opinion have served to eliminate the wearing of the veil. In the Soviet Central Asiatic republics thousands of women risked local reprisal, and hundreds gave their lives, in the finally successful struggle against this barbarous custom. Women's lot among minorities of the Soviet East has also been immensely improved by Soviet stress on maternal care and child care, on modern medical techniques, and on ordinary cleanliness and health.

Economically all racial and national groups of the USSR have made enormous headway. The czars consciously held back the economic development of minorities, so that their labor and raw materials could be better exploited; they sometimes even imposed tariffs on goods coming to western Russia from outlying parts of the empire. The Soviets have furthered the evolution of well-rounded economies in each Union republic. The great Five-Year plans reached out to the most distant and backward regions, investing huge amounts of capital, stimulating increased production in industry and agriculture, providing for the education of the native peoples in scientific methods and machine techniques. This policy has reaped high dividends in both local and national welfare, as can be seen from the invaluable role played by such peoples as the Azerbaidzhanians, the Tatars, the Uzbeks, and the Kazaks in the Soviet war effort.

The leadership of the Red Army well illustrates the multinational character of the Soviet state. Among the most prominent Soviet generals are Ivan Bagramian, an Armenian; Ivan Chernayakhovski, a Ukrainian, who died of wounds in the East Prussian offensive; Sabir Rahimov, an Uzbek; and Leo Dovator, a Jew, who was killed in action commanding a Cossack cavalry division. Among those holding the rank of marshal are Semyon Timoshenko, a Ukrainian born in Moldavia; Konstantin K. Rokossovski, of Polish origin; and Georgi K. Zhukov, a Russian. Generalissimo Joseph Stalin is a Georgian. The Georgians were severely oppressed by the czars, and the fact that Stalin has risen to the highest positions of leadership in Soviet Russia from within a formerly downtrodden minority symbolizes the genuineness of Soviet equalitarian policy toward all minorities. As a matter of fact, Stalin, more than any other Soviet leader, was responsible for the theoretical and practical development of that policy. His *Marxism and the National Question* is the authoritative Soviet book on the subject, and Stalin served from 1917 to 1923 as the first and only Soviet commissar of nationalities. The post was abolished in 1923, as no longer necessary.

In his book Stalin defines a nation as "a historically evolved, stable community of language, territory, economic life and psychological make-up manifested in a community of culture." He insists on the right of all such groups to self-determination, a point more recently emphasized in his enunciation, as premier, of Soviet war aims. The basic philosophy of the Soviet minorities policy as outlined in Stalin's volume and in other sources can be summarized under five headings: (1) *Eco-*

nomic. It is the Marxist theory that the fundamental roots of national and racial prejudice and persecution are economic. When these roots are eradicated through the elimination of poverty, depression, and unemployment, then different peoples no longer fear one another as economic competitors, and traditional hatreds and antagonisms tend to die out. According to the Soviet view, the planned socialist system of the Soviet Union has achieved these ends and has simultaneously unified the Soviet nations through the great common aim of building socialism. (2) *Scientific and biological.* Biology and related sciences show that there are no inherently superior nations or races, and inherently inferior nations or races. Not all peoples, however, are at equal levels of development. The Soviets assert, and claim they have proved, that even the most backward peoples can advance to high levels in a relatively short time. They believe that nations and races, like individual human beings within different ethnic groups, are very susceptible to education and other environmental influences. (3) *Ethical.* The professed ethical aim of Soviet socialism is the freedom and welfare of all individuals and peoples within the USSR irrespective of nation or race. According to the Marxists this goal can be achieved only in a classless society such as they claim they are establishing in the Soviet Union. In its promulgation severe measures and open discrimination were employed against the former exploiting classes, but never on the basis of ethnic divisions. (4) *Democratic.* Soviet theory and practice uphold the right of all national and racial groups to freedom and equality. The implication is that without full ethnic or racial democracy no country containing substantial minorities can be considered truly democratic. (5) *International.* The Soviet attitude of ethnic democracy extends to the whole world and embraces the ideal of all the peoples of the earth living in peace, freedom, and equality. The ideal of international human brotherhood is part of Soviet philosophy, though this feeling of good will of course does not apply to exploiting or war-making classes and groups.

The most signal failure in the Soviet minorities policy was in relation to the German minority within the USSR. Approximately 450,000 Germans had for many years their own autonomous Soviet socialist republic on the lower Volga River about 150 miles above Stalingrad. In September, 1941, when the Nazi armies were rapidly advancing, the Soviet government abolished this German republic on the grounds that a dan-

13

gerous proportion of its citizens were carrying on fifth-column work for Adolf Hitler. The territory was divided among adjoining regions, and its German population was moved to fertile lands in south central Siberia.

Various critics claim that there are other flaws in the efficacy of Soviet ethnic policy. The actual degree of autonomy possessed by the different ethnic groups in Soviet Russia is questioned, not only because of the strongly centralized controls of the Soviet government, but also because of the far-reaching influence and power of the Communist Party, which is active and well organized in every Union republic and other nationality division. There is genuine doubt, for example, as to whether any Union republic could really carry through its constitutional right of secession from the USSR. Again, some observers argue that, in view of the far-off communist goal of having the different national cultures freely merge into a single, unified civilization having a common language, the present program is a mere mockery. In reply to both these charges Soviet spokesmen cite the decree of January, 1944, issued by the tenth session of the Supreme Soviet of the USSR, which relaxed federal authority over the 16 Union republics and permitted them to set up their own commissariats of war and foreign affairs, thus voluntarily granting them increased autonomy. Other critics contend that in recent years, especially since the Nazi invasion, there has been a recrudescence of purely Russian nationalism and traditions. In view of the whole Soviet policy regarding nationalities, it would seem that the huge and populous Russian Republic has just as much reason to develop its cultural heritage as Armenia, the Ukraine, or Uzbekistan. Clearly the influence of this republic on the rest of the Soviet Union is very great. Since Russian is the common medium for international intercourse throughout the USSR, and since it is taught as a second language in most minority territories, an appreciation of Russian literature and culture is, of course, widespread outside the Russian Republic itself.

BIBLIOGRAPHY

Yarmolinsky, A., *Jews and Other Minor Nationalities Under the Soviets* (New York, 1928).

Chamberlin, W. H., "Babel Tower of Nationalities," *Soviet Russia: A Living Record and a History* (New York, 1931).

14

NATIONAL AND RACIAL MINORITIES

Kohn, H., *Nationalism in the Soviet Union* (New York, 1933).

Kunitz, J., *Dawn over Samarkand* (New York, 1935).

Smolka, H. P., *40,000 Against the Arctic* (New York, 1937).

Moore, Harriet, "The Nationality Policy of the Soviet Union," *Research Bulletin on the Soviet Union,* American Russian Institute, New York, June 30, 1937.

Halle, F., *Women in the Soviet East* (New York, 1938).

Webb, S. and B., "Problem of National Minorities," *Soviet Communism: A New Civilization* (New York, 1938).

Verbatim Report, Second Session of the Supreme Soviet of the U.S.S.R., August 10–21, 1938 (Moscow, 1938).

Mikhailov, N., *Land of the Soviets* (New York, 1939).

Chekalin, N., "Renaissance of Nationalities and the Consolidation of Nations in the U.S.S.R.," *The Communist,* New York, April, 1940.

Davies, R. A., and Steiger, A. J., *Soviet Asia* (New York, 1942).

Goodall, G., ed., *Soviet Russia in Maps* (London, 1942).

Stalin, J., *Marxism and the National Question* (New York, 1942).

Willkie, W., "Republic of Yakutsk," *One World* (New York, 1943).

Mandel, W., *Soviet Far East and Central Asia* (New York, 1944).

Stern, B. J., "Soviet Policy on National Minorities," *American Sociological Review,* New York, June, 1944.

Strong, A. L., *Peoples of the U.S.S.R.* (New York, 1944).

Jacobson, C., "The Jews in the U.S.S.R.," *The American Review on the Soviet Union,* American Russian Institute, New York, August, 1945.

Lamont, C., *The Peoples of the Soviet Union* (New York, 1946).

CHAPTER II

Physical Features

By HARRIET L. MOORE

T HE USSR occupies 8,400,000 square miles or one sixth of the habitable surface of the earth. It includes the eastern half of Europe and the northern third of Asia, stretching 6,000 miles from east to west and 1,800 to 2,800 miles from north to south. Except on the west, the borders of the Soviet Union for the most part follow natural water or mountain barriers. On the north the USSR is bounded by the Arctic Ocean (from west to east—the Barents Sea, White Sea, Kara Sea, Laptevykh Sea, East Siberian Sea, and Chukotsk Sea). On the east it is bounded by the Pacific Ocean (Bering Sea, Okhotsk Sea, and Japan Sea). On the south from east to west, the border runs along the Ussuri River by Korea (Chosen) and Manchuria; along the Amur River north of Manchuria; along the Tien Shan, the Sayan, Altai, and Pamirs Mountains, dividing it from the Mongolian Republic, China (Sinkiang Province), and Afghanistan; thence north of Iran, Turkey, and the Black Sea. The western boundary lies against Romania, Poland, Finland, and Norway (as a result of the armistice terms of September 29, 1944, ceding the Petsamo Province to the USSR).

In addition to the Continental expanse of the USSR, bounded as above, the USSR includes important islands in the Arctic and Pacific oceans and the Baltic Sea. The largest of these are Fridtjof Nansen Land, Novaya Zemlya, Vaigach, Kolguyev, Severnaya Zemlya, New Siberian Islands, Lyakhov Islands, and Wrangel Island, all in the Arctic Ocean; the Komandorskiye Islands, Shantarskiye Islands, Sakhalin, and

16

the Kuriles in the Pacific; and Saaremaa (Ösel) and Hiiumaa (Dagö) in the Baltic.

PHYSICAL GEOGRAPHY . . . The physical geography of the Soviet Union is characterized by its continentality. Although it is traditionally divided into a European and an Asiatic section, the geographical demarcation between the two is not significant, nor always agreed upon. Usually the line is taken to run south along the Ural Mountains and the Ural River to the Caspian Sea and thence west along the ridge of the Caucasus Mountains, so that the republics of Soviet Central Asia— Kazak SSR, Uzbek SSR, Turkmen SSR, Kirghiz SSR, Tadzhik (Tajik) SSR—and the republics of the Transcaucasus—the Georgian SSR, Armenian SSR, and the Azerbaidzhan (Azerbaijan) SSR—as well as Siberia can be considered in Asia. However, geographically as well as culturally, there is no sharp division between Europe and Asia along this line. Topographically, the greater part of the USSR can be divided roughly into three main parts: the great plains occupying the eastern part of Europe up to the Ural Mountains, the even larger lowlands lying east of the Urals as far as the Yenisei River, and the relatively mountainous regions of eastern Siberia from the Yenisei River to the Pacific. The lowlands are not more than 650 feet above sea level and occupy most of the western part of the country and the Arctic coast; the remainder of the flatlands are 650 to 6,500 feet in elevation in the east and southeast. In addition, there are sections below sea level north of the Caspian Sea, itself 85 feet below sea level, and southeast of the Aral Sea.

The mountains of the Soviet Union are grouped, geologically, as follows: those of the Tertiary Age are those of the Crimea, the Carpathian, Hindu Kush, Pamirs, Kamchatka, and Sakhalin mountain systems. These ranges contain evidence of former earthquakes and volcanic eruption. Kamchatka has active volcanoes even at present. Mesozoic mountains are located in the Far East between the Sea of Okhotsk and the Lena River. The Urals and the mountains of Kazakstan and the Tien range are the oldest and date from the Permian Age.

GEOLOGY . . . The structure of the earth within the territory of the USSR is very complex and varied. Various sections were formed in the pre-Cambrian period. Others underwent violent changes at a later period, as the earth's core shifted. There are two huge pre-Cambrian

17

massifs—the Russian and the Siberian. The Russian includes the wide plain of the European part of the USSR and that of the Baltic coast. It is almost completely surrounded by mountains of varying geological age. The ancient pre-Cambrian base of the Russian massif comes to the surface of the earth in the Scandinavian Peninsula, the Kola Peninsula, Finland, and Karelia, forming the so-called crystalline Baltic Shield. In the Ukraine, from the Pripet (Pripyat, Prypeć) River to the Azov Sea is another crystalline shield—the Azov-Podolsk Shield. Throughout the rest of the area, the massif lies deep beneath the surface, covered with thick strata of Paleozoic, Mesozoic, and more recent ages. The Siberian massif occupies the entire area between the Yenisei and the Lena and Aldan rivers. Its western edge has not been exactly located. On the east and south it is bounded by the Verkhoyansk Mountains and the eastern Transbaikal region; on the north it reaches the Laptevykh Sea and the mountains of the Taimyr Peninsula. The ancient pre-Cambrian base of granite, gneiss, and crystalline schists comes to the surface in three regions—around Lake Baikal, along the Yenisei ridge, and at the headwaters of the Anabar (Anabara), where it is called the Anabar Shield.

GLACIATION . . . During the Pleistocene Ice Age the southern border of the ice sheet ran from Zhitomir to Kremenchug, crossed the Dnieper (Dnepr) River, and passed through Poltava north to Bryansk and Tula, thence turning south almost to Stalingrad, then north again to cross the Volga east of Gorky, and thence west to Molotov. Then it passed northward to where the Scandinavian ice sheet joined with the Ural-Timan ice sheet, which reached as far east as the Ob River. Following the Ice Age, the area north and west of the Caspian Sea was covered by the Caspian and Black seas, which were for a period joined together through what is now the Azov Sea. During the glacial period a large part of the mountainous sections east and south of the east Siberian Plateau was covered by an ice sheet also, but the area covered, because of the drier climate, was not as great as in Europe.

HYDROGRAPHY . . . Although the Soviet Union has an exceedingly long coast line in the Arctic and on the Pacific, it is in effect virtually landlocked, because with few exceptions its outlets on the oceans are frozen for many months of the year. The exceptions are the Black Sea ports, Murmansk on the Kola Peninsula, which is warmed by the Gulf Stream, and Petropavlovsk on Kamchatka, which is warmed by the Japanese Current. The lakes, rivers, and seas of the Soviet Union are accordingly of extreme importance to its economy, despite the fact that for the most part they can be used only for internal communications. Because of climate conditions the rivers are frozen for a part of the year over most of their length, and they are subject to flooding with the spring thaws.

RIVERS . . . The Volga, which takes first place in Europe for length and for size of its basin, is the most important river of the European systems, draining a full third of the area west of the Urals. More than half of the river fleet of the USSR is on this system, which accounts for more than half of the freight carried by river. It is for this reason that new canal systems have been planned to link it with the Black Sea and the Baltic. The second most important river of the European section is the Dnieper, on the rapids of which was constructed the immense Dneprostroi hydroelectric station, serving the factories and farms of the surrounding area. The rivers of southern European Russia are subject to spring floods and tend to dry up during the hot summer months. Therefore, except for the largest, they are less navigable than those in the north.

Few rivers in the mountainous Caucasus are of importance except as sources of water power. On the northern slope of the mountains are the Kuban (Psishche) and Terek rivers; on the southern slopes the Rion, flowing into the Black Sea, and the Kura and Aras (Araks, Araxes), flowing into the Caspian.

The rivers of southeast European Russia are being developed for irrigation projects. This area of low rainfall has always been subject to severe droughts which seriously affected agricultural development. The Kuibyshev project on the Volga was planned not only to provide electric power but also to alleviate the danger of drought by providing a reservoir for a vast irrigation system.

Western Siberia has some of the greatest rivers in the world, including the Ob-Irtysh system and the Yenisei. They rise in the Altai and Sayan Mountains on the southwestern border of Siberia and empty thousands of miles north in the Arctic Ocean. Although they are frozen over for

19

many months of the year, they remain the major trade arteries of vast sections of northern Siberia. Moreover, the development of the northern sea route through the Arctic Ocean links these rivers with Europe and the Far East.

TABLE II. MOST IMPORTANT RIVER SYSTEMS	Length in miles	Area drained, 1,000 sq. mi.
Flowing into Baltic Sea:		
Western Dvina	633	32
Neman	580	38
Neva	46.5	97
Flowing into White Sea:		
Northern Dvina (and Sukhona)	802	158
Vychegda	688	46
Flowing into Barents Sea:		
Pechora	1,111	127
Flowing into Black Sea:		
Dnieper	1,417	194
Dniester	875	28
Flowing into Azov Sea:		
Kuban (and Ullukam)	583	20
Don	1,219	162
Flowing into Caspian Sea:		
Volga	2,287	531
Kama	1,260	201
Oka	916	94
Ural	1,571	85
Kura	939	72
Flowing into Aral Sea:		
Amu Darya (and Pyandzh)	1,557	196
Syr Darya (and Naryn) ...	1,773	84
Flowing into Arctic Ocean:		
Ob (and Katun)	2,508	934
Irtysh	1,841	412
Tobol	1,040	153
Ishim	1,122	53
Yenisei	2,360	1,042
Angara	1,149	193
Lower Tunguska	1,584	182
Olenek	1,497	95
Lena	2,644	932

The rivers of Central Asia are of special interest. None of them empties into the ocean. Some, including the Amu Darya (Oxus) and the Syr Darya, flow into the shallow and salty landlocked Aral Sea, and others, among them the Ili, into Lake Balkhash. Others, among them the Chu, Zeravshan, Murgab, and Tedjen (Tejend), rise in the high mountains and disappear into the sands of the Central Asian deserts, having lost all their water to irrigation and the oases of the desert. The Amu Darya is unique among the rivers of the USSR. In places it is so wide that the opposite bank is scarcely visible. Its thundering waters carry a yellowish-brown sediment and seem to boil up over the banks. Often these desert rivers change their courses and move into entirely different beds. But they remain the source of the richness of Central

Aldan	1,390	272
Vilyui	1,512	189
Kolyma	1,333	248
Flowing into Pacific Ocean:		
Amur (and Shilka and Onon)	2,699	709
Zeya	750	90
Ussuri (and Ulukhe)	528	72

Asia's agriculture, especially its cotton.

East Siberia and the Far East have two groups of rivers, those flowing into the Arctic Ocean and those flowing into the Pacific. The greatest is the Lena, draining into the whole of Yakutia. To this should be added also the important tributaries of the Yenisei, which rise in eastern Siberia: the Angara, a powerful river flowing out of Lake Baikal which is destined to be developed as a source of water power for the whole area, and the Tunguska rivers. The Amur is by far the most important river emptying into the Pacific. Taking its rise not far from Lake Baikal, it flows for more than a thousand miles along the southern border of the Soviet Union before it is joined by the Ussuri and turns north to empty into the Pacific at the Siberian city of Nikolayevsk. Not only is the Amur navigable for most of its length, but it is very rich in the variety and quantity of fish.

CANALS . . . Because of the relative flatness of the areas involved, the portages between the headwaters of many of the various river systems are not difficult and it has been possible to develop a system of canals linking them together. The most important of these are the Baltic-White Sea Canal, permitting ships to pass from Leningrad and the Baltic into the Arctic Ocean; the Moscow-Volga Canal, joining the Moscow and Oka rivers with the Volga, north of Moscow; and the projected Volga-Don Canal, which will join the Volga to the Black Sea. There is in addition the old system of canals joining the Volga to Lake Ladoga and the Baltic.

Lakes and Inland Seas.—The Soviet Union also has a large number of lakes and inland seas, the most important of which are the Caspian Sea, the Aral Sea, Lake Balkhash, Lake Issyk-Kul (Issy-Kol, Tuz-Kul, Temurtu-nor), Lake Khanka, and Lake Baikal in Asia, the latter, in eastern Siberia, being the sixth largest lake in the world and the deepest (5,711 feet). The only lake of any size in the Caucasus is the Sevan (Gokcha, Gok Chai), high on the Armenian Plateau, which is being developed as a powerful hydroelectric project.

21

TABLE III. MOST IMPORTANT LAKES AND INLAND SEAS	
	Area in sq. mi.
European section:	
Lake Ladoga	7,095
Lake Onega	3,822
Lakes Chud and Pskov	1,388
Lake Ilmen	424
Lake Beloye	463
Caspian Sea	168,893
Asiatic section:	
Aral Sea	24,601
Lake Baikal	12,146
Lake Balkhash	6,671
Lake Issyk-Kul	2,391
Lake Khanka	1,697
Lake Chany	1,003
Lake Zaisan	694
Lake Sevan	540

CLIMATE AND PRECIPITATION . . . Although the USSR, because of its size, has climate of all types except the tropical, 80 per cent of the country falls into the temperate zone. Only 4 per cent (in the Far East and the Caucasus) is subtropical, and 16 per cent is Arctic. Furthermore, for most of the country, winter, with freezing temperatures, is the longest season. Only the Atlantic Ocean has any moderating effect on the climate, and its effect is naturally limited primarily to European Russia. The Pacific coastal mountain ranges prevent the Pacific Ocean from having any marked effect on the climate in the east. The Arctic Ocean, on the other hand, is not cut off from the inland areas by mountains and has a very strong influence on the climate of a major part of the country. Proximity to the Atlantic and Gulf Stream controls the winter temperature levels, so that the January isotherms run from the northwest to the southeast.

In the European sections the lowest winter temperatures are on the lower Pechora and in the Urals (—8° F.), while the highest averages are in the northern Crimea (32° F.). In summer the highest average temperatures are on the lower Volga (July average 77° F.) and the coolest on the Arctic coast (46° F.). The whole northeastern part of European Russia has freezing temperatures by the end of November, and frosts begin in September.

Precipitation also varies with distance from the Atlantic. The greatest precipitation is in the area of Smolensk (25.6 inches), and the lowest on the steppes north of the Caspian (6.3 inches). The west slope of the Urals enjoys somewhat higher rainfall (24 inches) than the regions just to the west of the mountains. Because of the relatively low precipitation the snow cover plays an important part in the agriculture. In the north where the winters are long and the thaw is slow, the snow serves as a good source of moisture, but in the south where the snowfall is irregular and the spring thaw very rapid, because of the lack of trees, drought is likely to take place. The prevailing winds in northern Europe are western, and in the south are eastern.

The southern shore of the Crimea and the Black Sea coast of the Transcaucasus form a separate climatic zone with warm winters. The average January temperature in Yalta is 39° F. and in Batum 43° F. Likewise the precipitation is high—sometimes 98.5 inches in Batum, the highest in the country. But this region is small; the rest of the Transcaucasus is cut off by mountains from the warm air. These conditions make possible subtropical cultivation on the Black Sea coast.

Although the low Ural Mountains do not make a sharp climatic break between European Russia and western Siberia, the continentality of the climate is increased, with longer, colder winters and shorter, hotter summers. Even in southern Siberia winter temperatures of −40° F. are not unusual. Precipitation is also less in western Siberia. The central zone and the Altai regions enjoy somewhat more (19.7 inches) than the areas north of the 65° parallel and south of a line from Semipalatinsk to Kurgan (8 to 12 inches). Most of the precipitation is in the summer.

In Central Asia the climate is an unusual combination, considering the latitude, of very hot summers and relatively cold winters. Only the southernmost portions are free from frost. This situation is explained by the fact that the area is cut off from the south by high mountain ranges, but on the north the way is open from the Arctic. The prevailing winds are north and northeast. Because of the cold winters subtropical agriculture is impossible, except in a very few places, despite the great heat of the summer.

Eastern Siberia has the most severe climate of the whole country, because of its distance from the Atlantic and its access to the Arctic and the cold Sea of Okhotsk. The coldest regions of the earth are in eastern Siberia. The so-called Pole of Cold is in the Verkhoyansk region, where the average January temperature is below −58° F. and the thermometer is known to have reached −90° F. At near-by Oimyakon an unofficial record of −103° F. has been reported. On the other hand, in summer relatively high temperatures are reached: Verkhoyansk itself has as high as 92° F. in summer. The isotherm of —25° F. in January passes through Yakutia southward to the 55 parallel, and in most of the rest of eastern Siberia the January average is not above —4° F. Precipitation is lower than in western Siberia and is particularly low east of the Lena in the northeast Arctic sections, where it ranges from 6 to 8 inches. There is remarkably little snow in general, as most of the precipitation is in the summer. As a result, almost all of eastern Siberia is in the area of "perpetual frost," meaning that the ground never thaws beneath the surface. This causes surface swamps in the summer, as there is no drainage through the frozen subsoil.

The small area of the Primorsk belongs to a different climatic zone: that of the Pacific monsoons, which reach as far north as 58°. The monsoons bring much moisture, and they also lower the temperature levels. The average January temperature in Vladivostok is 10° F. as compared with 43° F. at Sukhumi, which is on the same latitude. Likewise the July average is 65.5° F. as compared with Yakutsk far to the north, where it is 66.4° F. Although there is comparatively little snowfall in the area, the summer rains are very great, sometimes resulting in serious floods in the Amur Valley. The greatest level of precipitation is on the southeast coast of Kamchatka, where it reaches 40 inches. The coastal areas are extremely foggy, especially in spring and summer.

SOIL, FLORA, AND FAUNA . . . The Soviet Union can be divided roughly into five zones with characteristic soil, flora, and fauna. These lateral bands, coinciding more or less with the climatic zones, are (1) the tundra, a strip running along the Arctic Ocean; (2) the forest zone, a wide band reaching from the westernmost European boundaries to the Pacific, including by far the largest part of the country and consisting largely of plains and coniferous forests; (3) the treeless steppe region south of the forest zone; (4) the southern semidesert and desert zone; and (5) parts of the zone of ancient subtropical growth and the southern mountain forests.

The Tundra.—Approximately 10 per cent of the Soviet Union, or about 887,000 square miles, is occupied by the tundra. Bordering the Arctic Ocean, this zone begins as a narrow strip in the northwest which gets wider toward the east until, in eastern Siberia, it reaches as far south as 60° N. It is typified by the absence of forests, as only plants with short roots can grow above the perpetually frozen subsoil. The annual average temperature is below freezing, and there is relatively little precipitation in this zone. The land is marshy in summer, and the shrubs and grasses grow in gnarled, tangled bunches to protect themselves from the severe winds. Almost all the vegetation is perennial, and growth is very slow. Moss, lichens, berries, and low shrubs are the principal types of growth, the Iceland lichen being the primary food of the northern reindeer. In the short summer there are bright flowers, growing in widely scattered clumps. The more northerly sections of the tundra are called the Arctic tundra and are even more rocky and barren, if not ice-covered. On the south the tundra merges gradually into the forest zone, and in the forest tundra there are low trees, including birches and other leafy plants.

The few animals and birds of the tundra include the reindeer, the lemming, the ermine and polar fox, the white and tundra partridge, and the polar owl. In the summer for a short period ducks, geese, swans, and other birds migrate to the tundra. Along the Arctic coast thousands of gulls, loons, and other sea birds congregate noisily and nest during the summer, but by September all except the partridge and owls have gone south. The tundra regions are plagued with gnats and mosquitoes in the summer. The rivers abound in fish.

The islands of the Arctic Ocean are even less endowed with life. They have a long four months of Arctic night, and on the New Siberian Islands the annual average temperature is as low as 1.4° F. Only mosses and lichens grow, and the polar fox and polar bear are seen from time to time.

The Forest Zone.—Stretching south of the tundra over a very large area consisting of approximately 4,240,000 square miles, or more than half the territory of the USSR, is the forest zone. It is the largest forest area in the world. This area can be divided into two parts: the northern and larger part called the taiga, in which the trees are coniferous, and the mixed forests of coniferous and deciduous trees of the south. In the taiga the most common trees are the spruce, the pine, and, to the east, the larch, the silver fir, and the cedar. In places deciduous trees such as birch, aspen, alder, mountain ash, and bird cherry are mixed in among the coniferous, especially in burned-over areas. The taiga covers the Ural Mountains almost completely. In Siberia it extends south to the 56° parallel, covering the Altai and Sayan Mountains and a large

25

part of the area east of Lake Baikal. In places the taiga is so tangled and marshy that it is hardly passable.

The belt of mixed forest south of the taiga covers almost all of European Russia from a northern boundary passing through Leningrad, Novgorod (Veliki-Novgorod, Holmgard), Yaroslavl, and Ivanovo (Ivanovo-Voznesensk), to the southern edge of the forest zone at Zhitomir, Kiev, Ryazan (Riazan), and eastward. The principal varieties of deciduous trees in the mixed forest belt are linden, oak, elm, maple, ash, and beech, but coniferous trees remain predominant. In the European sections the forest is widely cutover. In addition to the forests this zone has very large areas of swamp and peat bog. The taiga itself is more than half covered with swamps, especially in western Siberia. The soil of the forest zone is known as *podzol*. The animal life is similar throughout the area and includes elk, reindeer, deer, lynx, brown bear, badger, weasel, sable, and skunk. Wolves and foxes are also found throughout the zone.

The Steppe.—South of the forest zone is the steppe region, which stretches in an unbroken belt from the western frontiers to the Altai. It is characterized by its rich black earth, its fine grasses, and the absence of trees. The area of the steppe is about 964,000 square miles, or 12 per cent of the area of the USSR. This area, having a rich, humus, black soil, embraces some 250 million acres or two thirds of the cultivated land of the Soviet Union. There is no such huge expanse of black earth elsewhere in the world. There are two reasons for the absence of trees in this zone: first, the low precipitation, and, secondly, the fact that beneath the surface layer of black earth there are salts poisonous to the roots of trees. Consequently, only in river valleys, ravines, and other such places where these salts have been washed out of the subsoil do trees thrive. The steppe not only covers the flat area running through the central sections of the USSR, but it extends high up the slopes of the Altai Mountains; and in eastern Siberia there are isolated sections of steppe such as the Minusinsk and Abakan (Abakansk) steppes. The animals living on the steppe are fewer than in the forest. Some antelope are found in the Asiatic sections, and for the rest there are simply birds and small field animals.

Semidesert and Desert.—South of the steppe in the southeast of European Russia and in huge areas of Central Asia lies the zone of semidesert and desert lands. It occupies 1,500,000 square miles, or about 18 per cent of the area of the USSR. The semidesert occupies the northern half of this zone. Its annual average temperature is higher than that of the steppe and its precipitation less. The soil contains less humus, and the lack of water results, in many places, in the salts of the soil rising to the surface. In the very salty sections there is virtually no growth and the ground is bare. The desert sections are in the extreme southeastern part of Europe, just north of the Caspian, as well as in a large part of Central Asia between the Aral Sea and the mountain ranges on the frontiers. The largest sand deserts are the Kara Kum (Qara Qum), southeast of the Caspian Sea, and the Kyzil Kum, between the Amu Darya River and the Syr Darya River. Clay deserts are east of the Caspian and west of Lake Balkhash. The gray soil of these semidesert and desert areas has a high lime content, but it also contains some humus and is not unsuited to agriculture when there is irrigation. In addition to a few animals such as the antelope and smaller species such as the marmot and badger, the desert areas also have large lizards and many snakes.

The Subtropical Zone.—A very small corner of the USSR in the extreme south comprises the subtropical zone. In some parts it has been a region of luxuriant vegetation since before the Ice Age. This is true of the Colchis (Kolkhida) area on the Black Sea coast between Batum and Sochi, and on the Caspian Sea coast near Lenkoran. In other sections where the climate is less damp, the forests are not so thick and varied. Such is the situation in the Crimea, the remainder of the Transcaucasus, and the mountains of Central Asia. Together these sections total 190,000 square miles, or 2 per cent of the area of the USSR. In the Colchis the annual precipitation reaches 80–100 inches, and the average annual temperature is 57° F. In these areas tea, oranges, lemons, and olives are now grown. The soil is also subtropical, lacking lime but containing much clay from volcanic ash. Since ancient times humus has developed in forest areas, and the soil approximates the *podzol* type of the northern forest area. In the Transcaucasus there are many kinds of the larger animals such as deer, bear, and panther. In the Lenkoran area there are also tigers and hyenas.

The other chief area of ancient subtropical growth is the region of the Amur and the southern Ussuri regions of the Far East. Here too the

27

forests are tangled masses of rich vegetation, and the trees grow rapidly to a tremendous size. Much of the ground is swampy. The animal life is varied, and again tigers, deer, sable, panther, bear, and antelope are found.

In addition to the five zones described above, mention must be made of the Alpine vegetation in the high mountains. The tree line in the various ranges of the USSR differs according to the climate and precipitation, so that in the northern Urals it is only 1,000 feet above sea level, while in the Altai it reaches 8,500 to 9,500 feet in some regions, and in eastern Siberia and the Far East the mountains are wooded almost to their tops. The Alpine areas do not constitute a real zone and are scattered throughout the mountains of the country. The area totals some 270,000 square miles. It is for the most part rich in grasses and Alpine flowers, and serves as summer pasture for cattle, especially in the Caucasus and in Central Asia. Mountain sheep and goats, Manchurian deer, bear, and other mountain animals are found in these areas.

RESOURCES . . . The Soviet Union is very rich in natural resources. It has deposits of every type of mineral, nonmetallic ore, and rare metal. Its reserves of coal, oil, iron ore, and copper—basic to industrial development—are large. These resources are distributed widely throughout the country, but the areas of heaviest concentration are, for minerals, the Ural Mountains; for coal and iron ore, the Ukraine; for rare metals, the mountain system of Central Asia and the Far East; and for oil, the Caucasus. The USSR stands second to the United States in the size of its coal deposits (an estimated 1,654 billion tons as of 1938), and a large proportion of these deposits are anthracite. The main centers for coal are the basin of the Don (Duna) River, the Kuznetsk (Kusnetsk) Basin in western Siberia on the Tom River, and the Karaganda Basin in central Kazakstan. In oil reserves the USSR takes first place with an estimated 8,640 million tons in 1938. Its largest fields are in the Caucasus at Baku, Grozny (Grozni), and Neftegorsk. Next in size are the fields between the Volga and the Urals, known as "the second Baku" at Ishim. There is oil also in the Ukraine at Drogobych (Pol); in Kazakstan at Emba; in the Pechora Basin at Ukhta; and on Soviet Sakhalin. There are also some 26 billion tons of oil shale reserves in the USSR. Peat is likewise an important source of fuel in the USSR, which has the largest resources of this fuel in the world, estimated at

151 billion tons (dried). Peat deposits underlie large sections of central European Russia, especially Belorussia. The most important iron deposits are at Magnitogorsk, Baikal, and other localities in the Urals, at Krivoi Rog in the Ukraine, and at Kerch in the Crimea. When investigation of the Kursk Magnetic Anomaly in the early 1930's revealed tremendous reserves of iron quartzite at considerable depth, development of this resource was begun. Iron deposits are estimated at a total of 10,921 million tons. The most important copper deposits are in Kazakstan on the northern shore of Lake Balkhash at Kounrad, and other mines are being worked in Central Asia, in the Urals, and in the Caucasus, especially in Armenia. Important deposits of zinc, lead, and other nonferrous metals are found in various mountain systems, and gold also occurs in many places in the Urals, eastern Siberia, and the Far East, the most important centers being the Aldan and Kolyma (Kolima) fields. Platinum is mined in the Urals and in the autonomous republic of Yakutia in Siberia. Vanadium, wolfram, and molybdenum occur especially in the Caucasus, and the world's largest reserves of manganese (785 million tons) are worked at Nikopol in the Ukraine and at Chyaturi in Georgia. Tin is the one important metal that has not been mined in quantity, but deposits have been discovered in the far north and in Central Asia. Aluminum is produced from low-quality bauxite deposits near Leningrad at Tikhvin and in the northern Urals at Serov and elsewhere. On the Kola Peninsula at Kandalaksha there are rich nephelite deposits. The Soviet Union is extremely rich in certain nonmetallic minerals. In the Kara Bogaz (Qara Boghaz) Gulf in the Caspian Sea huge quantities of salts, especially Glauber's salt, are deposited. Potassium and magnesium salts in tremendous quantities have been discovered near Solikamsk in the northern Urals, putting the USSR in the first place as a producer of potash. In the Kola Peninsula there are gigantic deposits of apatite, estimated at 2,000 million tons, or 75 per cent of the known world reserves, along with nephelite. Phosphorites totaling 5.7 billion tons and chromites are also found in significant quantities. Asbestos is mined in the Urals in such quantities as to place the Soviet Union second in world production.

BIBLIOGRAPHY

Bolshaya Sovetskaya Entsiklopediya, in Russian (Moscow, 1936).
Mikhailov, N., *Land of the Soviets* (New York, 1939).

PART TWO

POLITICAL SCIENCE

CHAPTER III

The History of Russia
and the USSR

By VLADIMIR D. KAZAKÉVICH

Russia's history, or rather, the history of the peoples included in the USSR, who were joined together in one state by the Russians, begins long before the appearance of the Slavs as a distinct group. Traces of Stone Age culture are found on Soviet territory; and in the Caucasus, the Urals, the Altai Mountains, and Central Asia, bronze objects were produced in the second millennium B.C. By the middle of the first millennium iron had replaced bronze as a raw material for tools and weapons.

The peoples inhabiting parts of what is now Soviet territory often played an important role in the history of the ancient Mediterranean world, although geographically they formed only part of its outer fringe. As early as 1000 B.C. Haldian tribes in the Transcaucasian region were uniting to form a state, which by the eighth century had grown powerful enough to challenge, for a time successfully, the armed forces of Assyria. This state, known to the Assyrians as Urartu, was ruled by kings whose many slaves, the booty of victorious campaigns, built strong fortresses on steep cliffs and covered large sections of the dry plateau with a network of irrigation canals. The cuneiform script was used by the Haldians to record their many victories in battle, often over the Assyrians. Among the regions incorporated in the territory of Urartu was part of the land now occupied by Transcaucasian Soviet republics, where remains of their culture are found. The Assyrians finally conquered Urartu and demolished its capital on Lake Van (in modern Turkish Armenia). A later conquest by the Persians in the sixth century led to the complete disintegration of the state, whose name is echoed now only by Mount Ararat. The ancient Armenian kingdom which took the place of Urartu, with the aid of tribes occupying present-day Georgia and Soviet Armenia, so effectively opposed the Romans in the first century B.C. that the Senate had to send Pompey the Great (106–48 B.C.) to defeat the Armenian king, Tigranes II (r. 95–56/55 B.C.). After Pompey's victory Transcaucasia began to serve as a route for Roman trade with the Far East. In 329 B.C. Alexander the Great (r. 336–323 B.C.) penetrated into Central Asia, crossing both the Amu Darya and the Syr Darya rivers in what is now Soviet territory. After Alexander's death his soldiers maintained garrisons in Central Asia, and in this region Hellenistic culture flourished long after the collapse of Alexander's empire.

The Black Sea region was another important outpost of ancient civilization. The Scythians, a nomad people from the east, who occupied the steppes of southern Russia from about the eighth to the third centuries B.C., were known to the Greeks, who had planted colonies on the Black Sea shores as early as the seventh century. In Olbia (at the mouth of the river Bug), Chersonesus, Theodosia, Panticapaeum (all in the Crimea), and Tanais (at the mouth of the Don), the Greeks came into close contact with the Scythians, through whom they obtained the fish and grain produced by the native population of this region. Greek handicraft techniques strongly influenced native and Scythian artisans. In 512 B.C. the Scythians forced the great army of Darius I (r. 521–485? B.C.), king of Persia, to retreat out of the steppes across the Danube. In the fifth and fourth centuries B.C. the sea route from Athens to the Crimea was guarded as a life line by the Athenians, who depended on imports from the Black Sea for a large part of their grain supply. In the third century another nomad tribe, the Sarmatians, invaded South Russia and pushed the Scythians west to the Danube and south into the Crimea. The Greek colonies in the Crimea were thus threatened by a double danger. One of these colonies, which had formed the powerful kingdom of the Bosporus, suffered a combined attack from within and without in the second century B.C. A slave uprising with Scythian support led to the intervention of Mithridates VI Eupator (r. 120?–63 B.C.), king of Pontus in Asia Minor, and to the inclusion of the Bosporan kingdom in his expanding realm. When the Romans, after three savage wars, finally conquered Mithridates and his Armenian ally, Tigranes, in the first century B.C., the Bosporan ruler became a Roman vassal, and the Black Sea became a Roman lake, with Roman fortresses dotting its shores.

When Rome began to weaken in the third century A.D., a Germanic tribe, the Goths, penetrated toward the Black Sea, forming a Gothic kingdom in the Crimea and the Taman Peninsula in the Caucasian isthmus. In the fifth century the Huns, advancing from Asia, swept through this region, eliminating the Gothic kingdom. Under Attila, the "scourge of God" (r. 433?–453), they went as far as present-day France. The invasion of the Huns opened the way for periodic incursions from the east. In the sixth century the Avars marched in. About a century later the first migration of the Turks from the faraway Altai Mountains proceeded north of the Black Sea. The Magyars, also coming from Asia, crossed the Dnieper in 898 and settled later in present-day Hungary. Remnants of the Huns and other tribes formed the Bulgar kingdom on the Volga and Kama, whose name is preserved by quite a different people, the Bulgarians in the Balkans. In the eighth century the south of Russia was united in the Khazar kingdom, whose rulers adopted Judaism.

Around the Carpathian Mountains lived the Slavs. They multiplied and spread south, north, and east. To the Byzantine Empire they became a source of trouble as early as the fifth century. Probably in about the sixth century the Slavs began penetrating north along the rivers of Russia. With the Finnish tribes, who populated most of the forest region north of the steppes, they seem to have had no conflicts; their advance was an interpenetration, not a conquest. The Slavs began to dot the rivers with their settlements. The population of the Khazar kingdom probably already contained a goodly number of Slavs. Reaching the Baltic Sea, the Slavs formed by river connection what later became known as the road from the Vikings (in Scandinavia) to the Greeks (in Constantinople). By the beginning of the ninth century Slavic tribes that were still rather closely related stretched across all the vast countryside from the Black Sea to the Baltic.

At first hunters and fishermen, the Slavs later became primarily an agricultural people. Their simple tribal organization was expressed in the *veche,* or general assembly. By the ninth century, along the rivers, several towns had appeared, such as Kiev, Chernigov, Smolensk, Polotsk, Novgorod, and Staraya Rusa, around which farming took the shape of peasant communes.

To various empires these territories had served as colonial outposts; nomads had used the steppes of southern Russia as an avenue for invasion, settling for a few centuries, only to be dislodged by the next wave. The Slavs gradually populated the entire area and remained there.

THE KIEV STATE . . . In the ninth century the Vikings began to descend from Scandinavia. In western Europe they were known as Normans; among the Slavs, as Varangians. They came from the Baltic, went up the rivers, then dragged their smaller boats across the lands separating the river sources and launched them once more to go down the streams flowing south into the Black Sea. These Norse warriors quickly subjugated many of the river settlements of the Slavs, but they were few in number and were soon absorbed by the local population. The traditional first ruler of Russia was the Viking warrior Ryurik, who, according to later written accounts, established himself in Novgorod about 862 and died probably about 873. Thus began what Karl Marx described as the "Ryurikovich empire" or the "Gothic age" of Russian history.

The next ruler, Oleg, while holding Novgorod, established his seat farther south, at Kiev on the Dnieper. Mixed detachments of Vikings and Slavs raided the coast of the Black Sea and the Persian coast of the Caspian. The Greeks referred to the "Russians" and to "Varangians" interchangeably. After an attack on Constantinople Oleg signed a treaty (911 A.D.) with the Byzantine emperor. In 912 and 913 the Russians raided the shores of the Caspian Sea. The next prince of Kiev, Igor, reputed to have been Ryurik's son, equipped a large navy and in 941 carried out extensive raids in Greek waters, attempting to capture Constantinople, but the Greek Navy sank or burned most of his ships. (In 945 a treaty of alliance was negotiated.) In 943 the Russians again penetrated down the Caspian shores, but were beaten back by the Arabs. Merchant warriors, Russian or Varangian "guests," were frequent visitors in Constantinople, where special provisions were made not only for housing them but also for showing them the sights of the city; they were taken about by guides in small, unarmed groups, for the

Greeks took no chances on the city's being captured from the inside.

Igor's son, Svyatoslav, extended his rule to the Volga and penetrated the north Caucasus. The Kiev state now stretched not only from north (Baltic) to south (Black Sea), but also extended over the southern plains, the territory previously held by the Khazars. Svyatoslav also crossed the Danube and intended to transfer his capital into the Balkans. Not without difficulty did the Byzantine Greeks defeat Svyatoslav. In 971 he was forced to withdraw from the Balkans. On the way home he was ambushed and killed near the Dnieper rapids. His mother, Olga, had become a Christian. She was baptized in Constantinople (957) and had a church built in Kiev, but Svyatoslav had remained true to his warrior gods.

Christianity officially came to Kiev under Vladimir Svyatoslavich (d. 1015), later canonized by the church. In 987 the Byzantine Empire was threatened with a revolt in the Balkans and needed allies. Part of the deal between Vladimir and the Byzantine rulers was his acceptance of Christianity, particularly because the grand prince (as the ruler of Kiev began to be called) wanted to marry a Greek princess. In Kiev the old gods were thrown into the Dnieper, and the population was baptized wholesale in the same river by Greek priests (988); but in Novgorod resistance developed, and Vladimir had to use force. At first Christianity seriously affected only the upper layers of society. Among the masses of the people a duality of beliefs persisted for a long time. Still the official introduction of Christianity was a turning point in the development of the country. With the new faith came Greek priests, and with them the alphabet, an adaptation of Greek letters for Slavic use. Greek artisans and masons also came. Through religious ties the eastern Slavs became firmly linked to an older and much more advanced civilization, that of Byzantium. The Slavs in the west were also adopting Christianity about the same time, but they were joining the church of Rome. Thus the eastern and western Slavs became divided in matters of faith, an element of considerable importance in subsequent centuries.

In the Byzantine Empire little distinction was made between temporal and spiritual authority. Through the Greek clergy the emperor definitely expected to extend his temporal influence over the Kiev state. But the Kiev rulers fought for a native clergy. In 1051 a native was installed as metropolitan (head of the church) by a council of bishops in Kiev, but Constantinople refused to sanction the nomination. Up to the thirteenth century the Russian church remained in direct subordination to the patriarch of Constantinople. Even as late as 1389 the Greeks officially expressed indignation over the fact that the Russians seemed to accept the church, but not the power of the emperor. Although the seat of the highest church authority remained abroad, the plans of Byzantium to extend its political influence through religious channels did not materialize. The church in the Kiev state became a unifying factor in a now considerably extended and sometimes loosely held territory.

Under Yaroslav the Wise (Yaroslav Vladimirovich, r. 1019–1054) the territory of the state was expanded in the north along the Baltic shore and in the upper Volga region. The important role played by Kiev Russia in European affairs is attested by the marital connections of the grand prince's family. Yaroslav's daughter, Anna, was the wife of Henry I of France (r. 1031–1060) and ruled the country as regent after his death; another daughter, Elizabeth, married Harold III of Norway (r. 1046–1066); one of Yaroslav's granddaughters was married to the emperor of the Holy Roman Empire, Henry IV (r. 1056–1106). Two sons of the English King Edmund Ironside (d. 1016), driven from England by the Danish King Canute (d. 1035), found refuge in Kiev at Yaroslav's court. His heir, Vsevolod Yaroslavich (d. 1093), who spoke five languages, married a Greek princess, whose name was carried by Vsevolod's son and successor, Vladimir Vsevolodovich Monomakh (r. 1113–1125). Up to the early days of the eighteenth century, when the empire was established by Peter the Great, the "Hat of Monomakh" stood for the crown and was the symbol of central authority. Vladimir Monomakh married the daughter of Harold II, the last Anglo-Saxon king of England before the Norman conquest (1066). In the eleventh century Kiev Russia was the largest state in Europe and reached the pinnacle of its cultural development. The first body of written laws, later known as the "Russian Truth," was developed from a set of Yaroslav's rulings. Monks began writing *letopisi* (chronicles) of historical events. Greek artists and architects participated in the building of stone churches, notably in the construction of the cathedral of St. Sophia in Kiev.

The growth of the Kiev state posed new problems. Christianity brought with it monasteries, which acquired extensive lands operated with serf labor. Feudal relationships grew and expanded also around the large ruling family and its courtiers, all of whom began to acquire estates, and around many independent large landowners, the boyars. The land, previously worked by free peasants, now fell more and more into the hands of a variety of large landowners, and for the peasantry semiserf conditions were established. The peasantry fought both against losing its land and being attached to lands of others. In this struggle the princes, boyars, and monasteries were united by common interests. The city of Kiev had become a very large and prosperous trading center. The population often revolted against the "usurers" and the misdeeds and oppressions of the "prince's servants." In 1068 a revolt took place in Kiev, and when, in 1113, as a result of another such revolt, Vladimir Monomakh was asked to become grand prince, he put through such reforms as the setting of limits on interest charges. Internal social strife, caused by accentuated social stratification, was augmented by increasing raids of the nomads (first the Pechenegi, then the Polovtsy) from the steppes. Trade with the Byzantine Empire was being interrupted, and Kiev Russia began to decline.

Another factor contributing to this decline was the system of succession. The heirs of Ryurik regarded the country as one vast family estate. With the death of the senior member, the grand prince of Kiev, his oldest son, would receive Kiev, the most important city, as his "seat"; the next in line of seniority would be "seated" in the next most important city, and so on. The princes actually referred to the cities they occupied as "seats," and when one died, everybody had to change seats in accordance with seniority. This arrangement, peculiar to early Russian feudalism, led to endless strife, as members of the ruling house, each relying on his own armed men (*druzhinniki*) and large estates, supported by allies, fought to occupy the best "seats." The realm became split by endless armed feuds after the death of Yaroslav (1054). Vladimir Monomakh tried to reunite the country, but after his death (1125) the process of disintegration proceeded even faster. Nomads from the steppes were invited to help one side or another and often roamed the country at will, robbing all sides in the dispute. The great epic poem of the day by an author unknown to us, *The Tale of the Host of Igor,* depicting events of 1185, lays great stress on the plight of the country arising from feudal strife. The general disintegration of the state, decline of trade, impoverishment due to constant warfare and nomadic raids forced the population to migrate both west and north.

In the west, in Galicia, which was part of Vladimir's realm in the tenth century, there arose a new center, which in the twelfth and thirteenth centuries achieved a high stage of development. Prince Daniel (Daniil Romanovich) of Galicia, founder of the city of Lvov, even assumed in 1255 the title of king, after the western European fashion. The Galician principality was, however, constantly harassed by the Hungarians, Czechs, and Poles. To the northeast of Kiev there were dense forests, through which the nomads could not ride. There, beyond the forests, around the cities of Rostov, Suzdal, and Vladimir, another new center arose. From devastated Kiev the metropolitan of the Greek Orthodox Church moved to Vladimir. In 1147 Moscow was mentioned for the first time, as a princely estate on the river of the same name. Andrei Yurievich Bogolubski (the God-loving), prince of Vladimir (r. 1157–1174), attempted to unite the country from the north. He captured Kiev (1169) and tried to abolish feudal strife. But this first conscious advocate of centralized monarchy was far ahead of his times. The country was impoverished, economic ties between its various parts had weakened, and the advantages of unification were apparently no longer obvious to the population. Andrei did not receive the necessary support and was assassinated by the boyars. The Vladimir principality did flourish, however, for a time (at the end of the twelfth and the beginning of the thirteenth centuries), developing a new type of church architecture, the Vladimir-Suzdal style, and even establishing friendly ties as far south as Georgia.

In the middle of the twelfth century Novgorod separated itself from Kiev but continued to grow as the trading center of the north. In the summer the German tradesmen came by the sea to the river Neva; in the winter they traveled by sledge across Livonia. The city-state of Novgorod became a merchant and landlord republic, with the general assembly (the *veche*) hiring and firing princes, the leaders of the armed forces. Novgorod's colonies spread throughout the north, eventually reaching to the Urals. Both Novgorod and its sister city-state, Pskov, joined the Hanseatic League. Although the Novgorod republic resembled the medieval "free cities" of Europe, it must be noted that its wealth was derived from large landholdings as well as trade, and that feudal landowners (boyars) shared power with the merchants, which was not the case in the west.

With Kiev Russia breaking up into feudal principalities, very similar struggles between feudal lords and the centralizing authority of the sovereign took place in Georgia and Armenia. In Georgia the tendency toward unification won. The country was united by King David the Builder (r. 1089–1125) and became a formidable kingdom under Queen Tamara (r. 1184–1213), whose first husband was the son of Andrei, the ruler of Vladimir. In Tamara's reign there lived Shota Rustaveli, the great Georgian poet of the Middle Ages. Constant struggle between central authority and feudal separatism also went on in Armenia and Azerbaidzhan. The decentralization of what is now European Russia partly accounts for the inability of the population to withstand the great onslaught from the east that came in the thirteenth century.

UNDER THE TATAR YOKE . . . In 1206 a conclave of feudal lords proclaimed Timuchin the leader of the Mongolians, who then assumed the name of Genghis Khan. With this there began the great Mongolian conquests. Siberia was partially conquered in 1207; in 1211 there began the invasion of China; and then Central Asia was overrun, its cities devastated, and its centuries-old culture ruined. Azerbaidzhan, Armenia, and Georgia were subjugated next. In 1223 a Russian army advanced into the steppes and met the Tatars, as the Russians called the Mongols, near the Sea of Azov on the river Kalka. Lack of unity among the princes led to a crushing defeat of the Russians. The Mongols proceeded up the Volga but met with reverses from the Volga Bulgars and retreated through Central Asia to continue the conquest of China. In 1227 Genghis Khan died, having conquered Mongolia proper, north China, southern Siberia, Central Asia, and the Transcaucasus. His third son, Ugadei, became the Great Khan, and a grandson, Batyi, was given all the lands west of the river Irtysh in western Siberia, "as far as the hoofs of the Mongol horses could tread." In 1236 the Volga Bulgars were invaded and destroyed, disappearing forever out of history. In 1237 the principalities of northwestern Russia were invaded; in one month 14 cities were burned, including Moscow, and in the next year the grand prince fell in battle. The Mongolian horde moved south,

41

conquered the Crimea, and in 1240 approached Kiev. The princes fled, but the population decided to defend the city, which was, however, captured and destroyed. From there the invaders overran the Galician principality, crossed the Carpathian Mountains into Hungary, but met with defeat in the mountains of Czechia, where the Mongolian cavalry found it difficult to operate. Returning to the Volga steppes, the Mongolians, or Tatars, established their provincial capital, Sarai, near present-day Astrakhan.

[For Russia there began the period of the so-called Tatar Yoke. The country was devastated, and it is claimed by some historians that the population was reduced by one half. The cultural level of the nomadic conquerors was low, but they knew how to make use of the latest developments in military technique, which they took over from the Chinese. The Tatar rulers adhered to a rather loose type of empire organization but were interested in efficient tribute collection from all parts of their vast domain. Russian princes had at first to travel to the seat of the Great Khan in Mongolia to have their titles confirmed, which took several months. Later, when the Tatar empire began breaking up, the capital city of the Golden Horde (Sarai on the Volga) became the place where homage was paid and tribute delivered. Toward all religions and clergy the conquerors demonstrated a remarkable degree of tolerance and even encouragement, provided, of course, the particular church helped them to enforce their rule. Local rulers, among them the Russian princes, were also encouraged, provided they obeyed and produced the tribute. What two centuries before was the largest state in Europe (Kiev Russia), with dynastic ties all over the continent, was now not only split into many little principalities and devastated, but was also only a very minor part of a vast empire stretching all the way to the Pacific.

[Just prior to the Tatar invasion Constantinople was conquered by the crusaders, and a Latin empire was set up (1204–1261).] Thus the old center with which Kiev Russia had had such close cultural and religious ties changed its aspect profoundly. In the far north the Swedes, who had conquered Finland, now tried to cut off the sea lane from Novgorod through the Baltic and take into their hands the trade route to the west. In 1240 they landed in the river Neva but were defeated by Alexander (Aleksandr Yaroslavich), prince of Novgorod, who thereafter was known as Alexander Nevski (d. 1263). By that time the advance of the Germans eastward, which began under Charlemagne (d. 814) and continued under his successors across the Elbe River, had reached Russia. In the Baltic Sea German tradesmen were soon joined by brotherhoods of warriors, the knightly orders. In 1201 the German knights founded the city of Riga and began bringing in German settlers. In 1224 they captured the city of Yuriev (founded by Yaroslav the Wise), renaming it Dorpat. In 1237 two brotherhoods, the Teutonic Order and the Knights of the Sword, united. Through internal treason Pskov fell, and the enemy advanced toward Novgorod, on a crusade against the non-Catholic Russians. On April 5, 1242, the Russians, under Alexander Nevski, and the Germans met in battle on the ice of Lake Peipus. Alexander went out against the knights not only with his regulars, but also with a peasant militia. The knights were routed, put to flight, and the ice on the lake gave way under their heavily armored cavalry. Thus Alexander Nevski stopped both the Swedes and the Germans, but to the Tatars he consented to pay tribute voluntarily. The Tatars had not reached Novgorod, but the city decided to send tribute in order to forestall an invasion. Alexander went to the seat of the Great Khan and was received with honors. Alexander Nevski died on the way back from a second visit to the Tatars (1263), and was canonized by the church.

In the fourteenth century there proceeded a rapid expansion of Lithuania. Under Grand Duke Gedimin (r. 1316–1341) many formerly Russian lands fell to Lithuania. Under his son the process continued; the Lithuanians took Kiev and other Russian principalities. To the population this inclusion meant liberation from the Tatar yoke. Poland also expanded, and in the middle of the fourteenth century took over Galicia. When Yagailo of Lithuania (r. 1377–1392) married Queen Yadviga of Poland, the two countries formed a union (1385). The Lithuanians adopted the Roman Catholic faith, and the remaining Russian principalities were now confronted on the west by two united Catholic powers holding many Greek Orthodox lands recently Russian. The common German danger did compel some joint action. In 1410, near Tannenberg in East Prussia, a joint Polish-Lithuanian-Czech-Russian army defeated the German knights, who had renewed their offensive. But this joint action was only an episode; on the whole, the

43

new western neighbors were hostile, and centuries of strife between Russia and Poland-Lithuania followed.

In this period the eastern Slavs between the rivers Oka and Volga began to form into the Great-Russian nationality, those under Lithuanian rule developed into the Belorussian nationality, while in the south around Kiev and in Galicia, under Polish domination, there arose the Ukrainian nationality. Thus the eastern Slavs began to form the three basic nationalities, each with its separate language, which exist today. In the west the landowners assimilated easily with the Polish-Lithuanian landholders, mostly becoming Roman Catholics, while the peasantry held steadily to the Greek Orthodox faith of their forefathers. Later, when a new Russian state began to emerge around Moscow, there developed a tendency on the part of the Belorussians and Ukrainians for unity with the Great Russians.

What remained of Russia was, under the Tatars, more and more hemmed in on all sides by hostile powers. There were the Swedes in the north, the German knights and the Polish-Lithuanian state in the west, and finally, in the south, there appeared the Turks. When the Turks captured Constantinople in 1453, the encirclement of Russia was completed. For western Europe Russia faded from the scene for several centuries, and the progress of arts and sciences in western Europe remained almost unknown to the Russians. Both cultural and economic standards declined. The population engaged in agriculture, hunting, and fishing. Most necessities were produced in the household, trade was meager, and there was little money in circulation. Land belonged to the feudal lords, and among feudal landholders the monasteries were very important. Peasants paid for the use of land in kind to the noblemen, but since land was plentiful and labor scarce, it was to the interest of the noblemen to attach the peasant to the land. Thus semiserf relationships became more and more prevalent. The princes were quite independent of each other; by force of tradition one prince who "sat" in the city of Vladimir got a "license" from the Tatars to be grand prince. Only in the north, in Novgorod, trade continued to flourish, owing to the ties with the Hanseatic League. This city-state, nominally under the grand prince of Vladimir, assumed more and more the aspect of a feudal aristocratic republic, its richest feudal lord being the archbishop. The wealthier the city became, the stronger became the class conflict. In 1418 a revolt against the money-lending nobility in Novgorod was barely quelled by the church. Similar conditions prevailed in Pskov, which city split off from Novgorod but also remained nominally under the grand prince. To meet the demands of the Tatars for tribute, the princes had to extract from the peasants increasing amounts in taxation. This pressure forced the disjointed principalities to form alliances, and in the fourteenth century the allied princes established uniform custom duties for their domains. Thus the economic isolation of each principality began to lessen, indicating possibilities for assembling the realm.

THE RISE OF MOSCOW . . . Moscow became the capital of a minor independent principality toward the end of the thirteenth century. North of it the princes of the city of Tver (now Kalinin) were much stronger. The Tatars were apprehensive lest the grand prince in Vladimir might get too strong and were therefore not averse to helping other princes gain more power. Moscow first utilized this Tatar help against Tver. But the real rise of Moscow began under Ivan Danilovich (r. 1325–1341), called Kalita (the Money Bag). With the aid of a big Tatar army, Ivan subdued Tver and in 1328 became the grand prince, although he did not move his seat to Vladimir. The Tatars entrusted him with the collection of tribute from the entire realm. Ivan raised taxes well, built a good treasury of his own, and did not spare funds for presents and bribes in the capital of the Tatar Khan. The metropolitan of the Greek Orthodox Church moved his seat from Vladimir to Moscow. The church supported Ivan, blessed all his deeds, and even used the threat of expulsion from the church against those who opposed the Money Bag or refused to surrender his enemies to him or the Tatars. In Ivan's hands both the church and the Tatars became tools for aiding the growth of the Moscow principality, in which he established order and curtailed brigandage. When Ivan died, the foundation for the future unification of Russia around Moscow had been laid.

The influence of Moscow grew. Grand Prince Dmitri (Dmitrii Ivanovich, r. 1359–1389) replaced the old wooden walls around the city with stone ones. While Russian unity was growing, the Tatars were splitting up into several hordes. On September 8, 1380, a Russian army of 150,000 met the Tatars near the river Don, on Kulikovo field. The Tatars were defeated, and it was because of this victory that the grand prince became known as Dmitri Donskoi (i.e., of the Don). Two years later the Tatars returned and stormed Moscow, but failing to take the city by force, they broke a truce agreement, penetrated the town, and burned it. The grand prince had to continue paying tribute, but Russia now became aware that, by further unification, the country could eventually be liberated. The church and the grand princes of Moscow continued to work hand in hand, but the resistance of feudal princes to unification was not easily overcome. Basil II (Vasili Vasilevich, r. 1425–1462), the son of Dmitri Donskoi, fought a civil war for nearly 20 years, and Moscow changed hands several times. In 1446 Basil was taken prisoner by his princely opponents, blinded, and exiled. But to the blind sovereign, Basil "the Dark," rallied not only the church and the Moscow nobility but the people as well, and he was reinstated in Moscow.

In the second half of the fourteenth century the Tatar empire broke up. In Central Asia large feudal landlordism began to prevail. But a new leader united the nomads and set in motion another series of conquests and invasions. In 1370 Tamerlane (r. 1369–1405), known also as Tamburlaine, Timour, or Timur, established himself in Samarkand in Central Asia, conquered Georgia, defeated the Tatars of the Golden Horde (1395), destroyed their capital Sarai, and advanced into southern Russia. After approaching the border city of Elets, Tamerlane suddenly turned back, defeated the Turks in Asia Minor, and, capturing the sultan Bajazet (on the plain of Angora, where Pompey had defeated Mithridates, king of Pontus, in 66 B.C.), proceeded with fire and sword into Persia and India. Tamerlane, the conqueror who delighted in building pyramids of tens of thousands of human skulls after capturing cities, for some unknown reason decided not to invade Russia. Thus the young Moscow state, still struggling to achieve national unification, was spared a second Tatar invasion. After Tamerlane's death (1405) his empire fell apart. In the fifteenth century the Tatars nearest Russia separated into a Tatar kingdom of Kazan, on the middle Volga; others formed the kingdom of Astrakhan on the lower Volga; still others formed a third separate kingdom, that of the Crimean Tatars. The Tatars became Moslems, and the Crimean Tatars continued as vassals of the sultan of Turkey until the end of the eighteenth century.

The unification of Russia around Moscow was practically completed under Ivan (Vasilevich) III the Great (r. 1462–1505). The boyars of

Novgorod sought protection from the king of Poland, but in 1478 the city was absorbed into Ivan's realm, and Novgorod's "assembly bell," the symbol of its independence, was taken away to Moscow. The prince of Tver fled to Lithuania, and his principality, which once had rivaled Moscow, came under Ivan (1485). The process of unification under Ivan III went on much more swiftly and easily than before. The various parts of the country had already developed sufficient economic ties; the advantages of unification were becoming most obvious; and the grand prince enjoyed a good deal of popular support, particularly since many princely and nobility elements favoring feudal decentralization appealed for Polish-Lithuanian and Tatar aid.

In 1480, or exactly 100 years after the first successful challenge of the Tatar power by Dmitri Donskoi, came the end of Moscow's dependence on the Tatars: Ivan refused to continue paying tribute. On a tributary of the Oka River (the Ugra) the Russian Army faced the Tatars for several months, but the latter failed to attack. In 1502 the erstwhile powerful Golden Horde was smashed completely by the Crimean Tatars. The Ukraine and Belorussia were still outside the realm, but the Moscow state now embraced most of the Great Russians. In 1472 Moscow troops penetrated into the Perm region (now Molotov) inhabited by the Komi, and in 1500 an expedition was undertaken beyond the Urals. The Kazan Tatars acknowledged their dependence on Moscow, and after a three-year war with Lithuania (starting 1500), the city of Chernigov was recovered, and the German knights, now allied with Lithuania, promised to pay tribute to Moscow.

In 1472 Ivan III married Sophia Paleolog, niece of the last Byzantine emperor and a ward of the pope. Both the republic of Venice, with which Ivan established commercial relations, and the Vatican placed high hopes on this marriage. The German emperor proposed to grant Ivan the title of king, but the offer was turned down on the ground that Ivan did not need recognition. Venice and the Vatican also failed to exercise any political or religious influence in Moscow's affairs. Ivan established relations with Turkey and Persia. A Russian merchant from Tver, Nikitin, even penetrated into India (1467–1472). With Sophia came the Byzantine double-headed eagle, which remained on the coat of arms of Russia up to 1917. There also arrived numerous Greek advisers. The grand prince of Moscow now regarded himself as the suc-

47

cessor of the Byzantine emperor and viewed his capital as the new world center of Greek Orthodox Christianity, as the "third and last Rome." Several stone buildings were erected in Moscow at this time by craftsmen from Italy and Pskov. More elaborate court ritual was introduced; Ivan now sat on a throne, wore a crown (the Hat of Monomakh), and was no longer informal in his relations with the courtiers, as had been the custom of previous Moscow princes. The grand prince was now not "first among the equals" in his relations with other Russian princes, but was their ruler. The court was enlarged by the inclusion of several only recently independent feudal princes and their courtiers, many of whom did not like the new customs, blaming their introduction on Sophia Paleolog and the Greeks. But the church supported the throne and spoke of the divine right of the grand prince.

Moscow was becoming a trading center, and trade began to spread throughout the country. Indicative of the development of the money economy is the fact that landowners started to extract from peasants not only payments in kind but payments in money as well. Moneylending became prevalent—even Ivan's brothers were in debt to the Moscow merchants. A regular army was organized, divided into regiments, and equipped with artillery. This army was composed mostly of petty nobility, whose landholdings were dependent on their service. To insure the supply of agricultural labor for this "service" nobility, Ivan made it more difficult for peasants to move from the land of one lord to that of another. In 1497 a new law set aside only one day a year (St. George's Day, in November, after the harvest is in) when such migrations might take place—provided all debts were paid. Thus, although the country was being united, and feudalism as a dividing force was being eliminated, feudal socioeconomic relationships between landlords and peasants were being reinforced. To the old feudal princes and boyars, against whom the throne was strengthening the service nobility, one concession had to be made. They preserved the right not to serve under anyone whose family was less prominent than theirs. This made many aspects of administration most difficult. The church, which had played such an outstanding role in helping to unify the country, had become a landowner of great strength. When a movement arose within the church itself against the tremendous wealth accumulated by the monasteries, the throne took the side of the landed church interests. The position of the throne was not yet secure enough to challenge the wealth of the church.

Under Ivan's successor, Basil III (Vasili Ivanovich, r. 1505–1533), Pskov became part of the realm (1510). In the city of Ryazan the last independent feudal prince first plotted with the Crimean Tatars and then fled to Lithuania, and the city was taken over by Moscow (1521). In 1514 the Moscow troops took from Lithuania one of the oldest cities of the pre-Tatar invasion days, Smolensk.

In 1533 the three-year-old Ivan IV (Ivan Vasilevich, r. 1533–1584), later called by the Russians *Groznyi*—the Dread or the Severe (usually incorrectly translated into English as "the Terrible")—came to the throne. His mother ruled until 1538, when, apparently, she was poisoned. The old feudal elements now asserted themselves, and the young ruler was neglected and abused. At the age of 17 (1547) young Ivan proclaimed himself "czar," a Russian version of caesar, or emperor. The young ruler now concentrated on reforms directed to weakening the feudal elements, the princes and the big nobles (boyars), and strengthening the military service nobility. Administration of the country was centralized, administrators were put on a salary basis, and in local government the service nobility was given more power. However, the struggle with those who attempted to limit or share the power of the czar was not yet over. In 1564 one of Ivan's leading generals, Prince Andrei M. Kurbski (1528–1583), went over to the side of Lithuania. A most interesting correspondence between Kurbski and the czar ensued. The czar writes of the divine rights of kings, the prince replies by calling him a tyrant and accusing him of oppression (of the nobility). In 1565 the czar left Moscow and threatened to abdicate the throne in view of the prevalence of treason. As the price of his return he demanded broader powers with which to fight the boyars. The people of Moscow, the merchants and artisans, called the czar back, welcoming his intention to apply a reign of terror against the boyars. The realm was now officially divided into two parts, the one ruled by the czar directly, the other also ruled by him, but through the boyars. A special army (*oprichnina*) was recruited from petty noblemen, who received land from the czar. Its task was to eliminate treason. Members of leading feudal families were executed by the score. The head of the church, Metropolitan Philip, who pleaded for moderation, was jailed

49

and secretly done away with in captivity. In 1567 a vast boyar plot was discovered, and executions multiplied. The city of Novgorod and its archbishop wanted to secede and join Lithuania. The czar's troops stormed and looted the city, and Pskov also had to be militarily subdued. In 1571 the Crimean Tatars burned most of Moscow, but the next year, on a repeated raid, they were defeated, not by the czar's troops, but by the boyar generals. Treason was also discovered among the special troops, the *oprichniki,* which were abolished in 1572. What was in effect a civil war, conducted by Ivan against the remnants of feudal decentralization, consolidated the central authority of the czar, but also increased the power of the landed nobility as a class over the peasantry. The strengthening of the power of the throne was in the long run to the economic interest of the majority of the nobility, big and small, because the nobles could expand their landholdings and increase their power over the peasantry only through the support of the throne. Ivan strengthened autocracy, but also strengthened economically the broad landowning class, making conditions of servitude for the peasants much more severe.

During his long reign Ivan IV conducted long wars. During the reign of his father (Basil III) Kazan had allied itself with the Crimea and had broken off its dependence on Moscow. The service nobility needed more land, and the Kazan Tatars were a constant menace because of their raids. In addition, Kazan was on the road down the Volga to the Caspian Sea and also on the path to the Urals. In 1551 the Russians erected a city on the other side of the Volga, opposite Kazan, and the next year crossed the river and besieged Kazan. Well equipped with artillery and using foreign engineering aid, Ivan's troops blew up the walls and took the city on October 2, 1552. There followed the conquest of various non-Russian tribes living along the Volga, with more land grants to soldier noblemen and stricter attachment of peasants to the land. Local chieftains were often incorporated in the Russian service nobility. In 1555 the Russian penetration into Siberia, under the Cossack leader, Ermak (Yermak), resulted in the subjugation of western Siberia. In 1556 Astrakhan was taken, and the Russians emerged on the Caspian. An expedition to the Crimea down the Dnieper and Don followed, but this conquest had to be abandoned in view of the outbreak of the war in the north (1558). Thus under Ivan the Dread there began the expansion of Russia to the east, a process that continued into the first decade of the twentieth century. Ivan's conquests had another significance. Up to Ivan IV the princes of Moscow were trying to build a single national Russian state. Now, with the inclusion of the Volga Basin and parts of Siberia, the Russian state ceased to be a uninational state, and became multinational. This was an important new element in the history of the country. The reign of Ivan IV forms a dividing line between these two types of development of the state: national and multinational.

In the west Ivan was not successful. Although the German knights never really recovered from the defeat inflicted on them near Tannenberg in 1410, the Moscow state was still cut off from the Baltic by Lithuania and Livonia (the state of the knights). Lithuania, Sweden, Denmark, and Russia now all aspired to the territory of the knights. In 1558 the Russians went to war against Livonia, but their rapid initial successes involved Sweden, Poland, and Lithuania in the war. In pressing for annexation of all former possessions of the knights, Ivan was supported by a representative assembly of the nobility and clergy (*sobor*), which met in 1566. The danger from Russia prompted Poland and Lithuania to enter into a new union in Lublin (1569) under one elective king, thus strengthening considerably the Polish-Lithuanian state. The troops of Ivan proved incapable of defeating the western enemies with their superior training and equipment. Here the relative backwardness of Russia, due to the years of the Tatar subjugation and separation from the west, became quite obvious. The 25-year war (1558–1583) against Poland and Sweden brought no results. Russia did not succeed in breaking through to the sea in the west. This goal, to which Ivan devoted so much energy and labor, was destined to be reached only a century later, by Peter I.

Ivan IV was an intelligent and well-read man and had a sharp pen, but he was also cruel, suspicious, and temperamental. Educated contemporaries were particularly shocked by his brutality in suppressing the obstreperous high nobility. The people remembered him in their songs and tales as the czar who severely eradicated treason among the mighty. During his reign the first printing press appeared in Moscow, and the first printed book was published (1564), but a revolt of copyists smashed the press and forced the first printers to flee abroad. The conquest of Kazan was commemorated in Moscow by the erection of St.

Basil's Church, which still stands on Red Square. In 1553 the English, looking for a northern passage to India, by accident "rediscovered" Russia. Ivan established trade relations with England, founded the port of Archangel on the White Sea, and even had ideas of marrying Queen Elizabeth of England. By this time over 100 different crafts were practiced in Novgorod. The conquest of western Siberia offered great new trading possibilities, and the czar encouraged the merchant brothers, Yakov, Grigori, and Semyon Stroganov, in their trading ventures in the east. But the czar was also cruel and unreasonable; in a fit of temper he killed his son and heir. The lot of the peasantry grew more difficult; they were now firmly attached to the owners' land, being prohibited in 1581 from moving even on St. George's Day. Thus serfdom was made universal, legal, and complete; and those peasants who could not tolerate the burden fled to the borders, where they formed the armed settlements of freemen known as Cossacks. Internal peasant revolts now began to merge with revolts of conquered peoples. Having created a strong state against powerful opposition, Ivan had also sown the seeds of new social strife.

FOREIGN INTERVENTION AND PEASANT WARS . . . Ivan's successor was his son Fyodor (Fyodor I Ivanovich, r. 1584–1598), who behaved more like a monk than a sovereign. The actual ruler was the czar's brother-in-law, Boris Fyodorovich Godunov (1551?–1605), a man of considerable ability, who acquired prominence in the last years of Ivan IV's reign. The people regarded the new czar as feeble-minded. In 1589 the Russian Church, up till that time still formally under the patriarch of Constantinople, elected its first patriarch, thus severing its last, now purely nominal, ties of dependence. During Fyodor's reign Russia acquired from Sweden an exit to the Baltic (1595). When the czar died in 1598 the old Ryurik line was extinct, since another of Ivan's sons by a different wife was mysteriously murdered at the age of nine in 1591. Rumors blamed the murder on Godunov. Supported by the service nobility, Boris Godunov easily had himself made czar by acclamation. But his troubles had only begun. While Fyodor was still alive it had been decreed (1597) that any freeman who had worked for over six months for clothes and board automatically became a house serf (*kholop*). Serfdom was thus further expanded. In 1601 a famine broke out that lasted three years (1601–1603). Hungry peasants were raiding and looting. In 1603 a large detachment of peasants advanced toward Moscow under the leadership of Kosolap. Only with great difficulty, after a regular battle, did the czar's troops disperse the peasants. Peasants and house serfs fled by the thousands to the Don and the Ukraine. Thus opened up the period often referred to in Russia's history as the "troubled times."

In 1604 there appeared in Poland a young man who claimed—and apparently himself believed—that he was Dmitri, Ivan's son, whom the servants of Boris Godunov had allegedly failed to kill in 1591. He was received by the king of Poland, became a Roman Catholic, made territorial promises, and obtained the support of the Polish nobility. Entering Russia with a "volunteer" Polish detachment and some Cossacks, the false Dmitri, as he later became known, rallied all those dissatisfied with conditions in Russia. Although at first he suffered military reverses, unrest spread. In April, 1605, Czar Boris Godunov suddenly died, and in June the gates of Moscow were opened to Dmitri. In the spring of 1606 his Polish bride, Marina Mnishek, arrived with a large Polish guard. In May, 1606, an anti-Polish and anti-Catholic revolt broke out in Moscow, and the pretender was killed. Basil IV Shuiski (Vasili Ivanovich, r. 1606–1610), an old boyar, became czar, representing what remained of the feudal interests that Ivan had fought so hard.

Civil war now spread throughout the realm. Ivan Bolotnikov organized an army of serfs and Cossacks and barely missed taking Moscow. The service nobility first supported Bolotnikov, then switched over to Czar Shuiski. In 1607 the czar extended the number of years during which a runaway serf, if caught, had to be restored to his master from five years (the law of 1597) to fifteen years, but simultaneously he made all kinds of promises to the peasants to gain their support. On the Volga most of the subjugated national minorities revolted, and in the west appeared, in 1607, a false Dmitri II, who encamped near Moscow with a large army of Cossacks and Poles. Czar Shuiski appealed to the Swedes for aid, and Novgorod was occupied by a multinational mercenary army led by the Swedes. In the autumn of 1609 Poland officially declared war on Moscow and invaded Russia. The second pretender was no longer of any use to the Poles, who now advanced the claim of the king of Poland's son, later Wladislaw IV (r. 1632–1648), to the throne of Russia. The Polish nobility, having once united two states through a merger of crowns, now intended to unite three crowns—those of Poland, Lithuania, and Russia—on one head and build one Roman Catholic state, extending over all of eastern Europe. The boyars, frightened by the peasant war, began to pin their hopes on a Polish czar. In 1610 old Czar Shuiski was overthrown, and an interim government of "seven boyars" was set up. The latter, fearful of popular revolts, soon surrendered Moscow to the Poles. Although the Moscow state had now virtually fallen apart, the struggle was continued by the population.

Guerrilla warfare against the Poles spread. Smolensk held out against a siege by the main Polish forces for nearly two years. The patriarch (Hermogen) was imprisoned by the Poles, but his written appeal to rally the people for the defense of faith and fatherland was spread throughout all the cities. In 1611 a nobleman, Lyapunov, organized a people's army for the liberation of Moscow. This army, consisting of small noblemen and Cossacks, broke up over the question of land and serfs, and Lyapunov was killed. In the same year, in Nizhni-Novgorod on the Volga, the formation of a second people's army was begun. Its organizers were the merchant Kuzma Minin and Prince Dmitri M. Pozharski, who appealed to the entire country for money and men. The soldiers were fed and paid, and consisted not only of noblemen, Cossacks, and all kinds of city folk, but also of peasants, and even Tatars and many other non-Russians. In the early spring of 1612, when the people's army began moving in the direction of Moscow, money and men were coming in from all directions. In Yaroslavl a provisional government was set up. In August the army approached Moscow and engaged the Poles in battle. The Cossacks who were with the Poles first became passive and then joined the people's army. The battle was won, and the remainder of the Polish forces were besieged in Moscow, where hunger forced them to surrender on October 26, 1612. Moscow was liberated, and now the question of central authority had to be solved.

A representative assembly (*sobor*) was called; service nobility, townspeople, and Cossacks were in the majority; the boyars and clergy in the minority. It was first decided not to consider any foreign candidates to the throne. Finally, early in 1613, the choice fell on the 16-year-old Michael (Mikhail Fyodorovich) Romanov, politically an unknown quantity, whose family was related to Ivan IV and whose father had been forced to become a monk by Boris Godunov, taking the name

Philaret (Filaret). This is how the house of Romanov, which lasted until 1917, got its start. When Philaret returned from Polish captivity, he was elected patriarch; spiritual and temporal power were now held by father and son, respectively. But the fighting was far from over. After inflicting a defeat near Pskov (1615) on the famous Swedish military leader King Gustavus II Adolphus (r. 1611–1632), the Russians were in position to start peace negotiations, and with the aid of England and Holland peace with Sweden was concluded in 1617. With Poland an armistice was signed (for 14½ years) in 1618. Both deals involved territorial losses; Poland kept Smolensk, Sweden withdrew from Novgorod but regained the exit to the Baltic that had been obtained by Russia under Czar Fyodor. The upper layers of the Cossacks received increasing land grants and formed a Cossack nobility, which was more inclined to support law and order. Meanwhile, peasant and Cossack revolts continued, and the throne had to rely more than ever on the military service nobility. Drastic measures were undertaken to modernize the army. Regiments officered by foreign instructors and whole regiments of hired foreign soldiers were created. All this required money, and the major source of revenue was heavier exploitation of the peasant population. Moscow could not accept the loss of Smolensk and prepared for war. In 1632 Russian troops besieged Smolensk, led by the same Shein who defended the city so well in 1610–1611. The venture failed, and by a treaty of 1634 the Poles kept Smolensk but recognized the Romanov czar, thus abandoning their claims to the Russian throne. The Moscow state was gradually emerging from the "troubled times," or period of foreign intervention and peasant wars.

ON THE EVE OF REFORM . . . Alexis I (Aleksei Mikhailovich), the second Romanov czar (r. 1645–1676), was referred to as "the most quiet one," but his reign was filled with turbulent events. The country was still suffering from the aftermath of civil war, to which the burden of continued foreign wars was added. Since the throne was in constant need of funds, taxes were increased, particularly on the city population. Revolts followed, first in Moscow (1648), then in other cities. In its efforts to replenish the treasury and strengthen authority, the government appeared to be concentrating on the further expansion of serfdom. A runaway serf could now (1649) be forcibly returned to his master, regardless of when he was caught. Simultaneously capital punishment was introduced for crimes against the person of the czar, as well as severe penalties for insulting the sovereign. The throne was now surrounded by homage approaching that extended to a saint.

In the days of the Tatar yoke the church had been an important unifying element; it had aided in assembling the realm around Moscow and played an important role in the struggle against Polish intervention. Under Czar Michael Romanov (r. 1613–1645), while his father, Philaret, occupied the patriarchal throne, church and state were truly one. Under Alexis, however, the church came into conflict with the state and also developed an internal struggle. Patriarch Nikon, a most energetic man, undertook to reform the church ritual. This was to be accomplished by a revision of the church books, into which, during centuries of recopying, numerous changes had been introduced. Being an educated man, Nikon relied in this work on the advice of scholars, but his violent methods brought about a split in the church. Questions of ritual became matters of dogma: whether to cross oneself with two or three fingers became an important issue of faith. People were willing to die, and did die, for what they considered "the true old faith," as against Nikon's "innovations." The main defender of the "old faith," the archpriest Avvakum, a man just as outspoken as Nikon, was burned at the stake in 1681. His followers became known as the "old believers," a body that still exists. This more conservative form of worship appealed to many who found themselves in opposition to the throne and the Greek Orthodox Church for social and economic reasons. Thus the "schism" created an opposition church.

The czar supported Nikon's reforms and backed his punitive measures against the schismatics. But when Nikon began to advance the notion that the authority of the church is of a higher order than that of the throne, he soon came into conflict with the state. Following the example of Philaret, Nikon wanted to be addressed as "great sovereign"; he began to interfere in state and even military matters. All this ran counter to the traditions of Byzantine and Russian Christianity; Nikon was accused of "Latinism" and broke with Alexis. An assembly of bishops (*sobor*), with two eastern patriarchs in attendance, condemned Nikon (1666), and he was exiled as an ordinary monk, although his reforms of the ritual were upheld. Thus ended the attempt of the church to put itself above the state, which, together with the schism, weakened the church. The throne and the landowners wanted, of course, a strong church, but not so strong as to be a challenge to them, especially as the church was also a landowner in its own right. These events of the reign of Alexis may have been responsible for the relatively insignificant opposition that the church was able to muster against Czar Peter half a century later.

At the same time the war on the western borders continued, interrupted only by periodic armistices. The progress of this war was constantly hampered by insufficient funds and the attacks of other enemies. One of the reasons for the failure to recapture Smolensk in 1633 was the attack of the Crimean Tatars in the south. The Don Cossacks captured Azov from the Turks (1637), and even beat back a Turkish attempt to retake the city (1641), but upon orders from Moscow (1642) gave up Azov when the service nobility and the merchants made it plain that they could not provide the czar with means to go on with this war. In the west the Polish-Lithuanian state was now welded together more firmly (after the Union of Lublin, 1569), and the Polish landed nobility was increasing its power and expanding its landholdings. To the class conflict over land there was added, in Belorussia and the Ukraine, a religious issue. In the city of Brest a "union" (*unia*) of the Roman Catholic and Greek Orthodox churches was proclaimed (1596), sanctioned by the king of Poland, and the Polish landowners began to enforce this religious union on the Belorussian and Ukrainian population. Peasant revolts ensued, led by the Cossacks, who elected their chiefs (hetmans) and enjoyed a good deal of autonomy. After several such revolts all Cossack liberties were "for all time" abrogated by the Polish Diet (1638), and ten years of "golden tranquillity" followed. In 1648 the Ukraine rose under a new leader, Bogdan Khmelnitski, Ukr. Khmelnitzky (1593–1657). The intensity of the struggle was indicated by the fact that the Vatican granted absolution from sins to those who fought against the Cossacks, and the hard-pressed Khmelnitski even allied himself for a time with the old traditional enemies of the Cossacks, the Crimean Tatars. But the Polish-Ukrainian war of 1648–1651 demonstrated that the Ukraine could not defeat Poland alone. When Moscow offered (1653) to come to the aid of the Ukraine, Khmelnitski proposed to the Cossacks that they choose from among four sovereigns: the sultan (Turkey), the khan (Crimea), the king (Poland), and the eastern czar (Moscow). The Cossacks voted for the Greek Orthodox czar of the east. Russia now began a war to wrest from Poland not only the Ukraine but also Belorussia. Soon Smolensk was taken and the Russians occupied most of Belorussia, but Sweden entered the war on the side of Poland. After 13 years of fighting (1654–1667) both Russia and Poland were exhausted, and an armistice (for 13½ years) was signed. Smolensk was retained by Russia, and so were parts of the Ukraine and Belorussia, but only in 1686 did Poland cede Kiev to Russia "for all time." On the whole the results did not satisfy Russia; the peace with Sweden (1661) again did not grant Russia an exit to the sea, and Poland remained a formidable foe.

Czar Alexis did much to improve the Russian Army. The old militia consisting of petty noblemen was badly disciplined, and occasionally simply refused to fight. Already in the sixteenth century there were organized special troops equipped with firearms, the *streltsy*, who lived in Moscow and engaged in handicraft and retail trade between wars. But these troops often joined city revolts. Foreign mercenary regiments also proved unreliable, and Alexis created Russian regiments with foreign officers. Toward the end of his reign Alexis had 60 regiments trained according to western standards.

The czar was also constantly troubled by internal warfare. The large expenditures incurred in the war with Poland led, in 1654, to the issuance of copper coins (previously only silver had circulated). A rapid rise in prices followed, which led to what became known as the "copper revolt" in Moscow (1662). On the Volga and farther east the numerous non-Russian population staged several revolts, some of which were suppressed only with difficulty by the foreign-trained regulars. On the Don the Cossack settlements were being constantly augmented by serfs and others escaping from the more populated regions. In the spring of 1667 a big revolt of the poorer Cossack elements under the leadership of Stepan Razin spread from the Don to the Volga. Razin's forces first invaded Persia, sinking a large part of the Persian Navy on the Caspian, then took Astrakhan and began an expedition up the Volga (1670). The Cossacks, as they advanced, were joined by peasants in revolt, and Razin also appealed to the various non-Russian minorities to rise against the czar, which they did. To meet this new danger, which involved a very large territory, Czar Alexis had to mobilize the nobility in addition to the foreign-trained regiments. In 1671 Razin was defeated, captured, brought to Moscow, and executed on the Red Square. Razin's revolt was essentially a social war between peasants and Cossacks, joined by other dissatisfied elements, including non-Russian minorities and "old believers," on the one hand, and the landed nobility, the czar's boyars and administrators, on the other. This primarily serf revolution was chaotic, had no positive program, and did not manage to establish firm contacts with dissident city elements. The better-disciplined and organized forces of the central government suppressed the revolution methodically in one area after another. The Stepan Razin revolt was the first large-scale peasant war against the nobility; a century later (in the reign of Catherine II) another such war, led by Emelian I. Pugachyov, was again seriously to threaten the throne, and to fail for the same reasons.

In the reign of Alexis serfdom finally became all-prevailing and, although legally very different from slavery, in practice came to resemble it rather closely. At the same time the cities grew and manufacturing developed. A Hollander, Vinius, began mining iron ore near Tula in 1632; a glass factory was established near Moscow; and a distinct merchant class, receiving charters from the czar, began to be formed. The nobility and the city inhabitants were often called into representative assemblies (*zemski sobor*) to advise the czar. Such an assembly elected the first Romanov and met almost constantly during his reign. The higher nobility formed the boyar Duma, which was also a consultative body, over which the czar presided in person. Near Moscow a large foreign suburb arose, the "German settlement." At the court of Alexis a good deal of western influence made itself felt, but the population as a whole remained untouched by these Occidental innovations.

At the same time the eastward penetration continued. In 1632 what was later to become Yakutsk was settled; in 1652 a settlement, now the city Irkutsk, was founded near Lake Baikal. In 1643 an expedition was sent to the Amur, and in 1648 the Russians reached the Pacific opposite Alaska. On the Amur an armed conflict soon developed between the Cossacks and the Chinese, which led to the first Russo-Chinese treaty, signed in 1689.

Czar Alexis was both a very inquisitive man, interested in all kinds of western innovations, more advanced techniques, and even education in mathematics and the exact sciences, and at the same time a very cautious and deeply religious man, who spent much time in observing all types of traditional and religious ritual. The old and the new were curiously combined in this one person. The need for a thorough modernization of Russia seemed to have been obvious to several of the czar's advisers. For instance, Afanasi L. Ordin-Nashchokin (d. 1680) had plans for far-reaching reforms along western lines. Alexis listened, even went so far as to investigate personally some of the products of the west—for instance, he installed a theater in the palace. But the czar was reluctant to do anything drastic, and at the end of his long reign Russia was still on the eve of reform. Changes, long overdue, came later and all at once through his much more energetic son, Peter I, who was not at all tied to the traditions of the past.

THE GREAT REFORMER . . . Alexis was succeeded by his 14-year-old son Fyodor III Alekseyevich (r. 1676–1682), a youth weak in will and body. When Fyodor died his half brother Peter was proclaimed czar (1682). But there was a revolt in Moscow, and in the same year two boy czars were installed, the brothers Ivan V and Peter I (Pyotr Alekseyevich, r. 1682–1725), who later became known as Peter the Great, with their sister Sophia as regent. Her prime minister, Prince Vasili V. Golitsyn (1643–1714), was a well-educated man who engaged in conversations with foreigners about the need for basic reforms. In 1682 the genealogical books, on the basis of which it used to be decided who could serve under whom, were burned. In 1687 the Slavo-Greco-Latin Academy was established in Moscow. In 1686 the Poles finally signed an "eternal peace" with Russia, and an Austrian-Russian-Polish alliance was formed against the Turks. However, two expeditions (1687 and 1689) against the Crimean Tatars, vassals of the Turkish sultan, under Golitsyn, failed. Dissatisfaction with Sophia's rule was mounting. In 1689 the young Peter (b. 1672) overthrew his sister, removed his co-czar Ivan, and assumed full power.

While living in semiexile near Moscow with his mother during his sister's regency, Peter had not received the education traditional for a Russian czar. The youth engaged in war games with the boys of the adjoining villages and had friends among the foreigners. Gradually two youthful regiments were formed and trained as regulars according to western standards. Peter also found an old sailboat in a barn, and after

60

beginning to sail it on a lake, with the aid of his foreign friends, he decided that Russia must have a real navy on the big sea. At first Sophia was glad that Peter was "wasting his time" and not receiving a traditional education. Later she became worried by the military power growing about him. The two youthful regiments, later to become the first two regiments of the imperial guard (Preobrazhenski and Semyonovski), played a decisive role in Sophia's overthrow.

After assuming power the 17-year-old Peter became a frequent visitor in the "German settlement" near Moscow. Franz Timmerman from Holland instructed him in arithmetic, geometry, artillery. Patrick Gordon, an old Scottish general, told him about military campaigns, and the jolly Swiss, Francis Lefort, arranged parties. Peter journeyed to Archangel to take a good look at the sea. In 1695 he went south to take Azov from the Turks, but the expedition failed; only the two guard regiments fought well, and there was no navy. All that winter Peter spent building a navy at Voronezh, and in the spring of 1696, to the great surprise of the Turks, he sailed down the Don. Azov was besieged from land and sea, and taken.

In 1697 a large Russian mission went abroad, with Peter enlisted among its members as "Sergeant Peter Mikhailov." He visited Prussia; worked as a carpenter in Holland, learning the art of shipbuilding; went to France and England, where he even attended a session of Parliament; and then to Vienna. While studying arts and crafts, Peter did not neglect diplomacy. In Vienna he sounded out the emperor on another alliance against the Turks, and in Poland he made a deal with the king against the Swedes. In the summer of 1698, while Peter was away, four regiments of irregulars (*streltsy*) tried to capture Moscow and install Sophia as czarina. Gordon easily suppressed the mutiny, but Peter decided to hurry home and appeared near Moscow unannounced, ready for drastic measures in general. The next morning no one was allowed to kneel before the czar; during the reception Peter took a pair of scissors and began cutting off the beards of his visitors, and soon an order was issued prohibiting long sleeves and robes for men. The czar had decided to change everything and would brook no delays. Outside Sophia's window 195 rebels were executed, and executions went on throughout the city. The *streltsy* troops were disbanded and Sophia forced to become a nun.

61

In 1700 the "great northern" war against Sweden began. Poland and Denmark were allied with Peter. The first encounter with the Swedes, led by King Charles XII (r. 1697–1718), was disastrous, the Russians suffering a crushing defeat near Narva. Charles XII now devoted his attention to Poland, giving Peter time to organize a new army. One third of all the church bells were confiscated to make cannon, and conscription was introduced. In 1701 the Russians began to advance, soon reaching the Baltic. In 1703 St. Petersburg, the new capital, was founded on the banks of the Neva, and in the same year the first sea-going Russian man-of-war was launched. Peter was preparing for a naval war with Sweden. All this cost money, taxation stifled trade, and in 1705 the city of Astrakhan revolted and was subdued only after a siege. Cossack self-rule, formerly useful to Moscow as a frontier protection, now did not fit in very well with Peter's idea of a centralized and militarily powerful state. In 1707 and 1708 a Cossack revolt against the czar's administrators in the Don area had to be subdued by force. In 1708 an attempt by the Bashkirs to split off from Russia was defeated by the czar's troops. By 1711 all the popular revolts had been quelled.

In 1707 the Swedes, having defeated Poland, began their march into Russia. Instead of proceeding against Moscow, Charles XII turned south (1708) into the Ukraine. The Ukrainian hetman, Ivan S. Mazepa (1644?–1709) betrayed Peter and went over to Charles, but the population remained loyal and engaged in guerrilla warfare against the Swedes. In the fall of 1708 a large detachment of Swedes, coming with supplies for the king, was intercepted. The big battle took place in the following summer (1709) near Poltava in the Ukraine. The Swedish Army was annihilated, and Charles and Mazepa fled to Turkey. What was then considered the best army in Europe had received a crushing defeat; as a result of the Poltava victory Russia became the foremost military force. Poland and Denmark again entered into an alliance with Russia, soon to be joined by Prussia. In 1714 the young Russian Navy commanded by Peter achieved a decisive victory over the Swedish fleet near Hangö, Finland. Another naval victory in 1720 ensured Russia's mastery in the Baltic. The great northern war ended in 1721; Sweden's power was broken, and Russia was firmly established on the sea with the occupation of Vyborg (now Viipuri), Narva, Reval (now Tallinn), and Riga. In the same year Peter assumed the title of emperor (*imperator*), and in this way the Russian Empire came into being.

Thus the first major problem of foreign policy which Peter inherited, the Swedish or access-to-the-Baltic problem, was solved by him most decisively. He had less success with the second problem that had occupied his predecessors, the Turkish or access-to-the-Black Sea problem. After the victory of Poltava, the Russians marched against Turkey (1710). When Peter was surrounded by superior Turkish forces on the river Prut (1711), he returned Azov to Turkey, thus saving the army and obtaining peace. The Turks apparently did not realize the militarily critical situation into which Peter had let himself slide. Only a half-century later did the Russians establish themselves on the Black Sea. The third major issue of the past, the Russo-Polish struggle, now assumed a new aspect. With Poland's growing internal weakness Russia's role in Poland's internal affairs increased, Peter promoting a king of his own choice for Poland against a rival friendly to Sweden. In the east Russian penetration continued, though with varying success. A Russian military expedition into Central Asia was annihilated (1716), but the czar himself was successful in his campaign on the western shores of the Caspian (1722). Siberian penetration continued, and the Bering Straits were discovered (by a Dane of that name in the Russian service) in the course of an expedition prepared under Peter (1728–1730).

Peter made Russia into a first-class military and naval power. He established the imperial guard and an army of long-term conscripts from the basic Russian population, the peasantry. The army was 200,000 strong, excluding the Cossacks, and was divided into about 130 regiments. The Baltic fleet included 48 large vessels and numerous small craft. Like his famous adversary, Charles XII, the czar was a believer in mobile warfare, discarding the then traditional practice of "holding on" to fortresses. Bayonets were introduced for the infantry, earth fortifications erected on battlefields, closed battle formations adopted, and regimental artillery was used. The supply service was made mobile, and the tactics of scorching the earth before the advancing enemy introduced. Peter not only increased Russia's military power numerically, but he also placed the fighting skill of Russia's armed forces on a level equal to the best in Europe.

Having brought Russia back into Europe (as in the days of the Kiev state), Peter also introduced radical changes in the internal life of the country. The old boyar Duma no longer met, and the old formula, "the czar directed and the boyars decided," no longer applied; Peter now issued orders in his own name. A committee was created (1711) to be known as the "governing senate," which was both an executive and legislative body, with a "procurator-general" supervising, for the senate, all government institutions. The government was departmentalized (1718) into "collegiums" (first 9, later 12), in charge of foreign affairs, army, admiralty, finance, trade, manufacturing, mining, justice, etc. The country was divided into provinces: at first eight large ones (1708), and then fifty smaller ones (1719), with a uniform administrative setup. The governors and other officials were appointed by the czar.

All the nobility was welded into one body. The difference between the service nobility, with land tenure conditioned on services rendered, and the older landed aristocracy (boyars and princes) was disappearing. Service to the state on a salaried basis became compulsory for the nobility. One third was to enter the civilian service, two thirds the army and navy. In 1722 there was introduced the "table of ranks" classifying all functionaries, civilian and military, into fourteen ranks determined not by ancestry but by services performed. An entirely new stratum entered the nobility. Peter's closest collaborator and friend, Alexander D. Menshikov (1672?–1729), is said to have started out as a pie salesman; the dreaded procurator-general, Pavel I. Yaguzhinski (1683–1736), as a swineherd; and foreign affairs were managed by Peter P. Shafirov (1669–1739), a Jew who began life as a clerk in a store. Among the civilian and military functionaries, members of the old aristocracy and Peter's self-made nobility, often of most humble origins, were mixed with many foreigners who had entered the Russian service. Peter bestowed the western European titles of count and baron, in addition to the only previously existing Russian title, that of prince.

The old Church Slavonic script was modernized into a secular alphabet (1708) in which technical and historical works began to appear. The first Russian newspaper was published (1703) and the Julian calendar was adopted (1700), after which New Year no longer came on

September 1 and the years were no longer counted from the "creation of the world," as before. Youths of the nobility were made to study arithmetic, geometry, shipbuilding, and foreign languages, and severe whippings were inflicted on those who failed in these efforts. A theater was opened (1702) and later a museum, where "monstrosities and rarities" were exhibited by order of the czar. The building of St. Petersburg was carried on with foreign architects, who completely revolutionized the style of Russian building. The court had to dress in accordance with western customs, and Peter introduced social gatherings, called assemblies, at which attendance of both men and women was compulsory. The uniforms of the army and navy were patterned after those of Sweden and other European countries, and the Russian language absorbed many Dutch, English, German, and other foreign terms.

When in 1700 the patriarch (Adrian) died, Peter postponed the election of a new head of the church. The memory of Nikon's fight with Czar Alexis was still alive, and Peter did not want this experience repeated. In 1721 there was formed the "most holy governing synod," a committee of bishops (after the German Protestant pattern) that was to head the church. To this body was assigned an *oberprokurator*, a secular official appointed by the czar. Thus the emperor became in effect the head of the church, and the church itself a department of the government, which it remained up to 1917. To lower the prestige of the church Peter, although a believer himself, from time to time staged parodies on church functions, with street processions of drunks in bishops' vestments. Weakened by the schism and the unsuccessful fight against the throne under Patriarch Nikon, the church could not put up an effective resistance and, as an independent force, passed out of Russian history as long as the empire lasted.

Peter encouraged trade, manufacturing, shipbuilding, and mining. In 1721 merchants were allowed to purchase serfs, thus initiating "factory-serfdom." Toward the end of Peter's reign 240 manufactories were in operation, and in the 1720's occurred the first strike in Russia, in a Moscow wool-cloth manufacturing establishment. The first beginnings of manufacturing in the Urals were made. Peter also saw the possibilities offered by internal waterways, and the building of canals to connect rivers was begun in his reign. In 1703 the first foreign merchant vessel came to St. Petersburg; in 1724 the number of foreign ships arriving with merchandise was around 200. In his economic thinking Peter was a mercantilist, a strong believer in protective tariffs and in government participation and encouragement of trade and production. The first Russian writer on economic subjects, Ivan T. Pososhkov (1670–1726), was a contemporary and admirer of Peter.

A poll tax was imposed on the entire population, necessitating a census, which was carried out by the military authorities with an iron hand. The poll tax still further increased the power of the landowners over the peasantry, since the former were responsible for seeing that the tax was paid. In the cities merchants and artisans were organized into "guilds," into whose hands the city administration was placed, with the highest taxpayers playing the leading role.

The czar was a man of extraordinary energy, of unusual physical strength, and most versatile accomplishments. He not only studied constantly, but worked at numerous crafts. As a ruler his methods were often drastic and cruel. Even the senate was afraid of the czar's club, and his friend Prince Menshikov received many a beating. In his campaign against Russia's backwardness he was often crude. For instance, for "culture's sake" people were forced not only to study but to smoke and drink coffee, dance and be merry, visit the museum, and so on. The czar even entertained the notion that he was no mean dentist; he loved to extract teeth with pliers. Peter was a gay man and liked heavy drinking, his parties often lasting for several days. Reform, long overdue in all phases of life, now came all at once, like a flood breaking a dam. Peter wanted to eradicate backwardness everywhere, and in fighting bigotry and corruption he was particularly ruthless. He hated traditionalism of all kinds and refused to tolerate cowardice and dishonesty. Having "cut a window to Europe" by establishing himself on the Baltic, having made Russia an important European power, Peter upset all old customs and traditions, and his activity affected every class throughout the realm.

All this, of course, aroused opposition. Rumors were spread that Peter was "antichrist" and that the end of the world was at hand. Some of the clergy and the old boyar families encouraged these rumors. Having divorced and sent to a nunnery his first wife, a religious and tradition-bound noblewoman, Peter married a Lutheran peasant girl and crowned her empress (later Catherine I). His son by the first marriage, Alexis, was the hope of all those favoring a return to the past. Alexis fled abroad, seeking foreign aid, but was returned, tried, and condemned to death for treason. He died in jail, probably as a result of too ardent questioning under the whip. To the merchants, shipbuilders, manufacturers, and artisans Peter was a great czar. Rank, fame, and riches became wide-open to the ambitious and hardworking, and the self-made nobility also supported Peter, as did the new large conscript army and navy. The "old believers," his most bitter enemies, and all other adherents of the traditional past were far too disunited to challenge the emperor in earnest. Peter died in 1725, without leaving a direct heir or will, but having issued a law (1722) that the czar should appoint his own successor. He had established a strong, centralized nobility-and-merchant empire, and imposed western European forms, but at the end of his reign the lot of the enserfed peasantry had grown even harder. The great reformer died in the midst of his work, surrounded with the beginnings of the new arising everywhere amidst the old. He also apparently succeeded in splitting for a long time to come Russian thinkers and historians on the question of evaluating the significance of his eventful reign for the development of Russia.

RUSSIA IN THE EIGHTEENTH CENTURY . . . Peter's heritage fell into the hands of a series of sovereigns who were often surrounded by courtiers of limited ability, with the court squandering enormous sums on high living. The nobility of the capital, serving in the guards regiments, staged one palace revolution after another. In this period (1725–1762) of many rulers and several violent overthrows, the process of modernization begun by Peter was neglected.

Catherine I (r. 1725–1727), Peter's second wife, was put on the throne by his close collaborators and a threat of force by the guard. Then a compromise was arrived at between the "new nobility" and the old aristocracy, who together formed a "supreme secret council" to advise the empress. Under Catherine, the Russian Academy of Sciences created by Peter was officially opened (1725). The next czar was Peter II (Pyotr Alekseyevich, r. 1727–1730), a young grandson (b. 1715) of the great reformer. At first Menshikov did all the ruling and intended to make the czar his son-in-law. But soon Menshikov was exiled, and other families began to dominate the czar. When Peter II died the "supreme secret council" decided to invite Anna Ivanovna (r. 1730–1740), a niece of Peter the Great, to be empress, sidestepping Elizabeth, daughter of Peter I. The members of the council, all large landowners, were bent on limiting the power of the sovereign, as the nobility had succeeded in doing in England and Sweden. Anna was presented with a list of "conditions" and signed them, in effect transferring all power to the large landowners of the "supreme secret council." This caused indignation among the broader nobility layers, and the guard offered to support Anna against the council. The empress tore up the "conditions" and began to rule as an autocrat. Anna, a widowed duchess of Kurland, brought with her a strong German influence, exercised through Ernst J. Biron (1690–1772), a stubborn and uneducated man. The court and administration became Germanized, while the empress indulged in amusements. The Russian nobility who had saved Anna's autocratic prerogatives had to be paid off. Compulsory service for the nobility was limited to 25 years, and a special school graduated noblemen's sons directly into officers' ranks. However, the Russian nobility regarded Anna's reign (1730–1740) as tantamount to a German occupation. Together with Austria Russia fought Turkey (1735–1739), but in spite of large sacrifices failed to gain access to the Black Sea.

After Anna's death a three-month-old boy was proclaimed emperor, with Biron as regent. The latter was soon deposed with the aid of the guard, and the child emperor's mother, a princess of Braunschweig, became regent. In 1741 Elizabeth (Elizaveta Petrovna, r. 1741–1761), daughter of Peter the Great, with the aid of the guard overthrew the child czar and his mother, and became empress. She was also supported by the French, who were interested in terminating the "German yoke" in Russia. Under Elizabeth the privileges of the nobility were further expanded; landowners were allowed to exile serfs to Siberia without trial; and a nobility land bank was established. The empress tried to follow in the footsteps of her great father, but various amusements took up much of her time. Elizabeth was strongly anti-German in both internal and external affairs. Russia participated in the Seven Years' War (1756–1763) of France, Austria, and Saxony against Frederick II (r. 1740–1786), known as Frederick the Great of Prussia, who was supported by England. In 1757 the Russian Army won an important victory in Prussia, in 1759 Frederick was again very badly defeated, and in 1760 the Russians occupied Berlin. Prussia's position was hopeless, but in 1761 Elizabeth died, and the new czar, Peter III (Pyotr Fyodorovich, r. 1761–1762), an admirer of everything Prussian, promptly withdrew from the war, saving Frederick.

The first great Russian scientist, poet, and painter, Mikhail V. Lomonosov (1711–1765), was one of the outstanding figures of this period and was influential in the establishment of the University of Moscow (1755). The penetration to the east also continued. By 1732 the Russians were firmly established in Kamchatka. The Bashkirs revolted in 1735 and again in 1755, and the suppression of these revolts led to greater Russian interference in the affairs of Central Asiatic kingdoms.

Peter III, an eccentric prince of Holstein, concluded peace with Prussia and began to prepare for war with Denmark in the interests of the Holstein dynasty and Prussia. To appease the Russian nobility Peter issued a law on the "freedom of the nobility" (1762), releasing the latter from compulsory service in the army, navy, and administration. The existence of selfdom had been justified on the ground that the nobility had to serve the state and consequently the peasants had to serve the nobility. Now the nobility was released from compulsory service to the state, and rumors began to circulate that the law had a logical sequel, a provision freeing the peasants from serfdom, but that the nobility had suppressed that part of the law. The blatant pro-Germanism of Peter III, however, led to a plot by the Russian nobility against him. In the summer of 1762 the czar was overthrown and murdered. The guard elevated his wife, a petty German princess, to the throne as Empress Catherine II (Ekaterina Alekseyevna), later referred to as Catherine the Great (r. 1762–1796). Although not a Russian by birth, Catherine followed a pro-Russian policy and regarded the Russian nobility as her main base.

By the beginning of Catherine's reign everything had reached a state of decay. The treasury was empty, the army unpaid, ships and fortresses were falling apart, graft permeated everywhere, jails were full, and thousands of serfs were in revolt. Catherine was a believer in "enlightened absolutism." She corresponded with Voltaire and Diderot, wrote plays, and even participated in the publication of a literary journal. The empress created a commission to draft new laws, following the ideas of Montesquieu. The commission, consisting of noblemen and wealthy city people, met in Moscow (1767), but nothing came of it, as the nobility was interested primarily in a further broadening of its rights and privileges. Catherine herself, although she entertained some very advanced ideas, wanted also to protect her power by further strengthening the nobility, which had raised her to the throne.

Catherine resumed the policies of Peter the Great. The empire was expanded farther, and Russia began to play a very active part in European affairs. By this time the internal affairs of Poland had reached a high stage of disintegration. In 1763 an openly pro-Russian king was installed. By 1768 Russia practically dictated to the government of Poland. Other powers interfered in order to weaken Russia's influence. East Prussia was joined to Prussia, Austria took Galicia, and Russia acquired large parts of Belorussia. This was the first partition of Poland (1773). Russia's activities in Poland, plus prompting by France, caused Turkey to declare war. The first Turkish war (1768–1774) began by an invasion of Russia by the Crimean Tatars. Gen. Peter A. Rumyantsev (1725–1796) defeated the Tatars (1770) and then marched against the Turks beyond the Danube. The Russian Navy sailed around Europe into the Mediterranean and destroyed the Turkish Navy near the coast of Asia Minor (1770). All of the Crimea was occupied (1771), and by the peace treaty of 1774 Russia established herself on the Black Sea and the Crimea became "independent" of Turkey. In 1783 the Crimea was absorbed by Russia, and Potyomkin was building forts and trying to settle the steppes. Soon the second Turkish war began (1787–1791). In 1789 Gen. Alexander V. Suvorov (1730–1800) twice defeated the Turks; in 1790 he took the fortress of Izmail by storm, which decided the outcome of the war. By the peace of 1791 Russia was firmly entrenched on the Black Sea. During this war Sweden tried to regain her lost position of dominance on the Baltic (1788–1790) but failed. The border between the two countries remained unchanged. Thus under Catherine Russia was finally and firmly established both as a Baltic and as a Black Sea power, completing the original scheme of Peter the Great.

The misfortunes that were befalling Poland under its antiquated internal regime brought about the adoption of a liberal constitution in that country (1791). Prussia and Russia were now afraid that Poland would follow France's revolutionary lead. The Poles could not withstand the Russian Army, and in 1793 the second partition of Poland took place, large territories going over to Russia and Prussia. The Poles rallied under Gen. Thaddeus Kosciusko (1746–1817), a hero of the American Revolutionary War, but the Prussians took Cracow (1794) and in the same year the Russians were in Warsaw. In 1795 Poland was partitioned for the third time by Russia, Prussia, and Austria, and disappeared from the map of Europe as an independent state for over a century.

The partitions of Poland were accompanied by the final absorption of the Ukraine by Russia (with the exception of Galicia, which was taken over by Austria). The rule of the hetman, or the elective Ukrainian sovereign, was abolished (1764), the Dnieper Cossacks were suppressed (1775), the country was divided into provinces (1780), and the poll tax introduced (1783), together with the equalization of the Ukrainian and Russian nobility and the full establishment of serfdom. This process was paralleled by Ukrainian peasant revolts against the Polish nobility (1734 and 1768), which were suppressed by Russian troops.

Catherine feared peasant revolts, even when directed against Polish noblemen, not without cause. In 1773 a Don Cossack, Emelian I. Pugachyov, proclaimed that he was Czar Peter III whom his wife (Catherine) and the nobility had tried to kill, but allegedly without success. Pugachyov declared that he was going to grant freedom to the serfs, the freedom that the nobility were supposed to have deleted from the law of 1762. Although Pugachyov was obviously not the late Peter III, the people rallied to this "good czar." The revolt was joined by Cossacks, peasants, factory serfs, and oppressed national minorities, resulting in a full-fledged peasant war, very similar to that of Stepan Razin a century before under Czar Alexis. In 1774 Pugachyov besieged Kazan, and for a time it appeared that there was a threat to Moscow. However, the regular army defeated Pugachyov, who was captured and executed in Moscow (1775). The peasant war failed, but the entire foundation of serfdom, the basic social institution of the empire, had been openly challenged. Catherine was frightened, and so was the landed nobility.

As a result far-reaching measures were taken to strengthen the land-owning class (1775 and 1785). The entire local administration was to be rooted in the nobility, which received very wide self-government privileges. The administration assumed the aspect of a highly centralized government by the landowners. Catherine was referred to as the "nobility's czarina," and her reign as the "golden era" of serf-owning nobility. The empress granted much new land to the nobility and gave away about 800,000 serfs. In 1764 vast landholdings of the monasteries were confiscated. This measure served not only to increase very substantially the fund of land and serfs in the possession of the state, but also still further to increase the subjugation of the church to the state by materially weakening the monasteries, whose power had disturbed Russian sovereigns as early as the reign of Ivan III. Landowners received the right to exile peasants into chain gangs for "impertinence" (1765), and peasants were prohibited from filing complaints against landowners (1767). Serfs were sold on the open market, exchanged for hunting dogs, and one noblewoman is known to have tortured to death about 140 women and girls over a ten-year period. Factory serfs were made to work up to 16 hours a day and often rebelled. About half of all the peasants of Russia were now noblemen's serfs; the rest were owned by the state, by the imperial family, and by a special government department administering properties taken away from the church. Serfdom had reached its pinnacle.

The French Revolution (1789) profoundly disturbed Catherine, who now completely repudiated the Voltairian ideas of her youth. The cause of the king of France is the cause of all sovereigns—this became Catherine's slogan. At home the empress decided to fight all symptoms of "French infection." When Alexander N. Radishchev (1749–1802) published his *Journey from St. Petersburg to Moscow* (1790), the first Russian book attacking serfdom and autocracy, Catherine saw in the author a "villain worse than Pugachyov." Radishchev was first condemned to death, then exiled to Siberia. Another outstanding cultural figure of the day, Nikolai I. Novikov (1744–1818), the first to distribute books in Russia on a large scale, also went to Siberia. All that

72

was connected with the spirit of the French era of enlightenment was now persecuted in Russia. Just before she died Catherine was getting ready to send a large army into France to suppress the revolutionary "mutiny."

In spite of the reactionary turn after the Pugachyov uprising and the French Revolution, Catherine's reign was marked by an important cultural development. Several schools were opened, and the first significant Russian writers appeared, such as Alexander P. Sumarokov (1718–1777), Denis I. Fonvizin (1745–1792), and Gavriil R. Derzhavin (1743–1816). Drama and chamber music were cultivated. The extensive building of palaces and mansions helped to develop architecture. In military and naval science Russia began to occupy the leading place in Europe. In addition to Admiral Fyodor F. Ushakov (1743–1817) and General Rumyantsev, Catherine's reign produced a military leader of extraordinary ability in Field Marshal Suvorov, who in respect to many of his military arts was a precursor of Napoleon. During this period the population of the empire reached 37,000,000, and the army grew to half a million.

After Catherine's sudden death the throne went to her son Paul I (Pavel Petrovich, r. 1796–1801), an eccentric autocrat and, like his father, Peter III, an ardent admirer of all things Prussian. The army was reorganized after the Prussian fashion, the importation of books, and even of music, from abroad was prohibited, and the new emperor decided to discipline the nobility, as well as everybody else. During Paul's reign peasant revolts occurred in 32 out of 52 provinces. At first Paul withdrew from the war against revolutionary France; later he assumed the leadership of the Knights of Malta, who were dislodged by Napoleon Bonaparte, and the Russian Navy under Ushakov was active in the Mediterranean, where it won an important victory over the French (1798). Like his mother Catherine, Paul believed that Russia should have a firm naval foothold in the Mediterranean. In 1799 an alliance of Russia, England, Austria, and Turkey was formed against France. In the war that ensued Suvorov conquered northern Italy (while Napoleon was in Egypt) and then made his unprecedented march across the Alps. But Austria did not like Russia's victory in Italy, nor did England enjoy having Russian naval activities in the Mediterranean, and the alliance broke up. Paul wrote a letter to General Bonaparte and began preparing an expedition against India. In 1801 came the peaceful annexation of Georgia to Russia.

Paul's reversal of Russia's external policy, together with his eccentricities, set most of the nobility against him. In the spring of 1801 a group of guard officers killed the emperor. His son Alexander, a favorite grandson of Catherine, assumed the throne upon Russia's entry into the nineteenth century.

CONTINUED GROWTH AND BEGINNING OF DECLINE OF THE EMPIRE . . . Czar Alexander I (Aleksandr Pavlovich, r. 1801-1825) was a pupil of the republican-minded Swiss Frederic C. de La Harpe (1754–1838), but also a friend of Aleksei A. Arakcheyev (1769–1834), one of his father's most ruthless generals. Contemporaries spoke of the czar as "half a Swiss citizen, half a Prussian corporal." This duality was characteristic of his reign. The opening years witnessed many innovations. Merchants and other nonnoblemen were allowed to buy unsettled land (1801), noblemen were permitted to liberate their serfs with land (1803), a cabinet was created with several ministries (1802), and the senate became the highest judicial body of the empire (1802). A group of young personal friends of Alexander formed a "secret committee for the drafting of projects for reform." These reforms, however, did not go very far. More was done in the field of education, with universities opened (1805) in Kharkov and Kazan. The first years of this reign also witnessed the beginning of canal building, which went on for several years, and the opening of a bank in Moscow to finance commerce (1807). Trade and industry were growing, and the government had to take cognizance of this fact, but the crucial problem of serfdom remained untouched; only about one half of one per cent of all the serfs obtained freedom under the law of 1803. The ideas of reform were carried quite far by Mikhail M. Speranski (Speranskii, 1772–1839), privy councilor, who projected an elective Duma and a Cabinet responsible to this body. The nobility regarded Speranski as "a scoundrel, a revolutionary and a Cromwell." Only an upper house, the Council of State, appointed by the emperor, was formed (1810), and Speranski, the "dangerous reformer," who even wrote about "individual freedom" for serfs, was removed (1812).

While reformers and conservatives were struggling at court, the power of Napoleon was rising, and soon this issue overshadowed all

74

others. A new coalition against France included England, Austria, Sweden, and Russia, and in 1805 war broke out. In the same year the Russians suffered a defeat in the Battle of Austerlitz, fought by Alexander against the better advice of Mikhail I. Kutuzov (1745–1813), one of Suvorov's pupils. Two very bloody battles in 1807 (at Preussisch Eylau and Friedland in East Prussia) demonstrated that neither side could decisively defeat the other. In the summer of 1807 Napoleon and Alexander met in Tilsit and a treaty was signed. Russia was to join in Napoleon's "continental blockade" against England, a move that was ruinous to the nobility, for whom England was a market for grain and a source of manufactured goods. The peace of Tilsit led to a Russo-Swedish war (Sweden refusing to join Napoleon's blockade against England), in the course of which the Russians marched into Sweden across a frozen part of the Baltic Sea (1808). In Finland the nobility took Russia's side; and in 1809 the czar guaranteed Finland its constitution, became the "grand duke of Finland," and the country joined the Russian Empire. Alexander, czar and autocrat of all the Russias, was now a constitutional monarch in Finland.

The struggle with Napoleon continued in spite of the treaty of 1807. Russia began a tariff war against France; the "continental blockade" was not observed; English goods were coming into Russia on American and other neutral ships. In May, 1812, peace was signed with Turkey (war of 1806–1812), and that liberated considerable forces for use elsewhere. In June, 1812, Napoleon invaded Russia without a declaration of war, leading a coalition army recruited from all of Europe, with the exception of Spain, where large French forces were tied up in trying to subdue the Spanish people. The Russian Army was divided; both its wings began a retreat for a junction at Smolensk. While the junction succeeded (owing to the stubborn defense of Smolensk), Napoleon's forces were still overwhelming, and the retreat continued. Popular pressure forced Alexander to appoint Kutuzov commander in chief. Popular pressure also made it imperative for the new commander to give battle on the approaches to Moscow, near Borodino. Napoleon had more men there (130,000 to Kutuzov's 112,000), but the Russians had a slight advantage in artillery. After a most bloody battle, Kutuzov losing half his army, Napoleon failed to dislodge the Russians. But the retreat continued, Kutuzov deciding to abandon Moscow but to preserve the army. When Napoleon got to Moscow, the population had left and the city soon started to burn. The conqueror of all Europe found himself in a largely destroyed city with no supplies. Kutuzov marched farther inland, assembling troops and supplies. Winter was approaching, and Napoleon sent peace emissaries to the Russians, but these offers were rejected.

In the meantime the peasants rose against the invaders. Napoleon was threatened not only by Kutuzov's army, which he had failed to destroy, but by a peasant war that was severing communications and confining garrisons to the cities. The poet Denis Davydov and a few other officers, knowing of the fight of the Spanish guerrillas against the French, joined the peasants, so as to intensify the Russian guerrilla or partisan warfare. In October, 1812, Napoleon left Moscow, retreating back to Smolensk, harassed on all sides by armed peasants and Cossacks. Kutuzov followed in pursuit with the regular army. Smolensk was as empty of supplies as Moscow had been, and winter set in. The retreat became a rout; by the end of the year less than 50,000 crossed the Russian border on the way out—all that remained of an invading force of nearly 600,000. Kutuzov, who had halted the Russian advance, soon died, but Alexander continued the war into western Europe, and together with the Austrians and Prussians inflicted a great defeat on Napoleon near Leipzig, Germany (1813), and entered Paris (1814).

To the Russians the task of expelling Napoleon was a war of national liberation and has always been referred to as the "great fatherland war." The role played in it by the peasantry was of particular significance. The peasants helped free the country, but remained serfs. After 1812 serfdom became altogether an anachronism. Following the defeat and expulsion of Napoleon, Czar Alexander became the moving spirit of the Holy Alliance of European sovereigns, pledged to the principle of "legitimacy" and to wiping out all the achievements of the French Revolution. Alexander the liberal became a mystic, and General Arakcheyev became the unchallenged ruler. Alexander and Arakcheyev undertook to "militarize" the government serfs, or to combine army life and discipline with agriculture through the establishment of "military settlements." Revolts followed, and suppressions accompanied by flogging and exile to Siberia multiplied.

Poland had supported Napoleon, who had promised to aid in re-

76

establishing her independence. Serfdom was abolished in Poland (1807), but the peasantry did not receive any land. At the Congress of Vienna (1815) a large share of Poland was given to Russia, while Austria and Prussia kept other parts. Alexander became king of Poland under a "constitutional charter." Thus he was a constitutional monarch in another part of the realm, as well as in Finland. However, Poland remained divided, and the Polish nobility also objected to the non-inclusion in the "kingdom of Poland" (under Alexander) of Lithuanian and Belorussian territories. Belorussia was ruined by the war and experienced a very bad famine (1820–1821); the peasants were leaving the land to work in manufactories and canal construction. Earlier (1796) there had been established a Pale of Settlement for the Jews, barring Jews as traders from most of the empire, and in 1823 the Jews were expelled from the villages of Belorussia. In the Baltic provinces serfdom was abolished (1816, 1817, 1819), but the land remained the property of the German barons, and the peasants did not even receive full individual freedom. Agriculture and manufacturing were developing in the Ukraine, which was economically becoming more tightly linked with Russia. In the east the absorption of Georgia (1801) led to protracted warfare with Turkey and Persia for the Transcaucasian region. From Turkey Russia also took Bessarabia (1812), and from Persia the territory of present-day Azerbaidzhan (1813). In Siberia slavery was officially prohibited (1826), and Russian penetration continued, in many places practically eliminating the natives. Several Arctic expeditions were also sponsored by the government.

When Alexander suddenly died (1825) in the south of Russia, his younger brother Nicholas I (Nikolai Pavlovich, r. 1825–1855) was to become emperor, in view of the previous abdication of an older brother Constantine (Konstantin Pavlovich, 1779–1831). The fact that Constantine, who was in Warsaw, had renounced his right to the throne was not generally known, and an interim period of confusion developed. This opportunity was utilized by a group of revolutionaries. The wars against Napoleon had acquainted many officers with western Europe and its ideas, particularly those of the French philosophers of the eighteenth century and of the French Revolution. The first secret society of officers, favoring the abolition of serfdom and the introduction of a constitutional monarchy had (1816) only 20 members. Its suc-

77

cessor (1818–1821) had 200 members. Finally there arose a "southern society" (1821–1825) and a "northern society" (1822–1825). The leader of the former, Col. P. I. Pestel, favored a republic; in the northern society a project was drafted for a constitutional monarchy. Pestel had read Thomas Jefferson, and in the north American state constitutions had been studied. The death of Alexander brought these activities into the open. In December, 1825, the officers marched their troops to the Winter Palace in St. Petersburg, demanding a constitution. The armed uprising was poorly organized; the "dictator" designated to lead it did not turn up in the square; demands for a constitution were coupled with cries for Constantine, some believing that constitution (*konstitutsiya* in Russian) must be Constantine's wife. Nicholas subdued the uprising with artillery. Revolts in other towns were also crushed, five of the leaders of the "Decembrists" were hanged, and scores of others exiled to Siberia. These revolutionaries, most of whom were officers and noblemen, were as yet extremely far from the people, but their uprising was a challenge to the regime. It was taken as such by Nicholas I, who, in suppressing it, wanted to teach not only Russia but also Europe a lesson.

The new czar was a soldier bent on suppression of disorder. In 1830, following the July revolution in France, Poland rose, and the Polish Diet dethroned Nicholas as the king of Poland. For seven months the Poles fought off the Russians, but in 1831 Gen. Ivan F. Paskevich (1782–1856) took Warsaw. The constitution of 1815 was abrogated, the Polish Army disbanded, and thousands were exiled. In 1830–1831 a cholera epidemic in Russia led to rumors that the nobility was poisoning the peasants. Revolts spread in a number of provinces: in 1826–1834 they numbered 145; in 1845–1854 they reached the total of 348. When news of the 1848 revolution in France reached Nicholas, he said to the officers surrounding him, "Saddle your horses, gentlemen, there is a revolution in Paris." Nicholas aided Austria in suppressing the liberation movement in Italy and sent an army to crush the fight of Hungary for independence (1849). In domestic matters the slogan was "autocracy, orthodoxy, and nationalism"; internationally Nicholas I was known as the "gendarme of Europe." Not trusting the nobility after the Decembrist affair, Nicholas tried to create an all-embracing bureaucratic apparatus.

78

The wars in the east continued. After a war with Persia (1826–1828) Russia acquired a large part of Armenia; Turkey in the war of 1827–1829 lost more of the Black Sea coast and suffered a naval defeat in the Mediterranean (1827). This latter defeat indirectly aided the struggle of Greece for independence. Here the czar's role as a suppressor of revolutions came into conflict with his ambitions in the Near East. In the Caucasus a long war of conquest began (1834–1859). The mountaineers fought stubbornly for their independence under Shamil (d. 1871). In Central Asia the Russians were also advancing. The Near Eastern policy of Nicholas brought Russia into conflict with other powers, which resulted in the Crimean War (1853–1856) of England, France, Turkey, and Sardinia against Russia. Nicholas failed to obtain the aid of the sovereigns of Austria and Prussia, whom he had helped against revolution (1848–1849). The allies landed in the Crimea and took Sevastopol after an 11 months' siege. Before that the Russian Navy in the Black Sea under Pavel S. Nakhimov (1803–1855) destroyed a Turkish squadron (1853), but the navies of England and France, which included ironclad steam-powered vessels, the Russians could not overcome. Thus with the passing of wooden sailing ships Russia began to lose the position as a naval power acquired by her under Peter I. Her defeat in the Crimean War demonstrated that against the much more industrialized west, the serf empire could not compete. Although the first short railroad line was built in 1837, and in 1851 St. Petersburg and Moscow were linked by rail, the rest of the country had most inadequate means of transportation. At Sevastopol the soldiers and sailors fought heroically, but lack of transportation, antiquated equipment, and bad generalship caused Russia to lose the war. At the close of the eighteenth century Russia's and England's production of pig iron were about equal. In the first half of the nineteenth century Russia's production doubled, while that of England increased thirty times. The defeat in the Crimean War may be regarded as a turning point in the history of the empire, the beginning of its decline.

In spite of the reactionary nature of Nicholas' regime and the constant suppression of thoughts and writings, the period witnessed a considerable cultural advance. The founder of scientific literary criticism, Vissarion G. Belinski (1811–1848), the greatest Russian poet, Alexander S. Pushkin (1799–1837), the poet Mikhail Y. Lermontov

(1814–1841), the satirist Nikolai V. Gogol (1809–1852), the mathematician Nikolai I. Lobachevski (1793–1856), the surgeon Nikolai S. Pirogov (1810–1881), and the composer Mikhail I. Glinka (1804–1857) were laying the foundations of modern Russian culture. The great Ukrainian poet Taras G. Shevchenko (1814–1861), born a serf, laid the foundations of the modern Ukrainian language, as Pushkin did for the Russian language.

The next reign, that of Alexander II (Aleksandr Nikolayevich, r. 1855–1881), witnessed a number of changes. The most important, probably, was the abolition of serfdom in February, 1861. This reform did not satisfy the peasantry: [1] from 1861 to 1863 there occurred over 2,000 cases of peasant uprisings, in 400 of which the peasants resisted troops and were suppressed. In 1864 a new system of rural self-government (the zemstvo) was introduced, giving some outlet for local initiative on the part of merchants and noblemen in road building, on the part of the liberal intelligentsia in the establishment of social services. The entire judiciary was reorganized in 1864 by the simplification of court procedure, the introduction of trial by jury, and the establishment of an independent legal profession. Municipal administration was reorganized in 1870 by measures providing for city dumas (councils) composed of representatives of taxpayers and headed by an elective mayor. Universal conscription at the age of 21 was introduced in 1874, replacing the old professional peasant army with service of 25 years' duration by a force with much shorter service drawn from the entire population. This was the era of "great reforms," and Alexander II was generally referred to as the "czar liberator." Under the impact of the development of trade and industry the feudal structure of the empire was retreating and making concessions. Even the emperor acknowledged this by saying that it is better to liberate the peasants from above than have it happen from below. However, the very fact that changes could no longer be delayed (the Crimean disaster demonstrated this much even to the most conservative) prompted a much greater development of opposition elements, which regarded all these steps as halfway measures, and demanded far-reaching changes.

In 1863 Poland rose once more, and peasant revolts spread in Lithuania and Belorussia. Poland expected aid from England and France,

---

[1] See Chapter X, "The Economic System."

which she did not get, but it took 28 months to suppress the Polish revolt. After this the Russian government began to apply measures of forceful Russification in Poland. The military prestige of the empire had to be resuscitated, which was done through a series of conquests in Central Asia. Tashkent was taken (1865), Bokhara became a vassalage (1868), the khanate of Khiva was conquered (1873), one of the last strongholds of the Turkomans was taken by storm (1880), and by 1885 the conquest of all Central Asia was completed. In the west the empire was less successful. The Franco-Prussian war (1870–1871) gave Russia a chance to rearm on the Black Sea, a right denied to her by the Treaty of Paris (1856) that terminated the Crimean campaign. In 1873 Russia, Germany, and Austria entered into the "three emperors' alliance," prompted by the revolutionary threat of the Paris Commune (1871) and a common desire to stop revolutions. However, this belated revival of the Holy Alliance immediately faced difficulties, as Russia and Austria had conflicting interests in the Balkans, and the newly born German empire was a potential threat to Russia.

The Russo-Turkish War of 1877–1878 demonstrated once more what the earlier Crimean campaign had indicated: the technical and organizational backwardness of the empire as compared to the industrial west. Ideas of pan-Slavism reached their pinnacle in this war. Under Catherine II Potyomkin had developed plans for the conquest of Constantinople and the re-establishment of the Byzantine Empire. Nicholas I spoke of Turkey as the "sick man of Europe." Now a new war against Turkey was begun with the idea of liberating the "brother Slavs" in the Balkans and re-erecting the cross on St. Sophia in Constantinople, which the Turks had converted into a mosque. Advancing across the Danube, fighting in the mountains of the Balkans, the Russian soldiers showed great courage, but the Turks were better equipped, being supplied with modern arms from the west. When the Russians finally approached Constantinople, the English Navy sailed into the Sea of Marmora; Austria, supported by Germany, also took a hostile attitude. A preliminary peace was signed (San Stefano, 1878), but Russia was invited to a European congress, called by Bismarck in Berlin, where under the pressure of the powers she was made to relinquish most of her gains. Expansion of the empire farther to the west, under slogans of pan-Slavism, had failed. In 1879 Germany and Austria entered into an alliance; Berlin did not need the czar of Russia any more.

Among the educated sections of the population at this time two trends of thought stood out. There were the Westerners, who believed that Russia had not progressed sufficiently along the path laid out by Peter the Great. They wanted further westernization as a cure for Russia's backwardness. There were also the Slavophiles, who took an opposite view. According to them, Russia was diverted from her natural path of development by Peter, and the task of the day lay in regaining this indigenous Russian road. Both trends of thought developed radical thinkers, each opposing the existing regime for its own reasons. Meanwhile, in literature the influence of progressive writers was increasing: Nikolai G. Chernyshevski (1828–1889) and Nikolai A. Dobrolyubov (1836–1861) exerted a powerful influence as critics, and Nikolai A. Nekrasov (1821–1877), a liberal poet, wrote about the hard lot of the peasants. Although Russia was still a predominantly illiterate country, a very active public opinion developed in the cities which the government could not ignore.

Dissatisfaction took a variety of forms in the reign of Alexander II. Mikhail A. Bakunin (1814–1876), an anarchist nobleman, was active abroad advocating direct action. Many intellectuals put on peasant garb and went preaching against the czar among the people, which in most cases simply led to their arrest. The Narodniki (Populists), as this group was called, preached a direct transition to socialism, opposing the development of capitalism in Russia. Strikes multiplied in the 1870's, and the first revolutionary organization of workers appeared. The Narodniki were not predominantly noblemen, as were the Decembrists of 1825, but mostly intellectuals. From among them there was formed a terroristic organization, "The Will of the People," whose main efforts were concentrated on attempts to assassinate the czar. Several unsuccessful attempts on his life led the czar to consider further concessions, in the shape of a "limited constitution," but before this was accomplished Alexander II was assassinated by a bomb (March, 1881).

The new czar, Alexander III (Aleksandr Aleksandrovich, r. 1881–1894), was determined to stem the revolutionary tide. Agricultural workers quitting work were made subject to criminal prosecution (1886). Special judges were introduced for the peasantry (1889).

Local self-government was curtailed (1890). A wave of Jewish pogroms swept the Ukraine (1881), and educational restrictions for Jews were introduced (1887). In most non-Russian regions the policy of Russification was intensified, which fostered national liberation movements.

Russia's expansion in Central Asia sharpened relations with England. Through a number of treaties Russia and France entered into an alliance (1891–1893) directed against Germany. Russia had a treaty with both Austria and Germany (1881) and a "special" treaty with Germany (1887), but economically the interests of Russia and Germany were clashing more and more. Having failed to penetrate the Balkans, the empire tried to direct its ambitions eastward. The trans-Siberian Railroad was begun in 1891. Foreign capital was coming into Russia. From 1890 to 1900 foreign investments in Russian industry alone increased fourfold, reaching about half a billion dollars. The building of railroads was also conducted largely with foreign funds. Tariffs were raised (1891) and the gold standard was introduced (1897). Strikes multiplied; the textile strike of 1885 so frightened the government that fines levied on industrial workers were made payable not to owners of factories but to the government (1886). The revolutionary movement was broadening to include the working class. Although the first volume of Karl Marx's *Capital* was translated into Russian in 1872, only in 1883 was there formed by Georgi V. Plekhanov (1856–1918) the first circle of Russian Marxists. The first Marxist working-class organizations were established with the aid of Vladimir I. Lenin (Ulyanov, 1870–1924); and the Russian Social Democratic Labor Party was organized in 1898.

Nicholas II (Nikolai Aleksandrovich, r. 1894–1917), the last czar, began his reign with a continuation of the expansion in the Pacific area. The right to build a railroad through Manchuria was obtained in 1896, and Port Arthur on the China Sea was taken over in 1898, thus providing Russia with a warm-water port on the Pacific, which was soon connected by railroad with the rest of the empire. Russia's activities on the Pacific led to the Anglo-Japanese alliance (1902). Further commercial penetration into Korea finally brought the expansionist tendencies of the Russian Empire into armed conflict with Japan. Early in 1904 the Japanese attacked without declaring war. Port Arthur was

blockaded from land and sea; after an 11 months' siege the commanding general surrendered. The Baltic Fleet sailed all the way to the Far
East and was annihilated by the Japanese Navy in the Battle of Tsushima Straits. The Russian Army suffered defeat in the battle of Mukden (1905). Having directed its attention to the Far East in view of
its inability to cope with European powers, the empire now received a
decisive defeat at the hands of Japan. Peace was signed in Portsmouth,
New Hampshire, with President Theodore Roosevelt acting as media-
tor. Russia's expansion in the East was checked, Japan acquiring a
foothold on the continent. This war was tremendously unpopular in
Russia, and internal unrest began to rise as soon as it started.

The economic crisis of the early 1900's had hit the country hard.
Strikes spread not only through industry, but political strikes took hold
in the universities. In 1901–1902 a general strike in universities embraced 30,000 students. In an attempt somehow to redirect the movement, the government tried to organize through disguised agents its
own "conservative" labor unions (1901 and 1902). This, however,
soon became known, and the disclosure only strengthened the revolutionary movement. The peasantry also became increasingly active. In
1891–1892 there was widespread famine. From 1893 to 1900 there were
three years with local famines and two years of food shortages. In
1901–1902 there was again a famine. Strikers blacklisted by factory
owners were wandering through villages and talking to the peasants.
When, on top of all this, came the war with Japan, for which most
people put the entire blame on the personal ambitions of the czar and
his courtiers, the general dissatisfaction and unrest exploded in the
revolution of 1905.

THE TWO REVOLUTIONS: 1905 AND 1917 . . . In the revolution
of 1905 political parties assumed for the first time an important role.
The Social Democrats had formed a party in 1898 and at their Second
Congress (1903) split into a majority (Bolshevik) and a minority
(Menshevik) faction, but continued as one Marxist party for several
years. Successors of the Narodniki were the Socialist Revolutionaries
(1902), a non-Marxist revolutionary party that believed in individual
terroristic acts. In the 1890's there arose in Poland a liberal and a socialist party. In Belorussia there emerged an independent socialist
party. The Jews created their Social Democratic organization, the

Bund (1897). A Ukrainian revolutionary party was formed (1900) under strong Austrian influence, and in Georgia a party very similar to the Russian Socialist Revolutionaries was formed (1904). Thus various classes in the population began to express their aspirations in party form.

As the war with Japan progressed, the unrest increased. On January 22, 1905 (old calendar, January 9), which became known as Bloody Sunday, a very large demonstration of workers went to the Winter Palace in St. Petersburg to present demands. Troops killed over a thousand workers and wounded many more. This day shattered forever the workers' illusion that the czar "was above the struggle," that he could be appealed to for protection against the factory owners and officialdom. Strikes spread throughout the country. The Bolshevik faction of the Social Democrats favored direct working-class action in the struggle to overthrow the monarchy (Third Party Congress, April, 1905); the Mensheviks tactically favored the victory of a liberal revolution first, and even met separately. Bloody Sunday and the strikes had their counterpart in the villages; the peasants began rising and burning mansions. The peasants wanted more land—that is what the revolution meant to them. The Bolsheviks believed that a revolution could succeed only if there was a united effort of both the city and the countryside, differing in this from the Mensheviks, who stood for purity of proletarian action. In June, 1905, sailors of the battleship *Potyomkin* revolted in the Black Sea, raising the red flag. In the fall of 1905, immediately after peace with Japan was signed, a general strike swept the country. The czar saw that he had to make some concessions, and in October, 1905, a manifesto, prepared with the aid of Sergei I. Witte (1849–1915), president of the Council of Ministers (who had just concluded the peace with Japan), was issued, promising an elective Duma and various other reforms. But the revolutionary wave did not subside. In many cities there arose workers' councils (soviets), which demanded much more radical changes.

In Finland, where a Red Guard was organized, the czar was forced to re-establish the old constitution, which had been suspended in 1902. In Warsaw Polish revolutionaries demonstrated with banners inscribed "For our freedom and yours." In the Ukraine autonomy was demanded. In Belorussia there was a movement for a federation (1906) to consist of Belorussia, Latvia, Lithuania, and the Ukraine, with a joint Diet in Vilna. A Moslem congress in Kazan (1905) wanted equal rights. Georgians, Armenians, and the people of Azerbaidzhan rose; even in faraway Yakutia (Siberia) a union of national minorities was formed. In effect, all the nationalities of the multinational empire were set in motion, and in one or another form their movements began to merge with the revolution. To counteract this tendency the government tried to promote national animosities, and used anti-Semitism, with resulting pogroms, as a lever to sidetrack revolutionary ardor.

In November, 1905, Lenin returned to Russia after having spent some time abroad, and a month later he and Joseph V. Stalin (Dzhugashvili, 1879–) met for the first time in Finland. The Bolsheviks were getting ready for an armed uprising. In December, 1905, such an uprising took place in Moscow and in several other cities. However, the government still had many loyal troops and managed to bring more troops back in time from Manchuria. The uprisings in the cities were not properly co-ordinated with the peasant movement, and as a result the armed revolts were crushed and the revolution temporarily defeated. In the spring of 1906 elections were held for the first Duma, on the basis of a limited franchise. The Bolsheviks, believing that the revolutionary tide had not yet subsided, boycotted the elections; the Mensheviks participated. The strongest party in the first Duma was the Cadets (Constitutional Democrats), led by Professor Pavel N. Milyukov. At the Fourth Congress of the Social Democrats (Stockholm, April, 1906) the Mensheviks were in a majority, with Lenin and the Bolsheviks finding themselves outvoted. In spite of its relatively moderate political composition, the first Duma took up the agrarian question, and in July, 1906, the czar dissolved it. Unrest continued; in the course of 1906 troops were called out 2,559 times. Before calling a new election the prime minister, Peter A. Stolypin (1862–1911)—Witte had been dismissed as too moderate—put through his agrarian reform,[2] hoping to appease the wealthier layers of the peasantry. The Bolsheviks now reversed their stand and participated in the elections to the second Duma. The composition of this body proved to be considerably further to the left: instead of 18 deputies, the Social Democrats now had 65 (Bolsheviks and Mensheviks). In June, 1907, the second Duma

---

[2] See Chapter X, "The Economic System."

was dissolved and the Manifesto of October, 1905, virtually abrogated. The election law was changed, the rights of the Duma were curtailed, and the Social Democratic deputies sent to Siberia. At the Fifth Congress of the Social Democrats (London, 1907) the Bolsheviks were again in a majority. The June, 1907, Stolypin counterrevolution was now in full swing; the third Duma had 202 landlord deputies (46 per cent of the total). The strike wave subsided; many revolutionaries followed Lenin abroad; the intellectuals split into many factions, some wanting to co-operate with the government; a special brand of "frustration literature" appeared; the government's policy of forceful Russification of minorities was again in full swing; Finnish and Polish liberties again vanished.

In 1907 Russia and England reached an agreement on their mutual spheres of influence in Persia. Together with the Franco-Russian alliance (1893) and the Anglo-French understanding (1904), this agreement laid the basis for the Anglo-French-Russian entente against Germany (1914). But in 1909, when Austria-Hungary, with the support of Germany, annexed Bosnia and Herzegovina, Russia was still too weak to come to Serbia's defense. By 1910 the protracted economic crisis gave way to a prosperity period: foreign capital again poured in, and a very rapid "trustification" of Russia's industry and finance developed. The working-class movement also began to revive. In January, 1912, the Bolsheviks called a special conference (Prague) at which they formalized their split with the Mensheviks by constituting themselves as a separate party—the Russian Social Democratic Labor Party (Bolsheviks). The two groups had now become two parties, both considering themselves Marxist, but differing on the nature of party organization, on their attitude to the peasantry, to the national minorities, on tactics of revolutionary struggle, and on a variety of other issues. In April of the same year hundreds of strikers were shot on the Lena gold fields in Siberia. Trying to give an explanation in the Duma, the minister of the interior said, "Thus it was—thus it will be." Strikes and demonstrations spread throughout the country—the spirit of 1905 was reviving. The "strong man" of the government, Stolypin, had been assassinated in the previous year. The Bolshevik newspaper *Pravda*, edited by Stalin, appeared in 1912, and the May 1 strike in 1913 embraced half a million workers. But the fourth (and last) Duma elected

87

in 1912 was as conservative as the third. In 1913 a social security law was passed, and the Bolsheviks made important gains in the social security organizations. On May 1, 1914, over a million workers were on strike; in June this figure rose to a million and a half. The percentage of political strikes already exceeded that of 1905. The country was on the verge of another revolution when the First World War broke out.[8]

For a few months the war stopped the revolutionary movement, but when losses mounted and military reverses began, signs of unrest reappeared. From the outset the Bolsheviks opposed the war; most other Russian parties, including the Mensheviks, supported the government. However, Russia was technically unprepared to wage a big modern war: production became disorganized, prices were rising, agriculture suffered. In 1914 the czar introduced prohibition, and since the liquor business was a government monopoly, this at once unbalanced the budget. In 1915 and 1916 strikes began to multiply. Large revolts took place in Central Asia (1916) and were suppressed through extensive use of military force. The prestige of the monarch altogether faded away as a result of the scandals connected with the self-styled monk Grigori E. Rasputin-Novykh (1872–1916) whom the czar's family had befriended and who acquired an extraordinary influence in governmental matters. Representatives of the industrialists and the nobility were urging the throne at least to take conservative circles into its confidence. But the court saw revolutionary activities everywhere and trusted no one. The conservative fourth Duma became an oppositionist body. In December, 1916, the notorious Rasputin was killed by two princes and one archroyalist, who thus hoped to save the throne. Rumors of a forthcoming palace revolution, on the one hand, and of treasonable activities of the empress, on the other, were widespread. Food shortages in the cities and the general economic disintegration, particularly in the field of transportation, added to the confusion. Practically all classes were in opposition and the throne was isolated. In March (old calendar, February), 1917, the food situation in the capital reached a critical stage, and riots ensued. The Duma appealed to the czar to make concessions and save the dynasty. Nicholas II responded by dissolving the Duma, but in the streets of Petrograd (as St. Petersburg was known after 1914) the soldiers were joining the revolutionary

---

[8] See Chapter VIII, "Russia in the First World War."

crowds. The Duma refused to disperse and sent a delegation to Nicholas at the front. The time for concessions had passed, and on March 2 (new calendar, 15) the last czar and autocrat of all the Russias abdicated.

On the same day the Duma formed a provisional government with a large landowner, Prince Georgi E. Lvov (1861–1925), as prime minister and a number of Constitutional Democrats in the Cabinet; the member furthest to the left was Alexander F. Kerensky (1881–   ), Socialist Revolutionary. Practically simultaneously there was formed the Petrograd Soviet of Workers' and Soldiers' Deputies, consisting mostly of Mensheviks and Socialist Revolutionaries. Thus there arose at once a duality in authority: the provisional government was the center of authority but had insufficient actual power; the soviets, springing up all over the country and in the army, had the actual power but were as yet unwilling to exercise it fully. The provisional government took the position that the war must be brought to a victorious conclusion and that all basic questions would be solved by the Constituent Assembly, to be elected at some future date.

In April, 1917, Lenin returned from abroad, and the Bolsheviks advanced a list of demands (Lenin's *April Theses*), including a call for "all power to the soviets," overthrow of the provisional government, immediate nationalization of the land, and termination of the war. The Mensheviks regarded Lenin as having gone insane; those further to the right alleged that he was a German agent. But demonstrations against the provisional government grew, and on May 5 (18) a new Cabinet was formed, further to the left, including Mensheviks and Socialist Revolutionaries and increasingly dominated by Kerensky. The Bolsheviks were gradually gaining strength, although at the First Congress of Soviets (June, 1917) they had only 105 out of 1000 delegates. Economic disorganization was spreading: in May 108 factories closed, in June 125, and in July 206; unemployment was growing. On July 4 (17) mass demonstrations of workers, soldiers, and sailors were held in Petrograd under the slogan "All Power to the Soviets." The Bolsheviks considered an armed uprising premature, but since the people were moving, Lenin and the others deemed it their duty to lead. The uprising was crushed by Kerensky, and Lenin had to go into hiding in Finland. Early in August, 1917, the Sixth Congress of the party assembled illegally in Petrograd. The main report was given by Stalin. This congress admitted to the party Leon D. Trotsky (Bronstein, 1877–1940).

Kerensky, who had become prime minister of the provisional government on July 8 (21), apparently felt that the time had come to tighten up matters. In this he was supported by British and French representatives, who began to see that Russia might drop out of the war. But on the question of who was going to be the "man on the white horse" Kerensky and the commander in chief of the army, Lavr G. Kornilov, split, with the result that an armed conflict between the prime minister and the commander in chief ensued. Troops were marching on Petrograd (early September), and the Bolsheviks now rallied the working class of the capital against the openly counter-revolutionary move of Kornilov. With the aid of the proletariat, Kornilov was defeated. Kerensky became commander in chief (or persuader in chief, because he had very little actual power). Now the provisional government, headed by Kerensky, was isolated; first in July it had suppressed the Left, then in September, with the aid of the Left, it suppressed the armed forces of the Right, with the result that very little support now remained. The Bolsheviks, gaining a majority in the Moscow and Petrograd Soviets of Workers' and Soldiers' Deputies, again advanced the slogan, "All Power to the Soviets." Meanwhile, the front was disintegrating; the soldiers were going home, taking their rifles with them, to claim the land.

In October the Bolsheviks began to prepare an armed uprising with the object of seizing power and establishing a socialist state. But inside the Bolshevik group disagreement with Trotsky, Grigori E. Zinovyev (1883–1936), and Leo B. Kamenev (1883–1936) threatened to disrupt the undertaking. The committee in charge decided to start the uprising at once, even before the Second Congress of Soviets had assembled. On the morning of October 24 (new calendar, November 6) the uprising began, Lenin having returned to Petrograd in disguise. By the next day the city was taken over and the storming of the Winter Palace (headquarters of the provisional government) began at about 9:00 P.M., with the cruiser *Aurora* shelling the palace from the river. The Congress of Soviets opened on the evening of October 25 (November 7), with the storming of the palace still going on. Kerensky had

90

fled in the meantime, and at 2:10 A.M. the palace was taken. At 5:00 A.M. the Congress of Soviets approved the declaration written by Lenin to the effect that power had passed into the hands of the soviets. On the evening of the same day, October 26 (November 8), the Congress of Soviets approved, upon Lenin's motion, decrees for the conclusion of peace, for the nationalization of all land, and for the formation of the Council of People's Commissars. Russia had become a workers' and peasants' republic.

CIVIL WAR AND INTERVENTION . . . The first few months of the Soviet regime (November to February) were marked by a series of measures designed to destroy the old machinery of state. A workers' militia replaced the old police, new people's courts were created, a uniform citizenship for all was introduced, and ranks and titles were abolished. The church was separated from the state, and the school from the church; civil marriage was instituted; the spelling was simplified; and the old Julian calendar was discarded in favor of the Gregorian calendar of western Europe. In the economic sphere the first steps toward nationalization of finance and industry were taken.[4] Although the establishment of the Soviet regime was met by several strikes among professionals and office workers, and by brief local armed resistance, Soviet authority on the whole was rapidly extended throughout most parts of the former Russian Empire.

A Congress of Peasant Soviets, meeting in November, 1917, endorsed the first decrees of the Soviet government, and an agreement was concluded with the Left Socialist Revolutionaries, several of whom entered the government. In the same month elections were held for the Constituent Assembly, as scheduled under the provisional government, on the basis of lists of candidates drawn up before the October Revolution. The Assembly met in January, 1918, and refused to accept the declaration submitted to it by the Soviet government on basic measures already taken, such as the nationalization of land. Declaring that the Assembly "expressed the yesterday of the revolution," the Bolsheviks dissolved it (January 19). In the same month the Third Congress of Soviets enthusiastically endorsed all measures of the government.

One of the first measures of the Soviet regime was the "Declaration

---

[4] See Chapters X and XI, "The Economic System" and "Banking, Money, and Finance."

of the Rights of the Peoples of Russia" (November 2 [15], 1917), establishing the equality of all peoples; their right to self-determination, including secession; and the abolition of all national privileges and restrictions. The first commissar of nationalities was Joseph V. Stalin, a member of the formerly oppressed Georgian minority. In December, 1917, a decree was issued recognizing the independence of Finland, which wanted to go its own way. All over the territory of the former empire national governments were springing up. To many it seemed that the country was hopelessly falling apart. But Lenin asserted that a free union could arise only among free states; hence, in order to have peoples come voluntarily together, one had first to set them free, dissolve the old empire, and allow everyone to go his own way. Assertion of independence soon took two forms: either local anti-Bolsheviks or local Bolsheviks took power. Since there soon arose a struggle between those who supported the Bolsheviks (the Reds) and all types of anti-Bolsheviks (the Whites), various parts of the country began to pull together in accordance with their political coloration.

In December, 1917, when peace negotiations were begun, the terms demanded by Germany were severe. Lenin was for accepting them, but Trotsky and several others balked. Negotiations were broken off (February 10, 1918), and the Germans began to advance. On February 21, 1918, Lenin declared the socialist fatherland in danger; two days later came the first clash between volunteer detachments of Red Guards and the kaiser's troops; and February 23 is still celebrated as the birthday of the Red Army. After gaining much ground in their advance, the Germans finally agreed to reopen negotiations, and on March 3, 1918, peace was signed in Brest-Litovsk on very harsh terms. Internal trouble developed over ratification of the treaty. Both Left Socialist Revolutionaries and Left Communists opposed this peace, the latter group (including Bukharin) even advocating "consent to the possible loss of the Soviet power, which has now become purely formal." However, the Seventh Party Congress, opening March 6, upheld Lenin, and so did the Fourth Congress of Soviets. The Seventh Party Congress also changed the name of the party to the Russian Communist Party (Bolsheviks). In view of the catastrophic situation in foreign relations the capital was transferred from Petrograd to Moscow. The Germans occupied Kiev (March, 1918) and moved into the

Crimea (April). In Finland the Whites, with German aid, defeated the Reds and took Helsinki (April), and Romania occupied Bessarabia.

In spite of these reverses, the Bolsheviks had established their authority over large areas and were now beginning to consolidate their position and lay the groundwork for the building of socialism. Many of the economic measures introduced by Lenin met with opposition even within the party, particularly the policy of organizing "committees of poor peasants" to push the Soviet Revolution in the villages. Over this measure and the peace treaty of Brest-Litovsk, the Left Socialist Revolutionaries withdrew from the government. At the Fifth Congress of Soviets Lenin was upheld on these matters, and the first constitution of the Russian Soviet Federated Socialist Republic was adopted (July 10). On July 6 the German ambassador in Moscow was assassinated by a Socialist Revolutionary, and then the Left Socialist Revolutionaries organized an unsuccessful armed revolt in Moscow, which, it became known many years later, had the support of some individuals then in the Soviet government.

By the late spring of 1918 it also became increasingly clear that the Soviet regime intended to stay in power and work toward socialism. All those who enjoyed wealth and privileges in the past, as well as a variety of dissident radicals and "socialists," began to band together to oppose the Soviet regime more actively. The withdrawal from the First World War and the terms of the peace with Germany created violent resentment among the officers of the old army. All these factors, together with the intent of Russia's former allies to bring her back into their fold and into the war by any and all means, created preconditions for the civil war and intervention that started in the middle of 1918.

In May, 1918, Czechoslovak troops, organized from former prisoners of war to fight for the liberation of their country, clashed with local authorities while on their way to the Far East, where they expected to find ocean transportation to Europe. With their support a Socialist Revolutionary government was set up on the Volga. A White revolt took place in the city of Yaroslavl. On July 8, 1918, the former czar, Nicholas II, and his family were executed in Ekaterinburg (now Sverdlovsk) by a decision of the local soviet in view of the possibility of the occupation of the city by anti-Soviet forces. Murmansk and

93

Archangel were occupied by English and other forces of former allies, and a "Government of North Russia" was formed. In the Far East the Japanese landed with a large army of occupation. At the same time the Germans occupied Belorussia and the Ukraine and, together with their allies, the Turks, were active in the Caucasus. By the autumn of 1918 the Soviet regime was surrounded by enemies on all sides.

In the Ukraine the Germans set up Gen. Pavel P. Skoropadski (1873– ?) as hetman. After the German defeat in France this regime collapsed, but its place was soon taken by the Allied-sponsored Gen. Anton I. Denikin (1872–　　), first with a "volunteer army," later with the "armed forces of the south of Russia." In Finland the acceptance of a German prince as king had been arranged for, but with the defeat of Germany, the Finnish anti-Soviet leader, Baron Carl G. von Mannerheim (1867–　　), began to be sponsored by the Allied powers. For a short period the Allies even encouraged a German army in the Baltic area, thinking it would be useful as an anti-Soviet tool. The Volga and Omsk (Siberia) anti-Soviet regimes merged but soon were overthrown by Adm. Alexander V. Kolchak (1873–1920), who proclaimed himself "supreme ruler" of Russia. Thus by the end of 1918 civil war combined with foreign occupation raged all over the country. Soviet authority was preserved only in the center, which was for a time cut off from its main supplies of food and fuel. The efforts of all these diversified forces to eradicate the Soviet regime took the shape of three major military campaigns.

In March, 1919, the Whites under Kolchak began their advance from the Urals toward the Volga. By July they were repulsed, and the Red Army entered the Urals. Astrakhan was held, and a junction of Kolchak and Denikin forces was prevented. In the spring and summer of 1919 the Whites under Gen. Nikolai N. Yudenich (1862–1933) attempted to take Petrograd, aided by anti-Soviet Estonian and Finnish troops and the British Navy. In August, 1919, Yudenich was repulsed. Thus the first White campaign, with the Kolchak forces as the main spearhead from the east, failed.

The second campaign, with the main spearhead directed at Moscow from the south, began in the autumn of 1919. The offensive was started by the White armies of Denikin. On October 13 he took Orel and started marching toward Tula. At the same time Yudenich began a new advance on Petrograd. In the south Trotsky's plan for a flanking counterattack through the agricultural areas was rejected and Stalin's plan to counterattack directly through industrial areas accepted. The plan was based on the notion that in industrial areas the Red Army would have a preponderance of the population on its side, and also on the desire to deprive the Whites of industrial resources. A special cavalry army was created under Semyon N. Budyonny (1883–   ). The White tide was turned; in January, 1920, Rostov-on-the-Don was taken, and on March 27 Novorossisk, the last White stronghold, was cleared. The remnants of Denikin's army evacuated into the Crimea. The second attempt by Yudenich to capture Petrograd also failed, and on November 14, 1919, a major portion of his army surrendered. Thus the second major armed attempt to dislodge the Soviet regime also collapsed.

In the meantime the Red Army continued its advance east. In November, 1919, the capital of Kolchak's government, Omsk, was taken; in January, 1920, the Red Army entered Irkutsk. Soviet authority was being re-established in Siberia. Admiral Kolchak was taken prisoner, tried, and shot.

After a brief military respite early in 1920 there began the third major military campaign to destroy the Soviet regime. The main spearhead this time was directed from the west and consisted of the Polish Army, aided from the Crimea by the Russian Whites under Baron Peter N. Wrangel (1878–1928). In April, 1920, the Poles advanced into the Ukraine, occupying Kiev in May. The Red Army began a counteroffensive in June, liberated Kiev, and in mid-August stood at the gates of Lvov and Warsaw. The Poles asked to begin negotiations for peace (July 22) but soon broke off negotiations. French aid was arriving in Poland. After the Red Army had besieged Lvov, the advance into the industrial areas of Poland, urged by Klimenti E. Voroshilov (1881–   ), was not continued. It was Trotsky's and Mikhail N. Tukhachevski's (1893–1937) plan to lift the siege of Lvov and to divert all efforts toward taking Warsaw. Near Warsaw the Red Army was repulsed, but Poland did not have the strength to resume an advance on Moscow. In October, 1920, hostilities were halted, and in March, 1921, the peace treaty of Riga was signed, with western Belorussia and Galician Ukraine included inside the Polish border. Meanwhile, in the south the Wrangel forces emerged from the Crimea and began advancing north (July, 1920). In October they were repulsed and began withdrawing into the Crimea. The Perekop Isthmus was stormed and the Crimea occupied by the Red Army (November, 1920). Remnants of the Wrangel army fled abroad by sea. Thus the third and last major drive to overthrow the Soviet regime by force collapsed.

In 1919 and 1920 civil war continued in Central Asia. In February, 1920, the khanate of Khiva became a people's republic; in August, 1920, the emir of Bokhara was overthrown. Soviet regimes were established in Azerbaidzhan (April 27, 1920), in Armenia (November 29, 1920), in Georgia (February 25, 1921); Batum was not cleared of the Whites until March 19, 1921. To re-establish the Soviet regime in the Far East required not only a defeat of the Whites but also the expulsion of the Japanese Army of occupation. After a big battle near Volochayevka (February 10, 1922) Khabarovsk was taken (February 14, 1922), and on October 25, 1922, Vladivostok was entered by the Red Army. On the fifth anniversary of the October Revolution (November, 1922) the re-establishment of Soviet authority in the Far East was proclaimed.

The political victory (the taking of power) achieved by the Soviet regime in 1917 was now capped by a military victory. The White movement, made up of many different elements with only one point in common, their anti-Sovietism, was defeated, and the armed forces of foreign interventionists were expelled from the country. In the course of the civil war the Red Army grew to over 5,000,000. Many fighters, such as V. I. Chapayev (1887–1919) in the Urals, S. G. Lazo (1894–1920) in the Far East, N. A. Shchors (1895–1919), and G. I. Kotovski (1887–1925) in the Ukraine, became great popular heroes. Many battles and campaigns, such as the first defense of Tsaritsyn (now Stalingrad) under Stalin and Voroshilov in 1918, and the cavalry operations of Budyonny's horsemen, as well as many others, became part of the heroic past. But in spite of the military victory, the country was in a very bad economic state.[5] Although England, France, and Italy called off their economic blockade of Soviet Russia in January, 1920, most governments of the world remained hostile to the new regime, and the devastation brought about by the war led to severe famine. Furthermore, the western borders of the republic had undergone considerable

---

[5] See Chapter X, "The Economic System."

revision. In Finland, Latvia, Estonia, and Lithuania the local White forces had won; Poland, besides becoming a separate state, had acquired a substantial share of Belorussia; Romania held on to Bessarabia; and in the Transcaucasus territorial concessions were made to Turkey. Petrograd remained (within a few miles of the Finnish border) as an outlet to the Baltic, but otherwise the borders had been moved east, with a cordon of hostile new states separating Soviet Russia from the rest of Europe, thus in a sense reviving the situation that prevailed before the time of Peter the Great.

RECONSTRUCTION AND POLITICAL STRUGGLE . . . During the years 1918–1921 the enemies of the Soviet regime did not operate only on the military fronts. On August 30, 1918, the Bolshevik leader M. S. Uritski (1873–1918) was assassinated and Lenin was gravely wounded by a Socialist Revolutionary. The terroristic acts of the various brands of Whites were met by the Soviet regime through its own "red terror," organized and directed by Feliks E. Dzerzhinski (1877–1926), chairman of the "extraordinary commission to combat counterrevolution, sabotage, and speculation" (the Cheka). The Greek Orthodox Church excommunicated the government and all its agents, and fought actively against the regime. Meanwhile inner party struggles continued over various issues. At the Eighth Party Congress (March, 1919) Lenin had to overcome opposition from Nikolai I. Bukharin (1888–1938) and others on the peasant and national questions. This congress adopted a new party program, which reflected an important change in the attitude toward the middle peasants. At first tending to side with the White forces, this group, seeing that the victory of the Whites meant the return of big landlordism, began to swing around to the Soviet side. In order to encourage this tendency the party, which formerly relied mainly on the poorest peasantry, made certain concessions to the middle group. At the Ninth Party Congress (March–April, 1920), meeting after the defeat of Kolchak and Denikin, the party devoted much attention to plans for restoration of industry and transportation, and endorsed a long-range plan for the electrification of the whole country. Opposition developed in favor of "group management" instead of individual responsibility of managers.

Continuation of civil war in the summer and fall of 1920 interfered with the realization of the reconstruction program adopted by the Ninth Congress, but by the spring of 1921, with the end of hostilities with the Poles and the expulsion of Wrangel's forces, the party and the government were ready to deal with the now urgent economic problems. During the war it had been necessary to adopt a rigid policy of taxation and general regimentation in both agriculture and industry (the so-called policy of Military Communism [6]), but now that the pressing military danger was past, Lenin and others thought it necessary to ease up, especially to lighten the tax burden on the peasantry, so as to encourage food production. He also favored the voluntary aid of trade unions in reviving industry. Trotsky headed an intraparty opposition to this latter proposal, advocating instead a virtual militarization of the trade unions or the continuation of the rigid policies of the war period. The struggle over the trade-union question was widespread, but at the Tenth Party Congress (March, 1921) Lenin's policy prevailed. This congress voted to introduce a tax in kind, in place of the previously existing surplus-appropriation system in agriculture, thus leaving marketable surpluses in the hands of the peasantry. Private trade and small-scale private production were also allowed. This was the so-called New Economic Policy or NEP.[7]

An event that sounded the danger signal to the party and contributed to the decisions of the Tenth Congress was the revolt of the fortress of Kronstadt in the Baltic, where the slogan was raised: "Soviets without Communists." Marching across the ice to the island fortress, the Red Army crushed the revolt, the main significance of which lay in the fact that the struggle against the Soviet regime was adapting itself to Soviet forms and using pseudo-Soviet slogans.

Some opposed the NEP altogether, regarding it as a betrayal of the revolution. Others, at that time including Trotsky, Bukharin, Leo B. Kamenev, and Aleksei I. Rykov (1881–1938), demanded much greater concessions to private capitalism, believing the building of socialism (after the termination of the NEP) in one country alone to be impossible. The Eleventh Party Congress (March–April, 1922), the last in which Lenin took part, met when the economic situation had already improved somewhat. In his last speech to the country (before the Moscow Soviet in November, 1922) Lenin expressed the firm con-

---

[6] See Chapter X, "The Economic System."
[7] See *ibid.*

viction that "NEP Russia will become socialist Russia." In December, 1922, the First All-Union Congress of Soviets was held, at which a voluntary union was formed—the Union of Soviet Socialist Republics, then embracing four republics, the Russian (RSFSR), the Transcaucasian SFSR, the Belorussian, and the Ukrainian SS republics. In 1923 the first constitution of the USSR was adopted.

The Twelfth Party Congress met in April, 1923 (Lenin was unable to attend), and took up and rejected a number of proposals by Trotsky and others aimed at broadening and deepening the NEP. In January, 1924, the Trotskyite opposition was openly condemned at a party conference. On January 21, 1924, Lenin died. The Thirteenth Party Congress (May, 1924) upheld the decision of the January conference against Trotsky and the opposition. By this time the international situation of the USSR had begun to improve. In 1922 Soviet Russia was invited to participate, for the first time, in an international conference, held at Genoa, Italy. Although no satisfactory results ensued, Soviet Russia did enter into treaty relations with Germany (Treaty of Rapallo, April, 1922) and in 1923 successfully rebuffed a threatening ultimatum of Lord Curzon, British foreign secretary. In 1924 diplomatic relations were restored with England, France, Italy, and China.

Internally the economic situation continued to improve, but the dispute over the possibility of building socialism in one country also grew. Trotsky now advanced his theory of "permanent revolution." The Fourteenth Party Congress, meeting in December, 1925, decided over vociferous opposition on a program of socialist industrialization of the country. The year 1926 marked a turning point; the reconstruction period, and with it the NEP, were definitely coming to a close. Economically it became possible to advance, but full agreement was not yet at hand. In addition, difficulties developed in foreign relations. The headquarters of the Soviet trade mission in London was raided, and the British government broke off diplomatic and trade relations (May 26, 1927). Similar raids took place in Germany and China, and the Soviet ambassador to Poland was assassinated (June 7, 1927). At that time Stalin remarked that "something like a united front from [Foreign Secretary Austen] Chamberlain to Trotsky is being formed." The opposition demanded an open discussion of their program within the party. In October, 1927, after such a discussion, the matter was put to a vote in the party: 724,000 members voted for the policy of the Central Committee, the opposition getting 4,000 votes, or less than 1 per cent. In November, 1927, at the 10-year anniversary celebration of the revolution, followers of Trotsky and Zinovyev attempted to stage a public demonstration against the government. On November 14, 1927, the two were expelled from the party. The Fifteenth Party Congress, meeting in December, 1927, approved this step and expelled a whole list of followers of Trotsky and Zinovyev. Soon after the congress, most of the opposition recanted (with the exception of Trotsky) and asked for readmittance. The Fifteenth Party Congress not only laid stress on the necessity for industrialization, but called for the fullest development of collectivization of agriculture.

The beginning of large-scale industrialization brought forth a large public trial of old-time specialists involved in wrecking activities. This so-called Shakhty case indicated that the Soviet regime could not trust all the technical help carried over from the past but would have to train a new generation of specialists, friendly to the idea of socialism. Meanwhile, around the issue of collectivization of agriculture a new opposition emerged led by Bukharin and Rykov. This group opposed collectivization, as it were, from the right. In November, 1929, the party declared that belonging to the "rightist opposition" was incompatible with membership.

THE BUILDING OF SOCIALISM . . . By the time the Sixteenth Party Congress met (June–July, 1930) the drive for industrialization and collectivization of agriculture (the First Five-Year Plan) was in full swing. All the energies of the country were directed to one aim, the building of socialism. On the surface all opposition inside the party had disappeared; Trotsky was exiled abroad and seemed doomed to oblivion. The party, and to an increasing extent the country, looked on Joseph V. Stalin as Lenin's successor both in theoretical and organizational leadership.

In the summer of 1929 a conflict arose in Manchuria, where the Chinese Eastern Railroad (part-owned by the USSR) was seized by local Chinese authorities. Brief military action by the Red Army brought a re-establishment of the *status quo ante*. In October, 1929, diplomatic relations were resumed with England. But with the advent of the world economic crisis, international rivalries sharpened. In 1931 Japan began her career of aggression in Manchuria. The problem of preserving peace began to be more and more pressing.

At the same time trouble developed on the agricultural side of the First Five-Year Plan. Collectivization brought about a struggle with the wealthy peasants (kulaks), who opposed the program. On January 5, 1930, the party resolved to eliminate the kulaks as a class. Now the revolution was to take, in the village, the step it had already taken in the city: those living off other people's labor, even partially, were to be declassed. Although the kulaks numerically formed an insignificant minority, the struggle was intense. But when the voluntary principle in collectivization was violated in far too many instances, and abuses of all sorts accompanied efforts to introduce collectivization as rapidly as possible, widespread dissatisfaction arose. The situation became really grave, particularly when the peasantry began to slaughter cattle on a large scale. On March 2, 1930, by decision of the Central Committee of the party, Stalin's article, "Dizzy with Success," was published. The party and the government decided to call a halt on the perversions of the program which had arisen partly through the activities of enemies and partly through all kinds of "pig-headed left distortions," and which had reached such proportions that the entire program was endangered. This step proved to have been taken just in time. In some areas acute food shortages did arise, and the slaughter of livestock created a problem for several years to come. Although the first years of collectivized agriculture were marred by serious defects and social struggle of unusual intensity, recalling in some aspects the civil war of a decade before, still, in the course of the First Five-Year Plan, more changes took place and more advances were introduced in rural life than had occurred for centuries previously. An entirely new type of agricultural economy was emerging, that of collectively operated and mechanized agriculture—socialism had been extended to the countryside.

The Seventeenth Party Congress (January–February, 1934) met after a considerable interval and is referred to as the "Congress of Victors." The original program for industrialization had succeeded, and now Vyacheslav M. Molotov (1890–   ) and Valerian V. Kuibyshev (1888–1935) outlined to the congress far vaster plans for the future. Prominent members of former "left" and "right" oppositions one after another extolled the achievements of socialism in one country, which they had previously opposed on a variety of grounds. It appeared as if all intra-party difficulties had been overcome, and that the success of the party leadership under Joseph V. Stalin must be clear-cut and obvious to all. But on December 1, 1934, the Leningrad leader of the party, S. M. Kirov (1886–1934), was assassinated by an oppositionist. This led first to the discovery of two secret opposition centers; then a much more far-reaching plot was uncovered. In the autumn of 1936 the first large public trial was held; among those convicted and executed were Zinovyev and Kamenev. In January, 1937, a second public trial was held involving several followers of Trotsky, which also resulted in convictions and executions. In March, 1938, the third public trial took place; among those tried, convicted, and executed were Bukharin, Rykov, and several former people's commissars. All types of oppositionists, who had been overwhelmingly outvoted in open discussion in years past, had apparently merged in underground fashion, hoping to dislodge the government and party leadership, either through assassination or through connivance with hostile foreign governments or both. The scheme extended into the army, and Marshal Tukhachevski and several other commanders were executed (1937).

In spite of the gathering clouds of war the Soviet Union was making great strides forward economically and culturally. The completion of the First Five-Year Plan (1932) was followed by the Second Five-Year Plan (1933–1937). In 1936 a new constitution replaced the earlier document of 1923. This constitution, usually referred to as the Stalin Constitution or the Constitution of Victorious Socialism, reflected the altogether new conditions resulting from successful industrialization and the collectivization of agriculture. The second half of the 1930's witnessed a renaissance of historical studies and rapid progress in a variety of cultural and scientific fields. The standard of living was rising, new cities were being built, and specialists in many fields were being trained in increasing numbers. A new Soviet-educated generation was coming to the forefront everywhere. But the threat of war grew. In March, 1939, the Eighteenth Party Congress assembled to discuss not only the Third Five-Year Plan but also the threatening international situation.

THE USSR AND THE SECOND WORLD WAR . . . The Soviet republic was born during the First World War and received its first and gravest test in the civil war. The Soviet people were now engaged in building a new type of society and were vitally interested in not having this task interrupted by another war. With the advent of the fascist regime in Germany (1933) the problem of preserving peace became of primary importance. The Soviet Union joined the League of Nations (1934), and diplomatic relations, broken off since the October Revolution, were resumed with the United States (1933). In 1935 the Chinese Eastern Railroad in Manchuria was sold to the Japanese-sponsored local government, so as to avoid an armed conflict with Japan. Soviet diplomacy, through its then chief spokesman, Maxim M. Litvinov (1876–   ), tried to achieve collective security and prevent war. When Japan expanded her aggressive activities in China into a large war (1937), the USSR sent aid to China. When the Spanish government was faced with an armed uprising supported by foreign fascist powers (1936), the USSR also sent aid to the Spanish republicans. When Italy attacked Ethiopia (1935), the USSR advocated joint action by the powers to stop the aggressor. Soviet foreign policy regarded all these acts of aggression not as isolated incidents but as parts of one phenomenon, which if not checked collectively would plunge the world into a second world war. The Munich Conference (1938), to which the USSR was not invited, signaled the failure of the Soviet collective security policy. The point of view of "appeasing" fascism had won over the Soviet idea of collective security.

In the summer of 1938 the Japanese challenged the Red Army on the Soviet-Manchurian border, and the next summer they attempted to invade the Mongolian People's Republic, an ally of the USSR. In neither instance was war declared, or diplomatic relations severed, but both times the Japanese Army was beaten. In the summer of 1939 the Soviet Union attempted to reach a military understanding with England and France, but the negotiations failed miserably. After their breakdown the USSR accepted the offer of Hitlerite Germany to enter into a mutual nonaggression pact—not an alliance, as is so often incorrectly asserted. On September 1, 1939, the German Army invaded Poland. After the Polish government collapsed, the Red Army began to advance (September 17, 1939) toward the on-coming Germans, occupying western Belorussian and Ukrainian territories that had been included in Poland for nearly two decades. In November, 1939, after a plebiscite, these areas were incorporated in the Belorussian and Ukrainian SS republics. From

November 29, 1939, to March 12, 1940, the USSR fought a local war against Finland. After the Red Army had broken through a ring of Finnish fortifications on the Karelian Isthmus next to Leningrad, peace was concluded, with the Finnish border pushed to a safe distance from Leningrad. During this war the governments of England, France, and Italy aided Finland; the League of Nations expelled the USSR from membership; and the United States imposed a "moral embargo" on some exports to the USSR. The newly acquired territory, together with what used to be a Karelo-Finnish Autonomous SSR within the RSFSR, formed the twelfth Union republic, the Karelo-Finnish SSR (March 31, 1940). In June, 1940, Romania surrendered northern Bucovina, inhabited largely by Ukrainians, and Bessarabia, formerly part of Russia but seized by Romania in 1918. The thirteenth Union republic, the Moldavian SSR, was formed (August 2, 1940), embracing Bessarabia and the Moldavian ASSR, formerly part of the RSFSR. Lithuania became the fourteenth Union republic (August 3, 1940), Latvia the fifteenth (August 5), and Estonia was admitted (August 6) as the sixteenth republic. Thus all along its western border the USSR moved forward, toward Germany. In April, 1941, upon Japan's initiative, a nonaggression pact was entered into by the USSR and Japan. On May 6, 1941, Joseph Stalin assumed the post of chairman of the Council of People's Commissars (equivalent to that of prime minister). A member of the Central Committee of the party since 1912, a member of the political bureau of this committee since 1917, and general secretary of the party since 1922, Stalin was a member of the government only in the early days of the Soviet Revolution. Now the foremost political leader in the country returned to active government service. On the early morning of June 22, 1941, without a declaration of war, Hitlerite Germany attacked the Soviet Union.

The advancing enemy penetrated deeply inside the USSR, hoping not only to destroy its armies but also to cripple it economically. While the Red Army was retreating, an unprecedented evacuation of industrial facilities to the Urals, Siberia, and Central Asia from all areas endangered by the enemy was taking place. This migration of industry was accompanied by large movements of population. A complete picture of this evacuation in figures had not become available in 1945, but in the course of the Second World War the movement of industrial production and of population centers eastward, which began with the First Five-Year Plan, undoubtedly increased to a very considerable extent. In addition to very heavy military and civilian losses—figures were again lacking—the Second World War imposed much hardship on the entire population of the USSR. Again, as in the civil war and during the First Five-Year Plan, all activities were directed to one aim, this time toward the expulsion of the invaders and their ultimate destruction. The strenuous efforts made earlier, in industrializing the country and collectivizing agriculture, now proved not only to have been essential but also to have been accomplished just in time. The greatly expanded heavy industries, and particularly the new industrial centers, were able to supply the army with the mechanical equipment needed for modern warfare, which Russian industry was unable to do in the First World War. The existence of collective farming undoubtedly saved the day in a most difficult food situation, which arose when the enemy overran the richest food-producing areas. The nationality policy proved to have been particularly successful, as all the nations and national groups of the USSR contributed to the war with equal ardor, both at the front and in defense work. The eradication of treasonable activities—by drastic means, it is true, but several years before the war broke out—also proved most beneficial.

As soon as the country was invaded, the Greek Orthodox Church came out in support of the war and the government. Earlier the church had opposed the October Revolution; then a large part of the clergy was actively on the side of the Whites during the civil war; and, finally, many clerics resisted collectivization of agriculture. The clergy had fought the Soviet regime on all these issues and had lost decisively, but now in the face of grave danger to the country the church added its efforts to the defense of the fatherland. This change in the attitude of the church, and the aid that the church actually rendered, resulted in certain concessions from the government. With the permission of the government, election of a patriarch was held twice, in 1943 and in 1945.[8]

On the day the USSR was attacked, Winston Churchill stated that England would extend aid. In his first war speech (July 3, 1941) Joseph Stalin said that the Soviet Union would not be alone in this fight. Although still officially neutral, the United States extended lend-lease aid

---

[8] See Chapter XVIII, "Religion Under the Czars and the Soviets."

to the USSR (November 6, 1941). The Soviet Union participated in the joint declaration of the United Nations (January 1, 1942). In the summer of 1942 an alliance with England was concluded, and a joint Anglo-American-Soviet declaration on the opening of a second front in Europe was issued. Gradually the military coalition of the three big powers was more and more substantiated by joint action. A conference of foreign secretaries of the three powers (Moscow, October–November, 1943) decided on a number of war and postwar steps to be taken in common. The heads of the three governments met (Teheran, December, 1943), and definite joint military action was decided on. The USSR actively participated in the constantly growing number of international conferences.[9] The heads of the three governments met once more (Crimea [Yalta], January, 1945), issuing a declaration further emphasizing joint action to win the war and establish a durable peace. For the Soviet Union the Second World War resulted in a military partnership with England and the United States, and also in participation in the United Nations organization intended to secure the peace of the world. In the course of the war the Soviet Union concluded treaties of alliance with England, France, Czechoslovakia, Poland, and Yugoslavia.[10]

The first year of the Soviet-German war witnessed the shattering of the myth of invincibility of the German Army. The tide of the German advance was stopped near Moscow (December 6, 1941), Leningrad was besieged but could not be captured, and Rostov-on-the-Don was recovered. The three-pronged German drive was blunted and the blitzkrieg had failed. In the summer of 1942 the Germans and their allies were able to initiate only one offensive, in the direction of Stalingrad, succeeding also in penetrating the north Caucasus on the right flank of their main drive. The plan to go up the Volga and attack Moscow from the rear failed because of the heroic resistance of Stalingrad. In the winter of 1942–1943 the Germans suffered a decisive defeat near Stalingrad. The summer of 1943 witnessed the third and last attempt of the German Army to organize an offensive. In the battle of the Kursk salient the attack progressed only a few miles, and after that began the offensive of the Red Army, which continued with minor interruptions to the end of the war. In the Second World War the USSR made wide use of guer-

---

[9] See the next chapter.
[10] See *ibid.*

rilla action in the rear of the enemy, in co-ordination with the moves of the regular army. A form of warfare which arose largely spontaneously in the war against Napoleon in 1812 was this time initiated in organized fashion from the start of the enemy invasion.

The Soviet Union regards the Second World War as its second war for the fatherland, the first being that against the Napoleonic invasion. After the liberation of Poland and the Balkans, the capture of Budapest and Vienna, the last big battle took place before Berlin on the river Oder, with the largest concentration of tanks and artillery yet achieved by the Red Army. Berlin was taken (May 1, 1945) and a week later Germany surrendered unconditionally.

BIBLIOGRAPHY

Leroy-Beaulieu, Anatole, *The Empire of the Tsars and the Russians,* 3 vols. (New York, 1893–1896).

Kliuchevsky, V. O., *A History of Russia,* 5 vols. (New York, 1911–1928).

Hecker, J. F., *Russian Sociology* (New York, 1915).

Masaryk, T. G., *The Spirit of Russia,* 2 vols. (New York, 1919).

Reed, John, *Ten Days That Shook the World* (New York, 1919).

Rostovtzeff, M. I., *Iranians and Greeks in South Russia* (New York, 1922).

Schuman, F. L., *American Policy Toward Russia Since 1917* (New York, 1928).

Platonov, S. F., *History of Russia* (New York, 1929).

Chamberlin, W. H., *Soviet Russia—A Living Record and a History* (Boston, 1930).

Fischer, Louis, *The Soviets in World Affairs,* 2 vols. (New York, 1930).

Mirsky, D. S., *Russia, a Social History* (New York, 1930).

Miliukov, P. N., *Ocherki po istorii russkoi kultury,* vols. I–III (Paris, 1930–1937).

Mirsky, D. S., *Lenin* (Boston, 1931).

Yakhontoff, V. A., *Russia and the Soviet Union in the Far East* (New York, 1931).

Robinson, G. T., *Rural Russia Under the Old Regime* (New York, 1932).

Badayev, A., *The Bolsheviks in the Tsarist Duma* (New York, 1933).

Lobanov-Rostovsky, A., *Russia and Asia* (New York, 1933).

Pokrovsky, M. N., *Brief History of Russia,* 2 vols. (New York, 1933).

Stewart, G., *White Armies of Russia* (New York, 1933).

Bunyan, James, and Fisher, H. H., *The Bolshevik Revolution, 1917–1918* (Palo Alto, 1934).

Chamberlin, W. H., *The Russian Revolution, 1917–1921,* 2 vols. (New York, 1935).

Harper, S. N., ed., *The Soviet Union and World Problems* (Chicago, 1935).

Report of Court Proceedings by People's Commissariat of Justice of the U.S.S.R., *The Case of the Trotskyite-Zinovievite Terrorist Centre* (Moscow, 1936).

Stalin, J., and others, *The History of the Civil War in the USSR,* vol. I (New York, 1936).

Kliuchevskii, V., *Kurs russkoi istorii,* 5 vols., 4th ed., rev. (Moscow, 1937).

Report of Court Proceedings by People's Commissariat of Justice of the U.S.S.R., *The Case of the Anti-Soviet Trotskyite Centre* (Moscow, 1937).

——, *The Case of the Anti-Soviet "Bloc of Rights and Trotskyites"* (Moscow, 1938).

Lenin, V. I., and Stalin, Joseph, *The Russian Revolution, Writings and Speeches* (New York, 1938).

Shestakov, A. V., ed., *A Short History of the USSR* (Moscow, 1938).

History of the Communist Party of the Soviet Union (Bolsheviks), official text (New York, 1939).

Litvinov, Maxim, *Against Aggression*, speeches and documents (New York, 1939).

Pares, Bernard, *The Fall of the Russian Monarchy* (New York, 1939).

Istoriia SSSR, Lebedev, V. I., and others, eds., vol. I (Moscow, 1939).

——, Nechkina, M. V., ed., vol. II (Moscow, 1940).

Curtiss, J. S., *Church and State in Russia* (New York, 1940).

Khrestomatiia po istorii SSSR, Lebedev, V. I., and others, eds., vol. I, new ed. (Moscow, 1940).

——, Dmitriev, S. S., and Nechkina, M. V., eds., vol. II, pt. I (Moscow, 1941).

Pankratova, A. M., ed., *Istoriia, SSSR*, 3 vols. (Moscow, 1940–1941).

Graves, W. S., *America's Siberian Adventure, 1918–1920*, reprint (New York, 1941).

Potemkin, V. P., ed., *Istoriia diplomatii*, vol. I (Moscow, 1941).

Goodall, George, ed., *Soviet Russia in Maps* (Chicago, 1942).

Kafengauz, B., *Vneshniaia politika Rossii pri Petre I* (Moscow, 1942).

Kournakoff, S. N., *Russia's Fighting Forces* (New York, 1942).

Marx-Engels-Lenin Institute, *Joseph Stalin: A Short Biography* (Moscow, 1942).

Miliukov, Paul, *Outlines of Russian Culture*, 3 pts. (Philadelphia, 1942).

Moscow Patriarchate, *Pravda o religii v Rossii* (Moscow, 1942).

Stalin, Joseph, *The War of National Liberation*, pamphlet (New York, 1942).

Tarlé, Eugene, *Napoleon's Invasion of Russia, 1812* (New York, 1942).

Vasetskii, G., and Iovchuk, M., *Ocherki po istorii russkogo materializma XVII i XIX vv.* (Moscow, 1942).

Volgin, V. P., Tarlé, E. V., and Pankratova, A. M., eds., *Dvatsat piat let istoricheskoi nauki v SSSR* (Moscow, 1942).

Coates, W. P. and Z. K., *A History of Anglo-Soviet Relations* (London, 1943).

Kornilov, Alexander, *Modern Russian History*, new ed. (New York, 1943).

Manandian, I. A., *Tigran Vtoroi i Rim* (Erevan, 1943).

Marx-Engels-Lenin Institute, *Vladimir Lenin: A Political Biography* (New York, 1943).

Stalin, Joseph, *The War of National Liberation*, 2d collection, pamphlet (New York, 1943).

Vernadsky, George, *Ancient Russia* (New Haven, 1943).

Anderson, P. B., *People, Church and State in Modern Russia* (New York, 1944).

Dulles, F. R., *The Road to Teheran* (Princeton, 1944).

Grekov, B. D., *Kievskaia Rus*, 4th ed. (Moscow, 1944).

Pares, Bernard, *A History of Russia*, new ed. (New York, 1944).

Tarlé, E. V., *Krimskaia voina*, vol. I (Moscow, 1944).

Vernadsky, George, *A History of Russia* (New York, 1944).

Vipper, R. Y., *Ivan Groznyi*, 3d ed. (Moscow, 1944).

Vneshniaia politika Sovietskogo soiuza v period Otechestvennoi voiny, vol. I (Moscow, 1944).

CHAPTER IV

Foreign Affairs: Chronology

By VLADIMIR D. AND EMILY G. KAZAKÉVICH

ON NOVEMBER 7, 1917, Soviet authority was established in Russia as a result of the October Revolution (October 25 by old calendar, or November 7 by new calendar). Below is given a chronology of the more important events relating to the foreign affairs of the Soviet state from its inception to May 8, 1945.

1917

November 8—"Decree on Peace" adopted by 2d Congress of Soviets; addressed to governments and peoples of all belligerent nations.

November 15—"Declaration of Rights of the Peoples of Russia," decree of the Soviet government setting forth the basic principles governing its policy toward the different nationalities.

November 22—Soviet note to Allied ambassadors proposing immediate armistice on all fronts and opening of peace negotiations.

November 23—Publication of secret diplomatic documents of previous Russian regimes started.

November 27—German government accepts Soviet offer to negotiate armistice.

December 3—Opening of armistice negotiations with Central Powers at Brest-Litovsk.

Manifesto of the People's Commissariat of Nationalities "to all the toiling Moslems of Russia and the East," renouncing the colonial policies of previous Russian governments.

December 15—Representatives of Soviet Russia and Central Powers sign an armistice at Brest-Litovsk.

December 22—Peace negotiations opened at Brest-Litovsk.

English, French, United States representatives in Paris decide to aid all anti-Soviet forces in Russia.

December 23—Convention between France and England on the subject of activity in southern Russia signed in Paris.

December 31—Council of People's Commissars recognizes independence of Finland.

1918

January 8—Wilson's address to United States Congress, containing the Fourteen Points.

January 10—Representatives of the Ukrainian Rada (assembly) join peace negotiations at Brest-Litovsk.

January 14—British cruiser arrives at Vladivostok.

January 17—Japanese cruiser arrives at Vladivostok.

January 26—Romanian troops occupy Kishinev (Bessarabia); Soviet government breaks relations with Romania.

January 28—Revolutionary government formed in Finland; civil war breaks out.

February 8—Soviet troops take Kiev; Ukrainian Rada flees to Zhitomir.

February 9—Ukrainian Rada signs separate peace with Central Powers.

February 10—Soviet delegation breaks off peace negotiations at Brest-Litovsk; Trotsky's "No peace, no war" declaration.

February 16—Germans declare armistice ended as of noon, February 18.

February 17—Ukrainian Rada asks for German help against Soviets.

February 18—Council of People's Commissars agrees to accept German peace terms. German troops begin general advance into Russia.

February 21—Council of People's Commissars proclaims: "The socialist fatherland is in danger," as German offensive continues.

February 23—Soviet troops successfully resist German forces near Pskov—official birthday of the Red Army.

Council of People's Commissars accepts new German terms.

February 27—United States and other foreign embassies leave Petrograd for Vologda.

March 1—Germans take Kiev; Ukrainian Rada restored.

United States cruiser arrives at Vladivostok.

Soviet government of Finland signs treaty of friendship with Soviet Russia.

March 2—Murmansk soviet hands over control of economic and military affairs to Allied forces.

March 3—Treaty of Brest-Litovsk signed by Soviet delegation, taking Soviet Russia out of the First World War.

March 4—Germans occupy Narva.

March 5–9—Agreement between RSFSR and Romania on military and political matters, whereby latter agrees to evacuate Bessarabia in two months.

March 9—British land troops at Murmansk.

March 10–11—Soviet government moves from Petrograd to Moscow.

March 11—President Wilson's message to the Congress of Soviets, expressing sympathy with the Russian people.

March 14—Austro-Hungarian troops take Odessa.

March 15—Extraordinary 4th Congress of Soviets ratifies Brest-Litovsk Treaty.

March 18—Allied Supreme Council in London declares its nonrecognition of Brest-Litovsk peace.

French cruiser arrives at Murmansk.

March 25—Exchange of notes between Japan and Peking government on joint action against Soviet Russia.

March 26—Soviet-Czechoslovakian agreement for evacuation of Czechoslovak troops.

April 5—Japanese and British forces land in Vladivostok.

April 6—Soviet note of protest to Allied governments on Japanese intervention.

April 8—Germans occupy Kharkov.

April 9—Romania proclaims incorporation of Bessarabia.

April 14—Batum occupied by Turkish forces.

April 18—Soviet government protests Romanian seizure of Bessarabia.

April 20—Germans occupy Crimea.

April 22—Anti-Soviet authorities in Transcaucasia declare separation of that region from Russia.

April 29—Pavel P. Skoropadski proclaimed hetman of the Ukraine, with German backing.

Viborg, last stronghold of Finnish Soviet government, falls to German and Finnish White forces.

May 8—German and White Cossack forces take Rostov-on-the-Don.

May 23—Opening of peace negotiations between RSFSR and Ukrainian government of Skoropadski at Kiev.

May 24—American cruiser arrives at Murmansk.

May 27—Czechoslovak troops seize Cheliabinsk on Trans-Siberian Railway.

May 28—German control over railroads in Georgia established.

May 31—Czechoslovak troops take Tomsk; anti-Soviet "Commissariat of Western Siberia" established.

June 4—England, France, Italy, United States warn Soviet government that disarming of Czechoslovak detachments would be considered a hostile act.

June 7—Czechoslovak troops take Omsk.

June 8—Czechoslovak troops take Samara; formation in Samara of Socialist-Revolutionary government.

June 14—Soviet note protests presence of Allied warships in northern Russian ports.

Armistice signed with Skoropadski government at Kiev.

June 25—New landing of British forces at Murmansk.

June 28—Soviet note of protest on landing of British forces in Murmansk.

June 29—Czechoslovak troops take Vladivostok.

June 30—Anti-Soviet "Provisional Government of Siberia" replaces "Commissariat of Western Siberia."

July 6—Count von Mirbach, German ambassador in Moscow, is assassinated.

Anti-Soviet uprising in Yaroslavl.

July 25—Allied diplomats leave Vologda for Archangel.

August 2—Allied occupation of Archangel. Formation of anti-Soviet "Government of North Russia" at Archangel.

August 3—British troops arrive in Vladivostok.

August 4—British troops enter Baku.

August 6—Soviet note protests Anglo-French invasion.

August 7—Czechoslovak troops take Kazan.

August 9—French colonial troops arrive in Vladivostok.

August 11—Japanese troops arrive in Vladivostok.

August 16—United States troops arrive in Vladivostok.

August 26—General Anton I. Denikin's White forces in Kuban area take Novorossisk.

August 31—Anti-Soviet conspiracy, headed by unofficial British representative in Moscow, Bruce Lockhart, discovered by Soviet government.

September 4—Landing of American forces in Archangel.

September 7—Stalin telegraphs Lenin that Tsaritsyn (now Stalingrad) has been successfully defended from German-supported White forces of General P. N. Krasnov.

September 8–23—Anti-Soviet "All Russian Provisional Government" (Directory) formed at Omsk.

September 10—Red Army recovers Kazan from Czechoslovak and White forces.

September 15—Turks occupy Baku after departure of British.

October 7—Red Army recovers Samara from Czechoslovak and White forces.

October 30—Armistice between Turkey and the Allies permits entry of Allied warships into Black Sea.

November 8—Armistice proposal by Extraordinary 6th Congress of Soviets, addressed to "the governments of the United States of America, England, France, Italy and Japan, waging war against Russia."

November 11—Armistice between Allies and Germany, with clause providing that German occupation troops remain in Russia until Allies take over.

November 13—Soviet government annuls Brest-Litovsk Treaty.

November 17—British reoccupy Baku.

November 18—Admiral Alexander V. Kolchak takes power in Omsk as "Supreme Ruler of Russia."

November 22—Denikin's White Army lands in Crimea.

November 25–26—First Allied warships arrive at Sevastopol and Odessa.

November 27—Kolchak forces begin offensive west of Urals.

December 10—Red Army takes Minsk from German troops.

December 13—Rupture of relations between Poland and Soviet Russia.

December 14—Skoropadski flees to Germany; Kiev occupied by Ukrainian nationalist forces of Petlura.

December 15—British occupy Batum.

December 22—Soviet government recognizes independence of Lithuanian and Latvian Soviet republics.

December 24—Soviet peace proposals to Allies.

1919

January 2—Ludwig Martens appointed representative of People's Commissariat of Foreign Affairs in the United States.

January 3—Red Army takes Riga and Kharkov.

January 17—Soviet peace proposal to Allies.

January 22—Allied Supreme Council invites representatives of all Russian governments and groups to a peace conference at Prinkipo.

January 24—White governments refuse invitation to Prinkipo Conference.

January 29—Soviet offer to start negotiations with Poland.

February 4—Soviet government expresses willingness to attend Prinkipo Conference.

February 6—Red Army takes Kiev.

February 18—William C. Bullitt directed to go to Russia by United States Secretary of State Lansing.

March 8—Poles occupy Pinsk.

April 6—Mutiny in units of French fleet in Odessa.
Red Army enters Odessa after French evacuation.

April 10—Red Army enters Crimea.

April 16—French evacuation of Sevastopol. End of French intervention in south Russia.

April 19—Poles occupy Vilna.

April 26—Kolchak offensive stopped before reaching Volga River.

May 1—Soviet government demands evacuation of Bessarabia by Romania.

May 19—Start of Denikin offensive from southeast Russia.

June 12—Raid on the office of Ludwig Martens in New York.

June 13—Denikin forces enter Kharkov.

June 14—Kolchak, leader of White forces in Siberia, recognized by Allies as "Supreme Ruler of Russia."

June 26—American troops evacuate Archangel.

June 29—Denikin forces complete occupation of Crimea.

July 25—Soviet declaration of policy toward China.

August 22—Poles occupy Minsk.

August 31—Denikin forces take Kiev.

September 7—Peace negotiations with Estonia begun.

September 27—British evacuate Archangel.

October 11—White General N. N. Yudenich starts drive on Petrograd.

October 12—British evacuate Murmansk.

October 22—Yudenich pushed back from suburbs of Petrograd.

November 1—British troops leave Vladivostok.

November 8—Lloyd George's "Guildhall Speech" indicating the beginning of a turn in British policy toward Soviet Russia.

November 14—Kolchak's capital, Omsk, occupied by Red Army.

December 8—So-called Curzon Line drawn for the first time by Allied Supreme Council.

December 10—Vice Commissar of Foreign Affairs M. M. Litvinov sends peace proposals to Allied legations in Copenhagen, the ninth such offer since November 7, 1918.

December 16—Red Army takes Kiev from Denikin forces.

December 22—Soviet government invites Polish government to peace negotiations.

1920

January 8—Red Army takes Rostov-on-the-Don from retreating Denikin forces.

January 16—Allied Supreme Council decides to lift blockade of Soviet Russia and renew trade relations with Russian co-operative organizations.

January 28—Soviet government repeats invitation to Poles to open peace negotiations.

February 2—Peace treaty between RSFSR and Estonia.

February 7—Kolchak executed in Irkutsk.

February 20—Red Army occupies Archangel.

February 23—Red Army occupies Murmansk.

February 24—Allied Supreme Council announces readiness to encourage commerce with Russia but not diplomatic relations.

March 27—Red Army takes Novorossisk, last Denikin stronghold.

April 1—Last American troops leave Vladivostok.

April 4—Baron Peter Wrangel takes over command of White forces in south Russia from Denikin.

April 6—Far Eastern Republic established at Verkhneudinsk near Lake Baikal.

April 25—Allied Supreme Council announces decision to open trade talks with Soviet representatives.

Polish Army starts advance toward Kiev.

April 27—Red Army takes Baku; Soviet regime established in Azerbaidzhan.

May 6—Polish troops occupy Kiev.

May 7—Treaty between RSFSR and Georgia, recognizing latter's independence.

May 10—London dockers refuse to load munitions consigned to Poland.

May 31—British-Soviet trade talks open in London.

June 8—Wrangel's forces strike north from the Crimea.

June 12—Red Army recovers Kiev from Poles.

Publication of report of British Labour Delegation in Russia calling for removal of blockade and intervention and for recognition of Soviet government.

July 7—Announcement by the United States Department of State that previous restrictions impeding trade and communication with Soviet Russia are removed.

July 10—Poland appeals for Allied aid against Red Army.

July 11—British note proposing Allied intervention in Polish-Soviet conflict.

Red Army liberates Minsk from Poles.

July 12—General treaty between RSFSR and Lithuania.

July 14—British Trade Union Congress adopts resolution warning against British aid to Poland.

July 17—Soviet note to Allies expresses willingness to negotiate directly with Poles.

July 20—Allied ultimatum to Moscow threatening to support Poles in case Red Army invades Poland.

July 22—Poles agree to negotiate with Soviet Russia.

July 25—British and French missions, including Gen. Maxime Weygand, arrive in Warsaw.

July 31—Abortive peace negotiations with Poland open at Baranovichi.

August 2—Polish delegation returns to Warsaw.

August 5—Red Army nears Warsaw.

August 10—Note of United States Secretary of State Colby to Italian ambassador in Washington outlining United States policy toward Russia.

August 11—Peace treaty between RSFSR and Latvia.

France recognizes General Wrangel's White government in Crimea as the government of Russia.

August 15—Red Army repulsed near Warsaw; begins retreat.

September 2—Congress of the Peoples of the East opens at Baku.

September 21—Negotiations with Poland begun at Riga.

October 12—Armistice and preliminary peace terms signed with Poland at Riga.

October 14—Peace treaty between RSFSR and Finland.

October 27—Soviet proposals to Chinese government for settlement of outstanding questions with China.
November 9—General Wrangel decisively defeated by Red Army in Crimea.
November 13—Polish-Soviet conference reassembles at Riga.
November 29—Soviet regime established in Armenia.

1921

January 22—Ludwig Martens leaves New York for Soviet Russia under decision of United States Department of Labor of December 15, 1919.
January 24—Boundary treaty with Far Eastern Republic.
February 14—General treaty between Ukrainian SSR and Lithuania.
February 25—Soviet regime established in Georgia.
February 26—General treaty between RSFSR and Persia (Iran).
February 28—General treaty between RSFSR and Afghanistan.
March 16—Trade agreement between RSFSR and Great Britain.
  Treaty of Friendship and fraternity between RSFSR and Turkey (Anatolian Treaty).
March 18—Peace treaty of Riga, between RSFSR, Belorussian SSR, and Ukrainian SSR and Poland.
March 21—Maxim M. Litvinov's offer to United States to establish relations.
March 25—United States Secretary of State Charles E. Hughes refuses to consider the offer.
May 6—Provisional agreement between the RSFSR and Germany.
July 19—Soviet government protests exclusion from Washington conference on Pacific problems.
August 3—General treaty between Ukrainian SSR and Latvia.
August 19—Agreement with American Relief Administration on famine relief.
September 2—Provisional trade agreement between RSFSR and Norway.
October 13—Treaty of friendship between the Armenian, Azerbaidzhanian, and Georgian SSR's of the one part, and Turkey of the other; RSFSR participating.
November 5—Agreement between RSFSR and Mongolian People's Republic (Outer Mongolia) for the establishment of friendly relations.
November 25—General treaty between the Ukrainian SSR and Estonia.
December 3—Arrival in Washington, D.C., of special delegation of the Far Eastern Republic.
December 7—Provisional agreement between the RSFSR and the Ukrainian SSR of the one part, and the Republic of Austria of the other.
December 17—United States House of Representatives approves appropriation of $20,000,000 for Russian relief.
December 26—Preliminary agreement between RSFSR and Italy.
  Preliminary agreement between Ukrainian SSR and Italy.

1922

January 7—Allied Supreme Council, through Italian government, invites Soviet Russia to participate in financial and economic conference to be held at Genoa.
January 21—Treaty of friendship and fraternity between Ukrainian SSR and Turkey.

February 10–12—Far Eastern Republic and partisan troops take Volochaevka by storm from Japanese-supported White forces.

February 14—Khabarovsk occupied by revolutionary forces.

March 12—Armenian, Georgian, and Azerbaidzhanian SSR's form Transcaucasian SFSR.

March 30—Conference of Baltic countries at Riga, on Soviet motion, signs protocol declaring it would "fully support the principle of limitation of armaments in all States."

April 5—Supplementary treaty to Ukrainian-Latvian treaty of February 14, 1921.

April 10—Russian delegation at Genoa states its support of limitation of armaments.

April 10–May 19—Genoa Conference, first international gathering attended by Soviet representatives.

May 16—Treaty of Rapallo, general treaty between RSFSR and Germany.

June 5—Provisional treaty between RSFSR and Czechoslovakia.

June 6—Provisional treaty between Ukrainian SSR and Czechoslovakia.

June 12—Soviet proposal to Estonia, Finland, Latvia, and Poland to call conference at Moscow on reduction of armaments.

June, 15–July 28—Hague Conference; Soviet delegation proposes universal disarmament to prevent wars.

July 24—Japan announces intention to evacuate Siberia before October 30.

September 4—Representatives of Japan, Far Eastern Republic, and RSFSR open conference on Japanese evacuation.

September 25—Conference with Japanese breaks up; latter refuses to evacuate northern Sakhalin.

October 25—Japanese troops and remains of White armies evacuate Vladivostok.

November 13—National Assembly of Far Eastern Republic votes to amalgamate with RSFSR.

November 16—Soviet government proclaims incorporation of Far Eastern Republic in RSFSR.

December 12—Moscow Disarmament Conference ends without reaching agreement.

December 18—Soviet delegation submits proposal for control of Dardanelles and Bosporus at Lausanne Conference.

December 30—Treaty of federation concluded between RSFSR, Ukrainian and Belorussian SSR's, and Transcaucasian SFSR; 1st Congress of Soviets of USSR opens.

1923

April 23—Preliminary trade agreement between RSFSR and Denmark.

May 8—British note containing so-called Curzon ultimatum delivered in Moscow.

May 10—Assassination in Switzerland of Soviet representative to Italy, V. V. Vorovsky.

July 19—Ukrainian Commissariat of Foreign Affairs notifies representatives of foreign powers that foreign relations have been transferred to jurisdiction of the USSR.

July 21—Similar announcements made by Commissariats of Foreign Affairs of RSFSR, Belorussian SSR, and Transcaucasian SFSR.

August 14—Soviet representative signs Lausanne Convention on Dardanelles and Bosporus.

116

December 16—Foreign Commissar Georgi V. Chicherin's cable to President Coolidge proposing resumption of friendly relations.

December 18—United States Secretary of State Hughes refuses to enter into negotiations.

1924

February 2–8—Exchange of notes with Great Britain establishing diplomatic relations.

February 7—Exchange of notes with Italy establishing diplomatic relations.
Trade treaty and customs convention with Italy.

February 25–26—Exchange of notes with Austria establishing diplomatic relations.

February 15–March 10—Exchange of notes with Norway establishing diplomatic relations.

March 8—Exchange of notes with Greece establishing diplomatic relations.

March 15–18—Exchange of notes with Sweden establishing diplomatic relations.

March 15—Trade agreement with Sweden.

May 31—Treaty on the general principles for regulating questions between the USSR and the Chinese Republic.
Agreement with China on the Chinese Eastern Railway.

June 18—Exchange of notes with Denmark establishing diplomatic relations.

July 29—Protocol on the liquidation of the German-Soviet conflict.

August 4—Declaration concerning renewal of relations, made by the Mexican ambassador in Berlin.

August 8—Drafts of a general treaty and a treaty of commerce and navigation signed by British Prime Minister Ramsay MacDonald.

September 20—Agreement with Chinese authorities in Manchuria on the Chinese Eastern Railway and other matters.

October 25—Publication of the so-called "Zinoviev Letter" in London on the eve of the British general election; declared on the same day by the Soviet chargé d'affaires to be a forgery.

October 28—Exchange of telegrams with France establishing diplomatic relations.

November 21—British note to Soviet government on nonratification of draft treaties of August 8, 1924.

1925

January 20—Convention with Japan relating to fundamental principles of mutual relations.

April 4—Northern Sakhalin surrendered by Japan to USSR.

August 3—Agreement with Poland for settling frontier disputes.

October 12—General treaty with Germany.

December 15—Treaty on trade and navigation with Norway.

December 17—Treaty of friendship, nonaggression, and neutrality with Turkey.

1926

January 22—Soviet protest to Peking government obtains release of Soviet manager of Chinese Eastern Railway, arrested by Chinese Manchurian authorities.

February 16–April 17, 1927—Exchange of notes with Saudi Arabia on establishment of diplomatic relations.

April 24—Treaty with Germany concerning neutrality and nonaggression.

June 22–24—Correspondence with Iceland on establishment of relations.

July 19—Convention with Latvia concerning settlement of frontier disputes.

August 21–22—Establishment of diplomatic relations with Uruguay.

August 31—Nonaggression treaty with Afghanistan.

Protest by Soviet government to Peking government on order of Marshal Chang Tso-lin confiscating the merchant fleet of the Chinese Eastern Railway.

September 28—Nonaggression treaty with Lithuania.

1927

April 6—Raid on Soviet Embassy in Peking.

April 9—Note to Peking government demanding liberation of Soviet employees arrested in raid of April 6. Soviet Embassy withdraws from Peking pending satisfaction of demands.

May 4–23—International Economic Conference at Geneva with participation of USSR.

May 12—British police raid premises of Arcos Limited and Soviet Trade Delegation in London.

May 17—Soviet note to British government, protesting British raid on trade delegation.

May 25—Exchange of notes with Iceland on most-favored-nation treatment.

May 26—British note suspending relations with USSR.

June 2—Trade treaty with Latvia.

June 7—Voikov, Soviet plenipotentiary representative to Poland, assassinated in Warsaw.

August 8—Agreement with Estonia on procedure in settling border conflicts.

October 1—Treaty on guarantee and neutrality with Iran.

Customs convention and exchange of notes on trade relations with Iran.

October 8—Agreement with Sweden on status of Soviet trade delegation.

October 25—Soviet government protests exclusion from International Radio-Telegraph Conference in Washington, D.C.

November 30—Soviet disarmament proposal submitted by M. M. Litvinov at Geneva Preparatory Conference on Disarmament.

December 15—Severance of relations with Nanking government, following arrest of Soviet consul general and shooting of Soviet vice consul in Canton.

1928

January 28—Fisheries convention with Japan, granting Japanese subjects fishing concessions in Soviet waters in the Far East.

March 6—United States Treasury forbids Assay Office to accept Soviet gold.

March 15—Interruption of German-Soviet trade negotiations in connection with arrest of German engineers in Donets coal basin.

March 23—Soviet proposal for complete disarmament rejected at Geneva Conference. Soviet delegation submits proposal for partial disarmament.

April 14—Statement by United States Secretary of State Kellogg re-emphasizing U.S. policy of nonrecognition of the USSR.

May 18–July 5—Trial of 54 engineers, including three Germans, for sabotage of Donets coal mines.

August 27—USSR adheres to Briand-Kellogg Pact, renouncing war as an instrument for settling international disputes.

September 4—Exchange of notes with Lithuania on most-favored-nation treatment.

November 1—Treaty with Yemen on friendship and trade.

December 21—Protocol of Soviet-German negotiations, defining and developing provisions of October 12, 1925, treaty.

1929

February 9—Protocol with Estonia, Latvia, Poland, Romania, renouncing war.

March 10—Customs convention with Iran.

April 13—Customs and navigation convention with Finland, on customs supervision in Gulf of Finland, co-operation in the struggle against contraband, and on navigation rights.

May 17—Treaty on trade and navigation with Estonia.

May 27—Chinese authorities raid Soviet Consulate in Harbin.

June 11—Treaty on trade and navigation with Greece.

July 10—Soviet manager of Chinese Eastern Railway arrested and the Chinese take control of road.

July 18—Soviet government withdraws all commercial and consular representatives from China, after failure to settle incident of July 10.

October 3—Protocol providing for resumption of diplomatic relations with Great Britain.

November 17—Soviet troops begin advance into Manchuria.

November 26—Mukden authorities accept Moscow conditions for starting negotiations.

December 3—Preliminary protocol signed by Soviet and Chinese representatives.

December 17—Protocol renewing nonaggression pact of December 17, 1925 with Turkey.

December 22—Protocol on restoration of *status quo ante* on Chinese Eastern Railway.

1930

January 26—Mexico announces the recall of her diplomatic mission from Moscow.

February 1—Statement by Litvinov to the press on break with Mexico.

February 2—Pope Pius XI's letter to Cardinal Pompili on setting aside a special day of prayer to save the Russian people.

April 16—Temporary commercial agreement with Great Britain.

April 26—Attempt to blow up the Soviet Embassy in Warsaw.

July 16—Protest to Finland against expulsion of people across Soviet border.

July 25—M. M. Litvinov appointed commissar of foreign affairs.

August 2—Commercial agreement with Italy.

September 16—In reply to Soviet note, Finland charges USSR with border violation.

September 28—Note to Finland on border question.
October 7—Protest to Mukden on activities of White Russians in Manchuria.
October 11—Opening of Soviet-Chinese conference in Moscow.
October 20—Council of People's Commissars rules to retaliate against countries which impose restrictions on trade relations with USSR.

1931

March 16—Treaty of trade and navigation with Turkey.
March 26—USSR participates in Rome conference on world grain crisis.
April 28—Renewal of agreement of August 2, 1930, with Italy.
May 6—Nonaggression treaty of September 28, 1926, with Lithuania renewed for five years.
May 18—Litvinov proposes economic nonaggression pact to League of Nations commission for the study of a European Union, meeting at Geneva.
May 18–23—USSR participates in London Conference on world wheat production.
June 24—Treaty of neutrality and nonaggression with Afghanistan.
  Protocol on extension of nonaggression treaty of April 24, 1926, with Germany.
August 25—USSR endorses Geneva Convention of July 27, 1929, on the improvement of treatment of sick and wounded armed forces engaged in combat.
August 29—Protocol regulating juridical status of Soviet trade delegation in Lithuania.
October 27—Convention on settlers, trade, and navigation with Iran.
October 30—Protocol on extension for five years of nonaggression pact with Turkey.

1932

January 21—Treaty of nonaggression and peaceful settlement of disputes with Finland.
February 5—Nonaggression treaty with Latvia.
May 4—Treaty of nonaggression and peaceful settlement of disputes with Estonia.
May 28—Tariff protocol with Germany.
July 25—Nonaggression treaty with Poland.
August 13—Fishing agreement with Japan, regulating questions in connection with convention of January 23, 1928.
August 25—Col. Hugh L. Cooper, chief consulting engineer of Dneprostroi, and members of his staff decorated by Soviet government.
October 7—British note terminating temporary commercial agreement of April 16, 1930.
November 29—Nonaggression treaty with France.
December 12—Exchange of notes with Nanking government on resumption of diplomatic relations.

1933

February 6—Litvinov offers draft declaration on definition of aggression to general commission of Disarmament Conference.

March 12—Arrest of six British employees of Metropolitan Vickers, Ltd., in Moscow on charges of espionage and sabotage.

April 6—British Parliament votes bill for embargo on imports from USSR.

April 12–18—Trial of British engineers in Moscow.

April 19—British embargo on imports from USSR proclaimed.

April 22—Soviet government decree on retaliatory measures in answer to British embargo.

May 6—New commercial treaty with Italy.

May 29—Trade agreement and credit arrangements with Norway.

June 21—Draft protocol on economic nonaggression submitted by Soviet delegation to World Economic Congress.

June 28—Negotiations open for sale of Chinese Eastern Railway to Manchukuo.

July 1—British government lifts embargo on Soviet goods.
  Soviet retaliatory measures revoked.
  Prison sentences of British engineers commuted and engineers released.
  British government proposes resumption of negotiations for a trade agreement.

July 4—USSR, Romania, Czchoslovakia, Turkey, Yugoslavia sign convention on definition of aggression.

July 5—Convention with Lithuania on definition of aggression.

July 22—Finland adheres to convention of nonaggression.

July 28—Exchange of telegrams with Spain on establishment of diplomatic relations.

September 2—Treaty of friendship, nonaggression, and neutrality with Italy.

September 8—Temporary agreement with Greece, regulating transfer of payments for Soviet exports to Greece.

October 8—Soviet government publishes Japanese documents indicating Japanese plan to seize Chinese Eastern Railway.

October 10—President Roosevelt invites M. I. Kalinin, chairman of the Central Executive Committee of USSR, to send a representative to discuss outstanding questions between the United States and USSR.

October 17—Kalinin accepts United States invitation and announces that Litvinov will represent USSR in discussions.

November 16—Normal diplomatic relations established with United States by exchange of notes between Roosevelt and Litvinov at the White House.

December 4—New trade treaty with Latvia.

December 7—Soviet delegates withdraw from Tokyo conference on Chinese Eastern Railway.

1934

January 11—Provisional trade agreement with France.

January 14–16—Arrested Soviet officials of Chinese Eastern Railway released by Japan; negotiations on sale of Chinese Eastern Railway resumed.

January 21—Protocol with Turkey under which USSR grants Turkey an $8,000,000 credit for purchase of machinery in USSR.

January 24—United States Treasury lifts various restrictions hampering Soviet-American trade.

January 26—In report to 17th Communist Party Congress Stalin discusses Soviet foreign relations and notes Japan's refusal to conclude a nonaggression pact.

February 4—Exchange of notes with Hungary establishing diplomatic relations.
February 16—Provisional trade agreement with Great Britain.
March 28—Soviet government proposes to German government a protocol on preservation of the independence of Baltic States.
April 4—Nonaggression treaty with Lithuania extended until December 31, 1945.
    Nonaggression treaty with Latvia extended until December 31, 1945.
    Nonaggression treaty with Estonia extended until December 31, 1945.
April 7—Nonaggression treaty with Finland extended until December 31, 1945.
April 11—Germany rejects Soviet proposal of March 28, 1934.
May 5—Nonaggression treaty with Poland extended until December 31, 1945.
May 8—Trade agreement with Greece.
May 29—Litvinov's speech to general commission of Disarmament Conference, discussing reasons for failure to reach agreement on disarmament and proposing continuance of conference as a permanent organ for the preservation of security against aggression.
June 9—Exchange of notes establishing diplomatic relations with Czechoslovakia.
    Exchange of notes establishing diplomatic relations with Romania.
July 23—Exchange of telegrams establishing diplomatic relations with Bulgaria.
September 15—USSR accepts invitation of 30 countries to join League of Nations.
September 17—Exchange of notes establishing diplomatic relations with Albania.
September 18—Formal induction of USSR into League of Nations, with a permanent seat on the council; Litvinov's first speech before League Assembly.
October 31—Trade agreement with Estonia.
November 27—Mutual assistance agreement with Mongolian People's Republic.
December 5—Protocol with France providing for Franco-Soviet collaboration in negotiations for an east European pact.
December 7—Exchange of notes with Czechoslovakia on problems related to negotiations for an east European pact.
December 9—Protocol with France on conclusion of a new trade agreement.

1935

January–February—Border clashes on Manchukuo–Outer Mongolian frontier.
March 23—Agreement with Manchukuo on surrender of Soviet rights in Chinese Eastern Railway.
March 25—Trade agreement with Czechoslovakia.
March 26—Negotiations concluded at Tokyo for sale of Chinese Eastern Railway.
March 27–31—Anthony Eden visits Moscow, confers with Stalin, Litvinov, Molotov.
April 18—Litvinov's speech to extraordinary session of League of Nations on Germany's violation of the Versailles Treaty.
May 2—Mutual assistance pact with France.
May 15—Mutual assistance pact with Czechoslovakia.
June 25—Exchange of notes establishing diplomatic relations with Colombia.
July 1—Soviet ambassador at Tokyo protests long series of violations of Soviet territory by Japanese and Manchukuo forces.
July 13—Exchange of notes establishing diplomatic relations with Belgium.
    Exchange of notes with United States on tariff and trade.
August 25—United States note protesting activities of the Communist International.

August 27—Soviet reply to United States note.

New trade agreement with Iran.

September 5—Trade convention with Belgium.

October 13—Soviet protest to Japan over military invasions of Soviet territory by Manchukuo patrols commanded by Japanese officers.

November 7—Nonaggression treaty with Turkey extended for ten years.

December 27—Uruguay breaks relations with USSR.

December 31—USSR protests Uruguay's action to League of Nations.

1936

January 6—Trade agreement with France.

January 15—Trade agreement with Lithuania.

January 30—Protest to Japan on invasion of Soviet territory by Manchukuo and Japanese troops.

February 15—Soviet government announces closing of consulate general in Mukden.

February 17—Manchukuo protests to Mongolian People's Republic on alleged occupation of Manchukuo territory.

February 22—Soviet government informs Japan that it views "with serious concern" frequent clashes on Mongolian-Manchukuo border.

March 12—Protocol of mutual assistance with Mongolian People's Republic.

March 16—Publication of exchange of notes between Mongolian People's Republic and Manchukuo. Agreement on proposal to set up mixed commission to investigate border incidents.

March 17—In speech to League of Nations Council Litvinov protests German remilitarization of Rhineland.

March 19—Soviet Ambassador Ivan Maisky in London speech asserts that Franco-Soviet mutual assistance pact of 1935 "is open, even now, for Germany to enter."

March 26—Soviet-German trade discussions halted.

March 27—Armed clashes with Japanese-Manchukuo forces on both western and eastern Manchukuo borders reported.

March 29—Nonaggression treaty with Afghanistan extended for ten years.

March 31–April 1—Japanese and Manchukuo troops invade Outer Mongolia and are expelled.

April 7—Chinese government protests to USSR that Soviet-Mongolian mutual assistance pact is violation of Chinese sovereignty.

April 8—Litvinov denies Chinese charge.

April 9—Trade agreement with Germany.

April 11—Clash on Siberia-Manchukuo frontier reported.

Soviet and Japanese representatives both protest border violations.

April 14—Chinese government renews protest on Soviet-Mongolian pact.

April 28—USSR asks Japan to take measures to control activities of White-Russians in Manchukuo.

May 15—Maisky in London reaffirms Soviet interest in east European pact project of 1934, to include USSR, Germany, Poland, Czechoslovakia, and the three Baltic States.

May 25—Protocol extending fisheries convention with Japan.

June 22—Montreux Conference on control of Dardanelles opens, USSR participating.

July 1—Litvinov at Geneva attributes outcome of Italo-Ethiopian conflict to failure of League of Nations to apply sanctions.

July 3—Japanese patrol arrested on Soviet territory.

July 11—Trade agreement with United States of July 13, 1935, extended for one year.

July 20—Nine powers, including USSR, sign Montreux Convention.

July 30—USSR agrees to adhere to Three-Power Naval Treaty between Great Britain, France, and the United States.

August 3—Mass demonstration in Moscow pledges material aid to Spanish government through Central Council of Trade Unions.

August 5—USSR agrees to French proposal to join France, Britain, Italy, and Germany in pledge of noninterference in Spanish internal affairs (Non-Intervention Agreement).

August 13—Finland protests Soviet opposition to proposed commercial airdromes to be built in eastern Finland.

August 20—Exchange of ratifications of temporary trade agreement of October, 1935, with Belgium.

August 26—Protests by both Soviet and Japanese diplomats over border skirmishes.

August 29—Formal request to Norwegian government to expel Leon Trotsky for fomenting terroristic conspiracies and acts, including the Kirov assassination (December 1, 1934).

September 3—Norwegian government rejects Soviet request to expel Trotsky.

September 4—Japan notified that border incidents are endangering peace and the USSR will hold Japan responsible for future border incidents.

September 11—Norway notified that she will be held responsible for future political activities of Trotsky.

September 12—Hitler's Nuremberg speech on the Urals, Ukraine, and Siberia.

September 28—Litvinov at Geneva urges reform of League Covenant.

October 26—Soviet-Finnish border incident reported by Moscow.

November 25—Germany and Japan sign "Anti-Comintern Pact" in Berlin.

December 24—Trade agreement with Germany extended through 1937.

December 27—Trade agreement with France extended through 1937.

December 28—Fisheries convention with Japan extended for one year.

1937

March 23—Japanese Foreign Minister tells Parliament that the government does not intend to resume negotiations for a nonaggression pact with the USSR.

May 29—Litvinov at Geneva urges League to support Spanish government.

May 31—Litvinov defines Soviet position on disarmament to Bureau of the Disarmament Conference.

June 16—Agreement with Turkey to investigate and settle border incidents.

July 17—USSR and Germany sign bilateral naval agreements with Great Britain.

August 2—Protest to Japan on raiding and pillaging of Soviet Consulate in Tientsin by White Russians.

August 6—New commercial agreement with United States.

August 7—In answer to United States Secretary of State Hull's declaration on world peace, Litvinov restates Soviet principles on foreign policy.

August 21—Nonaggression treaty with China for five years.

September 6—Note to Italian government accuses Italian submarines of sinking two Soviet freighters in the Mediterranean.

September 10—USSR participates in Nyon Conference on piracy in the Mediterranean.

September 13—Japanese consular rights in Odessa and Novosibirsk withdrawn.

September 18—Litvinov at League of Nations Assembly denounces aggressor nations and urges aid to Spain and China.

September 26—Protest to Japan on bombing of Nanking.

September 28—Litvinov at Geneva urges that Spanish government be given full access to war materials abroad.

October 8—Trade agreement and commercial settlement agreement with Turkey.

October 16—Maisky at meeting of subcommittee of Non-Intervention Committee says nonintervention (in Spain) has become a "complete farce."

October 29—At similar meeting Maisky says USSR can no longer be responsible "for a policy of nonintervention which it considers to be unjust, futile and tending to encourage aggressors."

October 30—Protest to Japan on frontier violation by Japanese-Manchukuo troops.

November 3—Opening of Nine-Power Conference in Brussels on Far Eastern situation, USSR participating.

November 6—Italy adheres to "Anti-Comintern Pact."

November 8—Soviet ambassador in Rome states that USSR considers Italian participation in "Anti-Comintern Pact" an unfriendly act and an infringement of the Soviet-Italian Treaty of 1933.

November 18—Trade convention with Belgium extended for two years.

December 19—Note to Poland accusing Polish railroad officials of burning a Soviet train.

December 23—Trade agreement with Lithuania for 1938.

December 29—Fisheries convention with Japan extended for one year.

December 30—News agency TASS reports that USSR has sent and will continue to send some war supplies to China.

1938

January 3—Trade agreement with France extended for 1938.

January 26—Trade agreement with Estonia.

March 17—Litvinov in press statement, forwarded to London, Paris, Prague, and Washington, urges "practical measures" by the great powers to stop aggression.

April 18—Trade agreement with Greece for 1938.

April 28—Protocol with Finland defining the border.

May 14—USSR abstains from voting on League of Nations resolution to give Switzerland freedom from obligation to impose League penalties when other members do so.

June 25—Litvinov in speech at Leningrad says Soviet role on Non-Intervention Committee now is "to prevent the intervention of the committee itself in Spanish affairs on Franco's behalf."

125

July 6—Naval pact with Britain supplementary to agreement of July 30, 1936.
July 9—Protest to Finland on border violation.
July 13—Protest to Latvia on border violation.
July 29—Soviet-Japanese fighting on Changkufeng area starts.
August 6—Commercial agreement with United States extended for one year.
August 10—Truce arranged with Japan at Changkufeng.
September 21—Litvinov in speech to League of Nations Assembly reiterates intention of USSR to abide by treaty obligations to France and Czechoslovakia.
September 23—Note to Poland threatening denunciation of nonaggression treaty of 1932 if Poland attempts to invade Czechoslovakia.
September 30—Conclusion of Munich Conference on dismemberment of Czechoslovakia, to which neither Czechoslovakian nor Soviet representatives were invited.
October 4—Commissariat of Foreign Affairs denies reports that the Soviet government was informed of steps leading up to Munich agreement.
October 10—*Pravda* publishes letter of eleven prominent Soviet aviators accusing Col. Charles A. Lindbergh of spreading falsehoods about the weakness of the Soviet air force.
December 23—Trade agreement with Germany extended for 1939.
December 27—Exchange of notes with Finland on the definition of the border and the establishment of a border commission.

1939

January 3—Trade agreement with France extended for 1939.
January 11—Trade agreement with Estonia extended for 1939.
February 2, 9—Incidents on Soviet-Manchukuo border reported.
February 3—USSR discontinues direct representation in Hungary.
February 7—Agreements signed with Italy settling outstanding economic disputes and regulating trade relations.
February 11—Trade agreement with Latvia for 1939.
February 14—Trade agreement with Lithuania for 1939.
February 19—Trade agreement with Poland.
March 1—USSR withdraws from Non-Intervention Committee.
March 10—Stalin accuses foreign "politicians and pressmen" of inciting Germany to attack USSR.
March 18—Litvinov states that USSR considers German occupation of Czechoslovakia an act of aggression and refuses to recognize the incorporation of Czechia (Bohemia and Moravia) into the Reich.
March 21—Soviet communiqué announces proposal to Great Britain of a conference between France, Britain, Poland, Romania, Turkey, and USSR on situation following German occupation of Czechoslovakia. Communiqué also reports that the British government "found this proposal premature."
March 31—British Prime Minister Chamberlain announces British and French guarantee (without consultation with the USSR) to defend Poland against aggression.
April 2—Fisheries convention with Japan extended for 1939.
April 12—Lloyd George calls for a definite military understanding between Great Britain and USSR.

April 13—Chamberlain announces British guarantee (without consultation with the USSR) to Romania and Greece.

April 15—British ambassador asks USSR to make unilateral guarantee of Poland and Romania.

April 17—Soviet reply proposes: Anglo-Soviet-French alliance; a military convention; and guaranteeing of all states between Baltic and Black seas.

April 20—Poland informs Great Britain that her attitude toward passage of Soviet military forces over Polish territory is "negative."

May 1—Japanese Cabinet decides against converting "Anti-Comintern Pact" into a German-Italian-Japanese military alliance.

May 3—Chamberlain announces to Parliament Britain's readiness to consider an exchange of nonaggression pledges with Germany.

Germany offers nonaggression pacts to Norway, Sweden, Finland, Estonia, and Latvia.

Litvinov resigns as commissar of foreign affairs; Molotov appointed to replace him, while retaining post of chairman of Council of People's Commissars (premier).

May 10—Soviet communiqué characterizes British reply (of May 9) to Soviet note of April 17 as "one-sided," and restates Soviet proposals.

May 14—Soviet note to Great Britain reiterates proposals of April 17.

May 22—Italy and Germany sign a treaty of political and military alliance.

May 24—British Cabinet agrees in principle to a mutual assistance pact with France and USSR against further aggression in Europe.

May 27—British ambassador replies to Soviet note of May 14 and agrees to discuss a mutual assistance pact and a military convention, but restricting guarantee to Poland and Romania.

May 31—Molotov's speech outlining Soviet requirements for an antiaggression pact.

June 2—Soviet reply to Britain and France on latest British proposals (for a three-power mutual assistance pact) repeats request for the inclusion of the Baltic States.

June 5—Foreign Policy Committee of British Cabinet refuses to extend British guarantee to Baltic States bordering on USSR.

June 7—German-Estonian and German-Latvian nonaggression pacts signed.

June 15—Anglo-Soviet-French diplomatic negotiations begin in Moscow.

June 25—Conclusion of Soviet-Chinese trade agreement announced.

June 29—Zhdanov's article in *Pravda* accusing Britain and France of not wanting to come to any agreement.

July 11—USSR warns Japan against aggression in Mongolia, following fighting on Mongolian-Manchukuo border since May 6.

July 22—Negotiations with Germany for a trade agreement renewed.

August 4—Trade pact with United States extended for one year.

August 12—Anglo-Soviet-French military conference begins in Moscow.

August 19—Trade and credit agreement concluded with Germany.

August 21—Newly formed Egyptian Cabinet agrees to recognize USSR.

August 23—Nonaggression pact with Germany signed.

August 26—British and French military missions leave Moscow.

August 27—Soviet Defense Commissar Voroshilov attributes breakdown of Anglo-Soviet-French military conferences to unwillingness of Poland, backed by England and France, to allow the Red Army to enter Polish territory.

August 28—Large Soviet military operations begin against Japanese on Mongolian border.

September 1, 3—German Army invades Poland, Great Britain and France declare war on Germany.

September 6—British government announces termination of Anglo-Soviet naval agreement of 1937.

September 15—Japanese ask for armistice on Manchukuo–Outer Mongolian border, and hostilities cease.

September 17—Molotov informs the Polish ambassador that, in view of the collapse of the Polish state, the USSR cannot be bound by treaties with Poland, and announces that the Red Army has been ordered to cross the Soviet border in order to protect the lives and property of the western Ukrainian and western Belorussian population.

September 23—Diplomatic relations with Hungary restored.

September 28—Exchange of letters with Germany on agreement to draw up an economic program.

Treaty with Germany on "amity and the frontier between the USSR and Germany."

Joint Soviet-German declaration on the desirability of peace.

Soviet-Estonian mutual assistance pact providing for the stationing of Soviet armed forces on Estonian territory, and trade agreement.

October 3—Japanese war office report attributes Japanese reverses in recent "disastrous bitter battle" on Outer Mongolian border to superior mechanization of Soviet forces.

October 5—Finland invited to send plenipotentiary to Moscow to discuss "pending questions."

Mutual assistance pact with Latvia, with similar provisions to the one with Estonia.

October 10—Mutual assistance pact with Lithuania with similar provisions to the ones with Estonia and Latvia; under pact Vilna is returned to Lithuania.

October 11—Announcement in London of agreement to exchange British rubber and tin for Soviet timber.

October 12—United States note to USSR on desirability of maintaining Finnish independence.

Negotiations with Finnish delegation open.

October 15—Finnish delegation leaves.

October 16—Soviet reply to United States note on Finland.

Announcement of extension of trade agreement with Lithuania.

October 18—Trade agreement with Latvia.

October 23—Finnish delegation returns to Moscow.

October 25—Note to Great Britain protesting contraband regulations.

October 26—National Assembly of western Ukraine votes to join USSR.

Finnish delegation leaves for Helsinki.

October 29—National Assembly of western Belorussia votes to join USSR.

October 31—Molotov speech outlines Soviet proposals to Finland.

November 2—Finnish delegation returns to Moscow.

November 9—Second Soviet protest on British contraband regulations.

November 13—Finnish delegation leaves Moscow.

November 14—Belorussian Supreme Soviet votes to admit western Belorussia as part of Belorussian SSR.

November 15—Ukrainian Supreme Soviet votes to admit western Ukraine as part of Ukrainian SSR.

November 16—Agreement with Germany on exchange of Soviet and German nationals.

November 26—Note of protest to Finland on border incident.

November 28—USSR denounces Soviet-Finnish nonaggression pact and rejects Finnish reply on border incident.

November 29—Diplomatic relations with Finland broken.

November 30—Troops of the Leningrad Military District cross the Soviet-Finnish border.

December 2—Roosevelt calls for "moral embargo" on sales of American airplanes to USSR.

December 4—Soviet rejection of Finnish armistice proposals.

December 7—Mixed commission to delimit Outer Mongolian–Manchukuo border begins work.

December 10—United States government opens $10,000,000 credits for Finland.

December 14—USSR expelled from League of Nations on the motion of Argentina.

December 15, 20—United States State Department extends coverage of "moral embargo."

December 31—Two agreements signed with Japan: (1) on settlement of final payment for Chinese Eastern Railway, (2) extending fisheries convention for 1940.

1940

January 1—Announcement of British notification to League of Nations that Britain will aid Finland in struggle against USSR.

January 2—League of Nations notified that France is aiding Finland.

January 4—Final payment on Chinese Eastern Railway made.

January 5—Trade and navigation treaty with Bulgaria.

February 5—USSR expelled from International Labour Office.

February 6—Recruiting office opened in London for volunteers to fight in Finland.

February 8—Protest to France on raid of Soviet trade offices in Paris on February 5.

France rejects protest and announces concentration of 275,000 French troops in the Near East.

February 11—Red Army moves against main zone of Mannerheim Line.

March 1—United States government makes $20,000,000 loan to Finland.

March 12—Chamberlain announces to Parliament that British and French governments are prepared to aid Finland.

Daladier announces in Chamber of Deputies that 50,000 French soldiers have been ready since February 26 to leave for Finland.

March 13—Soviet-Finnish peace treaty signed.

March 25—Treaty of commerce and navigation with Iran.

March 27—Soviet ambassador to France recalled at request of French government.

March 31—Formation of the Karelo-Finnish SSR by decision of the Supreme Soviet of the USSR.

May 11—Trade and navigation treaty with Yugoslavia.

May 22—Note rejecting British terms that Anglo-Soviet trade negotiations be conducted on a war basis and that the blockade of Germany be recognized.

May 29—Protest to Lithuania on kidnapping of Red Army men.

June 9—Agreement with Japan on demarcation of Manchukuo–Outer Mongolian frontier in Nomonhan district.

June 10—Italy declares war on France and Great Britain.

Soviet-German agreement on "border incidents."

June 14—Note to Lithuania denouncing arrest of Red Army men and Lithuania's secret adherence to a Latvian-Estonian military alliance directed against the USSR, and demanding the immediate formation of a government willing and able to carry out the terms of the mutual assistance pact.

Komsomolskaya Pravda publishes letter by French soldier urging Frenchmen to fight for a "free, independent and traitorless France."

June 15—Lithuania accedes to demands in note of June 14.

June 16—Latvia and Estonia accede to similar Soviet demands.

June 17—New Lithuanian Cabinet formed.

June 20—New Latvian Cabinet formed.

June 21—Revolutionary government set up in Estonia.

France signs armistice terms with Hitlerite Germany.

June 24—Diplomatic relations with Yugoslavia established.

June 28—Trade treaty with Finland signed.

Publication of Soviet-Romanian exchange of notes on return of Bessarabia and cession of northern Bucovina to USSR.

July 21—New parliaments of Latvia, Lithuania, and Estonia, elected July 14 and 15, vote to petition USSR for membership.

July 23—United States Under-Secretary of State Sumner Welles condemns USSR for "annihilating" Baltic republics and says United States will continue to recognize Latvian, Lithuanian, and Estonian ministers.

July 27—New trade treaty with China signed.

July 28—Announcement of signing of commercial agreement with Afghanistan.

August 2—Supreme Soviet votes creation of the Moldavian SSR.

August 3—Lithuania admitted to USSR as a Union republic.

August 5—Latvia admitted to USSR as a Union republic.

August 6—Estonia admitted to USSR as a Union republic.

September 3—Trade agreement signed with Hungary.

September 5—Soviet-German agreement on German nationals in former Bessarabia and northern Bucovina.

September 8—Trade pact with Sweden signed.

September 12—German ambassador told USSR cannot remain indifferent to arrangements for regulating shipping on the Danube.

TASS news agency reports Soviet protest to Romania on border incident.

September 13—Mixed boundary commission formed to investigate Soviet-Romanian border incidents and define borders.

September 14—TASS news agency reports Romanian government's assurance of desire to preserve good relations with USSR.

September 18—Trade agreement with Denmark concluded.

September 27—German-Italian-Japanese alliance formed for mutual assistance with special article stating that relations of none of the three with the USSR are affected.

October 5—Arrangements with Great Britain for removal of British subjects fom Estonia, Latvia, and Lithuania.

October 15—TASS news agency issues denial that USSR was informed in advance of German intention to send troops into Romania.

President Roosevelt in press conference characterizes the USSR as a "friendly power."

October 17—Announcement that demarcation of new Soviet-Finnish frontier is completed.

October 26—Berlin and Moscow issue joint announcement of liquidation of previous Danube commissions and formation of new amalgamated Danube Commission, to include USSR, Germany, Italy, Romania, Bulgaria, Hungary, Slovakia, and Yugoslavia.

November 2—Soviet government rejects British protest of October 29 that Soviet participation in Danubian Conference at Bucharest is a violation of neutrality.

November 12—Hitler and Molotov confer in Berlin.

November 15—British Foreign Office announces offer of important diplomatic concessions to USSR in exchange for "a more benevolent attitude" on the part of the USSR.

November 22—TASS news agency issued denial that Hungary joined German-Italian-Japanese alliance with co-operation and approval of the USSR.

November 29—United States Under-Secretary of State Welles announces arrangements for establishing a United States consulate at Vladivostok.

December 5—Soviet government informs Japan that Soviet policy toward China remains unchanged in spite of Japanese recognition of Nanking government headed by Wang-Ching-wei.

December 6—Trade agreement with Slovakia.

December 25—Danubian Conference breaks up.

1941

January 4—Second part of Soviet-Chinese trade treaty signed.

January 10—Soviet Union and Germany sign three accords: a trade pact extending to August, 1942; an agreement on settlement of problems in the Baltic area; a frontier treaty.

January 12—Third part of Soviet-Chinese trade treaty signed.

January 13—TASS news agency issues denial that Soviet government has been consulted on or has agreed to any dispatch of German troops to Bulgaria.

January 20—Fisheries convention with Japan extended for 1941.

January 21—United States State Department lifts "moral embargo" on the USSR, introducing licensing system for all articles covered by "embargo."

February 3—Japanese-Soviet commission for a new fisheries convention appointed.

February 17—Conversation with Japan on a trade treaty opened in Moscow.

February 24—Trade agreement with Switzerland.

February 26—Two-year treaty with Romania on trade and navigation.

131

March 1—Ambassador K. A. Oumansky protests to United States against seizure of mail coming from the USSR.

Bulgarian note to USSR to the effect that Bulgarian government had agreed to dispatch of German troops into Bulgaria and that this action pursues peace aims in the Balkans.

March 3—Note in reply to Bulgaria stating that the USSR considers position taken by Bulgaria "does not lead to the consolidation of peace but to the extension of the sphere of war," and that the USSR cannot support Bulgaria in its present policy.

March 5—Statement in Finnish parliament by foreign minister to the effect that Soviet-Finnish relations are back to normal.

March 12—Exchange of notes with Thailand establishing diplomatic relations.

March 24—Joint communiqué with Turkey on neutrality.

April 5—Treaty of friendship and nonaggression with Yugoslavia.

April 10—Trade agreement with Norway.

April 12—Soviet statement disapproving of Hungary's participation in Germany's invasion of Yugoslavia.

April 13—Neutrality pact with Japan signed in Moscow.

May 6—Stalin becomes chairman of Council of People's Commissars (premier); Molotov becomes vice chairman.

May 9—USSR withdraws recognition from German-held Norway, Belgium, and Yugoslavia.

June 2—Agreement with Sweden on financial claims against Estonia, Lithuania, and Latvia.

June 22—Germany together with Romania and Finland invade the USSR; Winston Churchill pledges aid to Russia; Italy declares war on the USSR.

June 23—Slovakia declares war on the USSR.

June 24—Roosevelt promises aid to the USSR.

June 27—Hungary declares war on the USSR.

English military-economic mission arrives in Moscow.

June 30—Vichy government of France severs diplomatic relations with the USSR.

July 12—Anglo-Soviet agreement on joint action against Germany signed in Moscow.

July 18—USSR and Czechoslovakia sign an agreement of mutual assistance against Germany.

July 19—Great Britain and USSR send a joint warning to Iran on German activities in that country.

July 30—Polish-Soviet agreement on the resumption of diplomatic relations and joint action against Germany.

Stalin receives Roosevelt's personal representative, Harry Hopkins.

August 2—American-Soviet trade treaty extended for one year.

August 5—Diplomatic relations with Norway restored.

August 7—Restoration of diplomatic relations with Belgium.

August 10—Great Britain and USSR present a joint declaration to Turkey, pledging to observe its territorial inviolability and to aid in case of attack by a third power.

August 10-11—First All-Slav congress held in Moscow.

August 14—Military agreement concluded with Polish High Command.

August 15—Joint message from Roosevelt and Churchill received by Stalin, who states that he welcomes the idea of calling a conference of the three powers.

August 16—USSR and Great Britain sign a trade and financial agreement in Moscow.

Second joint warning to Iran by Great Britain and the USSR on German activities in that country.

August 20—Publication of a communiqué of the joint border commission of the Mongolian People's Republic and Manchukuo on the successful conclusion of its work.

August 23—Soviet ambassador in Tokyo told that shipping of war supplies from the United States to Vladivostok creates "a difficult situation for Japan."

August 24—Meeting of Jewish people held in Moscow; an antifascist appeal is addressed to the Jews of the world.

August 25—Molotov assures Japan that shipments of war supplies from the United States to Vladivostok need not disturb Japan; these imports are to fill Soviet needs in the West, and any interference with them will be regarded as an unfriendly act.

Iran is informed that Soviet troops are entering the country in conformity with the Soviet-Iranian treaty of 1921. Great Britain also informs Iran of the entry of its troops.

August 28—Newly formed government of Iran discontinues resistance to Soviet and British troops.

September 7—Women's antifascist meeting held in Moscow; appeal to women of the world.

September 10—German, Italian, Hungarian, and Romanian missions closed in Iran. Soviet Union sends protest to Bulgaria over the use of its territory by Germany as a base for war against the USSR.

September 16—Bulgaria assures the USSR that no unfriendly acts are taking place on its territory.

September 17—Bulgaria is told that her reply to the Soviet note of September 10 is unsatisfactory.

September 18—Molotov appointed Soviet representative for consultation on economic matters with United States and Great Britain in Moscow.

September 24—Soviet ambassador in London says USSR is in agreement with the basic principles of the Atlantic Charter.

September 27—Military agreement between Soviet and Czechoslovak high commands in Moscow.

Soviet ambassador in London and General Charles de Gaulle exchange letters.

September 28—A. Harriman and Lord Beaverbrook, heading United States and British economic missions to USSR, arrive in Moscow and are received by Stalin and Molotov.

Antifascist youth meeting in Moscow issues appeal to the youth of the world.

October 2—Joint statement issued on three-power conference, concluded October 1.

October 11—USSR warns Afghanistan on German and Italian activities in that country. Antifascist meeting of scientists in Moscow appeals to the scientists of the world.

October 13—British trade-union delegation arrives in Moscow.

October 15—Documents defining the border between Mongolian People's Republic and Manchukuo signed in Harbin.

October 19—Afghanistan deports German and Italian nationals.

October 23—Twenty Japanese soldiers attack a Soviet border post.

October 26—Statement issued in Moscow on the successful conclusion of the first session (held October 13–15) of the Anglo-Soviet Trade Union Committee.

November 3—Secretary of State Cordell Hull tells a press conference that the United States recommends that Finland discontinue military operations against the USSR.

November 5—USSR and Canada reach an agreement on the creation of a joint committee for armament production.

November 6—United States Department of State announces that a $1,000,000,000 loan is extended to the USSR under lend-lease.

November 8—Exchange of letters between President Roosevelt and Premier Stalin (October 30 and November 4) is published in Washington, D.C.

November 10—Litvinov appointed ambassador of the USSR to the United States.

November 11—First conference of German war prisoners, which issued a declaration to the German Army and people, announced.

November 14—Stalin and Molotov receive the ambassador of Poland. Litvinov, ambassador to the United States, appointed assistant people's commissar of foreign affairs.

November 18—People's Commissariat of Foreign Affairs issues statement on Soviet attitude toward Finnish government.

November 25—Soviet note to all powers with whom the USSR has diplomatic relations on the barbarous treatment of Soviet war prisoners by the Germans.

Finland, Croatia, Denmark, Romania, Slovakia, and Bulgaria, as well as the Japanese-sponsored Nanking government in China, add their signatures to the "Anti-Comintern Pact" already signed by Germany, Italy, Japan, Hungary, Spain, and Manchukuo. Pact extended for five years.

November 30—General V. Sikorsky, Polish premier and commander in chief, arrives in the USSR.

December 4—Soviet-Polish declaration on friendship and mutual assistance signed in Moscow.

December 6—Soviet troops begin counteroffensive near Moscow.

December 7—Litvinov arrives in Washington, D.C.

December 10—China declares war on Germany and Italy.

December 11—United States declares war on Germany and Italy.

December 21—Adolf Hitler appoints himself commander in chief of the German Army in the east.

December 29—Publication of an Anglo-Soviet statement on conversations held in Moscow between Stalin, Molotov, and British Foreign Secretary Anthony Eden.

December 31—Agreement on a 100,000,000 rubles loan to Poland signed. Soviet trade-union delegation arrives in London.

1942

January 1—United Nations declaration signed in Washington, D.C., by 26 powers, including the USSR.

January 7—Publication of Soviet note on pillage, destruction, and atrocities committed by the Germans in occupied Soviet territory.

January 8—Anthony Eden reports in Parliament on his visit to the USSR.

January 13—A conference of governments-in-exile of countries occupied by the fascists issues a declaration on war criminals; as an observer at this conference, the USSR expresses its solidarity with the declaration.

January 18—Germany, Italy, and Japan sign a military convention.

January 22—Agreement with Poland on a loan for the maintenance of Polish troops in the USSR.

Agreement with Czechoslovakia for a loan for the maintenance of the Czechoslovak brigade in the USSR.

January 23—Japanese foreign office states that Soviet-Japanese relations have not changed since Japan entered the war, that they are still guided by the neutrality pact.

January 25—Soviet press publishes appeal by the first conference of Romanian war prisoners in the USSR to the Romanian Army and people.

January 29—Treaty of alliance between the USSR, Great Britain, and Iran.

February 5—Agreement between the USSR and Canada relating to the establishment of consulates.

February 21—An agreement between the USSR and the Union of South Africa relating to the establishment of consulates.

February 22—Declaration of the first conference of Hungarian prisoners of war in the USSR, appealing for the overthrow of Hitler and the establishment of an independent, democratic Hungary.

February 26—In speech in New York Litvinov expresses Soviet desire to see all allied forces engaged in simultaneous action against Germany.

March 9—State Department imposes travel limits on Finnish representatives in the United States.

March 13—Free French mission received by Molotov.

March 20—Fisheries convention with Japan extended for 1942.

March 25—Greek patriots greet Premier Stalin on Greek "independence day."

March 27—It is announced in Washington that 10 days ago President Roosevelt sent out a letter instructing bureau heads to speed up the shipment of munitions to the USSR.

April 1—Trial of two Soviet citizens, charged with organizing an attempt on the life of the German Ambassador von Papen, starts in Ankara, Turkey.

April 4–5—Second All-Slav Congress in Moscow; appeals to all Slav peoples to rise for a war of liberation from Hitlerism.

April 14—Soviet press publishes an appeal to the German Army, signed by several hundred German war prisoners.

April 22—A monument to Lenin is unveiled in London.

April 27—Soviet Foreign Office issues a note about German atrocities and about the responsibility of the German authorities for these crimes.

May 21—Molotov arrives in London.

May 26—A 20-year treaty of alliance with Great Britain signed in London.

May 27—Prime Minister of Japan states in Parliament that Soviet-Japanese relations have not changed.

May 29—Molotov arrives in Washington, D.C.

June 4—Molotov departs from Washington, D.C.

June 6—United States declares war on Bulgaria, Hungary, and Romania.

June 11—Agreement signed in Washington between USSR and United States on mutual assistance in the war, superseding two previous agreements.

June 12—Publication of Anglo-Soviet statement on the alliance and White House statement on American-Soviet understanding with regard to creating a second front in Europe in 1942.

Agreement with Canada on direct diplomatic relations.

Roosevelt announces the creation on June 9 of a joint American-Soviet committee on production, resources, and food.

June 18—Molotov's report to the Supreme Soviet on foreign policy.

June 24—Soviet press publishes communiqué on Molotov's conversation with General de Gaulle in London.

June 25—Soviet press published a statement of the first conference of Italian war prisoners appealing to all Italians for a break with Germany and for the overthrow of Mussolini.

June 27—Agreement with Great Britain on financing deliveries of military supplies and other military aid to the USSR.

July 3–9—Visit of Czechoslovak minister of defense to Moscow.

July 10—Diplomatic relations established with the Netherlands.

July 16—Finland told to close all consulates in the United States by August 1.

July 31—Trade agreement between the United States and the USSR extended for one year.

August 2—Speech of President Beneš in England on necessity of opening a second front in 1942.

August 18—Publication of statements connected with Winston Churchill's visit to Moscow.

September 3—International students' congress opens in Washington, with three Soviet delegates participating.

September 8—Churchill reports in the House of Commons on the military situation and his trip to Moscow.

September 15—Bulgarian police loot the Soviet Consulate in Varna, Bulgaria.

September 23—Wendell L. Willkie received by Premier Stalin.

September 27—Publication of the Franco-Soviet statement, defining the attitude of the USSR to the Fighting France Movement and the French National Committee.

October 2—Soviet representative protests over arrest of Soviet tourist agency representative in Stockholm, Sweden.

October 5—Publication of Stalin's replies to the question on the second front posed by Associated Press correspondent in Moscow.

October 6—Soviet note of protest to Bulgaria over the holding of an anti-Soviet "exhibit" in Sofia.

An agreement is signed in Washington by representatives of the United States, USSR, and England on delivery of military supplies to the USSR.

October 7—President Roosevelt states that the United States is willing to co-operate with other powers in the creation of a joint committee for the investigation of crimes committed by representatives of aggressor nations.

October 10—Bulgarian government in replying to the Soviet note of October 6 denies that the exhibition in Sofia is anti-Soviet.

136

October 13—Agreement is reached on the exchange of ambassadors between the USSR and Australia.

October 14—Molotov's statement on the responsibility of war criminals sent to Czechoslovakian and French governments.

October 17—Establishment of diplomatic relations with Cuba and Luxembourg.

October 18—Commissariat of Foreign Affairs publishes statement on Albania.

October 22—Note of protest to Bulgaria on anti-Soviet activities.

November 2—Special committee appointed for investigation of crimes of enemy.

November 6—Stalin's speech containing statement on war aims of United Nations.

November 14—Publication of Stalin's replies to Associated Press correspondent's questions on Allied landing in North Africa.

November 17—Publication of data on organized pillage of objects of culture and art by the Germans.

November 19—Soviet counteroffensive at Stalingrad begins.

November 20—Moscow announces resumption of diplomatic relations with Mexico.

December 18—Joint declaration by several countries, including the USSR, on the extermination by the Nazis of Jewish population of Europe.

December 28—Protest to Sweden on violence against Soviet press representative.

1943

January 6—Joint declaration of powers, including the USSR, on the nonrecognition of property deals entered into by the fascist occupation authorities.

January 27—Soviet government accepts the offer of Uruguay to resume diplomatic relations.

February 4—Exchange of notes with Colombia on establishment of diplomatic relations.

February 25—Polish government in London issues statement on Soviet-Polish relations.

March 3—Soviet news agency TASS issues comments on Polish statement of February 25.

March 30—Soviet government accepts United States invitation to attend conference on postwar food problems.

April 25—Soviet government breaks relations with Polish government in London.

May 1—Stalin's reply to questions posed by New York and London *Times* on Polish question.

May 6—Statement by A. Y. Vyshinsky to the Anglo-American press on Soviet-Polish relations.

May 8—Union of Polish Patriots permitted to form a Polish division to fight the common enemy together with Red Army.

May 9—Appeal of Third All Slav Congress to the oppressed Slavs of Europe.

May 11—Molotov's note on slave labor in Germany.

May 18—Opening of the Hot Springs, Va., conference on postwar food problems. K. A. Oumansky appointed Soviet ambassador to Mexico.

May 19—Joseph E. Davies, personal representative of President Roosevelt, arrives in Moscow.

May 24—Statement by the chairman of Soviet delegation at Hot Springs, Va., postwar food problems conference.

May 28—Agreement with Czechoslovakia on the maintenance of Czechoslovak troops in the USSR.

June 3—Termination of the postwar food problems conference at Hot Springs, Va.

June 8—Congress of Union of Polish Patriots opens in Moscow.

June 14—Publication of the United Nations Relief and Rehabilitation Administration (UNRRA) project, worked out with the participation of the USSR.

June 24—British trade-union delegation arrives in Moscow for the third session of the Anglo-Soviet Trade Union Committee.

June 30—Exchange of notes establishing diplomatic relations with Abyssinia (Ethiopia).

July 19—Manifesto of the "Free Germany" committee issued in Moscow.

July 23—Publication of the results of the work of the third session of the Anglo-Soviet Trade Union Committee, held in Moscow, June 23 to July 22, 1943.

August 22—A. A. Gromyko appointed Soviet ambassador to the United States, relieving M. M. Litvinov.

August 26—Diplomatic relations established with the French Committee of National Liberation and with Egypt.

September 8—Congress of bishops of the Russian Orthodox Church addresses a message to Christians of the world urging all-out effort in the struggle against the Hitlerite hordes.

Italy surrenders unconditionally to the United States, Great Britain, and USSR.

September 12—Union of German Officers formed by antifascist prisoners of war in the Soviet Union.

September 26—Formation of a committee on Mediterranean affairs composed of representatives of the United States, USSR, and Great Britain, with the participation of the French Committee of National Liberation.

October 15—Donald Nelson, chairman of War Production Board, received by Premier Stalin.

October 18—Cordell Hull arrives in Moscow.

October 19—Three-Power Conference opens in Moscow.

November 2—Anglo-Soviet-American statement issued on the conference (October 19–30). Four-power declaration (including China) on general security. Three-power declaration on Italy and Austria. Declaration of the heads of the three states on responsibility of war criminals.

November 3—United States Senate adopts resolution favoring the Moscow four-power declaration on general security by 85 votes against 5.

November 4—Hull and Eden depart from Moscow.

November 18—Hull reports to Congress on the results of the Moscow Conference.

November 28—Roosevelt, Stalin, and Churchill meet at Teheran.

December 1—End of Big Three conference at Teheran; joint statement signed.

December 11—Eduard Beneš, president of Czechoslovakia, arrives in Moscow.

December 12—Treaty of friendship, mutual assistance, and postwar collaboration with Czechoslovakia.

December 14—Czechoslovak treaty, protocol attached to it, and speeches made at the signing published.

Information Bureau of Soviet Foreign Office gives out a statement "on events in Yugoslavia."

1944

January 14—Prime Minister of Mongolian People's Republic Marshal Chaibalsan arrives in Moscow.

First meeting in London of the European Advisory Commission created at the Moscow conference in 1943 for the study of questions arising in the course of the war.

January 15—Polish government in London issues statement on Soviet-Polish relations.

January 16—Soviet news agency TASS issues statement commenting on this London statement.

Publication of the report of the commission investigating the Katyn massacre.

January 17—Cordell Hull offers to mediate in Soviet-Polish matters.

January 19—Eden makes a statement in Parliament on Soviet-Polish relations.

January 22—All-Slav committee in Moscow issues appeal to Bulgarian people.

January 26—Soviet government declines Hull's offer of January 17.

February 1—Supreme Soviet approves constitutional amendment granting each of the 16 Union republics the right of separate diplomatic representation abroad.

February 5—People's commissar of foreign affairs appointed by the Ukrainian SSR.

February 6—Head of the Yugoslav government-in-exile tries to deliver to Soviet representative in Cairo a statement on General Mikhailovitch, which is not accepted by the Soviet representative.

February 14—Azerbaidzhan Soviet Socialist Republic announces its intention of appointing a minister to Turkey.

February 22—Commissariat of finance of the USSR issues a statement on the purchase of gold in countries not members of the United Nations. Statements on the same question are issued by the United States and Great Britain.

March 8—People's commissar for foreign affairs appointed by the RSFSR.

March 10—Yugoslav ambassador and military attaché in Moscow announce their break with Yugoslav government-in-exile and that they place their services at the disposal of Marshal Tito.

March 11—Agreement with Canada on shipments of military supplies in accordance with Canadian law of 1943.

Soviet government informs the Badoglio government of Italy of its willingness to establish diplomatic relations with that government.

March 30—People's commissar of foreign affairs appointed by Belorussian SSR.

Agreement with Japan on extension for five years of Soviet-Japanese fisheries convention and on return to USSR of Japanese concessions in the northern part of Sakhalin Island.

April 2—Moscow announces that Chinese troops have violated the borders of Mongolian People's Republic.

Upon crossing of the Romanian border by Soviet troops, Molotov makes a policy announcement.

April 13—Exchange of notes on the establishment of diplomatic relations with New Zealand.

April 16—Statement of A. Y. Vyshinsky on the situation in Italy.

April 22—Statement by A. Y. Vyshinsky on Soviet-Finnish relations.

April 23—Professor Oscar Lange of the University of Chicago arrives in Moscow.

April 28—Premier Stalin receives the Reverend S. Orlemansky, Roman Catholic priest, from Springfield, Massachusetts.

May 8—Exchange of notes on the establishment of diplomatic relations with Costa Rica.

Agreement with Czechoslovakia on the relations between the Soviet High Command and the Czechoslovak administration upon the entry of the Red Army on Czechoslovak territory.

May 12—United States, USSR, and Great Britain issue joint ultimatum to Hungary, Romania, Bulgaria, and Finland to abandon the Hitler cause.

May 16—USSR, Great Britain, and United States enter into agreement with Norway governing civil affairs during period of liberation.

May 21—Statement by Professor Lange on his visit to the USSR.

Third Anti-Fascist Youth Congress held in Moscow.

May 24—National Council of Poland in German-occupied territory sends representatives to Moscow.

May 25—Slav meeting held in London.

May 26—United States Department of State announces that the USSR has addressed a message to Japan on Anglo-American prisoners of war.

June 1—United States Vice President Henry A. Wallace delivers a speech in Irkutsk, Siberia.

June 3—Eric A. Johnston of the United States Chamber of Commerce speaks in Moscow before a luncheon meeting arranged by the People's Commissariat of Foreign Trade.

June 11—People's Commissariat of Foreign Trade publishes data on war supplies and goods received from United States, Great Britain, and Canada.

June 13—Stalin's statement on Allied landing in France.

June 19—Statement by Vice President Wallace on his visit to the USSR.

June 26—Soviet delegation to the Bretton Woods, New Hampshire, Monetary and Financial Conference arrives in Washington.

June 27—Finnish government announces its decision to go on fighting.

June 30—United States–Finnish relations severed.

Prof. Oscar Lange makes a radio address in New York on Soviet-Polish relations.

July 1—Bretton Woods Conference opens.

July 11—Relations with Denmark re-established.

July 13—D. Z. Manuilsky appointed people's commissar of foreign affairs of the Ukrainian SSR to replace A. E. Korneichuk.

July 19—Announcement of unofficial preliminary conversations between United States, Great Britain, and USSR on an international organization to secure peace, in conformity with the decision taken in Moscow on November 2, 1943.

July 21—Polish Committee of National Liberation formed by virtue of a decree issued in German-occupied Warsaw. A decree issued by this body on the formation of one Polish army from the troops fighting behind the German lines and those on Soviet territory.

July 22—Conclusion of the Bretton Woods Conference.

July 25—Statement by the People's Commissariat of Foreign Affairs on Soviet-Polish relations.

July 26—Agreement between Polish Committee of National Liberation on relations between the Soviet High Command and the Polish administration after the Red Army enters Polish territory.

July 27—Agreement with Polish Committee of National Liberation on relations between Polish administration and Soviet command.

August 3—Stalin receives Stanislaw Mikolajczyk and other representatives of the Polish government in London.

August 4—Diplomatic relations established with Lebanese Republic, formerly a French mandate.

August 8—It is announced that on August 6 and 7 joint conferences were held in Moscow between representatives of the Polish Committee of National Liberation and the Polish government in London.

Turkey releases two Soviet citizens held since 1942 for alleged participation in an attempt to murder the German ambassador.

August 10—Decree published issuing a general amnesty to Polish citizens convicted of crimes committed on the territory of the USSR.

August 11—Soviet statement on negotiations to be held in relation to the establishment of an international organization to secure peace.

August 14—German Field Marshal von Paulus, a prisoner of war in the USSR, issues statement advocating the overthrow of Hitler.

August 21—Conference on international postwar organization opens at Dumbarton Oaks, Washington, D.C.

August 22—Radio speech by King Michael of Romania on taking Romania out of the war.

August 23—New government formed in Romania.

President Roosevelt's speech to participants in the Dumbarton Oaks Conference.

August 24—Soviet statement on Romania.

August 26—Soviet government issues statements on "events in Romania" and "situation in Bulgaria"; armistice terms offered to Romania in April, 1944, are published.

Sofia radio states that Bulgarian government intends to follow a policy of "strict neutrality."

August 29—Delegates of the three major powers announce that preliminary agreement has been reached at Dumbarton Oaks.

Soviet announcement describes Bulgaria's declaration on neutrality as altogether inadequate.

August 30—Romanian armistice delegation arrives in Moscow.

September 1—New Cabinet in Bulgaria.

September 3—Armistice terms announced to Finland.

Finnish radio statement on armistice.

September 4—Radio statement from Bulgaria on "policy of strict neutrality."

September 5—Hostilities with Finland stop.

Soviet Union declares war on Bulgaria.

September 7—Soviet statement on "the break in Soviet-Bulgarian relations."

Finnish armistice delegation arrives in Moscow.

Hungary begins military operations against Romania.

September 8—Hostilities with Bulgaria stop.

Romania declares war on Hungary.

September 9—Agreement between Polish Committee of National Liberation and the Ukrainian SSR and Belorussian SSR on evacuation of population and property settlements.

New Cabinet in Bulgaria.

September 12—Armistice concluded with Romania.

Diplomatic relations established with Iraq.

September 13—Romanian armistice agreement published.

September 18—Notice of detention of several Romanian officials by Soviet forces published.

September 19—Armistice concluded with Finland.

September 20—Finnish armistice agreement published.

New Cabinet in Finland.

September 21—Notice of detention of several Bulgarian officials by Soviet troops published.

Finland severs relations with Hungary, Croatia, and Slovakia.

September 22—Agreement between Lithuanian SSR and Polish Committee of National Liberation on exchange of population.

September 27—Bulgaria breaks relations with Hungary.

September 28—Publication of the consent of Yugoslav authorities to the entry of Soviet troops on their territory in the interest of better prosecution of the war against Germany and Hungary.

September 29—Joint statement by United States, Great Britain, and USSR on Dumbarton Oaks published.

October 5—A. A. Zhdanov, chairman of Allied Control Commission, arrives in Helsinki.

Bulgaria announces decision to try all those guilty in bringing the country into war.

October 8—Publication of statement on meeting in London of Anglo-Soviet Trade Union Committee (October 2 to 6).

October 9—Churchill and Eden arrive in Moscow.

October 10—Publication of further material on Dumbarton Oaks Conference.

October 11—Bulgaria accepts preliminary armistice terms.

October 12—S. Mikolajczyk and other representatives of Polish government in London arrive in Moscow.

October 15—Bulgarian armistice delegation arrives in Moscow.

Regent Nicholas Horthy states on radio that Hungary wants an armistice.

Germans overthrow Horthy.

October 19—Churchill and Eden depart from Moscow.

October 20—Joint statement issued on Stalin-Churchill conversations in Moscow.

Publication of armistice agreement between Finland on the one hand and USSR and Great Britain on the other in reference to compensation of Anglo-Canadian concessionaires of nickel mines in Petsamo.

October 23—Provisional government of France recognized by USSR, England, United States, and Canada.

Gen. Col. F. I. Golikov appointed Soviet representative on repatriation of Soviet war prisoners and other citizens from Germany.

October 24—Soviet vice commissar of foreign affairs makes statement in Teheran on progress of negotiations on oil concessions.

October 25—Diplomatic relations resumed with Italy.

October 26—Armistice negotiations with Bulgaria begun in Moscow.

October 27—Churchill's speech in Parliament on results of visit to USSR.

Message from Norwegian government to Soviet government on the occasion of the beginning of Norway's liberation.

October 28—Armistice concluded with Bulgaria.

October 29—People's commissar of foreign affairs appointed by Estonian SSR.

Text of Bulgarian armistice published.

Soviet Union refuses to attend International Aviation Conference to open in Chicago on November 1.

November 1—Soviet government rejects the Swiss proposal of October 11 to establish diplomatic relations.

November 4—Allied Control Commission in Romania points out the unsatisfactory way in which certain provisions of the armistice of September 12 have been fulfilled.

November 7—Stalin's speech containing comments on results of Dumbarton Oaks Conference and classifying Japan as an "aggressor nation."

November 8—Vyshinsky arrives in Romania to check on the fulfillment of armistice terms.

November 11—Head of Swiss Department of Foreign Affairs resigns.

November 15—Stalin's statement to the mayor of Warsaw on future Soviet-Polish relations.

November 24—Trade delegation of the Mongolian People's Republic arrives in Moscow.

S. Mikolajczyk resigns from the Polish government in London.

December 2—General Charles de Gaulle arrives in Moscow.

Iran adopts a law prohibiting members of government to negotiate with foreigners on matters of oil concessions.

December 10—Treaty of alliance and mutual assistance with France. General de Gaulle leaves Moscow.

December 11—Exchange of notes establishing diplomatic relations with Chile.

December 12—Exchange of notes establishing diplomatic relations with Nicaragua.

December 15—Field Marshal F. von Paulus and 50 high-ranking German officers, prisoners of war in the USSR, appeal to the German people to rise against Hitler and his system.

December 17—Agreement with Finland on method of paying reparations.

December 18—Statement by E. R. Stettinius, Jr., on desirability of Soviet-Polish understanding.

Text of treaty of alliance with France published.

December 20—Anthony Eden comments favorably on Soviet-French treaty.

December 21—Provisional national assembly of Hungary appeals to the people to break with Germany and join the Red Army.

December 28—Provisional national government of Hungary declares war on Germany.

December 29—Soviet government hands to Bulgaria 11 individuals in its custody guilty of involving Bulgaria in war. The action is approved by United States and Great Britain.

December 31—Polish Provisional government formed in Lublin.

143

1945

January 1—Hungarian armistice delegation arrives in Moscow.

Secretary of State Stettinius states that the United States continues to recognize the London Polish government. Similar statement by the British Foreign Office.

January 4—A delegation from Lvov of the Ukrainian Orthodox Church (affiliated with the Roman Catholic Church) confers in Moscow with Soviet authorities.

January 6—Diplomatic relations with Provisional Polish government established.

January 13—Trade negotiations with Finland are started.

January 16—French trade-union delegation arrives in Moscow; a Franco-Soviet trade-union committee is formed.

January 20—Armistice concluded with Hungary.

January 22—Japan's foreign minister states in Parliament that Japan intends to "abide by policies of friendly relations with the Soviet Union."

January 25—Ambassador K. A. Oumansky killed in a plane accident in Mexico City.

January 27—Four republics, RSFSR, Ukrainian SSR, Belorussian SSR, and Lithuanian SSR, donate to the city of Warsaw 60,000 tons of bread.

January 30—Czechoslovakia establishes diplomatic relations with the Provisional government of Poland in Lublin.

January 31—Trade agreement with Finland.

February 1—Bulgarian court pronounces sentence on war criminals.

Provisional government of Poland moves from Lublin to Warsaw.

February 2—Congress (*sobor*) of Russian Orthodox Church opens in Moscow, with several representatives of other orthodox churches attending.

February 3—Gen. von Seidlitz, prisoner of war in the USSR, broadcasts an appeal to the Germans to end the war.

February 4—Second meeting of Roosevelt, Stalin, and Churchill opens near Yalta, in the Crimea.

February 6—World Trade Union Congress opens in London, with large Soviet delegation participating.

February 8—World Trade Union Congress decides to invite representatives of former enemy countries: Finland, Bulgaria, Romania, and Italy.

February 9—Statement of eight world leaders of the Orthodox Church issued in Moscow condemning the position of the Vatican on fascism.

February 11—USSR and Great Britain, and USSR and the United States sign agreements on matters pertaining to citizens of these countries, as well as prisoners of war, being liberated in Germany.

Joint statement of the Yalta Conference, signed by Roosevelt, Stalin, and Churchill.

February 13—Polish government in London denounces Yalta decisions.

Speech by head of Soviet delegation at World Trade Union Conference in London.

February 17—Vatican issues denial in reference to declaration made by representatives of Orthodox Churches in Moscow on February 9.

February 18—Publication of a letter of the patriarch of Romania thanking the Soviet government for protection given by the Red Army to monasteries.

Decision of the Council of People's Commissars to render aid in the rebuilding of Warsaw.

February 27—Churchill reports in Parliament on the Yalta Conference.

March 1—President Roosevelt reports to Congress on Yalta Conference.

March 4—Finland declares war on Germany.

March 5—United States Department of State issues invitation on behalf of USSR and other sponsoring powers to the San Francisco Conference on a world security organization.

March 8—Offer of Dominican Republic to establish diplomatic and consular relations accepted.

March 8–9—Exchange of letters between Premier P. Groza of Romania and Stalin on Transylvania.

March 11—Statement by A. Y. Vyshinsky to Romanian government on Transylvania.

March 13—Official return of Transylvania to Romania.

March 14—Diplomatic relations established with Venezuela.

TASS news agency denies rumors of negotiations between USSR and Vatican.

March 21—Soviet Union denounces Soviet-Turkish friendship treaty of 1925.

March 23—Guatemalan Congress recommends establishment of relations with USSR.

March 29—White House statement on the understanding with the USSR reached at Yalta on seating the Ukrainian SSR and Belorussian SSR at the San Francisco Conference.

March 31—United States and Great Britain reject Soviet request to invite Polish Provisional government to San Francisco.

April 2—Diplomatic relations with Brazil established.

April 5—Soviet Union denounces its neutrality treaty with Japan.

April 6—Marshal F. I. Tolbukhin's address in Vienna.

April 8—Publication of Turkish reply to Soviet denunciation of Soviet-Turkish friendship treaty.

April 10—Declaration of Ukrainian government on San Francisco Conference.

April 11—Twenty-year treaty of friendship, mutual aid, and postwar co-operation with Yugoslavia.

April 13—Trade agreement with Yugoslavia.

April 14, 15—Mourning for Franklin D. Roosevelt observed in the USSR.

April 14—In response to President Harry S. Truman's request, V. M. Molotov will attend San Francisco Conference.

April 17—Ottawa protocol on delivery of supplies to USSR signed by USSR, United States, Canada, and Great Britain.

April 18—Diplomatic and consular relations established with Bolivia.

April 19—United States refuses second Soviet request to invite Polish Provisional government to San Francisco.

Diplomatic relations established with Guatemala.

April 21—Treaty of friendship, mutual assistance, and postwar co-operation with Poland.

April 22—Molotov arrives in Washington.

April 23—Publication of warning to all German officials, signed by Stalin, Truman, and Churchill.

April 24—N. M. Shvernik, presiding at opening meeting of 11th Session of Supreme Soviet of the USSR, delivers a memorial address on the late President Roosevelt.

April 26—Speech by Molotov on second day of San Francisco Conference.

April 27—Ukraine and Belorussia seated; Soviet proposal to invite Polish Provisional government voted down at San Francisco.

Stalin announces meeting of American and Soviet troops in Germany. Similar statements by Truman and Churchill.

April 30—Molotov's motion to defer inviting Argentina voted down at San Francisco.

Statement to TASS by Col. Gen. F. I. Golikov on Soviet policy with regard to repatriation of Soviet citizens.

May 7—Molotov's press conference in San Francisco.

May 8—Field Marshal Wilhelm Keitel signs Germany's unconditional surrender in Berlin.

BIBLIOGRAPHY

IN RUSSIAN

Sbornik deistvuiushchikh dogovorov, soglashenii, i konventsii . . . (*Collection of treaties, agreements, conventions* . . . *in force*), vol. VI (Moscow, 1931).

Sabanin, A. B., ed., *Mezhdunarodnaia politika v 1930 godu* (*International Politics in 1930*) (Moscow, 1932).

——, *Ukazateli k deistvuiushchim dogovoram, soglasheniiam i konventsiiam* . . . (*Index for treaties, agreements, conventions* . . . *in force*), vol. I (Moscow, 1935).

Litvinov, M., *Vneshniaia politika SSSR* (*Foreign Policy of the USSR*), speeches and statements, 2d ed. (Moscow, 1937).

Rosenblum, B. D., comp., *Mezhdunarodnye ekonomicheskie konferentsii i soglasheniia, 1933–1935* (*International Economic Conferences and Agreements, 1933–1935*), pt. 2 (Moscow, 1937).

Mints, I., and Gorodetskii, E., eds., *Dokumenty po istorii grazhdanskoi voiny v SSSR* (*Documents of the History of the Civil War in the USSR*), vol. I (Moscow, 1940).

Potemkin, V. P., *Politika umirotvoreniia agressorov i borba Sovetskogo soiuza za mir* (*Policy of Appeasing Aggressors and the Struggle of the Soviet Union for Peace*) (Moscow, 1943).

Vneshniaia politika Sovetskogo soiuza v period Otechestvennoi voiny (*Foreign Policy of the Soviet Union in the Period of the Fatherland War*), vol. I, Documents and Materials, June 22, 1941–Dec. 31, 1943 (Moscow, 1944).

Mirovoe khoziaistvo i mirovaia politika (*World Economy and World Politics*), a monthly for 1944, and 1, 2–3, 4, 6 for 1945.

IN ENGLISH

Santalov, A. A., and Segal, Louis, eds., *Soviet Union Year-Book* (London, 1927 and 1930).

Schuman, F. L., *American Policy Toward Russia Since 1917* (New York, 1928).

Fischer, Louis, *The Soviets in World Affairs*, 2 vols. (New York, 1930).

Yakhontoff, V. A., *Russia and the Soviet Union in the Far East* (New York, 1931).

Korovine, E. A., *The USSR and Disarmament,* International Conciliation Series No. 292 (September, 1933).

Stewart, G., *White Armies of Russia* (New York, 1933).

Bunyan, James, and Fisher, H. H., *The Bolshevik Revolution, 1917–1918* (Stanford University, Calif., 1934).

Chamberlin, W. H., *The Russian Revolution, 1917–1921,* 2 vols. (New York, 1935).

Coates, W. P. and Z. K., *Armed Intervention in Russia, 1918–1922* (London, 1935).

American-Russian Chamber of Commerce, *Handbook of the Soviet Union* (New York, 1936).

Yakhontoff, V. A., *The Russian Empire and the Soviet Union in the Far East,* American Russian Institute Special Publication No. 3 (New York, December, 1936).

Lenin, V. I., and Stalin, Joseph, *The Russian Revolution* (New York, 1938).

Litvinov, Maxim, *Against Aggression,* speeches and documents (New York, 1939).

Kournakoff, S. N., *Russia's Fighting Forces* (New York, 1942).

Stalin, Joseph, *Leninism: Selected Writings* (New York, 1942).

Coates, W. P. and Z. K., *A History of Anglo-Soviet Relations* (London, 1943).

Dulles, F. R., *The Road to Teheran* (Princeton, 1944).

Konovalov, S., ed., *Russo-Polish Relations* (Princeton, 1945).

Research Bulletin on the Soviet Union, American Russian Institute (Jan. 15, 1936), vol. I, No. 1; (Dec. 31, 1937), vol. II, No. 12.

American Quarterly on the Soviet Union (April, 1938, to November, 1940), vol. I, No. 1, to vol. III, No. 2–3.

American Review on the Soviet Union (February, 1941, to August, 1941), vol. III, No. 4, to vol. IV, No. 3.

147

CHAPTER V

Government and Politics

By FREDERICK L. SCHUMAN

THE early principalities of Russia, like their western counterparts at the dawn of the feudal age, were for the most part organizations of power by landowners to protect their interests against invaders and to exact obedience and tribute from the tillers of the soil. This form of polity became general among the eastern Slavs with the transition from semibarbaric tribal life to territorial states, following the coming of the Norsemen along the Volkhov-Dnieper "water road" in the middle of the ninth century. The lowest class consisted of serfs or slaves. The ruling class was a nobility of boyars who originally were the councilors of the great princes, members of their bodyguards (*druzhina*), or courtiers (*dvoryane*). Ultimately, they were the "best people" (*luchshie lyudi*) who alone were entitled to bear arms and to own land and serfs. In the trading centers of the north and west, and to some extent elsewhere, there functioned, alongside of the rule of princes and nobles, a popular assembly or *veche* of all adult males. Government in primitive Russia thus combined elements of monarchy, aristocracy, and democracy.

These insecure communities were constantly assailed by Eastern invaders from the steppes and seldom enjoyed orderly union, despite the impressive power of the princes of Kiev between the tenth and twelfth centuries. All of them were profoundly influenced by their long subjugation (1238–1480) at the hands of the Mongol conquerors who swept over them out of Asia with fire and sword. During this period the grand princes of Moscow, while paying tribute to the khans, organized and

148

expanded their realm until they were finally able under Ivan III to cast off the Mongol yoke. In this process Muscovy (Moscow) became the political successor to the Mongol Empire of the "Golden Horde," which had its capital at Sarai on the lower Volga, near the present site of Stalingrad. Church and state were closely linked together against the pagan. The Muscovite princes became absolute monarchs who were able in the end to compel the unruly nobles to obedience. From the Mongols they borrowed the theory and practice of despotism, the idea of universal service to the state, procedures of taxation and census taking, a postal system, and many features of army organization.

Ivan III, surnamed the Great (1462–1505), married Sophia (Zoë), niece of the last Byzantine emperor and took unto himself the titles of caesar or czar, "autocrat," and "sovereign of all Russia." His work of unification and aggrandizement was carried further by Ivan the Terrible (Ivan IV, 1533–1584). The disorders of the "time of troubles" subsided with the election to the czardom by the Zemski Sobor (Assembly of the Land) of Michael (Mikhail Fyodorovich), first of the Romanovs, in 1613. His able successor, Peter the Great (Peter I, 1682–1725) assumed the title of emperor and continued the task of territorial expansion which Catherine the Great (Catherine II, 1762–1796) carried to even more impressive triumphs.

THE AUTOCRACY . . . This state, like its European contemporaries, was a divine-right monarchy in which power and wealth were enjoyed by a landed aristocracy. But its peculiar origins and retarded development gave it a unique character. While serfdom was waning in western Europe in the seventeenth century, it was consolidated and extended in Russia. From the time of Ivan the Terrible the power of the boyars was weakened through the establishment of a new aristocracy, the *pomiestchika*, whose members held their estates in return for service to the czar. The peasants on these lands, including freemen, were gradually reduced to serfdom, to the profit of the new landlords who, in turn, lacked the independence of the feudal gentry of the West and upheld, rather than resisted, the power of the crown. In the absence of any considerable middle class, representative institutions, both local and national, including the Zemski Sobor and the older Duma of the boyars, fell into decay. Before the emancipation of 1861 the great majority of the czar's subjects were illiterate peasant serfs. Before the revolution of 1905, the czar's government was an arbitrary despotism, with no constitution, no parliament, and virtually no public participation beyond the mir (village community) and the zemstvo (provincial assembly).

In this regime the czar, according to the fundamental laws, was an "unlimited autocrat" to whom obedience was "ordained by God Himself." He ruled his scores of provinces (*guberniyas* and *oblasts*) through governors appointed on the nomination of the minister of the interior. His chief agencies of national government were the Council of Ministers, composed of department heads; the Imperial Council of 100 appointed members, to whom were added in 1906 an almost equal number of elected members, with both groups consisting largely of wealthy landowners; a Senate (established by Peter the Great), composed of privy councilors and functioning as the highest judicial and administrative body; and the Holy Synod (also established by Peter the Great) of the Orthodox Church, dominated by the procurator of the Holy Synod, in effect a minister for ecclesiastical affairs. All these appointed officials were named by, answerable to, and removable by the czar alone, who was guardian of the church as well as head of the state. Legislation was prepared by the Imperial Council, but its members could only advise and never control the autocrat and his ministers.

BUSINESSMEN AND WORKERS . . . This archaic political structure, like the agrarian social order on which it rested, was not seriously challenged until commerce and industry fostered the growth of cities. This development was well advanced in England and the Low Countries in the seventeenth century and swiftly transformed western Europe and America between 1750 and 1850. In Russia it scarcely got under way before 1861 and then proceeded slowly and only with the aid of foreign capital. As in the West, urban capitalism gave rise first to an intermediate social stratum of burghers between nobles and peasants, and then to the division of this group into bourgeois entrepreneurs and factory workers or proletarians. As in the West, businessmen tended to embrace the ideals of nationalism and liberalism and to demand popular participation in government and constitutional restraints on absolutism. Workers lent willing ears to the spokesmen of internationalism and radicalism, including various schools of revolutionary anarchism and socialism. Both groups became the foes of czarism and of the aristocracy.

150

The aspirations of the liberal bourgeoisie found ultimate political expression in two party groups; the Constitutional Democrats or Cadets, seeking a parliamentary democracy, and the more conservative Octobrists, content with the Imperial Manifesto of October, 1905. Many workers, on the other hand, rallied to the support of the Socialist Revolutionaries (S.R.'s) or the Social Democrats (S.D.'s). The former were non-Marxist socialists who looked primarily to the peasantry for revolutionary action in the tradition of the earlier Narodniki or Populists. Some of the S.R.'s, like some of the members of the radical intelligentsia in the 1870's and 1880's, preached and practiced individual terrorism in an effort to weaken the autocracy through assassination.

The S.D.'s were Marxists whose leaders met in a secret Congress in Minsk in 1898 to found their party, devoted to the achievement of socialism through proletarian revolution. At the 2d Party Congress, held in Brussels and London in 1903, the delegates split into a moderate, reformist wing, then in the minority, and hence called Mensheviki, and an extremist wing, favoring a highly disciplined monolithic party, dedicated uncompromisingly to social revolution and a dictatorship of the proletariat. The members of the latter faction, led by Vladimir Ilich Ulyanov (alias Nikolai Lenin), then had a majority of the delegates and were, therefore, called Bolsheviki or men of the majority. During the early years of the century nothing could have seemed more fantastically improbable to most observers of Russian politics than the coming to power of this little group of obscure agitators and conspirators.

REVOLUTION DEFEATED . . . The results of the war with Japan (1904–1905) provided the enemies of the autocracy with their first promising opportunity to organize mass revolutionary action. An 11-point petition, drawn up at a conference of zemstvos representatives in November, 1904, demanded civil liberties and constitutional government. On Bloody Sunday, early in January, 1905, a peaceful demonstration of workers, bearing icons and singing hymns under the leadership of Father Gapon, was fired upon by troops before the Winter Palace with the loss of several hundred lives. A wave of strikes, peasant disorders, mutinies, and acts of political terrorism ensued. By autumn a political general strike was under way in many urban centers, under the direction of councils or soviets of workers' deputies in Moscow and St. Petersburg. After concessions by the government had appeased many

151

liberals, the authorities moved to crush the revolutionary radicals. They suppressed the St. Petersburg Soviet (the vice president of which was Leon Trotsky) and likewise destroyed the Moscow Soviet after bloody street battles. The year 1906 inaugurated a long period of repressions and reprisals directed by Prime Minister Peter (Pëter Arkadevich) Stolypin. His assassination (1911) did not alter the fact that the revolution had failed.

The failure was not unqualified. In the face of danger Czar Nicholas II (1894–1917) had issued the Manifesto of October 17, 1905, promising civil liberties and popular elections for a parliament which would have effective lawmaking powers and control over the ministers. The czardom thus became, paradoxically, a constitutional autocracy, but in the final arrangements the new assembly or Imperial Duma was weakened by a second chamber in the form of a recast Imperial Council. The franchise, moreover, was soon restricted (1907) by a complex system of indirect class elections which filled the third and fourth dumas with conservatives and reactionaries. In practice, the Duma was given no real control over legislation or appropriations and none at all over the ministry. The czar could veto all laws, could adjourn or dissolve the Duma at will, and, without consulting the Duma, could issue numerous executive proclamations (*ukazy*) having the force of law. The autocracy was no longer unlimited, but it was still an autocracy. The nobility and clergy now shared power with conservative businessmen, but most of the middle class and the mass of workers and peasants still had no direct voice in public affairs.

REVOLUTION TRIUMPHANT . . . The results of the war with the Central Powers (1914–1918) provided the enemies of autocracy with their chance to destroy it. The military defeats of 1915–1916 caused "dark forces" at the imperial court, headed by the czarina and her consultant, Rasputin, to indulge in treasonable intrigues. The assassination of Rasputin brought no change in the blindly reactionary attitude of the czar and his advisers in the face of mass misery, war weariness, and widespread demands for reform or revolution. Following strikes, riots, and mutinies, Nicholas II abdicated on March 15, 1917, and therewith brought to an end the dynasty of despots who had ruled or misruled all the Russias during the three centuries since the accession of Michael Romanov.

152

Pending the election of a constituent assembly, the symbols of power passed into the hands of a provisional government, consisting chiefly of Duma members and headed by Prince Georgi Lvov, with Pavel Milyukov, leader of the Cadets, as foreign minister and Alexander Kerensky, a leader of the S.R.'s, as minister of justice. But the substance of power all over the land passed to local soviets of workers', soldiers', and peasants' deputies who reflected mass demands for a democratic peace, for partition of the landed estates, and for the socialization of industry. Lenin and other Bolshevist leaders, who returned to Russia from Switzerland via Germany in mid-April, gained increasing influence in the soviets. Milyukov was forced to resign in May by Soviet opposition to his conception of war aims. By July the Cadets were out of the government. Kerensky became a nominal dictator amid a furious storm of controversy among Socialist Revolutionaries, Mensheviks, and Bolsheviks as to which brand of socialism should be adopted, and how and when it should be furthered. Kerensky suppressed a Bolshevist uprising in Petrograd in July, but in September was obliged to rely on Bolshevist support to thwart the effort of the reactionary Gen. Lavr Georgyevich Kornilov to seize power.

By autumn the Bolsheviks had a majority of the deputies in the soviets of Petrograd, Moscow, and various other cities. The former Menshevik, Leon Trotsky, who had joined the Bolsheviks in midsummer, became president of the Petrograd Soviet, with headquarters in Smolny Institute. Lenin preached, "Peace, Land, and Bread," "All Power to the Soviets," proletarian dictatorship, and conversion of the imperialist war into class war. Bourgeois liberals and aristocratic reactionaries were alike helpless in the face of growing popular support of Bolshevist demands. The Military Revolutionary Committee of the Petrograd Soviet organized the troops and workers of the capital into a Red Guard. Lenin decided that the blow should fall on November 7 (October 25, old style) when the Second All-Russian Congress of Soviets was to convene. On the appointed day the Red Guards seized public buildings, Trotsky proclaimed the end of the provisional government, Kerensky fled, and his supporters in the Winter Palace surrendered after a brief battle.

On the night of November 8–9, 1917, the Soviet Congress accepted the gift of power from Lenin, whose pleas for peace and for the abolition of private ownership of land were hailed with enthusiasm. The deputies adjourned after approving the establishment of a provisional workers' and peasants' government headed by a Central Executive Committee and a Council of People's Commissars (Sovnarkom) in which Lenin was president, Trotsky was commissar for foreign affairs, and later for war, Stalin was commissar for nationalities, and other Bolshevist leaders were named to the remaining posts. All over Russia authority was assumed by local soviets, under Bolshevist auspices, with little disorder. Bourgeois democracy became a lost cause. Its last hope, the long-heralded Constituent Assembly, elected in mid-November, had a heavy majority of non-Bolshevists among its members. They met for a day (January 18, 1918), refused to acknowledge the soviets, and were dissolved, unwept and unsung, by the Central Executive Committee. The imperial Russia of the landlords was dead. A democratic Russia of businessmen was powerless to be born. The great empire of the czars became Soviet Russia, ruled by the revolutionary Marxist leaders of the workers and peasants, and dedicated to the building of a new heaven and a new earth.

THE DICTATORSHIP OF THE PROLETARIAT . . . The new regime was not at the outset a one-party dictatorship. At the end of November, 1917, four Left S.R.'s were admitted to the Sovnarkom. The Right S.R.'s and the Menshevik S.D.'s might also have received representation had they been willing to join. There was no immediate socialization of industry nor any terrorization of the propertied classes. Lenin moved slowly toward socialism and appealed for the co-operation of former owners and managers. In March, 1918, at the Seventh Party Congress it was resolved to change the name of the party from Russian Social Democratic Labor Party (Bolshevik) to the Russian Communist Party (Bolshevik). The capital was moved to Moscow. A new party program declared that there could be no freedom for the bourgeoisie and that all its efforts to recover power must be suppressed. "This is what is meant by a dictatorship of the proletariat."

This initial tolerance of other socialist parties came to an end in the summer of 1918 when, as a sequel to the separate peace of Brest-Litovsk with Germany, the Left S.R.'s withdrew from the Sovnarkom and the Right S.R.'s, later joined by the Lefts and the Mensheviks, began to organize rebellion. The Allied blockade and intervention were initiated

154

at the same time. At the end of August S.R. terrorists assassinated M. S. Uritski and V. Volodarski and gravely wounded Lenin. The Cheka (Extraordinary Commission for the Suppression of Counterrevolution, Sabotage, and Speculation) then unleashed the Red terror against the enemies of the regime, who included most people of means, fighting to recover their properties, and most non-Bolshevik socialists, fighting for their own conceptions of socialism. There ensued (1918–1921) a long and bloody civil and foreign war. The imperial family was executed in Ekaterinburg (Sverdlovsk), July 16, 1918. Hundreds of thousands followed them to the grave, victims of Red or White terror or of the vicissitudes of battle, famine, and pestilence. In the anti-Soviet camp, liberals and socialists were soon ousted by the reactionary leaders of the White armies who received financial and military support from the Allies.

In this ordeal peasants as well as workers finally rallied to the Soviet cause and made possible the ultimate victory of the Red Army. As the price of its own survival the Soviet regime transformed itself into a one-party totalitarian dictatorship, which established a completely socialized economy in the name of "war communism." By the end of hostilities only half of the prewar farming areas was under cultivation. Industrial production was down to 15 per cent of its 1914 level. Lenin and his colleagues accordingly executed a "strategic retreat" in the form of the New Economic Policy (1921–1928) which permitted private trade for profit in agriculture and light industry. Once production was restored to prewar levels, the offensive against capitalism was resumed in the First Five-Year Plan (1928–1932). The competitive market was again abolished. Farming was collectivized in a second great agrarian revolution initiated in 1928, carried forward in the name of "class war in the villages" and accompanied by a ruthless liquidation of the *kulaks*, or wealthy peasants, who suffered the fate of the old aristocracy and bourgeoisie. The construction of a vast industrial plant was inaugurated in the name of "building socialism in one country." By the beginning of the Third Five-Year Plan in 1938, the Union of Soviet Socialist Republics had become a powerfully industrialized state, based solidly on social ownership of all means of production and maintaining full employment in a rapidly expanding economy.

THE COMMUNIST PARTY . . . This task, costly, at times heartbreaking, but in the end successful, was directed by the CPSU(B) or the Communist Party of the Soviet Union (Bolshevik). Members were carefully selected zealots, organized on Lenin's principle of "democratic centralism": full representation and free debate prior to the great decisions constituting the "party line"; iron discipline and unquestioning obedience once a decision was reached. The participants in this "vocation of leadership" were less politicians in the Western sense than spiritually consecrated men and women, dedicated to their cause with all the ardor of crusaders. The spirit, purpose, and problems of this unique brotherhood are well suggested by Lenin's words to the Eleventh Party Congress in 1922: "Communist principles, excellent ideals, are written large on you, you are holy men, fit to go alive to paradise, but do you know your business? . . . We must learn to begin anew again and again. . . . In the masses of the people we are as a drop in the sea and we can govern only if we adequately express what the people feels. . . . We shall not fall, because we are not afraid to speak of our weakness and will learn to overcome our weakness."

Quality rather than numbers has always been the goal in the recruitment of Communist Party members and in the periodical expulsions of the unworthy from the ranks. This army of the faithful numbered only 40,000 in April, 1917, and only 115,000 early in 1918. Not until 1929 were there as many as a million members, with less than half a million candidates. By 1934 there were almost two million members and a million candidates. The drastic purges of the following years reduced membership to 1,600,000 and candidates to 880,000 by March, 1939. Expansion during the war years brought members and candidates to 5,000,000 by V-E Day, with the party's junior auxiliary, the Young Communist League (Komsomol), having about 15,000,000 members, of whom half were enrolled during the war. Industrial workers have always constituted well over half of the party membership. All members pay small dues proportionate to their earnings.

The party functions through periodical All-Union congresses of elected delegates, which met annually between 1917 and 1925 (the Sixth to the Fourteenth). The Fifteenth Congress was held in December, 1927, the Sixteenth in June, 1930, the Seventeenth in January, 1934, and the Eighteenth in March, 1939, when it was decided that congresses should meet at least once every three years. No congresses were held during the war years. At the Eighteenth Congress, consisting of 1,567 voting delegates, representing 1,600,000 members in 113,000 local committees, changes of rules were adopted by which all applicants must be 18 years of age or over, must submit three recommendations from party members of three years' standing, and must have a probation period of one year. Periodical mass purges were abolished, though individuals remained subject to expulsion for violations of program, rules, or discipline. The new rules sought to safeguard members against unjustified expulsions, to protect their rights of criticism, and to promote intraparty democracy. The local committees also send delegates to district, city, area, regional (*rayon*), territorial (*oblast*), and republic congresses and likewise to All-Union conferences which, under the 1939 rules, are to meet annually. The executive organ of the Communist Party is the Central Committee of 71 members, elected by the congress and divided into various functional agencies, of which the most important in determining policy is the Politburo of 9 members.

THE CRISIS OF LEADERSHIP . . . In a one-party state political differences arise and are resolved not in a competition for public favor among parties but within the single party possessing a monopoly of legality. The history of the CPSU(B), both before and since its coming to power, is one of frequent clashes among factions regarding questions of strategy and tactics. Thus in 1918 the Left Communists, headed by Leon Trotsky and Nikolai I. Bukharin, opposed the Central Committee's decision to accept the Treaty of Brest-Litovsk. A 1921 resolution on "party unity" authorized the Central Committee to expel all members violating discipline or reviving factionalism. Lenin's death (January 21, 1924) led to a series of complex struggles for ascendency, polarized ultimately around Trotsky and Stalin. The latter was general secretary of the party and "boss" of the Politburo. He held no major governmental post until May 6, 1941, when he assumed the chairmanship (premiership) of the Sovnarkom. After Lenin's passing Trotsky became a vehement champion of world revolution, intraparty democracy, early and rapid collectivization and industrialization, and, in the end, forcible liquidation of the "Stalinist bureaucracy."

In 1927, following serious breaches of party discipline, Leon Trotsky, Leo Borisovich Kamenev, Grigori Evseyevich Zinovyev, Karl Bernardovich Radek, and other oppositionists were expelled from the party. Almost all recanted and were readmitted except Trotsky, who was exiled to Turkestan and then banished from the USSR in January, 1929. While abroad Trotsky made plans for a fourth International and for a new revolution in Russia to overthrow Stalin, whom he accused of betraying Marxism. Within the Soviet Union, Trotsky's followers, notably Zinovyev and Kamenev, made common cause with the Right Deviationists (Nikolai Bukharin, Aleksei I. Rykov), and both together, according to their later confessions, conspired with Nazi and other foreign agents.

The assassination on December 1, 1934, of Sergei M. Kirov, party leader of Leningrad, led during the next four years not only to a purge of one fifth of the party members but to numerous arrests, followed by sentences of imprisonment, exile, and death, and to a final "purge of the purgers" for abusing their authority. In a series of dramatic public trials (January, 1935; August, 1936; January, 1937; March, 1938) Kamenev, Zinovyev, Grigori L. Pyatakov, Bukharin, Rykov, G. Yagoda, N. N. Krestinski, and others were found guilty, on their own admissions, of plotting sabotage, assassination, and treason and were sentenced to death. In June, 1937, Marshal Mikhail N. Tukhachevski and seven other high Red Army officers were court-martialed for treason and executed. In December, 1937, Leo Kharakhan and other diplomats suffered a similar fate for allegedly treasonable dealings with Tokyo. Trotsky, then in Mexico (where he was to be assassinated by a disgruntled admirer, August 21, 1940), loudly proclaimed his innocence and avowed that Stalin had bloodily liquidated the "Old Bolsheviks" through a "frame-up" in order to consolidate his personal despotism.

A different conclusion is suggested by a consideration of the evidence in the public trials, the psychology of revolutionary conspirators, and the Nazi technique of disintegration. An oppositionist plot undoubtedly existed within the Communist Party and the Soviet military and civil bureaucracy. It was encouraged from Berlin and Tokyo in the hope of weakening the USSR and rendering it ripe for conquest. When it failed and was exposed, the chief conspirators, already demoralized by the successful building of socialism under Joseph Stalin's leadership, made abject confessions in a last effort to salve their consciences and to serve the cause to which they had devoted their lives. In destroying the future enemy's fifth column, the Soviet authorities purged or otherwise punished many whose guilt was questionable. But the measures taken helped to thwart Hitler's designs against the Soviet Union and thus

saved the United Nations from a common defeat. They also strengthened the party, the army, and the state, despite foreign opinion to the
contrary, and enabled the Soviet peoples to face the coming trials of war
and peace in unbreakable unity.

THE SOVIET CONSTITUTION . . . If the leaders of the party are
the actual rulers of the Soviet state, the state itself, as elsewhere, is an
elaborate apparatus of legislation, administration, and adjudication designed to elicit popular loyalty and obedience to those who rule. The
legal system and the courts are dealt with elsewhere. The governmental
machinery for formulating and executing the party program can best
be reviewed through a sketch of constitutional developments.

The first Soviet Constitution was prepared by the Third All-Russian
Congress of Soviets and by a drafting committee appointed by the Central Executive Committee. It was ratified by the Fifth Congress of
Soviets, July 10, 1918. This document of 90 articles was based in part on
the original Communist Manifesto of 1848. It sanctioned four levels of
soviet bodies for local government (territorial or *oblasts*, provincial or
guberniyas, county, and rural districts or *volosts*) and provided for an
All-Russian Congress of Soviets of a thousand members, indirectly
elected, who would appoint the Central Executive Committee of 200
members, who, in turn, would designate the Sovnarkom or Cabinet of
18 commissars. This constitution was limited in its application to the
RSFSR (Russian Socialist Federated Soviet Republic). Other Soviet
republics, with their own constitutions, came into being elsewhere. In
December, 1922, on Stalin's proposal, a treaty of union was drawn up
among the RSFSR, the Belorussian, the Ukrainian, and the Transcaucasian republics. A federal constitution, establishing the Union of
Soviet Socialist Republics was ratified by a new Central Executive
Committee, July 6, 1923, and given final approval by the Second Congress of Soviets of the USSR, January 31, 1924.

The Union thus formed was a federation of republics. Their number grew from 4 to 7 by 1929, with the admission of the Uzbek, Turkmen, and Tadzhik republics; to 11 by 1936 with the admission of Kazakstan and Kirghiz and the establishment of Georgia, Azerbaidzhan, and
Armenia as separate republics; and to 16 by 1941, with the incorporation of Lithuania, Latvia, Estonia, Moldavia, and the Karelo-Finnish Republic. As in the United States, the Union government has enumerated

159

or delegated powers and the constituent members have residual powers. The constitution of 1923 granted to the members the right of secession, subject to the approval of all the republics. It vested federal legislative powers in the All-Union Congress of Soviets, consisting of delegates sent by provincial and district congresses. The congress conferred actual legislative authority on a Central Executive Committee, composed of the Soviet of the Union of 451 members, representing the republics in proportion to population, and the Soviet of Nationalities of 136 members, comprising 5 from each of the member and autonomous republics and 1 from each autonomous region. These two bodies, meeting jointly, named the Presidium of 27 members and the federal Sovnarkom. Suffrage was denied to the former enemy classes. Only the deputies to local soviets were chosen by the voters, by a show of hands. All higher Soviet bodies were indirectly elected on a basis which overrepresented urban districts at the expense of rural districts.

These cumbersome and undemocratic features came to be regarded as undesirable, with the final success of socialist collectivization and industrialization. After prolonged public discussion a new federal constitution was adopted by the Eighth Soviet Congress, December 5, 1936. Soviet government rests upon this 1936 charter, as amended, and upon the constitutions of the republics, amended to conform to the new federal document. This fundamental law of 13 chapters and 147 articles abolished all class discriminations in suffrage and all forms of indirect and occupational representation. It provided for "universal, direct and equal suffrage by secret ballot" for all elections to all Soviet bodies, Union, republican, and local. The new national parliament or Supreme Soviet of the USSR, meeting twice a year in regular sessions, consists of the Soviet of the Union, with 647 members (1941) elected from districts with 300,000 inhabitants each, and the Soviet of Nationalities of 713 elected members, 25 from each member republic, 11 from each autonomous republic, 5 from each autonomous region, and 1 from each national region. The two chambers have equal authority. Legislation requires a majority in each. At a joint session they elect a Presidium of 42, constituting a kind of collective presidency of the Union, and the Sovnarkom, which is responsible to the Supreme Soviet and, in intervals between the latter's sessions, to the Presidium. With the Nazi invasion in 1941 a smaller "War Cabinet" was established in the form of a Committee for State Defense composed of Stalin, V. M. Molotov, K. E. Voroshilov, L. P. Beriya, and Georgi M. Malinkov.

The USSR remains a federation in which each member now has an unqualified right of secession (Article 17). The commissariats dealing with transportation, communication, and heavy industry are exclusively union or federal commissariats, while those dealing with light industry, agriculture, justice, health, etc., are joint union-republic commissariats, working with and through the corresponding commissariats of the republics. By the amendments of February 2, 1944, the commissariats of Defense and Foreign Affairs were transferred from the former to the latter category, with each republic now entitled to have its own commissariats in these fields and to enter into foreign relations and maintain its own military establishment. Federal law is enforced on individuals through national and local courts and prevails over republican law. In cases of conflict, however, the final decision does not rest with the federal Supreme Court, as in the United States, but with the federal Presidium, which also interprets the constitution. Amendments, similarly, do not require ratification by the republics but can be enacted (Article 147) by a two-thirds vote in each chamber of the federal Supreme Soviet. In the supremacy of the legislature, the lack of a clear separation of powers, the absence of a popularly elected chief executive, and the responsibility of the executive to the parliament, the Soviet Constitution follows the British rather than the American model.

THE CONSTITUTION IN PRACTICE . . . Loose analogies with Western political institutions are misleading, as are sweeping statements that the Soviet Constitution is "the most democratic in the world" or, conversely, is a mere fraudulent façade. The unique role of the Communist Party is not altered by the 1936 Constitution and is indeed expressly recognized (Article 126) in the statement that the party is "the vanguard of the working people in their struggle to strengthen and develop the socialist system." By Article 141, moreover, "the right to nominate candidates is secured to public organizations and societies of the working people: Communist Party organizations, trade unions, cooperatives, youth organizations and cultural societies." Since elections were suspended during the war, the practical operation of the constitution as a democratic charter has thus far been demonstrated only in the election of the federal Supreme Soviet, December 12, 1937, of the

161

Republican Supreme Soviets in June, 1938, and of local soviets in December, 1939.

In each case, only one candidate finally appeared on the ballot for each office. After an intensive nationwide campaign of education in civic duties, this so-called "Bloc of Party and Non-Party People" received the virtually unanimous endorsement of the voters. Of the deputies elected 81 per cent of those in the Soviet of the Union and 71 per cent of those in the Soviet of Nationalities were Communist Party members or candidates, with the remainder endorsed by the local Communist Party committee. Except for the insane and persons deprived of electoral rights by court sentences, all citizens 18 or over, regardless of sex, race, nationality, religion, residence, social origin, property status, or past activities (Article 135), have the right to vote and to be elected. But in actual voting the voters have no choice. Yet the conclusion scarcely follows that the Communist Party arbitrarily "dictates" the candidates with no reference to local desires. Many are nominated. All but one withdraws before the election. In this sifting process, accompanied by much group discussion, the preferences of the electors find expression.

Similarly the practice of making all votes unanimous in Soviet legislative bodies does not mean that all the lawmakers are mere rubber stamps. In enacting laws, as in electing legislators, long and earnest debate enables the party leaders to ascertain popular preferences, even though these may not always be followed. In the final action, which records a decision already reached informally, unanimity is the rule. These devices are widely at variance with Anglo-American notions of democratic government. In the USSR the forms of democracy are thrown over the persisting and unmistakable substance of dictatorship by the CPSU (B). Yet the forms represent a living ideal, and the substance may be regarded not unreasonably as a prelude to government by consent of the governed rather than its negation. In a peaceful world the Soviet leaders may well be less concerned with painting a portrait of complete unity for the benefit of foreign and domestic opinion and may be expected to let the winds of public controversy bring better ventilation to the house that Lenin built.

LIBERTY UNDER SOCIALISM . . . An impressive Bill of Rights is included in the 1936 Constitution) In the Marxist dispensation economic

162

security and opportunity are valued more highly than abstract political privileges. Duties to the community are as important as rights to be protected against the community. "Work," says Article 12, "is a duty and a matter of honor for every able-bodied citizen in accordance with the principle: 'He who does not work, neither shall he eat.' The principle applied in the USSR is that of socialism: 'From each according to his ability, to each according to his work.'" Other duties enumerated include observance of law, maintenance of labor discipline, honesty in public service, respect for the rules of socialist intercourse, protection of socialist property, and defense of the fatherland.

Personal and political rights include complete equality of sexes, races, and nationalities, with punishment provided (Article 123) for "any advocacy of racial or national exclusiveness or hatred and contempt." These rights are secure, for nowhere in the world is there a closer approach to the ideal of equality and brotherhood among peoples of all colors, languages, and nationalities than in the USSR. The customary civil rights of freedom of religion, speech, press, assembly, association, and inviolability of persons and homes are also guaranteed. But these are safe only within the limits of the current party line. The secret political police (originally, the Cheka, then the OGPU, and since 1934 a section of the N.K.V.D. or Commissariat of Internal Affairs) is no respecter of persons suspected of deviating from political orthodoxy.

Property rights guaranteed by the constitution include the right of collective farms to their land in perpetuity and free of charges, and the right of collective farmers to have small plots, with houses, livestock, poultry, and tools, for personal use (Articles 7 and 8). They also embrace the right of individual peasants and artisans to carry on personal labor "alongside of the socialist system of economy" and the right of all citizens to own and inherit personal property and to enjoy ownership of incomes from work as well as savings, houses, furniture, and articles of personal use and convenience (Articles 9 and 10). These rights would appear to be well observed and adequately protected.

A unique feature of the Soviet state is the realization of the social rights enumerated in Articles 118–121 of the constitution; full employment and payment for work by quality and quantity; rest and leisure through the seven-hour day, annual vacations with pay, sanatoria, rest-homes, and clubs; maintenance in old age, sickness and disability

163

through social insurance, and free medical service to all; and free public education. The economic and social organization of the USSR is such that these rights, some of which are merely ideals elsewhere, are concrete realities for all Soviet Union citizens, at least in peacetime. They represent the great human gains of the revolution. Whether they have been worth the cost in initial suffering, and in the relative absence of political and intellectual freedom, outsiders may debate. The Soviet people have shown in mortal combat with merciless foes that they deem no sacrifice too great to preserve what they have won and to carry socialism forward to a fuller and richer life.

The ultimate Marxist ideal of the "withering away of the State" and of the realization, beyond socialism, of the distributive principle of communism—"From each according to his ability, to each according to his needs"—is still far from fulfillment in the USSR. So long as the world remains one-sixth socialist and five-sixths capitalist, the ideal may remain forever unobtainable. But the Soviet state has built a new society which is classless in the sense that private ownership of productive property and the exploitation of man by man for private gain are abolished. It has likewise found the means of achieving economic freedom from fear and want and of providing employment in a constantly expanding economy for all able to work. The old freedoms of private enterprise and competitive political action have been sacrificed in the process. New opportunities in public enterprise and new satisfactions in community integration have offered compensations. In any event, a new civilization has come into being, based upon the conscious and rational direction of human destinies by intelligence and will. Whether its leaders and people can finally synthesize the best in the new and in the old remains to be seen in the years to come.

BIBLIOGRAPHY

Reed, J., *Ten Days that Shook the World* (New York, 1919).
Batsell, W R., *Soviet Rule in Russia* (New York, 1929).
Bunyan, J., and Fisher, H. H., *The Bolshevik Revolution* (Stanford, 1934).
Maxwell, B. W., *The Soviet State* (Topeka, 1934).
Chamberlin, W. H., *The Russian Revolution, 1917–1921*, 2 vols. (New York, 1935).
Central Committee of the Communist Party, *History of the Communist Party of the Soviet Union* (New York, 1939).
Florinsky, M. T., *Toward an Understanding of the U.S.S.R.* (New York, 1939).

Harper, S. N., *The Government of the Soviet Union* (New York, 1938).
Maynard, J., *The Russian Peasant and Other Studies* (London, 1942).
Pares, B., *A History of Russia* (New York, 1944).
Vernadsky, G., *A History of Russia* (New York, 1944).

CHAPTER VI

Jurisprudence

By JOHN N. HAZARD

D ISSOLUTION of the czarist court system was ordered by the new government of the Soviets on November 22 (old style calendar), 1917, in its first decree concerning the courts. By this same decree judges of newly created local courts were instructed to decide all cases in the name of the Russian Republic and to base their decisions and sentences on the laws of the deposed government insofar as these laws had not been abolished by the revolution and did not conflict with revolutionary conscience and the revolution's concept of law.

THEORY OF LAW . . . With the October Revolution the school of Marxist jurisprudence came to power. This school based its thinking upon sections in the *Communist Manifesto of 1848* in which Marx and Engels analyzed the jurisprudence of Europe. These theorists had written, "Your jurisprudence is but the will of your class made into law for all, a will whose essential character and direction are determined by the economic conditions of your class." They discarded any suggestion that law is above the state, having its source in reason or divine wisdom. They taught that law is but a tool of the state, an instrument of policy in the hands of the class which controls the state. Lenin stated the principle briefly in the words, "Law is politics."

Jurists in imperial Russia had followed their colleagues in most of Continental Europe in basing their jurisprudence largely upon the teachings of the "natural law" school of legal philosophers. As in other countries a vocal but small minority of jurists followed the teachings

166

of other major schools of Continental jurisprudence. The best known and most original of these dissenters was L. Iosifovich Petrazhitski (1867–1931), who called for the replacement of theories of "natural law" with a new separate juridical system which he called "the politics of law."

Petrazhitski taught, in essence, that law can be understood only as a subjective psychological experience, as an "emotion," which is distinct as a psychic phenomenon from cognition, feeling, and will. He believed that moral and juridical emotions, rather than pleasures or rational purposes, are guides to human conduct. He concluded that the existence of any authority is a sufficient basis for law. In so doing he liberated positive law from all necessary connection with the idea of the state.

Soviet jurists began early to restudy the history of law and to prepare texts for training a new generation of judges, prosecutors, and attorneys. P. I. Stuchka, as the second commissar of justice, was the principal legal theorist of the early years; he was followed in the late 1920's by Evgeni B. Pashukanis. These men and their students analyzed the works of Marx and Engels for historical material to support the class theory of the state and to define law as a tool of the class in control of the state. Stuchka's *The Revolutionary Role of Law and the State* appeared in 1921 and Pashukanis' *The General Theory of the State and Law* appeared in 1929. The second of these two textbooks traced the history of the state from the overthrow of the Gentile (tribal) constitutions—events which in Marxist thought ended the epoch of preclass society and marked the first appearance of the state—to the October Revolution in Russia.

The Soviet writers saw in each succeeding historical epoch a class state, controlled in turn by slaveholders, feudal lords, and bourgeoisie. They taught that their revolution had brought to power the proletariat, or the industrial workmen, supported by the poor and middle class peasants and the intelligentsia whose interests were akin to those of the proletariat.

Soviet legal theorists believed that only through a strong state in complete control of the proletariat would it be possible to achieve socialism, with a promise of economic democracy. They demanded a dictatorship of the proletariat, at least during the period of transition to a socialist economy, as a base upon which to build political democracy. They centered their attack upon private ownership of the means

167

of production—land, factories, forests, mines, livestock, and the means of communication and trade—as the source of power of the bourgeoisie against whom they had fought their revolution. Guided in their thinking by Nikolai Lenin's *State and Revolution,* written just before the revolution, they drafted the laws to place ownership of these sources of power in the proletarian state. They also drafted strict laws to protect this power, once it was achieved.

In looking ahead to the future of the Soviet state and law, Soviet jurists turned to Friedrich Engels for guidance. In *Origin of the Family, Private Property and the State,* Engels had analyzed the sources of power for each ruling class. In *Herr Eugen Duhring's Revolution in Science,* he had drawn conclusions as to the future of the state once the dictatorship of the proletariat had been established and in turn had abolished the source of class conflict. Engels said: "The first act in which the state really comes forward as the representative of society as a whole—the taking possession of the means of production in the name of society—is at the same time its last independent act as a state. The interference of the state power in social relations becomes superfluous in one sphere after another, and then ceases of itself. The government of persons is replaced by the administration of things and the direction of the process of production. The state is not 'abolished'; it withers away."

Pashukanis believed he was following Engels in teaching that the "withering" process would begin immediately after the revolution and would proceed by degrees as the heritages of the bourgeois epoch were wiped out. He encouraged new drafts of the criminal code, which appeared annually from 1930 to 1935 and had great influence on the teaching of law. These drafts sought to eliminate what he believed to be the vestiges of bourgeois law, such as the naming of specific penalties for specific types of crime—a practice he called the "dosage system"—and the differentiation between crimes committed intentionally, negligently, or without fault.

Civil law was also allowed to fall into the discard by Pashukanis, who treated it briefly at the end of courses and books on what he called "the law of economic administration." The essence of this theory was: since civil law is the regulation of human relations under the trading condition of capitalism, it will lessen in importance as the remnants of

168

capitalism disappear. He felt that the law of economic administration concerning the operation of government corporations which administered the property belonging to the state was the forerunner of the "administration of things," of which Engels had written.

Joseph Stalin warned against those who were preaching the gradual withering away of the state. He stated to the Sixteenth Communist Party Congress in 1930: "We are in favor of the state dying out and at the same time we stand for the strengthening of the dictatorship of the proletariat, which represents the most powerful and mighty authority of all forms of state which have existed up to the present day. The highest possible development of the power of the state, with the object of preparing the conditions for the dying out of the state; that is the Marxist formula. Is it 'contradictory'? Yes, it is 'contradictory.' But this contradiction is a living thing, and completely reflects Marxist dialectics." At his speech to the Extraordinary Eighth Congress of Soviets of the USSR, in 1936, he again sounded what was to become the keynote of Soviet legal thinking under the new constitution when he said, "We need stability of laws now more than ever."

The warnings of Stalin apparently went unheeded, for Pashukanis continued his teaching. But an article by P. Yudin in *Pravda*, January 20, 1937, denounced his teachings. He and his colleagues were removed from the faculties of the law schools, and their textbooks were withdrawn. Commissar of Justice N. V. Krylenko, who shared his opinions, recanted but was also dismissed. Next textbooks were demanded, reflecting theories more closely associated with current needs and based upon a new reading of the Marxist classics. For the next two years the official legal periodicals published the views of many men, usually with a footnote to the effect that the views were published for purposes of discussion and not as the views of the editors.

By 1940 these legal discussions began to bear fruit in the form of new texts, including Prof. S. V. Yushkov's *History of the State and Law, USSR*. The impression gained from reading Pashukanis is that the latter wrote his theory first and later embellished it with facts. Yushkov starts with facts and lets his readers draw their own conclusions, although from time to time he makes major points by using an adjective or phrase that highlights his moral, which is that the state is an apparatus of

169

class repression and law is the handmaiden of the governing class.

Andrei Y. Vyshinski also published important books. The 1940 edition of his standard work, *Agencies of Law in the USSR*, and his *Soviet Public Law* (1938) are the more important because Vyshinski is vice commissar of foreign affairs, prosecutor of the USSR, and the principal member of the section on law of the Academy of Sciences. In these books he develops Stalin's thesis of 1930 on the strong state. The following statement by Vyshinski summarized current thinking by Soviet jurists: "Soviet law is a combination of the rules of behavior, established in the form of statutes by the workers' government, reflecting their will. In their application they are enforced by the entire coercive power of the socialist state, for the purpose of protecting, strengthening, and developing relationships and procedures suitable and beneficial to the workers; for the purpose of completely and for all time destroying capitalism and its relics in economic life, social life, and in the consciousness of mankind; for the purpose of building a communist society."

In 1942 Vyshinski defined the Soviet state in a speech before the Academy of Sciences of the USSR: "The Soviet state, as a state of the proletarian dictatorship, must be a new type of democratic state for the proletariat and the propertyless, in general, and a new kind of dictatorship against the bourgeoisie." With these words he epitomized the two aspects of Soviet law: (1) the dictatorship against the bourgeoisie, implemented in laws intended to eliminate enemies and the ideologies and techniques by which the old regime held power; and (2) the democratic state for the proletariat, taking form in laws directed toward the creation of a new economic and social structure. The ultimate goal is the achievement of communism, when each shall give according to his ability and each receive according to his needs. To achieve this ultimate stage when the state as an instrument of compulsion shall have withered away, law must create a system of relations from which the new society may spring and must serve as a means of education toward the new society.

WRITTEN LAW . . . In directing the judges of the new revolutionary republic to base decisions and sentences upon the laws of the deposed government, but within the limitations of revolutionary thinking, the jurists who drafted the 1917 decree on the courts referred to a great body of law. Its history dates from the ninth century.

The *Russkaya Pravda* is considered the most important written source

170

of Russian law. Although its first version was written in the twelfth or possibly the eleventh century, its 50 concise articles are a register of customary law before that time, plus a few shorter laws of the princes, beginning with Yaroslav in the eleventh century. Its second version was much more voluminous and showed effects of Roman-Byzantine law and even some Germanic laws.

Local codifications were made in Novgorod in the middle of the fifteenth century and in Pskov at about the same time or earlier. Grand Duke Ivan Vasilyevich issued law for all Muscovy in 1497, under the title *Sudebnik*. It contained rules of procedure and criminal and civil regulations. It drew from the Pskov codification, the *Russkaya Pravda*, and from custom.

A voluminous codification of Russian law was published in 1648 by Czar Alexis, entitled *Ulozhenie Tsarya Alekseya Mikhailovicha*, containing all branches of court law. The influence of Roman-Byzantine law was strong.

The eighteenth century witnessed unsuccessful attempts to codify the laws of Russia. Not until 1832 was there published a new systematic collection of Russian laws; it was called *Svod Zakonov Rossiskoi Imperii*. The private law section exhibited a strong influence of French law.

The *Svod Zakonov* was declared in effect on January 1, 1835. All laws published subsequently were to be published in annual volumes as additions to the code. The original code filled 15 volumes and contained the law in eight categories as established by Mikhail Mikhailovich Speranski, whom Nicholas I had given the task of codification. These categories were (1) institutions; (2) duties and obligations; (3) government administration; (4) status and estates; (5) civil law and land survey; (6) state order, including the law of corporations, banking, and trade; (7) general order, including social welfare, health, and prevention of crime; and (8) criminal laws, including the code of criminal procedure. In the 1832 edition there were 42,000 articles, each containing a citation to the original act which served as the basis for the article.

Certain laws remained outside the *Svod*, such as the collection of military decrees, collection of maritime decrees, collection of local laws of the Baltic Provinces, civil code of the former principality of Poland, special laws in force in Bessarabia, and local laws of Finland. Also excluded were laws relating to state control and national education, laws of the royal court, and ecclesiastical law. The ecclesiastical law governing marriage was supplanted in many areas of the Caucasus and Asia by tribal customs or Moslem law.

A second edition of the *Svod Zakonov* appeared in 55 volumes, including laws in force to 1881; a third edition included later laws. Since serfdom and many other customs reminiscent of feudal Europe existed when the first edition was written, revisions were necessary as Russian economy and the social structure developed. In 1844 the criminal code was completely revised. In 1864 the court system was revised. In 1903 a new criminal code adopting the most advanced and liberal theories of the time was approved, but it was never published, except for the chapter on state crimes (treason). In the 1880's a commission was established to draft a new civil code. Its work reflected legal developments in advanced Western countries, but the code was never enacted.

The czar's abdication on March 15, 1917 (old style), brought no fundamental changes in the law. Even after the Bolsheviks seized power, new codes did not appear immediately. For some years the courts had only basic directives to guide them. Even prerevolutionary law ceased being a basis for decision, for the application of prerevolutionary law was explicitly forbidden in the People's Court Act of 1918.

Basic principles to be used in administering criminal law were published on December 12, 1919, followed by a criminal code, effective in the Russian Soviet Federated Socialist Republic on January 1, 1922. It was completely revised, effective January 1, 1927.

The RSFSR enacted a civil code, effective January 1, 1923, to provide laws applicable to the limited private production and trade which the New Economic Policy of 1922 permitted. With numerous amendments it is still in force.

Family law was taken out of the jurisdiction of the ecclesiastical courts immediately after the revolution, and the law of marriage and divorce was incorporated in a code dated December 22, 1918; a revised code became effective January 1, 1927. The later code included laws on adoption, guardianship, and the registration of acts affecting civil status.

Labor law was codified in 1918, and a new code, adapted to meet conditions of the New Economic Policy, became effective November 15, 1922. Law concerning workers on the land was developed in an early series of decrees and was enlarged into a land code, effective December

172

1, 1922. In 1928 the general basis for land operation in the USSR was published, and by decree of February 17, 1935, a model charter for agricultural artels was enacted to govern the organization and operation of collective farms. In large measure this model charter has become the land law of the USSR.

The RSFSR enacted a code for criminal procedure in 1922, with a new edition in 1923; it enacted a code for civil procedure in the same year. Independent statutes were enacted to cover special situations, such as the use of forests and mines, and the care of animals.

Each republic of the Union retained the right to enact legislation, subject to conformity with basic principles delegated to the Union in the Constitution of 1924. These delegated powers covered the development of a general plan for the entire national economy; the establishment of general principles for the development and use of the soil, mineral deposits, forests, and bodies of water; the direction of transport and telegraphic services; the direction of foreign trade; and the statement of general principles governing labor legislation. In conformity with these principles the various constituent republics enacted codes generally similar to those of the RSFSR, but varying to meet special conditions in each republic. The Union government enacted only a few codes such as those relating to patents, air law, and matters concerning the whole Union.

Transfer of jurisdiction over criminal and civil codes and codes of civil and criminal procedure was made to the federal government by the Constitution of 1936. Draftsmen began to revise all codes for enactment as laws of the Union, but their work was stopped by the Second World War.

Codes implement the Marxist theory of law. The criminal laws are designed to protect the state from socially dangerous acts; the code defines these as any act or omission that is directed against the Soviet authority or violates the order of things established by the proletarian dictatorship for the period of transition to a Communist regime. The code emphasizes the importance of the intention of the criminal, but it also declares illegal acts which the doer considered harmless but which led to consequences that he should have foreseen. Acts legally defined as crimes, but from which socially dangerous aspects have disappeared, are not punished; conversely, an act not defined as a crime but found to be so-

173

cially dangerous may be punished by analogy to some section of the code. In practice the use of this article was discouraged just before the Second World War.

Crimes against individuals are also punished by the code. These include crimes against life, health, liberty, and personal freedom as well as crimes against property, such as larceny, robbery, embezzlement, forgery, and willful destruction. The criminal law follows the basic principle of Marxism that personal freedom is possible only in the collective, and the pattern of the individual's life is developed accordingly.

Civil law carries out the principles of Marx regarding ownership of property. In a form which amounts to a law of government corporation, it provides rules for the administration of state-owned property. It also provides for the preservation of orderly processes in the use and protection of consumers' goods, which are privately owned. In performing this latter function the law provides for the acquisition, transfer, and deprivation of property, requiring always, however, that civil rights must be exercised in harmony with their social-economic purpose.

Procedural law is designed to guarantee that the innocence of the accused or of a defendant in a civil suit may be established if it can be proved. While procedures are in no sense as comprehensive in protecting the accused as those in Anglo-American law, they indicate an effort to protect the innocent, and they are strictly enforced; when they are violated there is a cause for reversal and remanding for a new trial. The law seeks to protect the individual from the arbitrary action of an individual state official. It does not, and under Marxian theory cannot, go farther and protect the individual from the state itself.

The rule of *stare decisis,* that is, to stand by (previous judicial) decisions, does not apply in Soviet law just as it is not followed in Continental western Europe. Previous cases are reported to judges as a guide, but each judge is free to decide the case before him with reference to nothing other than the statutes.

COURTS . . . The court system of the czarist government, dissolved by the first decree of the government of the Soviets, dated with few changes from the statute of November 20, 1864. Before that time justice in Russia had been administered through a judicial system established by Peter the Great, which followed the inquisitorial procedures of western Europe of his time. Both civil and criminal cases were tried in secret.

All proceedings were in writing. Judges were not confronted either with witnesses or even with the persons mainly involved until they delivered judgment. The courts had both judicial and executive functions. Five or more levels of courts existed. Judges were not trained professionally.

The 1864 decree of Alexander II established an entirely new system with two kinds of courts. There were (1) justice of the peace courts with jurisdiction over petty civil and criminal cases, and (2) general courts for more serious causes. The first were designed on the English model, and the second on the French.

Justices of the peace were elected in each section for three-years terms by the county assembly of landed nobility; they had to be persons with a university or secondary education or three years of practical service connected with judicial affairs, and they had to own a certain amount of land. Appeals from the justice lay to the Assembly of Justices of the Peace for the district, in cases of importance. Even in cases from which there was no appeal the assembly might by way of cassation review complaints and protests against legally binding judgments.

By amendment in 1899 the justices of the peace courts were superseded in 43 provinces of the empire. They were replaced by sectional *zemski* courts in the rural districts, and by municipal courts in the larger cities. County assemblies became the appellate courts. In 1912 the justice of the peace courts functioned in 35 provinces and the *zemski* and municipal courts in 66. A *zemski* court was presided over by a chief appointed by the provincial governor upon the advice of the county marshal of nobility, but the appointment had to be confirmed by the minister of the interior. Only provincial marshals of nobility or local noblemen were eligible for appointment; they had to meet land-ownership qualifications and have either a university education or one year of previous service in certain institutions connected with the supervision of peasants' affairs.

Municipal judges were appointed by the minister of justice. A university law degree was required and not less than three years' service in a judicial capacity not lower in rank than that of secretary of a circuit court.

Appeals from the *zemski* courts lay to the county assembly, composed of the county marshal of nobility, the county member of the circuit court, the municipal judges, and the *zemski* chiefs of the county. A Provincial Board had the power of judicial review over decisions by the county assemblies. Members of the Provincial Board were the provincial governor, the lieutenant governor, the provincial marshal of nobility, two special members, and the procurator and president of the circuit court.

The general court system was based on the circuit court. This had original jurisdiction over all serious offenses, which were excluded from the jurisdiction of the courts already enumerated. Judges were numerous, but the court was divided into sections of not less than three judges, each to hear cases, with or without a jury; a jury was provided only in cases where a verdict of guilty would include forfeiture of civil rights. Judges were appointed for life by the czar on nomination by the minister of justice; qualifications included a degree from a university law school and three years of service in the court as secretary. If the appointment was to the position of president or vice president of a court, the three years of service must have been as a judge or prosecutor.

Appeal lay to the judicial *Palata*, which had broad reviewing powers and the power of retrial. Three judges selected from the large membership of judges of every department heard the appeal. The judicial *Palata* had original jurisdiction over serious offenses against the government.

A Supreme Court of Cassation was created within the Senate with two departments—one civil and one criminal. Its function was not to decide cases on their merits but to insure that the laws of the empire were uniformly and correctly interpreted and applied. The czar appointed the senators on his own initiative. Jurisdiction extended to all legally binding judgments from which there was no further appeal. Interpretation of the law might issue, and cases reviewed might be returned for retrial.

The Soviets replaced the imperial courts with a system of two courts. These were (1) a people's court with a permanent judge and two cojudges who served in rotation, from which there was no appeal, and (2) a revolutionary tribunal to try counterrevolutionary cases; this had a president and six cojudges and there was no appeal from its decisions. Jury trials were abolished.

A soviet of people's judges was created to review by way of cassation cases originally heard by the people's courts. Members were elected at a conference of all people's judges in a province or city. This soviet was divided into colleges of three judges each. The colleges heard civil and criminal cases, and could reverse a judgment if a substantial violation of the law or procedure was found or if the judgment seemed manifestly unjust.

In a case in which the revolutionary tribunals rendered a verdict that the commissar of justice believed to be clearly unjust, he could recommend a new trial to the All-Russian Central Executive Committee. Later (in 1920) a Cassational Tribunal was instituted to assure uniform procedure in all revolutionary tribunals. It could reverse a decision but had to obtain confirmation of such a reversal from the Central Executive Committee. Finally (in 1921) a Supreme Revolutionary Tribunal received all powers of control formerly vested in the Cassational Tribunal.

A Judiciary Act was promulgated in 1922 when the new law codes were adopted. It abolished the system of revolutionary tribunals and revised the people's courts, creating a system which has continued with few basic changes to the present day. This is a people's court, a provincial court with original jurisdiction over important cases as well as cassational jurisdiction, and a Supreme Court with cassational jurisdictional over cases heard originally in the provincial court and with original jurisdiction over cases of major importance.

When the Union was organized in 1924, each republic retained its own court system. The constitution of the Union added only a Supreme Court of the Union. This had the right of review over the supreme courts of the republics and had original jurisdiction over civil and criminal cases when defendants were high officials of the Union charged with crimes in office, political crimes, or economic offenses, and over other cases of exceptional importance. To enter the Supreme Court of the Union civil cases had to concern the interests of two or more republics. On request of the Central Executive Committee of the Union, the court could also advise on the constitutionality of laws.

The only truly federal courts in the republics were created as the military tribunals, the railroad transport tribunals, and the water transport tribunals, which heard all cases arising in these spheres of activity, which involved the interest of the entire Union. These courts had two steps to the colleges of the Supreme Court of the Union.

When the Supreme Court acted as an interpreter of the laws, it sat as a body with at least three fifths of its 16 members present. To review cases from below, three judges sat as the court, one of whom might be a

177

cojudge not professionally employed by the court but selected from a panel named by the Central Executive Committee of the Union.

Until the new Union constitution was adopted in 1936, judges in all courts were named by the executive body in the area in which they sat. With the 1936 Constitution there appeared an extensive basic law on courts. Judges in the people's courts were to be elected by the people— not only the permanent judges for a three-year term but also the two co-judges to sit in rotation as juror-judges in each case. Judges in higher courts are named for five-year terms by the soviet in the area in which the court has jurisdiction. Legal education is not a prerequisite to elec-tion.

A Judiciary Act of 1938 now governs the organization and jurisdiction of courts within the basic principles of the 1936 Constitution. Federal and republic courts retain their distinguishing jurisdictions. Provincial and supreme courts of the republics and the Union lost their special tri-bunals which formerly handled counterrevolutionary cases. All cases are heard originally by a single professional judge and two cojudges sitting for short periods of time. These cojudges take the place of a jury but to-gether with the professional judge decide questions both of law and fact. Jurisdiction is determined by the nature of the crime or in civil cases by the character of the parties (government corporations, clubs, and trade unions have the right to be heard originally in provincial courts). In time of war all criminal cases in military theatres are tried by military tribunals. During the Second World War all the European part of the USSR was declared to be a military theater.

Trials are public unless they concern sex offenses or matters of diplo-matic or military concern. The accused has the right of counsel. Prosecu-tion is conducted by a state prosecutor, named by the state prosecutor of the Union, who is named in turn by the Supreme Soviet of the USSR for a seven-year term. His subordinates are responsible only to him and not to the republic in which they act.

A special committee continues to exist under a statute of 1934 within the Commissariat of the Interior with the right of administrative exile. This was the only remaining vestige of early administrative tribunals. Under it all cases involving penalties, other than exile to remote regions, in the event of social danger have to go before a court of law and be tried in accordance with procedural codes.

178

BIBLIOGRAPHY

Kovalevsky, M. M., *Modern Customs and Ancient Laws of Russia* (London, 1891).

Sigel, F. F., *Lectures in Slavonic Law*, Ilchester Lectures (London, 1902).

Engels, F., *Origin of the Family, Private Property and the State* (Chicago, 1902).

Sergeyevich, V. I., *Russkiya Yuridicheskiya Drevnosti*, in Russian (St. Petersburg, 1903).

Vladimirski-Budanov, M. F., *Obzor Istorii Russkovo Prava*, in Russian (St. Petersburg, 1909).

Petrazhitski, L. I., *Teoriya Prava i Gosudarstva*, in Russian (St. Petersburg, 1910).

Korkunov, N. M., *Lektsii po Obshchei Teorii Prava*, in Russian (St. Petersburg, 1909). Tr. by W. G. Hastings as *General Theory of Law* (New York, 1922).

Lenin, V. I., *State and Revolution* (New York, 1929).

Pashukanis, E. B., *Obshchaya Teoriya Gosudarstva i Prava*, in Russian (Moscow, 1929).

——, *Za Markso-Leninskuyu Teoriyu Gosudarstva i Prava*, in Russian (Moscow, 1931).

Zelitch, J., *Soviet Administration of Criminal Law* (Philadelphia, 1931).

Stuchka, P. I., *Revolyutsionnaya Rol Prava i Gosudarstva*, in Russian (Moscow, 1934).

Maxwell, B. M., *Soviet State* (Topeka, Kans., 1934).

Callcott, M. S., *Russian Justice* (New York, 1935).

Von Koerber, L., *Soviet Russia Fights Crime* (New York, 1935).

Hazard, J. N., "Soviet Law: An Introduction," *Columbia Law Review* (1936), XXXVII, 1236.

Marx, K., *Critique of the Gotha Program* (Moscow, 1937).

Marx, K., and Engels, F., *Communist Manifesto* (New York, 1937).

Vyshinski, A. Y., *Sovetskoye Gosurdarstvenoye Pravo*, in Russian (Moscow, 1938).

Hazard, J. N., *Soviet Housing Law* (New Haven, 1939).

Golunski, S. A., and Strogovich, M. S., *Teoriya Gosudarstva i Prava*, in Russian (Moscow, 1940).

Vyshinski, A. Y., *Sudoustroistvo v SSSR*, in Russian (Moscow, 1940).

Yushkov, S. V., *Istoriya Gosudarstva i Prava SSSR*, in Russian (Moscow, 1940).

Hazard, J. N., "Soviet Constitution: An Introduction," *Lawyers' Guild Review* (1943), III, 27.

CHAPTER VII

Diplomatic Relations
with the United States

By FREDERICK L. SCHUMAN

IN GEOGRAPHICAL situation, in diversity of populations, and in the rapid development of vast areas of virgin territory, the United States and Russia resemble each other more closely than any other two great world powers. They differ, however, more sharply than any other two powers in social systems and political practices, and this difference was not diminished by the Russian transition from czarist autocracy to the Union of Soviet Socialist Republics. These two powers have never been at war with each other but have fought as allies against the same enemies in the two world wars of this century. During most of the nineteenth century a tradition of friendship influenced popular attitudes and governmental policies in both countries. This friendship was founded neither on social similarities nor on official affinities which flourished in spite of differences. It rested rather upon a community of interests in world politics. In the earlier period both nations shared a common suspicion of Great Britain; later they shared a common fear of the ambitions of Germany and Japan.

EARLY RELATIONS . . . The Empress Catherine, while abhorring revolution, was not displeased by the effort of the American colonies to establish their independence from the British crown. Her proclamation of "armed neutrality" (March, 1780) was designed to defend Russian trading rights against the British Navy. In the following December the Continental Congress appointed Francis Dana as minister to St. Peters-

180

burg. He had instructions to seek diplomatic recognition and a treaty of amity and commerce. Dana, with the young John Quincy Adams as his secretary, arrived on the Neva in August, 1781, but soon discovered that the imperial Russian government had no intention of recognizing the United States. Two years later he returned home in disgust.

Not until 1794 did the United States have a consul in St. Petersburg. A decade later Czar Alexander I and President Thomas Jefferson were exchanging personal letters as fellow-liberals. In June, 1809, thirty-three years after the Declaration of Independence, diplomatic relations were established. André Dashkov was received as Russian chargé in Washington. The reception of John Quincy Adams as first American minister to the czar followed in October. American exports to Russia grew rapidly, largely at the expense of British merchants, whose goods were barred from all Europe under Napoleon's Continental System. British efforts to halt American commerce with the Continent led to war with the United States in June, 1812. French efforts to control Russian commerce led to war between France and Russia, also in June, 1812.

Alexander deplored the fact that the United States, in fighting his new ally Britain, was aiding his new enemy, Bonaparte. He therefore offered mediation. President James Madison accepted in March, 1813, and dispatched Albert Gallatin, J. Q. Adams, and J. A. Bayard to St. Petersburg on a peace mission. Upon arrival they found that London had rejected the czar's proposal. Both wars ended in 1814, however, one with the Treaty of Ghent and the other with the downfall of Napoleon. A minor quarrel over consular immunities led to an open rupture of American-Russian diplomatic relations in 1816. Thus the first phase of official contacts ended, as it had begun, with misunderstanding and disillusionment.

MID-NINETEENTH-CENTURY FRIENDSHIP . . . New frictions developed over Russian territorial claims south of Alaska and over Russian leadership in the Holy Alliance against Latin American independence. St. Petersburg yielded, however, after the promulgation of the Monroe Doctrine, and on April 17, 1824, the first American-Russian treaty was concluded. It fixed latitude 54°40′ as the southern limit for Russian colonization on the west coast of North America and provided for reciprocal freedom of navigation, fishing, and trade with the natives in the North Pacific. On December 18, 1832, a general treaty of navigation and commerce was signed. Under it trade and political relations pursued a normal course.

The Crimean War and the Civil War brought the two governments into closer collaboration. In the former, Britain, France, and Sardinia defended Turkey against Russia. In the latter, Britain and France expressed sympathy for the Confederacy and contemplated recognition and intervention. The czar's ministers feared possible Anglo-French intervention on behalf of the Polish rebels of 1863 and were grateful when the American Secretary of State, William H. Seward, refused to join in international protests against Russian atrocities in Poland. The two governments shared a humanitarian interest in the abolition of serfdom and slavery. They shared also a common political interest in crushing secession and in thwarting interference by other powers. In September, 1863, Russian squadrons appeared in New York and San Francisco. They were said to carry "sealed orders" to assist the United States if Britain and France came to the aid of the South, but the actual motive of their trip was to prevent the bottling up of the Russian fleet if another Anglo-Russian war broke out. Yet the gesture was popularly hailed as evidence of Russian solidarity with the Union.

In 1866 Assistant Secretary of the Navy Gustavus Vasa Fox carried to St. Petersburg on one of the new monitors a Congressional resolution of congratulation to the czar on his escape from an attempted assassination. Fox was entertained as cordially in Russia as the Russian admirals had been in the United States. On March 30, 1867, Seward and the Russian Minister Edward Stoeckl signed an agreement by which Russia sold Alaska to the United States for $7,200,000 in gold. Russians felt well rid of a remote and apparently worthless territory. Most Americans hailed the purchase of "Seward's icebox" as payment for earlier Russian friendship. Alaskan fisheries, furs, and gold soon made the purchase price seem absurdly small. New Russian-American agreements dealt with trade marks, extradition, and seal fishing in the Bering Sea.

FRICTIONS AND FRUSTRATIONS . . . By the turn of the century cordiality between the two nations had given way to discord. The United States championed the Open Door policy in China while Russia sought to keep foreigners out of the northeast provinces of the disintegrating Manchu Empire. When Tokyo challenged Russia to combat in Manchuria, American governmental and public sympathy was largely with

182

Japan. Secretary of State John Hay asked the belligerents to respect Chinese neutrality and expressed the hope that there would be no concessions of Chinese territory. In June, 1905, President Theodore Roosevelt, at Japan's request, offered mediation. Both contestants accepted. Roosevelt avoided a break in the peace negotiations at Portsmouth, New Hampshire, by persuading Baron Jutaro Komura and Minister Kogoro Takahira to forego a money indemnity and by inducing Count Sergei Y. Witte and Baron Roman R. Rosen to cede southern Sakhalin to Japan. The treaty of September 5, 1905, further provided for mutual respect of the Open Door and for Russian recognition of Japan's dominant position in Korea (Chosen) and the Liaotung Peninsula.

Revolution and reaction in Russia, 1904–1914, had repercussions in the United States. Over a million and a half Russian immigrants and refugees arrived in America during these years. More and more Americans condemned the repressions of the czar's regime and expressed indignation at anti-Semitic outrages. Washington repeatedly protested St. Petersburg's refusal to acknowledge acquisition of foreign citizenship by Russian emigrants and to accord equal rights to American naturalized citizens of Jewish origin seeking to revisit Russia. In December, 1911, the House of Representatives passed almost unanimously a resolution calling on the president to denounce the Treaty of 1832. The resolution pointed out the treaty's first article, pledging reciprocal freedom of travel, sojourn, and residence. On December 15 the president and State Department notified Russian Foreign Minister Sergei Sazonov that the treaty would be regarded as terminated as of January 1, 1913. The czarist regime attributed this rebuff to "Jewish influence" and refused to negotiate a new commercial treaty.

On October 1, 1914, Secretary of State William Jennings Bryan and Ambassador Georgi Bakhmetyev, last czarist envoy to the United States, signed a treaty for the advancement of peace. War between the Triple Entente and the Central Powers had already broken out in August. By the close of 1916 American exports to Russia (only $27,000,000 in 1913) were approaching the half billion dollar mark annually, and American investors were holding some $86,000,000 worth of czarist war bonds. The American ambassador to Russia, David R. Francis, had arrived in St. Petersburg in the spring of 1916, and had been so busy promoting business that he failed to foresee the political overthrow of czarism in 1917, which led to perhaps the most important social upheaval in human history. As Tyler Dennett puts it, "an embassy has always been an extremely poor place from which to study a revolution." Yet when the czarist government fell, President Woodrow Wilson and Secretary of State Robert Lansing welcomed the end of the autocracy and granted diplomatic recognition to the Provisional government on March 22, 1917. The United States declared war on Germany a fortnight later, and in his war message to Congress the president said of the new Russian government, "Here is a fit partner for a League of Honor."

The provisional government sent Boris Bakhmetyev to Washington as ambassador. In the early summer the United States sent a special diplomatic mission to Russia, distinguished but conservative in personnel, and headed by Elihu Root. It returned with optimistic reports about Russian loyalty to the Allied cause and about the prospects of Russian democracy. The American government lent $187,729,750 to the provisional government for war purposes. News of the overthrow of Alexander F. Kerensky by the Bolsheviks on November 7, 1917, was received in Washington with shocked incredulity. Ambassador Francis labeled the revolution "Disgusting! . . . but the more ridiculous the situation the sooner the remedy."

UNDECLARED WAR AND NONRECOGNITION . . . A tragedy of errors followed, largely from mutual misunderstanding and prejudice. The Soviet leaders requested recognition and peace negotiations. The White House and State Department refused to deal with them and strove to keep Russia in the war. Col. William B. Thompson and Col. Raymond Robins of the American Red Cross perceived the meaning and importance of the revolution and maintained contacts with the new regime; but Francis and his subordinates, viewing the Communists as madmen, sought to restore prowar sentiment in Russia. They failed to understand that the revolutionary government could have no reason for continuing to participate. In the Fourteen Points address of January 8, 1918, President Wilson asserted, "The treatments accorded to Russia by her sister nations in the months to come will be the acid test of their good will." No formal recognition of the new government was granted, however, though on March 11 Wilson sent a friendly message to the Congress of Soviets, in the hope of preventing ratification of a separate peace (already signed). Soviet ratification of the Treaty of Brest-Litovsk, the

184

repudiation of Russia's state debts, and the confiscation of foreign property were all received with displeasure in the United States.

In July, 1918, the United States, yielding to pressure from England, France, and Japan, reluctantly proposed Allied military intervention in Russia to aid Czechoslovak troops in rebellion against the Soviets in the Ural area and Siberia, to guard military stores at Murmansk and Vladivostok, and "to steady any efforts at self-government or self-defense in which the Russians themselves may be willing to accept assistance." Early in September about 4,500 American troops joined a larger number of British soldiers at Archangel and began to fight their way southward against the Red Army. At the same time 7,000 American troops under Gen. William S. Graves landed in Vladivostok to guard the Trans-Siberian Railway, over which military supplies were soon to flow from the United States to Alexander V. Kolchak's White Army. These troops fought no engagements with Red forces but were soon at odds with the Japanese, who, contrary to agreement, poured 70,000 soldiers into eastern Siberia in an apparent effort at occupation and annexation.

Intervention, coupled with a blockade of Soviet territory, soon turned into an armed effort to help the White armies overthrow Lenin's regime. Boris Bakhmetyev retained recognition in Washington as Russian ambassador and sent supplies to the anti-Soviet forces out of war funds borrowed earlier in the United States by the czarist government. Most congressmen and journalists accepted as true the fantastic horror stories issued by anti-Soviet propagandists, including the tale of the "nationalization of women." The imminent collapse of the Soviets was constantly predicted. Various peace efforts were made during the Paris Peace Conference, including the dispatch to Moscow of an American mission headed by William C. Bullitt (accompanied by Capt. Walter Pettit and Lincoln Steffens), but they came to nothing because the Allies expected a White victory in the Russian civil war. The defeat of Nikolai N. Yudenich, Kolchak, and Anton I. Denikin by the Red Army ended these hopes. By the end of June, 1919, the American troops in north Russia were withdrawn after suffering casualties of 244 dead and 305 wounded. British forces withdrew in October. On April 1, 1920, the last American troops left Siberia. The Soviet flag now flew over most of the old Russian Empire.

Soviet efforts to initiate normal relations with the United States were, however, unsuccessful. Early in 1919 Ludwig C. A. K. Martens presented to the State Department his credentials from Georgi V. Chicherin as Soviet diplomatic representative. They were refused. In June his New York offices were raided. In December, 1920, the secretary of labor ordered his deportation. Meanwhile the Polish and Red armies were at war, and Secretary of State Bainbridge Colby, in a note to the Italian ambassador (August 10, 1920) expressed opposition to any dismemberment of Russia but declared that the Soviet rulers could not be recognized since they ruled by "savage oppression," did not represent the Russian people, based their power "upon the negation of every principle of honor and good faith," and were seeking the revolutionary overthrow of other governments. Under the direction of Herbert Hoover the American Relief Administration raised $66,300,000 from public and private sources to aid victims of the Volga famine of 1921–1922. Yet the Warren G. Harding, Calvin Coolidge, and Hoover administrations adhered to the policy of nonrecognition on the ground that normal relations could not be maintained with a regime which repudiated debts, confiscated foreign property, and fostered revolutionary propaganda abroad.

During this period considerable trade developed between the two countries through the Amtorg Trading Company. The political interests of the United States and the Union of Soviet Socialist Republics, for example in relation to Japanese policy in eastern Asia, were often parallel, but the lack of official relations created legal and diplomatic difficulties. Boris Bakhmetyev retired as ambassador in June, 1922. On July 27, 1922, the United States granted diplomatic recognition to Estonia, Latvia, and Lithuania, though still championing Russian territorial integrity in other respects. President Coolidge (December 6, 1923) urged that America "go to the economic and moral rescue of Russia" only when "there appear works meet for repentance" and "evidence of returning to the ancient ways of society." Soviet proposals for mutual recognition continued to be rebuffed. Secretary of State Henry L. Stimson sought to invoke the Kellogg Pact in connection with Soviet-Chinese border clashes in Manchuria in 1929, and Litvinov rebuked him for offering advice to a government which the United States refused to recognize.

THE UNITED STATES AND THE SOVIET UNION . . . The United States did not grant diplomatic recognition to the Soviet Union until

November 16, 1933, sixteen years after the revolution. In a message of October 10 to President Mikhail I. Kalinin, President Franklin D. Roosevelt invited a discussion of questions of mutual interest. The threat of Japan and the rising menace of Nazi Germany dictated a *rapprochement* quite as much as considerations of commercial and diplomatic convenience. Maxim Litvinov came to Washington, and an exchange of notes was signed. The USSR pledged freedom of worship and legal protection to American citizens in the Soviet realm, waived all counterclaims for damages arising out of the Siberian expedition (the settlement of other debts and claims was left to later negotiations); promised noninterference with internal affairs of the United States; and agreed to prohibit the existence on Soviet territory of any organization aiming to overthrow the American political or social order. Ambassador Alexander Troyanovski was sent to Washington and Ambassador William C. Bullitt to Moscow.

This auspicious beginning, however, did not resolve all difficulties. Debt negotiations were begun, but collapsed on February 1, 1935; Washington contended that new loans requested by Moscow could not be granted until prerevolutionary debts had been paid. Moscow argued that increased interest charges on new loans should be accepted as payment on old debts. A one-year commercial agreement (since renewed annually) was concluded, however, in Moscow in July, 1935, pledging the USSR to purchase at least $30,000,000 worth of American goods in return for "most-favored-nation" treatment of Soviet exports to the United States. Secretary Hull sharply protested that the 7th Congress of the Comintern in Moscow in 1935 was a violation of the antipropaganda pledge. The Narkomindel sharply rejected the protest as irrelevant to the original agreement. Relations improved after January, 1937, when Joseph E. Davies went to Moscow as ambassador, but American distrust of the Kremlin arose again after the purge trials of 1936–1938, the German-Soviet Pact of 1939, and the Soviet war on Finland, 1939–1940.[1]

The German attack on the Soviet Union in June, 1941, changed popular attitudes, particularly after Soviet soldiers and civilians demonstrated their capacity to beat back the invaders. Lend-lease aid was made avail-

---

[1] See Chapter III, "The History of Russia and the USSR."

able to the USSR as a country whose defense was deemed vital to the defense of the United States, and after the attack on Pearl Harbor the two powers became allies against the European Axis.

The old tradition of Russian-American friendship was in large measure restored in the early 1940's under the impact of a joint struggle against common foes. As the war moved toward its end, both governments solemnly agreed to extend their collaboration after the war in a common effort to build a durable peace. No territorial disputes or economic rivalries stood in the way of this collaboration; nor did anything in the past experience suggest that two totally different social systems could not coexist and fruitfully co-operate in the same world. Some observers felt, however, that American fear of communism, especially if aggravated by another major economic depression, might translate itself into anti-Soviet attitudes and policies. Similarly it was feared that Soviet suspicion of the capitalist nations, especially if discord and rivalry continued to grow in central Europe and eastern Asia, might well translate itself into anti-American attitudes and policies. In any event the United States and the Soviet Union were the two largest and most populous nations of the world under unified and effective political control. They were also the two greatest centers of heavy industry. Therefore their future relations can spell weal or woe for all mankind. Those relations will be the acid test of American and Soviet statesmanship during the next generation.

BIBLIOGRAPHY

Dennett, T., *Roosevelt and the Russo-Japanese War* (Garden City, 1925).

Schuman, F. L., *American Policy Toward Russia Since 1917* (New York, 1928).

Graves, W. S., *America's Siberian Adventure, 1918–1920* (New York, 1931).

American Foundation, *The United States and the Soviet Union* (New York, 1933).

Davies, J. E., *Mission to Moscow* (New York, 1941).

Childs, J. L., and Counts, G. S., *America, Russia and the Communist Party in the Postwar World* (New York, 1943).

Willkie, W., *One World* (New York, 1943).

Lippmann, W., *U.S. Foreign Policy* (New York, 1943).

——, *U.S. War Aims* (New York, 1944).

Dulles, F. R., *The Road to Teheran* (Princeton, 1944).

Sorokin, P. A., *Russia and the United States* (New York, 1944).

CHAPTER VIII

Russia in the First World War

By SIR BERNARD PARES

O NE of the causes of the First World War was rivalry in the Balkans; Russian interests were in conflict with the interests of Austria and Germany. In 1866 Bismarck drove Austria out of Germany, and in 1871 he founded the German Empire. An essential part of his further policy was to take defeated Austria into alliance and to use this heterogeneous state, with a German sovereign and a largely German bureaucracy, to advance German interests in the Balkans. This he made clear in 1878 at the Congress of Berlin. Here, posing as an impartial "broker," he deprived Russia of the fruits of her victory in the war of 1877 with Turkey; he handed over the Serbian provinces of Bosnia and Herzegovina for military occupation by Austria, who had taken no part in that war. In contracting a Triple Alliance with Austria and Italy in 1883, however, he was careful to make also a "reinsurance" treaty with Russia. When Bismarck fell, Wilhelm II discarded this treaty.

Between 1908 and 1914 five crises threatened the peace of Europe, and four of them arose in the Balkans. In 1894 France and Russia had drawn together to counter the Triple Alliance. In 1907 the first step was taken towards an Anglo-Russian understanding. In the fifth crisis, which arose from the assassination of the heir to the Austrian throne in Bosnia, lately annexed to Austria, the real issue was Germany's claim that war between Austria and Serbia was no concern of Russia; Russian mobilization led to a German ultimatum and declaration of war. It was known a year and a half earlier that the Russian Army would in 1914 be undergoing a transition which would temporarily weaken it.

189

Russia, after her defeat by Japan in 1905, had passed through a period of great internal disorder, and revolution was again threatening at the moment of the German ultimatum; this fact, too, was well known to Germany. The German challenge, however, was followed by a general patriotic rally in Russia, which the czar should have utilized to come into union with his people. The Cabinet, which continued into the war, was almost equally divided between friends of the democracies and of internal reform and those who saw in Germany the one support for the decaying Russian autocracy. Army and people were at this time wholeheartedly for the war. Public pressure had brought military and naval improvements since the defeat by Japan, but munitions and transport were ludicrously inadequate. There were several able generals, and the Russian infantry soldier was as usual the hero of the fighting.

THE EARLY FIGHTING . . . When the Germans first marched on Paris, the Russians under Gen. Pavel K. Rennenkampf invaded East Prussia, and also in the south stood facing the whole Austrian Army. In a rash response to insistent French appeals, the Russians under Gen. Alexander V. Samsonov launched from Warsaw a second outflanking invasion of East Prussia. Two corps from the German Army in France were moved to meet this threat, with a critical effect on the battle of the Marne. Meanwhile, Gen. Paul von Hindenburg, called from retirement, with Gen. Erich F. W. Ludendorff as his chief of staff, stood between the two invading Russian armies, which failed completely to co-operate; attacking Samsonov at Tannenberg, the Germans surrounded the Russian center and eliminated it by superior artillery fire (August 26-30, 1914). Hindenburg then turned on Rennenkampf and drove him out of East Prussia (September 8–15).

The Austrians had meanwhile advanced on a convex front into Russian Poland. On the news of Tannenberg, the spirited Russian commander in chief, the Grand Duke Nicholas, called for a vigorous resistance; and throwing in strong outflanking reinforcements on both wings, the Russians drove the Austrians back over the frontier and more than half way through Austrian Galicia.

In October, and again in November, Hindenburg made a lunge at Warsaw in the center of the front, which had been left comparatively undefended. Each time he was foiled. In his second attempt, in the extremely complicated operations of Lodz, each side was on the point of

190

enveloping a large force on the other. In February, 1915, in furious fighting, the Germans pressed the Russians further back from the frontiers of East Prussia, but again they were foiled in their enveloping movement by the superb courage of the Russian infantry, to which Ludendorff later paid a willing tribute.

After all this fighting, the Russians occupied about as much enemy territory as their adversaries, but by the cruel arithmetic of this war they had paid in fighting men all that they lacked in munitions. As early as November the light-hearted war minister, Vladimir A. Sukhomlinov, who belonged to the reactionary camp in the Cabinet, informed the high command that munitions had practically run out and that no alleviation could be expected till spring. Yet in the early months of 1915 the Russians, virtually without artillery preparation and by infantry action alone, were storming their way through the deep belt of the Carpathian Mountains, and even entered the Hungarian plain with their calvary. Count Kálmán Tisza, the Hungarian premier, whose country house had fallen to them, hurried to Berlin with a warning of a separate peace. As a result, on May 2 an unprecedented concentration of heavy artillery under Field Marshal August von Mackensen was launched against the bulging and unprovided Russian front in the Carpathians. There could be no reply. Russian orders had gone out that no more than five shells a day were to be fired per gun, irrespective of what the enemy might do. The new German method of saturating a given front area with shells resulted in annihilation. The whole Russian front was pressed back—first in the south, then in the north, then in the center. Galicia was lost. On August 4 Warsaw fell. The retiring Russian center still bulged heavily westwards, and Hindenburg consistently tried to envelop it; but under the masterly maneuvering of Gen. Mikhail V. Alekseyev (Alexeiev), the threadbare Russian Army, often without shells and sometimes even without cartridges, its regiments shrunk to fantastic dimensions, always managed to get away. The official estimate of Russian front line losses in ten months of fighting was 3,800,000. In September the German advance was halted on a far straighter line passing through the Pinsk marshes, which was held until the revolution.

THE HOME FRONT . . . At that time the Russian public was passionately devoted to the first needs of the plain fighting man and was working hard to supplement the quite inadequate government provision.

The czar was also devoted to his army. The president of the Duma, Mikhail V. Rodzyanko, backed by the commander in chief, prevailed on the czar to set up a nationally representative organ of the government for the supply of munitions, and to summon the Duma to assist in this task. The lukewarm ministers were dismissed and replaced by men whom the country could trust. Thus the Cabinet was almost without exception of one mind with the Duma and the public. It looked as if the exigencies of the war might lead to complete constitutional rule.

These developments horrified the empress, who was obsessed with the wish that her sick son should come to the throne with undiminished autocratic powers. Unfortunately the empress, who lacked political sense, had a far stronger will than her husband. Experience justified the belief that her son, a hemophiliac, owed his survival through various medical crises more to hypnotic suggestions of the peasant Rasputin than to the best doctors. The public, however, knew Rasputin mainly as the chief character in a number of sexual scandals, which the empress obstinately refused to believe. She believed him to be a man of God sent in answer to her prayers, and even followed his recommendations regarding candidates for office. She persuaded the czar to take command of the army, and the government of the rear was left in her hands. The nation greeted the news with stupefaction. Nearly the whole Cabinet signed an urgent warning to the czar. The result was reprimand and ultimate dismissal. The Duma was prorogued (September 16, 1915).

There followed a return to the worst features of medieval rule. The empress, with her obsession that she was saving the autocracy, was the worst possible judge of candidates for office. Depending on the judgment and approval of Rasputin, whom no decent person respected, she appointed a succession of swindlers to govern the empire, and the state apparatus gradually stopped functioning. One of Rasputin's nominees in vain planned his assassination; another was known only for peculation. There were honest ministers, but they had no influence over the course of affairs; each, after giving a courageous warning, passed out of office.

DEFEAT AND REVOLUTION . . . Despite these extraordinary conditions, the Russian Army which the enemy almost regarded as defeated, made its last splendid rally. In the summer of 1916 the clever Russian general, Aleksei A. Brusilov, by surprise tactics reconquered hundreds

192

of square miles of lost territory. This was done by huge sacrifices of men, since munitions were almost lacking. Brusilov's victories dealt practically the final blow to the Austrian Army and brought Romania into the war on the side of the Allies. This was no gain, for the Romanian Army was at once overwhelmingly defeated by the Germans. The Romanians depended on the meager munition supply of the Russians, who had now to defend a greatly extended front.

All these conditions led straight to revolution. Rasputin frequently changed his protégés. The last of any importance, Alexander D. Protopopov, whom he raised to the all-important post of minister of the interior, was sick and entirely incapable. From this time on police reports emphasized the growth of propaganda in factories and barracks, though still without indication of leadership. In October a group of strikers was joined by troops sent to bring them back to duty. By the Constitution, or what remained of it, the summons of the Duma could no longer be deferred, and the Duma was practically unanimous in demanding reform. The prime minister, Boris V. Stürmer, was hissed, and at last the czar dismissed him, though he still retained Protopopov. On December 30, Rasputin, whose life had often been in danger, was assassinated by a group of conservatives, including members of the imperial family. By now nearly all the grand dukes had ceased to visit the imperial couple. The czar was sunk in apathy and his wife was helpless. In an atmosphere of mockery an Allied military council paraded through the capital in January, 1917.

The czar at last returned to the front, and on the same day disorders broke out in Petrograd. The immediate occasion was a bread shortage; the bread was there, but distribution was inept. Crowds passed along the streets, even carrying the red flag. Nicholas informed at headquarters, ordered immediate repression. The capital was crowded by an enormous garrison of 170,000, consisting of the last "combings-out" of conscription. Russian and Allied efforts had at last put arms in their hands. The only troops who could be trusted were the training squads.

On Sunday, March 11, the police fired on the people, and by noon the next day almost the whole garrison had joined the popular side. The Cabinet had been requesting dismissal, and now it dispersed of itself. Answering a call from the Social Democrat Alexander F. Kerensky, the revolting troops came and offered their allegiance to the Duma. They were soon joined by the bodyguard from the imperial palace at Tsarskoye Selo. There was no other leadership; the Duma had wished to postpone the revolution till after the war, and the revolutionary leaders were not in Russia; but the revolted troops met with no resistance. What was left of the autocracy fell of itself by its own rottenness. The Duma formed a provisional government and sent two of its members to demand the abdication of the czar. This had already been demanded by the army commanders, and he abdicated without demur (March 15). In view of his son's sickness, he abdicated against the established order of succession in favor of his brother Michael. The next day, in face of the threatening attitude of the capital, Michael avoided the succession. Such was the undistinguished end of the Russian monarchy (March 16, 1917).

The First World War continued a year and a half longer, but Russia practically played no further part in it. The war was entirely eclipsed by the revolution, which for Russians was of far greater importance.

If the Duma had not been made quite unrepresentative by a coup d'état of the czar in June, 1907, it might have still claimed authority. As it was, the new provisional government which it appointed was constantly overrun by the inevitable demand for radical change. This government, which never really governed, faced three tasks which, taken together, were impossibly great: to succeed, it must restore the shattered apparatus of state, give this apparatus an entirely new form, and keep Russia in the war. The final task was the last straw, though it was correctly believed that if Germany won the war, the Russian Revolution was as good as lost. This danger to the revolution appealed to the scantily educated public, but it had no appeal for the army, which had been destroyed and renewed three times over. Hence the impossibility of the task which later devolved upon Kerensky. It was not only in Russia that the war was to end the long period of European liberalism.

Nikolai Lenin and his principal colleagues did not reach Russia until a month after the czar's abdication (April 16, 1917). They did not make the revolution, but it was theirs to reap the fruits of it, for they alone had a clear idea of the new order which they were determined to establish. As Brusilov has stated, after the fall of the czar, the best of his officers was no more than "a squire in uniform." It was this that brought the Bolsheviks to power on November 7, 1917. The army had become a disorderly rabble, and one of the first steps was to open negotiations for an armistice. With no friends left, Russia was at the mercy of the Germans, whose terms were extravagant. By the Treaty of Brest-Litovsk (March 3, 1918) Russia surrendered practically all territory won since Peter the Great, including the conquest from Sweden of the gates of his new capital. The majority of the educated class refused to accept this sacrifice for an international ideal which they did not share and, as the war was not yet over, offered their help to Russia's former allies. This led to Allied armed intervention, which lost all point when Germany was defeated from the western side, and in all the warring countries the tired soldiers went home.

BIBLIOGRAPHY

Knox, Alfred, *With the Russian Army, 1914–17,* 2 vols. (London, 1918).

Ludendorff, Erich, *My War Memories, 1914–1918,* 2 vols. (London, 1919).

Letters of the Tsaritsa to the Tsar, 1914–16, with an introduction by Sir Bernard Pares (London, 1923).

Sazonov, S. D., *Fateful Years 1909–1916* (New York, 1928).

Pares, Bernard, *The Fall of the Russian Monarchy* (London, 1939).

CHAPTER IX

The USSR in the Second
World War

By SERGEI KOURNAKOFF

From the viewpoint of higher strategy the course of the war as it affected the Union of Soviet Socialist Republics can be divided into four periods.[1] The first period lasted seven months, from the initial German attack to the end of the Battle of Moscow; the second lasted a year, from the Battle of Moscow to the end of the Battle of Stalingrad; the third lasted six months, from the Battle of Stalingrad to the end of the Battle of Kursk; the fourth lasted twenty-one months, from the Battle of Kursk to the end of the final Battle of Berlin.

THE FIRST PERIOD . . . Germany attacked the Soviet Union with nearly 200 divisions, of which 170 were "pure German." No other German troops were engaged anywhere, except for the skirmishing in Libya by the British against three German divisions and a depleted Italian expeditionary force. British troops had pulled out of Greece in May. America was still virtually unarmed. Britain was slowly recovering from the so-called Battle of Britain. All Europe, with its 320,000,000 people and yearly production of 50,000,000 tons of steel, was Adolph Hitler's. The German Army could face eastward without having to look over its shoulder; the Soviet Union was politically and militarily isolated.

---

[1] This article was prepared only a few days after the end of hostilities in the Second World War. It was based on authentic but fragmentary data, as neither the details of many campaigns and battles nor complete figures on losses and trophies were as yet available. In the author's opinion, it will not be possible to formulate a completely satisfactory outline of the course of the war until after the process of sifting and studying the immense amount of material pertaining to the conflict has been completed, a procedure which will require several years.

The German High Command set itself the following strategic goal, or objective: to destroy the Red Army within three months and to force the USSR to capitulate before winter, 1941. (The term "strategic goal" may be defined as the objective of a war, or military campaign, set by the High Command, the attainment of which must bring decisive results.)

Territorially the objective was the capture of the Leningrad-Moscow-Kharkov-Rostov line, thus bringing about the utter paralysis of the Soviet transportation system. The Red Army was to be destroyed west of that line, thus making it unnecessary for the German Army to extend its communications beyond the 600-mile mark (Brest-Litovsk-Moscow). The attainment of that goal would also have cut the Murmansk route, made the Iranian route virtually impracticable, destroyed the Soviet Baltic Fleet, bottled up the Northern Fleet, and made the Black Sea Fleet almost useless by depriving it of its main bases, at least, so the Germans thought. Furthermore, the Soviet Union, deprived of 30 per cent of her population, of half of her food-producing area, 40 per cent of her coal, half of her steel and iron, was not expected by the Germans to be able to continue its resistance.

The 200-odd German divisions plunged forward in one strategic echelon, blitz-fashion. They beleaguered Leningrad; they took Kharkov; they captured Rostov (holding it for only a few days before being ejected); they reached the outskirts of Moscow. Vast as were the enemy armies attacking Leningrad, Kharkov, and Rostov, the direction of the main blow lay on the Brest-Litovsk-Moscow line. Here the blitz was stopped for the first time in September, east of Smolensk and two thirds of the way to the main goal, that is, Moscow. After that no blitz was possible. The result was a decisive delay which threw the Germans two months off schedule. Instead of opening the Battle of Moscow in August they were forced to start it at the beginning of October. They concentrated 51 divisions, of which 13 were armored, for the attack on Moscow. Three quarters of a million men, 1,500 tanks, 3,000 guns, and 700 planes attacked a perimeter of 300 miles, forging a pair of pincers aimed at the capital. In that battle the Germans had a numerical superiority of three to one in tanks, two to one in planes, better than two to one in guns, and one and a half to one in mortars.

At the eleventh hour the Soviet High Command, under Marshal

197

Joseph Stalin, delivered a blow in the north which frustrated the German maneuver to cut the Murmansk railroad and besiege Leningrad instead of blockading it (which is more than a fine point), struck a blow in the south which recaptured Rostov, and, finally, struck the big blow at the central grouping of the 51 German divisions, completely routing them and throwing them back as much as 250 miles in some sectors of the Moscow front. Moscow, Leningrad, and Rostov remained in Soviet hands; the Red Army was not only not destroyed but on the offensive; Soviet industry by a "miracle" of organization had been largely moved from the war theater hundreds of miles to the east. Part of the population of the occupied territory became partisans; another part was evacuated.

The German Army had failed in the attainment of its strategic goal. It had failed with its blitz method. Between November 16 and January 1, 1942—that is, during the Battle of Moscow—the Germans had lost 2,200 tanks, 14,000 motor vehicles, 2,000 guns and 140,000 killed (which means certainly another 400,000 wounded). Fifty of their best divisions were shattered, sustaining 50 per cent losses.

The Battle of Moscow made the Germans fail of the strategic goal of their decisive campaign; it destroyed the legend of German invincibility; it inflicted terrible human and material losses on them; it actually killed the blitz; it saved the Soviet Union and thereby the United Nations. After the Battle of Moscow the Germans dared no longer thrust directly at the Soviet capital, but advanced in a roundabout maneuver, a maneuver which, by the summer of 1942, brought them to Stalingrad.

THE SECOND PERIOD . . . In the spring of 1942 nothing outside the Soviet front threatened the Wehrmacht, because the front in North Africa absorbed only between three and six German divisions and ten Italian divisions of doubtful quality. The Germans mustered an overwhelming majority of their forces and again struck at the Red Army in a desperate new attempt to crush it. The offensive, however, instead of developing between the Baltic and Black seas, as in 1941, was limited to the southern wing, roughly between Oryol and the Black Sea. Of the available 256 German divisions the German High Command mustered 179 in the East plus 61 satellite divisions, or 240 in all. A front of 375 miles flared up in June, 1942, but only after the Germans had been delayed about two months by the epic defense of Sevastopol and by Marshal Semyon K. Timoshenko's counterblow in the Izyum-Barvenkovo sector.

Again, as in 1941, the Germans planned to advance in blitz tempo: July 25, Stalingrad; August 15, Kuibyshev; September 10, Arzamas; October–November, the attack on Moscow *from the east*. This time the Germans had to limit their offensive to the southern one third of the front; they did not dare attack Moscow head-on but had to pursue a roundabout course; and, finally, their blitz remained on paper. They were late at Stalingrad and never reached any of their other objectives.

Aside from the maximum objective (capture of Moscow from the rear), the Germans had immediate goals of limited strategic importance: they intended to capture the entire Donets industrial region, the wheat of the Don and Kuban, the oil of Maikop, Grozny, and Baku. They were trying to cut the artery of the Volga and thus deprive the USSR of Caucasian oil and of American materials being shipped through Iran up the Caspian and the Volga. Stalingrad became the strategic center of gravity of the whole campaign—the objective. It was also destined to become the zenith of the war. The Germans threw a total of about 60 divisions into the Don-Volga Battle. It began at the end of August, 1942 and lasted until the beginning of February, 1943.

Not even the most general description of this colossal battle, about which volumes will be written, can be given here. Suffice it to say that the Germans pushed a great spearhead to the Volga. This spearhead consisted of 22 of the best divisions Hitler had, a total of 330,000 men. When the Soviet double concentric pincers closed on November 24, 1942, after five days of offensive operations, one third of a million enemy troops were in the bag of a "super-Cannae" from which practically none escaped. (Cannae is a battle which Hannibal won over the Romans in 216 B.C. It is considered a classic of encirclement and annihilation.) The victory of Stalingrad was the signal for a series of Soviet offensive operations ranging from Leningrad (where the blockade was lifted) to the Sea of Azov.

The Germans did not achieve any of their strategic objectives and met with an unprecedented military disaster. After Stalingrad the German Army never successfully took the offensive on a strategic scale.

THE THIRD PERIOD . . . During the Battle of Stalingrad the Germans attempted to relieve their trapped Sixth Army Group with an attack by some 11 divisions from the southwest. The counterblow was a ghastly failure. During the third period of the war, preceding the Battle of Kursk, the Germans repeated that maneuver in February–March, south of the Donets. Here they succeeded in stopping the Soviet offensive which was aiming at the elbow of the Dnieper and in saving their own troops in the Donets Basin. This offensive between the Dnieper and Kharkov, in the early spring of 1943, was the last successful limited offensive of the German Army. It was successful in a strictly limited sense: it saved the German troops in the Donbas from a huge trap; it permitted the Germans to hold and exploit the mines of the Donbas for another eight months (until September, 1943); it checked the Soviet offensive which had rolled uninterruptedly from Stalingrad almost to the Dnieper, a distance of roughly 400 miles in three months; it recaptured Kharkov. After that, and up to the end of 1944, the Germans staged counterblows on a smaller scale at Uman, in the Ukraine; at Kiev; in Galicia; at Warsaw; in the Baltic region; at Avranches; in Normandy; in the Belgian Bulge; at Budapest; but not one of them succeeded in delaying their opponents more than for a few weeks, and most of them ended for the Germans in disaster. An analysis of these multiple operations of the Wehrmacht conclusively shows that after November 19, 1942, the German Army was unable successfully to take the offensive on a strategic scale. The three great German offensive blows were delivered roughly with 50 to 60 divisions at a time, in 1941 (Moscow), in 1942 (Stalingrad), and in 1943 (Kursk-Oryol); of these, the latter proved a complete failure. The counterblows mentioned before were conducted by the Germans with an average of between 12 and 20 divisions and, therefore, cannot be considered of strategic scope. Three big offensives and a dozen offensive-defensive counterblows—such are the highlights of the German operations in Europe after June 22, 1941. Of these 15 operations, 13 (three large ones and ten small ones) were directed against the Red Army and two small ones against the Western Allied armies. No German operation was successful after the Donets local counterblow in February, 1943 (not counting a small and temporary success at Kasserine Pass, in Tunisia). This is important to remember in considering the last German strategic offensive attempt in the summer of 1943, around the Kursk arc.

Concurrently with and immediately after Stalingrad, the Red Army had lifted the blockade of Leningrad and had recaptured Rostov, which had been lost to the enemy for the second time in 1942. It had pushed a salient beyond Kursk between the German-held strongholds of Oryol and Kharkov. The Germans were afraid of this great salient, which had been built up into a gigantic fortress. (They were right, because when the Red Army started rolling in early August, 1943, it ended up 21 months later, having gone 900 miles without stopping, 1,100 miles to the west, on the Elbe and the Muerz.)

The German High Command decided on a minimum and a maximum plan. The minimum plan envisaged nipping off the Soviet salient at Kursk and the destruction of the Soviet armies concentrated there. The maximum plan envisaged, in addition, a break-through of the Soviet front and a new march on Moscow. Just before this offensive the Germans, sensing that the Western Allies, bent on invading Italy, would not invade France, concentrated 207 German and 50 satellite divisions on the Soviet front. Just as the Western Allies were taking their first steps in Sicily, the storm broke over the Kursk salient.

Reviving the pincer pattern, 17 armored divisions and 21 infantry and motorized divisions struck at the Kursk arc from both flanks (from Oryol and from Belgorod.) No such concentration of tanks had hitherto been assembled. (It was matched and bettered only by the Russians during the Oder break-through in April, 1945.)

The German grand offensive lasted little more than two weeks and penetrated less than 20 miles in depth. Between July 5 and 14 the Germans lost 40,000 killed, 1,392 planes, and 2,919 tanks. As the battle developed toward its climax, the Germans threw in one fifth of the 250-odd divisions they had on the eastern front. A month after the start of the enemy offensive the Red Army had not only repelled it but had captured Oryol and Belgorod. The Western Allies captured Catania in Sicily on that very same day, August 5. The German front was broken through in the widest strategic sense of the word. The Soviet offensive spread from the Kursk Bulge to the Dnieper and up and down its course, from the Smolensk Gap to the Black Sea. Generally speaking, after Kursk the Red Army never stopped until it reached Berlin and Vienna, except to repel occasional German counterthrusts and for regrouping.

And now as to the amount of lend-lease materials received by the USSR up to the end of 1943, that is, the matériel that was used by the

Red Army during the campaigns of 1943. None could have been used at Moscow and very little in the days of Stalingrad and the 1942–1943 winter. Foreign Economic Administration Chief Leo T. Crowley reported (New York *Times,* March 12, 1944) that up to December, 1943, the USSR had received lend-lease valued at $4,241,000,000, or slightly more than one quarter of the total amount lent and leased by the United States to Allied powers.* This amount represented, so far as munitions of war go, 7,800 planes, less than 5,000 tanks, 33,000 jeeps, 173,000 trucks, and other materials such as machines, food, and special metals. A large part of this total did not reach the USSR in time for the Battle of Kursk. It is enough to turn back to the statistics of Soviet matériel losses during the first two years of the war to realize that this was a small, though welcome, addition to the Soviet arsenal. During the first two years of war, the Red Army lost 35,000 guns, 30,000 tanks, and 23,000 planes, and inflicted on the Germans the following losses: 56,500 guns, 42,400 tanks, and 43,000 planes.

THE FOURTH PERIOD . . . Following the victory of Kursk-Oryol-Kharkov, the Red Army offensive spread along the front and in one sweep reached and hurdled the lower half of the Dnieper and reached the upper Dnieper. In the fall it cleared the Donets Basin. In the winter it broke the Germans on the Leningrad front and reached the Narova and the Lake of Pskov. In the spring it reached the Dniester and crossed into Romania over the Prut and reached the Carpathians. It cleared the Crimea and recaptured Sevastopol. In early June it crushed Finland. Thus, by the time the western front was opened by the Western Allies on June 6, 1944, the Germans in the east had already lost everything they had been fighting for. They had been frustrated in the attainment of all their strategic goals in the USSR, both unlimited and limited. During this phase the Germans were keeping well over three quarters of their divisions in the east because they well knew that the Western Allies were not ready to do anything except continue to fight the slogging campaign in Italy, where they still faced the same 20-odd enemy divisions, with the Yugoslav Army holding almost as many divisions, and doing this with no tanks, a handful of planes, and no shipping to bring supplies.

During this phase of the war the aerial offensive against Germany

* Total lend-lease to Russia: $11,141,470,000. (Ed.)

202

from the west was only beginning to hamper the German industrial effort, but the Red Army could not possibly have felt its effects until the end of 1944 and the beginning of 1945, if then. For the study of the operations of the latter period (such as the Battle of the Vistula and the Battle of Hungary) shows very plainly that the Germans did not lack equipment. Indeed, during their defensive counterblow near Budapest around Christmas time, 1944, they were able to squander as many as 200 tanks a day during more than a week. An army which feels the industrial pinch cannot afford such lavishness.

Thus, up to the end of the second phase of the fourth period, that is, up to the moment of the commencement of the final drive from two sides, the Red Army had received only very scant assistance from any quarter and its emergence on a line running from Viborg (Viipuri) to Narva, Gomel, Sarny, Czernowitz (Cernăuti), and Odessa must be credited to the Soviet Union's own war effort.

The two-front war against Germany began at long last on June 6, 1944. This last phase was to last for 11 months. The invasion of France was followed 17 days later by the Red Army offensive across the Upper Dnieper (the Battle of Belorussia). While the Western Allies were battling in the Cotentin Peninsula (The Battle of the Hedgerows), the Red Army crashed from the Dnieper to the Bug and Neman, to the near approaches to Riga, to the Upper Vistula, and to the San. At the time of the Allied break-through at St. Lo in Normandy, the Red Army had cleared all Soviet territory except for the western half of the Baltic region and the southern part of Bessarabia.

The over-all line-up of enemy forces during this campaign was approximately this: 100 enemy divisions facing the Allies in western Europe, Italy, and Yugoslavia; at least 240 enemy divisions facing the Red Army on a curving 1,300-mile front from the mouth of the Narva (Gulf of Finland) to the mouth of the Dniester, not counting the still active front in Lapland, where action stopped only toward the end of October. The estimate of 240 enemy divisions operating on the eastern front in the summer of 1944 is based on the fact that the Germans themselves said they had 200 divisions between the Baltic and the Carpathians alone, as well as on the incontrovertible fact that in the battle of encirclement at Minsk in July and Kishinev-Jassy (Chisinau-Iasi) in August as well as in Kurland, the Germans lost close to 55 divisions encircled and annihilated, or blockaded and left to rot until they surrendered (in Latvia) in May, 1945.

After August 1, while the Allied armies were sweeping almost without opposition from St. Lo to the German border,[1] the Red Army was fighting for every town and village, for every marshy little river right up to the border of East Prussia and Czechoslovakia. While the Allies fought a counterblow by six German divisions at Avranches, the Red Army warded off a counterblow by thirty German divisions before Warsaw.[1]

While the Allies were marching, against little opposition, to the Elbe,[1] the Red Army effected its massive break-through on the Oder (end of April) and began the Battle of Berlin against 100-odd German divisions. Simultaneously, the East Prussian pocket was liquidated and the enemy defenses were broken through in Upper Silesia and in Austria.

The Red Army battered its way into Berlin a day before the British entered Hamburg and three days before Gen. George S. Patton roared into Linz. During the five days after the German capitulation (May 8), the Red Army fought a whole German army group across the western part of Czechoslovakia. The last shots of the war were fired on the eastern front on May 13, 1945.

THE SOVIET CAMPAIGN IN MANCHURIA . . . As agreed upon at the Yalta Conference, the Soviet Union declared war on Japan exactly three months after the capitulation of Germany, that is, on August 8, 1945.[2] Several hours after the official war declaration three Soviet army groups began to converge on the center of Manchuria from three sides, under the over-all command of Marshal A. M. Vassilevski. Marshal R. J. Malinovski struck from the west with his Transbaikal forces, across the Khingan Mountains toward Harbin and across the Gobi Desert toward the Great Wall of China. Gen. M. A. Purkayev struck from the north and along the Sungari River. Marshal K. Meretskov advanced westward across the difficult wooded hills of the Ussuri border from the Maritime Province.

Ten days after the start of hostilities, the famous Japanese Kwantung

---

[1] In the period between June 6, 1944 (D-Day) and August 25 (liberation of Paris) the Western Allies encountered savage resistance in northern France, chiefly from the German Seventh and Fifth Panzer armies. The invasion of southern France by the Western Allies, commencing August 15, was likewise fiercely contested. In mid-December the Germans could still mount in the north a large scale counterblow (Battle of the Bulge). After March, 1945, (Rhine breakthrough) the German high command recognized inevitable defeat in the west. (Ed.)

[2] Three days after the atomic bomb fell on Hiroshima, and the day before the second bomb obliterated Nagasaki. (Ed.)

army capitulated. Out of their Manchurian army, about 1,000,000 strong, the Japanese lost 594,000 officers and men taken prisoner, including 148 generals. The Japanese lost more than 80,000 officers and men killed. The Red Army captured 925 planes, 369 tanks, 1,225 field guns, almost 5,000 machine guns, 300,000 rifles, and proportionate quantities of other equipment. The Soviet Pacific Fleet sank 2 destroyers, 28 transports, 3 tankers, and a number of small vessels.

In this whirlwind operation the Red Army lost 8,219 men killed and 22,264 wounded.[3]

COSTS OF THE WAR . . . Tabulation of the costs of the war to the Soviet Union had not been completed in 1945. The battle losses of the Red Army for the first three years of the war were computed as follows: killed, prisoners, and missing, 5,300,000; planes lost, 30,000; tanks, 49,000; guns, 48,000. One could arrive at a close estimate of the total for the 47 months of the war by adding 20 per cent to these figures.

In addition to human losses, the USSR lost through destruction 1,710 cities and towns; more than 70,000 villages; 6,000,000 buildings; 31,850 industrial enterprises (destroyed or looted by the Germans); 98,000 collective farms; 7,000,000 horses; 17,000,000 head of cattle; tens of millions of sheep, pigs, and other livestock. Almost three quarters of a million square miles of Soviet territory were laid waste by the war.

CHRONOLOGY . . . A brief chronology follows of the principal events in the Second World War as they affected the USSR.

FIRST PERIOD

1941

June 22—Germany attacks the USSR.
July 3—Stalin in an order of the day outlines complete plan for total defense in depth.
July 19—Stalin appointed people's commissar for defense.
August 21—Siege of Leningrad begins (August, 1941 to January, 1944).
October 13—German assault on Moscow begins.
  Beginning of 250-day siege of Sevastopol.

[3] General MacArthur received the Japanese instrument of surrender at Manila, August 19, 1945. (Ed.)

November 16—Second and final German assault on Moscow begins.
December 6—*Red Army goes over to the offensive on Moscow front.*

1942

January 22—End of the Battle of Moscow.

SECOND PERIOD

1942

June 24—*Second German summer offensive begins in south.*
September—Beginning of Battle of Stalingrad.
November 19—*Soviet counteroffensive at Stalingrad begins.*
November 24—Encirclement of German Sixth Army Group at Stalingrad completed
November 25—Beginning of Soviet offensive on central front.
December 22—Beginning of Soviet offensive in the north Caucasus.

1943

January 18—First break in blockade of Leningrad.
February 2—End of the Battle of Stalingrad and capitulation of Field Marshal
   General von Paulus.

THIRD PERIOD

1943

March—End of the second Soviet winter offensive.
March 6—Stalin made a marshal of the Soviet Union.
July 5—*Germans start their third summer offensive at Kursk.*
July 23—*Having crushed the German offensive, the Red Army begins its own
   offensive in the Oryol and Belgorod direction.*

FOURTH PERIOD

1943

October–November—Battle of the Dnieper.
November 6—Kiev liberated.

1944

January 14—First Soviet offensive blow of the 1944 campaign (at Leningrad-
   Novgorod, January 14–February 29). Blockade of Leningrad completely lifted.
February–March—Second Soviet offensive blow (Ukraine). Carpathians reached.
April–May—Third Soviet offensive blow (Crimea). Sevastopol liberated on May 9
   after three-week siege.

206

May—Fourth Soviet offensive blow (Karelia).
June 23—Fifth Soviet offensive blow (Belorussia).
July–August—Sixth Soviet offensive blow (western Ukraine).
August 20—Seventh Soviet offensive blow (Bessarabia-Romania). Bucharest captured August 31.
September–October—Eighth Soviet offensive blow (Baltic region).
October—Ninth Soviet offensive blow (Hungary-Yugoslavia). Belgrade liberated October 20.
   Tenth Soviet offensive blow (northern Finland-Norway).

1945

January 15—Beginning of Soviet offensive on the Vistula.
January 17—Warsaw liberated. March to the Oder begun.
January–April—Battle for East Prussia, culminating with the capture of Koenigsberg on April 9.
February 13—Budapest captured.
April 13—Vienna captured.
April 23—Battle of the Oder opens.
May 2—Berlin captured.
May 8—German armed forces capitulate in Berlin.
May 13—Last shots fired in Czechoslovakia against German army group which refused to capitulate on May 8.
August 9—Soviet Union enters war against Japan exactly three months after capitulation of Germany, as agreed upon at Yalta.
August 18—Japanese Army in Manchuria and Inner Mongolia lays down its arms.
August 23—Last order of the day issued by Generalissimo Stalin (372d victory order of the day of the war).

TOP SOVIET COMMANDERS IN THE SECOND WORLD WAR

. . . Heading the list of the Soviet commanders is Generalissimo Joseph Stalin, who was in over-all supreme command of the armed forces throughout the war. He was also chairman of the State Defense Committee, and people's commissar for defense. Below are given the names of his commanders, with their rank, and the campaigns in which they distinguished themselves.

G. K. Zhukov, Marshal of the Soviet Union; Moscow (1941)—Stalingrad—Leningrad (1943)—Kursk—Podolia—Carpathians—Vistula—Oder—Berlin.

I. S. Konev, Marshal of the Soviet Union; Moscow (1941)—Kharkov—Dnieper—Bessarabia—Vistula—Silesia—Czechoslovakia.

K. K. Rokossovski, Marshal of the Soviet Union; Moscow (1941)—Stalingrad—Kursk—Belorussia—Warsaw—East Prussia—Pomerania.

F. I. Tolbukhin, Marshal of the Soviet Union; Stalingrad—Donets Basin—Crimea—Sevastopol—Bessarabia—Romania—Bulgaria—Yugoslavia—Vienna.

R. J. Malinovski, Marshal of the Soviet Union; Stalingrad—Ukraine—Odessa—Romania—Hungary—Czechoslovakia—Far East.

A. M. Vassilevski, Marshal of the Soviet Union; Stalingrad—Summer campaign 1943—Sevastopol—East Prussia—Far East.

L. A. Govorov, Marshal of the Soviet Union; Moscow (1941)—Leningrad—Finland—Estonia.

K. Meretskov, Marshal of the Soviet Union; Volkhov—Karelia—Far East.

K. E. Voroshilov, Marshal of the Soviet Union; Leningrad (1941)—later on special military-political missions—training reserve armies.

S. M. Budyonny, Marshal of the Soviet Union; Ukraine (1941)—later training reserve cavalry units.

S. K. Timoshenko, Marshal of the Soviet Union; Moscow (summer 1941)—Ukraine (1942)—reported severely wounded in 1942—Kishinev-Jassy (1944).

A. I. Yeremenko, General of the Army; Northwest (1941)—Stalingrad—Northwest—Crimea—Latvia—Silesia.

N. F. Vatutin, General of the Army; Don—Kiev—Zhitomir. Died soon after the liberation of Kiev.

I. D. Chernayakhovski, General of the Army; Kursk—Kiev—Belorussia—Lithuania—East Prussia. Killed in battle in East Prussia, early 1945.

M. A. Purkayev, General of the Army; Moscow—Kalinin front—Far East.

V. I. Chuikov, Colonel-General; Commander of the famous 62d Army at Stalingrad which he led to Berlin via Zaporozhye—Odessa—Lublin—Posnan. Nicknamed "Tenacity."

N. N. Voronov, Chief Marshal of Artillery; commanded artillery concentration at Stalingrad as well as in later campaigns.

A. A. Novikov, Chief Air Marshal; commanded air concentrations at Stalingrad, Kursk, Koenigsberg, Berlin, and in the Far East.

P. S. Rybalko, Marshal of Tank Troops; Voronezh—Kharkov (February, 1943)—Kiev—Lwów—Silesia—Berlin—Czechoslovakia.

N. G. Kusnetsov, Fleet Admiral; Commander in Chief and People's Commissar of the Navy.

A. G. Golovko, Admiral; Commander of the Northern Fleet.

V. F. Tributz, Admiral; Commander of the Baltic Fleet.

F. S. Oktyvabrski, Admiral; Commander of the Black Sea Fleet.

I. S. Yumashev, Admiral; Commander of the Far Eastern Fleet.

BIBLIOGRAPHY

Carroll, W., *We're in This with Russia* (New York, 1942).

Kournakoff, S. N., *Russia's Fighting Forces* (New York, 1942).

Werner, M., *Great Offensive* (New York, 1942).

Werth, A., *Moscow War Diary* (New York, 1942).

Graebner, W., *Round Trip to Russia* (New York, 1943).

Werner, M., *Attack Can Win in '43* (Boston, 1943).

Voytekov, B., *Last Days of Sevastopol* (New York, 1943).

Kerr, W., *Russian Army* (New York, 1944).

Skomorovsky, B., and Morris, E. G., *Siege of Leningrad* (New York, 1944).

Stowe, L., *They Shall Not Sleep* (New York, 1944).

Lauterbach, R. E., *These Are the Russians* (New York, 1944).

Werth, A., *Leningrad* (New York, 1944).

Allen, W. E. D., and Muratov, P., *Russian Campaigns* (London 1945).

Galaktionov, M., "Strategic Objective," in Russian, *Znamya*, Russian magazine (Moscow, 1945).

Kournakoff, S. N., *What Russia Did for Victory* (New York, 1945).

Martin, J. S., *Picture History of Russia* (New York, 1945).

Simonov, K., *Days and Nights* (New York, 1945).

Stalin, J., *Great Patriotic War of the Soviet Union* (New York, 1945).

PART THREE

THE SOCIAL SCIENCES

CHAPTER X

The Economic System

By VLADIMIR D. KAZAKÉVICH

BASIC PRINCIPLES OF SOVIET ECONOMY

As a result of the October Revolution of 1917 the economic system of the Soviet Union became markedly different from that of any other country. It became a socialist system of economy in which private ownership of the means and instruments of production was abrogated (see Article 4 of 1936 Constitution). To quote the constitution directly (Article 6): "The land, its natural deposits, waters, forests, mills, factories, mines, rail, water and air transport, banks, post, telegraph and telephones, large state-organized agricultural enterprises (state farms, machine and tractor stations and the like) as well as municipal enterprises and the bulk of the dwelling houses in the cities and industrial localities, are state property, that is, belong to the whole people."

Socialist property (Article 5) exists either as state property (the possession of the whole people) or as co-operatively or collectively held property (the possession of a collective farm or of a co-operative association). The constitution permits (Article 9) small private economy, provided it is based on personal labor and precludes the exploitation of the labor of others. Economic life in the USSR (Article 11) is determined and directed by the state national plan. To work is a duty for all able-bodied citizens; "he who does not work, neither shall he eat" (Article 12).

The Socialist motto is: "From each according to his ability, to each according to his work." In a communist economy the motto would be: "From each according to his ability, to each according to his needs."

213

Since the Soviet economy cannot yet produce in sufficient quantities for distribution "according to need," there is no communism as yet, although the only existing political party in the country is the All-Union Communist Party (Bolshevik), and the stated goal of this party is the achievement of a communist economy. Soviet leadership regards the socialism of today as the first step toward a future communist economy. Such an economy, to be able to satisfy everyone's needs, will have to be an economy of abundance, which the Soviet economy of today admittedly is not. It is still an economy of scarcity, but in its operation according to a central plan, based on social ownership of the means of production, it differs radically from economies whose operation is based on the incentive of private profit.

Socialism in Russia was made possible by the October Revolution, but did not arise immediately after the revolution. The 1918 constitution of the Russian Socialist Federated Soviet Republic had a programmatic aspect; in dealing with economic matters, it often spoke in the future tense as did the first Union constitution of 1923. Only in the 1930's was the socialist character of the economic system definitely established. Hence the Constitution of 1936 speaks of economic matters in the present tense and is commonly referred to in the Soviet Union as the Stalin Constitution or the Constitution of Victorious Socialism. To obtain a clear picture of the Soviet economy one must trace its evolution; one must, in fact, begin with Russian economy before the revolution.

INDUSTRY BEFORE 1917 . . . Although the country was predominantly agricultural, it would be wrong to assume that no industry existed in czarist Russia. Various types of handicraft production had existed for centuries. In the reign of Ivan III (r. 1462–1505) cannon were already being made. Czar Peter I (r. 1682–1725) encouraged the development of mining in the Urals, shipbuilding, and merchant capital in general. In the battle for Moscow (near Borodino) against Napoleon on August 26, 1812, the Russian artillery was numerically superior to that of the French. From the days of Czar Peter to about 1850—as long as men-of-war were sailing ships built of wood—Russia was also a formidable naval power.

During the nineteenth century Russia began to lag behind other nations, particularly after the Industrial Revolution had introduced machine production in the West. During the Crimean War (1853–1856)

214

the technical superiority of Western equipment and transportation became particularly obvious. The abolition of serfdom laid the ground for the development of modern industry and transportation. Toward the end of the nineteenth century, with the beginning of large-scale imports of foreign capital, the construction of railroads and of modern industrial establishments was definitely under way.

Modern machine industry had arrived in Russia, and because its arrival was late, it started at a rather high level. In 1866, of the workers employed in large factories (those employing more than 100 workers), more than 27 per cent worked in factories employing 1,000 or more workers; in 1879 the percentage was 40; and by 1890 it had risen to 46. By 1903 large factories, while representing in European Russia only 17 per cent of the total number of factories and works, employed 77 per cent of all the workers. In 1890 the average number of people employed per establishment in Russian factories or mines having 1,000 or more employees each was larger than the average for Germany in 1895 by more than 600 workers. The influx of foreign capital during the first decade of the twentieth century caused a further rapid expansion of industry; the value of industrial production rose from 4.7 billion rubles (as of the 1926–1927 price level) in 1900 to 10.3 billion of the same rubles in 1913.

Nevertheless, Russia remained backward in comparison with other industrial nations. In 1913 the per capita output of electric power was one seventeenth that of the United States and one fifth that of Germany. The per capita output of pig iron was one eleventh of that in the United States, one eighth of that in Great Britain, a similar fraction of that in Germany, and one fourth of that in France. The Russian per capita output of steel in 1913 was one eleventh of that in the United States, one eighth of that in Germany, one sixth of that in Great Britain, and one fourth of that in France. In spite of the expansion from 1900 to 1914, Russia was not catching up but falling further behind. The per capita pig iron production of Russia was one eighth that of the United States in 1900; in 1913 it was only one eleventh. Though in 1900 it was one sixth of Germany's production, by 1913 it was only one eighth.

Prerevolutionary Russia had a textile industry, produced wool and leather goods, engaged in mining, and even manufactured her own locomotives. But production of agricultural machinery was backward, the

215

chemical industry was nearly nonexistent, automobiles, electrical appliances, and machine tools were not manufactured. In total industrial production Russia occupied in 1913 the fifth place in the world. Modern industry had reached Russia, but the country remained backward as compared with the great industrial nations of the world in terms of quantity production; and in terms of its own economic resources it was very poorly developed.

AGRICULTURE BEFORE 1917 . . . In 1861 Czar Alexander II liberated 21.3 million male serfs, together with their families. The peasants received not only freedom but some land. This land went not to individual peasants outright but to the village commune, supposedly restoring the prefeudal independence of the peasantry. Land received by the village commune and that retained by the nobleman often formed one economic unit; hence legal emancipation did not necessarily terminate the economic dependence of the peasants on the noblemen. On the contrary, the abolition of serfdom often benefited the nobleman by creating a pool of cheap wage labor. The peasants had to pay for the land they received and were given 40 years to complete their payments. Some two billion rubles were thus paid between 1861 and 1905.

The income of the peasants was small, while Russia's increasing grain exports placed the peasant communal economies, with their medieval methods of production, in a constantly growing dependence upon world prices for agricultural commodities. Although the nobility were mortgaging and losing their estates, large landlordism persisted. The last czar, for instance, personally owned over 100 million acres. In 1905, in European Russia, 699 large landlords averaged 80,000 acres apiece, while 12.3 million peasant households averaged only 30 acres, half of them enjoying the use of less than 22 acres.

Large landlords farmed with tenant labor but increasingly used wage labor and agricultural machinery. Well-to-do peasants also frequently employed labor. The middle peasants did tenant labor for landlords and barely made a living from their allotments in the commune, with only an insignificant marketable surplus. Poor peasants could make both ends meet only by selling their labor power. Caught between a survival of semiserf conditions, on the one hand, and modern capitalism with its commercial production and money obligations, on the other, the peasantry was breaking up into economic layers. The village commune, with its strip system of land cultivation, became more and more an anachronism.

Meanwhile, the landed nobility were declining economically and Russia's autocracy was confronted with the problem of finding a new social and economic base on which to rely. In 1906 P. A. Stolypin (1863–1911), one of the last energetic statesmen of czarist Russia, attempted to break up the village communes and create a large class of independent farmer-owners, several million strong, a conservative yeomanry that would serve to stem the revolutionary tide. As a result of Stolypin's reform about half a million such farms appeared.

Large grain exports abroad, on which the financial solvency of the Russian state depended, were a strong incentive for higher agricultural productivity. But this very fact accelerated the economic stratification of the peasantry, the vast majority of whom were not in position to introduce improvements. General backwardness of production methods led to frequent crop failure and famines, but grain deliveries to the world market had to continue. In the First World War Russia, the largest single grain-producing area in the world, began to experience food shortages. The peasants were justly land hungry. The only solution they saw for all their difficulties was to get more land. To them the Revolution meant land.

THE WORKING CLASS BEFORE THE REVOLUTION . . . Although large-scale modern machine industry, and with it a modern industrial proletariat, did not arise in Russia until the last quarter of the nineteenth century, the beginnings of the industrial working class go back to a much earlier period. In 1721 Peter I decreed that merchants could buy serfs from the landed nobility for work in manufactories. In 1767, in 498 manufacturing establishments, 39.2 per cent of the labor consisted of freemen, 60.8 per cent of serfs. By 1825, in 5,261 manufacturing establishments, more than half (54.4 per cent) of 210,600 workers were freemen. By 1860, the year before the abolition of serfdom, 565,100 workers were engaged in Russia's 15,338 manufacturing establishments. Amidst a serf economy an industrial proletariat was being formed.

After the abolition of serfdom the working class grew more rapidly. By 1897, when large-scale capitalist production had already arrived in Russia, there were 39,109 manufacturing establishments, employing 2,098,200 workers. In 1900, in large factories subject to government factory inspection, 1,692,300 workers were employed; by 1914 this figure had risen to 2,282,100.

After the abolition of serfdom the peasants who swelled the ranks of factory labor did not immediately sever all ties with the country. Many at first were seasonal workers, returning to the countryside in the summer. Gradually the number who remained in the city all year round increased. In 1910, of the 1,076,400 who were registered as peasants in St. Petersburg, 10.4 per cent went to the country during the summer. Just before the revolution 47.8 per cent of the factory workers in European Russia were fully divorced from the land; although 31.3 per cent still had some property interest in land, only 20.9 per cent were actually involved in agricultural production.

The fact that the industrial proletariat was becoming hereditary is illustrated by the growth in the number of workers whose fathers were also workers. In 1908, in the Moscow province, 52.4 per cent of the men and 38.8 per cent of the women among laborers 20 to 25 years old were sons and daughters of workers. Older groups showed a lower percentage, and the percentage among women was lower through all age groups than among men. The urban population of Russia was growing: in 1863 it was just above six million people; by 1914 it had reached some eighteen and a half million. By the time of the revolution the Russian proletariat included many second-generation workers and probably quite a core of third-generation workers.

Among factory workers the level of literacy was also relatively high. In 1897, among the male workers, 56.5 per cent were literate, as against some 30 per cent for the population as a whole. In 1918, among the workers of Russia, 79.2 per cent of the men and 44.2 per cent of the women were literate. An interesting fact is that many of them were self-taught, acquiring literacy outside of schools. A sample taken as early as 1883–1884 shows that slightly over one third of the literate workers were self-taught.

To sum up: for a good while before the revolution Russia had an industrial working class, whose roots went back deep into the period of serfdom. This class was growing; it was becoming increasingly detached from the land; a substantial share of it consisted already of children of workers; and the level of literacy among the proletariat was high in comparison with the rest of the population, the large majority of whom were peasants. It may also be added that these workers wanted better working conditions; they wanted the right to organize their own trade unions; since 1905 they had been predominantly anticzarist, and many of the literate workers wanted socialism.

THE FIRST YEARS OF SOVIET POWER . . . On the night of the October Revolution (November 6–7, 1917) a decree was adopted by the Congress of Soviets, upon Lenin's motion, declaring all land, urban and rural, to be public property. In December, 1917, banking was nationalized, payments on coupons were suspended, and deals in stocks and bonds were terminated. In January, 1918, all bank guarantees were annulled as well as all internal and external loans; a few days later all bank capital was confiscated and bank stock declared void. In April, 1918, all stocks and bonds were subjected to registration with the authorities. During the same month foreign trade was declared a state function and the government monopoly of foreign trade was established. The sugar industry was nationalized in May and the oil industry in June of the same year.

A general nationalization decree was issued on June 28, 1918, that affected over 1,100 corporations with capital over 3 billion rubles. The decree embraced about three quarters of all large industry. Several other decrees followed, and by October, 1919, the Supreme Council (Soviet) of National Economy (VSNKh) was operating 2,522 large industrial enterprises; by April, 1920, this number rose to 4,141 enterprises with 933,000 workers. On November 20, 1920, all enterprises with over five employees (operating with mechanical power) and with over ten employees (operating without mechanical power) were nationalized. Thus three years after the October Revolution the nationalization of industry was virtually completed.

Nationalization meant a threefold process: first, the transfer of ownership or title from private owners to the public; second, the establishment of a government monopoly in the activity taken over; third, the introduction of a new system of economic operation—production for use rather than for profit. Apparently the Soviet authorities originally intended to switch over from a privately owned to a publicly owned economy more or less gradually and in a most orderly fashion. Some of the early decrees were quite elaborate, furnishing time limits, providing partial compensation to small shareholders, etc. All this met with

219

practically universal opposition from property owners, large and small.

With the outbreak of civil war (summer of 1918) and the acceleration of monetary inflation, shorter and more drastic decrees followed in rapid succession. With the Soviet Republic blockaded on all sides, and with most of the country occupied by its internal and external enemies, there ensued the so-called period of military communism. Money had become nearly worthless. Whatever production remained was used to service the numerous military fronts. Cities were often on the brink of starvation. The few remaining articles of consumption were rationed. Thus the military exigency of the civil war threw the country back to a great scarcity of goods. It was highly organized scarcity, with the scant available necessities of life allotted mainly in return for work essential to the war effort or for the care of children. In view of the military aspect of the period and the political issue involved in the civil war, this period became known as military communism—at best a colorful misnomer. After three years of civil war the Soviet regime achieved a military victory; the White forces were defeated and the forces of foreign interventionists were expelled, but at the cost of terrific economic devastation of the country.

RECONSTRUCTION . . . The period of reconstruction began with Lenin's announcement of the adoption of the New Economic Policy (the NEP) in March, 1921. Under the NEP, land, both rural and urban, remained public property. Heavy industry and transportation also remained nationalized. Petty manufacturing, the production of consumers' goods, and retail trade were thrown open to private enterprise. But all the key positions, the "commanding heights" in the political and economic organization of the state, were reserved exclusively for adherents of socialism, that is, for members of the Communist Party. The NEP was described by Lenin as a "strategic retreat," or "a respite" before a new advance.

Civil war, blockade, foreign intervention, and famine had brought privation and ruin. By 1920 the value of industrial production had declined to 1.4 billion rubles, as against 10.3 billion for 1913. The national income dropped to 8.0 billion rubles by 1921, as against 21.0 billion for 1913 (all in rubles of 1926–1927 prices). Transportation facilities were particularly damaged during the civil war years, and the feeding and heating of cities became most difficult problems. The ravished countryside

220

required a reduction in the tax burden. Consumers' goods of all kinds were extremely scarce. Despite its aim of socialist planning, the government had neither the material means nor the personnel to organize satisfactory production and distribution of articles of consumption. Hence the "respite," or "retreat."

Private enterprise was enlisted to help the country get back on its feet, to help create the material means for a new advance toward socialism. Nationalized enterprises (for the most part small) were leased out. Private entrepreneurs rented about 52 per cent—of these 30 per cent went to former owners; the rest were leased by co-operative groups. Private foreign capital was invited to come in and participate in the operation of even large enterprises. These joint undertakings of the Soviet government and foreign capitalists were known as "concessions" (to foreign capital). On the whole, foreign capital did not avail itself of this opportunity to any considerable degree. At their peak the "concessions" accounted for only about 4 per cent of the production of Soviet large industry.

Some of the noblemen's landed estates were turned into state farms, but peasant agriculture remained primitive. Artisans engaged in petty commodity production for the market. A government pledged to socialism was running a mixed economy, containing both private and public ownership. In 1924–1925 the socialized sector accounted for 81 per cent of industrial production. Retail trade was 42 per cent in private hands, but only 5 per cent of wholesale trade was private. Economic life was reviving, although slowly. In October, 1925, heavy industry amounted to only 43 per cent of all industrial production, and iron and steel production was still below the 1913 level. Eighty-nine per cent of all industrial equipment was still prerevolutionary, and machine building itself amounted to only 8 per cent of large industrial production.

Lenin had already said in 1922 that the NEP was soon to be ended, because it was then well on the way to the accomplishment of its purpose. He died in January, 1924, and so did not witness the turn. As soon as the government began to accumulate some surpluses, it was in position to invest in new production. In 1926 both the value of industrial production and national income for the first time exceeded the previous record levels of 1913. The reconstruction period was coming to an end, and with it the NEP, the "concessions," private trading, and the mixed

221

economy. The country was now ready to take the next step forward, to socialism.

THE NATURE OF SOVIET PLANNING . . . This step had to be carefully prepared, since it involved changes both in the institutional setup and in methods of operation. During the course of nationalization enterprises that had passed to public ownership had been subordinated to central offices. There was, for instance, a central office for lumber production, another for fisheries, and so on. This form of organization proved inefficient, and in the early 1920's enterprises were combined in "trusts," a term borrowed from the United States. Government-owned "trusts" now began to operate throughout the country, each performing one or more functions. In the 1930's direct supervision by the commissariats in charge of various branches of the economy began to increase. Toward the end of this decade the USSR developed a very large Council of People's Commissars, or "cabinet." Unlike any comparable body in the world, the Council of People's Commissars includes "cabinet members" for the paper and cellulose industry, river transport, the coal, oil, electrical, heavy-machine-building, machine-tool, and rubber industries, and so on. In several localities industrial production forms a "combinat," which often operates under more than one commissariat because of the diverse nature of its production. Thus the form of organization of industry in the USSR has changed more than once.

As early as 1918 Soviet leaders had begun laying the foundation for a planned economy. The Supreme Council of National Economy (VSNKh), under which the central offices for various types of economic activities operated in the early days, was an initial move in that direction. In 1920 a state plan had been worked out for the electrification of Russia (the Goelro), in which Lenin had taken great personal interest. In February, 1921, the State Planning Commission (Gosplan) was set up; it was considerably expanded and reorganized in 1923. This was a technical body; above it was a sort of economic cabinet, the Council of Labor and Defense (STO). The latter body decided what was to be done, and experts of the Gosplan worked out how to do it. All these efforts were largely experimental. The first attempt at unified planning was not launched until 1925. Sets of annual "control figures" were issued for various types of production, but these proved to be only approximations of actual accomplishments. Experience indicated clearly that only

222

the most thorough, co-ordinated planning of each step in the production process, industry by industry, could introduce real planning. After nearly three years of preparatory work by the Gosplan, such an all-embracing program was finally launched in 1928: the First Five-Year Plan.

It is important to understand what the word "plan" means in these circumstances. On the basis of public ownership of the means and instruments of production a blueprint is made of what is to be achieved. This must include a detailed inventory of human and material resources available, an appraisal of the location of raw materials and of the problems of transporting them, and an estimate of the time necessary to deliver finished products to their destination. Each industry has to be synchronized in all these respects with other branches of production. On a nationwide basis it has to be calculated how much of the general surplus (accumulated by the state) is to be invested where, how long certain enterprises are to be subsidized from the general budget, when they should start contributing to it, and how much. On a nationwide scale planning is a gigantic cost-accounting task—Lenin once said, "Socialism is accounting." Thus the Soviet Union has developed a new professional skill, that of the planner, who is usually a young man or woman with engineering and accounting training.

As long as the economy remained both private and public (under the NEP), no such scheme could operate. The distribution of consumers' goods through the channels of private trade was a free market element that could not itself be planned and that tended to upset planning calculations in other spheres of the economy. It therefore had to give way to government-owned and co-operative stores. Agriculture also had to be entirely reorganized. No general plan could operate while the country's food supply depended on the vicissitudes of crop raising by millions of individual households with antiquated production methods. As long·as retail trade and agriculture were outside the socialized sector of the economy, one had to rely on forecasts, or guesses, as to what would happen in these fields—no comprehensive plan was possible.

The basic feature of Soviet planning is that it does not rest on the forecasting of wholly or partly uncontrollable trends. Soviet planning is the antithesis of such forecasting. It is based on public ownership and on control—as complete as possible—of all the factors. Blueprints are only half the story. The other half is the execution of the plan. In this process things have constantly to be changed and readjusted, not only annually, but quarterly and monthly, in response to changing capacities and requirements of the entire economy and of local bodies. It is a dynamic process involving the active participation, not only of the central planning authorities, but of millions of people in the various localities.

INDUSTRIALIZATION UNDER THE FIVE-YEAR PLANS . . . Under the First Five-Year Plan (1928–1932), completed nine months ahead of schedule, the main emphasis was on the development of a heavy-industry base. That meant iron and steel production. Another task of this plan was to lay the groundwork for extensive production of all types of agricultural machinery to service the newly organized collective farms.[1] Finally, the First Five-Year Plan laid the groundwork for establishing new industrial centers in the Urals, in western Siberia, and elsewhere, in order to terminate the irrational concentration of most industrial facilities in the western part of European Russia. All this necessitated very heavy capital investments. An unprecedented share of the national income was plowed back into construction of means of production rather than into production of consumers' goods; this of course involved considerable hardship. By the end of the First Five-Year Plan the value of the output of producers' goods nearly tripled, while that of consumers' goods increased only about 84 per cent. Unemployment had disappeared by 1931, and the Soviet Union has ever since experienced a shortage of labor.

During the Second Five-Year Plan (1933–1937) the building of producers' goods industries continued. The output of producers' goods increased almost two and a half times, while that of consumers' goods (including foods) doubled. The disparity between the rate of growth of the two branches of production was, however, not so great as in the first plan. The Second Five-Year Plan stressed the development of motor production (largely trucks, tractors, and airplanes) and the manufacture of electrical appliances.

The Third Five-Year Plan, scheduled for completion in 1942, provided for further tremendous advances in all branches of production. It was to lay particular stress on the development of fuel and power

---

[1] See Chapter XII, "Agricultural Development."

224

bases and on the expansion of the chemical industry. By 1942 producers' goods industries were to be expanded by 203 per cent and consumers' goods industries by 169 per cent. Production of means of production was still scheduled to expand more rapidly than that of industries manufacturing articles of general consumption, but the disparity between the rates of growth was smaller than in the previous five-year period, and much smaller than in the First Five-Year Plan. The Third Five-Year Plan was interrupted by the fascist invasion on June 22, 1941. It had originally envisaged much improvement in the local self-sufficiency of industrial centers, particularly in fuel, but also in many types of manufactured articles of consumption. It had also projected a vast housing development. Just before the outbreak of the Second World War, Soviet leadership was already talking in terms of a 15-year plan, to terminate in the fifties, at the end of which the per capita output of various basic products in the USSR would have caught up with the per capita production of those products in the most advanced industrial countries.

The era of the Five-Year plans resulted in a fundamental change of the entire Soviet economy. In 1913 the share of industry in total production (agricultural and industrial combined) was 42.1 per cent. In 1928 it was 54.5 per cent, but in 1937 it had risen to 77.4 per cent. The socialized sector of the economy accounted in 1928 for only 44.0 per cent of the national income; in 1937 the corresponding figure was 99.3 per cent. State-owned and co-operative trade accounted for 77.5 per cent of all trade in 1928, but in 1937 there was no private trade in the usual sense of that term.

This transformation was not only qualitative (from private to public), but also quantitative. In 1913 Russia accounted for 2.6 per cent of the industrial production of large nations, the United States for 38.2 per cent; in 1928 the Soviet Union's share was 3.1 per cent and that of the United States 46.3 per cent; but in 1937 the USSR produced 13.7 per cent and the U.S.A. 41.9 per cent. In quantity of production, the Soviet Union in 1937 occupied the second place in the world, being exceeded only by the United States. In 1937, when the USSR accounted for 13.7 per cent of the total industrial production of the five great powers, England's share was 9.3 per cent, Germany's 11.6 per cent, and France's 5.7 per cent. This Soviet expansion is best demonstrated by the following figures:

VALUE OF INDUSTRIAL PRODUCTION AND THE NATIONAL INCOME [2]		
(In billions of rubles of 1926–1927 prices)		
	Industrial	National
Year	production	income
1913	11.0	21.0
1928	16.9	25.0
1929	21.2	28.9
1930	27.2	35.0
1931	34.2	40.9
1932	38.8	45.5
1933	42.0	48.5
1934	50.6	55.8
1935	62.1	66.9
1936	80.9	86.0
1937	90.2	96.3
1938	100.4	105.0

In 1940 the national income was 125.5 billion rubles, or nearly six times as great as in 1913 (or 1926). This industrial expansion was accompanied by a considerable rise in the efficiency of production. In 1928 an English industrial worker produced per year, on the average, about 1.9 times more than a Soviet worker; a German worker produced 2.2 times more, and an American worker about six times as much. In 1937 the average production of a Soviet industrial worker per year was somewhat higher than that of an English worker, a fraction less than that of a German worker, but still only two fifths that of a worker in the United States.

The very rapid industrial expansion in the Soviet Union was not accompanied by a corresponding railroad expansion. Soviet railroad mileage did not even double between the years 1926 and 1940. With a territory two and a half times as great as that of the United States, the USSR had, in the late 1930's, only about one quarter as much railroad mileage. The density of traffic on this mileage was very high (in 1937 the Soviet railroads handled a volume of freight traffic approximately 60 per cent of that handled by Class I railroads in America), but the country was still under-railroaded.

During the years under discussion the Soviet Union moved toward urbanization. Only about one tenth urban (and nine tenths agrarian) before the Revolution, the country had become about one third urban in 1939. The change in class composition of the population is best shown by the following figures:

---

[2] See the author's article in *Science & Society*, No. 4 (1941), V, 385–389.

SOCIAL COMPOSITION OF THE POPULATION [3] (In percentages of total population)		
	1928	1937
Workers and employees	17	35
Collective farmers and handicraftsmen organized in co-operatives	3	55
Individual peasants and unorganized handicraftsmen	73	6
Private traders and rich peasants (kulaks)	5	0
Students, armed forces, pensioners, etc.	2	4
	100	100

COLLECTIVIZATION OF AGRICULTURE . . .

Soviet agriculture did not expand as rapidly as industry. The value of agricultural production was 12.6 billion rubles in 1913, 13.1 billion in 1928, and 19.8 billion in 1937, as measured in rubles of 1926–1927 prices. The major change in Soviet agriculture was qualitative. This partly explains why the national income rose from 1926 to 1940 only about six times, while there was a nearly ten-fold increase in industrial production. In 1927 the Soviet Union still had over 24 million individual peasant households. By 1938 such households numbered only 1.3 million. The bulk of the peasantry was now organized in 242,400 collective farms (kolkhozy). These farms (see Articles 8 and 7 of the constitution) are co-operative enterprises enjoying permanent use (not ownership) of the land. The members of a collective farm own jointly its facilities except for most of the mechanical equipment, which is rented from state-owned machine and tractor stations (MTS). There were 6,358 of these stations in 1938. The individual members of a collective farm may also possess subsidiary establishments, which they operate with their own labor. State or soviet farms (sovkhozy) also exist; there were 3,961 of these in 1938. These are agricultural "factories" employing wage labor and using state-owned machinery and equipment. Excluding state farms, 93.5 per cent of all the peasant households in 1938 were in collective farms, working 99.3 per cent of the arable land. In 1937 collective farms contributed 62.9 per cent to total agricultural production. The share of soviet farms was 9.3 per cent, subsidiary establishments of members of collective farms accounted for 21.5 per cent, similar establishments of workers and employees produced 4.8 per cent, and the remaining private owners were responsible for only 1.5 per cent of the total. Thus production on individually owned farms had declined to insignificant proportions.

[3] From a report by V. M. Molotov, March, 1939.

By 1938 the Soviet Union had about half a million tractors, compared with approximately 1.5 million in the United States. Tractors in the USSR are rented out constantly, however, and each is used about four times as intensively as one in the U.S.A. Thus, with only one third as many tractors, the Soviet Union has already reached a higher degree of mechanization of agriculture. The mechanization of agriculture released millions of people to the cities for work in industry. More scientific methods of farming increased total agricultural yields and stabilized yields from year to year. What used to be peak harvests became average ones. The average annual grain production for the entire country in the five years 1933–1937 was 40 per cent higher than the annual average for 1910–1914, and the average yield per unit of land was 25 per cent more during the later period than during the earlier. The constant threat of famine, which had visited the Russian countryside every few years for centuries, was now removed.

Collectivization of agriculture extended the industrial revolution from the cities to the villages. Mechanization, scientific methods, and all the advantages of the division of labor were for the first time applied to agriculture in an organized and systematic manner. The collectivization of agriculture, achieved under the First Five-Year Plan, extended the revolution economically to the countryside by creating an entirely new type of production relationships in agriculture. Without this agricultural revolution the creation of a vast industry and the establishment of a planned economy, that is, the building of socialism, would have been impossible.

OBJECTIVES OF SOVIET ECONOMY . . . The Soviet economic system still produces less per capita than is produced in the older industrial countries. The Soviet regime won political power in 1917. It won militarily in the civil war that followed and in the Second World War. It still remains for it to win economically, that is, to achieve under the socialist mode of production as high or higher per capita production of basic commodities and consumers' goods as is achieved in England or the United States. Hence the motto "to catch up and surpass" has been, and will probably remain for some time to come, one of the main Soviet slogans. The extensive construction program launched in the late twenties had only begun to bear its first fruits when increasingly greater quantities of resources had to be diverted to defense; and the invasion of 1941 reoriented the entire economy to war production. Soviet construction was interrupted, but with the end of hostilities, plans were immediately laid to resume the former trend.

THE POLITICAL ECONOMY OF SOCIALISM . . . One may now restate exactly how the Soviet economy differs from that of other countries. It is a socialist economy, with the means of production owned socially. The laws of political economy operate in the Soviet Union, but not exactly in the same way as elsewhere, and socialism has created new politico-economic premises, or laws. The very existence of state-owned and state-operated industrial production is a new economic premise. Collectivized agriculture is another new and different phenomenon. The presence of these two factors makes possible the existence of the third, namely, the planned direction of the national economy.

In the Soviet Union the role of the state is not only quantitatively greater than elsewhere, but also qualitatively different. Production and distribution, capital accumulation and investments are all planned and conducted through the mechanism of the state. The investment of surpluses accumulated by society as a whole is a public function, not a private function. The Soviet economy is not subject to the compulsion of what is known elsewhere as the law of the average rate of profit. Capital can be invested, if larger issues warrant, without immediate expectation of returns and even independently of yield in the distant future.

Since Soviet economy is still one of scarcity, the sum total of goods and services (those that are not free) available for consumption is divided among individual members of society on the basis of socially useful work done by them. Since degrees of skill and productivity vary from person to person, compensation (mostly monetary) is also unequal. The labor theory of value still operates in modified fashion in the USSR, but not as an independently determining factor. The quantity of socially necessary labor-time embodied in a commodity serves as the starting point in cost calculations on the basis of which prices are planned. The final price of goods is determined by the exigencies of the over-all plan.[4] Thus value is a measuring rod in the hands of the planners, but is not the final determining element. In the Soviet economy, moreover, the law of value plays a role in only a limited sphere; since land is not subject to

---

[4] See Chapter XI, "Banking, Money, and Finance."

purchase or sale, the movements of the principal tools of production are determined by plan, and labor power is also not a commodity, as it is elsewhere. Thus the basic determining element is the plan; value is a measuring rod, but the law of value does not operate alone and spontaneously.

Since there are no private owners and all capital accumulation is public and planned, no situation can arise where the supply of goods would exceed the effective monetary demand. In other words, the Soviet economy, if properly planned, cannot have an economic crisis. One of the difficulties has been in just the opposite direction. With a greater expansion of producers' goods industries than of consumers' goods industries, the effective purchasing power of the population constantly exceeds the available supply of consumers' goods. Another difficulty since industrialization began has been the shortage of labor, as already stated. Planned economic activities have developed at a faster rate than the training of new personnel or than the natural growth of the population.

Although the economy is evolving toward its declared goal, a classless society, and although exploitation of man by man has been abolished, the population still consists of two classes and one stratum. That is, there exist two basic socioeconomic groups having different relations to the means of production. However, it is a unique feature of the Soviet economy that these classes do not conflict with each other, but collaborate. There is the working class, in which the workers on Soviet farms are included, operating with plant, tools, and equipment owned by the state. The second class is the peasantry, now predominantly collective farmers, who are cooperative owners of their collective farm property, but who rent most of the machinery they use from the state. The relations to each other and to the tools of production are different in these two cases, hence the two classes. Then come the professional workers, who service the two classes mentioned above. The professional workers are a stratum, but not a class, because they have no independent economic base.

The higher the mechanization of the countryside, the greater the efficiency of agriculture, and the greater the number of those who can leave the country for the city. The growth of industry, in turn, provides more and cheaper goods for the countryside. Thus the interests of the two economic classes, workers and peasants, do not conflict, but supplement each other. The age-old economic conflict between city and country is thus resolved.

Some elements of private production still persist in Soviet society, but they become less significant each year. The collective farm economy still includes a private factor, namely, production by individual collective farmers for their own use or for sale, in addition to what they all produce as a group. This is, however, not a private sector operating alongside of the public economy, as in the days of the NEP, but a private element inside the socialized economy, subordinate to it and dominated by it.

It has been asserted by some that the Soviet economic system is simply an economy with an unusual quantity of government economic activities, and that therefore it is merely a form of "state socialism," not a different system. Others have asserted that in the Soviet Union the government simply replaces private ownership and operates as if it were a private owner—that the result is a form of "state capitalism," not a different system. All available evidence shows that neither of these assertions is true, but that the USSR has an economy qualitatively different from any and all other economies. It is a new and different economic system, a socialist economy.

BIBLIOGRAPHY

GENERAL

Marx, Karl, *Capital,* 3 vols. (Chicago, 1921).

Lenin, V. I., "Karl Marx" in *Collected Works,* vol. XVIII (New York, 1930).

American-Russian Chamber of Commerce, *Economic Handbook of the Soviet Union* (New York, 1931).

Eckardt, Hans von, *Russia* (New York, 1932).

Stalin, Joseph, *Leninism,* 2 vols. (New York, 1933).

Leontiev, A., *Political Economy* (New York, 1935).

American-Russian Chamber of Commerce, *Handbook of the Soviet Union* (New York, 1936).

Lenin, V. I., *Selected Works,* 12 vols. (New York, 1935–1938).

Vyshinsky, A. Y., ed., *Sovetskoe gosudarstvennoe pravo* (Moscow, 1938).

Webb, Sidney and Beatrice, *Soviet Communism: A New Civilization,* 2d ed., 2 vols. (New York, 1938).

Mikhailov, Nicholas, *Land of the Soviets* (New York, 1939).

Arutinian, A. A., and Markus, B. L., eds., *Razvitie sovetskoi ekonomiki* (Moscow, 1940).

Granovsky, E. L., and Markus, B. L., eds., *Ekonomika sotsialisticheskoi promysh-lennosti* (Moscow, 1940).
"Statistics on the Soviet Union," *American Review on the Soviet Union*, No. 2 (June, 1941), vol. IV.
Stalin, Joseph, *Leninism: Selected Writings* (New York, 1942).
The Constitution of the USSR, pamphlet (New York, 1943).
Political Economy in the Soviet Union, pamphlet (New York, 1944).

PREREVOLUTIONARY RUSSIA

The Industries of Russia, prepared for the World's Columbia Exposition in Chicago, 5 vols. (St. Petersburg, 1893).
Olgin, M. J., *The Soul of the Russian Revolution* (New York, 1917).
Mavor, James, *Economic History of Russia*, new ed., 2 vols. (New York, 1923).
Zagorsky, S. O., *State Control of Industry in Russia During the War* (New Haven, 1928).
Antsiferov, A. N., and others, *Russian Agriculture During the War: Rural Economy* (New Haven, 1930).
Robinson, G. T., *Rural Russia Under the Old Regime* (New York, 1932).
Rashin, A. G., *Formirovanie promyshlennogo proletariata v Rossii* (Moscow, 1940).
Lenin, V. I., "Razvitie kapitalizma v Rossii," in *Sochineniia*, 4th ed., vol. III (Moscow, 1941), (excerpts in English in *Selected Works*, vol. 1).

SOVIET RUSSIA, FIRST DECADE

Heller, A. A., *The Industrial Revival in Soviet Russia* (New York, 1922).
Ten Years of Soviet Power in Figures (Moscow, 1927).
Soviet Union Year-Book (London, 1927).
Nearing, Scott, and Harding, Jack, *The Economic Organization of the Soviet Union* (New York, 1927–1928).
Dobb, Maurice, *Russian Economic Development Since the Revolution* (New York, 1928).
Burns, Emile, *Russia's Productive System* (New York, 1931).

THE FIVE-YEAR PLANS

Chamberlin, W. H., *The Soviet Planned Economic Order* (Boston, 1931).
Hoover, Calvin, *Economic Life of Soviet Russia* (New York, 1931).
Social Economic Planning in the USSR, report of the Delegation of the USSR to the World Economic Congress in Amsterdam, 1931.
State Planning Commission of the USSR, *The Second Five-Year Plan* (New York, 1935).
Summary of the Fulfilment of the First Five-Year Plan, 2d ed. (New York, 1935).
Socialist Construction in the USSR (Moscow, 1936).
Sotsialisticheskoe stroitelstvo SSSR (Moscow, 1934, 1935, 1936).
The Land of Socialism Today and Tomorrow, reports and speeches (Moscow, 1939).
Second Five-Year Plan, statistical summary, in *Planovoe khoziaistvo*, No. 5 (1939).
Sotsialisticheskoe stroitelstvo Soiuza SSR (1933–1938. gg) (Moscow, 1939).

SSSR i kapitalisticheskie strany (Moscow, 1939).

Varga, Eugene, *Two Systems* (New York, 1939).

Kazakévich, V. D., "Contrasting Two Economic Systems," *Science & Society*, No. 1 (Winter, 1941), vol. V.

——, "The Economic Strength of the Soviet Union," *Science & Society*, No. 4 (Fall, 1941), vol. V.

Voznesensky, N., *The Growing Prosperity of the Soviet Union*, pamphlet (New York, 1941).

Leontyev, A., *Work Under Socialism and Capitalism*, pamphlet (New York, 1942).

Ropes, E. C., "Soviet Industries in the Urals," *Foreign Commerce Weekly*, May 23, 1942.

Dobb, Maurice, *Soviet Economy and the War* (New York, 1943).

——, *Soviet Planning and Labor in Peace and War* (New York, 1943).

SOVIET AGRICULTURE

Selskoe khoziaistvo SSSR (Moscow, 1936).

"Sotsialisticheskoe selskoe khoziaistvo Soiuza SSR," *Planovoe khoziaistvo*, no. 7 (1939).

Sovetskoe krestianstvo (Moscow, 1939).

Rochester, Anna, *Lenin on the Agrarian Question* (New York, 1942).

Laptev, I., "Collective Farm Income and Differential Rent," *American Review on the Soviet Union*, No. 3 (May, 1943), vol. VI.

Batyzev, V. M., and Sitnin, V. K., *Finansovaia e Kreditnaia Sistema SSSR* (Moscow, 1945).

CHAPTER XI

Banking, Money, and Finance

By VLADIMIR D. KAZAKÉVICH

B ANKING, money, and finance are not as a rule an independent economic development; they are an institutional structure serving a general economic setup and usually reflecting its basic characteristics. This was true of Russia before the revolution and it is true of the Soviet Union. Since the economic system of the USSR is quite unlike that of other countries,[1] the financial system there also differs considerably from financial arrangements in other states.

In Russia banking is not a new thing. Two state-owned banks were opened in 1754, one for the landed nobility, the other for commerce. The state-owned central bank of Russia was founded in 1860. In 1864 the first private joint-stock bank got under way. By January 1, 1914, there existed 47 private commercial banks with 743 branches. There were also state-owned savings banks (over 8,000 in 1912), co-operative banks, and mutual credit societies. Russian banking in the days of the empire was marked by a rather greater participation of the state than in other countries and by a large influx of foreign capital. On December 13, 1917, following the October Revolution, banking was nationalized. The great currency inflation that developed during the years of civil war wiped out all monetary values. In the early 1920's the Soviet regime had to make a new financial start.

A new state bank (Gosbank) was organized in 1921. Several other banking institutions soon appeared. The capital was subscribed either

---

[1] See Chapter X, "The Economic System."

by the state or by state-owned institutions. Some of the new institutions served regions; others specialized in particular types of financing. None of them was privately owned, but the new institutional structure outwardly resembled the old prerevolutionary setup. Methods of financing were similar, also. The publicly owned banks extended credit, discounted bills, dealt in all types of credit documents. Ownership of the banking mechanism was now in different hands, but old financial techniques persisted, and the staffs of the new banks included many individuals with previous bank experience. The big change in Soviet banking came at the end of the reconstruction period with the launching of the First Five-Year Plan. The banking and credit reforms of 1930–1932 created a new type of banking mechanism designed to service a socialist economy.

A reshuffling of the institutional structure resulted in the following setup. The state bank of the USSR (Gosbank) remains the central bank. This is both a bankers' bank and a short-term credit institution, with several regional head offices and over 3,000 branches. Credit for longer terms is handled by four institutions: a bank for capital construction of industry and electrification (Prombank), a bank to finance agriculture (Selkhozbank), a bank for financing co-operative societies (Vsekobank), and a bank for financing municipal construction (Tsekombank). All these institutions operate branches and agencies. There were also over 41,000 savings banks in 1941. Thus in the 1930's the Soviet Union segregated financial functions into separate institutions, reducing the likelihood of intermingling short-term and long-term obligations and the consequent danger of freezing bank portfolios. It must be remembered, of course, that all these institutions are publicly owned; the USSR has no privately owned banking institutions.

Mortgage banking as such does not exist in the USSR. Where there is no private ownership of land, urban or rural, there can be no land mortgages. Since all industry is publicly owned, there is no long-term bonded indebtedness, outside of government bonds sold to individuals and institutions. Agricultural financing takes the shape of short-term and intermediate credit. Capital formation in the Soviet Union is a state budgetary problem. Funds out of the state budget are invested in publicly owned industry, and from most industries funds flow back into the public treasury. Neither industry nor agriculture has any outstanding bonded indebtedness, and in industry there are, of course, no private stockholders.

Because of the credit reforms of the early 1930's, the methods of extending credit also differ from earlier methods and from those prevailing elsewhere. In most countries banks usually finance sellers of goods. The seller receives in payment for his goods the buyer's note, or promise to pay, and discounts it with his bank. In the Soviet Union it is the buyer who obtains credit from the bank, paying the seller at once either in cash or through a deposit transfer on the books of the bank. This practice of Soviet finance eliminates not only the credit document, but also the flow of such documents between banks and other institutions. What is known in the United States as the money market thus disappears. This change was introduced over the protest of rightist oppositionists, who did not want to see the financial apparatus entirely subordinated to planning.

The criteria for lending, as applied by Soviet banks, are not only the traditional maxims of credit analysis, but also the *plan,* which is the primary credit test. The borrowing enterprise operates in accordance with a *plan;* the first question the banker has to decide is whether or not the client is warranted to borrow within the terms of his *plan,* that is, in the light of the client's record and prospects in the fulfillment or nonfulfillment of his *plan.* The second question has to do with the banker's own financial plan: to what extent does a requested loan fit in with the banker's planning assignments? "No plan, no credit" seems to be the motto of Soviet finance. This basic characteristic of Soviet finance distinguishes it from all other types of finance. Its implications go beyond the issue of government versus private ownership of banking facilities and beyond issues related to the extent of government regulation or participation. It is a qualitative feature peculiar to a socialist economy. Soviet planning is not merely economic; it is social and economic. The point of departure in economic operations is the notion of planned costs and not the idea of private profit. In other words, the motivation of a Soviet bank in extending credit might be one that could exist only in an economy based on public ownership of the means of production with corresponding social objectives. The state uses its banking and credit institutions as a mechanism for the extension, withholding, and allocation of credit; thus directing with its financial rudder the fulfillment of the plan in production and distribution. This is referred to in the USSR as "control by the ruble." Paradoxical as it may seem, the immediate necessity for sound banking is greater in the Soviet Union, a socialist country, than anywhere else in the world.

Prices of commodities do not play the same determining role in the USSR as elsewhere. The price of an article in the Soviet Union is the result of planned costs (raw material, labor, overhead), to which may be added, also according to plan, such elements as a planned surplus and a turnover tax. The price of the article is thus the final result of a planned process. It is feasible, if deemed socially desirable, to sell goods below cost of production, making up the "loss" from the budget. Goods may be sold at cost, when they could easily have yielded a "profit" for the state. Still other articles may be sold at what would seem an "exorbitant profit" for the state. The criterion is always the long-range social and economic plan. Late in 1944, for instance, prices of consumers' goods were lowered in Moscow as a preholiday bonus to consumers. Prices are thus devices to record transactions and regulate consumption, but not an independent and determining factor, as in the rest of the world.

Since prices are expressed in money and all financial institutions deal in money units, the next problem to consider is money. The monetary unit in the Russian Empire was the ruble; the coins were mostly silver and copper. In 1769, under Catherine II, the first paper money, the assignat, was issued by the state. It soon depreciated, and by 1810 one silver ruble was worth four assignat rubles. A fixed rate between silver and paper was established in 1839 (3.5 assignat rubles to one silver ruble) and the assignats were withdrawn. New paper money ("credit notes") was issued, but it in turn depreciated as a result of the Crimean War (1853–1856). Not until 1897 did Russia adopt the gold standard and with it a stable currency. The gold ruble contained 11.94792 grains of fine gold. During the first World War the inflationary spiral began once more. By October, 1917, currency in circulation equaled 12.01 (with July 1, 1914, as 1), and retail prices stood at 10.20 (with 1913 as 1). The civil war that began in 1918 accelerated the process of inflation. By the second half of 1921 one gold ruble exchanged for 11,300 paper tokens, and the price level equaled 48,758 (with 1913 as 1). The hyperinflation finally wiped out completely all old values expressed in money. Stabilization on a new level was achieved in 1924 on the basis of a new unit, the *chervonets*, containing 119.4792 grains of fine gold, or equaling ten gold rubles. The old ruble was thus in a sense re-established, despite the protest of leftist oppositionists, who objected to having any monetary unit whatever. The functions of the new ruble represented a considerable departure from previous monetary practice.

As elsewhere, currency in the USSR is a medium of exchange—goods and services are exchanged for rubles. As elsewhere, money is the standard of deferred payments—contractual obligations involving payments and a time element are expressed in terms of money, or in rubles. As elsewhere, money is used for bank reserves. Certain differences, however, must be noted. Reserves of the state bank of the USSR (Gosbank) consist not only of money and gold but also of silver and platinum; that is, they are on a broader basis than the monometallic principle of most other central banks. When one considers money as a standard of value, one finds another important difference. Values are formed in the process of planned production, the monetary expression of these values does not arise independently in the market, but is itself a planned phenomenon. Soviet money, the ruble or *chervonets,* is primarily a unit of account and not an independent automatic standard of value, as is metallic commodity money elsewhere.

Soviet money in circulation is related to the turnover of goods and services within the country. It is a planned and managed currency for internal use only; it neither circulates nor is quoted abroad. The purchase rate of rubles in terms of foreign currencies is purely arbitrary and has remained unchanged since the mid-1930's. This rate has no connection with the relationship between price levels in the USSR and those in any other country. Abroad, the USSR deals in foreign currencies obtained through the sale of its goods. Although the USSR keeps a reserve of gold and other precious metals, it does not redeem its money in specie. Since the Nazi regime, a new manifestation of the fascist phenomenon, arose in Germany, no figures on the gold reserve of the Soviet Union have been published. As the second largest gold-mining country in the world, after British South Africa, the USSR must have accumulated a considerable gold reserve. Some guesses place it as high as five billion dollars. The Soviet Union preserves the forms of a metallic money base, probably because the rest of the world adheres to gold; it accumulates a gold reserve, probably because one can always pay for goods with gold in any part of the world; but at the same time its currency system is a managed money system, divorced as completely as possible from price levels or monetary changes anywhere outside its borders. Because all foreign trade has been a state monopoly since April, 1918, the entire inflow and outflow are planned and go through one agency. There are no foreign investments in the USSR, and there is no Soviet bonded indebtedness outstanding abroad. The problem of foreign exchange, in the usual sense of the term, is nonexistent, as both the visible and invisible balance of international payments is but an outgrowth of the planned operations of the monopoly of foreign trade. Prewar Soviet financial dealings abroad did not involve the internal currency at all. They were subordinate to the necessities of trade; they were a means of serving an end, but not of formulating that end. In all these respects Soviet money is unique among the currencies of the world.

Before the revolution Russia was a debtor country. The services of the external debt were met through grain exports. The inflow of foreign capital into Russia, particularly for railroad construction, was heavy and increased greatly after 1900. From 1900 to the outbreak of the First World War approximately two billion dollars of foreign capital became domiciled in Russia. During the First World War the Russian government became heavily indebted to its allies. The state budget, balanced previously through revenue from the liquor (vodka) monopoly, suffered severely from the introduction of prohibition in 1914. Even before the overthrow of the czar (March, 1917), the internal budgetary situation of the Russian state was most unsound, and the external indebtedness grew so vast that it is hard to see how Russia could have met it. All government indebtedness of the old regime was invalidated by the October Revolution; enterprises owned by foreigners were nationalized with the rest of industry, and equities owned by foreigners and expressed in the old ruble were obliterated by inflation. Financially the Soviet regime started, in a sense, with a clean slate.

Soviet state budgets include the budgets of all publicly owned enterprises, that is, industry, mining, transportation, etc. From the expenditure side of the budget, funds flow back into production. Investment, or capital formation, is a public function, not a private one. Before the First Five-Year Plan, capital investments from the state budget amounted to 26.5 billion rubles. Under the First Five-Year Plan (1928–1932) investments rose to 51 billion and under the Second Five-Year Plan (1933–

1937) to 115 billion; for the Third Five-Year Plan (1938–1942) they were expected to reach 181 billion. In 1940 investments equaled 38 billion rubles, and in 1941 they were to be 57 billion. For 1944 the budget envisaged a capital investment of 20.8 billion rubles, in addition to 16.0 billion to be spent on rehabilitation of liberated areas. During the Second World War military expenditures were of course very high. The 1941 budget envisaged an expenditure of 70.9 billion rubles for defense, but actual military expenditures of that year seem to have come to 91.5 billion. The defense item began to increase after the Nazi regime came to power in Germany. In 1934 defense expenditures for the first time exceeded one tenth of the budget. In 1940 defense still cost less than one third of total disbursements, and in the 1941 budgetary estimate, slightly over one third. The invasion came in June, 1941. Actual defense costs for that year were over 40 per cent of all expenses, and in 1943 defense formed close to 60 per cent of all expenses. The 1944 budget estimate allotted approximately 53 per cent of all expenses for defense. Out of a budgetary estimate of 245.6 billion rubles for 1944, defense expenditures were to equal 128.4 billion, but it is worth noting that "social and cultural services" (education, public health, and social services) got the highest figures so far recorded in Soviet budgets, nearly 47 billion rubles, or close to 10 billion more than in 1940.

Budgetary revenue is built up from taxes and through plowing back into the budget revenue from publicly owned enterprise. The turnover tax is the main Soviet tax; it is collected at the source and included in the final price of the commodity. Revenues from state enterprises come next. There is also an individual income tax, increased considerably since 1941. Sales to the public of government bonds of the lottery variety and of interest-yielding bonds to institutions bring in further revenues. It is an interesting fact that the Soviet state budget was balanced throughout the thirties and continued to be balanced in wartime. The war seems to have been financed by the USSR as nearly as possible on a pay-as-you-go basis, through special taxes, drives to reduce production costs (35 billion rubles were thus saved in 1943), mobilization of free resources of enterprise (20 billion in 1943), and even cash gifts to the government (13 billion in 1943). Public loans, the first of which was floated in 1922, continued under the Five-Year plans and as a measure of war finance, but they are resorted to much less than in other states. In the first two and a half years of the Second World War borrowings from the public comprised 38.6 billion rubles, while a special tax yielded 33 billion. By the end of 1944 the internal government indebtedness of the USSR must have amounted to something like 110 billion rubles.

No figures being available on money in circulation, it was impossible to say whether the currency was overexpanded in 1944 or not. The likelihood is that through price control and rationing of all goods, probably more thorough in the USSR than in any other country, monetary inflation was prevented. The Soviet Union may have come out of the war with a very small internal debt, perhaps amounting to less than half its annual budget, with the service charges forming an insignificant percentage of annual expenditures. The pay-as-you-go policy of financing the war undoubtedly worked great hardships, and the devastation in human and material resources brought about by the invasion by Germany and her allies was undoubtedly very great, but financially the Soviet Union seemed to have emerged from the Second World War in a healthier position than most other belligerents.

BIBLIOGRAPHY

Michelson, A. M., Apostol, P. N., and Bernatzky, M. W., *Russian Public Finance During the War* (New Haven, 1928).

Kohn, Stanislas, and Meyendorff, A. F., *The Cost of the War to Russia* (New Haven, 1932).

Reddaway, W. B., *The Russian Financial System* (London, 1935).

Hubbard, L. E., *Soviet Money and Finance* (New York, 1936).

Arnold, Arthur Z., *Banks, Credit and Money in Soviet Russia* (New York, 1937).

Rovinskii, N. N., and others, *Gosudarstvennyi biudzhet Soiuza SSR* (Moscow, 1939).

Arutinian, A. A., and Markus, B. L., eds., *Razvitie sovetskoi ekonomiki* (Moscow, 1940).

Granovsky, E. L., and Markus, B. L., eds., *Ekonomika sotsialisticheskoi promyshlennosti* (Moscow, 1940).

Kazakévich, V. D., "Financing War and Reconstruction," in *The U.S.S.R. in Reconstruction* (New York, 1944).

CHAPTER XII

Agricultural Development

By LAZAR VOLIN

WITH an enormous crop area of about 340 million acres and over half its population engaged in agriculture, the Soviet Union is one of the leading agricultural countries of the world. Although the USSR has been losing its predominantly agrarian character in recent years as a result of a rapid industrial development, nevertheless agriculture has continued to be the backbone of Russian economic life.

The agricultural pattern of a country is shaped by the interaction between the land and its people—between natural environment and social and economic institutions. The two natural factors that most affect agriculture are soil and climate. The Soviet Union is characterized by a great diversity of soils, distributed in rather well-defined geographical zones or belts.[1] Beginning in the extreme north, a great zone of tundra extends southward from the shores of the Arctic, the Barents, and the White seas. South of the tundra lies a belt of forest-tundra soils which, according to Leonid I. Prasolov, Soviet soil authority, constitute about 15 per cent of the total area of the country. Next come the *podzol* and marshy soils of the coniferous forest zone of northern Russia, which account for more than half of the total area of the country. Farther south still are various types of *chernozem* or black soils, which cover much of the wooded steppe and steppe zones of the central and southern European part of the USSR and of southwest Siberia and northern Kazakstan. Beyond these are the soils of the dry steppes, which are much more extensive in the Asiatic than in the European part of the country. These

---

[1] See Chapter II, "Physical Features."

soils merge into the desert types prevalent especially in Soviet Central Asia. Finally, there is distinguished also a group of subtropic soils in the humid subtropics of Transcaucasia (mainly on the eastern coast of the Black Sea). The soil formations of the high mountains of the Caucasus and Asiatic Russia are also separated into a distinct group.

By far the most important of all these soil belts is that of the fertile *chernozem,* or black soils, which form the natural foundation on which Russian agrarian economy has largely developed. This belt comprises roughly three fourths of the total estimated land available for crops, or 371 million acres. In contrast, the much less fertile *podzol,* or "nonblack soil" zone, is more than four times as large, yet has only one fourth as great an estimated acreage available for crops.

So important is the distinction between the two soil belts—the *chernozem* or black, and the *podzol* or nonblack—that it has long served as a basis for a broad, economic, regional division of the country. The black soil belt was often called the producing area and the nonblack soil belt the consuming area; the former was the granary or surplus-producing region of Russia, while in the latter agriculture was of secondary importance.

Nevertheless, with proper use of fertilizer much of the nonblack soil area is well fitted for agricultural production, particularly of flax fiber, potatoes, and various root crops. It is suited also for livestock raising, which would provide the manure necessary to maintain the fertility of the soil. A solid physical basis therefore exists for the expansion northward of Russian agricultural production. Such an expansion became the goal of the Soviet government in the 1930's, when a program was started to "convert the consuming area into a producing area" by developing farming even in the Arctic region.

The climate, in fact, is a smaller obstacle to agricultural production in the more northern regions, and less of a boon in the south, than many people believe. In the northern and north central regions, low temperatures and sometimes excessive moisture hamper agriculture; but in the south and more especially southeast, moisture deficiency hinders production. The subtropical region of Transcaucasia and much of the southwestern Ukraine have ample rainfall and therefore constitute exceptions. In the north temperature deficiency is in some measure compensated by more favorable sunlight conditions during the growing season. It was found possible to grow a number of crops, even in the Arctic region, by planting varieties which mature rapidly. However, the frost-free growing season is rather short even in the south. In Kharkov, for instance, it is 150 days long or only slightly longer than in Duluth, Minnesota. As far south as Krasnodar, North Caucasus, there are 190 days frost free, or about the same as in Omaha, Nebraska. In Moscow, a frost-free season of only 130 days corresponds to that of the northern part of North Dakota.

In a large part of the black soil area farming is carried on under semi-arid conditions of low and variable precipitation. Here harvests are uncertain from year to year because droughts are frequent, and in their wake often came severe famines with many attendant miseries. The Soviet government has given much attention to the drought problem. In 1938 a comprehensive government program was announced for combating drought conditions in the districts of southeastern Russia which had suffered most. This program involved better adaptation of the crop system to the climate and the use of various moisture-conserving practices, including the use of tree shelter belts.

AGRICULTURE BEFORE 1917 . . . In social and economic structure, Russian agriculture until the 1930's followed a pattern of individual, small, peasant farming. Small-scale peasant agriculture predominated even before the revolution of 1917. In that year the peasant farmers owned over 70 per cent of all farm land in European Russia (exclusive of Poland and Finland). This land came to them through allotment and purchase after they were emancipated from serfdom in the 1860's. They also leased in 1917 a considerable proportion of the 30 per cent of farm lands which remained in large estates. Siberia was almost entirely a land of peasant farming.

However, the peasants had to pay a heavy price to landlords, not only for land recently purchased, but also for the holdings allotted at the time of emancipation. Peasant holdings in the more fertile districts of the black soil area, where land was valuable, were often smaller than those cultivated by peasants when, as serfs, they could devote only part of their time to their own farming. Moreover, it was generally the worst and most inconveniently situated land, often lacking pastures or meadows or forests, which had been allotted to peasants. Access to it was sometimes only through land belonging to large estates, and the

244

peasant was forced to enter upon new leases if he wished to avoid fines for trespassing. Rentals were often exorbitant. Thus, new grievances were added to old resentments of the peasants against their former masters. It was a firm traditional belief among Russian peasants that all land belonged to them by right, that they were cheated at the time of emancipation, and that estates should be distributed among those who actually tilled the land.

A cardinal feature of the land tenure system was that the serf, upon emancipation, did not become a full-fledged proprietor of his holding. In most of Russia the land title was vested in a special organization, the mir or rural commune. The mir was responsible not only for allotting the land to its cultivators but also for collecting taxes and redemption payments for the estate owner. The mir allotted land for cultivation to each peasant family, usually according to the number of males in the family, and this land was as a general rule repartitioned either periodically or at irregular intervals. A peasant's holdings, moreover, were not ordinarily a single tract of land, resembling the typical American farm, but a number of separate strips scattered about the whole land area of his commune. Because of this system of repartitional tenure, the Russian peasant did not develop the strong sense of private property that goes with individual stable ownership of land under hereditary tenure. He saw no reason why all the fields in neighboring estates—the land which he or his ancestors had tilled as serfs, and which he now farmed as a renter or as a hired laborer—should not go into the common pool of mir land.

The rapid growth of population in European Russia (over 90 per cent between 1871 and 1914) aggravated this land hunger of the Russian peasant. Industrialization progressed too slowly in Russia to absorb the growing population as in western Europe. The mir system, also, favored large families and tended to preserve ties with the land among city workers. Although emancipation gave an impetus to migration into less densely settled southern and southeastern regions, little was done officially to relieve the pressure of rural overpopulation in the central agricultural districts until almost the end of the century, when the Trans-Siberian Railway was built. Then a large colonization movement into Asiatic Russia was encouraged.

Nothing much was done during the nineteenth century to improve farm techniques among the peasants, though results were excellent when such an effort was seriously made. For example, in the 1890's tame hay and cultivated grasses were introduced into the crop rotation system in north central Russia, particularly in the Moscow province, in order to remedy a great shortage of livestock forage. For the most part, however, the peasant of central Russia followed the "three-field system" of rotating a winter grain (usually rye), a spring grain (oats), and fallow. In the east and south no regular rotation was practiced; land was cropped continuously until its fertility was exhausted, and then permitted to remain idle for many years at a time.

As a result of all these factors the economic difficulties of the Russian peasant increased constantly. Smoldering peasant discontent flared into open revolt after the Russo-Japanese War of 1905, which weakened the Russian autocracy. The government was able to suppress the peasant uprising and embarked in 1906 on a series of sweeping agrarian reforms associated with the name of Prime Minister Peter Arkadevich Stolypin.

Agricultural extension work, rural resettlement, farm credit (especially loans to purchase land which many uneasy estate owners were anxious to sell to the peasants after the events of 1905), consolidation of the scattered mir strips into larger single fields—these and other agricultural reforms received much attention from the government during the years 1906 to 1914. The main objective of the czarist government in all these reforms was to abolish the repartitional mir tenure and to create a class of prosperous individual peasant proprietors. This class would comprise only a minority of the rural population, which the government hoped would stand as a bulwark against any new agrarian revolution with its demand for wholesale expropriation of estate land.

SOVIET AGRICULTURE . . . The overthrow of the monarchy in 1917 brought this policy to an end. A peasant revolt followed, this time successful. The liquidation of the landlord system was sanctioned by early Soviet agrarian legislation. The peasants divided up not only the estates but even the larger peasant holdings. They used for this purpose the traditional repartitional mechanism of the land commune, the mir, which the czarist government tried so hard to destroy during the decade preceding its overthrow.

During the so-called regime of war communism (1918–1921) farm products were forcibly requisitioned, private trade was prohibited, and the first attempts at agricultural collectivization were initiated, but the individualistic character of the small-scale peasant agriculture was substantially strengthened when this policy was abandoned. The New Economic Policy, or NEP, which supplanted war communism, restored the free market for agricultural products, substituted taxes for the requisitioning of crops, and granted farmers considerable freedom of choice regarding land tenure, though land remained legally the property of the state and was not subject to sale or mortgage. However, Soviet legislation now permitted limited leasing of land and the employment of hired labor, which were previously prohibited. Considerable agricultural and general economic recovery followed the introduction of the NEP.

In the late 1920's, Soviet agricultural policy took a more important new turn. Its principal new objective was to liquidate individual peasant agriculture and to develop large-scale, socialist types of farming. The Bolsheviks believed that large-scale production methods would work as well in agriculture as in industry. They had also been in considerable conflict with the peasantry, and the conflict was primarily responsible for the decision to collectivize agriculture. In its aim of rapid industrialization of the country, the government was anxious to obtain at low prices the largest possible supply of grain and other agricultural products for the needs of state industries and the rapidly increasing class of industrial workers, as well as for export.

Government-controlled prices of agricultural products, particularly grain, were held at low levels, and manufactured products were high-priced. Moreover, there were frequent shortages of manufactured products. Under these conditions the peasants, particularly the more prosperous ones, were unwilling to sell their surpluses and frequently even went so far as to curtail production. An intense mutual hostility grew up between the soviets and the more prosperous peasants, the so-called *kulaki.*

The new system of collective agriculture, coupled with the policy of liquidating or uprooting the *kulaki,* had to weather a number of severe shocks. The famine years of 1932–1933, which took a heavy toll of human life, were most critical. Collective agriculture, however, became an integral feature of Soviet planned economy in peace and war.

247

SOVIET FARM UNITS . . . There are three distinct types of Soviet farm units: (1) the collective farm or *kolkhoz* (plural, *kolkhozy*), (2) the state farm or *sovkhoz*, and (3) machine-tractor stations or MTS. By far the most important of these is the *kolkhoz*, which is an association of formerly individual peasant farmers, a sort of producers' co-operative, operating under government control and direction. Only the land, the livestock (with some qualifications discussed below), and the farm machinery are collectivized or pooled together.

In other words, land in the USSR is no longer broken up into individually owned holdings, large and small. Individual holdings in the Soviet Union have been combined into broad areas suited to large-scale, modern, mechanized methods of cultivation and harvesting, and to large irrigation systems where these are necessary. The households which have thus pooled their holdings live in their own dwellings in villages, just as they did before collectivization, each village usually comprising the members of one or more *kolkhozy;* and from these centers the peasants go out every day to work on the farm, which they collectively own and operate with the assistance of, and under the direction of, the government. According to Article 8 of the Soviet Constitution, "The land occupied by collective farms is secured to them for their use free of charge and for an unlimited time, that is, in perpetuity." Each peasant family is entitled, if land is available, to a plot of 0.6 to 1.2 acres and in some regions to 2.5 acres for a kitchen garden.

The basic law governing the organization, function, rights, and obligations of the *kolkhoz* is embraced in a model charter issued in 1935. According to the charter the *kolkhoz* is a self-governing organization. It elects its officers by majority vote and manages its own affairs, within limits set by government plans and regulations. In practice, however, government officials have been in the habit of appointing, dismissing, and transferring officers of the *kolkhozy* at will. The government concerns itself directly with problems of seed and forage supply, timely and efficient sowing and harvesting, proper care of livestock, crop rotation, internal organization of the farm unit, and many others. The acreage to be sown to different crops, and even yields per acre, are dealt with by national plans, which establish the goals for various republics and provinces of the Soviet Union. Local goals are set up by republican and provincial authorities.

248

The state is a partner in collective farming and has the first claim on production. A *kolkhoz* must deliver to the government at low fixed prices a specified quantity of crops and livestock products per unit of land. To these taxes in kind must be added payments in kind to state machine-tractor stations. The government received 26 per cent of the *kolkhozy* bumper grain crop in 1937 and 34 per cent of the smaller 1939 crop. After the obligations to the state are met, seed supplies are assembled for next year's sowing, and other reserves required by law are set up, the remainder is available for distribution, in cash and in kind, by the *kolkhoz* to its members. Distribution is made on a sort of piecework basis, according to the quantity, skill, and quality of the work performed; work is measured in special units called "labor days." The peasants are residual claimants to the income of the *kolkhozy,* and there are distinct variations in the earnings of individuals and families of the same *kolkhoz* as well as among different *kolkhozy* during the same season.

Collective farmers often found it advantageous to work on their little plots and tend their few animals rather than to work in the collective fields, especially if they had the opportunity to sell their produce on the limited private market in a neighboring town. *Kolkhozy* members have a legal right to do so, provided they sell their products at the market and do not use the services of a middleman. In 1937 this personal farming by members of the *kolkhozy* was estimated at over a fifth of the total agricultural production. In 1939 the government decided to curb the extension of this type of farming, which competed with collective farming, by fixing a minimum required time for each member to devote to collective work. Members of collective farms, both men and women, who consistently fall below the minimum, are liable to expulsion and loss of their little plots of land.

From the standpoint of labor management, the members of a collective *kolkhoz* farm were usually divided into so-called brigades, each including several scores of workers under a foreman. A definite area of land to be cultivated or a certain number of livestock to be tended is assigned to each brigade. For crops such as sugar beets, or cotton, which require much intensive labor, a brigade is further subdivided into smaller working units, called *zveno.*

On July 1, 1938, there were altogether 242,400 *kolkhozy.* On them worked 18,847,600 families, or 93.5 per cent of all peasant families.

Membership in the various *kolkhozy* ranged from less than 15 families to over 500; the average for the whole country was 78. The average land area per *kolkhoz* in 1938 was 3,800 acres; it ranged from as low as 830 acres in Moscow province to many thousands of acres in the eastern steppe regions. The average *kolkhoz* planted about 1,200 acres to crops exclusive of individual plots; the range was from less than 400 acres in northern and northwestern European Russia to over 4,000 acres in the middle and lower Volga region. The *kolkhozy* accounted in 1938 for 86 per cent of the total crop area; members' plots totaled 4 per cent. The 1,300,000 individual farming families which still remained in 1938 sowed only 2,200,000 acres, or less than 1 per cent of the total sown area.

The *sovkhoz*, unlike the *kolkhoz*, is a farm entirely owned and operated by the state. There are nearly 4,000 of the state farms in the Soviet Union, and their workers and employees are paid wages just as factory workers are. The first state farms were organized during the early years of the Soviet regime, from estates which the peasants had not already seized. A new impetus to the development of state farming was given by the grain crisis of 1928–1929, when the government encountered great difficulties in collecting grain from the peasants. The government decided then to establish large mechanized state grain farms, primarily on uncultivated land in the drier areas of the Union. Later, during the collectivization campaign, there arose a severe livestock shortage. The government established large-scale state farms to grow livestock. Similar ventures in state farming were made in other branches of agriculture.

The state farms were at first unwieldy and suffered from excessive specialization and from inefficient utilization of tractors and combines. These problems were met during the 1930's through subdivision, transfer of some land to the *kolkhozy*, and emphasis on diversified farming. In 1938 only 9 per cent of the crop area was in state farms.

The mechanization of agriculture made great strides in the USSR. The number of tractors increased from 26,700 at the end of 1928 to 148,500 in 1932 and 483,500 in 1938. While there were practically no combines in 1928, in 1932 there were 14,500, and in 1938, 153,800. The number of trucks on farms increased from less than 1,000 in 1928 to 14,200 in 1932, and 195,800 in 1938. Whereas, at the end of 1932, mechanical power accounted for less than a fourth of the total power resources in Russian agriculture, by the end of 1937 it approached two thirds.

250

Tractors, combines, and other important farm implements are owned, not by the *kolkhozy*, but by the state machine-tractor stations. These supply the necessary machinery and operators to the *kolkhozy* on the basis of annual agreements. For the services of the machine-tractor stations, the state is paid in kind by the *kolkhozy* at specified rates per hectare of the work done; these rates vary with the officially determined crop yields in a district.

The machine-tractor stations usually have repair shops for tractors and combines, and also staffs of mechanics, agronomists, and officials to provide technical assistance and direction of the *kolkhozy*. Tractor drivers are paid by the *kolkhozy* on the basis of "labor days" earned, as are other collective farmers, except that minimum amounts of grain and cash per "labor day" are prescribed by law. Combine operators are paid by the machine-tractor stations.

In 1939 there were nearly 6,500 machine-tractor stations, with over 400,000 tractors and 140,000 combines. Smooth operations of tractors and combines were interfered with by frequent breakdowns and stoppages due to poor care, inefficient repair work, great turnover and inexperience of the operating personnel, and other causes. In 1938, 75 per cent of spring plowing, 72 per cent of fall plowing, 44 per cent of spring sowing, 66 per cent of cotton planting, 95 per cent of sugar-beet planting, 50 per cent of winter sowing, and 45 per cent of the harvesting of grain and legumes were done by the machine-tractor stations for *kolkhozy*.

CROPS . . . Table IV showing the distribution of the Soviet crop area indicates that wheat is the leading crop. Although spring-sown varieties predominate and their acreage increased by 25 per cent between 1928 and 1938, winter (fall-sown) wheat acreage more than doubled during this period. Winter wheat is grown mostly in the south (Ukraine, Crimea, Caucasus, and Central Asia) and spring wheat in the east (lower and middle Volga, western Siberia, and Kazakstan). Next to wheat as an important bread grain is rye, which is almost entirely a winter-grown crop. The rye acreage has been steadily declining and rye is grown primarily in regions where soil and climate are less favorable for wheat. Northern and central European Russia is a typical rye region. Rye is also grown east of the Volga as a hardy winter and drought-resistant crop.

Oats is the important feed grain; its acreage increased despite a large reduction in horses. The area under barley, a highly important export crop before the First World War, declined in the 1920's, but increased in the 1930's. Corn is relatively unimportant.

In general, grain acreage diminished in proportion to other crops as farming became more diversified. Between 1928 and 1938 the actual acreages sown increased in all seven of the important grain crops except rye, but the proportion of the total acreage of these cereals among all crops declined from 79 per cent to 72 per cent. Potatoes, legumes, sugar beets, flax, and cotton all showed increased acreages, and there was also a very large increase in tame hay and other forage crops. The tendency has been toward the intensive cultivation of wheat (especially winter wheat), potatoes, and various industrial crops.

Much effort has been devoted to increasing crop yields. Crops are more carefully chosen for rotation; the fallow is now plowed earlier than formerly; and there has been an increase in fall plowing for spring sowings. There has also been great improvement in seed stocks. In 1938, 67 per cent of the total grain acreage was planted with seed of pure strains. The supply of mineral fertilizers increased from 234,000 metric tons in 1928 to 3,216,000 in 1938. In contrast with these

TABLE IV. CROP AREA 1928 AND 1938, AND PERCENTAGE 1938 IS OF 1928 °

Crop	1928 Million acres	1938 Million acres	Percentage 1938 is of 1928
Winter wheat ...	15.3	36.0	235.3
Spring wheat ...	53.2	66.5	125.0
All wheat	68.5	102.5	149.6
Rye	59.6	52.3	87.8
Oats	42.6	44.2	103.8
Barley	18.0	22.8	126.7
Corn	10.8	6.4	59.3
Millet	14.1	9.7	68.8
Buckwheat	7.2	5.2	72.2
Potatoes	14.0	18.2	130.0
Legumes	2.4	6.2	258.3
Vegetables	5.0	5.0	100.0
Sugar beets	1.9	2.9	152.6
Sunflower seed ..	9.6	7.8	81.2
Castor beans ...	.1	.6	600.0
Flaxseed	.9	.9	100.0
Flax for fiber ...	3.4	4.6	135.3
Hemp	2.3	1.6	69.6
Cotton	2.4	5.1	212.5
Tame hay	5.6	17.7	316.1
Other forage crops	4.0	17.2	430.0
Other crops	6.8	7.5	110.3
All crops	279.2	338.4	121.2

° From *Posevnye Ploshchadi SSSR*, 1939. Office of Foreign Agricultural Relations, United States Department of Agriculture.

improvements, Soviet agriculture, according to numerous official reports, suffered serious harvesting and storage losses. Weeds, the eradication of which requires great effort, have hindered production.

Collectivization encountered its greatest difficulty in the field of animal husbandry. Many of the peasants slaughtered much livestock before they were liquidated as *kulaki* or joined the *kolkhozy*. Poor care and shortage of feedstuffs on the new collective and state farms also contributed at first to a high animal mortality. Horses decreased between 1928 and 1933 by about half and cattle by nearly half. Sheep and goats decreased by two thirds and hogs by more than half. By 1938, however, cattle had increased to nearly 90 per cent of their 1928 number and hog numbers exceeded the 1928 figure by 18 per cent. There were still 30 per cent fewer sheep and goats.

TABLE V. LIVESTOCK NUMBERS, JUNE–JULY 1928, 1933, 1938 *

Kind	June–July		
	1928 Million head	1933 Million head	1938 Million head
Horses	33.5	16.6	17.5
Cattle	70.5	38.4	63.2
Sheep and goats	146.7	50.2	102.5
Hogs	26.0	12.1	30.6

* From *Zhivotnovodstvo SSSR*, 1940. Office of Foreign Agricultural Relations, United States Department of Agriculture.

Except for horses, which were 90 per cent collectivized, most livestock was in 1938 still individually owned by peasants. In 1939 the government laid greater emphasis on building up collectivized herds by requiring the *kolkhozy* to deliver livestock products on the basis of acreage.

To meet the greatly increased need of collectivized and mechanized agriculture for technical and managerial personnel and skilled workers in the Soviet agriculture, large numbers of students were trained in agricultural subjects at various levels. In 1938–1939, there were over 60,000 students in agricultural institutions of the college level, nearly 140,000 in agricultural high schools, and about 600,000 training as agricultural workers in special schools and courses. Graduates from agricultural colleges increased from less than 2,000 during the years 1909–1913 to over 40,000 during the period 1933–1937.

Much attention was given to agricultural research. The number of agricultural experiment stations increased from 44 in 1913 to 303 in 1938, to which must be added 87 agricultural research institutes of various types. The total number of research workers in all these institutions increased from 250 in 1913 to 9,800 in 1938. Agricultural research extended even to the *kolkhozy,* on which there were in 1941 over 12,000 agricultural laboratories.

TABLE VI. LIVESTOCK NUMBERS ON JANUARY 1, 1938, BY TYPES OF FARM AND OWNERSHIP *

Type of farm and ownership	Horses million head	Cattle million head	Sheep and goats million head	Hogs million head
Kolkhozy (communal herds)	12.4	14.8	22.8	6.3
State farms	2.0	3.7	7.0	2.8
Members of *kolkhozy*	0.8	25.1	30.7	12.8
Other individually owned livestock ..	1.0	7.3	6.1	3.8
Total	16.2	50.9	66.6	25.7

* From *Zhivotnovodstvo SSSR,* 1940. Office of Foreign Agricultural Relations, United States Department of Agriculture.

BIBLIOGRAPHY

Tulaikov, N. M., "Agriculture in the Dry Region of the U.S.S.R.," *Economic Geography* (January, 1930), vol. VI.

Robinson, G. T., *Rural Russia Under the Old Regime, a History of the Landlord-Peasant World and a Prologue to the Peasant Revolution of 1917* (New York, 1932).

Timoshenko, P., *Agricultural Russia and the Wheat Problem* (Palo Alto, Calif., 1932).

Ladejinsky, W., "Collectivization of Agriculture in the Soviet Union," *Political Science Quarterly* (March and June, 1934), vol. XLIX.

Volin, Lazar, "Agrarian Collectivism in the Soviet Union," *Journal of Political Economy* (October and December, 1937) vol. XLV.

Ladejinsky, W., "Soviet State Farms," *Political Science Quarterly* (March and June, 1938), vol. LIII.

Michael, L. G., "Cotton Growing in the Soviet Union," *Foreign Agriculture* (August, 1938), vol. II.

Hubbard, L. E., *Soviet Agricultural Economics* (London, 1939).

Michael, L. G., "Soviet Ukraine—Its People and Agriculture," *Foreign Agriculture* (July, 1939), vol. III.

Volin, Lazar, "Peasant Household Under the Mir and the Kolkhoz in Modern Russian History," *Cultural Approach to History,* Caroline F. Ware, ed. (New York, 1940).

——, "Russian Peasant and Serfdom," *Agricultural History* (January, 1943), vol. XVII.

CHAPTER XIII

Industry Under
the Soviet Government

By ERNEST C. ROPES

WHEN the Soviet government nationalized industry and began to operate hundreds of diversified plants and factories through agencies organized for the purpose, it inherited very few manufacturing establishments from the czarist regime. These were limited in kind, and were located in only three or four districts.

Most prerevolutionary factories made textiles, and the textile industry had grown fast. It had started with home spinning and weaving of home-grown flax; then cotton was imported and later it was produced in Russia. Large-scale production was limited to cheap qualities of linen and cotton goods, and to woolen army uniforms. An industry with more varied products was ferrous metallurgy, based in the Ukraine on the tremendous resources of coal and iron in the Donets Basin, and in the Urals on a few deposits of remarkably pure iron ore, which was smelted with wood charcoal. There were also the famous oil industries of the northern and southern Caucasus and of the north Caspian. Forests were distributed all over the Russian Empire, yet Archangel was the only place where lumbering had become an industry. The manganese of the Caucasus and the platinum of the Urals were known all over the world. The fisheries of the Caspian and the Far East had the elements of industrial organization, but had not progressed far.

Almost all these "infant industries" in prerevolutionary Russia were started and managed by foreign investors and directors. The oil wells

255

were Swedish (Nobel), French, and British. Nonferrous metal mines were British. Coal mines in the Donets were Belgian. Though the textile industry was largely Russian, a number of large mills were controlled by the British.

These industries were largely concentrated in European Russia, in or near Petrograd (Leningrad), in Ivanovo-Voznesensk, and in a few cities of the Donets district. Oil and manganese were in the Caucasus; Archangel was a lumber export port; and in the Urals a few mining enterprises, owned by foreign firms, supplemented the small coal and iron production of that area.

On this relatively small industrial foundation, which in no respect supplied the needs of the country, the Soviet government, after several years of revolution and civil war, undertook to erect a modern, diversified industrial economy, sufficient to satisfy all the requirements of the growing population. It was necessary at the same time to construct an adequate transport system, to modernize old cities and build new ones, and to prepare for defense against attack.

The easiest steps were naturally taken first, in districts with ample natural resources, trained manpower, and some previous industrial development. The area that best met all these requirements lay on the Black Sea, between the Dnieper and Don rivers; it later became famous as the Donets Basin. Here were enormous stores of good coking coal, of high-grade iron ore (the Krivoi Rog deposits), and of good manganese ore (at Nikopol). With the avowed object of ending "the technical and economic dependence of the USSR on capitalist countries," and ultimately of providing Soviet citizens with a high standard of living, the government, in the period 1923-1928, devoted its largest budgetary appropriations to the restoration and expansion of industry, not only in the Donets area but also in the Leningrad and Moscow districts. Foreign engineers and technicians were engaged on a contract basis to help introduce the most advanced industrial methods.

During this period the idea of a planned economy was developed and applied in constantly increasing degree. A government planning agency (Gosplan) was formed; its purpose was to plan and co-ordinate the expansion of mining, industry, transportation, and agricultural production throughout the USSR, in accordance with the potentialities and needs of each region. In 1928 the First Five-Year Plan of economic development was adopted, to be followed by two other plans, the third of which was interrupted by the German invasion in 1941.

Soviet reports on the First and Second Five-Year plans give a clear picture of the theory and practice of Soviet economic planning, and of the results attained by this method of estimating and plotting the possible rate and direction of development of the productive forces of the country, including human.

Soviet writers also credit the system of economic planning with the material and psychological preparedness of the country to resist the German attack, to recover from initial enemy successes, and finally to drive out the invaders. Economic planning has also proved its worth in the reconstruction of reoccupied areas, and it will undoubtedly guide the expansion eastward of Soviet industry and agriculture; this is already well advanced and was stimulated during the years of war.

The basis of Soviet planned economy is the immense and still largely undeveloped natural resources of the country. Industry, accordingly, is continuously projected into the future, as these resources are uncovered, charted, evaluated, and, when promising, developed. Building on the investigations of the Academy of Sciences in czarist times, Soviet geological, geophysical, and other scientific exploring parties have continued the search, even during the war, for new subterranean riches worth exploiting, either for local use or for national distribution. As new minerals are found, mines, smelters, and factories are built. Industries have expanded with such remarkable rapidity in the USSR that they bid fair to cover the entire country, in a few years, not only from west to east, but also from south to north, culminating in a series of industrial centers along the Arctic Ocean.

Coal and oil for industrial fuel are the backbone of modern industry, and Soviet industrial engineers first sought to uncover ample reserves of these two mineral products. The coal field of the Donets area was well known before the revolution, but the Soviet government multiplied and modernized the mines and extended the limits of the field underground as far east as Rostov-on-Don. The total estimated coal reserves in the USSR in 1938 were 1,654,000,000,000 metric tons, and the Donets field is the largest field to have been thoroughly explored. Donets anthracite and coking coal is equal to the best in the country, and until the Second World War it was shipped all over the European USSR and abroad.

South of Moscow, around Tula and Kaluga, is another coal field, containing large reserves of lignite, suitable after treatment for fuel, and also a source of chemical by-products. This field has been exploited for many years. No other large deposits have been found in European USSR, though the Ural district is well supplied with coal, and during the 1940's many new mines were sunk and put into operation. The new field in Kazakstan, at Karaganda, was intensively utilized to fuel Ural plants, and coking coal came from the Kuznetsk field farther east. The extent and reserves of the Kuznetsk field have not yet been fully mapped, but they are known to be huge. Other coal deposits are already being exploited for local industry in the Caucasus (Tkvibuli, Tkvarcheli), in Pechora near the Arctic Ocean, in Central Asia at Angrena, Shor-Su, and Kugitai in Uzbekistan, and at several discovered points in Tadzhikistan and Kirghiz. The Far East is well supplied with coal: at Cheremkhovo near Irkutsk, Bureya in Birobidzhan, Sangarkhaya on the Lena River, and Suchan near Vladivostok, known deposits are sufficient for any future industrial development in these districts.

Oil has also been found at many points in the USSR besides the well-known fields at Baku, Maikop, and Grozny in the Caucasus, and at Emba on the Caspian Sea. The oil deposits at Pechora extend northeast to Vorkuta and perhaps farther. Oil has also been discovered southeast of the Ural chain, at Ishimbayevo, and northwest along the Kama and Volga rivers; Soviet geologists class this chain of fields as a "Second Baku." Kirghiz has many producing wells, Uzbekistan has one at Khandak, and Tadzhikistan has one at Nefteabad. On Sakhalin production is steadily growing, and promising traces of oil have been located at several points along the Arctic littoral.

With an ample supply of coal and oil within reasonable hauling distance of present and future industrial consumers, it has not been necessary to utilize the enormous supplies of peat and oil shale which stretch from west to east across European USSR, from the Estonian Republic to the northern Urals, or the huge supplies of natural gas in several oil-fields; these have been exploited only on a small scale for the production of electric power. What is imperative for modern industry, however, is an ample supply of iron, coupled with large quantities of manganese, chromium, and other alloy metals, and of copper, lead, zinc, tin, nickel, and several other non-ferrous metals.

The Krivoi Rog mine in the Ukraine, with other known reserves at Kursk and Kerch, was sufficient to supply a tremendous expansion of ferrous metallurgy in the Donets and Crimean areas. In the Urals, also, old iron mines have been reopened, modernized, and greatly expanded in output. Perhaps the most important act of the Second Five-Year Plan was to start exploiting the vast deposits of magnetite at Magnitogorsk in the southern Urals; the use of these deposits increased greatly during the Second World War. Not far from the Kuznetsk coalfield much iron was found in the Gornaya Shoriya Mountains, and also near Minusinsk and Biisk. Two other deposits were discovered near Irkutsk, another one south of Ulan Ude, and several smaller ones in the Far East. Still others will probably be discovered as this area develops.

Manganese is mined near Krivoi Rog, at Nikopol, but the highest grade ore is found at Chyaturi in the Caucasus. Other deposits were located before 1941 at Marsyatsk, and at Dzhezdin in Kazakstan. These amply supplied the Ural and eastern steel mills when Nikopol and Chyaturi were unavailable because of the German occupation.

Russia and the whole USSR is rich in copper, but the amount mined has never covered the demand and imports have always been necessary. The Gosplan has discovered many new deposits, however, and wartime production exceeded all previous records. The old mines in the Urals, at Krasnouralsk, Kirovgrad, Revda, Pyshma, and at other points expanded production, and the new smelter at Balkhash, drawing on Kounrad and Dzhezkasgan ores, is the largest in the USSR. Additional mines in the Caucasus, the Buryat-Mongol Republic, and in Central Asia, at Almalyk and elsewhere, have added to the total production.

Of chromites, like manganese important as ferroalloy metals, the USSR has an abundance, chiefly in the Urals. But of tungsten and molybdenum, also alloy metals, many deposits are still unexploited, and imports have always been required. It is the same with nickel, though mines at Monchegorsk (Kola Peninsula), Ufalei, Khalilovo (Urals), and Norilsk, when they reach full production, may meet all demands.

The USSR has an abundance of zinc and lead in the Urals and eastward. Little tin has been produced so far, although rich deposits in the

Far East are reported, which will add to the small output of the mines at Olovyannaya and Khapcheranga, near Chita. Other useful metals, such as mercury, antimony, vanadium, tantalum, niobium, platinum, iridium, and gold and silver, are to be found in quantities which may ultimately permit export.

The USSR has large reserves of many other minerals, some of which are now produced in quantity. There are literally mountains of apatite and nepheline at Kirov on the Kola Peninsula north of Leningrad, and great phosphate deposits at Karatau in Kazakstan. From the latter are made phosphate fertilizers and other chemical products. The largest potash deposit in the world is at Solikamsk in the northern Urals, where carnallite and sylvinite are measured in billions of tons. There is a salt deposit at Usolye. The northern Urals also have large reserves of high-grade bauxite and asbestos, both necessary for modern industrial production. Other minerals found in quantity in several districts are magnesite, sulphur, fluorspar, corundum, graphite, and mica, all of which have many uses in modern industry.

The Soviet Union has stores of every variety of building materials. There are many kinds of rock, including limestone for cement; clays, with fireclays prominent; gypsum; and of course many varieties of sand for concrete, glass, and many other purposes. As for timber, the largest forest stands in the world are distributed over the entire country; only a few steppes, the Central Asiatic deserts, and the area north of the Polar circle are treeless.

An important natural resource is water power, in which this huge country, with its many rivers, is reported to be richer than any other. Only a fraction of the horsepower available has been utilized, and that since the revolution. The first hydroelectric installation was on the Volkhov River near Leningrad; it was later supplemented by two dams and stations on the Svir River. Two other stations have been built on the Arctic river Niva on the Kola Peninsula. A number of stations provide power to industries and agriculture in the Caucasus from the Rion, Kura, Zanga, and other smaller rivers. Finally, several rivers in Central Asia, the Chirchik, Irtysh, Chu, and Syr Darya, and some of the irrigation canals in that area, have been harnessed.

Two hydroelectric enterprises, however, dwarf all others in the USSR; the first, on the Dnieper River in the Ukraine, was completed in 1932. It had a capacity of 850,000 kilowatts and provided power for many new industrial cities in the vicinity. It was destroyed by the Germans but in 1945 was being restored. The second was still uncompleted. It involves harnessing the great Volga River and making its waters available for power, navigation, and irrigation, from far upstream to the mouth at Astrakhan. The first dam, at Rybinsk, was barely completed when the Second World War stopped work there. The plan, however, calls for resumption and completion of the project as early as possible. Many other hydroelectric stations in various parts of the country are also planned.

The list of natural resources would not be complete without mentioning many agricultural products for which Russia has long been famed. Foremost is grain, many varieties of which are raised for food and feed in practically every region, including the Far North. The so-called technical plants, however, have more industrial importance. These include textile fibers, such as cotton, flax, hemp, kenaf, kendyr, and ramie; and also various oil-seed plants, such as sunflower, hemp, flax, rape, poppy, and soybeans. The latest additions to the list of technical plants are the natural rubber-bearing plants *kok-sagyz* and *tau-sagyz,* and Eucommia and guayule, which have already been acclimated and planted over large areas.

It is evident that the Soviet Union has all the resources necessary to develop a modern industrial state. These are distributed in many regions, and the known reserves of materials are sufficient to supply hundreds of large plants for an indefinite time. Soviet planners at first envisaged a few giant industrial cities, producing a great variety of products, but this policy was later replaced by one of decentralization. Accordingly, after the first period of reconstruction there was a shift eastward in federal budgetary investment, from the European USSR to the Urals and points east of that range, where materials were locally available for basic ferrous metallurgy, the foundation of all other industry. Even before 1941 a whole series of industrial towns and districts had grown up in the east. Each new site was chosen according to local metal or mineral reserves. During 1941–1944 this process was accelerated by the necessity of supplying growing armies with larger quantities of war goods. It is only now becoming clear how rapidly the Ural district was transformed to a point where it could replace the factories and mines

261

temporarily lost to the Germans. Many facts about the expansion of war manufacturing east of the Urals, along the Trans-Siberian Railroad to the Pacific, and throughout the Central Asiatic republics, have not yet been disclosed. Enough is known, however, to enable one to list by general districts the many kinds of industry that have been established. These, of course, concentrated at first on war products, but after the war they will contribute to the needs of the growing population of the USSR.

FERROUS METALLURGY . . . All coincidences in the USSR of coal and iron deposits in close proximity, considered ready for exploitation, are utilized to produce iron and steel semifinished or finished goods. The largest district of this kind in European USSR is in the southern Ukraine. Here, before the German invasion, thousands of different products were turned out. The region was equipped not only with hundreds of modern-ized, mechanical coal mines, but also with blast furnaces, open-hearth furnaces, and electric furnaces, which turned out over half the total Soviet output of iron and steel. By the use of the manganese of Nikopol, ferromanganese was produced. A number of other ferroalloys and special steels were made in furnaces drawing on Dnieper hydroelectric power and on power produced in numerous large coal-fueled stations. The latest blast furnace blown in, at Kerch, produced ferrovanadium from ores naturally rich in vanadium.

A list of the ferrous products turned out in great industrial cities of the Ukraine would run into thousands, but a few may be named: rolled products of all kinds; pipe and wire; locomotives and railroad cars; farm tractors, lathes, and machine tools of many types; electrical machinery; agricultural machinery in great variety; large turbogenerators, steam and water; and airplanes. Undoubtedly many forms of munitions were also manufactured, though no information on this subject is available.

When the German invasion forced the evacuation of the Ukraine, all the machinery that could be moved was transferred to the Ural district, and production was multiplied in the many industrial cities there. Old coal and iron mines were expanded, new plants and furnaces were built, and the manufacture of war material was rapidly increased, until in 1943 it was estimated to equal in value and quantity all produced in 1940 in the USSR. Since then with the added production of the eastern metallurgical centers, the output of goods has exceeded previous records, though the turnout of steel has dropped as a whole. New centers of iron and steel production have greatly increased their production, notably in the Kuznetsk Basin district and at Magnitogorsk in the southern Urals. In the former district new plants have been erected at Stalinsk and other cities; at Magnitogorsk large iron and steel castings, rolled shapes, sheets and rails, and many other products are turned out in large quantities. Other products of Ural industrial cities are steel railroad cars, tractors, river ships, internal combustion motors, and many forms of war material, including tanks, guns, and shells. Important cities are Sverdlovsk, Chelyabinsk, Novo-Tagil, and Molotov. The many iron and steel plants at Sverdlovsk manufacture all the kinds of products made in the famous Krupp works in Germany. At Petrovsk-Zabaikalsk and Komsomolsk east of Kuznetsk are steel mills, but few details are known of their output. Ulan-Ude has a large new locomotive and car building plant, Komsomolsk a steel mill and shipbuilding yards, Khabarovsk a new steel plant, and Vladivostok a rolling mill. It is a well-known fact that the Soviet government has long been strengthening its Far Eastern industry in anticipation of war in the East, though details of this particular development have not been disclosed.

NONFERROUS METALLURGY . . . The deposits of the various nonferrous metals in the USSR are so numerous and scattered that only a few cities have grown up around mines, and few industrial plants are concentrated near smelters. There are exceptions, however. The Nikopol manganese mine is part of the Donets industrial district, and several copper and zinc mines have been developed in the Urals (Krasnouralsk and Kirovgrad for copper, Chelyabinsk for zinc). A great bauxite mine explains the concentration of wartime aluminum manufacture at Kamensk in the Urals; much machinery was taken there from the Dnieper dam cities, and production now exceeds any prewar figure for the country. The numerous plane factories evacuated eastward in 1941 consume all production of this metal. The town of Balkhash, on Balkhash Lake in Kazakstan, was built there because of copper. Several other smelters exist in the Urals, at Kyshtym, Revda, and elsewhere.

THE CHEMICAL INDUSTRY . . . Soviet planners early saw the need to develop a chemical industry based on native raw materials, and early Soviet exploration uncovered great stores of materials, needing only recovery and treatment to become hundreds of products useful to

263

industry and agriculture. The results, as listed in the Third Five-Year Plan for the chemical industry, show that the USSR has already become an exporter of chemicals instead of an importer, though the expansion in this field, in terms of future possibilities, seems hardly to have started. The table below shows the progress made in a few important items of chemical manufacture:

Product	1913	1927–28	1932	1937
Soda ash (1,000 metric tons)	161.0	180.0	288.3	529.0
Superphosphate (1,000 metric tons)	63.0	154.9	614.0	1432.0
Apatite concentrates (1,000 metric tons)	...	....	156.5	1157.6
Potash fertilizers (1,000 metric tons)	...	....	78.5	1585.0
Plastics (1,000 metric tons)	...	0.3	3.5	13.8

In accordance with the Soviet custom, when possible, of erecting "combinats," a series of interrelated plants to include all stages of manufacture, new cities and plants have grown up near large deposits or sources of materials. Thus, the town of Kirov was built near the phosphate mountain at Khibiny, and plants have been erected to treat the rich ores mined there for superphosphate and other products. A second chemical town is Solikamsk, which works up potash salts; a third in the vicinity is Usolye, using the old salt deposits. Sulphur production, formerly drawing only on the pyrites roasters in the Urals, has been increased by the output of the large sulphur deposits in the Kara Kum Desert and elsewhere. Nitrates are produced in the northern Urals and at Chirchik. Soda and other salts are turned out from evaporated Caspian waters at Kara Bogaz-Gol. A field of production with possibilities for wide expansion has been found in the recovery of coke-oven fumes, from which a whole gamut of coaltar products can be fashioned; petroleum wastes are also used increasingly for by-products. Beginning with the Donets Basin, coke-chemical plants have spread to all coal fields except those in the Far East, while plants have also been erected in connection with the gasification of coal at Gorlovka and elsewhere. A very modern development has been the construction of several plants to turn coal into gasoline and other oil fuels, at points distant from oil fields but rich in solid fuel.

The Soviet chemical industry includes paint and varnish, rubber, plastics, matches, and many other products in which chemical processes dominate production. Progress in all of these was rapid before the war, and was intensified during the war. Chemical institutes work in close contact with the industry and are constantly engaged in devising new processes or improving old. Particular success was attained in the manufacture of synthetic rubber, at Yaroslavl and elsewhere, and in the production of fertilizers, sulphur, and soda products. Plastics and artificial fibers are scheduled for postwar expansion, as is the dyestuffs industry.

Soviet large-scale industry manufactures too many products even to list here, but the subjoined tables cover the principal branches and give figures denoting the progress made since the revolution. Of particular importance is the machine-building industry, on which great emphasis was placed in peacetime. Conversion to war production was rapid in this industry, although many entire plants had to be moved eastward, to towns in the Urals and beyond. A separate table lists many products never before produced in Russia, but now the daily output of hundreds of mills. Figures are also given for the production of fuels and some metals, and of important consumers' goods. Though published statistics stop with 1938, the figures indicate progress up to that year and suggest lines of manufacture undoubtedly expanded during the war. The location of many mills and plants is not fully known, but they are doubtless in old and new cities in the Urals, and in eastern and southern Asia, where there are vast stocks of raw materials. Thus, steel and rolling mill production at Kuznetsk and in the Far East has been raised far above previous records; textile mills have been built in the cotton belt of Central Asia; Kazakstan has been intensively industrialized and the process is continuing, with new steel mills being constructed at Karaganda and fertilizer plants in the south; a new tractor plant at Rubtsovsk has started operation.

New oil fields in Kirghiz send trains of tank cars north to refineries. Along the Trans-Siberian railroad every city has become a beehive of new industry. Among many new plants and mills are the first locomotive plant, the first packing houses, and the first beet-sugar mills to be built in Asia. It is safe to predict that this eastward march of industry, of which only a few high points can be mentioned, will continue for many years after the war; as industry grows, there will undoubtedly be a great growth in population both by natural increase and colonization. Many scholars believe that Soviet Asia will become a great center of human population and industry.

It remains to mention what has been accomplished in the region north of the Arctic Circle, where low temperatures and long winters had always discouraged explorations and settlement. In developing the Kara Sea shipping route, a search was made for coal, which was found at a number of points along the Arctic coast; further investigation discovered fluorspar, salt, nickel, and other valuable minerals, and unestimated quantities of gold. As a result industrial construction has already begun. At two points it has made rapid strides: at Norilsk, east of the Yenisei River, where a "nickel town" has risen in the barren tundra, and along the Kolyma River. Here gold mining is several years old, and the recovery of gold and other metals has stimulated considerable town building, though the details are not yet known. The Kara Sea route is now a safe water highway; ships are protected by radio and weather stations and are convoyed by icebreakers. On shore are ample bunkering facilities of local fuel, while cargoes of valuable ores will soon supplement the lumber vessels which have for fifteen years regularly visited the mouths of the Ob, Yenisei, and Lena rivers.

In this outline of the growth and expansion of Soviet industry, emphasis has been laid on branches which make producers' goods and transport material. The ultimate value of an industrial machine lies, of course, in its ability to supply the population of a country with adequate consumption goods, and with machines that increase the supply of foodstuffs. The second section of Table VII gives figures for agricultural machine output that indicate advances in this field since the revolution. The third section covers consumers' goods, in which progress has been even more startling: only one of the sixteen classifications listed here was even represented in 1913; since 1921 factories have sprung up all over the country, and many articles are produced in the millions.

Yet the production even of basic materials in 1938 was far short of the needs of the growing population, and in most of the important indexes of industrial production the USSR stood below all other industrial countries in per capita output. During the war all manufacturing facilities

TABLE VII. PRODUCTION OF CHIEF BRANCHES OF SOVIET INDUSTRY

Kind	Unit of Measure	1913	1929	1933	1938 (prelim.)
Electric power	Million kw.-hr.	1,945	6,224	16,357	39,600
Coal	Mill. met. tons	29.1	40.1	76.3	132.9
Petroleum and gas	Mill. met. tons	9.2	13.8	22.5	32.2
Peat	Mill. met. tons	1.7	6.9	13.8	26.5
Iron ore	Mill. met. tons	9.2	8.0	14.5	26.5
Manganese ore	Thous. M. tons	1,245.3	1,409.2	1,021.3	2,272.8
Pig iron	Mill. met. tons	4.2	4.0	7.1	14.6
Steel	Mill. met. tons	4.2	4.9	6.9	18.0
Rolling mill products	Mill. met. tons	3.5	3.9	5.1	13.3
Chemical products	Million rubles	450	619	2,283	6,715
Cement	Thous. M. tons	1,520	2,232	2,710	5,696
Paper	Thous. M. tons	197.0	384.9	506.1	834.1
Cotton textiles	Million meters	2,224.0	2,996.0	2,732.0	3,491.0
Woolen textiles	Million meters	103.0	100.6	86.1	114.0
Footwear (excluding felt and rubber)	Million pairs	8.3	48.8	99.4	213.0
Sugar, granulated	Thous. M. tons	1,346.8	1,282.6	995.3	2,519.5
Fish, catch	Thous. M. tons	1,018.0	956.4	1,303.0	1,560.0
Machine Building Industry					
Metalworking and machine building industries	Million rubles 1926–27 prices	1,446	3,349	11,283	33,613
Transport machinery:					
Automobiles	Thousands	.....	1.4	49.7	211.4
Including trucks	Thousands	.....	1.3	39.5	184.4
Main-line locomotives in units of E and SU types	Number	418	602	941	1,626
Heavy locomotives FD, SO, IS types	Number	.....	.....	22	1,025
Freight cars in 2 axle units	Thousands	14.8	15.9	21.6	49.1
Machines for heavy industry:					
Metalworking machines	Thousands	1.5	3.8	21.0	53.9
Rolling mill equipment	Thous. M. tons	.....	.....	6.5	17.2
Coal cutters	Number	.....	59	372	1,110
Steam boilers	Thous. sq. meters	28.0	126.4	197.3	240.4
Locomobiles	Thous. horsepower	.....	16.8	26.9	84.3
Diesel engines	Thous. horsepower	35.1	69.2	92.4	261.8
Agricultural machinery:					
Truck-type tractors	Thousands	.....	0.2	2.1	32.2
Tractor ploughs	Thousands	.....	3.6	67.2	72.8
Tractor cultivators	Thousands	.....	1.6	19.5	64.8
Grain combines	Thousands	.....	.....	8.6	22.9
Grain cleaners	Number	.....	.....	28	3,831
Consumers' Goods					
Sewing machines	Thousands	.....	.....	265.8	502.5
Watches, pocket and wrist	Thousands	.....	.....	102.9	635.0
Clocks, alarm	Thousands	.....	.....	439.9	506.2
Cameras	Thousands	.....	.....	115.4	207.5
Radio receiving sets, tube	Thousands	.....	.....	22.0	202.4
Loudspeakers	Thousands	.....	.....	372.8	1,355.1
Phonographs	Thousands	.....	.....	99.3	843.5
Phonograph records	Thousands	.....	.....	2,121.8	66,797.6
Pianos	Thousands	.....	.....	4.1	14.0
Stringed instruments	Thousands	.....	.....	645.9	2,206.2
Concertinas	Thousands	.....	.....	44.2	177.0
Electric lamps (up to 150 watt)	Millions	2.9	.....	45.0	82.1
Electric flatirons	Thousands	.....	.....	181.0	483.7
Electric teapots	Thousands	.....	.....	73.7	187.5
Electric plates	Thousands	.....	.....	6.5	297.3
Bicycles	Thousands	.....	.....	132.4	385.6

were concentrated on war production, and the supply of peacetime goods for the population was cut to the vanishing point. Even during the war, however, plans were laid for a large peacetime increase in the manufacture of consumption goods, beginning with textiles and foodstuffs. Postwar industrial expansion will probably be greatest in the eastern Asiatic provinces, where the population has been doubled by the evacuation of workers from the west and by colonization. A later development will be the exploitation of the known resources of the taiga and the tundra, and of the Arctic littoral. Soviet planned industrialization may well make even more extraordinary progress during the next 10 years than during the last 15 years.

BIBLIOGRAPHY

Dobb, Maurice, *Russian Economic Development Since the Revolution* (New York, 1928).

Mikhailov, Nicholas, *Land of the Soviets* (New York, 1939).

Ropes, E. C., ed., *Russian Economic Notes, 1928–1940.*

Sotsialisticheskoye stroitelstvo SSSR (Moscow, 1935, 1936, 1939).

Yugov, Aaron, *Russia's Economic Front for War and Peace* (New York, 1942).

CHAPTER XIV

Communications:

Railways, Highways, Air

By ANDREW J. STEIGER

UNLIKE the United States, which has the densest network of rail and motor roads in the world, the Soviet Union still offers great prospects for expansion of internal railways and motor highways. Since this immense country is situated almost wholly north of the 40th parallel, climate limits river transport to the warm season. Highway transport has been limited both by shortage of motor trucks and the scarcity of hard rock for road building. Although based primarily on soft schist and sandstone, the vast Russian plains offer certain advantages in railroad construction. For example, very few tunnels need be built; the main Soviet railways from the western border to Lake Baikal do not pass through a single tunnel. Some natural obstacles to railroading, such as limited water supply from hard winter frosts, frozen subsoil, and desert areas, are being overcome by forestation and through using condenser-steam-type locomotives. Russian railways, which carry four fifths of the country's total freight, have therefore assured prospects for future development.

Construction of the Russian railway system began in the nineteenth century. The 16-mile Tsarskoye Selo line from St. Petersburg to Pavlovsk was completed in 1838. The second line, the 200-mile Warsaw-Vienna railway, began operating in 1848, twenty-three years after the world's first railway was built in England. In railway construction Russia lagged very far behind the United States, where the first railway was laid in 1829 and the first transcontinental line, the Union Pacific, was opened in 1869. The Trans-Siberian was not completed until after 1900. This is the longest continuous railway in the world. In connecting Leningrad and Vladivostok, 5,435 miles apart, its roadbed covers about one and three-quarters times the distance between New York and San Francisco.

In European Russia the Nikolayev line between St. Petersburg and Moscow was opened in 1851. During the next half-century the railway system leading from Moscow expanded to Nizhni Novgorod (Gorky), to Kursk, and into the Ukraine; and a through line was opened between Odessa and the Baltic. Between 1881 and 1913 new trackage was laid at the average rate of 881 miles per year; the highest rate of expansion, 1,787 miles per year, was reached between 1893 and 1902. The Russo-Turkish War of 1877–1878 had demonstrated Russia's weakness for defense, and after 1880 the czarist government increasingly extended state control over the railway system. By 1913 the government had invested 2,000,000,000 rubles in buying existing lines and in building new ones. The Russian railway network then totaled 43,798 miles, of which the state controlled 67 per cent.

The railways of czarist Russia were in general designed for exporting grain and raw materials through Baltic and Black Sea ports and for importing manufactured goods from western Europe to inland cities. Odessa, on the Black Sea, and the ice-free Baltic ports were the chief railheads in European Russia, and the Trans-Siberian was first laid to ice-free Port Arthur on the Pacific. The railway from Petrograd to Murmansk, the far northern ice-free port, was not completed until 1917, under pressure of a great need for war supplies from England. At about the same time the railway to Archangel, on the White Sea, was also completed. The Trans-Caspian line from Krasnovodsk to Samarkand, opened in 1888, and the Orenburg-Tashkent Railroad, completed after 1900, had been built to carry cotton from Central Asia to the textile factories of European Russia. Thus the early Russian railway system served primarily the nation's economic needs, but it was also useful for national defense. Few rail lines crossed the western border in an east-west direction. Even these offered little help to invaders from western Europe because the Russian tracks were laid five feet apart, in contrast with the standard gauge (four feet eight and one-half inches) of western Europe and America.

Such were the main features of the Russian railway system in 1917, when the Soviet government was founded. In 1918 the Soviets lost about 7,500 miles of railway when Poland, Bessarabia, and the Baltic States were separated from the Russian state. This reduced the total railway mileage to 36,300 miles. New construction by the Soviets increased the mileage to 53,000 in 1937.

Under the czars most railway construction was in European Russia, where no place south of Leningrad and west of the Volga lies farther than 35 miles from a railway. Most of the new railway construction under the Soviets has been in the eastern areas. In the early 1930's they built a 500-mile line from Kazan on the Volga to Sverdlovsk in the Urals. They completed the 896-mile Turkestan-Siberian Railroad in 1930. In the same period they constructed a 751-mile branch line from the Trans-Siberian south to the Karaganda coal basin and the Lake Balkhash copper plant, and a 140-mile spur from Temrez to Stalinabad. In the Soviet Far East they finished double-tracking the Trans-Siberian on a sector 1,865 miles long. By 1940 they had also completed the 673-mile Moscow-Donbas trunk line and the Amolinsk-Kartaly and Kizlyar-Astrakhan lines. The 2,000-mile long Amur-Baikal trunk line, or northern Trans-Siberian, seems to have been completed from Taishct to Bodaibo. Between 1940 and 1943 the Soviets built the 1,154-mile northern Pechora railway from Konosha via Kotlas to Vorkuta, the region of rich coal deposits called by Russian writers the Arctic Donbas.

During the Second World War about 200 other miles of new railway were laid in Central Asia, and a few hundred miles of spur trackage were driven into new industrial centers in the Urals and Siberia. Although the Soviets have been developing railways to serve the growing eastern industries, trackage is still far less dense in the east than in the Moscow region and the Ukraine, where it averages 51 miles per 1,000 square miles. Eastern trackage varies from three to seventeen miles per 1,000 square miles, and there is still need for considerable expansion.

Within two decades Russian railways were twice devastated by war. Between the period 1914 and 1920 about 3,700 bridges were demolished, 1,200 miles of track were destroyed and effective locomotives were reduced from 23,000 to about 4,000. The German invaders of 1941 seized about 20,000 miles of Russian railways, chiefly in the Ukraine. Most of this trackage was seriously damaged during the German retreat of 1942–1943, but the Soviets reported in July, 1944, that they had restored more than 18,000 miles of track and over a thousand large and medium-sized bridges, totaling 60 miles in length. Reconstruction was aided by lend-lease shipment of 1,500 American locomotives, 540,000 tons of rails, as well as freight cars, car wheels, and axles.

In addition to steam railways the Soviets have nearly 2,000 miles of electrified lines. These include the Kola Peninsula division of the Murmansk Railroad, about 300 miles of the Ural rail network, and the 300-mile Donbas-Krivoi Rog line. Beginning with the Baku-Sabunchi line in 1926, suburban electric railways have been opened out of Moscow, Leningrad, and other large cities.

The Soviets produce rolling stock in their own locomotive and car building works; the figures for 1939 were 1,626 locomotives and 49,100 railway cars. Between 1927 and 1937 these plants supplied 236,700 freight cars, 9,400 passenger cars, and 9,370 locomotives. The annual output of locomotives increased from 458 in 1927, to 1,215 in 1937. Between 1913 and 1931 the total rolling stock on Russian railways increased as follows: locomotives from 16,315 to 18,300; passenger cars from 25,300 to 27,200; and freight cars from 401,600 to 516,000.

Russia's oldest locomotive works were founded at Bezhitsa (in the 1840's) and at Kolomna (in 1863); the Kolomna plant originally made structural steel for railway bridges. Both plants had to be moved east in 1942, but when Bezhista and Kolomna were liberated from German occupation, production was resumed at both places. Before the war the Kolomna plant produced passenger engines able to travel 93 miles per hour, some of which were used on the Moscow-Leningrad Red Arrow express. Voroshilovgrad, also occupied by the Germans for a time, is another center of Soviet locomotive manufacture; so is Leningrad with its famous Putilov engine works. The great new center for freight car manufacture is Nizhnei-Tagil in the Urals.

In developing railway transport the Soviets have borrowed ideas from the United States. Most Russian freight cars, like the American, have four axles; the European freight cars have two axles. One fourth of the cars in use in 1938 had automatic couplings. The new types of locomotives have 50 per cent higher traction power than the older types, and are equipped with mechanical stokers. The drawbar traction power

272

of Russian locomotives in 1934 was 12.5 tons for freight and 8.61 tons for passenger trains. Locomotives working on condenser steam are able to run 620 miles without stopping for water and save 20 per cent on fuel; 406 of these were built in 1938; Soviet industry also produces electric locomotives, which operate on 3,000-volt direct current.

The modernization of Soviet railways was accompanied by an increase in total traffic, which to keep pace with industrial growth had to be stepped up faster than it was possible to build new lines. Although railway mileage increased only from 36,300 in 1913 to 53,000 in 1937 (about 50 per cent), the traffic run increased from 41 billion metric ton-miles in 1913 to 370 billion metric ton-miles in 1939 (560 per cent). This means that Soviet railways are intensively exploited. Russian freight transport in 1913 was only 13.5 per cent of freight transport in the United States; in 1936 it was 63.4 per cent. The annual load carried per mile in operation rose from 689,000 metric ton-miles in 1913 to 2,589,000 metric ton-miles in 1937. During the same period this index remained relatively static in Germany and the United States, where motor transport came to bear an increasing proportion of the traffic load.

Coal, oil, ore, and metal account for 42 per cent of the volume of freight traffic, and the daily haul of a freight car increased from 45 miles in 1913 to 61 miles in 1930. By 1937 the freight being moved per mile of track was more than twice the highest figure recorded in the United States; and although railways in the United States have superior equipment, Soviet freight moved on the average only two miles per hour more slowly than freight in the United States. During the wartime evacuation of Ukrainian industry, Soviet railwaymen set new records. Average daily carloadings in the Ukraine in 1939 were 30,000; in August and September, 1941, they were 80,000. Trainloads of 14,000 tons, the equivalent of a 350-car train, were moved, and 5,000-ton loads were common, double the maximum peacetime schedules. Average daily carloadings on Russian railways showed an increase from 27,400 in 1913 to 89,900 in 1937. Annual passenger traffic rose from 185 million revenue fares in 1913 to 1,178 million in 1938.

In total railway mileage the Soviet Union ranks second only to the United States. The Soviet railway network has about one quarter the mileage of railroads in the United States. The American system has not appreciably expanded since 1913, whereas the Russian system expanded

50 per cent between 1913 and 1937. Further expansion will probably occur in the eastern areas of the Soviet Union and in Asia generally. Any good railway atlas of the globe reveals that of the world's 760,000 miles of railways, about one half are in the Americas, chiefly in the United States. A third are in Europe, and less than one fourth are found in the continents of Asia, Africa, and Australia combined.

The vast size of the USSR is suggested by the fact that it takes three and one-half days to travel north by rail from Odessa, on the Black Sea in the south, to Murmansk on the Barents Sea, a trip almost as long as from New York to San Francisco. Transcontinental express trains make the trip from Leningrad east to Vladivostok, on the Pacific, in nine and one-half days. But to cross central Siberia northward, from Mongolia north to the Arctic Ocean, it requires two weeks by river boat down the Yenisei River.

In the west, railways link the Soviet Union with Poland, the Baltic States, and Romania. In the south and east five Soviet railways cross the frontier into Turkey, Iran, and Mongolia; two other lines enter Manchuria. There is no access by rail into western China, which is reached by motor highway.

In contrast with the United States, where 95 per cent of the railways are privately owned, there are no privately owned railways in the USSR, where all public carriers are nationalized. Railways are operated by a commissariat, subordinate to the Council of Peoples' Commissars. Formerly, the railways commissariat administered all forms of transport, having subordinate departments to manage waterways, airways, and highways.

In the late 1930's the waterways were put under two separate commissariats, one for inland waterways, the other for the merchant marine. Soviet airways are now administered by a special commission, appointed by the Council of Peoples' Commissars and directly responsible to it. Motor truck transport, which is still of local importance only, is directed by the individual Union republics. During the war a special transport committee was set up in 1942 to bring the administration of rail, marine, and river transport under a co-ordinated national traffic plan.

HIGHWAYS . . . Vehicular roads in the Soviet Union still resemble those in the United States before the mass production of automobiles forced the development of national highways. Between 1914 and 1941 surfaced highways in the United States increased from 250,000 to 1,596,000 miles. Meanwhile, in the Soviet Union, a country three times the size of the United States, surfaced highways expanded from 12,500 miles in 1914 to 64,200 miles in 1938. Only 2,400 miles were asphalted; the rest were surfaced with gravel or cobblestone. Most of the 840,000 miles of Soviet roadways were natural dirt or prairie roads. In new highway construction the lack of hard rock limits foundation material to sand or river gravel. In the Ukraine, where even pebbles are rare because the river sources are not in mountains but in marshland, the motor road from Kiev to Chernigov had to be paved with brick.

There are no paved transcontinental highways in the USSR radiating from Moscow. Motor highways link the capital with Leningrad, Minsk, Yaroslavl, Gorky, and Tula, and permit intercity trucking; but in the Urals in 1940 there were not more than a hundred miles of paved road outside the rising urban centers. Through the Pamirs a 469-mile motor highway now links Osh to Khorog. In the Soviet Far East, a motor road runs 620 miles from Bolshoi Niever station on the Amur Railroad north to the interior of Yakutia; another runs from Nogayeva on the Okhotsk Sea several hundred miles north across the mountains to the upper Kolyma River. There is a 500-mile strategic motor road between Vladivostok and Khabarovsk. Plans are discussed for building a transcontinental motor road parallel to the Trans-Siberian Railway.

Although through motor roads are rare, intracity and farm-to-city trucking has been well developed, and trucks are used more and more to deliver farm and factory goods to railway depots and boat stations. The motor truck peak of the Soviet Union totaled 760,000 machines in 1938, as against 18,700 in 1928 and 8,800 in 1913. In 1943, 18,000 motor trucks were reported in operation in Moscow, 6,500 in Kuibyshev, and 6,650 in Sverdlovsk.

Rather than restore all war-demolished railways, the Soviets are considering a plan to shift from railway to motor transport for short hauls of 30 to 40 miles. Thirty per cent of the railway depots in the devastated areas handled no more than one freight car daily under normal operation, and the Russian academician, V. Obraztsov, suggested that the traffic they formerly handled could be economically shifted to container and trailer trucks such as are used in the United States. When wrecked freight stations are rebuilt, convenient platforms are added for truck haulage, and overpasses and underpasses are constructed at railway crossings. In 1937 only 2 per cent of the total Soviet freight in ton-miles was handled by trucks, but prewar plans called for them to carry 6 per cent of the total freight load by 1942.

The war gave Soviet Russia great experience in the trucking operations necessary to supply fast-moving mechanized armies. Many thousands of new drivers were trained, and the auto park was greatly enlarged by captured German lorries and by lend-lease shipments from the United States, which up to March, 1945, had sent to the Soviet Union 406,000 motor vehicles. To increase the war supply of Soviet-made motor cars, a new automobile factory was built in the Urals, adding its output to that of plants established earlier in Moscow, Gorky, and Yaroslavl. Soviet automobile production, which began in 1929 with 1,390 machines, had in 1937 increased the annual output to 200,000 machines; 70 per cent of these were trucks.

In November, 1943, the noted explorer, Sir Hubert Wilkins, commented on the importance of the new "web-ways of tractor roads" developed in Russia to give access to remote territories in the Far North and Siberia. Soviet war aid to China was transported over such roads. A new motor road crosses the Soviet-Iranian frontier south of Ashkhabad, following the old east Persian camel route from Bajgiran to the railhead at Zahidan on the border of Baluchistan. Opened during the war, it brings Russia's southern border to within a week's road-rail journey of India.

Professor Semyonov Tian-Shanski once said of czarist Russia that in a third of the vast realm transportation depended on dogs and reindeer; in a sixth of the country on camels; in nearly half, on horses and oxen; and in certain southern areas, on mules, asses, and buffaloes. Despite the great improvements in transportation made by the Soviets, the remark still holds some truth, especially for remote regions.

WATERWAYS . . . For centuries the great river systems of Russia have been arteries of transport, commerce, and conquest. In the middle sixteenth century the power of Moscow expanded along the Volga to control the Persian trade route down to Astrakhan. Subsequent conquests extended czarism's sway over the valleys of the Don and Dnieper, and the Russian Empire overran Asia along the east-west tributaries of the great Siberian rivers—the Ob, the Yenisei, the Lena, and the Amur. As Great Britain rose through control of marine trade routes, Russia grew through successive conquest of trade routes that followed the river systems of eastern Europe and northern Asia. The Russians with good reason speak of "Mother Volga."

Although there are many important Russian rivers, their use for transport is limited to the warm season and to predominantly north-south communication, especially in Asia. The north-flowing Siberian rivers are frozen during seven or more winter months. Moreover, during the arid summers of Central Asia, the glacier-fed Amu Darya and Syr Darya rivers become shallow streams, and many other Russian rivers dry up in the late summer months. Most Russian rivers either flow into the ice-bound Arctic Ocean or empty into the inland seas like the Aral, the Caspian, and the Black seas. The Dvina runs into the frozen White Sea, the Amur into the Okhotsk Sea; while the small Neva, once an important link in the Hanseatic trade with Novgorod, falls into the Baltic Sea. No great river navigable the year round flows from the heart of Russia out into the open ocean.

Despite their limitations, the rivers of the Soviet Union are being intensively utilized for seasonal transport. In 1939 there were 56,170 miles of internal waterways in operation. The total traffic run in 1938 was about 23 billion metric ton miles, one tenth the load carried by the railways that year. In 1913 one third of Russia's freight load was carried by waterway; rail transport has been expanded much more rapidly than transport by water. Half the total cargo carried by water is timber moved in rafts and barges. Timber is always moved by water, when feasible. During 1944 the plan was to ship by barge or raft the equivalent of 10,000 carloads daily during the timber-floating season. During 1943 the shipment by water of firewood into Moscow released 50,000 railway cars for military supply duty. To eliminate the long rail haul which brought Siberian timber into the treeless plains of Central Asia, timber is now cut in the Tien-Shan Mountains and rafted down the Central Asian rivers.

One quarter of the water-borne freight consists of minerals and construction materials; grain and coal also make up a large portion. The Volga remains the country's chief waterway, along which pass Baku oil and Donets coal. Although new rivers such as the Piassina, the Yana, the

Indigirka, and the Kolyma have been opened to navigation in northern Siberia, the freight carried on all the Siberian river systems—the Ob, the Yenisei, and the Lena—accounts for only one fourteenth of the country's total river-borne cargo, which in 1938 was 66,600,000 metric tons. In the same year 68,100,000 passengers were carried on all Soviet internal waterways, a threefold increase over 1929. Trips averaged 30 miles per person.

To increase the usefulness of their internal waterways the Soviets have built canals to link the main river systems of European Russia. The 80-mile Moscow-Volga Canal, completed in 1937, diverts the upper Volga River to Moscow, thus linking the capital with the Caspian, and when the projected Volga-Don Canal is finished, Moscow will be connected by water with the Black Sea. Meanwhile a rail service shuttles traffic around the 30-mile unfinished section of the Volga-Don Canal. Barges drawing eight and one-half feet can now pass between Moscow and the Caspian. The Baltic–White Sea Canal, completed in 1933, is 142 miles long and connects the Gulf of Finland with the White Sea via Lakes Ladoga and Onega. Vessels of 1,250 tons can pass through this canal from northern waters to Leningrad. Since the Mariisk Canal, completed in 1808, connects the Volga headwaters with Lake Ladoga, Leningrad and Moscow are also linked by waterway. Soviet journals have repeatedly discussed a project for creating an artificial lake to unite the headwaters of the Pechora and Kama rivers. It would then be possible for vessels to sail from the Caspian via the Volga basin to the Arctic seas. Another projected canal system would link the upper Kama with an east-flowing tributary of the Ob river system and open a modern waterway into Siberia.

The state boundaries of the USSR extend 40,600 miles. Of these, 30,000 miles are washed by sea, for the most part icebound. The country's great natural handicap has been a vast coastline opening mainly on the Arctic Ocean. For centuries northern sea communication was impossible between European Russia and its Pacific possessions. In 1932 the Soviet icebreaker *Sibiryakov* made the trip from Archangel eastward via the Bering Strait to the Pacific Ocean during a single navigation season. This historic trip opened up the northern sea route between the Atlantic and the Pacific. In the summer of 1934 the icebreaker *Litke* made the same voyage in reverse direction from Vladivostok to Archangel. New ports, such as Port Igarka, Dickson Island, Tiksi Bay, and Providence Bay, have been built along the Arctic shores as freight stations to handle incoming supplies for northern Siberia and outgoing raw materials—furs, salt, gold, ores, and timber. During 1939, when the northern sea route was first officially opened for commercial traffic, 104 vessels sailed in this great Arctic sea lane, transporting more than 100,000 tons of freight. Eleven vessels made the through passage, which is safeguarded by a system of 50 polar service stations. About 40 icebreakers, ranging up to 12,000 tons in size, keep the sea lanes open during the summer for convoys of freighters.

The Arctic provides the shortest sea route between European Russia and the Soviet Far East. Freight shipped from Odessa to Vladivostok via the Suez Canal travels 13,264 miles; via the Panama Canal it travels 14,177 miles. The distance is cut to 6,835 miles via river and canal to Murmansk and through the Arctic Sea the rest of the way to Vladivostok. Many war supplies during the Second World War went from America to Russia through the Soviet's northern sea route. The shortest route from either New York or Seattle to Archangel is via the Arctic seas. From each city the distance is about 6,000 miles. The one route passes through the north Atlantic and eastward; the other through the north Pacific and westward through the polar seas. The voyage from New York to Bandar Shahpur on the Persian Gulf, a port on another supply route to the Soviet Union, is 14,500 miles.

Before 1941 the Soviets had built new seaports at Belomorsk on the White Sea, Nogayeva on the Okhotsk Sea, and Sovietskaya Gavan on the Tatarskiye Strait. These new ports, like Murmansk and Archangel in the north, and like Chapayev (Guriyev) and Krasnovodsk on the Caspian, became big transit centers for war supplies to the Soviet Union after the German blockade closed the Baltic and Black seas. Among Russian seaports, only Batum on the Black Sea, Petropavlovsk on the Bering Sea, and Murmansk on the Barents Sea are ice-free the year round. All other ports are on inland seas or are icebound part of the year. Leningrad is frozen from late November or early December to April. Vladivostok can be kept open by icebreaker.

In 1938 Soviet vessels carried sea-borne cargo totaling 30,400,000 metric tons, an increase of about 350 per cent over 1929. In 1938 the traffic run was about 24 billion metric ton-miles, slightly above that for the river-borne cargo. In the same year 3,100,000 passengers were carried on sea-borne vessels, double the passengers carried in 1929. In 1938 dock operations at Soviet sea ports were 55.2 per cent mechanized.

AIRWAYS . . . Civil airways not only link all the main urban centers of the Soviet Union but reach out over great stretches of trackless wilderness into the remotest districts of Asia and the Arctic. In 1944 the major air routes totaled more than 86,800 miles. Soviet airlines spanned more space than any other form of internal transport—railways, roads, or waterways. By express train the trip from Moscow to Vladivostok takes about nine days. The air trip requires only two or three days. Tbilisi (Tiflis), in Georgia, is one day's flight from Moscow, but three and a half days by rail. In Central Asia planes fly in three hours from Stalinabad to Khorog, formerly 30 days apart by road.

Soviet civil airlines were inaugurated in 1922 with scheduled flights on 148 miles of airway. Volunteer aviation societies (later merged into the All-Union Society of the Civil Air Fleet) promoted the development of internal airlines, which expanded most rapidly during the decade following 1928. Early in this decade the Soviets established their own aircraft industry, and by 1932 they had become independent of other countries in manufacturing motors and planes.

All the major Soviet cities have been linked by a national air communication system. Airdromes are equipped with night lights for round-the-clock flying. Local airways have also been widely developed to serve collective farm districts and outlying centers. Soviet aircraft are extensively utilized for aerial mapping, geological survey, forest fire service, ambulance duty in emergency cases, and for combating crop pests and malarial mosquitoes. Between 1929 and 1938 all airways under the Soviet Civil Air Field Administration expanded from 11,562 to 71,500 miles—58,300 miles of which were national lines and the rest were interlocking local lines. In 1938, 45,500 tons of freight and mail carried by airplanes in the Transcaucasus, Central Asia, and Kazakstan exceeded the total air transport of Germany, France, and England. Air passengers carried on Soviet planes increased from 9,300 in 1929 to 292,700 in 1938. In addition to lines under the Civil Air Fleet Administration the chief administration of the northern sea route in 1938 operated in the Far North of Siberia about 7,700 miles of airways, which in that year carried 338 tons of freight, 203 tons of mail, and 12,270 passengers.

A tremendous feat of Soviet aviation occurred in 1937, when four large transport planes landed at the North Pole to found the famous scientific research station that drifted nine months through the polar basin on an ice floe. In the same year Soviet airmen made two nonstop flights across the North Pole from Moscow to the west coast of the United States, breaking all previous records for distance. A Soviet flyer had made an earlier pioneer flight (in 1936) over the Alaska-Siberian route from Los Angeles to Moscow via the Bering Strait. North American aviators had also experimented extensively with Arctic flying, and in November, 1942, the Allied northern air route was established to ferry lend-lease war planes from the United States via Alaska and Siberia to the fighting fronts in the Soviet Union. Of approximately 10,000 American-built planes sent to Russia between 1941 and August 1944, about half were flown by this route. The Arctic air ferry route was called "not only the longest aerial lend-lease channel, but the safest."

In a study of postwar air routes the Brookings Institute has rejected the idea that the North Pole is the coming aerial crossroads of the world. Pan-American's proposed world-girdling air routes tend likewise to avoid the polar regions; their projected 6,408-mile line from New York to Moscow goes via Iceland, Oslo, Stockholm, and Leningrad, while their projected 6,831-mile route from Seattle to Canton, China, passes via Alaska and the Aleutian Islands. However, George A. Bleyle of the Wright Aeronautical Corporation said in April, 1944, that "planes are being readied" to fly across Arctic routes between the world's great cities. Planes would have to fly only 7,700 miles from New York to Chungking via the North Pole, compared with 11,700 surface miles via San Francisco and Honolulu. The Arctic route between New York and Moscow is only 4,700 miles, against 5,800 miles via Cherbourg and Berlin.

Since aircraft require surface installations only for landing and taking off, express and local airlines may follow variant routes. Local service flights between cities may skirt the uninhabited Arctic areas, but fast stratoliners in the intercontinental express service can pass directly across the polar regions, which offer the shortest flying distances between world centers in the northern hemisphere.

Before the Second World War the Soviet Union operated the following international air routes: Moscow to Stockholm; Moscow to Prague; Moscow to Kabul in Afghanistan; Alma Ata to Chungking; and Ulan

Ude in Buryat Mongolia to Ulan Bator in the Mongolian People's Republic. During the war an airline was operated from Moscow to Teheran in Persia. Here it connected with the international airlines developed by the United States Army Transport Command, which operated 140,-000 miles of world-circling airways in 1944, some of its eastward lines reaching from America via Africa and the Middle East into India and China. Over this air cargo system of the Middle East, Soviet platinum was exchanged for Chinese mercury after the Soviet Union lost many mercury deposits through German occupation.

Soviet airways are all state-owned and operated. There are no private lines. Moreover, the Soviets reject as dangerous to the national interest the principle of unrestricted global freedom of the air. The Soviet authority, Professor A. Voskresenski, has phrased this attitude as follows: "Free and unregulated flights over foreign countries open dangerous possibilities of misuse and aggression against the national interests of separate states, possibilities of reconnaissance and spying, of violating customs laws and other frontier regulations." He contends that no plan for international postwar civil aviation can succeed without "correct understanding and consideration of the interests and role of the Soviet Union."

The USSR covers a sixth of the earth, including the heart of the Eurasian continent, and sits astride the most direct air routes between Europe and Asia, and between North America and Asia. The Soviet air transport system, therefore, must necessarily be a vital link in any sound system of global airways.

POSTAL SERVICE . . . The Russian civil postal service dates back to Peter the Great, whose *ukase* of 1721 merged the czarist *yamskaya* courier mails with the "merchant" post. Historically, Russia's postal system originated with the Tatars, whose khan in the thirteenth century organized the country's first long-distance courier mails, the term *yamskaya* deriving from the Tatar word for "road." Accordingly, all the early postilions in Russia were called *yamsheks* or dispatch riders, and the delivery system was literally a postal one, mails being horsedrawn by 20- to 30-mile stages, from one halting post to the next.

About 1800 there were in Russia 3,222 postal stations, with 33,840 horses. Mails were delivered along post roads exclusively between the big cities—Moscow, Petersburg, Smolensk, Astrakhan, and towns beyond the Volga along the old trans-Siberian post road. Mails passed about once or twice a week, urgent czarist decrees going by special mail *troikas,* or three-horse carriages.

In the vast territory of the czarist empire by 1913 there were 12,800 post offices located in cities, and in big villages. Where railroads were built, railway mail was initiated. Since rail lines usually followed the old post roads, rural areas not covered under the older system were not generally reached by railway mail. Moreover, since mail service was a big source of czarist income, new post offices were opened only where the mails handled could carry the expense with a profit to the state.

After 1913 the Russian postal service experienced considerable change. Delivery by motor road and airway came into existence. Rural mail service was expanded by opening branch post offices in some 30,000 villages, and by adding rural letter carriers, an institution resembling the American free rural delivery system. In Table VIII are the available facts on Soviet Russia's postal service facilities.

TABLE VIII. POSTAL SERVICE

	1913	1937	1938	1940
Post offices	12,800	....	43,400	......
Post office branches ...	7,168	....	29,400	......
Rural mail carriers	none	....	154,600	......
Public mail boxes	25,000	180,000	......	......
Letters carried	536,000,000	1,466,000	......	......
Newspapers, magazines	358,000,000	....	......	6,000,000,000
Mail routes (in miles)				
Railway	36,625	....	......	70,625
Motor road	none	109,000	......	......
Rural cart road	106,000	350,000	......	......
Waterway	20,000	127,500	......	......
Airway	none	72,000	......	......
Air mail (in tons)	....	....	10,700	......
			(203 tons in the Arctic)	

Soviet Russia, an active member of the International Postal Union founded last century, in 1927 initiated the first international air mail conference. In Soviet Russia, as elsewhere, mail delivery contracts have been a powerful stimulus to the growth of civil airways. In this sense the role of air mail is comparable to that of railway mail in railroad expansion, and it is noteworthy that the first single tariff postage stamp came into existence in England in 1840, in Russia in 1845. These dates correspond closely to the inauguration of railway mail service. In 1940 Soviet Russia marked the Postage Stamp Centennial by issuing a small album of international stamps showing the life and voyages of Columbus. It was titled, *What Postage Stamps Tell Us About the Discovery of America*, and illustrates the educational value the Soviet authorities attach to philately.

TELEPHONES AND THE TELEGRAPH . . . In the evolution of modern communications the railways generally followed the older post roads, and with their rise came the almost coincident opening of electric telegraph lines, in turn usually parallel to railways. Every railway post office became also a telegraph station. In origin Soviet Russia's telegraph lines differ little from those of other nations except that in certain instances the telegraph line preceded the railway, in one notable instance by 40 years. The telegraph line across Siberia follows a route east from the Urals not substantially different from that of the old Siberian post road, along which the great through railway was laid around 1900. As early as 1861 there was through wire service to Irkutsk, near Lake Baikal, in eastern Siberia, over a line later extended to the Pacific.

Only in 1940, however, was the parallel trans-Siberian telephone line opened to bring Vladivostok within phone call distance of Moscow. In this same year, 1940, via a reinforcer station at Khabarovsk, north of Vladivostok, radio-telephone communication was opened through the Soviet Far East between Moscow and San Francisco. The 5,450-mile telegraph-telephone trunk line across Siberia is the longest in the world; formerly this distinction was held by the 3,920-mile trunk wire between Halifax and Vancouver in Canada. Being a vast country, Soviet Russia had in 1940 about one fifth of the world's total seven million miles of communication wire lines, of which the United States had one third. But in number of telephones installed Soviet Russia ranks behind Canada, as seventh in the world.

The same trend toward expansion in rural areas observed in the postal service marks the growth of the telegraph-telephone system. The available facts are presented in Table IX.

284

TABLE IX. TELEGRAPH-TELEPHONE FACILITIES

	1913	1935	1938	1940
Wires, length in miles .	314,000	1,265,000	....	1,562,000
Bronze and bimetallic wires	......	55	....	....
Telephone wires, length in miles	......	......	....	600,000
Telegraph keyboards ..	8,225	11,881	....	....
Telegrams handled	......	......	....	128,000,000
Telephones installed ..	......	......	1,272,500	....
Urban phone centrals ..	......	3,463	....	....
Mounting capacity	290,000	742,000	....	....
Automatic switchboards	......	55	....	....
Automatic capacity ...	......	274,700	....	....
Rural telephones (in 1929 —6,300)	......	......	108,500	....
District centers linked to provincial capitals, by telegraph (in 1929— 70 per cent)	......	3,125	96 per cent of total	....
by telephone (in 1929 —32 per cent) ...	......	2,627	89 per cent of total	....
Villages linked by phone to district centers (in 1929—15 per cent) .	......	41,289	77 per cent of total	....
Machine tractor stations linked by phone to district centers	......	3,812	5,551 or 87 per cent	....
State farms, same phone link	......	4,172	....	....

Soviet Russia's telephone industry is relatively new, and during the war it was aided by lend-lease from the United States. Up to April, 1944, the United States supplied 850,000 miles of field telephone wire and 275,000 field telephones to the Red Army. Technical aid in rehabilitating the tele-tele system in Russia is being given by the American International Telephone and Telegraph Corporation.

RADIO . . . Radio communication in Soviet Russia originated in 1922, when a 12-kilowatt broadcast station was opened in Moscow. Broadcasts are state-sponsored, and scheduled program broadcasting began in 1924, the same year in which a law was passed permitting private possession of receiving sets. This privilege was suspended during the Second World War for security reasons; but the suspension did not mean discontinuance of radio broadcasting or listening. The characteristic listening point at present is the loud speaker connected by wire to a central receiver that serves a network of loud speakers installed variously in apartment rooms, factory halls, city squares, or farm houses. Control of the central receiver is vested in a committee elected by the local subscribers. In 1940 there were 10,000 such wired networks servicing over five million listening points. An expansion program for the networks in 1945 called for an additional one million loud speakers.

Wartime expansion of broadcast facilities saw the opening in 1943 somewhere "in the east" of what Russian writers called the "most powerful transmitter in the world." The new station evidently supersedes the once "most powerful" 500-kilowatt station opened in Moscow in 1933. Likewise, during wartime the Soviet radio became a soldiers' mail carrier, transmitting to and from the front more than 2,000,000 letters.

The weak link in Soviet Russia's radio system is inadequate listening equipment for its almost 200,000,000 citizens. The country had, in 1944, about 15 set-producing factories, but they were then mostly serving the military. At the same time Soviet radio spokesmen were sounding an alarm in the press about the lack of listening facilities, especially among the rural population. The country's 2,000 rural district transmitters were then broadcasting only from a half hour to one and a half hours daily, giving primarily news to supplement the irregular local press. In the large urban centers powerful stations broadcast continuously, giving programs of news, music, and drama in 70 native languages, chief of which is Russian, and in 28 foreign languages, chiefly European.

The available facts on radio facilities are presented in Table X.

TABLE X. RADIO FACILITIES

	1935	1938	1940
Large urban transmitters (in 1929—41) .	....	83	126
Radio-tele transmitters	252	....	....
Local rural transmitters	520	....	2,000
Wired listening networks	6,860	....	10,000
Listening points (in 1929—40,000)	1,834,700	3,300,000	5,500,000
Urban	1,543,000	....	....
Rural	290,700	....	....

BIBLIOGRAPHY

American-Russian Chamber of Commerce, *Handbook of the Soviet Union* (New York, 1936).

Bolshaya Sovetskaya Entsiklopediya, in Russian (Moscow, 1936).

Socialist Construction in the USSR (Moscow, 1936).

American-Russian Institute, *Indices of Socialist Construction in the Union of Soviet Socialist Republics* (New York, 1936).

Mikhailov, Nicholas, *Land of the Soviets* (New York, 1939).

Molokov, V., *Soviet Civil Aviation* (Moscow, 1939).

Obraztsov, V., *The Railroads of the USSR* (Moscow, 1939).

Vassilev, S. A., "Transportation Problems of the USSR" in *USSR Economy and the War* (New York, 1942).

Williams, Albert Rhys, *The Russians* (New York, 1943).

Cressey, George B., *Asia's Land and Peoples* (New York–London, 1944).

Hershey, Burnet, *Skyways of Tomorrow* (New York, 1944).

Mandel, William, "Soviet Transport" in *Soviet Russia Today,* January–February, 1944.

CHAPTER XV

The Development
of Social Institutions

By ROSE MAURER

M ANY social institutions of czarist Russia at the beginning of the
twentieth century were little beyond a feudal level of development. Compared with those of Europe generally, they were backward
and were changing very slowly. Moreover, they varied in character
widely from region to region; for the czars believed that perpetuating
hostile differences, according to the historical principle of "divide and
rule," facilitated·the problem of ruling the numerous nationalities of
which the population of the country is composed.[1] The coating of repressive Russification was spread thinly over some and thickly over other
sections of the various non-Russian peoples.

Since 1917 the various nationalities have been encouraged to develop
their own languages, customs, and institutions according to their own
varying historical traditions, the degree of variation, however, being
limited by their common commitment to socialism. The aim has been, to
quote the slogan which was promulgated throughout the country, the
creation within each Soviet republic of a culture "national in form; socialist in content." A striking similarity in the kind and functioning of
social institutions is accordingly found throughout the USSR, cutting
through a kaleidoscopic variety of traditions and customs.

In the Soviet Union social institutions, whether economic, cultural,
political, or domestic, are all characterized by the rapidity with which

[1] See Chapter I, "National and Racial Minorities."

288

they change, by their close interconnection, and by their development in directions determined conseiously by common agreement and stated in public documents. Soviet men, women, and children have been taught to expect and welcome modifications, in line with predetermined goals, and to believe that all society undergoes continuous change. Within their own lifetimes they have seen their country change from capitalist to socialist society; and they are taught that present efforts are directed toward a change from socialist to communist society.[2]

Soviet social institutions are planned in accordance with certain fundamental theses, humanist and materialist in character: (1) that man is perfectible, and that social institutions determine the extent and also the rate of his development; (2) that nature is understandable without invoking supernaturalism, and that social institutions must agree with, and change with, the findings of science; and (3) that the values which individuals seek include security, health, brotherly love, and the development of aesthetic and rational capacities, and that social institutions must be judged in terms of their effectiveness in promoting these values.

Because the direction of social change is specifically stated and planned in the USSR, social institutions must be so geared into the over-all plan as not to nullify one another's efforts to achieve the values mentioned above: the cinema, for example, must not undo what schools are accomplishing; industry must not develop in a way that undermines the family; sports clubs must not vitiate the work of health clinics; and vice versa, of course.

Maladjustments that appear from time to time among Soviet institutions are publicly criticized in the press. The entire population is encouraged to expect and demand this high degree of integration among all social institutions. This does not imply that these institutions develop uniformly. The Five-Year plans themselves emphasize different institutions at different periods.

The nature of Soviet society has led to the creation of many new institutions, and to the enlargement of familiar ones to unique proportions. Among the new social institutions are the collective farms, the machine-tractor stations, the soviets, the factory "Red Corners" (factory Red Corners began as reading corners and have expanded into separate

---

[2] See Chapter XX, "Soviet Philosophical Thought."

—often quite elaborate—clubrooms), and the Prophylactoria for Former Prostitutes; while day care for children below school age has become an integral part of the Soviet educational and health program. On the other hand, since there are no college fraternities, no opposition political parties, no commercial sports, no privately owned factories—these and many other institutions can form no part of the Soviet social structure. These major changes in the kind and functioning of social institutions led Beatrice and Sidney Webb, in *Soviet Communism; a New Civilization*, to conclude that the USSR of the mid-1930's represented a fundamentally new type of society.

While all institutions in any society are social institutions, only those will be discussed in this article which are not treated elsewhere in this volume under separate titles.

THE FAMILY . . . The diversity of religions and nationalities in czarist Russia was paralleled by wide variations in the family's role and in family structure and relationships. The Khevsurs of the Caucasus, for example, had clans and clan feuds, and also the notorious institution of *samrevlo* for the isolation of mothers during childbirth. Among the Chukchi of the far north aged parents committed enforced suicide. Child marriage, bride purchase, and polygamy were customary among the Uzbek, Kirghiz, and other Moslem people. Among the Slavic peoples of European Russia there existed not only the customary European monogamous family but also legalized prostitution and legal barriers to marriage between individuals of different religious faiths. The unifying principle underlying this diversity was the general notion of male supremacy, and the consequent subservience of woman to her father, husband, brother, and son. The *Domostroi*, or family code, drawn up in the sixteenth century by the priest Sylvester, court chaplain to Ivan IV; the *Shariat* which regulated life for the Moslems; and czarist laws were alike in emphasizing the inequality of husband and wife.

Patriarchal authority began to weaken in western Russia during the nineteenth century with the advent of industrialization and the abolition of serfdom; for when factories began functioning, women, many of them serfs freed from rural bondage, began working in factories for strangers instead of working at home for fathers and husbands. It was these workers who most strongly supported the demand for greater recognition of women's rights in Russia. An active role in this regard was also played by women who went outside czarist borders to study and came into contact with more advanced attitudes toward women.

With increasing industrialization after the revolution, the family completely lost its old role as an economic unit dominated by the male head of the family. Moreover, as collective farms were organized, the contribution of each individual, whether man or woman, to agriculture was separately reckoned and recompensed. These economic changes were preceded and accompanied by legislation based on the principle of women's "equal rights with men in all spheres of economic, public, cultural, social, and political life" (federal constitution, Article 122).

The theory that women's potentialities for development are comparable with men's was not challenged, although the practice in the early Soviet years often fell short of the theory. No theory concerning the family found similar unanimity; sharp controversy surrounded the question in the early 1920's. Although extremists declared the family outmoded, Lenin and his followers held only that the family should be relieved of some of its responsibilities. Public laundries, restaurants, nurseries, kindergartens, clinics, and similar institutions, Lenin urged,[3] would make it possible for women to utilize their new opportunities for self-development, and would allow them to participate in the development of their country. "Every cook must learn to run the state," said Lenin, and this phrase became a national slogan.

The family was never "abolished" in the Soviet Union. Its ties weakened during the years of internecine strife following the First World War but grew stronger as Soviet economy strengthened, and as rifts between the younger and older generations were sealed by a joint acceptance of socialism. The Soviet family, once it was relieved of part of its responsibility for education and physical care, was able to resume partial responsibility on a new level of economic security. Preschool child care has relieved most working mothers of part of their responsibility for children between the ages of 4 weeks and 7 years. Eleven million women were employed in 1940, and 19 million more were members of collective farms. In wartime they outnumbered men workers and farmers. Factory, farm, and neighborhood nurseries and kindergartens, to which young children may be entrusted (voluntarily and at a low fee), provide day care under the direction of doctors, nurses,

---

[3] See Clara Zetkin, *Lenin on the Woman Question.*

teachers, dietitians, and recreational workers. Such scientifically run institutions feed, change, bathe, and instruct young children, and also give them their naps and provide them with proper recreation, in their mothers' absence. A parallel program of adult education taught formerly illiterate parents to co-operate closely with schools and preschool institutions in their children's education, with clinics, school doctors, and sports counselors in their children's physical development, and with playwrights, musicians, and other artists in their children's cultural growth. One hundred and forty of the 748 theaters in the Soviet Union in 1938 were theaters for children. The stated aim of the Soviets was to establish love and respect between parents and children upon mutuality of interests, rather than upon tradition and precept, and they claim that this effort has proved increasingly successful. As woman's economic, cultural, and political horizons broadened, relations between husbands and wives tended toward equality in fact as well as in law. Property considerations were increasingly separated from marital relationships. Prostitution had almost completely vanished by 1941, for the economic basis of prostitution had been removed, and former prostitutes were rehabilitated in special medical-labor institutions called Prophylactoria for Former Prostitutes. Monogamy, which Friedrich Engels termed the only form of family under which individual sex-love can develop, became effective for both husbands and wives. It was also planned that the family should no longer face disintegration through loss of work on the part of the wage earner, through sickness, eviction by landlords for nonpayment of rent, domestic tensions resulting from hardship and insecurity, and other economic strains. The family was rather reinforced and stabilized by the liquidation of unemployment in 1930, by the economic independence of its adult members, by sickness and maternity benefits, and by medical services provided by the state without charge, and old-age pensions relieved elderly parents of some of their dependence upon their married children. The higher birth rate recorded as Soviet economy was strengthened in the mid-1930's must be related also to the specific institutional aids which permit women to combine home and career. The Soviet Union encourages large families and has, particularly since the loss of population resulting from the Second World War, decreed various economic and prestige rewards for motherhood.

Job abundance, and the prestige attaching to work, reduced property considerations in the choice of a mate and increased the role of the romantic love factor. The emphasis on ethnic equality also removed nationality, race, and religion as limiting considerations in founding a family. Under these conditions, according to Soviet observers, the family itself became a living exponent of the society's ideals, instilling in children a respect for women, work, other races and nationalities, mutual aid, science, learning, and culture generally. These developments gradually permeated the entire Soviet Union, although the Moslem peoples were markedly slower than others in accepting the new view of women and the family. The affirmative Soviet estimate of family influence is seen in the encouragement of the adoption of orphans to limit the number of children who must live in institutions.

The first Soviet marriage law (December 18, 1917) separated the functions of church and state as regards marriage, and required registration of marriage by secular authorities. Church marriages have never been banned in the Soviet Union; they are regarded as extralegal personal matters. Years of civil war, 1918–1920, followed by unemployment, increased the breakup of the family begun by the long years of separation caused by the First World War, and men tended to avoid marriage and its concomitant responsibility for offspring. (Legal responsibility for children born out of wedlock had been established, but it was more easily evaded.) Women demanded the right of legal abortion to avoid bearing children whom they might have to support alone, and in 1920 this right was granted, over the protests of the medical profession. Abortion remained legal until 1936. By that time new attitudes favoring the stability of marriage had been built up by the disappearance of unemployment, by the cultural and political development of women, by the establishment of more and more nurseries and other family aids, and by the constant lauding of the family in the Soviet press. The Second World War, threatening home and children, intensified feelings of family devotion. The Soviets stressed these feelings in posters, plays, and stories designed to intensify the war effort against the invader, and established evacuation centers, new clinics, orphan homes, and other institutions for the protection of children in order to relieve the fighting men of worry about their families back home. The 1927 marriage code of the Russian Soviet Federated Socialist Republic had placed *de facto* marriage on a par with registered marriage, and in this respect, as in

293

many others, most of the Soviet republics had followed suit; but in 1944 a new federal law restored the original distinction between registered and unregistered marriages, and provided for marital and parental obligations only in the case of registered, or legal, marriage. Government allowances for children born out of wedlock now provide the economic protection incumbent upon parents until this law was passed.

Provisions for divorce in the Soviet Union have closely followed the pattern of the marriage laws. They have changed frequently to conform with rapidly changing conditions, and their avowed aim has been to strengthen family life. The first decree regulating divorce (December 19, 1917), like the early decree on marriage, abolished church control. In the government office, ZAGS (Registration of Civil Acts), divorce by mutual consent could be immediately obtained, and in the courts the request for divorce on the part of one spouse could be recorded whether or not the other spouse responded to the summons. The courts, with their new personnel, could not handle the large number of cases resulting from desertion, and the 1927 divorce provision was designed to deal with this situation. ZAGS was permitted to record all divorces, and to send notification (the famous postcard) after the fact. To the courts was left jurisdiction over cases involving dispute about marital property and the custody of children. While the 1917 and 1927 laws sought to end the old concept of the indissolubility of marriage, Soviet leaders had no intention of allowing easy divorce to become a substitute for the vanishing practice of prostitution. The 1927 provision was misused by a small number, but its demoralizing effect was widely felt. The 1936 federal law sought to correct this situation. While ZAGS recorded divorces, the recording had to be preceded by summons of both spouses. As a further deterrent to what the law frankly termed "a lightminded attitude toward the family and family obligations," divorces were written into the passport which each Soviet citizen carries, and divorce fees were raised to 50 rubles for the first divorce, 150 for the second, and 300 for others. On July 8, 1944, both cost and procedures were made even more deterrent: locally elected People's Courts inquired into the motives of every divorce petition and sought to effect a reconciliation, and the power to grant divorce was reserved to higher courts which could charge either or both applicants from 500 to 2,000 rubles.

Serious thought before marriage and divorce is now enjoined upon

294

Soviet men and women; changing economic and cultural conditions—literacy, economic security, awareness of children's needs—have, in the Soviet view, made such deliberation possible. An increasing number of institutions are designed to strengthen woman's position in society and hence in the home. A decree in 1944 made it obligatory to include day-care institutions for preschool children in all industrial construction plants. This Five-Year Plan projected for the years 1946 to 1950 inclusive will operate within a condition of serious labor shortage, and further Red Army demobilization is not expected to reduce the economic opportunities of Soviet women in the immediate postwar years.

HOUSING . . . Buildings in imperial Russia ranged from tent, or *yurta*, of nomadic peoples east of the Caspian, and the crude hut of Ukranian peasants, with its earthen floor and its walls of clay mixed with straw, to the superb architecture of Central Asian mosques and palaces dating back to Tamerlane. The small log or frame house characterized the cities of European Russia. Despite the increasing importance of cities in the country's economic life as industrialization proceeded, municipal engineering was at a primitive level. Street paving, lighting, and sewage and water supply systems were backward and compelled most city dwellers to undergo daily hardships. The expansion of urban population from 3,400,000 in 1851 to 26,800,000 in 1914 was not accompanied by commensurate housing construction. The resulting congestion was reflected in the report of a survey in 1912 which revealed almost two thirds of the Moscow population occupying half a room or less. While high rents accounted for part of the crowding—a two-room apartment in Moscow when wages were averaging some 25 rubles monthly is reported to have cost 14 rubles, or 56 per cent of an average salary—there was a housing shortage in absolute terms, necessitating the use of cellars, corners of rooms, and barracklike lodging houses. Traditions of privacy were, accordingly, not highly developed among the Russian people.

When the Soviets nationalized the better dwellings, which constituted about half the total housing space, and redistributed the rooms, there was an improvement in accommodations for many urban dwellers; the percentage of the Moscow population occupying half a room or less is reported to have been reduced, by 1923, to 36. This was only a first step in a solution which obviously required extensive new construction.

Building proceeded slowly until the Five-Year plans began, and some losses were sustained through the serious disrepair into which many dwellings had fallen. Yet the Soviets were able, between 1923 and 1941, to double their housing space. New construction figured progressively larger in each plan: the First Five-Year Plan saw the addition of 27,-000,000 square meters of floor space while the third plan called for 35,000,000.

The amazingly rapid rate of urbanization, and the high average annual increment of population (1.23 per cent between the two censuses of 1926 and 1939), due largely to a lowered death rate, account in large part for the fact that conditions of crowding have remained characteristic throughout the years of Soviet power. In 12 years the urban population more than doubled, reaching 56,000,000 by January, 1939. The migration from country to town was planned, and was smaller in volume than it would have been if urban women by the million had not joined the labor force. Even so, peasants entering the new factories often found themselves obliged to live in "corners," in barracks, in various shelters originally contemplated as temporary. The Soviet housing problem was complicated, of course, by the fact that the country faced so many building shortages concurrently. Because the Soviets felt that hospitals, schools, factories, and places of recreation could not wait, construction had to be undertaken along many lines at once and with a laboring force almost totally unfamiliar with modern building methods. Also, raising the standards of backward nationalities, which included the settling of millions of nomads, necessitated building homes for millions who had never before figured in any housing program.

While crowding still existed in 1941, when the building program was interrupted by the war in many parts of the country, it was relieved by many places of relaxation, including workers' clubs, theaters, and sports stadia, and meanwhile standards in related matters had been improved. Electric light, sanitary inspection, running water, paved streets, greenery, indoor plumbing, planned cities with superior locations and facilities, rents based not only on kind of accommodation but on income, tenant-elected house committees (*domkomy*)—these factors differentiated the Soviet housing picture from what had preceded it.

In cities the majority of apartment houses belong to the local government (the city soviet). However, a considerable number were constructed by industrial enterprises for the use of their personnel, and still others were co-operatively owned.

In rural areas the establishment of the collective farm changed the housing situation in certain respects. Collective barns taught the farmer not to share his home with his livestock. The erection of public buildings, including schools, theaters, hospitals, and administration centers, created new standards and stimulated farmers to supersede the earthen floors of their huts with washable flooring. Household equipment, such as sheets and individual dishes, made their appearance for the first time in millions of farm homes. Electricity, thanks to the nationwide electrification program insisted upon by Lenin in 1920, became a common convenience. However, in rural and urban areas alike, small kerosene stoves continued as the prevalent cooking apparatus. With the wartime discovery of new supplies of natural gas, this situation is expected to change rapidly.

The Second World War deeply aggravated the Soviet housing shortage. The scorched earth policy and damage by Nazi bombs, artillery, and deliberate destruction reduced many villages and whole cities to rubble. Soviet authorities estimate that 25 million of their people were deprived of their homes. Schools, hospitals, factories must also be rebuilt by the tens of thousands. As the invader was pushed back, however, architects and engineers were taken off camouflage, air raid, and fortification work and set to tasks of reconstruction. The problem of reconciling short-range and long-range requirements proved to be a difficult one, and because of the immediate need, one- and two-story houses became the dominant motif in the housing pattern. Emphasis was laid, in city and village alike, on small privately owned homes, the building of which was financed by long-term government loans, amounting in 1944 to 260,000,000 rubles; in 1945 the allocation for such loans was increased by 25 per cent. The land, being state property (all land in Soviet Russia is public domain), continued to be made available without charge. Article 7 of the federal constitution had guaranteed the collective farmer's right to own his dwelling, and many urban dwellers had also built *dachi*, or summer homes, in the country; but the construction of small homes in cities had been relatively rare. War veterans are given

297

such housing privileges as priority in building materials, extension of the loan repayment period, and the right to reoccupy their prewar apartments without payment of rent for the period of military service.

FOOD . . . Accustomed to periodic famine and having almost no food industry, imperial Russia was characterized by a meager diet in which soup and porridge predominated. Caviar and pancakes were foods for the wealthy. Consonant with generally low hygienic standards, the handling of food was on a primitive level. In the cities, except for the few palatially baroque shops which dealt mainly in imported delicacies, retail trade was carried on in badly lighted, filthy huts, or *lavki*. Lack of a modern distribution network was to create great difficulties when, under the Soviets, the urban part of the population, which depends on retail purchases, increased so rapidly. There was a scarcity of experienced store clerks, almost no mechanical equipment for slicing, adding, and so on, and no tradition of "service"; and consequently queues were caused not by goods shortages alone. Gradually a network of retail food stores was built up, urban stores reaching a total of 125,000 by 1936, rural stores numbering almost 150,000. Trade in the villages is largely carried on through consumers' co-operatives; in the cities government stores, run by various commissariats, such as those of trade, food, and local industry, predominate. In 1940 consumer goods production was 7 per cent above 1939 and 33 per cent above 1937, while the 1941 plan called for a 9 per cent increase over 1940; and this increase was reflected in the increase of retail trade in government and co-operative shops. In 1937 retail turnover amounted in value to 126,000,000,000 rubles; in 1938 it amounted to 10 per cent more; and in 1940 it totaled almost 175,000,-000,000 rubles. The 1941 plan called for a turnover of 197,000,000,000 rubles, and the 1942 plan for 206,000,000,000 rubles. These figures did not include sales in still another retail outlet, the collective farm markets in which farmers could sell products whether collectively or individually raised. In 1938 sales in these collective farm markets, where prices were not fixed by the state but were held in check by the degree of availability of goods in government and co-operative shops, amounted to almost 25,000,000,000 rubles.

Before 1935 the Soviet people had known only a few years when foods were not rationed, and these years, 1923–1929, were characterized by wide-scale unemployment which severely reduced purchasing power.

298

After 1935, however, when rationing was abolished because food had become more plentiful, purchasing power kept increasing. Unemployment had ceased to exist in 1930 and until 1941, when the Nazis attacked, there was a steadily rising wage fund; it was almost 72,000,000,-000 rubles in 1936 for 25,800,000 workers and employees and 124,000,-000,000 rubles in 1940 for 30,400,000 workers and employees. Also, the monetary income on collective farms rose to 14,200,000,000 rubles in 1937, and 18,300,000,000 rubles in 1939. New prices were established after rationing was abolished, and during the ensuing period of rising wages, employment, and production they remained stable or decreased. (Price rises reported in 1940 by various foreign observers seem to have been restricted to certain perishable items, as wartime prices of bread and other staples appear to be almost identical with prices set late in 1935.)

Food was available in increasing abundance in the years before the Nazi invasion. Mechanized agriculture and scientific livestock breeding were rapidly filling up the granaries and animal pens which had been depleted by crop failures and the destruction of cattle in the collectivization struggles, persisting until the early 1930's. The new large grain harvests meant that more than enough raw material was available for the mechanized bakeries which the Soviets had built in large numbers. With abundance, virtuosity in the preparation of bread appeared, and the favorite food of the Soviet people took varied and fantastic shapes. Quality was better, with finer wheat used, and sanitation was at a high level except in transport from store to home, as the paper shortage prevented wrapping. Abundant and low in price also were potatoes, cabbage, carrots, and pickled cucumbers. Meat and dairy products remained scarce. The diet of rural dwellers, with Soviet encouragement of livestock and poultry ownership by farmers, is undoubtedly more varied than that of the average worker, although the Stakhanovite with higher pay than average vied with farmers in the consumption of fish, meat, eggs, and butter. Severe rationing characterized the years following 1941. Wartime losses of 17 million cattle, 20 million pigs, 27 million sheep and goats will be reflected on Soviet tables for years to come. Nutrition research and consumer education, combined with large-scale cooking (school and factory meals), are mitigating factors in this situation.

CLOTHING . . . The clothing industry was poorly developed in czarist Russia. In 1913 a little over 8,000,000 pairs of boots and shoes were produced in factories. Reliance was upon the individual craftsman, rather than upon the factory, with the result that the majority of the vast peasant population never owned a pair of shoes; coarsely woven bast sandals were the usual substitute. The wealthy sought clothes as well as food from abroad. Coarse, shapeless garments were characteristic for the masses in rural and urban areas alike, those of the latter being more somber in tone. In the countryside there was great contrast between daily garments and the traditional costumes worn for festivals. Lack of soap and of changes of clothing resulted in unhygienic habits of wearing garments for long periods of time. Among some peoples of the country superstition sanctified necessity. Health hazards were increased also by religious and other customs in the matter of apparel. The heavy enshrouding *paranja* worn by women of Central Asia, with the *chachwan,* a rough horsehair net beneath it, often resulted in eye disease and general debility. Among some mountaineer women of the Caucasus, tightly laced leather garments were common, and contributed to a high tuberculosis rate among them.

In the matter of clothing the Soviets faced, as in food and shelter, a combination of shortages and low consumption standards. By the mid-1930's marked quantitative gains were evident in the supply of clothing, but the great improvements in quality made in housing and food were largely absent. In matters of style, variety, and durability, the Soviet clothing industry, particularly where women's apparel is concerned, still had much to learn. Soviet men continued to wear the traditional *rubashka,* its high neck usually cross-stitched and its full folds worn outside the trousers. Because this garment can be worn without a jacket it has virtues in summertime which will probably ensure its retention in the Soviet Union and possibly its spread to other lands. The cap continued as the most common masculine headgear. Leather or sheepskin jackets, heavy shoes or felt boots (*valenki*), together with the cap, gave Soviet men a sturdy woodsman's appearance, not unbecoming, and put them in a more advantageous position, in general, than women, whose clothing, selected with a view to more finesse of texture and variety of color than that of men, remained more evidently shoddy. The problem of adequate quantity was enlarged in the Soviet Union by this shoddiness, which necessitated frequent replacement. Also, while public laundries had been set up in large though insufficient numbers, dry-cleaning plants were few, and their scarcity had an unfavorable effect on attempts to preserve garments and raise standards of cleanliness.

The Soviet clothing industry has been built up on a base of domestic raw materials, and factories have been established close to the raw materials, reducing transportation costs. Soviet Central Asia not only increased its cotton and silk cultivation but in the new factories, formerly denied to the region by Moscow merchants who feared competition, began to manufacture goods several times greater in value than the agricultural yields of the area. Between 1913 and 1939 total production of raw cotton increased more than threefold in the Soviet Union and that of flax fiber almost doubled. The manufacture of consumer goods did not match these increases; however, cotton textiles in 1938 were 50 per cent above 1913 production, while knit goods showed a fourfold increase. Factory production of leather shoes increased from the 8,300,000 pairs of 1913 to almost 165,000,000 in 1938, about one pair per capita. Amicable relations with the peoples of the Far North resulted in increased fur catches, and scientific breeding in Kara-Kalpakia and other republics has multiplied the total yield of valuable fur. The Soviets have built up a fur-finishing industry and no longer need to send furs abroad to be dyed and dressed. Furs, therefore, are no longer too expensive for home consumption; in 1935 it was estimated that 60 per cent of Soviet furs were being sold on the domestic market, the rest being exported, largely to the United States.

As in the matter of food, the Soviets established prices in relation to clothing that differentiated between basic needs and what, in a shortage situation, were deemed luxuries. No Soviet citizen, therefore, suffered from cold; but relatively few could afford silk dresses or fancy shoes. Pricing also aided in developing institutions deemed desirable by the Soviets. Sports clothes, for example, were kept low in price to encourage athletics.

Wartime conversion of industry drastically reduced the production of consumer goods. Even handicraft co-operatives manufactured military supplies. Urgent need marks the area which had been overrun by enemy troops, and has been met in some part by shipments of used clothing gathered by Russian War Relief, an American organization which in 1945 assumed the title of American Society for Russian Relief. American clothing manufacturers have aided Russia in resuming mass production of juvenile garments by sending samples and patterns.

LABOR LEGISLATION . . . The most notable advance in living standards in the Soviet Union before the German attack was registered in cultural opportunities (schools, books, newspapers, theaters, cinemas, concerts, and exhibits), in civic participation, and in health care. Improvement in working conditions contributed to this advance. The amount of leisure time available for study and recreation increased when the working day was shortened to seven hours for the vast majority of workers in the Soviet Union, and mechanization of production demanded a smaller expenditure of physical energy, leaving vigor for the workers' participation in health-building sports activities. On the other hand, mechanization and progressive pay rates both created pressure in the direction of technical study, and the Soviet citizen's day was sometimes uncomfortably full. This was a temporary situation, of course, bound up with a heritage of technological backwardness and, until 1940, large but still insufficient opportunities for technical education before workers engaged in production.

When Soviet labor legislation refers to "workers and employees" it means not only laboring and professional staffs of urban enterprises but agricultural workers on state farms (*sovkhozy*) and in machine-tractor stations (MTS). (Members of collective farms operate within the provisions of the Model Rules of the Agricultural Artel.) Each constituent republic of the USSR adopts its own code of labor law, but the federal government has within its power, according to the constitution (Article 14, t), "establishment of the principles of labor legislation"; most of the important provisions concerning hours, social insurance, and so on are thus centrally set, ensuring similarity of working conditions throughout the vast sweep of Soviet territory.

Because of this universality, the Soviets claimed for their workers "the shortest working day in the world." The normal working day, which had been fixed at eight hours soon after the establishment of Soviet power, was reduced to seven hours by the early 1930's, but restored again to eight hours in June, 1940, because, it was claimed, of the war threat. Overtime had been severely limited in peacetime; during the war three hours a day overtime became permissible (paid at time and a half). The working day was four hours for those minors 14 to 16 who were granted special permission to work, and, for adults, four to seven hours for night work, hazardous trades, for nursing mothers, etc. It should be noted that protective legislation for women is regarded by the Soviets as not only consonant with the principle of sex equality but as a fundamental prerequisite to the realization of that principle. After June, 1940, work was based on a seven-day week (six days of work followed by one day of rest) instead of the six-day week in effect after 1932, when it superseded the five-day week which the Soviets had tried for three years. In addition to 52 rest days a year, and six holidays (January 22, May 1 and 2, November 7 and 8, December 5), there is a paid vacation of two weeks to one month (with additional days in hazardous trades, difficult climatic conditions, etc.). A money substitute for vacation was instituted in wartime; pregnant women were still given vacation time, however, in addition to paid maternity leave, after the adoption of a decree in July, 1944, to that effect. Vacations were restored in 1945 for all workers except those in certain branches of industry deemed vital by the highest federal executive organ.

Places of work are generally new or rebuilt, and incorporate health safeguards (ventilating systems, showers, etc.) regarded as essential by research organizations (the various institutes for labor hygiene and occupational disease). Labor inspectors, of whom there were 5,124 in 1938, are appointed by the trade unions after state examination. Physicians participate too, as every enterprise with 250 or more workers must have a medical center on the premises. While "self-criticism" in the Soviet press reveals that enforcement is not complete, the system of free medical care and sickness insurance operates as a check to encourage adherence to the labor code provisions. Working with the salaried labor inspectors and health authorities is a vast body of voluntary labor inspectors, elected by each unit of 20 trade-union members.

Relevant to the matter of living standards is the Soviet conception of the place of occupation as a center of learning and recreation as well. Of great significance in the individual's daily life is the opportunity to combine earning a living with cultural activity. For the Soviets it is one of the devices designed to "eliminate the difference between mental and physical labor." Study circles, concerts, lectures, and plays are part of the factory day, with the premises (Houses of Culture, "Red Corners," libraries, etc.) usually owned or supervised by the trade unions.

The Soviet government guarantees the right to work and increasingly favorable working conditions, but it also requires a commensurate sense of obligation on the part of workers. The abundance of jobs typical of planned economy makes discharge useless as a penalty for lateness, absenteeism, or any other violation of "labor discipline," the mainte- nance of which is declared (Article 130 of the constitution) to be the duty of every citizen of the USSR. Labor discipline, defined by the *Political Dictionary* (Moscow, 1940) as "the conscientious, scrupulous relation of the individual to his work," should not be confused with com- pulsory labor. With the exception of certain periods (the early period of war communism, the Second World War) and certain categories, in- cluding graduates of technical schools and higher institutions who are committed to work in their chosen profession for a certain number of years, not exceeding five, Soviet citizens can choose whether to apply for work. Social pressure, educational stimuli, and material need make the decision an affirmative one for the vast majority, and they then come within the jurisdiction of the labor codes. These codes enlarged the authority of factory directors and industrial commissars in the matter of labor mobility when the threat of war in 1940 increased the serious- ness of labor shortages. With more than a million boys and girls grad- uating annually from the vocational schools established in that year, however, the shortage of skilled labor can be expected to be overcome shortly, and the code provisions eased.

PUBLIC ORGANIZATIONS . . . A wide network of mass voluntary organizations exists in the Soviet Union to help implement the basic ob- jective of improved living standards.

Trade Unions.—Protecting the worker in his relation to manage- ment are the Soviet trade unions, which conceive as their purpose the promotion of productivity, upon which depends betterment of working conditions and the raising of wage scales. By 1940, 25,500,000 out of the country's 30,400,000 workers and employees be- longed to almost 200 unions organized on industrial lines. (Collective farmers are not subject to the labor codes nor eligible to join the trade unions.) Soviet trade unions, with their constitutions, elections, shop meetings, production conferences, and co-operation with local and national government, are regarded in the USSR as a vital force in the development of democratic processes. The large funds at the disposal of trade unions (members pay 1 per cent of their monthly earnings and employing enterprises must contribute twice that amount) encourage a wide interpretation of trade-union activities, such as rest homes, study courses, and the labor press. Limitations on management's right to fire workers are set forth in the labor codes (Article 47 of the Russian Soviet Federated Socialist Republic code), and any dispute in this connection as well as other grievances are handled by the Conflicts Commission in each plant, composed of equal numbers of labor and management representatives. Standing committees in the unions include those on Wages, Labor Protection, Welfare, Education and Recreation, Production and Inventions, and Social Insurance. They involve in their functioning hundreds of thousands of volunteers called "activists."

Social insurance benefits are administered largely by the trade unions, whose members and families are entitled to full payment of the benefits in each situation, while those who do not belong to trade unions are eligible to only half the amount. The fund consists of compulsory contributions by industrial and other enterprises, ranging from 3.7 to 10.7 per cent of the amount of their payroll, the precise contribution depending upon the amount of benefits likely to be paid out in the particular industry. (In the case of collective farmers, elected officers of government-subsidized mutual aid societies administer old-age, disablement, and other pensions under the supervision of Social Welfare commissariats.) Among the items of social insurance falling within trade-union jurisdiction are cash benefits during temporary illness (including pregnancy leaves, for which women are eligible after seven months' employment), superannuation pensions for those who are entitled to retire but who continue to work, funeral expenses, special diets, baby layettes, and nursing grants, as well as various disbursements for housing improvement and the maintenance of rest homes, research centers, and other institutions of importance in sickness and accident prevention. The scale of benefit payment is determined by federal decree, however, and the trend, as in wage payment, is in the direction of doing away with "leveling" or equalitarianism (uravnilovka). By making the illness benefits a percentage of the wage, with differentiations according to length and continuity of employment, degree of hazard, and character of output (shock-worker, Stakhanovite, etc.), social insurance in the Soviet Union is not only a security medium but a device for stimulating more conscientious and productive work. Old-age pensions also provide greater reward for the more productive worker; generally they vary between 50 and 60 per cent of average earnings. Since January, 1939, the pension is payable regardless of whether the man or woman continues at work. Administration of the payments for those who do retire is a function of the Soviet Welfare Commissariat (SWC) in each republic, a department which also handles that part of the social insurance fund affecting totally disabled workers and survivors of deceased workers.

The amount of money available for social insurance purposes has constantly increased. By 1941 the social insurance budget was 10 billion rubles, some 2 billion more than in 1935. Furthermore, in contrast to the earlier year when about one fourth of the fund went to repay the cost of medical aid rendered by the health commissariats, the fund has since 1937 been relieved of such expenditure. Health care is now financed mainly by allocations from the budget of the USSR (in 1940, 9,000,-000,000 rubles, or over 5 per cent of the total budget).

While the Social Insurance Fund has been relieved of responsibility for supporting certain institutions, such as preschool and health care, and while its unemployment benefits are completely suspended, its obligations have increased in other directions, notably since the decree of July 8, 1944, which increased maternity leave payments to eleven weeks and more, and increased layette grants from 45 rubles to 120 rubles. Also, during the war years increasing numbers of disabled veterans entered industry and became eligible for wage payments during sickness. (Other aid to disabled veterans—pensions, job training, placement, maintenance of invalid homes, provision of artificial limbs—is administered by the Social Welfare commissariats, which rely heavily upon trade-union co-operation. Such aid is financed by the Soviet government and does not draw upon the Social Insurance Fund.)

The Soviet security system thus provides assistance for practically every event and emergency that can affect the earning power of its working and professional population: illness, pregnancy, accident, old age. Article 120 of the constitution makes security an essential part of governmental guarantees: "Citizens of the USSR have the right to maintenance in old age and also in case of sickness or loss of capacity to work." Because the expenses involved are borne by the government or by industry and agriculture, the amounts paid out in benefits and services may be regarded as socialized wage, i.e., additions to the individual's income which leave his money wage free for the satisfaction of other needs. This fact, and also the adjustment of rent to the wage earner's income, obviously makes calculation of real wage in the Soviet Union a more complicated process than in other societies. And totally elusive of statistical calculation, although an undeniable factor in living standards, is the psychological atmosphere created by social institutions devoted to the elimination of "rainy day" fears and serving to diminish differentiations in living standards among various income groups.

Sports Societies.—Trade unions are not only among the most important public organizations in the Soviet Union but under their auspices various other institutions, including sports societies, are widely developed. Using the many playing fields, gymnasia, and stadia constructed during the plan periods, were, by 1941, 60,000 sports clubs with 12,000,000 members. Many more millions, while not club members, responded with increasing interest to the deliberate efforts of the government (through the All-Union Committee on Physical Culture and Sports), and of youth organizations, collective farms, and defense societies, to make participation in sports a mass phenomenon. The only professional athlete in the Soviet Union is the graduate of a physical-training college who teaches athletics in the schools. Most of those who compete in the skiing, skating, swimming, track, and other meets are workers, students, farmers, of all ages and both sexes. There was no slackening of interest in wartime as shown in the participation of 9 million men and women in the 1943 cross-country races. It was not until Germany had been defeated, however, that the spectacular annual sports parade in Moscow was resumed on Physical Culture Day, August 12.

Defense and Humanitarian Societies.—Membership in sports clubs and in the civilian defense organization overlaps. *Osoaviakhim* (Society for Co-operation in Defense and in Aviation-Chemical Construction) makes the acquisition of sports skills a major part of its work in the defense training, which, until the war made it compulsory, was a

307

voluntary activity for millions of Soviet civilians. By 1941 when the Soviets were invaded, over 8,000,000 men and women, and children 13 to 16, had qualified, with the aid of *Osoaviakhim*, for the "Ready for Labor and Defense" badge awarded by the government. (Badges, titles, awards, are in the USSR part of a complex system of prestige substitutes for money incentives, although the latter continue to be used as well, often in combination.) This badge bespoke not only sports proficiency but a knowledge of first aid. Many of the holders could also extinguish incendiary bombs and cope with the problems of bomb debris and contamination. As guerrilla fighters and as workers in bombed cities, *Osoaviakhim* members were to find practical use for this defense knowledge. The membership, which grew to 13 million in the war, expanded its activities to include scrap metal collection, aid to families of soldiers, contributions in money and kind to the Defense Fund, and sewing clothing for the Red Army.

The Union of Soviet Red Cross and Red Crescent Societies, which is a member of the International Red Cross Committee at Geneva, joins together the mass voluntary humanitarian organizations of the 16 constituent republics of the USSR. (Azerbaidzhan, Tadzhikistan, Uzbekistan, and Turkmenia, with their predominantly Moslem populations, choose, as do Turkey and Iran, to use the crescent rather than the cross as their symbol.) In 1918 after the abolition of the imperial Red Cross, its Soviet counterpart was established and devoted itself to relief work during the civil war, helped cope with famine and epidemic in the early 1920's, and then performed medical missionary work among the Kirghiz, Kazaks, and various underprivileged peoples. In the mid-1930's defense activities were emphasized, and when the Nazis invaded, the Soviet Red Cross units had eight million members. Another two million joined during the war and participated in first aid, blood donorship, epidemic prevention, and the care of war invalids and orphans.

In each Soviet republic voluntary societies of the blind and of the deaf and dumb, aided by government subsidies, have organized special nurseries, boarding homes, study courses, clubs, and libraries, and have promoted research to perfect aids in fitting the handicapped for a life of useful labor. While the number of blind had been decreasing because of preventive work (eyes dispensaries, hygienic precautions, reduction of trachoma, glaucoma, syphilis), war injuries again expanded the membership during the Second World War and made essential the expansion of public organizations of this kind.

Women's Organizations.—Because trade unions are so dominant a part of the Soviet institutional picture, and since it is through them that doctors, engineers, and other professional personnel maintain scholarly and recreational contacts, separate associations for this purpose do not hold the same important place as in other countries. Housewives, however, are not members of trade unions and have formed various clubs, committees, and movements to facilitate joint activity. Women's clubs were a characteristic feature of the Soviet East, particularly in the 1920's, for by excluding men and ensuring privacy, they were able to shield girls and women threatened by their menfolk, whose hegemony was endangered by new laws. In these clubs, which took varied forms from the Red Yurta which followed nomad tribes to organizations housed in impressive urban structures, the fight for women's rights was encouraged by legal advice, by campaigns against such institutions as the veil and child marriage, and by instruction of women in the abc's, in trades, in child care. As the Five-Year plans affected Eastern thinking, the women's clubs became less isolated from masculine society and began giving lectures and entertainments to which men were invited; in many districts it was the first time that men and women had sat in the same public room.

While these clubs continued to function as cultural centers, their significance was overshadowed later by the Wives' Movement, a development of the plan periods, which spread across the whole Soviet Union. Although this movement was particularly encouraged for housewives, its participants included many women engaged in industrial or professional work. Those in the Wives' Movement sought to better the working and living conditions of the men and women in their husbands' places of occupation. The movement was a further extension of the volunteer activity which characterizes Soviet society and was regarded as significant not alone for the tangible improvements resulting in factories, shops, army barracks, and other such quarters, but for the effect upon family life. Husband and wife found a sense of common effort, and many of the participants became so interested in their volunteer jobs that they chose to enter the ranks of working and professional women themselves. A notable wartime woman's organization was the Women's Anti-Fascist Committee established in Moscow.

BIBLIOGRAPHY

"Marriage," *Bolshaya Sovetskaya Entsiklopediya*, vol. VII (Moscow, 1927).

Smith, J., *Woman in Soviet Russia* (New York, 1928).

"Child Welfare," *Bolshaya Sovetskaya Entsiklopediya*, vol. XXI (Moscow, 1931).

Soviet Law on Marriage, government publication (Moscow, 1932).

"Women's Movements," *Bolshaya Sovetskaya Entsiklopediya*, vol. XXV (Moscow, 1932).

Conus, E., *Protection of Motherhood and Childhood in the Soviet Union* (Moscow and Leningrad, 1933).

Halle, F., *Woman in Soviet Russia* (New York, 1935).

Kingsbury, S. M., and Fairchild, M., *Factory, Family and Women in the Soviet Union* (New York, 1935).

Fediaevsky, V. M., and Hill, P. S., *Nursery School and Parent Education in the Soviet Union* (New York, 1935).

Webb, B. and S., *Soviet Communism: A New Civilization*, vol. II (New York, 1936).

Sigerist, H., *Socialized Medicine in the USSR* (New York, 1937).

Krupskaya, N. K., *Soviet Woman* (New York, 1937).

"The Development of Soviet Domestic Trade," *Research Bulletin on the Soviet Union*, New York, Sept. 30, 1937.

Williams, A. R., *The Soviets* (New York, 1937).

Hazard, J., *Soviet Housing Law* (New Haven, 1939).

Gosplanizdat, *Socialist Construction* (Moscow, 1939).

Land of Socialism Today and Tomorrow, Communist Party proceedings (Moscow, 1939).

Somerville, R., "That Soviet Standard of Living," *American Quarterly on the Soviet Union*, New York, April, 1940.

——, "Soviet Hours Law," *ibid.*, New York, April, 1941.

——, "Problem of Labor Turnover," *American Review on the Soviet Union*, New York, June, 1941.

——, "Osoaviakhim Spells Soviet Civil Defense," *ibid.*, New York, August, 1941.

Voznesensky, N., *Growing Prosperity of the Soviet Union* (New York, 1941).

Blumenfeld, H., "Regional and City Planning in the Soviet Union," *Soviet Culture in War Time* (San Francisco, 1943).

Dobb, M., *Soviet Planning and Labor in Peace and War* (New York, 1943).

Maurer, R., *Soviet Children and Their Care* (New York, 1943).

——, *Soviet Health Care in Peace and War* (New York, 1943).

Serebrennikov, T., *Woman in the Soviet Union* (Moscow, 1943).

Smith, E., *Organized Labor in the Soviet Union* (New York, 1943).

Somerville, J., "Dialectical Materialism," *Twentieth Century Philosophy* (New York, 1943).

Engels, F., *Origin of the Family* (Hottingen-Zurich, 1844; New York, 1944).

Maurer, R., "Recent Trends in the Soviet Family," *American Sociological Review*, Menasha, Wis., June, 1944.

——, *Soviet Women* (New York, 1944).

——, "Restoring the Disabled Veteran and His Family," *USSR in Reconstruction* (New York, 1944).

——, "New Soviet Family Laws," *Soviet Russia Today*, New York, Sept., 1944.

CHAPTER XVI

Medicine and Health

By HENRY E. SIGERIST

T HE USSR made a new departure in medicine by establishing a complete system of public medical services available to all the people free of charge. The Constitution of 1936 grants citizens of the USSR "the right to maintenance in old age and also in case of sickness or loss of capacity to work. This right is ensured by the wide development of social insurance of workers and other employees at state expense, free medical service for the working people, and the provision of a wide network of health resorts at the disposal of the working people" (Article 120). A health plan is part of the general economic and cultural plan of the nation.

As early as 1864 Russia had established a system of public medical services for rural districts; it was financed through taxation and administered by the Zemstvo. Although the program was inadequate, particularly among the national minorities, it was a progressive step and laid the foundation upon which the Soviets developed their health system. Despite emergency conditions at the time of the October Revolution, the Military Revolutionary Committee in Petrograd set up a medical division. In February, 1918, a Medical Council was established, and on July 11, 1918, upon Lenin's initiative, the first People's Commissariat of Public Health was founded, with N. A. Semashko as first commissar. This was a new type of administrative health agency. Medical progress was very difficult during the years 1918–1922. Civil war, blockade, foreign intervention, famine, and epidemics unparalleled since the Middle Ages had completely disorganized the country. The commissariat had to concentrate its efforts on providing medical services to the Red Army and on fighting epidemics, particularly typhus. In 1922 the work of reconstruction along socialist lines began. The chief task was to provide medical facilities and services to the working population in town and country, not only in the European section of Russia but all over the USSR. Medical personnel and hospitals inherited from czarist days were completely inadequate, and the thirteen medical schools, all located in European Russia, were too few to satisfy the demand. New medical schools had to be founded, particularly among the national minorities where instruction would be given in the native languages. New schools, however, required new teaching personnel that had to be trained first. In spite of all difficulties, in 1928—only seven years after the civil war—the number of physicians had been increased from 19,785 in 1913 to 63,162; the number of general hospital beds from 142,310 to 217,744; of maternity beds from 6,824 to 27,338; of rural health stations from 4,367 to 7,531; of women's and children's consultation bureaus from 9 to 2,151. In 1913 free nursery facilities were available for only 550 children, while in 1928 there were permanent nursery facilities for 62,054 and seasonal ones for nearly 200,000 children. The groundwork was laid; the future task was to expand the system and improve its quality. This was done systematically through the Five-Year plans, during which the health budget increased from 660,800,000 rubles in 1928 to 9,433,000,000 in 1938 and 11,980,000,000 in 1941. All health facilities were increased (see Table XI) and standards were universally raised.

ADMINISTRATION . . . All health activities are administered by the people's commissariats of public health of the constituent republics and their subsidiary organs (commissariats of autonomous republics, health departments of *oblast,* or province, *krai* or region, city, and *rayon* or district. The Constitution of 1936 created a new health agency, the All-Union People's Commissariat of Public Health. It is the central federal health agency, and the All-Union commissar of health is a member of the Council of People's Commissars. The commissariat establishes health policies, directs and co-ordinates the work of the health commissariats of the constituent republics, and administers medical institutions that serve the Union as a whole.

The commissariats are in charge of sanitation and the control of communicable diseases. Sanitary inspection is one of their very important functions. They also control such agencies as hospitals, health centers, rural health stations, nurseries, sanatoria, health resorts, and pharmacies, and the services rendered by these institutions. The training of medical personnel is under the control of the commissariats. Medical schools increased in number from 13 in 1913 to 51 in 1941—training 106,000 students. In addition to the medical schools, the country in 1945 had twelve dental schools and nine pharmacy schools. Medical students, after completing a ten-grade school or its equivalent, pursue a five-year course, supplemented by several years of rural practice. Rural physicians take postgraduate courses lasting several months every three years. Middle medical personnel, that is *feldshers* (medical assistants), midwives, nurses, and pharmacy assistants are trained in 985 schools.

The commissariats are further responsible for producing the equipment required for the health work of the nation. They, therefore, control medical and pharmaceutical industries and all industries producing medical instruments, appliances, and other commodities.

Health administration is carried out democratically under the broad participation of the entire population and of the medical workers. Special committees of the Medical Workers Union are in constant touch with the commissariats, and no decision concerning medical workers is made without consultation. Each commissariat has a special bureau to examine complaints. Factories, farms, and other working places have health committees that co-operate closely with the health agencies in planning health and in carrying out health measures.

Until 1937 medical services for wage earners were financed primarily from social insurance funds. After 1937 services were financed increasingly from general state funds, and social insurance money was used for special services, such as special diets or treatments in health resorts.

THE PROMOTION OF HEALTH . . . The central purpose of Soviet health activities is to promote health and prevent illness. A vigorous campaign of health education is carried out permanently throughout the country. Children in nurseries are taught sound health habits, and parents are reached through the nursery. Health education continues in the schools of all grades and in youth organizations. Millions of workers take their chief meal in the factories, and this practice has made it possible to improve dietary habits. The educational activities of health committees reach large numbers of people. The health educational program has been unusually successful because it went hand in hand with education in citizenship. The Soviet view is that health and sickness are not a private matter, and once the citizen became aware of his responsibility toward the community, health education fell on fertile ground.

The widespread development of physical culture also has contributed greatly to health. The All-Union Council of Physical Culture is appointed by the Council of People's Commissars and is directly responsible to it. Millions of people in town and country have trained under its guidance, and over 6,000,000 men and women have received badges to certify that they have passed a prescribed number of tests. All training is under medical supervision.

Health is also promoted through the systematic organization of rest and recreation. Not only do workers have vacations with pay, but many institutions beneficial to health are available to them for vacations: rest homes, vacation camps, health resorts—in the country, at the seaside, and in the mountains. Medical personnel are attached to all such institutions, so that minor ailments can be remedied before serious illness develops.

THE PREVENTION OF DISEASE . . . General sanitation was very backward in czarist Russia; the country had frequent devastating epidemics of smallpox, cholera, dysentery, typhoid fever, typhus, relapsing fever, and similar diseases. Malaria was endemic in the Caucasus and many other sections of the country. During the civil war it spread as far north as the Arctic zone. It has been a tremendous task to improve the sanitation of dwellings and to construct new water and sewage systems over such a vast area. Much remains to be done, but there has been great progress, and water-carried diseases have diminished considerably. Vaccination is universal and smallpox has disappeared. Other immunization work is increasing, and such diseases as diphtheria, scarlet fever, whooping cough, and typhoid fever have been reduced considerably. Typhus has ceased to be a problem. Widespread antimalarial measures in subtropical sections and the rising standard of living have reduced the incidence of malaria.

Special measures have been developed to protect those who for physiological or social reasons are particularly threatened. From the very first, motherhood, infancy, and childhood received special protection. All discriminations against women were abolished, and legal pro-

315

tection was extended to pregnant and nursing women. The country now has 5,803 women's and children's consultation bureaus where women can obtain advice and aid for themselves and their children on all physiological and pathological problems. Over half of all children are born in maternity homes.

It is the responsibility of the trade unions to protect labor and to create the best possible working conditions, a task in which they co-operate closely with the health authorities. The work is administered by the councils of trade unions of the constituent republics under guidance of the All-Union Council of Trade Unions. The unions collect and spend vast social insurance funds contributed by the employing agencies. One of their tasks is to protect workers against accidents and disease. Strict labor inspection is carried out by sanitary inspectors and specially trained labor inspectors; in every plant and shop these officials are aided by workers' delegates elected by their fellow workers. Every case of occupational disease must be reported and is investigated by specialists. The unions support over 40 research institutes for the protection of labor; equipped with laboratories and clinical divisions, many of these have budgets of several million rubles. Workers receive physical examinations at regular intervals prescribed by law. In harmful industries workers must be examined once every six months, or even once every four months.

MEDICAL CARE THROUGH MEDICAL CENTERS . . . The Soviet Union has tried to create a social organization that makes the maximum use of modern technology in every field. In medicine the plan was to form medical centers, through which organized groups of physicians, general practitioners, and specialists could care for public health. The idea is for each individual to obtain all health services needed, preventive, diagnostic, and curative, from his own medical center. In 1941 the country had 13,461 urban and 13,512 rural medical centers. These are administered by health departments, and in the cities they are connected either with working places or residential districts. Three types of medical center are distinguished. The *ambulatorium* is a small medical center staffed by not more than 14 physicians, serving about 10,000 people. The *polyclinic* is a large medical center prepared to handle all cases that do not require hospitalization. Some polyclinics are staffed with up to 200 physicians and serve groups of over 100,000 people, but a later tendency is toward smaller medical centers serving about 50,000 people. In addition to these two types of medical center, there are specialized dispensaries for the prevention and treatment of such diseases as tuberculosis, cancer, mental diseases, skin and venereal diseases, goiter, and malaria. The whole organization is not rigid but is adapted to local requirements; the goal is to make all services available to everyone.

The same principle prevails in providing medical services to the rural population. The large state farms have medical centers and hospitals similar to those in the cities. The problem is more complicated in the villages of collective farms, and a somewhat different system had to be developed. Just as several collective farms are served with agricultural machinery from a tractor station located at a strategic point, a group of collective farms is served by a rural medical center that combines ambulatorium and hospital and is staffed with general practitioners and specialists. The individual villages also have rural medical stations staffed with *feldshers,* nurses, and midwives, and sometimes with physicians and dentists. Many villages have small maternity homes constructed with the aid of government subsidies. The rural medical centers supervise and co-ordinate the work of the rural medical stations. Rural health work is administered by the Department of Health of the *rayon.*

All physicians are salaried, and salaries are determined by three factors: experience, responsibility, and hazard. This is why rural physicians have salaries 10 to 20 per cent higher than those of urban doctors in corresponding positions. All doctors have at least four weeks' vacation a year with full salary and opportunities for postgraduate training. Private practice has never been forbidden but it is negligible.

During the First Five-Year Plan 75 per cent of all medical students were women. The percentage decreased somewhat after 1932, but increased again during the Second World War, and there can be no doubt that the number of women engaged in medical work will exceed the number of men in the very near future. Women are holding leading positions in every field of medicine.

REHABILITATION . . . The USSR has done pioneer work in the field of rehabilitation. Every effort is made to reintegrate a former patient into society and to prevent skilled workers from dropping to the ranks of unskilled labor through physical disability. Most factories have

TABLE XI. Growth of Medical Facilities in the USSR, 1913–1941

		Units	1913	1928	1932	1938	1941
Hospital facilities (nonpsychiatric)	City	Beds	93,223	158,514	256,158	450,694	491,543
	Village	Beds	49,087	59,230	116,075	153,129	169,888
	Total	Beds	142,310	217,744	372,233	603,823	661,431
Psychiatric facilities	City	Beds	36,240	30,016	39,945	66,265	73,992
Maternity hospitals	City	Beds	5,192	18,241	26,984	74,480	75,612
	Village	Beds	1,632	9,097	16,673	60,323	66,261
	Total	Beds	6,824	27,338	43,657	134,803	141,873
Sanatoria and health resorts		Beds	2,000	36,100	63,300	102,000	132,000
Urban medical centers		Institutions	1,230	5,673	7,340	12,645	13,461
Rural medical centers		Institutions	4,367	7,531	9,883	11,594 *	13,512
Tuberculosis dispensaries and stations		Institutions	43	498	498	925	1,048
Venereal disease dispensaries and stations		Institutions	12	800	683	1,351	1,498
Women's and children's consultation centers	City	Institutions	9	1,383	2,126	3,103	3,499
	Village	Institutions	.....	768	1,162	1,765	2,304
	Total	Institutions	9	2,151	3,288	4,868	5,803
Permanent nurseries	City	Capacity	550	53,748	257,659	460,911	554,448
	Village	Capacity	.....	8,306	342,519	280,568	299,598
	Total	Capacity	550	62,054	600,178	741,479	854,046
Seasonal nurseries	Village	Capacity (in thousands)	10.6	195	3,929.1	3,242.3	4,045.6
Physicians		Total	19,785	63,162	76,027	112,405	130,348
Health budget		Total (in millions of rubles)	.....	660.8	2,540.0 †	9,433.0	11,960.0

* On Jan. 1, 1938.
† For 1933.

kitchens, supported from social insurance funds. Many large factories have special workshops where the conveyor belt moves more slowly. Disabled craftsmen join co-operatives where they can continue their work with government aid. Stipends are provided for the re-education of disabled individuals. Rehabilitation work was greatly increased under the pressure of the Second World War, but it is carried on in peace as in war as an important part of the general health program.

RESEARCH . . . The All-Union Commissariat of Public Health is advised in scientific matters by the Medical Research Council, which includes the leading medical scientists of the nation. Attached to the commissariat are over 20 All-Union scientific research institutes, each devoted to a special field of medicine such as nutrition, tuberculosis, venereal diseases, or tropical medicine. All have large budgets and are provided with laboratories and clinical divisions. Foremost among them is the All-Union Institute of Experimental Medicine (VIEM), one of the world's great medical research centers.

Other medical research institutes are attached to the commissariats of the constituent republics and to municipal health departments or similar agencies, and all medical schools take an active part in the scientific life of the country. In 1941 the Soviet Union had 223 medical research institutes staffed with 19,550 scientists.

Important contributions have come from the USSR in many fields of medical science, including physiology (I. P. Pavlov, K. M. Bykov, L. S. Stern), pathology (A. D. Speranski, A. A. Bogomolets), transplantation of tissues (V. Filatov, A. V. Vishnevski), general surgery (T. I. Yudin), neurosurgery (N. N. Burdenko, N. I. Propper-Grashchenko), and virus diseases (A. Smorodintsev, V. D. Solovyov).

BIBLIOGRAPHY

Newsholme, Arthur, and Kingsbury, J. A., *Red Medicine: Socialized Health in Soviet Russia* (New York, 1933).
Semashko, N. A., *Health Protection in the USSR* (London, 1934).
Sigerist, H. E., *Socialized Medicine in the Soviet Union* (New York, 1937).
American Review of Soviet Medicine (New York, 1943–   ), vol. I ff.

CHAPTER XVII

Educational System

By JOHN SOMERVILLE

IN CONSIDERING Soviet education, the reader should bear two ideas carefully in mind. First, the aims and objectives of a given system of education are as important as the details of school structure and pedagogic procedure. Second, the process of education itself, of communicating information, of influencing opinions and beliefs, of building habits and character, does not take place exclusively, or perhaps even primarily, in the classroom. Thus to understand and judge education in any society, one must consider not only the school system but all the avenues and agencies of educational influence, such as the press, radio, screen, theater, and general environment. In a sense, the goals or objectives of education are more important than anything else, since the value and meaning of methods are inseparable from the ends and aims which they serve. In the main, the aims of education in any society are expressed in the ethical and social ideals which command general allegiance in that society. Here, of course, one must take account of the preponderant trend rather than isolated exceptions, and practice rather than mere preachment.

Education in imperial Russia was, broadly speaking, under the spiritual dominion of the Orthodox Church and under the political dominion of the autocracy. The main feeling of the czarist regime was that not much was to be gained, and perhaps a good deal could be lost, by any large development of public education. A. S. Shishkov, minister of education under Czar Alexander I, went so far as to state, "Knowledge is useful only when, like salt, it is used and offered in small measure, according to the people's circumstances and their needs. . . . To teach the mass of people, or even the majority of them how to read will bring more harm than good." More often than not, unquestioning obedience to the wishes of the autocracy was gained through darkness rather than through public enlightenment. For the vast majority of people, the ethical ideals of the church came into play to help them bear suffering and oppression, rather than to point the way to intellectual development or materially improve conditions of life.

In order to state the fundamental aims and objectives of Soviet education, we must refer to the basic philosophy, especially the ethical and social principles, called socialist humanism, to which it is committed These may be found in the writings of Nikolai Lenin, Karl Marx, Friedrich Engels, Joseph Stalin, Maxim Gorky, and others, and in the laws, policies, and practices actually operative in the country at large. The ideals which dominate the educational process in the Soviet Union, taken in terms of their content as standards of individual behavior and character, are essentially the generally accepted standards of the ethical traditions of Western civilization. It is well to note that the materialist emphasis in Soviet ethics (as a part of its general philosophy of dialectical materialism), does not involve a rejection of ethical values like unselfishness, charity, brotherly love, peace, honesty, truthfulness, and the other basic precepts expressed, for instance, in the Bible. Like many other naturalistic ethical philosophies, socialist humanism, while advocating these ethical standards, regards them as man-made, and as mandatory by virtue of their demonstrable value in the light of human reason rather than as divinely ordained. Thus, the concept of a future life with rewards and punishments is rejected. The Soviet viewpoint is that people generally can be educated to see the necessity of conforming to such moral standards on the basis of their human values in this world, without invoking the hope of reward or the threat of punishment in a life after death.

Socialist humanism manifests an immense confidence in human nature, an unbounded faith in the possibilities of development of human beings, if given proper educational environment. There is no concept of an elite, or of the inherent inferiority or superiority of groups or races. Hence, in the Soviet Union it is an offense punishable under the criminal code to exercise any kind of arbitrary discrimination, segregation, quota, or disqualification based on race, color, or sex in regard to educational, economic, professional, residential, or other opportunities. The operating premise is that all people are worth educating. Hence, peacetime education has not only been free of charge at every level throughout the country, but stipends have provided living expenses for most students beyond the secondary level. Modifications in this system introduced during the Second World War are discussed below.

The ideals of life taught by socialist humanism are connected in more than one sense with education. They not only supply goals for education; education itself is one of the chief goals. Central in these ideals are intellectual development and cultivation of the emotions, knowledge of and participation in the arts and the sciences. This emphasis is evident from the earliest days. Lenin, while pointing out that education helps build communism, stressed that education for communist ideals meant the fullest possible education. In a speech to youth (*Tasks of the Youth Leagues*) he said:

> You would be making a great mistake if you attempted to draw the conclusion that one can become a communist without acquiring what human knowledge has accumulated. It would be a mistake to believe that it is sufficient to learn communist slogans. . . . If a communist took it into his head to boast about his communism on the basis of readymade conclusions obtained without a great deal of serious and hard work, without understanding the facts which he must examine critically, he would be a very deplorable communist. Such superficiality would be decidedly fatal. If I know that I know little, I will strive to learn more; but if a man says that he is a communist, and that he need know nothing thoroughly, he will never be anything like a communist.

Educational and cultural development is constantly played up by every avenue of public influence. The prestige attaching to the word *kultura* (culture) among people of the USSR is very great. Health and economic security are looked upon as the natural accompaniments of higher cultural development, and all these values are looked upon as finding their natural function and fruition in socially useful work. The conception is that the more education and training a person has, the more socially valuable work at higher professional and technical levels he or she will be able to do, and the more enjoyable that work will be to the doer. Powerful propaganda exhorts everyone to take advantage of opportunities for "raising his or her qualifications." Such opportunities are free of economic or other artificial barriers.

There is no leisure class in the USSR, and no avenue of influence which promulgates the idea that a life of leisure has social prestige. The contrary idea is driven home. Socially useful work at increasingly higher levels of competence is looked upon as the naturally satisfying outlet of man's abilities and capacities, and also as a duty. In this regard, the constitution of the USSR quotes the Biblical injunction: "He who does not work, neither shall he eat" (Chapter I, Article 12).

One of the basic ideals involved in the social development from socialism (the initial or lower phase of communism, now regarded as attained) to communism proper (not yet fully attained) is expressed as "the eradication of antagonisms between mental and physical labor." This ideal envisages a more satisfactory fusion of bodily and mental elements in the life activity of the individual. Instead of manual workers who lack cultural development, and intellectual workers who lack physical development, each group feeling alien to the other and suffering from the lack of what the other possesses, the aim is to build richer personalities, more balanced individuals who will be more versatile, more productive, and healthier in every sense. One of the pedagogic concepts central in school practice, discussed below, that reflects and implements this aim is called polytechnization.

A distinguishing characteristic of socialist humanism is its high degree of articulation with social institutions—its emphasis on the close relation between ethical theory and social practice. The position taken is that an indispensable requisite in the ethical improvement of the great majority of people is to set up on a large social scale those economic and cultural arrangements through which the opportunities, resources, and facilities for leading the higher cultured and enlightened life will actually be available to them. Soviet thinkers hold the view that any realistic ethical program must involve the construction of a type of society which can guarantee economic security at the level of qualifications, and offer complete education and health care entirely free of economic, race, or sex barriers. This is the operational meaning of socialism in terms of the interplay of educational ideals and social practice in the Soviet Union.

METHODS AND AGENCIES . . . School Structure. The accompanying diagram (see Chart I) gives the principal divisions, according to age levels, of the school structure in the USSR in 1944. The services of the nursery (*yasli*) may be utilized as early as the fifth or sixth week

CHART I. SCHOOL STRUCTURE—USSR

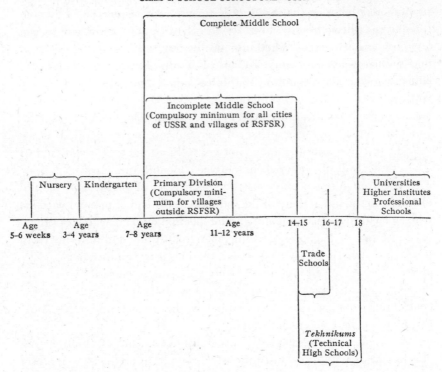

after birth, but they are not compulsory. The three-year-old child is eligible for kindergarten (*detski sad*). Compulsory schooling begins at seven to eight. The first four years, or primary grades (*nachalnaya shkola*), are the compulsory minimum in villages outside the RSFSR (Russian Soviet Federated Socialist Republic). These four years plus the next three constitute the Incomplete Middle School (*Nepolnaya Srednaya Shkola*) or Seven-Year School. This is compulsory in villages and cities of the RSFSR and in all cities outside the RSFSR. Pupils who have completed these seven years have several choices. They may go on for three more years of the general cultural course, and thus finish the Complete Middle School (*Polnaya Srednaya Shkola*) or Ten-Year School; this makes them eligible for all sorts of university work and professional training. Or they may enter a *tekhnikum*, a kind of technical high school, for three or four years of training in a special field, which

324

may be anything from music or painting to textiles or steel production. Or they may enter one of the shorter course trade schools for extensive training up to two years. These are the chief opportunities within the regular school structure. There are also various courses and opportunities in correspondence work and in adult education, a great many of which are brought directly to the individual in his or her working establishment.

EXPANSION OF EDUCATIONAL FACILITIES . . . It must be borne in mind, however, that this picture is a dynamic one, subject to rapid developments in the light of large-scale plans. From the beginning of the Soviet regime, the rate of expansion of educational facilities and opportunities at all levels has been exceptionally rapid, though only the poorest sort of educational coverage of the population was inherited from the czarist regime. In 1913 illiteracy was still 70 to 80 per cent; there were fewer than 8,000,000 pupils in primary and secondary schools, and fewer than 300,000 in technical and higher institutions. By 1928 illiteracy had been reduced to 44 per cent, and enrollment had risen in the categories mentioned to more than 11,000,000 and 600,000 respectively. By 1935 illiteracy had been further reduced, while the other figures had jumped to 26,000,000 and 2,500,000, respectively. In 1939 there were 31,000,000 pupils in primary and secondary schools; in 1941, 35,-000,000. Illiteracy had dropped to less than 20 per cent according to the census of 1939.

The Nazi attack upon the Soviet Union in 1941 interrupted plans to make the Ten-Year School the general minimum. Average school attendance, of course, considerably exceeds the compulsory minimum. It should perhaps be emphasized that attendance in preschool institutions is not compulsory; it is only a myth that children in the USSR are arbitrarily taken from their parents and brought up in state institutions. Nursery facilities are administered by the Commissariat of Health, not that of Education, and they may be planned and built by any institution, such as a factory, a farm, or a university, which needs their services. Likewise, all vocational or technical schools, *tekhnikums*, and many higher institutes are under the control and administration of whatever commissariat has jurisdiction over the field within which the given type of work falls.

Though there is no central All-Union Commissariat of Education in the USSR, each republic having its own commissariat, that of the RSFSR, which is the most populous and technically advanced republic in the Union, serves in practice as a kind of model for the others. For higher education there is an All-Union Committee on Higher Schools, entrusted with problems of general supervision. The immediate control over any given higher institution, however, is exercised by the commissariat having responsibility for the given field of work.

TUITION FEES AND STUDENT STIPENDS . . . Before the Second World War, the Soviet Union had attained a position unique in the history of education. Not only was all education, from primary grades through university or professional school, completely free of tuition payment, but most students beyond the secondary level (around 90 per cent in 1939), including technical students within the secondary level (around 85 per cent in *tekhnikums* in 1939) received stipends for general living expenses. The impact of the war, as well as increases of income for various groups, caused certain changes in the fee system. Because of the sharply increased need for trained personnel in fields directly connected with the war effort, new vocational schools were set up with especially attractive stipend arrangements beginning at the age of 14 to 15. At the same time most students in fields not directly connected with the war effort were obliged to pay tuition fees beyond the Seven-Year School. Exempt from the ruling were students with grades of the *otlichnik* or "excellent" level (A's in two thirds of their studies, B's in all others). Students in this category may claim stipends as well as free tuition, where needed, in higher institutions and technical secondary schools. A similar provision applies to demobilized and wounded Red Army men and to children of Red Army men.

Under peacetime conditions there is no compulsion for students to enter any particular field of training or work. However, students pledge themselves, upon completing any technical or professional training, to practice for a period up to five years in the area where they are most needed at the time.

COEDUCATION . . . Until 1943 the general rule was coeducation at all age levels in the USSR. Partly influenced by the needs of the war situation, which necessitated a sharper division of tasks and of training between boys and girls, and partly as a result of psychological investigations, an exploratory program was entered upon involving separation of the sexes in many city institutions at the age levels within the Ten-Year School. Professor Evgeni Medynski of the Lenin Pedagogical Institute in Moscow explains the Soviet position on this matter as follows:

> Coeducation hinders the adaptation of the school program to the different rates of physiological development of boys and girls. It prevents adequate treatment of certain psychological differences, and the necessary differentiation of training of boys and girls for practical activities. Under coeducation the composition of intermediate and senior classes of secondary schools becomes very heterogeneous, negatively influencing the efficiency of the instructional program.
>
> The full equality of women's rights and the general availability of education has been completely achieved during the quarter of a century that has elapsed since the Soviet Revolution. The number of schools has vastly increased. In all towns and industrial settlements universal compulsory seven-year secondary education has been introduced.
>
> In view of all this, and with the object of eliminating the shortcomings inherent in coeducation, in all capitals of the USSR and in large industrial centers and cities (72 cities in all), as of 1943, segregated education of boys and girls has been introduced in all of the ten classes of secondary schools by means of establishing separate schools for boys and girls. This was preceded by six months of experiment at segregated teaching in several Moscow schools during the spring term of 1943, yielding good results. In all other towns and in rural localities junior and senior secondary schools continue coeducation.
>
> As distinguished from prerevolutionary times, this segregated education provides for an identical level of general-educational knowledge for boys and girls, and involves no segregation in any extra-school activities. The principals of the schools concerned declared that during the first six months the principle of segregated education introduced in 1943–44 showed up favorably as indicated by achievement.[1]

THE ABOLITION OF RACE AND SEX DISCRIMINATION . . .

The provision of the constitution (Chapter 10, Article 123) that makes it a criminal offense to exercise any form of discrimination or disqualification on grounds of race in "all spheres of economic, state, cultural, social and political life" applies directly to entrance into educational institutions. There is a like guarantee of equality of rights for women (Article 122). Such guarantees extend also to employment opportunities in occupations and professions, and to rates of pay. A woman can be barred only from those fields or types of work wherein it is scientifically demonstrable that she would undergo harm or injury on account of her sex

---

[1] *American Sociological Review*, No. 3 (June, 1944), XI, 291.

LITERACY . . . It is difficult to state precisely the degree of literacy in a large population. The last full-scale census of czarist times (1897) placed the rate of literacy at about 24 per cent. According to the latest Soviet federal census (1939) the rate of literacy for the country as a whole was about 81 per cent. Some authorities claim that literacy increased considerably between 1897 and 1914, but there are no adequate statistics, and there was no expansion of educational facilities sufficient to affect the rate of literacy very greatly. If there were gains, most of them must have been wiped out by the time the Soviets came to power, through war, famine, and general social disintegration—conditions which were particularly severe in their impact on the youth. In view of the vast number of people involved, the many geographical and traditional obstacles which had to be met, and the short period of time, the extension of literacy under the Soviet regime is recognized as remarkable.

PEDAGOGY AND CURRICULUM . . . While czarist education reached too few people, even at the grade-school level, the qualitative level of czarist instruction and training for the few who received a full education was high. Some Russian universities before the First World War were among the best in the world. Soviet pedagogy has undergone sweeping and rapid changes during its short history. At first, influenced by the Dalton plan and by American ideas having their source largely in the work of John Dewey, it attempted a complete application of progressive methods. A modified project method, with emphasis on group work, had considerable vogue. It was felt, however, that these methods did not obtain satisfactory results. They were sharply criticized for failing to instill a proper sense of system and discipline in the young, and for not providing a solid foundation of necessary knowledge.

The backbone of general education in the USSR is the Ten-Year School. Its curriculum is fairly standardized throughout the country. The principal studies in the primary grades are arithmetic and simple geometry, the native language (Russian also, in the non-Russian republics), nature study, geography, social science, polytechnized labor, music, art, and physical culture. By the time the pupil has reached the fifth class at the age of 12, he has begun a foreign language. As he goes on in secondary work, further subjects, such as history, literature, algebra, trigonometry, physics, chemistry, biology, logic, psychology, military studies, and other special subjects are added. There are relatively few electives within the first ten years. *Tekhnikums* offer a good deal of general education in addition to the technical training in the field of specialization.

While some of the advanced studies in the Ten-Year School and the *tekhnikum* would correspond to what Americans call college work, a great deal of what Americans would refer to as higher education takes place in "institutes" devoted to special areas of study, as well as in multifaculty universities. However, in all institutions of higher learning, the student, no matter what his specialty, receives general cultural training. For example, at least a year of philosophy is compulsory, including not only the principles of dialectical materialism, but all schools in the history of philosophy from pre-Socratic times to the present. World history, art, and literature are widely studied, and American authors like James Fenimore Cooper, Edgar Allan Poe, Henry Wadsworth Longfellow, Walt Whitman, Jack London, and Mark Twain, and contemporary writers like Theodore Dreiser, Upton Sinclair, Ernest Hemingway, John Dos Passos, and Sinclair Lewis are well known. The great masters of the past in all fields of art and culture are probably as well known and respected by the Soviet public as by the general public of any other country.

POLYTECHNIZATION . . . A basic emphasis that has been very significant throughout practically the whole history of Soviet education is upon what is called polytechnization. This concept derives ultimately from the whole socialist idea of the labor school, which goes back to the days of Marx and Engels and even earlier. The idea that is stressed is the value of scientific and technical training, not at the expense of the arts and cultural pursuits, but in fusion with them. Polytechnical education in the Soviet Union does not mean simply vocational or trade training in its narrower sense. It means a grasp of science and technology in terms of their immense significance in modern society, a grasp of the basic forces of economic production upon which the life of man depends. Put in other words, the child is taught the significance and value of the labor process in all its different senses. Concerning the nature of the polytechnical school, Nadezhda K. Krupskaya, widow of Lenin and an educationist of considerable standing in her own right, said: "This does not mean a school in which one studies several trades, but rather

329

a school where children learn to understand the essence of the laboring processes, the substance of the labor activity of the people, and the conditions of success in work. It is a school where children learn to know the extent of their powers." [2]

The objectives of polytechnization are implemented concretely by tool, shop, and laboratory work, and by personalized interaction between the school and neighboring institutions, such as farms, factories, and hospitals. Each visits the other; each helps in concrete ways in fulfilling the tasks of the other; each submits certain problems to the other. The polytechnical approach in higher curricula means an enrichment of scientific and technical subjects by showing their vital connections with human problems and cultural values, and a more realistic treatment of the arts and humanities by relating them to the actual life and life work of people. Another manifestation of this emphasis is that technical schools and higher institutes generally are under the control of that commissariat which has jurisdiction over the field of work in question. The aim is to place the institution of professional or occupational training in as close contact as possible with actually functioning institutions in the same field of work.

PEDOLOGY . . . Great reliance was at one time placed on the field of study known in the Soviet Union as pedology. This field was defined as follows by Albert Pinkevich, a leading figure in Soviet education during the 1920's and early 1930's. "This science is concerned with the psychological and physical development of the child from birth to maturity. It studies the biology and psychology of human growth. Pedagogy takes the findings of pedology and utilizes them in the organization of methods for promoting the desired physical and mental development of the child." [3]

The pedological approach did not prove satisfactory. It was criticized for relying too much on early psychological testing as a basis for separating pupils into different groups and schools, and for disposing of the child in accordance with such tests rather than in the light of the classroom teacher's knowledge of him and his daily work. The abandonment of pedology in the middle 1930's also reflected newer trends in psychol-

---

[2] Quoted by Albert Pinkevich in *The New Education in the Soviet Republic* (New York, 1929), p. 200.
[3] *Ibid.*, p. 7.

ogy, not confined to the Soviet Union. It is now seen that much earlier testing was too mechanical, narrow, and rigid to deal adequately with the full nature and personality of the child.

NON-RUSSIAN NATIONAL SCHOOLS AND CULTURES . . . The historic policy of the czarist government toward the 150-plus indigenous racial and national minorities in the Russian Empire was one of "Russification," which meant the attempt to impose the Russian language and Russian culture on all peoples throughout the empire. Russian was made the language of public life and the official language of instruction throughout the regular school system. In contrast, the Soviet government has followed a policy of encouraging diversity of cultures within the economic and political framework of socialism, under the principle of "culture national in form and socialist in content." The constitution of the USSR specifically provides that instruction in schools be conducted in the native language (Chapter 10, Article 121) in those regions where it is desired. Thus instruction has been offered and textbooks have been printed in more than 70 languages. Up to 1937, no fewer than 74 alphabets have been created for linguistic groups without a written language. Extensive government support and subsidies have been given to native theaters, museums, and other art centers.

SCHOOL GOVERNMENT AND EXTRACURRICULAR ACTIVITIES . . . Under the czarist regime, student participation in school government, and even student clubs and other activities, were discouraged. The following are typical of numerous regulations established by the minister of instruction:

> 14. Within the buildings, courts, and grounds of the university the organization of students' reading-rooms, dining or food clubs, and also theatrical representations, concerts, balls, and other similar public assemblies not having a scientific character is absolutely forbidden.
> 15. Students are forbidden to hold any meetings, gatherings for deliberations in common on any matter whatsoever, or to deliver public speeches, and they are likewise forbidden to establish any common funds whatever.[4]

In the early days of the Soviet regime educational experimentation was extreme and variegated. Students, even in secondary schools, were given so much power in school government that their authority often seemed to overshadow that of teaching staff and administration. Some

---

[4] Quoted by Beatrice King in *Changing Man* (New York, 1937), p. 15.

of these conditions are vividly pictured by N. Ognyov in *The Diary of a Communist Schoolboy*. This system was criticized on the ground that it failed to promote education results of positive value. The evolution has been toward increasing the authority of teachers and directors, but the participation of students at all levels in school government is also fostered and valued. A 1932 decree of the Commissariat of Education of the RSFSR stated that self-government by school children is directed toward the aims of:

(a) raising the level of general knowledge; (b) an extension of the polytechnical outlook and knowledge; (c) acquisition of skills, the planning of studies and manual work; (d) the strengthening of conscious discipline; (e) fulfilling of social duties; (f) carrying on in an organized way out-of-school (mass cultural) work; (g) improving the children's health.[5]

There are class committees of students and a governing joint Pupils' Committee of students and teachers. This committee takes part in handling problems of discipline and of poor academic work through enlisting the co-operation and support of other students. Clubs and teams, known as circles and representing all forms of artistic expression, cultural activity, and physical culture, are very popular among students. Supplying funds for facilities, directors, and guides is an important part of school budgeting.

BUDGET AND FINANCE . . . In 1914–1915 there were about 8,000,-000 students in elementary and secondary schools; in 1941, about 35,-000,000. Budgetary outlay on education rose proportionately, mounting steadily since the Soviet regime came to power. In 1928–1929, the first year of the Five-Year plans, the allocation for education was about 1,000,000,000 rubles; in 1941–1942 it was about 26 times that amount. In 1932 the educational expenditures for the whole country were 21.2 per cent of the total budget. In 1937 they were 26.1 per cent of the total.

ADULT EDUCATION . . . Adult education facilities, like all other education facilities, were very meager under the czars. The Soviet regime has stressed adult education and has provided a large network and variety of facilities. The liquidation of mass illiteracy was a huge undertaking in adult education. In this field the tendency has been to bring educational facilities to working establishments, to rouse greater

---

[5] *Ibid.*, p. 94.

interest, to make the instruction more realistic, and to save time. Courses and lectures are frequently given by radio. On January 1, 1933, there were about 50,000 clubs receiving adult education services, nearly 2,000 "culture homes," 34,000 "reading huts," and over 32,000 "mass libraries." In 1941 there were about 10,000 secondary schools for adults, with an attendance of about one and a half million people. The armed services are also an active center of education, where much systematic instruction, not confined to technical subjects, is given. In a country with compulsory military service of two to five years, this policy has considerable effect.

LIBRARIES AND MUSEUMS . . . In 1941 there were about 77,000 public libraries in the USSR. Of these, about 43,000 were for the general reader, 6,000 were technical, 3,000 were children's libraries, and over 20,000 were traveling libraries, which carried reading matter by truck, wagon, sledge, camel, and reindeer to farmers and other workers in outlying localities. In czarist times there were about 15,000 general libraries. One of the largest libraries in the world is the Lenin State Library in Moscow; it has nine and a half million volumes, and issues over four million books annually to about 825,000 people.

About 70 special schools, *tekhnikums*, and institutes train library personnel. Libraries were an important instrument in liquidating illiteracy, and they are centers for many adult education programs. In addition to state libraries for the general public, extensive library systems are operated by the central commissariats to serve their working establishments, and by trade unions and the Red Army. With literacy, expanded education, and increased library facilities, there has arisen an enormous demand for books, which are supplied to the public at very low cost. Since 1918 some 9,000,000,000 books have been published in over 100 languages. Before 1941 about 45,000 new titles a year were published; the yearly output in volumes was about 25 million.

The number of museums in Moscow has increased from 87 to over 200. This is typical for the country at large. Besides the ordinary types of museum there are many others devoted to various aspects of social life: for example, life in the 1840's, the czarist army, children's playthings. Museums are centers for social propaganda, and traveling museums service outlying farms and working establishments. The tendency has been to turn away from the conception of museums as static collections of objects toward a dynamic conception that museum exhibits should present objects functionally in their relationships with history and daily life.

THE PRESS, THE THEATER, AND THE RADIO . . . The most distinctive educational characteristic of the popular arts in the Soviet Union is the deliberate co-operation between them and the agencies of formal education in terms of general goals and standards. Commercial influences are absent, and there is a general freedom from the psychologically deleterious overemphasis on sex, crime, and horror themes. Popular magazines devoted to murder and other sensational crimes or to sex exhibitionism do not exist. Nor does the screen produce much that could be called a vulgarized exploitation of sex themes. The radio is free from horror serials and from commercial announcements. Children seldom find themselves in the position of being educated in one direction by the school and in other directions by agencies outside the school. The Soviet educator can usually count on the co-operation of other avenues of influence. In general, the psychological and ethical standards dominant in the classroom are also dominant in the popular arts. This point is of great significance in judging the operation of education in the society as a whole.

FREEDOM . . . In the Soviet system there is no freedom for organized antisocialist teaching. The viewpoint taken is that the ideals of socialism, such as economic security, full health service, complete education, and freedom from race or sex discrimination are of maximum democratic significance, and that they cannot be attained in practice except by large-scale government measures and long-time planning. Soviet writers maintain that freedom to teach against these objectives would jeopardize the freedom of the majority to attain a fuller material and cultural life, which in their interpretation is the most basic of democratic freedoms.

While all organized educational processes must operate within the aims of socialism, there is freedom for criticism in regard to the ways and means of attaining these gains. There is abundant opportunity for critical discussion and differing viewpoints regarding methods and operating conditions of this or that plant, factory, farm, or school, and regarding the effectiveness or shortcomings of the administration concerned. In Soviet newspapers, journals, and wall newspapers, and in periodic meetings for "criticism and self-criticism," the methods and practices of administrative superiors are sharply criticized by those of lower rank. Children and adults are educated in this atmosphere of "criticism and self-criticism." Major decisions of social policy are frequently preceded by widespread public discussions, as in the case of the marriage and divorce laws, and the new Constitution in 1936.

However, when the decision has finally been made, and official action has been taken, freedom of discussion in regard to the decision itself is considered at an end. Discussion is then confined to ways and means of carrying out the concrete plan with which the decision has usually been implemented. The principle seems to be that all should have a voice in making the plans, but once the plans are made, all should cooperate in their fulfillment.

BIBLIOGRAPHY

Ognyov., N., *The Diary of a Communist School Boy* (London, 1928).

Pinkevich, A. P., *The New Education in the Soviet Republic* (New York, 1929).

Harper, S. N. *Making Bolsheviks* (Chicago, 1931).

Ilin, M., *New Russia's Primer: The Story of the Five Year Plan* (New York, 1931).

Williams, F. E., *Russia, Youth, and the Present-Day World* (New York, 1934).

Lenin, V. I., "The Tasks of the Youth Leagues," *Selected Works*, vol. IX (New York, 1935–1938).

King, Beatrice, *Changing Man: The Education System of the U.S.S.R.* (New York. 1937).

Turosienski, S. K., *Education in the Union of Soviet Socialist Republics and in Imperial Russia*, bibliography (Washington, D.C., 1937).

Levin, D., *Children in Soviet Russia* (London, 1942).

Maurer, Rose, *Soviet Health Care in Peace and War* (New York, 1943).

Medynski, E., "Schools and Education in the U.S.S.R.," *American Sociological Review* (June, 1944), vol. IX.

CHAPTER XVIII

Religion Under the Czars

and the Soviets

By SIR BERNARD PARES

T HE East Slavs, or Russians, were pagan until 989 A.D. They had no priestly caste but they had certain rites of burial and many other religious ideas which later blended with peasant Christian beliefs. Their gods were the forces of nature. In 989 Vladimir I of Kiev, after a careful examination of various forms of belief accessible to him, decided as an act of statesmanship to accept, from Constantinople, the Orthodox or Eastern form of Christianity. His people soon became quite reconciled to their new religion, especially through the emotional appeal of its wonderful church music. Unlike Latin Christianity, the Orthodox belief did not place the pope above all sovereigns; the church devoted itself to illustrating the existence of another world, the spiritual, always side by side with the temporal. The monks of the Monastery of the Caves outside Kiev served as state employees and envoys and drew up the first chronicles with a fidelity which set a high standard for later historians.

In 966 the adjoining Polish kingdom had accepted Latin Christianity from the pope. The Poles historically regarded themselves as the frontier guardians of western Europe and civilization, and the difference of con fession has been one of the principal sources of discord between Poles and Russians down to our own times.

The Orthodox Church took firm root in Russia and deeply satisfied the instincts of the people. It is to be noted that in the adaptation of Greek church law to Russia, the changes were mostly in the direction of humanity and leniency, with also a greater consideration for women. The church was a great pioneer in Russian colonization, and the ascetic hermitages and monasteries in the wilds were followed up by the peasant population. But the church never even attempted such an organization of social services as was to be found in western Europe. During 240 years of subjection to the Tatar conquerors (1240 to 1480), when for a long time there was no single accepted secular authority, the church served as the one unifying force in the country and the chief hope of final deliverance.

As little Moscow in the backwoods grew up into authority, and through subservience to the conquerors was able to offer tranquility to the roving peasants, the church made its home there and in every way forwarded Moscow's influence and power.

By an accidental lack of competitors for local sovereignty through several reigns, Moscow developed a new order of succession from father to son—instead of from brother to brother as elsewhere—which favored long and quiet reigns, and this was supported by the church.

But the monasteries, losing their first ascetic spirit, developed into rich land-owning communities, and the church wealth, as in medieval western Europe, aroused sharp criticism and controversy. The Reformation did not seriously touch Russia: dissent was little developed, and the church never made any serious attempt to challenge the secular power.

On the contrary, the temporal power received a great accession of strength from the conquest of Constantinople by the Moslem Turks in 1453. This event brought the original home of Greek Christianity into bondage. The pope then appealed for a reunion of Christendom, and offered the niece of the last Byzantine emperor in marriage to Ivan the Great of Moscow. Ivan accepted the lady but emphatically rejected reunion, and Moscow thus became the champion of liberation for the Christian subjects of the sultan. This development was reflected in Russia in a heightened court ceremony on Byzantine lines and in the claim that Moscow was now the third and last Rome. In Russia the temporal power rose higher and higher above the spiritual.

In 1596 something happened outside the frontiers of Moscow which was to cause her much trouble later. The Polish state then included a large Russian population, of the Ukrainian and White Russian branches, who were Orthodox. They vigorously resisted Catholic propaganda. An arrangement, called the Church Unia, was made in Poland by which they could escape persecution if they accepted papal supremacy even though they retained the Orthodox form of belief and worship, which was now rechristened "the Eastern Rite." Only a portion of the Russians in Poland accepted this compromise, and they were henceforth called Uniats. The rest looked to Moscow for liberation.

On the other hand, in 1598, when the Patriarch Jeremy of Constantinople was on a visit to Moscow, a fifth Orthodox patriarchate was established there. This was on the eve of the end of the dynasty of Ryurik, and the new authority came just in time to serve as a pivot for national unity during the succeeding Time of Troubles (1605–1613), when no czar was accepted by all the country. The Russian Church played a valiant part in this period. The fortified Monastery of the Trinity and St. Sergius successfully stood siege for a year while the Catholic Poles held the Moscow Kremlin and came near to imposing a Polish czar on Russia. Letters from this monastery and from the captive Patriarch Hermogen in the Kremlin brought a great national host of the peasantry to Moscow to drive out the Poles. The new sovereign, chosen in 1613, by a widely elected national assembly, the first of the new dynasty of Romanov, owed his choice in part to the fact that he was the son of another patriarch, Philaret (Filaret). For the next two reigns the patriarch practically enjoyed an authority equal to that of the czar and was also styled sovereign.

Under the second Romanov, Aleksei I Mikhailovich, a serious schism (*raskol*) arose in the Russian Church. Alexis' counselor and almost cosovereign, the Patriarch Nikon, wished to erase mistranslations from the Greek from the church books, but he did this with such violence that a considerable section of the church fought back, even sometimes to the point of death, and finally parted company with the official body. Nikon owed his victory only to the secular power. From this time on there was a rebel church, which often supported other rebel movements. The significance of the split was infinitely heightened by the fact that during this reign serfdom was finally legalized and riveted on the mass of peasant population, which in its own way continued to be deeply religious.

This isolation of the official church and its complete subjection to the

338

temporal power was carried much further in the next reign by Alexis' son, Peter the Great (1682–1725).

The church strongly opposed Peter's radical innovations, and its primitive backwardness was one of his principal obstacles to reform. He found distasteful the rival authority of the patriarch, and when Adrian died in 1700 he allowed the office to lapse by appointing no successor. Instead he put church affairs permanently under a commission entitled "The Holy Synod," whose every action was watched by a lay official whom he described with brutal frankness as the "czar's eye." This arrangement was continued up to the revolution of 1917 and does much to explain the reaction against official religion which followed immediately afterwards. The official church was robbed of all independence. In a sense the community of believers, like the mass of the peasantry, had gone underground. Quite accurate was the summary of a peasant in 1908: "The State has got wrong with the community and has dragged the Church with it." Another illuminating comment was made by the last French ambassador to the czars, Maurice Paleologue: "This people is more religious than its Church."

The Russian clergy were divided into the "White" clergy or monks, and the "Black" or parish priests. The latter, who were ordinarily very poorly educated, were close to the peasantry. They not only might marry but had to be married—often to the daughter of an outgoing predecessor, and these marriages were by no means unsuccessful. A widower could not remarry, and he became eligible for monkhood and promotion. The bishops were taken exclusively from the White clergy, more often than not trained in the higher monastery schools. In or near the larger towns were famous monasteries which served as episcopal residences and seats of administration. To these were attached schools of church vocal music, sung in many male parts without accompaniment, in which some outstanding musical reputations were achieved. The great monasteries were also the centers of icon painting, which had many traditions and rules, and was always one of the finest Russian arts. These religious pictures aim at portraying beauty less than suffering and character, and the Russian painters often went far beyond the Byzantine originals. But the Russian Church did little to continue its early role as the center of culture in the country, and the monasteries ordinarily became nests of obscurantism.

Russian religion may be said to have recognized two parallel orders, the one of priests and the other of prophets. In regard to the latter, there was a tradition throughout Russian history of self-commissioned "Men of God," who abjured ordinary human needs to wander barefoot over the country; sometimes at critical moments they interfered in public affairs with bold warnings even to czars themselves. These wanderers (*stranniki*) were especially revered by the peasants, and unfortunately they served as model for the notorious charlatan Rasputin-Novykh. Under its official uniformity Russian religion also embraced a number of strange beliefs which almost defied classification.

The French Revolution, with the long wars and the closer contact of Russia with Europe that followed, set many minds at work. Patriotism flared up in all classes in the "Fatherland War" of defense against Napoleon in 1812. The top layer of society, which in Russia almost monopolized education, absorbed many new ideas while in service in the Army of Occupation in France after 1815. The disgrace of serfdom was in all thoughts, and it led to the rising of the Decembrists in 1825. This was easily crushed, and leadership for reform passed to the growing professional class, who were now filled with discontent. From neighboring Germany, which lay in a bondage like that of Russia, a series of great thinkers from Immanuel Kant to Georg W. F. Hegel fired the minds of young Russians. Hegel asked what contribution each national culture could contribute to world thought, and in the stifling reaction under Nicholas I (1825–1855) Russian thinkers found difficulty in giving any answer.

Two schools of thought arose. The Westerners could see hope only in assimilating the most progressive ideas of western European progress, which included a strong reaction against religion. The Slavophiles, on the other hand, were deeply religious, and they looked for a kernel of culture in Russian peasant institutions, especially in the collective spirit of the traditional village community, the mir. To the teaching of the old Greek ascetics they added the collective spirit of the peasant masses. They eschewed the individualistic departure from this spirit which arose in the west with the Reformation, and they believed that collective Russia had a great deal to say some day to the world. For them the object of life was not merely to think but to be. They were essentially Russian: they were inaccessible to Catholic influence and did not proselytize.

340

In these qualities and in their teachings they resembled, by an extraordinary trend of history, the Anglicans in England.

The Slavophiles were as free and independent in thought as the Westerners, but they were deeply religious. The Westerners can best be described as religious atheists; for atheism is itself essentially an expression of religious thought. Russian thought is basically religious, and every adaptaton which it borrows from Europe naturally takes a religious tinge. Russian philosophy is idealistic on the lines of Plato. The great Russian writers of the nineteenth century—and they will bear comparison with the writers of any other country—were all religious. The two greatest, Tolstoy and Dostoyevsky, had spiritual advisers who lived holy lives of self-discipline in famous monasteries. It might be said that in every educated and thinking Russian there lies the germ both of the Slavophile and of the Westerner.

The friendship with England, which in 1914 became an alliance, was much more a reality in Russia than in England. England was the political model of all four Dumas (1906–1917). A great wave of liberalism had swept the educated classes and with it a powerful movement for religious liberation. The last notable lay official who acted as the "czar's eye," K. P. Pobedonostsev (1881–1908), made religion almost a mere matter of drill. In 1905 the Orthodox opposition nearly achieved its goal of summoning a church council on a congregational basis and restoring the patriarchate as the symbol of church independence. The First World War saw many outstanding expressions of the religious spirit, and the fall of the monarchy in March, 1917, was regarded by Russian churchmen as the end of Byzantinism. The Church Council was called, and the patriarchate was re-established. The laws drafted for the impending Constituent Assembly by the provisional government accorded full freedom to all the many diverse religions of the state.

It was well that the Russian Church, as soon as it was freed of the dead weight of czardom, did so much to purify itself on the eve of its greatest ordeal. The international Bolsheviks, devoted to world revolution, returned from exile pledged to a purification of another sort—to the extinction of religion, which they regarded simply as a kind of opiate used by capitalists to keep the masses in bondage. Marx had reversed the teaching of Hegel by placing matter before spirit. Church property of course shared in the general nationalization; churches now

341

had to be leased back from the government by communities of believers. Freedom of conscience and of religious worship were guaranteed. Persons were not punished for religious belief alone, but belief was to be cut at the source by prohibiting religious teaching outside the home. This intention was dramatized by two trials scheduled for Easter, 1923. During the Western Holy Week, which that year preceded the Russian by one week, the highest Catholic dignitaries were put on trial and met the challenge with unanimous courage. The Polish Catholic Archbishop Jan Cieplak was condemned to death and his principal lieutenant, Monsignor Konstanty Budkiewicz, was actually martyred. The outcry from western Europe and America and the fear of losing recently concluded trade treaties drove the Soviet government to retreat. The Catholic archbishop was liberated and the Orthodox Patriarch Vasili B. Tikhon was never put on trial; but neither of them long survived his ordeal.

The frontal attack was never renewed. Anatol V. Lunacharski, the Soviet minister of education, who had been only half-hearted in the matter, now undertook to spread atheism by propaganda, which was by no means effective. Before his retirement he declared, "Religion is like a nail; the harder you hit it the deeper it goes into the wood." The young remained cut off from any regular religious teaching, and all that was formal in adherence to religion disappeared of itself, but the core of Russian religion was strengthened in those who had to pay in indirect ways for their belief.

The battle against religious belief was now entrusted to a sincere and intelligent atheist, a friend of Stalin's youth, E. Yaroslavski, who discontinued all measures of violence but encouraged a Union of the Godless, of which he was president. In 1929 he was aided by state action. Freedom of religious propaganda was deleted from the constitution (April 14) and by a comprehensive law of April 8 the church was denied legal existence and debarred from any activities other than the performance of worship. This was the reply to its attempt to participate in the excellent social services instituted by the government. Antireligious museums were opened, and antireligion became an active part of the compulsory school curriculum. This measure tended to defeat itself, for it emphasized the vitality of religion. Indeed that quality of Russian thought which always gave an idealist character to any lessons

342

borrowed from abroad tended to turn Marxism itself from a materialism to an idealism; it has been pointed out that the contest became a battle between two idealisms, each finding something to respect in its rival. Indirect oppression of the ministers of all cults only brought them nearer to the masses and tended to replace former distinctions of belief by something like a common religious front. In 1937 Yaroslavski himself, in his instructions to his followers, rated more than one half the population as sincerely religious—a proportion which might have been envied in other countries; he declared that his own antireligious organizations had "fallen to pieces" (*raspalis*).

By this time Stalin's bid for the co-operation of the Western democracies against the threat of German invasion reduced the antireligious laws more and more to a dead letter. The war itself, with the alliance of the United Nations against Hitler, completed the process. Substantial alleviations for religion followed fast on each other. Priests received the franchise; icons could again be produced and sold; the great church feasts became national rest days; Sunday was restored; and the "godless" magazine was suspended. Following the dissolution of the Comintern on May 22, 1943, the patriarchate, which had been suspended since the death of Tikhon in April, 1925, was restored with the concurrence of Stalin on September 4, 1943, and training colleges for priests were again established in Russia.

BIBLIOGRAPHY

Gumilevsky, D. G., *Geschichte der Kirche Russlands* (Frankfurt, 1872).
Maynard, John, *Russia in Flux* (London, 1941).
Timashev, N. S., *Religion in Soviet Russia* (New York, 1942).
Anderson, P. B., *People, Church and State in Modern Russia* (New York, 1944).

CHAPTER XIX

The Armed Forces

By NICHOLAS COROTNEFF

THE first armed forces of ancient Russia were the household troops or the bodyguard (*druzhina*) maintained by each ruler during the Kiev period (882-1132). The country was divided into several principalities under the princes of the Ryurik dynasty. The *druzhina* was formed of professional warriors, bound to the prince not by allegiance but by a time agreement, and the warriors jealously guarded this "right of departure" at the expiration of a contract. Thus the contingents were fluid and unstable and in the ninth and tenth centuries were mainly foreigners, Scandinavians predominating. Later, native warriors gained ascendance. As the prince had to provide arms, upkeep, and pay, the number of men in a *druzhina* rarely exceeded a thousand. In war a general levy of militia was called, based on a "communal" principle of liability to service, each village or township providing a certain quota of self-armed and self-provisioned men.

Records tend to show that at times of grave danger, such as were created by frequent invasions of Eastern nomadic hordes in the tenth and eleventh centuries, the levies amounted to total mobilization. As horse breeding in Russia was not yet developed, the militia were foot soldiers, only *druzhinas* being mounted. In the roadless and sparsely populated country, the infantry, burdened with large trains, was usually dependent on river transport.

In the tenth and eleventh centuries, when the Kiev princes maintained unity and co-ordination of military effort, these armed forces were adequate to cope with incessant attacks and forays of invaders, among

344

whom the most dangerous and ruthless were the Polovtsy. With the decline of Kiev the progressive dismemberment of the state and growing feuds among the princes weakened the national military power. Even when a common foe brought the princes into the field together, the inherent handicaps of coalition warfare frequently led to military disasters. Against the perfectly integrated war machine of the Mongols, whose mounted armies combined power and speed, the disjointed foot levies had no chance; the Tatars overran Russia during two winter campaigns (1237–1240). Novgorod was the only large community to escape the invasion and was able under the leadership of Alexander Nevski to fight off the Swedes (1240) and to administer a crushing defeat to the Teutonic knights near Pskov (1242). The calamity of long Tatar domination (1237–1480) demonstrated the need for strong national authority and a unified military force, and the rise of Moscow provided the nucleus of a national army. In 1380 Dmitri Donskoi gathered under the banners of Moscow an army variously estimated at 150,000 to 400,000 men; with it he decisively defeated an equally large Tatar force in the battle of Kulikovo. Under his successors the armed strength of Moscow continued to grow, evolving a peculiar system of military feudalism. At first loose and fragmentary, it achieved full development under Ivan III and Ivan the Terrible, and the army structure permeated the whole state structure.

Large grants of land were given to the nobility in exchange for permanent military allegiance; thus was eliminated the former tendency of the *druzhinas* to change employers. According to the arable land he controlled, every landowner had to keep a certain number of men in readiness to report with him at the first call to his district center—all mounted, fully armed, and provisioned.

In cities and townships, part of the population, upon voluntary enlistment, was given plots of land, houses, small annual grants of money, and exemption from certain taxes. Those who enlisted obligated themselves and their sons to military service in wartime, but they were free to engage in trade or commerce in peacetime, except for one or two months of military training a year. These town troops, a distinct semi-professional military class, formed the infantry—pikemen and musketeers (*streltsi*) and the rank and file of artillery and service troops.

In a somewhat similar way the Cossacks, first mentioned in 1444, served as town cavalry in the border regions west and east of the Don. Arms, ammunition, and equipment for the town troops were provided by the state. A few units of foreign mercenaries and auxiliary troops of Tatars also served for pay. The mounted arm grew steadily from the beginning of the Moscow period, and by the end of the fourteenth century the cavalry constituted more than two thirds of the army. In the fifteenth century whole cavalry armies began to appear, and the role of infantry became negligible. With the growth of town troops, however, a revival of infantry took place.

Russian army tactics up to the end of the fifteenth century bear considerable resemblance, on the whole, to the tactics of Western medieval armies, though Russian arms and equipment were decidedly inferior. Protective armor never progressed beyond the stage of reinforced mail, and a great deal of this armor was imported from the West and the East. On the other hand, the Russian medieval tactics were often more flexible and better articulated than tactics in the West. Armies in the field formed in five tactical bodies instead of three (vanguard, main body and rear guard) as in the West; left and right flanks were separate formations. Notable also were the careful and judicious husbanding of tactical reserves and the prominent development of the element of surprise. In the eastern regions of Russia the tactics naturally followed a more Oriental pattern. Scattered and fluid cavalry formations were used, and mounted archers were employed on a large scale.

Artillery, imported from western Europe, appeared at the end of the fourteenth century. The Russians proved adept in its use and it quickly assumed an important role, especially in the defense of towns. The first ordnance works were founded by Ivan III under the supervision of foreign gunmakers. In 1550, at the siege of Kazan, Ivan IV had a powerful siege train, cleverly employed and supplemented by extensive use of mining galleries.

Russia did not share greatly in the development in western military art brought by the Renaissance, when tactics of all arms were improved and standing armies were introduced, although some of the new developments were borrowed, or imported by foreign mercenaries. The chaotic conditions created by the great crisis of 1602–1612 (Time of Troubles) reflected most unfavorably on the state of the armed forces. The devastation and ravages of the Time of Troubles weakened the

346

country's military potential; great quantities of irreplaceable material were destroyed, and the budding armament industry was shattered. At a time when powerful Western neighbors kept Russia virtually isolated, the backward military leadership at home kept the armed forces frozen in the medieval stage, both tactically and technically. Yet to compete with the growing efficiency of European armies, the importation of foreign mercenary troops and of Western military instructors was greatly accelerated. The army became a motley assortment of (1) purely foreign units; (2) regiments designated as "of foreign drill" (Russians trained by foreign officers in Western fashion); and (3) of still other Russian units which trained and fought in the national manner of the fifteenth and sixteenth centuries (called regiments "of Russian drill"). Such disparities rendered the antiquated administrative machine even more cumbersome.

Another glaring weakness was the stubborn adherence to a peculiar command system originated in the previous century. Higher commanders—of armies and their component bodies—were appointed according to a system of ranking based not on personal merit but on military genealogy, i.e., on the service records of their families, going back for generations. With time, the ranking tables became more and more complex, and interminable dissensions and squabbles arose between the appointees, sometimes on the very field of battle. By the middle of the seventeenth century the system had become a monstrous absurdity, and it was abolished in 1682.

Although at this time the field strength of a fully mobilized army exceeded 200,000, it was admitted that probably not more than 20,000 could be considered entirely reliable. A drastic reform of the whole war machine was the only solution. This task was accomplished by Peter the Great, who created the first regular standing army in Russian history. The nucleus of the new army was two regiments—Preobrazhenski and Semenovski, formed in 1687, which later became the Imperial Guard. They were armed, clad, and drilled in the European fashion and were commanded by foreign officers.

After more than a decade of experimentation, the true foundations of the new military system were laid in 1699, when three divisions of nine regiments each were formed along the same lines. They were recruited on the principle of compulsory military service for all classes. The institution of mercenary troops was abolished; thus the army had become truly national. Perhaps the greatest shortcoming of Peter's system was the principle of life-long enlistment, which tended to encourage a caste organization and precluded the gradual formation of trained reserves. The long war with Sweden (1700–1721) was a formidable test for the young army, pitched against one of the best armies of Europe. After a crushing defeat at the Battle of Narva (1700), Peter's strategy of avoiding decisive battles but of seasoning the army in harassing tactics of active defense and guerrilla warfare, reaped excellent results. The great victory of Poltava (1709) put Russia on the map as a European power.

At Peter's death, the field army had grown to 49 infantry and 33 cavalry regiments, with about 150 guns. Counting special garrison forces and territorial formations, the army numbered about 220,000 men. Administration was concentrated in the College of War—a small body of officials headed by a presiding member, with decisions reached by vote. An important part of Peter's military reforms was the creation of an adequate industrial basis for the war machine. The few existing armaments works were expanded, and new ones were opened in central Russia and in the Ural region. The army was assured an abundant supply of weapons and equipment, without dependence on foreign imports. The basic Service Regulations of 1716, followed by others, established high standards of discipline and training among Russian soldiers.

Under Peter's inept successors the army continued to grow numerically. Foreign techniques and tactics were borrowed indiscriminately, but there was little or no progress. Unstable political conditions caused a deterioration among the higher commanding personnel. However, Peter's military machine proved sturdy, and in the Seven Years' War (1756–1763), despite frequent incompetency of the high command, the rank and file were more than a match for the well-drilled troops of Frederick the Great. The Prussian Army was routed at Kunersdorf (1759), and in the following year Berlin was captured by a cavalry raid. By the end of the war the total strength of the army exceeded 300,000.

Several important reforms came during the reign of Catherine II. The enlistment term was changed from life to 25 years and for some regions to 15. Cossack formations were greatly increased (to about 50

348

regiments), raising the effectives to 400,000 men. A group of capable and energetic commanders, led by Rumyantsev and Suvorov, came to the fore. Suvorov's brilliant offensive tactics, based on mobility, speed, and surprise, brought Russian arms a string of victories in the Polish and Turkish wars (1768–1794), and in the Italian campaign of 1799. Suvorov's teachings and his intensive training, based on the principle that "every soldier must understand his maneuvers," left an indelible imprint on the following generation of commanders.

During the short reign of Paul I (1796–1801), an ardent admirer of Frederick the Great, the Prussian influence became paramount. Although several sound reforms took place in the army's administration, mechanical drill and parade-ground exercises achieved disproportionate prominence. The Napoleonic wars (1805–1807, 1812–1814) swelled the army to 600,000 men. Under Alexander I the collegiate system of administration was replaced by a Ministry of War. After the war of 1812, however, the executive power was concentrated in the newly established post of chief of the imperial staff; the minister of war retained authority only over supplies and economic administration. In the last years of Alexander's life the tendency revived of attaching excessive importance to the niceties of drill, parade ceremonials, and guard duty, reaching its zenith during the reign of Nicholas I. Numerically, the army grew to 27,000 officers and 968,000 men. But this huge force had a field strength of only 29 divisions. The rest were garrison troops and the Corps of Internal Guard.

The reign of Alexander II was a period of reforms. The war of 1812 had clearly demonstrated the inherent weaknesses of the military machine. Although actual army numbers decreased to 650,000, field strength grew to 48 divisions. Numerous other reforms were introduced in the economic administration of the army and in military education. The conscription bill of January 1, 1874, gave Russia a modern draft system. Lowering the enlistment term to five years permitted the gradual formation of trained reserves and a more flexible utilization of manpower. The basic foundations of Alexander II's military system survived until the beginning of the First World War, though with numerous changes and alterations.

The main outlines of the military system just before 1914 can be indicated as follows: Theoretically, every able-bodied male 21 to 33 was subject to conscription, with quite numerous exceptions and exemptions. The largest category of exemptions was to breadwinners, that is, to sons constituting the sole support of their families. For political reasons certain non-Slavic groups, such as the aborigines of Turkestan and the Finns, were permanently exempted, though they had to pay a special tax. The number of conscripts called annually was usually determined by the imperial Senate in accordance with recommendations made by the minister of war. The annual quota varied somewhat. It was about half a million men in the period preceding the First World War, and a considerable expansion had been planned when war broke out. The enlistment term was three years for infantry, artillery, and engineers; four years for the cavalry. Later a man remained 14 to 15 years with the first reserves and 4 more years with the second reserves. Cossacks were liable to practically life-long service, alternating between periods of active service and service in territorial reserves. Numerous privileges were granted for educational background; university graduates served in the line little more than a year.

For military purposes Russia was divided into 14 districts, each in the charge of a district commander equal in status to an army commander in the field. In 1914 the army had 357 infantry and 129 cavalry regiments. Artillery numbered 4,868 guns. During the First World War Russia mobilized about 15,000,000 men, reaching a peak strength of 280 infantry divisions and 286 cavalry regiments. A weak armament industry impeded the growth of artillery, and during the war Russia had to depend largely on the import of arms and ammunition from the Allied countries.

THE RED ARMY

The first armed forces of the November Revolution were the Red Guards—militia formations of industrial workers, sailors of the Baltic and Black Sea fleets, and improvised guerrilla detachments of peasants, demobilized soldiers, and Cossacks who banded together in the winter of 1917 to fight the Germans in the Ukraine, the Don, and the northwestern regions. To integrate these inchoate forces, numbering possibly 40,000 to 50,000 men, into an army was the first supremely urgent problem of the Soviets. The civil war was imminent and in its wake loomed the specter of foreign intervention. The task of creating a new revolutionary army of workers and peasants out of the wreckage of the old army, at a time when transport and supply were disorganized and the masses were war-weary and defeatist, was further complicated by a scarcity of trained commanders.

The official birthdate of the Red Army was February 23, 1918. It was established on that day as a volunteer force by a decree of the Soviet of People's Commissars. The new army, in Lenin's words, was "to be created of the most class-conscious and organized elements of the working classes," and it was intended to be the army of the world proletariat. The principle of volunteer enlistment proved short-lived, as internal conditions steadily worsened. Compulsory recruitment began on June 29, and the total male population of ages 18 to 40 became liable to military service. By the end of 1918 the Red Army numbered about 300,000 men. Over 20,000 were officers of the old army. Some of these enlisted voluntarily; others joined under the threat of proscription. In a further effort to increase the number of trained officers, over 120,000 former noncommissioned officers were appointed as subalterns in charge of platoons and sometimes companies. Numerous short-term command courses were opened to train new personnel.

The deep distrust and antagonism felt toward the officers' corps during 1917 continued unabated, and in order to fuse the heterogeneous elements of the new army the institution of political commissars, first introduced into the army by the provisional government, was greatly expanded and given enlarged powers. The decree of July 10, 1918, defined the commissars as "guardians of the revolution," to be recruited from "irreproachable revolutionaries, devoted to the cause of the proletariat . . . to whom the fate of the army is entrusted." Although the planning of military operations was left to the commanders, no orders they issued were valid unless countersigned by the respective commissar. A duality of command was thus inevitably created; and although the political and administrative work of the commissars helped greatly during the civil war to improve co-operation between the socially disparate and often conflicting elements of the army, objections to this hampering of command were voiced from the very first. For years the institution of political commissars was one of the most controversial issues in the Red Army. As the political scene changed, the corps of commissars underwent many changes; their powers fluctuated frequently until they were finally abolished in November, 1942.

Before the main structure of the new army was completed, it had to face the stern test of war; but from the Red Army's initial disasters to the concluding victories, its combat efficiency constantly improved. An effective, often ruthless discipline was gradually forged in the fighting lines, if not in the rear units. More potent even than the commissars in improving discipline were the communistic party cells which were introduced into every unit before the end of the civil war. The number of Communists in the army reached 208,000 before the war ended; they discharged military duties with fanatical zeal, and the majority fought in the ranks with great courage. Buttressed by this determined minority, the expanding Red Army overcame continuous internal stresses caused variously by rifts between officers and the ranks, by the individualism and anarchism of former guerrilla leaders, and by the lack of revolutionary enthusiasm among many of the peasantry who were the main source of manpower. Early in the war, desertion was the scourge of the army, depleting the ranks by hundreds of thousands. Gradually it was curbed by a relentless and systematic policy of arresting deserters and returning them to the front lines.

The outbreak of the Polish war in the spring of 1920 created a second front, and transport and supply facilities were strained to the breaking point. The state economy and the whole civil life had to be shaped and regulated by war, and by fall the Red Army reached the total of 5,300,-000 men. The armistice with Poland in October, followed by the defeat of General Wrangel's forces in the Crimea, brought the war to a close.

Victory in the civil war ensured the survival of the Soviet state, though it was surrounded by nations which it considered potential enemies. It was necessary to maintain a powerful military establishment, but since little or no postwar planning had been possible during the civil war, the country emerged from the war with no defined national military policy and no unified military doctrine.

The next four years were a transitional period for the Red Army. Demobilization proceeded swiftly. During 1921 the army was reduced from 5,300,000 to 1,400,000; in 1922 it was further diminished to 800,000, and in 1923 to 612,000 men. The training system and the whole organizational structure were upset; the crisis was aggravated further by the economic disruption and ruin brought about by the war. The army suffered acute shortages of shelter, food, and equipment; living standards were much lower than during the war.

In formulating a comprehensive military policy, Soviet leadership was sharply divided between advocates of a large standing army and those who advocated a citizen army of territorial militia, plus a small kernel of regular formations. The final solution, reached in 1924, was a compromise. The standing army was reduced to 562,000 men, roughly equal in numbers to a yearly conscription class, with a field strength of 29 infantry and 12 cavalry divisions. The term of enlistment was set at two years for the basic army; three for aviation, coastal defense, and frontier guards; four years for the navy. Territorial militia formations, numbering about 850,000, provided 41 infantry and 4½ cavalry divisions. The militia units consisted of (1) small permanent cadres, subject to the same enlistment terms as the regular army, and (2) alternating annual contingents of men serving a total of from eight to eleven months, according to the branch of service, over a period of five years. The reserves were divided into two categories. In the first the age limit was 35; in the second it was 40. The annual military budget from 1924 to 1925 was 395,000,000 rubles.

The establishment of a stable military system improved internal conditions of the Red Army, and a period of far-reaching reforms started under the able leadership of M. V. Frunze, appointed commissar of defense in 1924. In the following three years the system for training commanding personnel was greatly improved. The short-time command courses of the civil war era were supplanted by military schools with courses of three and four years' duration. Existing academies for higher military learning were enlarged, and new ones were created for different branches of service. Thousands of civil war commanders, retained in the army after demobilization, were sent to these academies for much-needed training. The material conditions of the army were gradually bettered, while a new stress on rigorous discipline corrected the postwar laxity and enhanced the authority of the commanders. Orders no longer required countersignatures of the commissars, although these retained full authority in the field of political education.

Throughout the whole army, but especially in the formation of the commanding cadres, class origin now played a decisive role. Peasants and workers were moving to the fore. The majority of old army officers were mustered out, although over 4,000 remained, many of whom were in high staff and command positions. To attain homogeneity in the army structure, cultural standards for officer candidates were temporarily lowered; this situation was later corrected by the tremendous growth of the Soviet educational system.

The greatest weakness of the Red Army still lay in its lack of modern technique and equipment, in almost complete absence of mechanized forces and aviation. The Soviet strategic and tactical doctrine evolved during this period rejected definitely the idea of the supremacy of the defense, a doctrine prevailing among the Western armies after the First World War. Instead, Red Army leaders visualized future war as primarily a war of movement and maneuver, with possible periods of stabilized positional warfare in certain sectors. They advocated, therefore, a bold strategic offensive and mobile tactics of encirclement and annihilation, secured by a strong defensive base organized in depth. For this broad conception the technical means of the Red Army were inadequate. Because of civil war experience, cavalry was considered the strategic arm, as a kind of substitute for mechanized forces. Nevertheless, the country's weakness in industrial potential and its inadequacy for modern warfare were keenly realized and frankly admitted.

The First Five-Year Plan, inaugurated in 1928, opened a new era for the Red Army in creating a powerful armament industry. Technical progress was prodigious during these years. Since the size of the army remained the same throughout the five years, the improvement was primarily qualitative—new arms and the new technique were better mastered and exploited. By 1934 the Red Army's mechanized forces and aviation were qualitatively equal to any in western Europe.

The army was now ready for numerical expansion. In March, 1934, the commissariats of Army and Navy were reorganized into the Commissariat of Defense, with sweeping powers over the armed forces; the Revolutionary Military Council was abolished. (Later, in 1938, a Supreme Military Council was set up, headed by Stalin.) The standing army was raised to 940,000 men, its first increase in size for a decade. In 1935 it was further expanded to 1,300,000. These were increases in the standing army only; the territorial militia was thus relegated to a second place, and in 1939 the militia system was abolished altogether. Accord-

354

ing to Marshal Voroshilov, "The territorial system began to conflict with the defensive requirements of the state as soon as the principal imperialist powers started to increase their armies, and adherence to the old system was no longer possible."

The growth of the Red Army in the years 1934–1939 is reflected in the defense budget. It rose from 395,000,000 rubles in 1924, to 5,000,000,000 in 1934, to 14,800,000,000 in 1936, and to over 34,000,000,000 in 1939. Besides structural changes and reforms affecting every branch of service, a new factor of prime importance during this period was the Osoaviakhim—a voluntary organization for defense training, whose manifold activities permeated the whole fabric of Soviet life. Its membership exceeded 12,000,000 by 1939. On a mass scale it trained army marksmen, parachutists, machine-gunners, drivers, and technicians. Through mass sports and prearmy training the physical health of young people was improved sufficiently to warrant lowering the draft age from 21 to 19, beginning with the draft of 1937. In 1935 permanent officer ranks similar to those of the old army were introduced, and a new rank of marshal of the Soviet Union was created.

The purges and trials during the First and Second Five-Year plans afflicted the army, particularly in 1937, when eight high commanders were tried and executed, and numerous shifts and dismissals followed in the ranks of lower commanding personnel. The internal stresses and political dissensions of this period brought the commissars back into power; they again held a responsibility equal to that of commanders, and political personnel was increased throughout the army. At the same time increasing emphasis was laid upon the national character of the armed forces. A new military oath of allegiance, introduced in January, 1939, recognized this trend by rejecting the international clauses of previous oaths. The Red Army ceased to be "the army of the international proletariat"; its sole task was the defense of the country.

The new military service law of September, 1939, reflecting the Constitution of 1936 and abandoning the principle of class distinction, made all male citizens liable to service regardless of social origin. This statute also increased the enlistment term for the navy from four to five years and for noncommissioned officers in all basic arms from two to three years; and it extended reserve status to the age of 50.

The estimated strength of the Red Army had now risen to 2,000,000 men. The motorization quotient had increased to 13 h.p. per man, as compared with 3 h.p. in 1930. Other figures, quoted by Marshal Klimenti E. Voroshilov to the Eighteenth Congress of the Communist Party in March, 1939, showed that in five years the tank forces had increased by 108 per cent, aviation by 130 per cent; the artillery arm had become the most powerful in Europe; the growth of divisional artillery and of technical troops had increased the size of the rifle division (of the triangular type) from 13,000 to 18,000 men.

The first battle tests for the new Red Army came in 1938–1939. The undeclared border war with Japan reached its peak in the battle at Hassan Lake in August, 1938, and at Khalkin Gol a year later. In the latter, about 60,000 troops participated on each side, and the Japanese suffered a decisive defeat. Tanks and artillery played an important part in this victory. The march into Poland in September, 1939, was more a logistical than a tactical problem, since little actual fighting occurred.

An acid test for the Leningrad sector of the Red Army was provided by the Finnish campaign of 1939–1940. After a slow start the tactical performance of the troops involved improved, and in the closing stage of the war the Mannerheim Line was breached in impressive style. However, this campaign disclosed some important tactical deficiencies in training and leadership. In May, 1940, the new commissar of defense, Marshal Semyon K. Timoshenko, inaugurated another period of reforms and drastic changes in training methods. The main reforms were toward improvement of tactical standards and leadership of the small units (platoons, companies, and battalions), and toward eradication of routine training methods, of adherence to classroom instruction instead of field work, and of excess paper work. Large-scale maneuvers were abandoned; they were replaced by tactical field exercises, using formations no larger than a division.

The object of this new training was to recreate the realities of the modern battlefield, to reproduce battle conditions as closely as possible. The basic tactical operations of small units in defense and offense were worked out with the closest attention to every detail and with lavish use of live ammunition. Separate training of different arms was practically abolished, since teamwork and flexible co-operation of all arms were considered the foundation of modern tactics, with infantry and artillery recognized as the mainstay of the battle team. Night combat and prolonged operations in extreme cold were prominently featured, and the troops were toughened by intensified physical training and long marches over difficult terrain. Altogether, the period between the Finnish campaign and the German invasion on June 22, 1941, was probably the most arduous in the peacetime life of the Red Army. The new tactical concepts and training methods proved of inestimable value in the war that followed.

THE NAVY

The history of the Russian Navy begins with Peter the Great. The only battleship before his time, the *Oryol*, was built by Czar Alexis to combat pirates and protect trade in the Caspian Sea; it was burned during a Cossack rebellion. Peter started extensive shipbuilding in 1696, and after 1713 the young navy played a prominent role in the war with Sweden, during which Russia won an important naval victory in the Battle of Hangö (1714). By the end of Peter's reign, the navy numbered 40 ships of the line, 10 frigates, and over 100 smaller craft. A series of successful naval actions was fought during the Turkish and Swedish wars of the reign of Catherine II; the destruction of the Turkish fleet at Chesmé in the Aegean Sea is especially notable. The early nineteenth century, when the main Russian effort was concentrated on expanding its land forces, was a period of neglect and retrogression for the navy. Nicholas I built up the navy somewhat, and in the war of 1853–1856, the Black Sea Fleet gave an excellent account of itself. After the advent of steam and ironclads, Russian industrial lag hampered the development of shipbuilding on a large and modern scale; by the end of the nineteenth century, although numerically the navy was large, many ships were obsolete in design and armor. Russia paid dearly for this technical inferiority in the Japanese war (1904–1905), especially in the disaster at Tsushima. Russia's defeat in this war led to a large program of expansion, which continued until the outbreak of the First World War. In 1914–1917 the Russian Navy numbered 19 battleships, 16 cruisers, over 100 destroyers, and about 50 submarines, with many more under construction. After the revolution most of the Black Sea Fleet was sunk by its crews to escape surrender to the Germans.

In 1945 the strength of the Red Fleet was not exactly known. A considerable number of destroyers, submarines, minesweepers, and other smaller craft were probably built during the Five-Year plans. In 1939 three battleships of the "third international" class were laid down; these were 35,000-ton vessels carrying nine 16-inch guns, twelve 6-inch, and 24 smaller guns, with a speed of 30 knots. One was apparently destroyed in dock at Nikolayev in the fall of 1941, before the town fell to the Germans. According to Jane's *Fighting Ships*, three battleships of 1911 vintage, *Marat, October Revolution,* and *Paris Commune* (23,000 to 26,000 tons) are still in service. Among the cruisers the most modern are six ships of the *Kirov* class (8,800 tons). Destroyers of all types and ages numbered 90 to 100. Over 200 submarines and many torpedo boats were listed as under construction. Only one aircraft carrier was known to be in service and several more were laid down just before the war, according to unofficial estimates. According to *Lloyd's Register* (1939) the merchant marine numbered 716 vessels with a total tonnage of 1,315,766. Personnel numbers are not exactly known, but the crews are well trained and efficient.

BIBLIOGRAPHY

IN ENGLISH

Jane, F., *The Russian Imperial Navy* (London, 1898).
Berchin, Michel, and Ben-Horin, Eliahu, *The Red Army* (New York, 1942).
Kournakoff, S. N., *Russia's Fighting Forces* (New York, 1942).
Basseches, N., *The Unknown Army* (New York, 1943).
Parry, Albert, *Russian Cavalcade* (New York, 1944).
White, D. F., *The Growth of the Red Army* (Princeton, 1944).
McMurtrie, F. E., ed., *Jane's Fighting Ships: 1945* (New York, 1945).

IN RUSSIAN

Kiskovatov, N., *Istoriya odezhdi i vooruzheniya Rossiiskikh voisk,* 30 vols. (St. Petersburg, 1842–   ).
Golitsyn, N., *Russkaya voyennaya istoriya* (St. Petersburg, 1878).
Maslovski, D., *Zapiski po istorii voyennovo iskusstva v Rossii* (St. Petersburg, 1891–1892).
Petrov, N., *Russkaya voyennaya sila,* 2 vols. (Moscow, 1898).
Russian General Staff Officers, *Istoriya Russkoi armii i flota,* 15 vols. (Moscow, 1911).
Voyenno-Morskaya entsiklopediya, 19 vols. (1911–1916).

PART FOUR

THE HUMANITIES AND SCIENCE

CHAPTER XX

Soviet Philosophical Thought

By JOHN SOMERVILLE

IN ONE sense, the Soviet Union represents an attempt to construct a social system on the basis of an explicit philosophy of life. An understanding of this philosophy, called dialectical materialism, may throw considerable light on the temper, objectives, and policies of the Soviet system as a whole.

While there is always a margin between goals and actual attainment, between plans and fulfillment, only a knowledge of the guiding principles will lead to a proper understanding and evaluation of the complex scene of changing patterns and policies of Soviet developments.

In general, Soviet philosophers stress the human values and objectives attainable in this world and this life. They do not conceive of human values as having either a supernatural source or a supernatural fulfillment. This view of life is historically connected with the long tradition of naturalistic and humanistic thought which goes back to the "physicalistic" thinkers of pre-Socratic times, a tradition which emerged so powerfully in the eighteenth-century materialism of the French Enlightenment. Philosophic materialism must not be confused with sensualism or cynicism.

The dialectical materialism which gives perspective to all Soviet culture represents a fusion of several elements: the general orientation and outlook of French materialism, the dialectical concept of scientific method worked out by Georg W. H. Hegel (1770–1831), the social analysis of Karl Marx (1818–1883) and Friedrich Engels (1820–1895), and the specific experience yielded by Russian problems and conditions as reflected in the work of leading figures like Nikolai Lenin (Vladimir I. Ulyanov, 1870–1924) and Joseph Stalin (Iosif V. Dzhugashvili, 1879–   ).

GENERAL WORLD VIEW . . . As a theory of reality or the universe, Soviet materialism assumes that the order of nature, in all its immensity and complexity, is real in its own right, and that the requirements of logic and reason do not necessitate or even permit the assumption of any realm prior to or beyond the eternal order of nature. This theory leans heavily on the Spinozistic principle that if the universe, as the totality of existence, has no beginning, it could have no creator. While it does not deny the existence of abstract ideas or moral values, it sees matter as the root and foundation of these and of all forms of existence. The detailed analysis of matter is left to the physical sciences. What is insisted on philosophically is that matter is not created by mind, but that mind is a complex outgrowth of matter. Contrary to idealism, the position held is that ideas are neither prior to nor independent of things, but are reflections of things. Stress is laid on the infinite qualitative richness of the material order and on its unlimited potentialities of growth and development.

The term "dialectical" signifies change or movement of an extreme kind—expressed logically, it means movement between contradictories, or, from A to non-A. That is, all existence, at whatever level, is characterized by change. The process of change is a continuous one in which gradual and quantitative accumulation gives rise to sudden qualitative transitions, followed by further quantitative changes at the new level, and so on. Soviet thinkers make great use of this concept in handling social problems. It is the methodological key to their whole analysis of society. (*Capital,* for example, is a treatise in historical economics wherein Marx tries to show how capitalist society arose upon the breakdown of a previous system, what changes are taking place within capitalism, and how these changes accumulate to presage a qualitative transition to socialism.) This fundamental pattern of universal change is expressed in the three basic laws of dialectics, worked out originally in abstract idealistic terms by Hegel and reworked into a materialist context by Marx and Engels. These are:

(1) *Law of strife, interpenetration, and unity of opposites.* This law asserts that anything which exists is a fusion of interpenetrating, dif-

362

ferently acting elements or forces, a fusion which represents a unity, but a dynamic, changing unity which finally breaks up. The unity is not static even while it is a unity; it is in process of continuous change because of the fact that its constituent parts are oppositely acting forces or elements. Hence it is felt that the formalistic law of identity (A is A) does not do justice to the complexity of existence, since there is no such thing as a self-identical A. During any instant of time, however small, the given A is changing into non-A in all of its parts. Its "nature" is to become what it is changing into as well as to be what it is changing from. Consequently, the dialectical formula is: A is A and also non-A.

(2) *Law of the transition or transformation of quantity to quality.* This law expresses the fact that changes taking place in any given existence at first represent gradual increases or decreases in the qualities present in the existence. However, after a certain point is reached in the gradual quantitative accumulation, a sudden precipitation of new qualities, which were not present in any degree in the previous state, takes place. Water becomes steam or ice, the egg a chicken, the seed a plant, the brush strokes a figure, the letters a word, the words a sentence, the sentence a hypothesis, the hypothesis a conclusion. Engels in *Dialectics of Nature* expresses the significance of this law by saying that all quantitative changes sooner or later precipitate qualitative changes, while the only known way to effect qualitative changes is by means of the accumulation of quantitative changes.

(3) *Law of negation of the negation.* Each qualitatively new state is regarded as a negation of the preceding state, and this law expresses the fact that the series of qualitative transitions is endless. At each new qualitative level, the strife of opposites ensues, the quantitative changes accumulate, and they move to a new synthesis.

Soviet thinkers are emphatic in pointing out that these laws of materialist dialectics are not asserted *a priori* but represent the generalization of scientific evidence, of observation, and experiment from every quarter. Nothing has been found immune to change; empirical findings show that the essential nature of existence is not static but dynamic. The *Bolshaya Sovetskaya Entsiklopediya,* the most comprehensive and authoritative reference work in the USSR, states in its article entitled "Dialectical Materialism, vol. 22, p. 154: "Not a single principle of dialectics can be converted into an abstract schema from which, by purely logical means, it would be possible to infer the answer to concrete questions." The principles are to be taken as "a guide to activity and scientific research, not a dogma."

METHODOLOGY . . . As laws of thought or methodological directives, the principles of dialectics point to the central importance of taking account of changes, of remembering that quantitative changes become qualitative. They give the mind of the thinker a dynamic rather than a static orientation, adding to the conceptual framework the fundamental dimension of evolution. To think dialectically means to think historically, to think in terms that not only accept change, but suggest the necessity of seeking its patterns, of discerning the elements and forces moving within the given subject matter, and the types of struggle or conflict which mark its evolutionary path.

In other words, it is not only that "state" in which any given subject matter exists at a given time that is important, but also the rate and direction of changes taking place. Dialectical materialists claim that the principles of dialectics express more faithfully than those of formal logic the basic nature of scientific method and the implications of its achievements, inasmuch as science has progressively demonstrated the pervasiveness of motion, growth, expansion, qualitative development, evolution. Their feeling is that the historical method of approach proves most fruitful in social and cultural studies, enabling us to gain greater predictability and thus to increase our range of social control.

SOCIAL AND POLITICAL PHILOSOPHY . . . In accordance with this orientation, the specific social philosophy within dialectical materialism is called historical materialism. It represents an attempt to approach basic problems of human society historically, and in terms of observable phenomena in cause-effect relations. Thus Soviet thinkers hold that historical materialism is primarily a body of sociological method; that it offers a basic methodological framework and conceptual apparatus for all social studies, among which are included aesthetics and ethics. The basic problems to which this theory addresses itself may be stated as follows: What are the chief social causes underlying the movement of human history so far? What are the principal factors causing the rise, development, and passing away of historical epochs, cultures, civilizations?

364

What is presented in answer to these questions may be called a hypothesis in historical sociology, according to which some of the leading roles in the drama of human history so far have been played by the following factors: the forces and relations of production, that is, the types of tools, powers, and technics by which people have produced the means of living; the basic economic relations that they have entered into and legally sanctioned in the process of production and exchange; the classes which have grown up in relation to possession, control, and use of the forces of production; and the struggles into which these classes have entered.

The view taken is that the legally sanctioned economic relations of any society must conform to the nature and possibilities of use of the tools of production. In like manner the general social superstructure of cultural and domestic life will have a certain consonance with the methods and relations of production. But the technics of production, and hence, economic possibilities, undergo gradual change and modification. The point is reached where, in order to utilize these new possibilities and demands, the economic relations must be more and more altered, which in turn means that the legal and political system must be altered. These adjustments have involved conflicts, violent and otherwise, including international wars, civil wars, and revolutions, as well as clashes of philosophies, ideologies, and schools of thought.

A class is defined as a group of persons having such a common economic relationship to the means of production as brings them into conflict with another group possessing some other common economic relationship to the means of production. The principal pairs of classes in human history so far are seen as slave owners and slaves, feudal lords and serfs, capitalists and proletariat. Their various struggles over the means of life are viewed as the chief dynamic of history. These struggles, beginning on the economic level, come to involve the whole range of social institutions because the whole way of life is in question. All peoples and institutions are viewed as playing a part in these struggles, although it may not be a conscious or direct part. Literature, art, and philosophy reflect and influence them, although it may be unintentionally.

While it is recognized that the moral forces of the cultural superstructure, such as ethical and religious ideas, can influence the economic base, it is held that the influence of this base upon the superstructure (that is, upon its history, the direction of its changes) is by far the more powerful. The processes of influence are reciprocal but not equal.

Soviet thinkers emphasize that their historical view involves neither a personal condemnation of any ruling class, nor a wholesale condemnation of any social system. They hold that each succeeding system was a great progressive step beyond the preceding one. They do not view social systems as in timeless competition, but in historical interconnectedness. Thus, in their view, capitalism gives way to socialism only when the former has broken down, or has generated problems which it cannot solve but which can be solved by socialism. When societies reached the point, in past historical experience, where problems arose that could only be solved by a transition to a new form, revolutions were usually precipitated. A peaceful transition is recognized as possible, if not probable, and revolutions are regarded as justified when there is no other way of fulfilling the needs and demands of the majority of the people.

The system of social life operating in the USSR is called socialism, as distinguished from communism proper. Sometimes socialism is referred to as the first or lower phase of communism. In order to understand the basic features and over-all structure of Soviet socialist society, as well as the further stage toward which its plans are being laid, close attention must be given, not only to the economic but to the general social implications of the term socialism as distinguished from communism. Socialism in the economic sense relies upon collective ownership of the means of production, in a completely planned and controlled economy, for the abolition of class antagonism, the elimination of the business cycle, and the end of mass involuntary unemployment. Culturally, socialism seeks the progressive elimination of artificial barriers to education and health care (implemented in the Soviet Union by full-scale national health insurance, and, before the Second World War, by free education, with stipends to students beyond the secondary level). Socially, it makes race or sex discrimination illegal by constitutional provision and legal enforcement. These material guarantees of an economic, educational, cultural, and racial nature are basic in what Soviet thinkers call socialistic as opposed to formalistic democracy.

The construction of socialism, regarded as virtually completed at the outbreak of the Second World War, has always been considered by Soviet thinkers as a process dominated by the aims and values of democracy, and resulting in the extension of democracy to the several spheres of social life. In their view the objectives of socialism, considering the state of chaos and disintegration following the collapse of czarist society and the aftermath of the First World War, could have been attained only by large-scale, long-time planning which could count on the co-operative efforts of all. Under these conditions, they say, the need for attaining socialism was a matter of national life or death comparable to the crisis of a war situation, and, hence, no political party could have been permitted to organize in opposition to the basic objectives of socialism. Soviet social thinkers felt that they had to choose between freedom for antisocialist parties on the one hand, and freedom of their people from economic insecurity, race and sex discrimination, disease, and ignorance, on the other hand. In choosing the latter kind of freedom, they felt they were making a far greater contribution to democracy under the historical conditions with which they were faced than they could have made by choosing the former.

Any state or government is viewed as having two principal functions—administration of things and the power to invoke force against persons, a power implemented by police, jails, prisons, army, navy and the like. This latter aspect of the state is what Soviet thinkers refer to as a dictatorship. They have not developed the doctrine of a personal dictator, like the Nazi *führerprinzip*, which justifies the arbitrary rule of a single individual on the ground of his superior strength of will, scorning majority decisions and contemptuous of mass opinion. Soviet thinkers hold that every state is a dictatorship to the extent that it possesses or uses the apparatus of physical dictation. As they see it, the vital question is: In the interests of what group, primarily, is the apparatus of state force used? In terming their own state a dictatorship of the proletariat or of the working class, the meaning they wish to convey is that it is a government using its power in the interests of the working class, which they conceive of as a majority group, to construct a type of society, socialism, in which classes and class antagonisms no longer exist. In Nazi and Fascist social philosophy, the term dictatorship is used as the opposite of democracy, which is sharply condemned in principle.

Whether or not the objectives of socialism could actually be attained in one country surrounded by capitalist countries was the chief issue which divided the camp of Stalin from that of Trotsky. Trotsky's position, which seemed to be a literal adherence to the earlier position of Marx, was that it was possible to attain such difficult and large-scale objectives as those noted above only if the leading countries of the world participated simultaneously in the undertaking. From his viewpoint, the fundamental strategy should have been to plot a world revolution rather than to plan for the construction of socialism in the USSR. Stalin argued that Marx's whole method pointed to the fact that he wanted his teachings to be taken dialectically rather than dogmatically—that is, as subject to further development in the light of changing conditions. Stalin and his followers held that if Marx had lived in the twentieth century he would have seen that the construction of socialism could be successfully carried through in one country, and that it was rendered historically necessary and possible because of the uneven course of development of world capitalism since Marx's day, as pointed out and emphasized in the work of Lenin. The attainment of socialist objectives through the Five-Year plans was considered the decisive validation of the Stalinist approach.

Communism proper, or the higher phase of communism, which is conceived of as a qualitative development beyond socialism, is defined, economically, as a system of unrestricted abundance in which it will be possible to apply the slogan formulated by Marx (*Gotha Program*): "From each according to ability, to each according to need." Socialism is marked by the economic formula: "From each according to his ability, to each according to his work" (constitution of the USSR, Chapter 1, Article 12). That is, under socialism there is a guarantee of continuity of employment at the level of qualifications, but it is still a money and wage economy in which consumption possibilities are largely determined by wages and market prices. However, it is considered that when scientific and technical possibilities are fully utilized, the resulting potential of productivity will be so great that, if it is not artificially restricted by a competitive market subject to waves of depressed purchasing power, or diverted into destructive war channels, there will be sufficient abundance for anyone to have what he can really use. It is anticipated that improved machinery can eliminate labor that is mere drudgery, and that socially useful activity, motivated by interest, training, and prestige, as well as by human necessity, will be generally regarded as one of the normal satisfactions of life. A money economy would no longer be needed, and possession of sufficient quantities of economic goods would no longer be either a problem or a source of social power.

When basic economic needs are thus met, it is stated that it will become possible to solve further problems that cannot be fully solved under socialism. Most frequently mentioned in this connection are the eradication of antagonisms and lags between town and country, and between mental and manual labor. From the point of view of mental and physical health, and the promotion of aesthetic values, it is felt that better planning of cities and countryside is needed, in which there will be a more even distribution of economic and cultural goods, less backward isolation on the one hand and less unhealthy overcrowding on the other. In like fashion, it is felt that it will become possible to adjust and enrich conditions of work so that there will not be large groups of "manual" workers suffering from lack of mental development, or large groups of "brain" workers suffering from lack of physical development. The objective is a more versatile, longer-lived individual of richer personality.

The fulfillment of such objectives presupposes, of course, great extension of facilities for education, training, and health care. When such facilities are fully utilized, and when an economy of unrestricted productivity is worldwide, the repressive or dictatorial apparatus of state power (police, jails, army, navy, and the like) is expected, in Engels' phrase, to "wither away." Soviet thinkers believe that people will learn to live in such a way as to solve the problems that arise without invoking a special apparatus of state force, particularly since the historic reasons that called such an apparatus into existence at the time of the transition from tribal communal to slave society, namely, the rise of private property in the means of production, and hence, classes and class antagonisms, will have been eradicated.

Traditional Marxian thinkers, up to and including Lenin, generally took it for granted that communist objectives must await attainment until all the principal countries of the world participate co-operatively in the construction of that type of society. However, during the 1930's, the leading thinkers of the Soviet Union, including Stalin, began to develop the concept that most basic features of communist society can, after the successful construction of socialism in one country, be attained in that country through further large-scale planning. The chief exception

369

is the "withering away" of the state, which, it is recognized, could occur only on a world-wide basis. Most Soviet thinkers felt, just before the Second World War began, that their country had virtually completed the construction of socialism and was prepared to begin planning for its further development into most of the basic features of communism.

ETHICS . . . There is, of course, implicit in the foregoing discussion of Soviet social and political objectives a general sense of direction and standards in ethical values. The specific body of ethical teachings characteristic of Soviet thought is called socialist humanism, or Soviet humanism. The term humanism is used to indicate the belief that humanity, mankind, is the source and the agency of fulfillment of moral codes and ideals of a better life. Soviet humanists reject the concept of a supernatural source of ethical commands and the belief in life after death wherein rewards or punishments are dispensed. They use the term socialist or Soviet to emphasize the thesis that the type of society itself under which people live determines, in large measure, what proportion of them will be able to lead the higher life.

The Soviet view is that, although humanistic ideals of brotherhood, peace, and cultural enrichment were historically elaborated in the ancient world, the actual slave society which prevailed prevented their attainment by all but a few people, and even then in a somewhat dubious sense, since slavery limits not only the higher striving of the slaves but the ethical claims of the slave owners. A like situation is seen in serf-lord relationships under feudal society. In the Soviet conception, the residual historical meaning of the modern humanism which broke away from narrow medieval patterns was that the higher life of cultural development, of assumption of social responsibilities, of leading and guiding position, was no longer confined to the class of hereditary aristocrats. At the same time, the gates were not actually opened to all. Practically speaking, it was the rising bourgeoisie to whom this humanism meant a real opportunity, since the type of society, capitalism, which succeeded feudalism, gave to this class the actual power, and the prerequisites for that education and training without which the higher ethical life remains for most people merely an ideal. While capitalism thus increased the number of those who could actually hope to possess and utilize the means and agencies of personal development which would lead to a cultivated life, it still left conditions of economic underprivilege and insecurity,

370

racial and other discriminations, which adversely affected the prospects of higher development for large masses of people. The thesis stressed by Soviet thinkers is that only when economic security, health protection, full education, and freedom from discrimination are guaranteed for all people, will it be possible to say that the practical conditions underlying the good life are really available to everyone. They feel that the great ethical contribution of socialist society lies in the attainment of these conditions.

Humanism, in the Soviet outlook, implies an almost unlimited confidence in what can be accomplished through co-operative social action and by the development of man's natural capacities. While it is thus profoundly optimistic, it considers that its optimism is securely grounded on a scientific estimate of historical probabilities, and it sharply rejects sentimental utopianism. No undercurrent of frustration or bitterness about the universe runs through this humanism. In line with the general dialectical world view, the totality of existence, while regarded as impersonal, is also seen as a limitless source of future possibilities of development. The Soviet view of ethics, in stressing the interconnectedness of operating moral values with social institutions, the historical extension of ethical practice as a function of the historical evolution of types of society, illustrates and bears out the dialectical and historical methodology, while its reliance upon human rather than superhuman forces carries out the basic orientation of its materialism.

AESTHETICS . . . The predominating philosophy of art in the Soviet Union is called socialist or Soviet realism. Art is defined as a reflection of reality—a reflection possessed of aesthetic properties. This reflection, it is held, need not be literal, and, to be of any great value, must be much more than a mirror image. The dialectical approach to art emphasizes the proposition that, to render any reality faithfully, the artist must somehow include or suggest the dimension of change, development, evolution. In the end, according to the laws of dialectics, every reality is dynamic: if the artist would be true to his subject matter, he must not portray the content of a present moment as if it were static or existed in a vacuum. The living present is something rooted in the past and branching out into the future. Each art has its own qualitative richness, its own aesthetic appeal, its own manner of rendering reality, but the Soviet viewpoint insists that it is reality that is being rendered. While forms are

371

infinitely variable, there must be a solid basis of content. Thus, mere aesthetic by-play, without any sense of responsibility to the conditions of objective reality (the tendency called "formalism" by Soviet critics), is condemned as sharply as the barren variety of photographic realism (the tendency they call "naturalism").

As a theory of art criticism, the main task of socialist realism was to overcome the approach which predominated in the field of literary and aesthetic discussion in the USSR up to the 1930's, now referred to as the method of "vulgar sociology." This tendency considered a work of art— a novel, for instance—as primarily a reflection of the "class consciousness" of its author. Hence, it was argued that an author of aristocratic background, or one who professed a historically reactionary social philosophy, could not be a great artist, nor could his works have any significance for a socialist society. Socialist realism, however, developed in terms of the thesis that it is the work of art that must be judged, not the professed philosophy or the family background of the artist. In this connection, great emphasis was laid on both Marx's evaluation of Balzac and Lenin's analysis of Leo Tolstoy. Although Balzac, who proclaimed himself a Royalist and a Catholic, was in philosophic outlook as far as possible from a Marxian position, his artistic work was considered surpassingly great as a faithful and aesthetically powerful reflection of the dynamic social reality with which he was dealing. In fact, the view taken was that the social forces which Balzac so vividly portrayed actually showed society to be moving in a direction quite different from that anticipated by his explicit philosophic views. Similarly, regarding Tolstoy, Lenin scouted the idea that Tolstoy as a noble was unable to portray with artistic truth the social reality of peasant problems. Lenin maintained that Tolstoy's work was a magnificent reflection of the struggle of classes and the nature of the forces that were working to a resolution, although he considered the novelist's own position in relation to the struggle and its outcome to be historically and pragmatically ineffectual.

The materialist philosophy of art does not deny or belittle aesthetic values and artistic creation, but, rather, emphatically affirms them. As in the field of morals, what is in question is not the values themselves, but their source and functioning. Soviet materialism sees aesthetic emotions as a natural functioning of the developed human being rather than as something mystical or inexplicable. Art is seen as both a product of subjective richness and a reflection of something which has objectively real status. The effort is to approach art as a natural part of society and to approach the whole question of standards of beauty as a changing pattern connected with social evolution.

HISTORICAL DEVELOPMENT OF PHILOSOPHY IN RUSSIA . . .
As modern Russia became culturally more closely connected with western Europe in the eighteenth century, a substantial tradition of philosophic thought developed which was at once distinctively Russian, yet integrally related to the general movement of European thought. Outstanding figures like M. V. Lomonosov (1711–1765) and A. N. Radishchev (1749–1802) had considerable influence in a progressive democratic direction in relation to the basic social and political problems of eighteenth-century Russia. Radishchev's *A Journey from St. Petersburg to Moscow* was particularly effective in stimulating and guiding the work of the leading philosophic liberals of nineteenth-century Russia. Prominent among these were A. I. Herzen (1812–1870), V. G. Belinski (1810–1848), N. G. Chernyshevski (1828–1889), N. A. Dobrolyubov (1836–1861), and D. I. Pisarev (1840–1868). Social and political problems, arising principally out of the institution of serfdom (including its aftermath) and out of the repressive policies of the autocracy, were particularly acute in nineteenth century Russia. A great deal of philosophic work was directed toward these problems; their existence also served to direct Russian attention to western European social philosophy. Strong influences came from the materialist thinkers of the French Enlightenment, from later social thinkers like Auguste Comte (1798–1857), and from German philosophers like Georg W. H. Hegel (1770–1831) and Ludwig A. Feuerbach (1804–1872). Utopian socialists like François M. C. Fourier (1772–1837), Claude H. de R. Saint-Simon (1760–1825), and Robert Owen (1771–1858), and later socialists like Marx and Engels also influenced Russian thought.

The general position of the nineteenth-century Russian thinkers mentioned might be termed, in its social outlook, revolutionary democracy with a leaning toward socialism; in its ontological viewpoint, a tendency toward the scientific materialism of the time. However, the first prominent Russian philosophical thinker who could be called a Marxist in the strict sense is Georgi V. Plekhanov (1857–1918), whose early work greatly influenced young Lenin.

The historical development of Soviet philosophy after the revolution was marked by two critical controversies on the issues of mechanism and of idealism. The first controversy took place in the 1920's. It involved the question whether mechanism, especially as that doctrine had been developed in the physical sciences, should be regarded as an adequate concept of philosophic materialism. Prominent mechanists, like K. A. Timiryazev, Timyanski, Stepanov, and P. B. Axelrod, were somewhat suspicious of philosophic theorizing in general and of Hegelian dialectics in particular. They felt that science rather than philosophy should be stressed, and, within science, the mechanist viewpoint. The group opposed to the mechanists was led by A. M. Deborin, who argued that there must always be a place for philosophy in addition to the specific sciences, and for the dialectical method as a basic directive common to all fields. The antimechanists pointed out the mechanistic science was progressively losing its hold upon scientists themselves, under the impact of new work in physics, chemistry, biology, and related fields.

In 1929 the controversy came to a head in the debates of the Second All-Union Conference of Marxist-Leninist Scientific Institutions, made up of 229 delegates from scholarly institutions throughout the country. All the leading figures on both sides presented their views, and the conference passed a resolution which acted as a kind of semiofficial condemnation of mechanism on the ground that this tendency underrated the importance of philosophy and misconstrued the method of materialist dialectics.

However, it seemed to an increasing number of thinkers that, although Deborin's group was right in its critique of the mechanists, it had not itself reached any satisfactory level of work, particularly in relation to the momentously developing field of social problems in the Soviet Union. The feeling was that in attempting to overcome the shortcomings of mechanism, Deborin had gone too far in the idealistic (antimaterialist) direction; that he was constructing a philosophic theory unconnected with scientific developments and divorced from social problems. Deborin's critics emphasized first, the need, not for a philosophic theory separated from scientific work, but for a philosophic theory organically

374

connected with the sciences, integrating their results and helping in the selection of problems and hypotheses. The second part of the criticism applied this judgment particularly to the area of social problems. It was argued that neither the mechanists nor the Deborin group had paid sufficient attention to the developing social situation, which had, indeed, reached the point where some of the most critical decisions in Soviet history had to be made—for example, whether to abandon the New Economic Policy (NEP) and begin national planning for full-fledged socialism, and whether to take the plunge into full-scale collectivization of agriculture. M. B. Mitin and P. Yudin led in the philosophic criticism of Deborin for having contributed so little toward clarification of basic social problems. The shortcomings of the Deborinite group were termed "menshevising idealism," by which was meant that type of divorcement of theory from practice in the realm of social problems which had been characteristic of the Menshevik (minority) wing of the prerevolutionary Russian Social Democratic Labor Party, a group to which Deborin had once belonged.

In the latter part of 1930, at a three-day philosophic conference which met in Moscow, the whole issue was threshed out, with reports and discussions by all the interested parties on both sides. Deborin acknowledged the shortcomings of his philosophic program and methodology, and the conference concluded that a new vigor and realism were needed to give proper scope and direction to philosophy.

Contrary to widespread impression, sale of the works of mechanists and "menshevising idealists" was not banned in the USSR, nor were the criticized philosophers imprisoned or executed. The case of Nikolai I. Bukharin (1888–1938) probably served to give currency to various misapprehensions. His earlier philosophic work was criticized, and he was executed after the trials of 1936-1937. Bukharin, however, was accused of, and admitted, overt treasonable acts in concert with foreign powers inimical to the USSR, acts which, upon detection, would necessarily have involved any individual in criminal proceedings.

TEACHING AND RESEARCH IN PHILOSOPHY . . . Considerable emphasis is laid upon the study of philosophy in higher institutions in the USSR. There is a compulsory minimum of one year, which includes not only the principles of dialectical materialism but a survey of the history of philosophy from the pre-Socratics to the present day, with

375

readings from the original sources of all the leading schools of thought. The dominant approach to the writings of the past is not one of polemical rejection but of historical evaluation. There is a wide circulation of philosophic classics in the USSR in low-priced, large-scale editions. The number of such works published in the USSR has risen sharply since the revolution. Table XII gives some comparative figures.

TABLE XII. Philosophical Works Published		
	From 1897 to 1916. Copies in thousands	From 1917 to 1938. Copies in thousands
Aristotle	1	78.3
Voltaire	65	228.6
Hegel	5	200.5
Diderot	2	139.1
Spinoza	8	55.2
Feuerbach	10	44
Bacon	0	23
Holbach	0	79.4
Helvetius	0	67.5
Democritus	0	10

In addition to the researches of graduate students and teachers of the subject, a great deal of work in philosophy is produced through the Institute of Philosophy connected with the social sciences division of the central Academy of Sciences in Moscow. This body is staffed by a score or more of mature scholars devoting full time to research without teaching responsibilities. Other scholars participate on a temporary or part-time basis in various projects initiated by the Institute.

The Institute of Philosophy, like all working establishments in the USSR, has its Five-Year Plan, which is broken up into annual plans. Although there are individual projects, emphasis is placed upon co-operative effort and the utilization of collective research resources. Among recent and current projects of the Institute are the *Kratki Filosofski Slovar* (*Brief Philosophic Dictionary*) which sold more than two million copies within a few years after publication in 1939, and a seven-volume *History of Philosophy*, three volumes of which appeared in the early 1940's.

BIBLIOGRAPHY

Lenin, V. I., *Materialism and Empirio-Criticism* (New York, 1927).
——, *State and Revolution* (New York, 1932).
Engels, Friedrich, *Anti-Duhring* (New York, 1935).

——, *Ludwig Feuerbach and the Outcome of Classic German Philosophy*, containing *Marx's Theses on Feuerbach* (New York, 1935).

Lenin, V. I., *Filosofskie Tetradi* (*Philosophical Notebooks*), in Russian (Moscow, 1936).

——, *Theoretical Principles of Marxism* (Moscow, 1936).

——, *Essays on Leo Tolstoy* (Moscow, 1936).

Mitin, M., *Boyeve Voprosy Materialisticheskoi Dialektiki* (*Controversial Issues of Materialist Dialectics*), in Russian (Moscow, 1936).

Gorky, M., *Culture and the People* (New York, 1939).

Engels, Friedrich, *Dialectics of Nature* (New York, 1940).

Plekhanov, G., *Essays in Historical Materialism* (New York, 1940).

Rosental, M., and Yudin, P., eds., *Kratki Filosofski Slovar* (*Brief Philosophic Dictionary*), in Russian (Moscow, 1940).

Stalin, J., *On Dialectical and Historical Materialism* (New York, 1940).

——, *Leninism* (New York, 1942).

Somerville, John, "Dialectical Materialism," *Twentieth Century Philosophy*, ed. Runes, D. D. (New York, 1943).

CHAPTER XXI

The Russian Language

By ERNEST J. SIMMONS

THE Russian language is the most important branch of the Slavonic family of languages in the Indo-European group. It is spoken by the most numerous of the Slavic races (the Great Russians), and is an excellent key for understanding the other Slavonic tongues, such as Bulgarian, Serbo-Croatian, and Slovenian. Polish and Czech are also in the Slavonic family, though both have been influenced more by Latin than other Slavonic languages, hence have deviated further from the original Pra-Slavonic. Russian itself should be carefully distinguished from Little Russian or Ukrainian, and from White Russian. Properly understood, Russian, the language of the Great Russians, is simply one of the eastern group of the Slavonic languages, which includes also Ukrainian and White Russian.

The morphological and syntactic development of Russian is made somewhat difficult to trace historically by the fact that Old Bulgarian, spoken by tribes along the Volga, became the ecclesiastical and literary language and remained so until the seventeenth century. Very early, however, the local spoken Russian of Kiev influenced Church Slavonic (Old Bulgarian) in both pronunciation and vocabulary, and in turn Church Slavonic affected the vernacular. Church Slavonic elements may still be observed in the Russian language, especially in phonetic and morphological peculiarities in words connected with intellectual and religious life. Church Slavonic, in a considerably modified form, of course, has remained the language of the Russian Orthodox Church: the Scriptures were written in it, and it was the language of church services up to the latest times. Thus, the history of Church Slavonic resembles the history of Latin in the Roman Catholic Church.

The earliest written literature, chronicles and judicial documents, employed a language that was an admixture of the vernacular and Church Slavonic. In the fourteenth century Moscow displaced Kiev as a cultural center, and the local speech of Moscow, a combination of southern and northern dialects, influenced the written language. But Church Slavonic still continued to influence the written language, though on a diminishing scale, until the eighteenth century. At that time, the great scientist, philologist, and poet, Mikhail V. Lomonosov, pointed out in his *Russian Grammar* the dependence of the literary language on Church Slavonic, a fact that had not been scientifically studied before. The literary language now began to fall more in line with the spoken language. Toward the end of the eighteenth and the beginning of the nineteenth century, especially through the efforts of Nikolai M. Karamzin and Alexander Pushkin, a literary norm was established.

CHARACTERISTICS . . . Russian is an extremely rich language, and by virtue of its structure it is capable of expressing the subtlest nuances of thought. Only a great people, said Ivan S. Turgenev, could possess such a language. As a member of the Indo-European family, Russian has developed in much the same way as other members of this family. As an inflected language, it resembles Latin and Greek in morphology. The alphabet can be mastered in one lesson. Both Russian and Church Slavonic use the same alphabet, except that Peter the Great simplified the letters of Russian in 1708 by bringing them into closer conformity with the easier Latin letters of the west. Thus there are a current form known as the "civil alphabet" and the Church Slavonic alphabet, which is called *Kirilitsa*. The civil alphabet was simplified still further after the 1917 revolution. There had been 36 letters, not counting the *ë*, which is not a separate letter and rarely occurs in this form except in grammars and texts intended for foreigners. In 1918, the Soviet government issued a "Decree on the Introduction of the New Orthography," which rejected as redundant four letters of the old alphabet. Hence the present alphabet has 32 letters. The decree effected further simplification: the hard sign was abolished at the end of words; a clarifying differentiation was introduced for spelling certain prefixes before unvoiced consonants; useless variations in the genitive endings of adjectives, pronouns, and

379

participles were abolished; uniformity was given to the two nominative and accusative plural endings of all three genders; the masculine and neuter form of the third person plural pronouns was substituted for the old feminine form; the masculine and neuter form of the word "one" replaced the old feminine form; the genitive singular of the feminine personal pronoun became the same as the accusative. All these changes unquestionably made for simplification, and at the time this article was written Russian had become one of the most nearly phonetic languages in Europe.

The pronunciation of Russian is not difficult. The chief obstacles for a person speaking a western European language is his tendency to make soft combinations hard. Before *e* and *i*, and before vowels beginning with *y*, such as *ya*, *ye*, and *yo*, all consonants, especially the dentals, are palatalized; that is, they are sounded not with the top of tongue pressing against the back of the teeth, but by touching the palate with the tongue higher up. Another difficulty is the hard *l* before *a*, *o*, and *u*. This is not pronounced as in English with the tip of the tongue at the root of the teeth, but rather with the tip of the tongue just touching the teeth; the uvula then vibrates, producing a kind of guttural *l* similar to a guttural *r*. Other sounds offer no particular difficulties. However, a real obstacle for non-Russians learning the language is the variation in stress in Russian words. No definite rule for placing the stress is possible as in other Slavonic languages such as Polish and Czech. The stress is not always placed in the same position in the inflected forms of a single word. A few helpful generalizations regarding stress may be stated: (1) the stress in long (attributive) forms of an adjective is that of the nominative singular; (2) pronouns are usually stressed on the case endings; (3) the majority of nouns are stressed throughout as in the nominative singular. Incorrect stress may sometimes lead to misunderstanding, especially in pairs of words which are spelled alike but stressed differently. Accurate handling of stress in Russian words can come only after long experience with the language.

Russian has comparatively few sounds which do not occur in English, and the variations in sound represented by each letter are usually regular. One peculiarity of the sound system is that there are two sets of vowels: hard vowels and soft or "jotated" vowels. Pronunciation of a hard vowel varies according to whether it is stressed or unstressed and, if unstressed, according to its position in regard to the stressed vowel in the word. A soft vowel, whether it appears initially, or follows another vowel, has the same range of sounds as the corresponding hard vowel but is preceded in each case by the sound "jot." There is a system of vowel mutation governed by definite rules, and also a regular system of consonant mutation, which likewise has its own rules.

The Russian noun has three genders, two numbers, and six cases (a seventh, the vocative, exists only in a few survivals). The genders are declined differently, but their plurals are virtually identical except for the genitive case. The neuter singular differs little from the masculine, but the feminine declensional forms are entirely different. A peculiarity in inflection is that words with soft endings are declined soft throughout. And there are many variations in the genitive and prepositional cases, owing chiefly to a confusion of the historic o and u declensions. During historic times Russian lost many of its grammatical forms, which can still be studied in Church Slavonic. One of these is the dual, which still exists in a sense after the numerals "two," "three," and "four," when the noun stands in the genitive singular, because that form frequently corresponded to the nominative dual.

In Russian the attributive is transformed into the corresponding adjective or participle. Hence Russian is richer in adjectival forms than the languages of the West. Numerals are fully declined and are quite difficult. Although the nominal declension is complex, its syntactical application is rather simple, since an abundance of cases, each with a distinct function, obviates certain difficulties which are present in a language without grammatical endings.

The verb system is an interesting combination of simplification and complexity. Little has survived of the intricate structure of the verb system in Church Slavonic, with its aorist and multiplicity of past tenses. Only one unconjugated past is left. The ordinary future is a compound of I shall and the infinitive, but in a large class of verbs the present does duty for the future. There are two conjugations, a wealth of participial forms, and gerunds from the old masculine nominative singular. As though to compensate for this relative simplicity in the conjugational system in a highly inflected language, a curious mechanism exists by which these few verbal forms are able to express by means of aspects most of the shades of meaning expressed in English through the tense

381

structure. That is, the five tenses of the Russian verb are divided into two groups called the imperfective and perfective aspects. The imperfective aspect has three tenses: past, present, and future. The perfective aspect has only a past and a future. Each verb has two infinitives, from one of which the imperfective aspect is derived, from the other the perfective. The two infinitives are closely related. One may be formed from the other by (1) the addition of a prefix, (2) by the expansion of one infinitive through insertion of a syllable, or (3) by the alteration of a vowel preceding the infinitive ending. For a few verbs the two infinitives come from different stems. The imperfective tenses indicate iterative and durative actions; the perfective tenses indicate instantaneous actions, or single and complete actions. The perfective aspect sometimes indicates also the performance of the action for a short time, or the beginning of the action, which is itself an instantaneous action. With such an instrument for nice distinction in meaning, it may be readily seen that Russian is capable of distinguishing shades of thought beyond the capacities of most languages. Needless to say, long training is necessary in order to make full use of the fine distinctions in the use of the aspects of the verbs.

Russian does not ordinarily use the passive voice, and it has a very simple way of expressing the subjunctive with an unconjugated past tense and the addition of a particle. A reflexive is also used, which does not differ from the rest of the verbs, except for the addition of the unchanged reflexive ending.

BORROWINGS . . . The influence of Church Slavonic (Old Bulgarian) on spoken and written Russian has already been pointed out. Other foreign influences may be noted. Tatar has contributed names for many Oriental objects, such as weapons, garments, jewels, and some terms concerned with government. A few words have come from Finnish, and from the more refined literary Polish came a good many words dealing with manners. Many Dutch and German words were imported after Peter the Great "opened his window on Europe." By the eighteenth century, with the full cultural rapprochement with the West, numerous words had been introduced; most of them were French, but some were English and German. Since then, new loan words from international scientific terminology have entered the Russian language. Since 1917, the Soviets have evinced a partiality for American words, not a few of them slang.

Despite its rather formidable grammar and unfamiliar alphabet, the Russian language is simple and direct and admirably suited to every purpose that a modern language serves. Its literature, both prose and poetry, is among the great literatures of the world. It is spoken by more than a hundred million people, and as the principal language of the Soviet Union its importance in international intercourse will certainly increase.

BIBLIOGRAPHY

DICTIONARIES

Sreznevski, I. I., *Materials for a Dictionary of Old Russian Language*, 3 vols. (St. Petersburg, 1890–1912).
Dictionary of the Russian Language, 4 vols. to the letter L (St. Petersburg, 1895).
Dal, V. I., *Explanatory Dictionary of the Living Great Russian Language*, 4 vols. (St. Petersburg, 1904–1909).
Preobrazhenski, A. G., *Etymological Dictionary of the Russian Language*, to the letter S (Moscow, 1910–1916).
Pavlovski, I. Ya., *Russische-Deutscher Wörterbuch* (Riga, 1911).
Alexandrov, A. A., *Russian-English and English-Russian*, 2 vols. (New York, 1929).
Ushakov, D. N., *Explanatory Dictionary of the Russian Language*, 4 vols. (Moscow, 1934–1940).
Segal, L., *New Complete Russian-English Dictionary* (New York, 1942).

GRAMMARS

In Russian

Sobolevski, A. I., *Lectures on the History of the Russian Language*, 4th ed., (St. Petersburg, 1908).
Shakhmatov, A. A., *Sketch of the Earlier Period of the History of the Russian Language* (Petrograd, 1915).
Durnovo, N. N., *Sketch of the History of the Russian Language* (Brno, Czechoslovakia, 1924).
Vinogradov, V. V., *Contemporary Russian Language*, 2 vols. (Moscow, 1938).
Shakhmatov, A. A., *Sketch of the Contemporary Russian Literary Language* (Leningrad, 1941).
Abakumov, S. I., *Contemporary Russian Literary Language* (Moscow, 1942).

In English

Forbes, N., *Elementary Russian Grammar* (Oxford, 1919).
Birkett, G. A., *A Modern Russian Course* (London, 1937).
Semeonoff, Anna, *A New Russian Grammar*, 4th ed. (New York, 1941).

PRONUNCIATION

Trofimov, M. V., and Jones, D., *The Pronunciation of Russian* (Cambridge, 1923).
Bogoroditski, V. A., *Phonetics of the Russian Language*, in Russian (Kazan, 1930).
Boyanus, S. K., *A Manual of Russian Pronunciation* (London, 1935).

CHAPTER XXII

Literature: Old and New

By ERNEST J. SIMMONS

MEDIEVAL literature appeared somewhat late in Russia; the first documents date from the eleventh century, about 50 years after the introduction of Christianity. They were in Church Slavonic, which St. Cyril and St. Methodius created as a written language in the ninth century. Church Slavonic resembles Old Bulgarian. Slavonic remained the language of the Russian Orthodox Church and was used for all literary purposes until the seventeenth century, when it was displaced by the vernacular. Printing also was long delayed; the first book was published in 1564, and printing did not come into general use until the eighteenth century.

The earliest literary remains are connected with the flourishing cultural development of Kiev, which lasted until about 1200. Religious writings, mostly sermons, were inspired by Byzantine Greek models. But some highly original examples of pulpit oratory have come down to us, such as the excellent *Eulogy on St. Vladimir* by Ilarion, metropolitan of Kiev (d. 1053), and the ornate and eloquent sermons of Cyril, bishop of Turov (twelfth century). The account of a pilgrimage to the Holy Land by Abbot Daniel the Palmer (twelfth century) is highly informative, and its whimsically realistic revelations of ecclesiastical trickery recall Chaucer's charming narratives.

Most remnants of early secular literature are chronicles (*letopisi*). These exist only in later compilations, although contemporary entries go back to about 1040. The chronicles contain valuable material for re-

384

constructing the ancient history of Russia, and some have considerable literary merit. One of the best is the *Chronicle* imputed to Nestor, twelfth-century monk and author, which includes some delightful tales of mingled history and popular lore. Another notable secular piece is the *Instructions to His Children* of Vladimir Monomakh, grand prince of Kiev (1113–1125), a document of wise and pious counsel. A considerable body of purely imaginative literature was probably written during the Kiev period, but the only substantial piece to survive is *The Word of the Campaign of Igor* (twelfth century), discovered in 1795 and first published in 1800. This prose poem tells of the disastrous expedition of Prince Igor against the nomadic Polovtzy of the south. The work occupies a unique place in ancient Russian literature, and its unknown author was clearly a writer of great talent. The rich imagery, diction, and beautiful lyric interludes compare favorably with the best western European medieval verse. Later fragmentary remains in similar vein have been preserved, some of them describing the Battle of Kulikovo (1380), but they are pale imitations of *The Word of the Campaign of Igor.*

After the downfall of Kiev, there was a period of strife between the several city states, and not until the rise of Moscow were conditions again favorable for literary creation. The results, even then, were poor, since the new literature was ecclesiastical—Byzantine in spirit and monotonously formalized in style. Many sermons and lives of saints were written, and churchmen kept up the official chronicles. There were a few interesting exceptions. The *Domostroi* is generally ascribed to Sylvester, adviser to Ivan IV, the Terrible (1530–1584), although it was probably written earlier. Essentially a description of household management, this work reveals in stark detail the family pattern of the age: the father is a swaggering lord of creation, to whom mother, children, and servants owe absolute obedience. The most famous among polemical and historical writings is an exchange of letters between Ivan the Terrible and his former general Prince Andrei Kurbski (1528–1583). These show the czar's talents as a controversialist and master of biting invective. The most significant Muscovite literary performance came from the pen of the Archpriest Avvakum (1620–1681), the leader of the Old Believers in the church schism of the time. In several epistles Avvakum encouraged his followers to oppose religious and cultural innovations, but his chief work is his *Life* (1673), written in the vernacular and revealing a courageous personality and a masterful and original style.

FOLK LITERATURE . . . Russia has one of the richest folk literatures of Europe, kept alive through centuries by oral transmission. No doubt its remarkable vitality rested partly on the fact that until 1917 illiteracy was the rule rather than the exception among the masses of the population. One very important genre of Russian folk literature is the *byliny* —long narrative poems in unstanzaed, stressed verses. The themes are either historical events, usually related to the siege of Kazan (1552), or the legendary feats of heroes, such as Ilya of Murom. The *byliny* were intoned by professional folk reciters. The oldest extant texts were recorded from oral recitations by Richard James, an Englishman, in 1620. A second collection, attributed to Kirsha Danilov, was taken down in the middle of the eighteenth century in Siberia and first published in 1804. Later scholars have made collections. M. A. Rybnikov collected many (1861–1867), mostly from the fishermen of northern Russia, where there is a long tradition of *byliny* recitations. *Spiritual Verses* (*Dukhovnye stikhi*), somewhat related to the *byliny* in style, were recited by wandering religious mendicants; they were much influenced in subject matter by Byzantine apocryphal literature. There are also many and splendid folk songs about wedding ceremonials, harvest, death, feast days, superstitions, etc. Perhaps the richest branch of Russian folklore, however, is its folk tales (*narodny skazki*). The tales resemble western European fairy tales, except that in Russian prose folk tales the fairy does not appear. As narratives they are highly original, artistic, and charming, with all manner of supernatural figures and events. There are many published collections, but among the earliest and the best are those by Alexander N. Afanasyev, or Afanasev (1870) and Nikolai Y. Onchukov (1903). Other departments of folk literature are the charms (*chastushka*)—each is usually a song of four rhymed lines—and popular dramas based on seventeenth- and eighteenth-century literary sources. Folk literature greatly influenced the work of several great Russian poets, Alexander Pushkin particularly, and its themes and imagery have been woven into Russian ballet and opera. Soviet scholars have manifested a renewed interest in the country's rich folklore, and many collections and learned investigations of this material have been made.

EIGHTEENTH-CENTURY LITERATURE . . . Peter the Great (1686–1725) opened a window to western Europe, and the whole country felt new energizing influences. Peter abolished the old Church Slavonic script and simplified the alphabet; some of the changes were suggested by Latin script. The vernacular came into use as the written language, although it continued for some time to be heavily influenced by Old Church Slavisms and foreign loan words and expressions.

Ukrainian and White Russian scholars and clerics now began to introduce a Latinized scholasticism into Muscovite Russia. The forerunner of this development was Simeon of Polotsk (1629–1680) who made many translations from Latin and published books of rhymed didactic verse. Two prelates of Ukrainian extraction and education, however, were more original as men of letters. They were St. Demetrius Tuptalo, metropolitan of Rostov (1651–1709), and Feofan Prokopovich, archbishop of Novgorod (1681–1736), both of whom wrote plays. Prokopovich was also the greatest orator of his day; his *Spiritual Reglement* (1718) advocated the liberal reforms of Peter the Great.

Peter, whose feverish activity was directed toward practical improvement in Russia, cared little for culture as such, and imaginative literature did not flourish during his reign. A historian of the time, V. N. Tatishchev (1686–1750), forecast with some truth that it would take Russia seven generations to catch up with civilization in the West. A book typical of the literature in Peter's reign is *On Indigence and Wealth*, by Ivan Pososhkov (1670–1726), a work erroneously thought to have anticipated the economic ideas of Adam Smith (1723–1790).

The reigns of Anna Ivanovna (1730–1740) and Elizabeth Petrovna (1741–1761) did little to promote literature. For the first time, French neoclassicism began to exercise a marked influence on Russian letters, as seen in the Horatian satires of Prince Antiokh Kantemir (1709–1744) and in the dull odes of Vasili Tredyakovski (1703–1769), whose real contribution to literature was an able treatise on prosody. Mikhail Lomonosov (1711–1765) was of infinitely greater stature. He is generally regarded as both the founder of modern Russian literature and the father of Russian science. In intellectual and artistic versatility, he was a kind of Russian Goethe. The language of his majestic odes sounds strikingly modern, and his pioneer studies in literary criticism and prosody were very important for his day.

387

It has been said that Peter the Great created new bodies for the Russians, but Catherine the Great (1762–1796) put souls into them. Certainly her reign surpassed Peter's in encouraging cultural development. In a modern sense, during this period, Russian drama really began. It was initiated by Alexander Sumarokov (1718–1777), also an able literary critic and excellent songwriter. Under the neoclassic influence of Voltaire (1694–1778) Mikhail Kheraskov (1733–1807) won the title of Russian Homer with his vast epic poems: *Rossiada* (1779) on the taking of Kazan by Ivan the Terrible, and *Vladimir* (1785) concerning the introduction of Christianity into Russia. Both of these long narrative poems were very popular in their day, but their only saving grace for a modern reader is a kind of sprightly dullness.

Better poets than Kheraskov wrote during Catherine's reign. The greatest was Gavrila Derzhavin (1743–1816). His *Ode to God*, written in the favorite genre of the age, even surpassed Lomonosov's poetry, particularly in the splendor of its imagery. Of a lower order, but still highly competent poetry, were the clever fables of Ivan Khemnitser (1744–1784) and a very popular adaptation by Ippolit Bogdanovich (1742–1803) of La Fontaine's *Psyche*.

Although the French neoclassical influence was dominant during Catherine's lifetime, English and German influences also played a part. Several satirical journals appeared. Catherine herself seems to have started the first one in 1769. It was called *All Sorts and Sundries,* and was inspired by the English journals *Tatler* and *Spectator* of Joseph Addison and Sir Richard Steele. The freemason and pietist Nikolai Novikov (1744–1816) edited a number of satirical journals, in which he boldly criticized social conditions, and in 1773 the empress suppressed all the journals. Catherine affected liberalism only up to the point where it grew critical of her regime. She also suppressed the *Journey from St. Petersburg to Moscow* (1790) and imprisoned its author, Alexander Radishchev (1749–1802). This book attacked both serfdom and autocracy, and Soviet scholars now regard it as the starting point of revolutionary thought in Russia.

A foremost literary figure of Catherine's time was Nikolai Karamzin (1766–1826), whose most significant service was in reforming the literary language. This reform lay in the direction of eliminating Church Slavisms and in following French syntactic and stylistic models. A group of literary conservatives unsuccessfully opposed these reforms. Their leader, Admiral Alexander Shishkov (1754-1841), argued for the preservation of archaic forms. Under Karamzin's influence and practice, modern Russian literary prose took shape, a monument of which is his well-known work, A *History of the Russian State*, 12 vols. (1818–1826). Influenced by Jean Jacques Rousseau and the eighteenth-century English writers, Samuel Richardson and Laurence Sterne, Karamzin also introduced the sentimental movement into Russian literature. His charming *Letters of a Russian Traveler* (1791) and his tremendously popular sentimental tale, *Poor Liza* (1792), are both in this vein. The most talented followers of Karamzin were Vasili Zhukovski (1783–1852) and Konstantin Batyushkov (1787–1855). There is little trace of sentimentality in Batyushkov, for his models were French and Latin elegiac poets and Torquato Tasso; his verse is classical in form. Zhukovski, however, added to the new sensibility the influence of English and German romantic writers. His mood is primarily elegiac, and his few original lyrics are among the best in Russian. Much of his fame rests on his extraordinary talent for translation; in this art he is hardly surpassed by translators in any language. Some of his versions of English poems are better than the originals, and he made splendid translations of Indian, Persian, and Greek epic poetry.

THE GOLDEN AGE OF POETRY . . . The bulk of literature written during Catherine's reign slavishly followed French, German, and English models. There was little originality, for Russian writers were still serving an apprenticeship to the authors of western Europe. In the first forty years of the nineteenth century, however, Russian literature came of age in a wonderful flowering of poetry both original in form and peculiarly native in content.

The towering genius of the period was Russia's greatest poet, Alexander Pushkin (1799–1837). Influenced at first by neoclassical eighteenth-century French poets, he soon fell under the romantic spell of George Byron. Finally, he struck his own original manner, which was essentially realism in a form lucid and classical. His earliest long poem was *Ruslan and Lyudmila* (1818–1820), a semi-ironic and light romance. A series of verse tales followed—*The Prisoner of the Caucasus* (1820–1821), *The Robber Brothers* (1821), *The Fountain of Bakhchisarai* (1822), and *The Gypsies* (1824)—all more or less inspired by Byron's

Eastern verse tales. Meanwhile, in 1823 he began writing his master-piece, which he did not complete until 1836. This was *Evgeni Onegin*, a novel in verse. He also wrote several plays, a wonderful series of folk tales in verse, other long poems, including the inimitable *Bronze Horseman* (1833), a substantial body of prose, and the finest collection of lyrics in Russian. His early death in a tragic duel shocked the country and left unfulfilled, despite his great achievements, the career of a poet who belongs among the foremost writers of the world.

The Pushkin Pleiad was a group of poets of real distinction who were contemporary with Pushkin. The most talented of them was Evgeni Baratynski (1800–1844), a profoundly intellectual poet who aspired to a fuller union with nature. In striking contrast was the bright, clear, convivial poetry of Nikolai Yazykov (1803–1846). Others in the group were Denis Davydov (1784–1836), author of many fine poems on war and love; Prince Peter Vyazemski (1792–1878), a witty poet and acute critic; Baron Antony Delvig (1798–1831), Pushkin's close friend and the author of a few chiseled lyrics; Kondrati Ryleyev (1795–1826), executed as a leader in the revolt of the Decembrists, who left a sheaf of noble and eloquent civic poems; Dmitri Venevitinov (1805–1827), whose few philosophical poems promised a lofty poetic future if he had lived; and Fyodor Glinka (1786–1880) whose verse combined deeply religious devotion with marked simplicity. An older poet, apart from the Pushkin Pleiad, was the greatest Russian fabulist, Ivan Krylov (1768–1844). His first book of *Fables* appeared in 1809, and he continued to write fables for years. The enormous popularity of his verse arose from its sound common sense and his perfect mastery of words.

A very great genius of this age was Mikhail Lermontov (1814–1841). At his best he rivals Pushkin, although he was at his best only in a few perfect lyrics, in certain parts of his verse tales, and in his unsurpassed narrative romantic poem, *The Demon* (1829–1833). He, more than Pushkin, deserves the title of the Russian Byron, though he was outgrowing that manner when he died. The Golden Age of Russian Poetry closed with Fyodor Tyutchev (1803–1873) and Aleksei Koltsov (1808–1842). Koltsov was an uneducated and plodding admirer of Pushkin. His attempts at philosophical poetry are mediocre, but his simple lyrics on the realities of peasant life, the first poetry of this kind in Russian, are excellent. Tyutchev is one of the three or four greatest figures of Russian

390

poetry. His verse began to appear as early as 1836, but critical recognition came much later. His poetry is essentially metaphysical and is based on a pantheistic conception of the universe. Its prevailing pessimism derives from a constant dualism—a struggle between chaos and cosmos. His diction is faultless, and the love lyrics of his later years are cast in perfect eighteenth-century classical style. Many years passed before Russia produced a body of verse in any way comparable to that of the first forty years of the nineteenth century.

EARLY PROSE FICTION . . . Little prose fiction of distinction was written in Russia during the early nineteenth century. Karamzin's *Poor Liza,* already mentioned, dates somewhat earlier. Vasili Narezhny (1780–1825) wrote *A Russian Gil Blas* (1814) in the realistic English and French picaresque tradition, and a little later Faddei V. Bulgarin (1789–1859) wrote *Ivan Vyzhigin* (1829) in a similar vein. Sir Walter Scott's popularity in Russia inspired historical romances of some merit. Mikhail N. Zagoskin (1789–1852) wrote *Yuri Miloslavski* (1829); Ivan I. Lazechnikov (1792–1869) wrote *The Last Recruit* (1831), *The Ice House* (1835), and *The Heretic* (1838); and Pushkin wrote *The Captain's Daughter* (1836). The Byronic prose tales of adventure of Alexander A. Bestuzhev (1797–1837)—pseudonym Marlinski—won wide popularity. The fiction of Prince Vladimir Odoyevski (1804–1869) and of Aleksei Veltmann (1800–1869) was less obviously romantic. Yet a romantic Byronic hero did not keep Lermontov's prose masterpiece, *A Hero of Our Times* (1840), from being a realistic and acute psychological study of human nature.

The greatest fiction writer of this period was Nikolai V. Gogol (1809–1852), who combined the romantic and the realistic as his special quality. Much in his early collections of short stories, *Evenings on a Farm Near Dikanka* (1831) and *Mirgorod* (1835), is sheer romanticism, but in some early stories and in later tales he combines the romantic with an unusual power for realistic portraiture. After finishing his well-known play *The Inspector-General* (1836), he began work on his great masterpiece *Dead Souls.* Here with realism and sharp satirical intent he creates a series of unforgettable characters and reveals the vulgarity and ugliness of provincial life. The last years of Gogol's relatively short life were darkened by religious mania that undermined his creative powers.

391

THE RISE OF THE INTELLIGENTSIA . . . Partly under the philosophical influence of Friedrich W. J. von Schelling and Georg W. F. Hegel, a kind of intellectual revolution took place between 1825 and 1840 that resulted in the formation of a class known as the *intelligentsia,* which later played so important a part in Russian political and social thought. By 1840 this movement had divided into two sharply opposing groups—the Slavophiles and the Westerners. The Slavophiles, strongly nationalist, advocated a return to the virtues and traditions of old Russia; they sanctioned the Orthodox faith and the autocracy of the czar. Important Slavophile leaders were the brilliant religious thinker and poet, Aleksei Khomyakov (1804–1860), the brothers Konstantin Aksakov (1817–1861), and Ivan Aksakov (1823–1886). The leader of the Westerners was the great literary critic, Vissarion Belinski (1810–1848), who felt that Russia's salvation lay in assimilating the progress of western Europe. The romantic idealism of Belinski's early critical writing changed later to a demand for a literature of social significance and reform. His famous contemporary, Alexander Herzen (1812–1870), was also a Westerner. Herzen was obliged to leave Russia early in life, and he carried on from abroad, through journalism, a political war against the Russian government. Herzen had artistic talents, and although most of his writing was political and social his brilliant autobiography, *My Past and Thoughts* (1852–1855), and his didactic novel *Whose Fault?* (1847) have high literary merit.

Belinski established a tradition in literary criticism that was followed ably by Nikolai G. Chernyshevski (1828–1889), Nikolai A. Dobrolyubov (1836–1861), and Dmitri Pisarev (1840–1868). They carried still further Belinski's emphasis on social significance in literature, their principal criterion of value in art being its utilitarian value. Dobrolyubov's famous article, *What Is Oblomovism?* (1858), amounts to a criticism of Russian life at the time. The radical trend begun by the Westerners became more emphatic about 1870 with the rise of the Populists (*narodniki*); they stressed service to the people as the only possible atonement for the sins committed by the educated class against the serfs. Their principal leader was the critic Nikolai K. Mikhailovski (1842–1904). Few figures of notable literary ability were in the camp of the Slavophiles. The critic Apollon Grigoryev (1822–1864) was an exception, for his best work is deeply imaginative and keenly perceptive. Nikolai Strakhov

(1826–1896) was an able though less profound critic, and the critical and philosophical writing of Konstantin N. Leontyev (1831–1891) showed excellent literary talent.

THE REALISTIC NOVEL . . . The classical Russian school of realism in fiction stems from Pushkin, not only from his prose tales but also from his novel in verse, *Evgeni Onegin*. Pushkin's style, his realistic descriptions of life on provincial estates, and such character creations as Evgeni and Tatyana all left a deep imprint on later fiction. In some ways Gogol was a continuator of Pushkin, though he also had great originality, especially in style and characterization. His humorous types are delightful, and the oppressed character of his famous tale, *The Cloak* (1836), illustrates a new "philanthropic trend" in Russian fiction. One of the earliest writers to reflect the influence of Gogol was Vladimir Sologub (1814–1882) in his book *Tarantas* (1844), a satirical account of a journey from Moscow to Kazan.

Soon appeared the great followers of Pushkin and Gogol, all of whom became known beyond Russia. One of the earliest was Ivan A. Goncharov (1812–1891). Belinski hailed his first novel, *A Common Story* (1847), as a vital contribution to the new realistic school, but his masterpiece *Oblomov* (1858) became a national classic. The hero Oblomov is a clear descendant of Pushkin's Evgeni, and he became a symbol of sloth and ineffectiveness—faults which exist in Russian character despite generous aspiration and a high sense of values.

An older man, Sergei Aksakov (1791–1859) found his proper medium in literature rather late in life, under the influence of Gogol. He published *A Family Chronicle* (1856), *Recollections* (1856), and *Years of Childhood of Bagrov—Grandson* (1858). All are essentially reminiscences of his own life and that of his grandparents, though they undoubtedly contain a large fictional element. They are masterpieces of realistic narrative. The author's remarkable objectivity, his pure prose style, and the freshness and vividness with which he recreates scenes of nature have hardly been equalled in Russian fiction.

The crown and glory of the realistic novel were the three giants Ivan Turgenev (1818–1883), Fyodor Dostoyevsky (1821–1881), and Lev (in English, Leo) Tolstoy (1828–1910). Modern criticism considers Turgenev the least able of the three; he is obviously a continuator of Pushkin. His first substantial work, *A Sportsman's Sketches* (1847–1852), was poetic in style and showed sympathetic understanding of the oppressed serfs. In his two next novels, *Rudin* (1855) and *A Nest of Gentlefolk* (1858), appear Turgenev's favorite "weak hero" and "strong heroine" types—their obvious inspiration is Pushkin's Evgeni and Tatyana. In *Rudin,* particularly, Turgenev, who was a Westerner, also showed his predilection with social problems. In *On the Eve* (1860), Turgenev tried to rid himself of the "superfluous" man type of character and create an active hero. The critics were quick to point out that the new hero, Insarov, was a Bulgarian and not a Russian. The author's final answer to the demands of the critics for an active hero was Bazarov, in his masterpiece *Fathers and Sons* (1861). Radical critics, however, condemned Bazarov as a caricature of a revolutionist. Deeply offended, Turgenev spent most of his later life abroad, and although he continued to write, his later work fell off in power. Turgenev's novels are rich in human experience and social significance; his gallery of heroines, as well as his style, is among the best in Russian fiction. His chief fault was an inability to come solidly to grips with life.

Dostoyevsky was another kind of writer, quite outside the traditional development of Russian realism. His chief debt was to Gogol, who had pioneered in philanthropic fiction; Dostoyevsky followed Gogol's lead in his preoccupation with the downtrodden and oppressed. Thus the hero of his first tale, *Poor Folk* (1846), is a miserable copying clerk, like the hero in Gogol's *The Cloak.* But unlike Gogol, who developed characters through external details, Dostoyevsky analyzes his characters from within. He is primarily interested in their souls. After publishing a series of short stories, Dostoyevsky was exiled in 1849 to Omsk, for association with a radical group; he did not return to St. Petersburg or begin writing again until ten years later. *Crime and Punishment,* published in 1866, won him widespread fame, and the great novels that followed, *The Idiot* (1869), *The Possessed* (1871), and *The Brothers Karamazov* (1880), made him one of the most celebrated authors in Russia. His novels have been discussed endlessly in Russia and abroad; critics have found everything in them from grotesque, sensational misrepresentation of real life to the revelation of a new Christianity. His titanic characters, such as Raskolnikov, Prince Myshkin, Stavrogin, the Karamazov brothers, and the holy Zosima, undoubtedly reflect his own spiritual tragedy in the search for God. His attempts to find solutions and harmonies for his characters never seem to have the same profundity and terrible realism of their tremendous conflicts and tragedies. Yet in his novels the fusion of the philosophical and imaginative fabric is complete, and his intense inner psychological analysis of characters is unique in world fiction.

In both manner and subject matter, Leo Tolstoy reverts to the Pushkin tradition of realism, but, unlike Turgenev, he was not primarily concerned, in his artistic works written before his spiritual change in 1880, with contemporary problems of social significance. Yet the orginal stamp of this colossal genius was placed on everything he wrote. His early works, such as *Childhood* (1854), *Boyhood* (1856), and *Youth* (1856), have the peculiar flavor of Aksakov's charming reminiscences, but they reveal a realistic grasp on the experiences of life and a potential power of character analysis far beyond the talents of the older writer. These qualities reach their height in *War and Peace* (1865–1869) and *Anna Karenina* (1875–1877). Modern realism has never equalled the achievement of *War and Peace*. Each of the more than five hundred characters has a distinct personality and speaks a distinct language. A Russian critic remarked that even the dogs in the book are individualized. Truth and simplicity, the two canons of Tolstoy's artistic faith, are scrupulously observed. And these same attributes, as well as the author's ecstatic love of life, appear throughout *Anna Karenina*. After his spiritual struggle and conversion about 1880, Tolstoy professed to turn his back on art. Nevertheless, apart from the voluminous critical, moral, and religious works that he wrote after 1880, he produced a considerable body of imaginative literature of great merit, such as *The Death of Ivan Ilyich* (1886), *The Kreutzer Sonata* (1889), *Hadji Murad* (1896–1904), and *Resurrection* (1896–1904); he also wrote several plays. Toward the end of his life he abandoned the psychological and analytical manner of his great period for a simple narrative style that would appeal to the masses. However, everything that he wrote, before and after his conversion, bore the indelible trace of his magnificent talent.

LATER NINETEENTH-CENTURY LITERATURE . . . There were other nineteenth-century realistic novelists, not in the same class with the giants, yet writers who have won a high place in Russian literature. The best novels of Aleksei F. Pisemski (1820–1881) are *The Petersburgher* (1853) and *A Thousand Souls* (1858); the first depicts uneducated people with rugged virtues and moral strength, and the second is a satire on genteel life. Pisemski's heroes and heroines are vigorously drawn, both in his novels and in his plays. One of the great satirists in Russian literature is N. Shchedrin (real name Mikhail E. Saltykov, 1826–1889). His *Golovlev Family* (1876) is a satirical masterpiece, a social novel that portrays the sordid and crass lives of the ruble-hunting lower provincial gentry. Among many radical journalists and novelists of the 1860's, the only outstanding one is Gleb Uspenski (1840–1902); his best work, *The Power of the Soil* (1882), portrays peasant life with humor and great sympathy.

A conservative rare for these times in literature, Nikolai S. Leskov (1831–1895) was the author of minor classics. His *Cathedral Folk* (1872) is an amusing chronicle of provincial life. In novels and many short stories, he paints a canvas of Russian life, its saints and sinners, always with bright colors, a strong sense of humor, and in a style rich with folk idioms. Drama too claims a high place in later nineteenth-century literature but the same can hardly be said for poetry. The poets were torn between the necessity of writing verse that reflected the civic problems of the day and of indulging in the poet's eternal search for truth and beauty. In trying to fulfill this double mission Apolloni N. Maikov (1821–1897) and Yakov P. Polonski (1819–1898) succeeded only moderately well. Count Aleksei Tolstoy (1817–1875), perhaps the greatest Russian writer of nonsense verse, also wrote exquisite lyrics and excellent dramas. The most celebrated realistic poet of the period, much read in Soviet Russia, was the radical writer, Nikolai A. Nekrasov (1821–1877). His narrative poems *The Pedlars* (1863), and *Who Can Be Happy in Russia?* (1873–1876), are filled with keen, good-humored, shrewd satire and remarkable verbal power, always with undertones of poignant protest. Afanasi A. Fet (1820–1892) was as conservative as Nekrasov was radical; his short, condensed lyrics are very beautiful.

FICTION AND POETRY (1880–1900) . . . The towering shadow of Leo Tolstoy dominated fiction from 1880 to 1900. An early member of the new generation which he influenced was Vsevolod M. Garshin (1855–1888), the fame of whose brief, creative life rests on his collected short stories. The most notable of these stories, particularly *The Red Flower* (1889), reveal a moral sensitivity and an infinite sympathy for the victims of man's inhumanity.

Among many minor novelists, the only one remembered is A. I. Ertel (1855–1908). His long novel, *The Gardenins* (1898), is still interesting; its picture of family life on a huge estate shows the influence of Tolstoy. Vladimir G. Korolenko (1853–1921) was a writer of quite a different type. He was exiled to Siberia for radical activities, and he drew upon his experiences there in his tales. In stories like *Makar's Dream* (1885) he combines a delightful humor with a kind of radical idealism.

Korolenko's great rival was Anton P. Chekhov (1860–1904), whose first collected tales met with immediate success when they were published in 1886. His mature period, however, began in 1889, with the publication of *A Dreary Story*. Here we find that mutual lack of understanding among characters and the psychological development of a mood that combine to form the "Chekhovian state of mind" so characteristic of his best-known tales, such as *The Duel, Ward 6,* and *In the Ravine.* These same qualities, along with deeper symbolic overtones, reappear in his famous plays.

Little excellent poetry was written during this decade. The most popular of the civic poets was Semyon Nadson (1862–1887). His brief creative life was dedicated to themes of reform, but he lacked imaginative power and originality of expression. His wide success must be attributed to his smooth, highly quotable, effortless verse. His rival for popular favor was A. N. Apukhtin (1841–1893), whose poetry is filled with a hedonist's regret for the lost pleasures of youth. The verse of Vladimir S. Solovyov (1853–1900) rose above this undistinguished level. A brilliant philosophical thinker and a clever writer of nonsense verse, he was yet capable of embodying profound mystical experiences in beautiful lyrics.

FICTION AFTER CHEKHOV (1900–1910) . . . Since radical movement of the 1880's and 1890's was driven underground by the czar's secret police, it could find no legal expression in literature. Yet a new force, Russian Marxism, had entered the struggle against autocracy, aided by a growing proletarian class. After the disastrous 1905 revolution, the Duma was established, yet the high hopes of the revolutionists were blasted. A deep disillusionment with the whole radical movement followed, reflected in literature in antipolitical individualism, in the growth of aestheticism, and, in some fiction, in the growth of eroticism.

For a time the two most popular representatives of the new manner in

397

fiction were Leonid N. Andreyev or Andreev (1871–1919) and Mikhail P. Artsybashev (1878–1927). Andreyev had two styles, the restrained, logical style of such celebrated short stories as *The Seven That Were Hanged* (1908), and the shrill, rhetorical style of *The Red Laugh* (1904). In general, the underlying theme of his fiction and plays was physical death and the annihilation of society, morals, and culture. Artsybashev echoed the same theme and added that of sexual emancipation in his enormously successful and somewhat pornographical novel, *Sanine* (1907).

In striking contrast was the fiction of Maxim Gorky (pseudonym of A. M. Peshkov, 1868–1936), who raised his voice on behalf of the lost men and women of Russia's lower depths and at the same time liberated Russian realism from its rather conservative tradition. Although Gorky began to publish long before the 1917 revolution, he lived to become the titular head of Soviet literature, which he profoundly influenced both by example and criticism. Gorky's early stories, published in two volumes in 1898, reveal the cruelty and ugliness in the lives of lowly creatures he met on travels through southern Russia. The novels and plays of his second period—*Foma Gordeyev* (1899), *Mother* (1907), *Matvei Kozhemyakin* (1911)—mainly depict the vicious life of provincial Russia and the unhappy lot of oppressed workers. In his last period he devoted himself largely to superb volumes of recollections. After the Soviets came to power appeared his huge masterpiece, *The Life of Klim Samgin* (1927–1938), which presents the history of Russian life between 1880 and 1917. He draws a dark, cruel, and ugly picture, but rising above the gloom there is always a ray of hope for a better and happier country.

Around Gorky and his publishing firm, Znaniye, were grouped writers who reveled in outspoken realism and went as far toward revolutionary protest as the government would permit. Two of them, Vikenti Veresayev (pseudonym of Vikenti V. Smidovich, 1867–   ) and A. S. Serafimovich (1863–   ), are popular in Soviet Russia through novels sympathetic with the ideals of the revolution. Serafimovich's *Iron Torrent* (1924) is especially popular. Some influence of Gorky appeared in the fiction of Alexander I. Kuprin (1870–1938), whose novel *The Duel* (1905) made him famous overnight. *Sulamith* (1908) and *Yama* (1910) were also quite popular, but they were less powerful. A finer artist was

I. A. Bunin (1870–   ), who first won notice through verse but who achieved his greatest fame as a novelist. Perhaps his best work is *Sukhodol* (1911), a story of the disintegration of a landowning family.

THE SYMBOLIST MOVEMENT . . . There was one important reaction in the 1890's and 1900's to writers such as Andreyev and Gorky, and to the dominance of social significance and nihilistic thought in literature. It took form in a definite turning away from city morality to aestheticism, from duty to beauty. Most participators in the new movement were brilliant intellectuals like Dmitri S. Merezhkovski (1865–1941) and his talented wife, Zinaida Hippius (1869–   ), N. M. Minski (1855–1937), and V. V. Rozanov (1856–1919). Merezhkovski is best known for his trilogy of historical novels (*Julian the Apostate*, 1896; *Leonardo da Vinci*, 1902; and *Peter and Alexis*, 1905), but he also played the philosopher and prophet, developing a curious antithetical approach to religion and morality. Rozanov was a critic and thinker of considerable power; his best works were *Solitary Thoughts* (1912) and *Fallen Leaves* (1913).

This emphasis on aesthetics and mysticism provided an easy transition to the remarkable symbolist movement, partly an offshoot of western European French symbolism. Valeri Bryusov (1873–1924) established the movement with a collection of poems published in *The Russian Symbolists* (1894). Though a weaver of gorgeous imagery, his verse often seems chill and premeditated. The early symbolist Konstantin D. Balmont (1867–1943) was a more natural poet, yet there is more sound than sense in such volumes as *Under Northern Skies* (1884) and *Let Us Be as the Sun* (1903). *The Cypress Chest* (1910) by I. F. Annenski, and *Cor Ardens* (1911) by Vyacheslav I. Ivanov (1866–   ), were regarded in their day as fine collections of symbolist verse; the former was compressed, subtle, and precise; the latter, ornate and metaphysical. One of the most remarkable authors of the whole symbolist movement was Fyodor K. Sologub (pseudonym of Fyodor Kuznich Teternikov, 1863–1927). He was a refined poet, but is still better known for his famous novel, *The Little Demon* (1907)—its hero Peredonov has become a symbol of concentrated nastiness. Perhaps the most original, and the most difficult, of the symbolists was Andrei Bely (1880–1934), whose real name was Boris N. Bugayev. He was a brilliant critic and poet, but he too is best known for his novels, particularly *Petersburg* (1913) and *Kotik*

Letayev (1920). His style in the latter suggests the works of James Joyce. An author often associated with Bely, both as symbolist and prose stylist, is Aleksei M. Remizov (1877–   ), whose tales (*The Story of Stratilatov*, 1909; *The Fifth Pestilence*, 1912) are of ugly provincial life, and are written in an ornamental and highly mannered prose.

In general, symbolist literature pointed in two clear directions—an aesthetic direction, emphasizing refinement of form, and a religious-mystical direction that usually involved the creation of dream worlds, often realistically described. Both tendencies fused in the work of the greatest of the symbolist poets, Alexander A. Blok (1880–1921). His early poems (*Verses about the Beautiful Lady*, 1904) tell the history of the author's mystical "love affair" with a beautiful lady, who continued to haunt Blok's later poems as he went through a long period of black despair. After 1917, he considered the revolution as a cleansing fire that would purify the soul of Russia. This attitude found expression in his greatest poem, *The Twelve* (1918), which is a miracle of revolutionary mysticism and metrical harmony. His radical enthusiasm later gave way to disillusion and chronic despair, and he died in 1921. He was perhaps the greatest Russian poet since Lermontov.

LITERATURE AT THE BEGINNING OF THE 1917 REVOLUTION

. . . Blok's *The Twelve* was in a sense the swan song of symbolism. The opposition was centered in two new groups: the acmeists, led by the excellent poets, N. S. Gumilyov (1886–1921) and Anna Akhmatova (1888–   ), and the futurists, the chief adherents of which were Igor Severyanin (1887–1942), Velemir Khlebnikov (1885–1922), and Vladimir V. Mayakovski (1893–1930). The futurists demanded the destruction of all literary traditions in the name of a new flesh-and-blood art that would banish the pale aestheticism of the symbolists and the dry academism of classical writers. In the shadow of this blatant revolt, Soviet literature began, and it was the immensely talented futurist poet, Mayakovski, who first set his impress on the new movement.

After 1917 Mayakovski devoted all his ability and energy to the revolution; his inspiration was the "social command" that he thought every Soviet poet must obey. He wrote many short pieces and plays, but his chief fame rests on several long narrative poems (*150,000,000*, 1919; *Vladimir Ilyich Lenin*, 1924; and *Good*, 1927). He employed very remarkable sound effects and all the typographical tricks of the broken line. No Soviet poet has been more honored than Mayakovski. His only rival in popularity during those early days was Sergei A. Esenin (Yesenin, 1895–1925), who regarded himself as the "last poet of the village." He had a fine lyric gift, but was unable to adapt himself to the new order.

Out of the confusion and conflicting literary demands during the early years of revolution and civil war, certain definite tendencies began to appear. In 1917 the Proletcult was formed to direct the fight for a proletarian culture on an international scale. Two schools of thought promptly arose: (1) the moderate group, supported by prominent government officials and certain writers known as "fellow-travelers," who argued that it was impossible to create a proletarian literature by official decree, and that much of value could still be learned from bourgeois art and culture; and (2) the extremists, soon known as the "On Guard" group, who supported the idea of a government literary dictatorship and called for an uncompromising class-literature. A resolution of the Central Committee of the Communist Party in 1925 declared in favor of the moderate school, and for a time the fellow-travelers were left free to write much as they desired.

THE BEGINNINGS OF SOVIET FICTION . . . No Soviet fiction of any consequence was written until about the time of the New Economic Policy (1922–1928). The predominant themes of this early fiction were the stirring events of the revolution and civil war, in which many of the young authors had participated. One of the first successful novels to depict revolutionary violence was A Bare Year (1920), by Pilnyak (1894–   ), whose real name was Boris A. Vogau. The Armored Train (1922) and The Partisans (1923), by Vsevolod Ivanov (1895–   ), treat guerrilla warfare in Siberia. Ivanov's characters are vivid, though astoundingly primitive in their emotions and actions. The extremely popular book Chapayev (1923), by Dmitri Furmanov (1891–1926) is an almost documentary narrative of the famous peasant partisan, Chapayev, who commanded a division that saved Uralsk from the White forces. Red Cavalry (1926), by Isaak Babel (1894–   ), is more romantic in its treatment of violence; it is a collection of stories based on the author's experiences with Marshal Semyon M. Budyonny's Cossacks.

On the whole, this early fiction eschewed the psychological analysis of the great nineteenth-century Russian novelists and concentrated on straightforward realistic narrative. Soon, however, Soviet novelists began to appear who wrote on themes of revolution and civil strife, much in the manner of Leo Tolstoy, Dostoyevsky, and Chekhov. One of the first was Konstantin A. Fedin (1892–   ). His novel, *Cities and Years* (1922–1924), of a self-centered intellectual who eventually betrays the revolution, aroused considerable interest. The flavor of Fedin's novel suggests Chekhov, and the spiritual doubt of his hero echoes Dostoyevsky. Dostoyevsky is even more in evidence in the fiction of Leonid M. Leonov (1899–   ), especially in his psychological development of character (see *The Badger*, 1925; and *The Thief*, 1927).

Critics praised Leonov's fiction as a bridge between Soviet realists and classical writers of the past. In a sense the two periods are linked even more strongly in the work of Aleksei N. Tolstoy (1882?–1945), a leading literary figure of Soviet Russia. Perhaps his most distinguished novel is *The Road to Calvary* (1921–1942), which pictures Russia before, during, and after the revolution. The first novel of Alexander A. Fadeyev (1901–   ), *The Rout* (1926), shows the obvious influence of Leo Tolstoy in psychological insight and unrestrained realism. Fadeyev shows intimate knowledge of Siberia in *The Rout* and again more extensively in his longest and best novel, *The Last of the Udegs* (1929).

FICTION DURING THE FIRST FIVE-YEAR PLAN . . . Under the First Five-Year Plan (1928–1932) a new attempt was made to regiment literature. The Russian Association of Proletarian Writers (RAPP) fell under control of the critic L. Averbakh and a few close supporters, who dictated that the only themes suitable for Soviet writers were industrial reconstruction and agricultural collectivization under the Five-Year Plan, treated against a background of the class struggle. The results of this "planned literature" were for the most part unsatisfactory. Discontent became so great that in 1932 a government decree dissolved RAPP, and this extreme form of literary dictatorship came to an end. A general association of Soviet writers was set up to which all, Communists and non-Communists, were freely admitted.

Although most literature produced during the First Five-Year Plan hardly rose above the dull level of official propaganda or skillful reporting, a few novels had superior merit. Fyodor V. Gladkov (1883–   ) had in 1927 anticipated the kind of fiction encouraged under the Five-

Year Plan with his enormously popular *Cement*. In 1933 he published *Power*, a story of the men and women who built Dneprostroi. In *Sot* (1930) Leonov depicts the establishment of a paper industry, and in *Skutarevski* (1933) he describes a large-scale electrification project. In both books he bores the reader with countless scientific technicalities. Yet in both he shows a typical Dostoyevskian concern for the "inner man" and his spiritual doubts. The subject of industrial construction provided the theme for Pilnyak's fine novel, *The Volga Flows into the Caspian* (1931). *Time, Forward!* (1933) by Valentin Katayev (1897–   ) is still more lively and artistic. The theme is the competition of shock brigades in pouring cement, and the story is told with verve and excitement.

Mikhail A. Sholokhov (1905–   ), one of the greatest Soviet novelists, reached artistic maturity during this period. He began his long epic of Cossack life, *And Quiet Flows the Don*, in 1926, but he interrupted it to write *Soil Upturned* (1932–1933), the best novel on the theme of agricultural collectivization during the First Five-Year Plan. Sholokhov finished *And Quiet Flows the Don* in 1940; the book covers eight years of its hero's experiences and development during the First World War, the revolution, and the civil war. It is an intensely moving story of a man's weakness and strength and reflects the influence of Leo Tolstoy's wonderful sense of realism and simplicity of character delineation.

Meanwhile, up to this point there was no lack of criticism of Soviet life in fiction. Satire aimed against the vices, foibles, and absurdities of Soviet officials was freely tolerated, provided it did not attack the accepted principles of the new order. Among the best known satirists in fiction are E. I. Zamyatin (1884–1937), Ilya Ehrenburg (1891–   ), and Mikhail A. Bulgakov (1891–1940). Katayev's *The Embezzlers* (1928) is a delightful satire on two naïvely peculating Soviet officials. A number of humorous, popular satires were written by that devoted pair of collaborators, Ilya Ilf (d. 1940) and Evgeni Petrov, whose real name was Evgeni P. Katayev (1903–1942). The most widely read Soviet humorist, however, is Mikhail Zoshchenko (1895–   ), who has published about ten volumes of short stories and novels. Beneath his humor there is always a deft criticism of the abuses of Soviet life.

Nor were ethical problems—the conflict of the new communist conscience and ideals with traditional views of sex, love, marriage, and the

403

family—neglected in fiction produced during the First Five-Year Plan and even earlier. Two older writers who wrote on such problems were S. N. Sergeyev-Tsenski (1876–   ), and Panteleimon Romanov (1884–1936). Yuri Libedinski (1898–   ), in his later works, concerns himself with ethical and social problems, especially in his finest novel, *The Birth of a Hero* (1930); and so does Yuri Olyosha (1899–   ) in his much discussed novel, *Envy* (1927).

SOVIET POETRY . . . Mayakovski's insistence in the years after 1917 on the socialist function of verse deeply influenced later Soviet poetry. Young authors followed his advice to write poetry that grew out of their participation in social creation and life. Poets, however, like the novelists, were soon split into factions by the conflicting demands made by their communist conscience and by "social commands." Demyan Bedny (1883–1945), an older writer regarded as a kind of poet laureate in the early days of the revolution, was untroubled by these conflicts; much of his ephemeral verse was satirical and humorous commentaries on Soviet daily life.

Many of the young proletarian poets under Mayakovski's influence, however, often lost themselves in the factional strife. They professed contempt for Russian bourgeois literature of the past; their devotion was to the Communist Party and its aims. One of the first of them, and for a time the most popular, was A. I. Bezymenski (1898–   ). He wore his Party card, he declared, not on his sleeve, but in himself; he asserted, in one of his best-known volumes of verse, *That Is How Life Smells* (1924), that his only real concern was for proletarian realities. After the dissolution of RAPP in 1932, Bezymenski and his strident leftism lost favor. Others among this group of young proletarian poets were Alexander Zharov (1904–   ), Nikolai Ushakov (1899–   ), Mikhail Golodny (1903–   ), Ivan Doronin (1900–   ), and Mikhail Svetlov (1903–   ). Vasily Kazin (1898–   ) was more talented and wrote in a more genuine proletarian vein. The chief follower of Mayakovski is Nikolai Aseyev (1889–   ). He honored his master's memory in a long poem, *Mayakovski Begins* (1940), which strengthened Aseyev's position as one of the foremost poets of Soviet Russia.

Constructivism, a somewhat vague movement that developed out of futurism, has Ilya Selvinski (1899–   ) for its principal poetic adherent. Somewhat influenced also by this movement was Eduard Bagrit-

404

ski (1899–1934), a highly talented poet with a fine lyric gift. The "poet's poet" of Soviet Russia, and certainly one of the most distinguished figures in literature, is Boris L. Pasternak (1890–   ), who began his career under the influence of the Futurists. His long narrative poems, such as *Spektorski* (1926) and *The Year 1905* (1927), seem uncongenial to his special lyric style, which is more in evidence in his shorter pieces. He is very much of an individualist, and although his language is often obscure and unorthodox in its syntactical structure it is brilliantly successful in rhythmical effects. An entirely different poet, though sometimes thought of as Pasternak's chief rival, is Nikolai Tikhonov (1896–   ). From the time of his earliest verse tales *(The Horde,* 1922; *Mead,* 1923) to his later ballads on civil-war themes and his recent poems, Tikhonov has developed his art in an independent fashion, largely as a medium for treating romantic subjects realistically.

In general, Soviet poets have lagged behind fiction writers; they seemed unable to adapt themselves as easily to the new demands made upon literature by the state. The discipline of verse is more severe, and it takes a longer time for forms to crystallize and for faith to take root in the poetic consciousness. The Second World War brought to fuller realization the earlier promise of poetry. Something of a renaissance took place in Soviet war poetry; the older poets are being paced by newcomers such as Konstantin Simonov and Alexander Tvardovski—the latter gained fame even before the war by his brilliant long poem *Muravia Land.* There has been a definite transition from the often difficult, futuristic language of prewar poetry to a simple, uninvolved poetical style, especially in many of the lyrics and ballads on war themes.

SOVIET LITERARY CRITICISM . . . After the 1917 revolution, the old schools of historical-comparative and religious-philosophical literary criticism gave way to sociological and Marxist criticism, which examined literature from the point of view of social and economic evolution. Even earlier a less purely Marxian approach had been formulated by such critics as Georgi V. Plekhanov (1857–1918), V. M. Friche, P. S. Kogan, V. L. Lvov-Rogachevski, and A. A. Bogdanov. Bogdanov became the principal theorist of the Proletcult and was the author of *Art and the Working People* (1918).

This early Marxian literary criticism split into a Right wing (Leon Trotsky, Vyacheslav P. Polonski, A. Voronski, I. Lezhnev, and A. V.

Lunacharski), and a Left wing (G. Lelevich, G. Gorbachev, and L. Averbakh). Both wings accepted the doctrine of historical materialism, and the critical method of both groups was to interpret literary works through an analysis of the economic and social structure of society. Their differences largely lay in the relative importance of these factors. V. Pereverzev and his followers proposed a variation in the Marxian approach: they maintained that literature became essentially a manifestation of the economic productive process in which every aspect of an author's creative art inevitably will reflect the economic laws of the period in which a writer lives. This approach was quickly condemned as a vulgarized kind of Marxism.

The most serious opponents of the Marxists in literary criticism were the formalists. Most of them are men of brilliant scholarly attainments, and their published works are confined largely to investigations of poetic speech and problems of style (consult B. V. Tomashevski, *The Theory of Literature*, 1925; I. Vinogradov, *The Struggle for Style*, 1937; P. Medvedev, *Formalism and Formalists*, 1934). Their general thesis is that a work of art is the sum of the devices in it, and that "form creates its content."

Since 1932, the universal touchstone of Soviet literary criticism has been "socialist realism." The interpretation and application of the term vary. In its primary sense, socialist realism means a realism that is socialistic, reflecting socialist realities and a socialist mentality. Some later Soviet critics insist, however, that socialist realism must rest on socialist humanism.[1] This concept is intended to broaden and ennoble the aims of art. Thus Soviet literature inspired by socialist realism is essentially optimistic: it confirms existence as activity, it strives to integrate literature and life, and it directs the creative present towards a more creative future.

RECENT TRENDS IN SOVIET LITERATURE . . . Since 1932 there has been less emphasis in Soviet literature upon themes dictated by "social commands," and greater emphasis upon permanent values and universal constants of human behavior. Although in the fine novels of, let us say, Nikolai Ostrovski (1904–1936), such as *Those Born by the Storm* (1936) and *How the Steel Was Tempered* (1937), a communist con-

---

[1] See the explanation of socialist humanism in Chapter XX.

science is still omnipresent, the works of many other novelists give way to more commonplace emotions and human values.

Enthusiasm has increased for historical fiction in which a Marxian approach is employed to reinterpret the past in the light of the present. Historical documentation is usually very careful and scholarly, and some of the novels are very interesting. In the brilliant historical novel *Peter I* (1929–1934), A. N. Tolstoy treats the period of the famous czar as one of transition, symbolically parallel to the period of tremendous upheaval in Soviet Russia. Other noteworthy examples of this genre are *Stepan Razin* (1927) by Aleksei Chapygin (1870–   ); *Tsusima* (1934) by A. Novikov-Priboi (1877–   ); and *The Brusilov Breakthrough* (1941) by Sergeyev-Tsenski. The historical novels of Yuri Tynyanov (1894–   ) are quite different. They attempt to re-create literary figures of the past and the age in which they lived *(Kukhlya,* 1925; *The Death of Vasir Mukhtar,* 1929; *Pushkin,* 1934). In most historical novels the patriotic motif is strong, not in a chauvinistic sense, but rather as an emphasis upon the unity and heroism of the past that must be reborn in the socialist present as a warning to potential foes of the Union.

During the Second World War this muffled note of warning became a fierce cry of patriotism. Two themes predominated in numerous war stories, poems, and plays that appeared after June, 1941: love for the socialist fatherland and infinite hatred for the enemy. There was still another note also in most of the war literature, a note of optimistic faith in the future. This faith has always been an inalienable part of Soviet literature.

BIBLIOGRAPHY

REFERENCE WORKS, LITERARY HISTORY, AND CRITICISM IN RUSSIAN

Skabichevski, A., *History of New Russian Literature, 1848–1893* (Moscow, 1893).
Brockhaus and Efron, *Encyclopedia* (St. Petersburg, 1890–1907).
Engelhard, N., *History of Russian Literature of the 19th Century* (St. Petersburg, 1902).
Brockhaus and Efron, *New Encyclopedia* (St. Petersburg, 1910–1917).
Vengerov, S. A., ed., *Russian Literature of the 20th Century, 1890–1910* (Moscow, 1914–1915).
Peretts, V. N., *Methodology of Russian Literature* (Moscow, 1922).
Piksanov, N. K., *Two Centuries of Russian Literature* (Moscow, 1924).
Vladislavlev, Ivan, *Russian Writers of the 19th to 20th Centuries* (Moscow, 1924).

Kogan, P. S., *Literature of the Great Decade* (Leningrad, 1927).
Voronski, A., *Literary Types* (Moscow, 1927).
Gorbachev, G., *Contemporary Russian Literature* (Leningrad, 1928).
Polonski, V., *Outline of Contemporary Literature* (Moscow, 1930).
Lunacharski, A. V., ed., *Literary Encyclopedia* (Moscow, 1929–1939).

LITERARY HISTORY AND CRITICISM IN ENGLISH

Vogüé, M. de, *Russian Novel* (London, 1913).
Waliszewski, K., *History of Russian Literature* (New York, 1900).
Brückner, A., *Literary History of Russia* (London, 1908).
Baring, Maurice, *Outline of Russian Literature* (New York, 1914).
Mirsky, D. S., *History of Russian Literature* (New York, 1927).
Lavrin, Janko, *Introduction to the Russian Novel* (London, 1942).
Simmons, E. J., *An Outline of Modern Russian Literature, 1880–1940* (Ithaca, N.Y., 1943).
Kaun, A., *Soviet Poets and Poetry* (Berkeley, Calif., 1943).
Struve, Gleb, *Twenty-five Years of Soviet Russian Literature* (London, 1944).

ANTHOLOGIES OF RUSSIAN LITERATURE IN ENGLISH

Wiener, Leo, ed., *Anthology of Russian Literature from the Earliest Period to the Present Time* (New York, 1902).
Deutsch, Babette, and Yarmolinsky, Avrahm, *Russian Poetry* (New York, 1927).
Coxwell, C. F., trans., *Russian Poems* (London, 1929).
Graham, Stephen, ed., *Great Russian Short Stories* (New York, 1929).
Cournos, John, ed., *Short Stories out of Soviet Russia* (New York, 1929).
Reavey, George, and Slonim, Marc, eds., *Soviet Literature: an Anthology* (New York, 1934).
Fen, Elizabeth, trans., *Modern Russian Stories by Soviet Writers* (London, 1942).
Montagu, Ivor, and Marshall, Herbert, eds., *Soviet Short Stories* (London, 1942).
Shelley, Gerard, trans., *Modern Poems from Russia* (London, 1942).
Bowra, C. M., ed., *Book of Russian Verse* (London, 1943).
Cournos, John, ed., *Treasury of Russian Life and Humor* (New York, 1943).
Guerney, B. C., ed., *Treasury of Russian Literature* (New York, 1943).
Yarmolinsky, Avrahm, ed., *Treasury of Great Russian Short Stories* (New York, 1944).

CHAPTER XXIII

Drama and the Theater

By ERNEST J. SIMMONS

ALTHOUGH the Russian theater has earned a high reputation in western Europe and America, Russia has never produced a body of dramatic literature comparable to Elizabethan drama or that of the great age of Corneille, Racine, and Molière in France. Nor is Russian drama as a whole comparable to the notable body of Russian realistic fiction. Yet some Russian plays merit a place beside the outstanding dramas of world literature, and a number of others are nearly as great.

The earliest Russian drama was imported from the West. Latin school dramas on religious themes were introduced into west Russian schools before 1600 and reached Moscow shortly afterward. Most of these dramas were influenced by the medieval miracle and mystery plays. When not performed in the original Latin, they were translated from Latin or from Polish. The only originality in the Russian adaptations is in the comic interludes, where Ukrainian types—the Cossack, the clerk, and the braggart Pole—were introduced. Prelates and clerics brought this school drama from Kiev to Moscow, and before long strolling bands of student actors took it out of the schools and began performing in many parts of Great Russia. The school drama, however, never became widely popular. For one reason, it soon met the rivalry of a second importation from the West—secular plays of German origin. These had a great influence on the history of Russian drama.

A German Lutheran pastor, Johann Gottfried Gregori, living in the German suburb of Moscow, gave the first impetus to this new dramatic development during the reign of Czar Aleksei (1645–1676). In 1672

409

Gregori organized a troupe of actors to perform before the czar. For repertoire he drew upon printed collections of the plays of German strolling companies which he had known in his youth. These plays in turn had been largely borrowed from the repertoire of companies of English actors performing in Germany. Among the plays selected by Gregori for translation and performance were *The Comedy of Queen Esther and the Haughty Aman* (acted in 1672) which was very likely based on an English interlude and *Temir Aksakovo* (acted in 1674), which unquestionably had as its ultimate source Christopher Marlowe's *Tamburlaine the Great.*

Under this new impetus, Simeon of Polotsk wrote a play in rhymed syllabic verse, *Action of the Prodigal Son,* and in the last years of the seventeenth century the rhymed school drama became predominant. But under Peter the Great secular prose plays translated from the German again came into vogue, supplemented by translations of a few of Molière's dramas. Public theaters were opened, and the old school plays were now played only in the seminaries and academies.

There is little literary worth in any of the early prose drama, but some literary merit and originality can be claimed for the verse drama. The verse plays of St. Demetrius Tuptalo of Rostov and of Feofan Prokopovich (1681–1736) were real contributions to Russian drama. In the *Nativity Play* of St. Demetrius, for example, the dialogue of the shepherds before the apparition of the angels is most attractive for its quality of quaint humor in dealing with things solemn and holy. *Saint Vladimir* (1705) by Prokopovich, a tragi-comedy on the theme of the introduction of Christianity into Russia, is almost classical in conception, and the verse represents the highest poetic level achieved at this time.

EIGHTEENTH-CENTURY DRAMA . . . The continuous history of both the Russian theater and the drama really begins with Alexander P. Sumarokov (1718–1777) during the reign of Elizabeth (1741–1761). Sumarokov's tragedy, *Khorev,* though influenced by outside sources, was the first Russian play. It was acted before the empress in 1747. To encourage this dramatic development, Elizabeth established the first permanent Russian theater (1756) at St. Petersburg, with Sumarokov as director. Its leading actor was a Yaroslavl merchant, Fyodor G. Volkov (1729–1763), who had earlier organized a local troupe of players. Volkov began the great tradition of Russian acting; he was soon ably sup-

410

ported by the famous tragic actor, Dmitrevski (1734–1821), who is said to have studied under Garrick. Excellent acting rendered the poor plays of Sumarokov acceptable, as was so often to be the good fortune of later Russian dramatists. Sumarokov wrote several comedies and tragedies, but they are for the most part slavish imitation or mere adaptations of French neoclassical pieces. Critics called him the "Russian Racine," a sobriquet which perhaps bears less of compliment than implication of plagiarism. He even adapted *Hamlet* but proudly denied strict adherence to his famous model, declaring: "My *Hamlet,* except for the monologue at the end of the third act and the praying of Claudius, hardly resembles the tragedy of Shakespeare." Yet Sumarokov's efforts have won him the title of "father of Russia drama." He did much to popularize in Russia the best plays of Pierre Corneille, Jean B. Racine, Molière, and Voltaire.

The new interest in drama and theater was furthered by Catherine the Great (1762–1796), who dabbled in playwriting herself. She wrote several satirical comedies, something that passes for a translation of *The Merry Wives of Windsor,* two historical plays that are classified as "imitations of Shakespeare," and still another play that was inspired by *Timon of Athens.*

Little good tragedy was written during Catherine's reign, except for *Vadim* (1789) by Yakov Knyazhnin (1742–1793), which breathes a revolutionary spirit of political freethinking. Comedy, still largely influenced by the French neoclassical manner, but now with a firmer grasp on the realities of Russian life, predominated. Knyazhnin, an imitator of Voltaire, was a prolific writer of comedies, which on the whole are superior to his tragedies. They usually make excellent theater, but are not first-rate in character drawing and dialogue. Perhaps his best comedies are *The Queer Fellows,* a satire on Russian Gallomania, and *An Accident with a Carriage,* a bold satire on serfdom. Even better as dramatic satire is the famous comedy *Chicane* (1798) by Vasili Y. Kapnist (1757–1823). This play is a vicious attack on officers of the law, who are painted as thieves and extortioners. Worthy of mention also are the comedies and comic operas, particularly *The Miller Wizard, Quack and Matchmaker* (1799), of Alexander A. Ablesimov (1742–1783).

The greatest dramatist of the eighteenth century was Denis Fonvizin (1744–1792). His reputation rests upon two comedies, *The Brigadier-*

411

General (1766) and *The Minor* (1782), which have won him a place among the foremost Russian playwrights. Both are in prose and reflect the influence of neoclassical French comedy, although Fonvizin's immediate model was the Danish dramatist Ludwig Holberg, whom he had read in German. *The Brigadier-General* is a social satire directed against the fashionable French semieducation so prevalent in Russia at the time. It is well constructed and full of carefree amusement. Fonvizin's masterpiece, *The Minor,* is more serious, though less well constructed. This too is a social satire, and in the typical neoclassical fashion contains a conventional and uninteresting subplot. Attention is centered on the main plot and the vicious members of the Prostakov family: the domineering bully of a mother, her sheepish husband Prostakov (Mr. Simpleton), her furious brother Skotinin (Mr. Brute), and her son Mitrofan, who typifies brutal selfishness. The satire of the comedy is directed against the crude, barbaric natures of uneducated country gentry. Both character drawing and dialogue are superior and strike a realistic note that was to be heard again in the best comedy of the nineteenth century.

DRAMA DURING THE FIRST HALF OF THE NINETEENTH CENTURY . . . At the turn of the century there was little progress in the development of drama. French neoclassicism gave way to a taste for sentimental plays, but no original work of value was written in this vein. Ivan A. Krylov (1768–1844) wrote two rather successful satiric comedies, but the two most popular plays on the Russian stage were translations from the German melodramatist, A. F. F. von Kotzebue. The outstanding native dramatist of the early nineteenth century was Vladislav Ozerov (1770–1816). His sentimental verse tragedies, such as *Fingal* (1805) and *Dmitri of the Don* (1807), owed their tremendous success to superb acting by Catherine Semenova, one of Russia's greatest tragic actresses.

During the first half of the nineteenth century four famous authors wrote plays; two of them wrote plays of supreme merit. Two of these authors, Alexander S. Pushkin (1799–1837) and Mikhail Y. Lermontov (1814–1841), were primarily poets. The third, Nikolai V. Gogol (1809–1852), was essentially a novelist, and only the fourth, Alexander S. Griboyedov (1795–1829), was solely a dramatist. Pushkin's first and longest play, *Boris Godunov* (1825), was an experiment—an attempt to write a Russian Shakespearean tragedy as a departure from the prevalent

412

French neoclassical form. It is a historical play on the theme of Czar Boris Godunov, written in blank verse. Despite scenes of real dramatic beauty and occasional passages of stirring poetry, the play was not one of Pushkin's most mature performances. It has never won a secure place on the Russian stage. Pushkin's so-called "little tragedies," *Mozart and Salieri* (1830), *The Feast During the Plague* (1830), *The Covetous Knight* (1836), and *The Stone Guest* (1836), are more interesting and on a much higher level of perfection. They were not intended for acting but were rather essays in the understanding of character and of dramatic situations: as such they leave little to be desired, either as poetry or drama. Mikhail Y. Lermontov (1814–1841) had less merit than Pushkin as a dramatist. As a mere youth he wrote three prose plays that deal with high-strung passions and melodramatic situations. His verse play, *The Masquerade* (1835), has more worth, but it is too melodramatic and the characters barely come alive. The play was revived with some success in Soviet Russia.

There are critics who insist that Nikolai V. Gogol's (1809–1852) *Revizor* or *The Inspector-General* (1836) is the greatest play in the Russian language. Certainly it is one of the greatest. The general theme, supplied to Gogol by Pushkin, of the hero who is mistaken by the people of a town for a government inspector, is developed with unerring art from beginning to end. As a piece of theater, it is perfectly constructed. Gogol's originality, against the background of contemporary drama, is shown by the complete absence of the traditional love element and of any sympathetic characters. The play is a moral satire directed against corrupt and despotic officials. The characters are superbly drawn, and the dialogue with its comic intensity is the most effective, with perhaps one exception, in the whole range of Russian drama. The lasting popularity of this play rests in part on an underlying symbolism which makes the speech and actions of its characters timeless despite their local application. Less known but almost as great is Gogol's comedy *Marriage* (1842), which has more exuberance and pure fun in it than the *Revizor*.

The reputation of Alexander Griboyedov as one of the greatest Russian dramatists rests on one play, *Woe from Wit*, which he wrote in Tiflis in 1822–1823. The play belongs to the French neoclassical school of comedy and recalls at once the manner of Molière. Like Fonvizin, who wrote in the same vein, Griboyedov stresses characters and dialogue at

413

the expense of plot, which is loosely constructed. But in characterization and dialogue in comedy, only Fonvizin and Gogol can be compared to him. The dialogue is unique in Russian drama. It is in rhymed iambic verse of variable length, but the author never allows a rebellious metrical form to spoil the effect of everyday conversation. The dialogue is full of brilliant wit, epigrams, and repartees, and it has provided more clever quotable lines than any other single work in Russian literature. Its characters, such as Famusov, Molchalin, Repetilov, and the famous hero Chatski, have become household words for the universal human traits that they represent.

DRAMA DURING THE SECOND HALF OF THE NINETEENTH CENTURY . . . The remarkable realistic development in fiction during the second half of the nineteenth century was accompanied by a similar realistic movement in acting and in playwriting. The famous actor Mikhail Shchepkin (1787–1863) had already established the great tradition of Russian realistic acting, which was eventually developed into a theory of theatrical art by the celebrated actor and producer K. S. Stanislavski (1863–1938), in his great Moscow Art Theatre, founded in 1898. In its later development Russian scenic realism concentrated on social realism, on truth to the particular, on the least universal and most individual aspects of a given social milieu. All this found its first complete expression in original drama in the plays of Alexander N. Ostrovski (1823–1886) the greatest professional Russian dramatist.

Between 1847 and 1886 Ostrovski wrote about forty plays in prose and eight in blank verse. Although of unequal merit, this collection is the most remarkable body of dramatic work in Russian. Dramatists like Griboyedov and Gogol may surpass him in literary genius, but Ostrovski created a school of Russian drama. With few exceptions, his plays are neither tragedies nor comedies; they are best described as "tragicomedies." Though not a master of language, his dialogue is always adequate. Nor is he much of a psychologist, yet his characters have the individuality and uniqueness that we recognize in our fellow creatures. Where he is supreme is in the breadth, the grasp, and variety of his vision of Russian life and in his ability to re-create this life on the stage.

The subject matter of his early and most characteristic plays is the life of Moscow and provincial merchants, and the lower strata of the official world. Ostrovski's first play, *The Bankrupt* (1849), was a sensational success, and it revealed at once his peculiar and rather original technique. He presented only unsympathetic characters, and he boldly discarded the ancient tradition of comedy—the poetic justice that punishes vice. His realism avoids both caricature and farce; it is based on solid first-hand knowledge of the life described. He resorted to no theatrical tricks in order to achieve effects. All these traits were strengthened in the successful plays that soon followed—*The Poor Bride* (1852), *Poverty Is No Crime* (1854), and *The Profitable Post* (1857). The play generally considered his masterpiece is *The Storm* (1860). It is the most poetic piece he ever wrote, a great poem of love and death, of freedom and thraldom. The inevitable tragedy of the heroine grows out of the dark, oppressive forces of Russian provincial life at that time. Notable later plays are *Enough Simplicity in Every Wise Man* (1868), *The Forest* (1871), and *Wolves and Sheep* (1877).

The only two contemporary dramatists who appoach Ostrovski's art are Alexander V. Sukhovo-Kobylin (1817–1903) and Aleksei F. Pisemski (1820–1881). The best of the former's three plays is *Krechinsky's Wedding* (1855), a pure comedy of picaresque intrigue, in which the rogue triumphs over the stupidity of the virtuous character. The two chief rogues, Krechinsky and Rasplyuyev, are among the most memorable in Russian dramatic literature, and the play has a secure place in Russian repertoire. The two other comedies, *The Affair* (1869) and *The Death of Tarelkin* (1869), are brutally cynical satires. Pisemski, essentially a novelist, began his dramatic career with comedies. But his most memorable work is one of the great tragedies in Russian dramatic literature, *A Hard Lot* (1860). The subject concerns the seduction by a squire of the wife of one of his serfs; the husband murders his wife and gives himself up to the law. The human conflict between the squire, who is legal master of the husband, and the husband, who is legal master of his wife, is worked out powerfully with a tragic inevitability that is classical in quality.

The great realistic novelist, Ivan S. Turgenev (1818–1883), ranks perhaps next to Pisemski as a playwright, though some critics give this position to Leo Tolstoy for his dramatic works. Early in his career, Turgenev thought he might devote himself entirely to drama. His plays belong to the years 1843–1852. They are largely experimental gropings after an adequate form of expression. The most actable is *The Provincial Lady*

(1851), a light comedy with delicate characterizations. *A Month in the Country,* a more interesting play, is a psychological study on the old theme of rivalry in love between a mature woman and a young girl. In its undramatic nature it is a forerunner of Anton P. Chekhov's plays.

In the extensive literary production of Leo (Lev) Tolstoy (1828–1910), drama was merely incidental. Yet he wrote several plays, one or two of which have an enduring place in the great dramatic literature of Russia. He succeeded though he possessed few of the essential qualities that make a dramatist. On the lighter side are *The Contaminated Family* (1863), a delightful satire on the young generation and a little masterpiece of character drawing and dialogue; the *First Distiller* (1886), a humorous antiliquor morality play; and *The Fruits of Culture* (1889), an amusing social comedy which satirizes the vogue of spiritualism. But the best known and greatest of his plays is *The Power of Darkness* (1887), a realistic tragedy of peasant life. The play embodies a favorite conviction of Tolstoy, the evil-begetting power of every evil action. Although superfluous details clutter up the action, there are great moments in the play, particularly the impressive third act where we see Nikita enjoying the first joyless fruits of his initial crime. Two more plays of Tolstoy are worthy of comment: *The Light That Shines in Darkness* (begun early in the 1880's and continued in 1900–1902 but never finished), and *The Living Corpse* (1900). The first draws on Tolstoy's life, for it concerns a Tolstoyan moralist surrounded by an unsympathetic family. *The Living Corpse,* in point of view, is rather unique for Tolstoy; it reflects the mellow attitude of a kindly old man, free from Tolstoy's customary dogmatic moralizing and full of sympathy for the abandoned drunkard in the play and even for the proud society mother. The dialogue in both these plays is remarkably true to the society speech of the time.

The second half of the nineteenth century saw a revival of metrical historical plays largely under the belated influence of Pushkin's *Boris Godunov.* In general all these plays are characterized by mediocre blank verse and by failure, despite often careful research, to catch the flavor of old Russia, from which most of the themes were drawn. The movement was begun by the poet Leo A. Mei (1822–1862) in his *Maid of Pskov* (1860), a conventionally pretty drama of the time of Ivan the Terrible. Between 1862 and 1868 Ostrovski also tried his hand at a series of chronicle plays; these often dramatize history interestingly, but the verse is flat and the characters are wooden. The best of these historical dramatists is Aleksei K. Tolstoy (1817–1875) whose famous trilogy, *The Death of Ivan the Terrible* (1866), *Czar Fyodor* (1868), and *Czar Boris* (1870), deserves its high reputation. The historical material is skillfully handled, the character drawing is adequate and sometimes brilliant, and the blank verse is superior to that in other contemporary historical plays.

DRAMA AND THEATER ON THE EVE OF THE REVOLUTION

. . . The founding of the Moscow Art Theatre in 1898 by Stanislavski and Vladimir Nemirovich-Danchenko ushered in a new development in Russian theater and drama. One of the first productions of the new theater in 1898 was Chekhov's *The Seagull*. Anton Pavlovich Chekhov (1860–1904) had written his first play *Ivanov* in 1887 and had followed up its success with several one-act comedies. In 1895 he wrote *The Seagull*, which was acted the next year in St. Petersburg. The performance was an utter failure, for neither director nor actors understood the play, and Chekhov vowed to abandon drama. Stanislavski's performance, however, in 1898, was a triumphant success, and Chekhov turned with new energy to writing plays. There soon followed *Uncle Vanya* (1900), *The Three Sisters* (1901), and *The Cherry Orchard* (1904), all of them striking successes. These four plays constitute Chekhov's theater and represent quite a new direction in drama, although their undramatic nature had been partly anticipated by Ostrovski and Turgenev. There is no subject matter in Chekhov's plays, no plot, no action. In certain essentials the plays resemble his short stories. In a sense there is no hero or heroine; all the characters are equal. And the dialogue Chekhov employs is admirably suited to the expression of one of the favorite ideas of his tales—the mutual unintelligibility and strangeness of human beings who make no effort to understand each other. Further, his plays are steeped in emotional symbolism, and the dominant note is one of gloom, depression, and hopelessness. Stanislavski's style of directing suited perfectly the peculiar nature of Chekhov's plays and undoubtedly accounted for a good deal of their initial success on the stage. The Moscow Art Theatre specialized in naturalistic realism, dispensed with all theatricality, abandoned the "star" system of acting, and concentrated on bringing out the inner biography of each character.

417

Chekhov's highly original drama quickly inspired imitators, but almost all imitations of Chekhov are bad. One of the first imitators was Leonid Andreyev (1871–1919), who wrote about a dozen plays, several of which are still played. His Chekhovian realistic plays of Russian life, such as *Towards the Stars* (1906), *Days of Our Life* (1908), *Anfisa* (1910), and *Gaudeamus* (1911), are very poor Chekhov. He showed more originality, however, in another group of plays, which are symbolical dramas in a conventional setting, such as *The Life of Man* (1907), *King Hunger* (1908), *Black Masks* (1909), *Anathema* (1910), and *He Who Gets Slapped* (1914). *The Life of Man* and *He Who Gets Slapped* won considerable success both in Russia and abroad. There is a curious avoidance of real life in his plays, and the rhetorical prose and gaudy colors weary both the ear and eye. But their melodramatic effects often make for good theater, and for a time their philosophy of vanity, death, and the falseness of everything human had vogue. There is something of the Chekhovian atmospheric details in the plays of Mikhail P. Artsybashev (1878–1927) although he was additionally influenced by Strindberg. His psychological problem dramas, including *Jealousy* and *War*, are rather crude but they act well.

Maxim Gorky (Maksim Gorki) (1868–1936) whose dramatic efforts continued well into the period after the 1917 revolution, began as a patent follower of Chekhov. He wrote fifteen plays, but only two or three won outstanding success on the stage. His first play, *The Petty Bourgeois* (1901), was a bitter picture of a middle-class family and a revolutionary engine driver. It was eclipsed by *The Lower Depths* (1902), which won sensational fame in Russia and abroad. This play is a penetrating study of different types of human derelicts in an underground night's lodging. Gorky's dramatic system resembles Chekhov's. The four acts, undivided into scenes, the absence of action, and the exaggerated development of conversations on the meaning of life—all these suggest Chekhov. The conversations particularly, but also the extraordinary realism of the settings and the unique characters, won unbounded applause for *The Lower Depths* especially abroad. Succeeding plays, *Suburbans* (1904), *Children of the Sun* (1905), *The Barbarians* (1906), *Enemies* (1907), *Vassa Zheleznova* (1911), won no great success. However, *Yegor Bulychev and Others* (1932) was extremely well received in Soviet Russia. Its theme is the death of a capitalist on the eve of the revolution.

SOVIET RUSSIAN DRAMA AND THEATER . . . Theatrical development in Soviet Russia has continued and even surpassed the finest traditions of the prerevolutionary period; the Russian theater today is perhaps the most vital in the world. Recognizing the educational and cultural value of the theater, the Soviet government gave every encouragement to the theater arts, and millions of people who had never witnessed a play before became constant theater-goers. There has been a great expansion and development of theatrical schools, theories of acting and staging, and other phases of the theater. The Moscow Art Theatre took a new lease on life after 1917, and other now famous theaters developed individual theories of dramatic art—the Meyerhold Theatre, the Vakhtangov Theatre, the Kamerny Theatre, and the Realistic Theatre.

Playwriting has hardly kept pace with the art of the theater, yet the Soviet plays written since 1917 are not markedly inferior in quantity or quality to those of any other nation in western Europe or America during the same period. Soviet drama, like fiction or poetry, has mirrored the swift political, social, and economic changes in the Union of Soviet Socialist Republics. Most of the dramatists first on the scene, such as Aleksei N. Tolstoy (1882?–1945), K. A. Trenev (1878–   ), Anatol V. Lunacharski (1875–1933), B. S. Romashev (1895–   ), and Sergei M. Tretyakov (1882–   ), belonged to the intelligentsia, and some had written plays before the revolution. Several novelists who also wrote plays belong to this group and some have gained a permanent place in the Soviet theater. Varied tendencies, futuristic, romantic, and realistic, feature the plays of the early Soviet period.

A second group of dramatists, some of proletarian origin, wrote plays mainly on civil war themes. These were frequently poorly executed propaganda plays. Among them are *The Echo* (1924) and *The Storm* (1926) by V. N. Bill-Belotserkovski (1884–   ), and *The Band* (1924) by F. V. Gladkov.

Playwrights with postrevolutionary training make up the third group; a few of them have written plays of enduring worth. Of particular significance are Alexander N. Afinogenov (1904–1941) Vladimir M. Kirshon (1902–   ), Nikolai F. Pogodin (1900–   ), and V. V. Vishnevski. Some of their outstanding plays are Afinogenov's *Fear* (1931) and *The Town of Dalekoye* (1935); Kirshon's *Bread* (1931); Pogodin's

Tempo (1930) and *Aristocrats* (1935); and Vishnevski's *First Cavalry Army* (1930).

The tendency in Soviet drama, as in fiction, has been more and more toward realism, and attempts were made to treat the problems and conflicts that grew out of the changing Soviet life. Straight propaganda plays, such as V. V. Mayakovski's *Mystery-Bouffe* (1921) and *The Bedbug* (1929), and Sergei M. Tretyakov's *Roar China!* (1926)—the last a crude drama of foreign imperialism—soon wearied the audiences. A few of the civil war plays, especially the *Armored Train* (1927) of V. V. Ivanov (1895–   ), Mikhail Bulgakov's (1891–1940) *Days of the Turbins* (1926), and Trenev's *Lyubov Yarovaya* (1926), were well constructed and well acted.

A portion of the great body of literature written during the First Five-Year Plan was drama. The plays of this period suffered from the monotonous and didactic propaganda patterns enforced by the dictatorial heads of RAPP (Russian Association of Proletarian Writers), who required writers in all literary forms to contribute their skill to the tremendous drive for industrial reconstruction and agricultural collectivization. A few of these forthright propaganda dramas, however, were good plays; for example, Afinogenov's *Fear*, which attempts to solve in terms of individual and not mass psychology the moral problem of revolutionary terror. N. F. Pogodin's *Tempo* (1930) and V. M. Kirshon's *Bread* (1931) were also superior to the average Five-Year Plan dramas, despite shortcomings in construction and dialogue.

In more recent Soviet drama the realistic trend has continued. Effective anti-Nazi plays appeared both before and after the Nazis came into power. Many of the later Soviet plays show deeper understanding of the individual's problems in a collectivist society. The didactic element has not been eliminated, but dramatists are growing more concerned with the causes and effects of universal human behavior. Contemporary dramatic concern with the past of the Russian people is reflected in historical plays, often dramatizations of famous novels, such as Leo Tolstoy's *War and Peace* and Aleksei N. Tolstoy's *Peter I*. This trend continued after the German invasion of 1941; other plays treated immediate war themes with stark realism. Among these were Konstantin Simonov's *The Russian People*, Leonid Leonov's *Invasion*, and Alexander Korneichuk's *The Front* and *Guerrillas of the Ukrainian Steppes*.

420

BIBLIOGRAPHY

REFERENCE WORKS, HISTORY AND CRITICISM OF THE DRAMA AND THEATER, IN RUSSIAN

Prygunov, M. D., *The Russian Stage During the Last Forty Years, 1880–1920* (Karan, 1921).

Znosko-Borovski, E. A., *Russian Theatre at the Beginning of the 20th Century* (Prague, 1925).

Redko, A. Ye., *The Theatre and Evolution of Theatrical Forms* (Leningrad, 1926).

Yakovlev, M. A., *Theory of Drama* (Leningrad, 1927).

Beskin, E., *History of the Russian Theatre* (Moscow, 1928).

Vsevolodski, V. N., *History of the Russian Theatre* (Leningrad, 1929).

Novitski, P. I., *Contemporary Theatrical Systems* (Moscow, 1933).

Rafalovich, V. Y., ed., *History of the Soviet Theatre* (Leningrad, 1933).

Kirpotin, V. Y., *Prose, Dramaturgy, and the Theatre* (Moscow, 1934).

Yuzovski, Yu., *Performances and Plays* (Moscow, 1935).

Vsevolodski, V. N., *Anthology of the History of the Russian Theatre* (Moscow, 1936).

HISTORY AND CRITICISM OF THE DRAMA AND THEATER, IN ENGLISH

Wiener, Leo, *Contemporary Drama of Russia* (Albany, N.Y., 1924).

Mirsky, D. S., *Contemporary Russian Literature, 1881–1925* (New York, 1926).

London, Kurt, *The Seven Soviet Arts* (London, 1927).

Mirsky, D. S., *A History of Russian Literature* (New York, 1927).

Markov, P. A., *The Soviet Theatre* (New York, 1934).

Houghton, Norris, *Moscow Rehearsals* (New York, 1936).

Macleod, Joseph, *The New Soviet Theatre* (London, 1943).

Simmons, E. J., *An Outline of Modern Russian Literature, 1880–1940* (Ithaca, N.Y., 1943).

Struve, G., *Twenty-five Years of Soviet Russian Literature, 1918–1943* (London, 1944).

BIBLIOGRAPHIES OF ENGLISH TRANSLATIONS OF RUSSIAN PLAYS

Wiener, L., *Anthology of Russian Literature*, 2 vols. (New York, 1902).

——, *Contemporary Drama of Russia* (Albany, N.Y., 1924).

Mirsky, D. S., *Contemporary Russian Literature, 1881–1925* (New York, 1926).

——, *A History of Russian Literature* (New York, 1927).

Noyes, G. R., *Masterpieces of the Russian Drama* (New York, 1933).

Dana, H. W. L., *Handbook on Soviet Drama* (New York, 1938).

CHAPTER XXIV

Music and Composers

By NICOLAS SLONIMSKY

R ussian music is at least one thousand years old. The first folk melodies of European Russia date from the tenth century; Asiatic Russia did not come into the national cultural complex until centuries later.
The most ancient Russian folk songs are entirely *sui generis;* for the
first great alien influence, from Byzantium, was a factor affecting Russian religious music only. Russian folk song collectors have gathered
and published so much authentic musical material during the last century and a half that the record of traditional Russian folk songs is now
remarkably complete.

Peter Sokalski (1832–1887), in his book *Russian Folk Music in its
Melodic and Rhythmic Structure* (Kharkov, 1888) summarizes the essential characteristics of ancient Russian folk songs in these four points:
(1) the melodic motion of Russian folk songs is predominantly descend-
ing; (2) the range of folk modes varies from as narrow as a fourth to as
wide as an octave and a fourth; the older the song, the narrower the
range; (3) the intervals of the fourth and fifth determine the modula-
tion to the new keys; (4) in ancient Russian folk music, only three tones
are used, a whole tone, and a tone and a half, adding up to the interval
of the fourth.

The rhythm of Russian folk songs is determined by characteristic
groupings of two short notes followed by a long note—the most familiar
example is the *Song of the Volga Boatmen*. As for metrical arrangement
of musical phrases, Russian folk songs have a large incidence of uneven
metrical units (such as 5, 7, or 11) to a musical phrase. Great Russian

composers have used such typical time-signatures as 5/4 (Glinka), 7/4 (Borodin), and 11/4 (Rimski-Korsakov).

The first collection of Russian folk songs, *Collection of Simple Russian Songs With Notes,* was compiled and published (1782) by Vasili Trutovski, a singer at the court of Catherine the Great. A more important collection was made by the Russianized Czech Ivan Prach, of 150 songs noted down for him by Nikolai Lvov, a musical amateur. Its publication in 1790 found immediate response, and a second edition appeared in 1806. The famous Italian composer Giovanni Paisiello expressed amazement at the beauty of these songs created by simple peasants, and Ludwig van Beethoven incorporated themes from them in his String Quartet, Opus 59, which he dedicated to Count Andreas Razumovski, the Russian ambassador to Vienna. More songs were collected and classified during the nineteenth century. The most significant collection was by N. Palchikov (Moscow, 1888); he published 125 melodies with texts, all gathered in the village Nikolayevka, in Ufa Province. Palchikov gives as many as eight versions of each song, enough to permit general deductions as to the chief characteristics of Russian folk music. Harmonizations of Russian folk songs published by Balakirev (1886), Rimski-Korsakov (1877), Tschaikovsky [Chaikovski] (1868), Lyadov (1894), and others further increased the interest in the subject.

The beginning of scientific musical ethnography was made by Evgenie Lineva, who was first to use the phonograph in recording Russian folk songs. She published, in 1905 and 1912, two volumes of transcriptions of Russian folk songs under the general title *Peasant Songs of Great Russia in Folk Harmonizations Transcribed from Phonograms.* Each song begins with a solo, and is followed by a chorus in which the basic melody is freely embellished. The choruses usually have two or three individual parts, but Lineva found some four-part singing. She believed that Russian folk music is essentially polyphonic, but there is no proof that the ancient songs were anything more than single musical phrases, without secondary parts. The later polyphony of peasant choruses may have been the influence of part singing in the church choirs.

Musical ethnography continued to advance after the 1917 revolution. Numerous collections of regional songs have been published under the auspices of the Academy of Sciences, in the folklore series of the Institute of Anthropology, Ethnography, and Archeology. For example, two substantial volumes of songs from the relatively small region of the Pinega River basin were published in 1937. Revolutionary songs of czarist times are included in the collection *Russkaya Narodnaya Pesnya* (*Russian Folk Song*), published in Moscow in 1936.

INSTRUMENTS . . . Folk music is deeply rooted in Russian folklore. In *The Tale of the Campaign of Igor* dated about 1200, the legendary figure Bayan, is a musician: "Bayan, as he recited the strife of bygone times, sent out ten falcons after a flight of swans, and the one that was first overtaken began her song. But in truth, brethren, not ten falcons did Bayan loose on the swans, but his wise fingers did he lay on living strings, and they by themselves sang the glory of the princes." The stringed instrument that Bayan played was the ancient *gusli*, a sort of zither or horizontal harp, with ten or more strings and a wooden sound chest. The *gusli* is no longer in practical use. Rimski-Korsakov introduced a part for *gusli* in his opera *Sadko*, to evoke the atmosphere of old Russia, but the part is usually performed on the harp. Other ancient stringed instruments are the *domra* (similar to the guitar, and played with a plectrum), and the *gudok* (a three-stringed instrument with a pear-shaped body, and played with a string bow). The *domras* were revived in Soviet Russia, and are often included in modern orchestral compositions.

In the Ukraine, the *domra* is known under the name *kobza* or *bandura* (from the Polish *pandura*). The popular balalaika is in all probability a development of the *domra*. In the eighteenth century, the balalaika assumed its familiar triangular shape. It usually has three strings and is plucked like a guitar, without a plectrum. An ensemble of balalaikas, organized by V. Andreyev early in this century, gave many successful concerts in Russia and abroad.

Among Russian wind instruments, the following are typical: the *rog* (diminutive, *rozhok*), a hunting horn; the *dudka*, a vertical flute; the *zhaleika*, a double reed with a single mouthpiece—the two pipes are connected at an angle; and the *svirel*, a Panpipe composed of several reeds of different lengths, bound together. The nomenclature of these instruments varies according to locality and period. Finally, there is the Russian bagpipe or *volynka*, probably so named because of its supposed origin in the district of Volynia. It consists of a goatskin bag and two pipes. The *volynka* is referred to in the proverbial phrase, *zatyanut volynku*, "to strike up the bagpipe," meaning to begin a tedious tale.

424

A most remarkable development of Russian primitive instruments was an orchestra of hunting horns (*rog*), initiated by Simeon Narishkin in 1751. Forty-nine hunting horns of different sizes were manufactured, ranging from three inches to the enormous length of 24 feet. The largest horn produced the note of low A under the bass clef staff. Each member of the ensemble could play only one note, and patient rehearsing was required to perform even a simple polyphonic composition. A German resident of St. Petersburg, Jacob von Stählin (1709-1785), described hearing a successful performance in his interesting memoir, *Nachrichten von der Musik in Russland* (1770); his account was republished, in Russian translation, in *Musikalnoye Nasledstvo* (*Musical Heritage,* Moscow, 1935).

Ancient Russian percussion instruments were drums, metal bars, and bells. The most interesting instrument is the *buben* (tambourine). A huge *buben,* called *nabat,* was so large that it took four horses to carry it and eight men to operate it.

SKOMOROKHI . . . The first musical entertainers mentioned in Russian history were the *Skomorokhi,* or minstrels, who are spoken of, as early as 1068, in Nestor's chronicle. Nestor (1056–1114), Russian monk and chronicler, complained that entertainments by the *Skomorokhi* drew the people away from God; that churches stood empty while the populace amused themselves by playing on the *gusli* and blowing trumpets. According to thirteenth-century sources, the *Skomorokhi* played Panpipes (*svirel*), string instruments (*gudok*), and the tambourine (*buben*). In the fifteenth century, they introduced a new type of entertainment, the puppet theater, which ultimately developed into the popular carnival play *Petrushka.*

The *Skomorokhi* were so popular in medieval Russia that numerous villages in Central Russia were named Skomorokhovo. As this popularity spread, the opposition of church and lay authorities grew stronger. Czar Alexis (1645–1676) took drastic measures against the *Skomorokhi.* In his decree of 1649, he ordered ruthless persecution of the "godless *Skomorokhi* with their *domras* and *gusli,*" and instructed police to destroy all musical instruments found among their possessions.

Very little is left of the musical compositions sung by the *Skomorokhi;* Nikolai F. Findeisen, in his valuable two-volume work, *Sketches of Music History in Russia from the Most Ancient Times to the End of the Eight-*

eenth Century (Moscow, 1928), cites a few songs and verses preserved in oral tradition.

CHURCH MUSIC . . . Parallel to the development of folk music, the church established the foundations of formal musical learning. The pioneers were Greek and Bulgarian clerics who introduced Byzantine chant into Kiev after the Christianization of Russia. As early as the eleventh century, texts with musical notation, derived from the Byzantine system of neumes, were in use in the Kiev churches and monasteries. In the thirteenth century, the Russian system of notation, known as *znamenny* (from *znamya*, sign) or *kryuki* ("hooks," from the angular shape of the notes), emerged as a native version of the Greek system. In 1551, Ivan the Terrible (1530–1584) established schools for teaching musical notation for use of church choirs. He had some knowledge of music and wrote several religious chants himself. Later still, the eight modes of the Russian *znamenny* chant were organized according to typical melodic figures, called *popiyevki* (singing patterns). About 1700, the five-line notation, current in Europe, was universally adopted in Russian churches.

The first beginnings of polyphonic choral music date from the early eighteenth century. In 1713, Peter the Great (1672–1725) formed a choir of sixty singers, and Russian noblemen organized private choruses. These so-called *capellas* (from the Italian word *cappella*, meaning chapel or choir) developed into the Russian choirs which became famous for their fine qualities and virtuosity. The *capella* founded by Peter the Great is still flourishing in Leningrad.

The father of Russian religious music in the polyphonic style was Dmitri Bortnyanski (1751–1825), who studied in Italy, where he acquired the technique of part writing. Maxim Berezovski (1745–1777) wrote during his short life (he committed suicide at the age of 31) many sacred works of high quality. Aleksei Lvov (1799–1870), author of the czarist national anthem, also composed sacred music, and wrote a treatise on the structure of Russian religious songs. Later both Peter Tschaikovsky (Chaikovski) and Alexander Grechaninov contributed to Russian music, writing in a free contrapuntal style.

SECULAR MUSIC . . . The initial impetus to secular music was given by the Italian musicians who were invited to Russia in the eighteenth

426

century by the empresses Anna Ivanovna, Elizabeth Petrovna, and Catherine the Great. They included several world-renowned names: Francesco Araja, Vincenzo Manfredini, Giuseppe Sarti, Baldassare Galuppi, Tommaso Traetta, Giovanni Paisiello, Domenico Cimarosa, and others. These Italians were largely responsible for the flourishing state of opera and ballet in St. Petersburg during the second half of the eighteenth century. They acted as choir masters, teachers, concert players, and composers. The first opera with a Russian text, *Cephalus and Procris*, was composed by Francesco Araja (c. 1700–c. 1770) on a libretto by Alexander Sumarokov (1718–1777), and produced in St. Petersburg in 1755. Its serious defect is inaccurate conformity with the prosody of the libretto; Araja had poor knowledge of the Russian language.

Under the influence of Italian music, several Russian-born composers wrote operas during the reign of Catherine the Great. Among them were Evstigney Fomin (1761–1800), the author of the opera *Amerikantsy* (in the sense of Indians), depicting a romantic story in Mexico; and Vasili Pashkevich, composer of the opera *Fevey*, of which Catherine the Great wrote the libretto. The *Kalmuck Chorus* from the opera *Fevey* is the earliest example of orientalism in Russian music.

THE NATIONAL SCHOOL . . . By the beginning of the nineteenth century, Russian music had evolved to a point where it was feasible to establish a national style of composition. The Russian art song, in the folklore manner, was cultivated by Alexander Alyabyev (1787–1851), Nikolai Titov (1800–1875), and Alexander Varlamov (1801–1848). Aleksei Verstovsky (1799–1862) wrote an opera on a Russian subject (*Askold's Tomb*, 1835), which in spite of its Italianate idiom has some Russian traits.

The acknowledged founder of the Russian national school of composition was Mikhail I. Glinka (1804–1857), who is to Russian music what Alexander Pushkin is to Russian literature. Glinka integrated the elements of Russian musical folklore into a musical language that can be called genuinely national. His first opera was produced in 1836, under the title *A Life for the Czar;* he had originally named it *Ivan Sussanin*. The subject was taken from Russian history, and Glinka developed it in a purely national manner, especially in the songs and choral passages. His second opera *Ruslan and Lyudmila* (1842), from Pushkin's poem, is remarkable for its brilliant color. Glinka's symphonic dance, *Kamarin-*

427

skaya, was the earliest example of orchestral treatment of Russian dance rhythms. In his songs and ballads, the vocal line of Russian songs received its perfect expression.

The music of Alexander S. Dargomyzhski (1813–1869) differs greatly frrom Glinka's. Less brilliant in color, it is rich in musical characterization. Dargomyzhski's opera *Russalka (The Mermaid,* 1855) retains the traditional division into arias, but is written in a distinctly Russian folklore style. In his posthumous opera *Kamennyi Gost (The Stone Guest,* 1868), Dargomyzhski appears as an innovator: he abandons Italian models in favor of operatic realism and replaces conventional recitative with vocal declamation.

THE MIGHTY FIVE . . . Both Glinka and Dargomyzhski remained little known outside Russia, but with the great symphonic and operatic works of Tschaikovsky, Rimski-Korsakov, and Musorgski Russia became a powerful factor in the general course of music history. The spirit of nationalism in Russian music was accentuated when five Russian composers known as the *Moguchaya Kuchka* (literally, "a mighty heap") formulated a set of musical aims. These composers were Balakirev, Borodin, Cui, Musorgski, and Rimski-Korsakov, and the epithet was bestowed on them by the Russian critic Vladimir Stasov (1824–1906). The individual talents and the contributions to Russian national music by these five composers were far from equal. César A. Cui (1835–1918), a military engineer who wrote several operas in a conventional romantic style, could not be included among the "Mighty Five" except by accident. Mili A. Balakirev (1837–1910) played the role of spiritual head of the group and did much to inspire his companions with the ideals of Russian national art. But he wrote little, and only his Oriental fantasia, *Islamey,* survives the test of time. It is more appropriate, therefore, to speak of the "Mighty Three" of Russian music: Borodin, Rimski-Korsakov, and Musorgski. It is interesting that not one of them was a professional in the narrow sense of the word. Borodin was a professor of chemistry, Rimski-Korsakov was a naval officer, and Musorgski was a government employee.

Of the three, Nikolai Rimski-Korsakov (1844–1908) was the most prolific. In his many operas, he re-created the spirit of Russian folklore and history. Russian legends and folk tales are reflected in *Snegurochka (Snow Maiden,* 1882) and *Sadko* (1894); and Russian history in *Tsar-*

skaya Nevesta (*Czar's Bride,* 1893). He wrote operas to two fairy tales by Pushkin, *Czar Saltan* (1899–1900) and *Zolotoi Petushok* (*Le Coq d'or,* or *The Golden Cockerel,* 1906). Rimski-Korsakov's religious opera *Skazanye o Nevidimom Grade Kitezhe* (*Tale of the Invisible City of Kitezh,* 1907) shows the influence of Wagner's *Parsifal.* In the symphonic field, *Scheherazade* (1881) was epoch-making in its colorful treatment of musical material.

Alexander P. Borodin (1833–1887) was partly an orientalist. His symphonic sketch *In the Steppes of Central Asia* (1880) utilized elements of Russian orientalism, which appears also in the famous *Polovtzian Dances* from the opera *Prince Igor,* completed posthumously by Rimski-Korsakov and Glazunov. In a purely Russian style, Borodin created an epical work in his Second Symphony (1870), which without an explicit program, paints a panorama of Russian *byliny* (epical chronicles).

Modest Musorgski (Moussorgsky, Mussorgsky, 1839–1881) was regarded by contemporaries as an erratic genius with inadequate technical equipment for the tasks he undertook. In historical perspective, however, he seems the greatest of the "Mighty Five" in boldness of musical invention and in profound understanding of the essence of Russian national folklore. Many of his harmonic procedures anticipate developments of modern music. Musorgski's greatest work is the opera *Boris Godunov* (1869). It is usually performed in the version prepared by Rimski-Korsakov, in which certain crudities of orchestration and unconventional harmonic progressions are smoothed out. Recently Musorgski's original score was restored, and the opera has been performed as composed, in Russia and abroad. Dmitri Shostakovich also undertook reorchestration of *Boris Godunov* in 1941. Musorgski's opera *Khovanshchina* (on a historic subject) was begun in 1873, and completed by Rimski-Korsakov. In his short opera *Marriage* (1868, after Gogol's play), Musorgski applies the modern treatment of operatic dialogue. His piano suite, *Pictures at an Exhibition* (1874), is remarkable for variety of characterization from light humor to grandiose tonal painting. The suite has become extremely popular in the orchestration by the French composer, Maurice Ravel.

The cause of nationalism in Russian operatic music was ably served by Alexander Serov (1820–1871), author of *Vrazhya Sila* (*Enemy Power*), produced posthumously in 1871 and still in the Russian theatrical repertoire. Serov's music, however, lacks the revolutionary originality of Musorgski and the effectiveness of Rimski-Korsakov's operatic panoramas. Similarly lacking in force are the numerous operas of Anton Rubinstein (1829–1894), who left a mark on Russian musical culture as the first great Russian pianist and as founder of the St. Petersburg Conservatory (1862). His opera *The Demon* (1875, after Mikhail Y. Lermontov) and his effective piano pieces enjoy great popularity. Anton's brother, Nikolai Rubinstein (1835–1881) was also a celebrated pianist and founded the Moscow Conservatory in 1866.

RUSSIAN ROMANTICISM . . . The unique and solitary figure of Peter Ilich Tschaikovsky, or Chaikovski (1840–1893) dominates Russian symphonic music of the second half of the nineteenth century. Tschaikovsky stood aloof from his musical contemporaries and developed a style intensely individual, subjective, and often morbidly introspective. Although his music is unmistakably Russian, Tschaikovsky rarely resorts to literal quotations of Russian folk songs (as in the finale of the Fourth Symphony). His nationalism lies in his extraordinary power to create a peculiarly Russian mood by expressing his own inner sentiments. From Tschaikovsky's pessimism, his predilection for minor keys, and his choice of titles (*Chanson triste, Sérénade mélancolique,* etc.) some interpreters of Russian music have concluded that the "Slavic soul" is inexpressibly sad. This conclusion appears unwarranted. Much of Tschaikovsky's own music is joyful, though the programmatic designs of his symphonies are invariably dark and somber. The Fourth and the Fifth symphonies express the inexorability of fate and the futility of struggle. The spirit of the Sixth Symphony (*Pathétique,* 1893), which Tschaikovsky conducted in St. Petersburg a few days before his death from cholera, is one of dejection. The musical quotation from the service for the dead, in the first movement of the *Pathétique,* is characteristic of the composer. Tschaikovsky's symphonic poems (*Romeo and Juliet,* 1869; *Francesca da Rimini,* 1876) are romantically somber, but the music itself has great vitality. Tschaikovsky's operas, *Eugene Onegin* (1878) and *La Pique-Dame* (*The Queen of Spades,* 1890), both after Pushkin, are extremely popular in Russia, as are his ballets, *Lac des cygnes* (*Swan Lake,* 1876), *La Belle au bois dormant* (*The Sleeping Beauty,* 1889), and *Casse-Noisette* (*The Nutcracker,* 1892).

430

ST. PETERSBURG AND MOSCOW SCHOOLS . . . Tschaikovsky and the "Mighty Five" greatly influenced the development of Russian music during the late nineteenth and early twentieth centuries. Tschaikovsky's followers cultivated the romantic type of symphonic, operatic, and vocal music. The center for music nationalists of the modern school was St. Petersburg, where the "Mighty Five" had flourished, while the stronghold of the romantic school was Moscow, where Tschaikovsky had taught at the conservatory.

The heir of the nationalist School of St. Petersburg was Alexander Glazunov (1865–1936); he wrote eight symphonies, violin and piano concertos, and chamber music, but no operas. As director of the St. Petersburg Conservatory (1906–1927), Glazunov played an important role in the education of the new generation of Russian composers. Anatole Liadov, or Lyadov (1855–1914), not a prolific composer, distinguished himself principally by short symphonic poems (*Baba-Yaga, Kikimora*) in the Russian folklore manner. Nikolai Tcherepnin, or Cherepnin (1873–1945) is known chiefly for his songs in Russian style.

The greatest representative of the Moscow school was Sergei Rachmaninov (1873–1943); his most enduring works are his piano compositions, which greatly elevated Russian pianistic style. His Piano Concerto in C minor, No. 2 (1901) is a classic of piano literature. His songs, poetic and lyrical, are in the Tschaikovsky tradition. Rachmaninov spent the last twenty-five years of his life abroad, chiefly in the United States, and his work of this period is less significant than his earlier music. Anton Arenski (1861–1906) wrote effective piano and chamber music in a style resembling Rachmaninov's, and Vasili S. Kalinnikov (1866–1901) is remembered for his romantic First Symphony.

Sergei I. Taneyev (1856–1915), Nikolai Medtner (1880–   ), Alexander Grechaninov (1864–   ), Mikhail M. Ippolitov-Ivanov (1859–1935), Reinhold Glière (1875–   ), and Sergei Vassilenko (1872–   ) in general follow the Moscow school, with some stylistic departures toward the nationalists. Taneyev was a great master of counterpoint and wrote a monumental treatise on contrapuntal technique. Few of his compositions (a symphony, chamber music, songs) achieved popularity. Medtner wrote almost exclusively for piano, and his style is a modern adaptation of Chopin and Brahms. After the revolution, Medtner left

431

Russia in 1921 and settled in London in 1936. Grechaninov composed several operas, which follow the nationalist school in using subject matter from Russian epical legends. His songs and choral works reflect Russian romanticism. Grechaninov left Russia in 1925 and settled in the United States in 1939, where he continued to compose. Glière combines features of the nationalist school with romantic elements. Vassilenko adheres stylistically to the Moscow school, with some kinship to the nationalists in his operas.

Vladimir I. Rebikov (1866–1920) merits a place in the history of Russian music. At first a follower of Tschaikovsky, he was later attracted to modernism. He was the first Russian composer to use the whole-tone scale, not as an incidental device, but as a basic thematic structure.

RUSSIAN MODERN MUSIC . . . The first true modernist of Russia was Alexander Scriabin, or Scriabine (1872–1915). His early piano works were strongly influenced by Chopin and his orchestral music owed much to Wagner. But Scriabin outgrew these influences to develop his own highly individual technique of composition. He moved from the harmonies of Liszt and Wagner to a style of composition in which tonality almost ceases to exist and dissonances supplant concords. As a new harmonic basis Scriabin made use of a six-note chord, which he called the "mystic chord." Religion and philosophy were important in Scriabin's aesthetics, and his major works bear such indicative titles as *Le Divin Poème* (*The Divine Poem*, 1903); *Le Poème de l'extase* (*The Poem of Ecstasy*, 1907–1908); and *Le Poème du feu* (*The Poem of Fire*, 1909–1910). In *The Poem of Fire* (also known as *Prometheus*), Scriabin included a part for a *clavier à lumières*, an instrument designed to produce sequences of colored lights. This color keyboard proved impractical, however. Shortly before his death, Scriabin made sketches for a pantheistic work called *Mystery*, in which he intended to unite all arts. Scriabin's music stands outside Russian national culture as a purely musical development of modern times, yet his technical innovations and his explorations in the field of new sonorities have deeply influenced the new generation of Russian composers.

The modern period of Russian national music is associated with the name of Igor Stravinski (1882–   ). Stravinski's early works continued the tradition established by Rimski-Korsakov, with whom Stravinski had studied. The use of color in instrumental treatment and the programmatic depiction of Russian fairy tales, characteristic of Rimski-Korsakov's last period, are the mainstays also of Stravinski's early compositions. His *L'Oiseau de feu (The Fire Bird,* 1910) is a colorful symphonic panorama of Russian folklore. His *Petrushka* (1911) portrays the scenes of the Russian carnival. Both scores were written for Sergei Diaghilev's Ballet Russe in Paris. After their production, Stravinski went abroad; he became a French citizen in 1934, and lived in France until 1939, when he went to the United States. Paradoxically, Stravinski became the acknowledged leader of Western modernism through works which are intensely Russian. His most revolutionary score is *Le Sacre du printemps (The Rites of Spring,* 1913), which is a modernistic representation of the rituals of pagan Russia. In this composition, Stravinski broke away from tradition and introduced polytonal and polyrhythmic innovations of unprecedented boldness. After 1924, Stravinski's style changed toward neoclassicism. His works of this period are based on pseudoclassical formulas (the ballet, *Apollo Musugètes,* 1927; the opera-oratorio, *Oedipus Rex,* to a Latin text, 1928; *Symphonie des psaumes,* 1930), or are pasticcios of music by other composers (*Le Baiser de la fée,* [*The Kiss of the Fairy,* 1928], a ballet based on Tschaikovsky's themes).

Several Russian composers living abroad were commissioned to write ballets for Diaghilev's Ballet Russe. The most prominent is Sergei S. Prokofiev (1891–   ). He returned to Russia in 1933, after an absence of 16 years, and identified himself with Soviet music. Of the younger men, Vladimir Dukelski (1903–   ), Nikolai Nabokov (1903–   ), and Igor Markevich (1912–   ) wrote effective ballets in the neoclassical manner, which were produced by Diaghilev.

SOVIET MUSIC . . . The period after 1917 provides the musical historian with many contrasts. The political revolution did not signalize developments of extreme leftism in music. Ultramodernists attempted to discard the musical heritage of the past and to inaugurate a new revolutionary type of music, but such attempts were doomed to failure from popular distaste. Adherents of proletarian music were equally unsuccessful in attempting to emphasize mass appeal and revolutionary subject matter. A compromise was effected in the formula of socialist realism, which postulates an art "socialist in content and national in form." Changing trends in Soviet musical aesthetics ran parallel with changes in the political and social structure of the Soviet Union. The development of Soviet music may be subdivided into three phases (1) the initial period, from 1917 to 1921, marked by the spirit of absolute innovation; (2) the period of conflicting trends, from 1921 to 1932, signalized by the rise and fall of proletarian music; (3) the period of socialist realism in music, after 1932.

The atmosphere of famine and civil war during the early years of the Soviet regime did not encourage creative composition. Yet concert life continued, and the new audiences of soldiers and workers eagerly patronized the opera, ballet, and symphony. Revolutionary ideology had little effect on the repertoire, although there were attempts to inject a social note into familiar operas. Giacomo Puccini's *Tosca* was rewritten as a story of the Paris Commune and Giacomo Meyerbeer's *The Huguenots* was changed to *The Decembrists;* but after a few performances, the old libretti were restored.

The first operas on Soviet subjects were *Za Krasni Petrograd* (*For Red Petrograd,* 1926) by Arseni Gladkovski (1893–   ) and Vladimir Prussak, and *Ice and Steel* by Vladimir Deshevov (1889–   ). The libretto of the first treated the Petrograd campaign of 1919, and the second opera was about the Kronstadt rebellion of 1921. Neither was successful. More interesting was *Severny Veter* (*The North Wind,* 1930) by Leo Knipper, an opera on the subject of the civil war and intervention. The first really successful Soviet operatic composer was Ivan Dzerzhinski (1909–   ). The subject of his first opera was Mikhail Sholokhov's famous novel *Tikhi Don* (*And Quiet Flows the Don*). It was produced in Leningrad on October 22, 1933, and had instantaneous success. His second opera, *Podnyataya Tselina* (*Soil Uprooted*), also after Sholokhov, was staged in Moscow on October 23, 1937, and proved equally successful. Other operatic composers of significance are Oles Tchishko (1895–   ), author of the opera *Battleship Potemkin* (1937), and Tikhon Khrennikov (1913–   ), who wrote the opera *Brothers* (1936), based on an episode from the civil war. The Ukrainian composer Boris Lyatoshinski (1895–   ) composed an opera *Shchors,* on the life of a Ukrainian civil war hero of that time.

Though the early years of the revolution saw few radical departures in composition itself, there were many daring innovations in musical science and in performance. In Moscow, a conductorless orchestra, called *Persimfans* for Pervi Simfonicheski Ansamble (First Symphonic Ensemble), was organized in 1922 as a protest against autocratic conductors. For five years it presented numerous classical and modern works. In 1922 the Soviet engineer Leon Theremin (1896–   ) demonstrated in Moscow the first electronic instrument, the *thereminovox*, capable of unlimited variation of pitch and tone color. A later development in electronic instruments was the *emiriton*, or electric piano, built in 1943 by a grandson of Rimski-Korsakov.

With the re-establishment of communications with western Europe, Russian musicians became acquainted with the new music of Germany and France. The Association of Contemporary Music in Leningrad, formed in 1927, was active for several seasons in presenting works by European modernists. Machine music, as exemplified by Arthur Honegger's (1892–   ) symphonic poem, *Pacific 231*, had its adepts in Russia. Vladimir Deshevov wrote *The Rails*, which imitated the noise of a railroad train in motion; Alexander Mosolov (1900–   ) composed the industrial ballet *Zavod* (Factory), which for realistic effect included a metal sheet in the orchestration. On the theme of Soviet industrial development, Prokofiev wrote a ballet called *Le Pas d'acier (The Age of Steel,* 1925), which was produced in Paris by the Ballet Russe.

In opposition to the modernists a powerful movement arose in favor of a special type of proletarian music. The Russian Association of Proletarian Musicians (RAPM) issued a manifesto in 1924, proclaiming the principles of proletarian music. It opposed all "progressive" trends in modern music, and all types of Western urban art, including jazz, in favor of revolutionary themes, in the tradition of Beethoven's Third Symphony (*Eroica*). After several years of propaganda and controversy, which threatened to end creative activity in Russian music, the RAPM was dissolved by governmental decree on April 23, 1932. This date was a landmark in the evolution of Soviet ideology in music.

Proletarian music was discredited and now Stalin's formula of socialist realism ("socialist in content, national in form") was applied to music, within the framework of national art. A new crisis came in January, 1936, when the Moscow newspaper *Pravda* in two articles severely criticized the composer Dmitri Shostakovich, first for "leftist deviation" and "naturalism" in his opera *Lady Macbeth of the District of Mtsensk* (1930–1932), and second for "oversimplification" in treatment of a Soviet theme in the ballet *Svetly Ruchey (The Limpid Stream,* 1934).

435

The articles posed the problem of defining socialist realism and of drawing a clear line of demarcation so as to prevent the fallacy of "naturalism" or "oversimplification." The Shostakovich case became a *cause célèbre* in the annals of Soviet music, because of the stature of the composer and his place in Soviet art.

Dmitri Shostakovich was born in Leningrad in 1906 and grew up almost entirely under Soviet life; his talent developed with the evolution of Soviet ideology in general aesthetics. His early works were satirical in character. His opera, *The Nose* (1927–1928), based on a tale by Nikolai Gogol, featured such effects as drunken hiccoughs, imitated by harp and violins, and the sound of a razor on the face. The part of the principal character, the Nose, was to be sung by a performer with his nostrils stuffed with cotton wads. There was an octet of eight janitors singing eight different advertisements. The opera was produced as an experimental spectacle in Leningrad on January 13, 1930.

The ballets of Shostakovich have the same satirical vein. In *The Golden Age* (1929–1930) there is a discordant polka which satirizes the Geneva disarmament conference. There is a similar satiric strain in his symphonies. His First Symphony in F minor, written at the age of nineteen, has become a standard piece of orchestral repertoire in Russia and abroad. The Second Symphony in F Minor and the Third Symphony, named *May First*, were less successful. After the rebuke administered by *Pravda*, Shostakovich abandoned programmatic music and returned to pure symphonic composition. His Fourth Symphony remained in manuscript, but his Fifth, played in November, 1937, at the festival celebrating the twentieth anniversary of the Soviet Revolution, received tremendous acclaim, and Shostakovich regained his place as a foremost Soviet composer. The Sixth Symphony (1939) was less successful, but the Seventh (1941), written during the siege of Leningrad, became world-famous. This work depicts the struggle of the Soviet citizen against the invader, and its triumphant finale foretells the inevitable victory. In 1943 Shostakovich wrote his Eighth Symphony, and in 1945 the Ninth Symphony. The Soviet government twice awarded Shostakovich the Stalin Prize of 100,000 rubles, once for his Piano Quintet (1940) and again for the Seventh Symphony.

In recent years the national element has grown very strong in the works of Soviet composers. Prokofiev, since his return to Russia in 1933, has written many compositions in this vein. Among them are the cantata *Alexander Nevsky* (based on the score of a film of the same name, which glorifies the repulse of the Teutonic Knights by the Russian Prince Alexander in the year 1242) and the opera *War and Peace* (after Tolstoy's novel), completed, 1941–1942, during the Second World War. He wrote a symphonic suite entitled *1941*, and the *Ballad of an Unknown Boy* (1943), a cantata about a young guerrilla fighter who died for his country. Yuri Shaporin (1890–   ) has written two patriotic cantatas: *Na Pole Kulikovom* (*On the Kulikov Field*), commemorating the Russian victory over the Tatars in the fourteenth century, and *Skazanye o Bitve za Russkuyu Zemlyu* (*Chronicle of a Battle for Russian Land*), composed in 1944, on the subject of the war against the Nazis.

Older Soviet composers have successfully adapted themselves to the new themes. The most important are Reinhold Glière (1875–   ), Sergei Vassilenko (1872–   ), Maximilian Steinberg (1883–   ), and Mikhail Gnessin (1883–   ). Glière excels in monumental symphonic and operatic subjects; Vassilenko writes romantic music; Steinberg, a disciple and son-in-law of Rimski-Korsakov, continues the tradition of the Russian national school; Gnessin writes music based on Hebraic motives.

Nikolai Myaskovski (1881–   ), the greatest symphonist of modern Russia, occupies a unique position. He has composed 24 symphonies, most of them during the Soviet period. Despite his predilection for somber and individualistic moods, Myaskovski's symphonies are highly regarded by Soviet musicians, and he is the acknowledged dean of Soviet composers.

Aram Khachaturian (1903–   ), an Armenian composer, wrote symphonies, concertos, and chamber music, notable for sincerity of emotional expression. His wife, Nina Makarova (1908–   ), became known as one of the most talented women composers in the Soviet Union. Other important names in Soviet music are Boris Asafyev (1884–   ), author of numerous operas and ballets, who wrote music criticism under the name Igor Glebov; Leo Knipper (1898–   ), author of nine symphonies; Alexander Krein (1883–   ), composer of effective stage music; his brother Gregory Krein (1880–   ), and Gregory's son, Julian Krein (1913–   ), who wrote instrumental music in a romantic vein; Vissarion Shebalin (1902–   ), an able symphonist; Alexander

437

Veprik (1899–   ), who wrote music inspired by Jewish folklore; Dmitri Kabalevski (1904–   ), composer of several operas, symphonies, and concertos; Mikhail Starokadomski (1901–   ), who wrote in a neoclassical manner; Valeri Zhelobinski (1912–   ), who wrote effective piano music; and Vano Muradelli (1908–   ), Caucasian-born composer who attracted attention by his strongly individual symphonic writing.

Popular music is encouraged in the Soviet Union. Modern folk ballads, marches, and even the syncopated music classified as "Soviet jazz," are widely sung and played. The most successful composer of light music in the period immediately succeeding the Second World War was Isaak Dunayevski (1900–   ), who received a Stalin Prize in recognition of his achievement. Soviet "mass songs" have a strong flavor of Russian folk music. Some of them have in fact become folk songs: for example, *Polyushko Pole* (*Meadowland*) by Knipper; *Katyusha* (*Katherine*) by Blanter; and *Provozhanye* (*Farewell*) by Zakharov. A marching song by the band leader A. V. Alexandrov, *Gimn Partii Bolshevikov* (*Hymn of the Bolshevik Party*), was proclaimed by government decree (March 15, 1944) the national anthem of the Soviet Union, in place of the *Internationale*. New words for it were written, stressing the national and patriotic character of the country's credo.

BIBLIOGRAPHY

Montague-Nathan, M., *A History of Russian Music* (London, New York, 1914).

Rimski-Korsakov, N. A., *My Musical Life* (New York, 1923; new ed., 1936).

Sabaneyev, L. L., *Modern Russian Composers* (New York, 1927).

Findeisen, N. F., *Otcherki po Istorii Muzyki v Rossii* (*Studies in the History of Russian Music*), in Russian, 2 vols. (Moscow, 1929).

Orlov, G., *Muzikalnaya Literatura* (Leningrad, 1935).

Abraham, Gerald, *On Russian Music* (New York, 1939).

——, *Eight Soviet Composers* (London, New York, Toronto, 1943).

Slonimsky, N., "Soviet Music and Musicians," *Slavonic Review* (December, 1944), vol. XXII.

Sovetskaya Muzyka, a Russian periodical (Moscow).

See also the biographies, in English, of individual Russian composers, notably Tschaikovsky, Musorgski, Rubinstein, Scriabin, Rachmaninov, and Shostakovich.

CHAPTER XXV

Art: Painting and Sculpture

By LOUIS LOZOWICK

A FEW ancient Russian monuments date from the pre-Christian period, but the information about them is scant and their artistic value is too slight to discuss, outside the field of archaeology. The history of Russian art, therefore, begins with the introduction of Christianity in the tenth century. The Christianization of Russia took a century, just as the process of westernization covered a later century. Byzantine art, like the art of western Europe, later, was only gradually accepted and assimilated, and it was modified by various influences, including the historically varying national determinant. It is the latter quality that gives unity and continuity to ten centuries of Russian art.

With Christianity came Byzantine literature, art, philosophy, and social institutions. Kiev soon became one of the most prosperous states in Europe and a leading cultural center. With the missionaries and preachers from Byzantium came Greek artists, who produced numerous mosaics, frescoes, and icons for Kiev, Vladimir, and Novgorod, and who taught their skills to the Russians. The Russians were apt pupils, but almost from the first they added touches of their own to the lessons learned. Ancient Russia carried on a lively intercourse with many other states and regions besides Byzantium; and while the Byzantine heritage in art remained paramount until the eighteenth century, it was modified at various times by the art of the Caucasus, Italy, Persia, India, and western Europe, and by the folk art of Russia itself. The ancient empire began falling apart even before the Mongol invasion early in the thirteenth century, and many separate cities, including Vladimir, Tver, and Pskov had developed clearly marked styles. The most important style centers, however, were Kiev (eleventh-thirteenth centuries), Novgorod (fourteenth-fifteenth centuries) and Moscow (sixteenth-seventeenth centuries).

The early Kiev period lasted from the baptism of the Emperor Vladimir I (956?–1015) to the Mongol invasion; it left mosaics, a few striking frescoes, and icons in the Cathedral of St. Sophia in Kiev, the Cathedral of Chernigov, the Church of Nereditsa of Novgorod, and the Dmitriev Cathedral of Vladimir. Most monuments from this period were destroyed by the Germans in their Second World War invasion. Artistic work of the Kiev period very closely resembled its Byzantine prototypes. Most of it was, in fact, produced by Byzantine masters. The compositions contain few figures simply drawn, and convey an air of solemnity. Favorite subjects were Jesus, the Virgin, the church fathers, the apostles and, by way of rare exception, chariot races and other games at the hippodrome of Constantinople, pictured in St. Sophia at Kiev. Figures are conventionalized, as in all Byzantine art, but some have a strong illusionistic quality. The colors are subdued, almost monochrome. When the Mongol invasion in the thirteenth century isolated Kiev from Byzantium and destroyed many of its monuments, the artistic hegemony passed to Novgorod, the only center not engulfed by the invasion.

Between the fall of Kiev and the rise of Moscow, Novgorod was the most important community in old Russia. Its artists continued to work in the Byzantine tradition which received an added impetus from the second renaissance of Constantinople. Their greatest achievement, however, lay in the building on the Byzantine foundation of a national art as expressed in the frequent use of national saints, in folk ornamentation, in bits of national genre, and architecture, in greatly enriched colorfulness with the generous employment of red, yellow, and green so characteristic of Russian folk art, and in functional innovations connected with the iconostas, a partition between the church altar and the worshipers. The iconostas grew in size, in the course of several centuries, from a low screen to an enormously high wall covered with row upon row of icons. These were arranged in strict order and represented local saints, the Trinity, the apostles, the prophets, and others; since the iconostas was viewed upward and from a distance, both colors and composition had to be varied. The outline was emphasized; the design

440

was made broad and simple; figures were elongated; colors were flat.

Ancient Russian art reached its apogee in the fourteenth and fifteenth centuries. Politically these centuries saw the struggle against the Tatar yoke and Teuton aggression, and the beginnings of a unified greater Russia under Moscow. Andrei Rublev (c.1370–1430) is the greatest name of the period. One of his very few remaining authentic icons is the *Old Testament Trinity* (early fifteenth century). It is the most famous single work of art between the tenth and eighteenth centuries, vying perhaps only with the icon, *Our Lady of Vladimir,* which is said to have been brought from Constantinople to Kiev in the eleventh century. The *Trinity* is an outstanding example of compositional subtlety, rhythm, and brilliant harmony of complementary and contrasting colors.

The next great name is Dionysios (early sixteenth century), who is known especially for his frescoes at Ferapont monastery. His figures are elongated, their gestures mannered; the tonality is a mixture of colors and tints. He was the forerunner of a trend.

With the consolidation of Moscow under Ivan III and Ivan IV and the conquest of Novgorod, Moscow became the center for all schools and styles. In this interpenetration of schools, each lost its identity. Rublev and Dionysios are as much of Novgorod as of Moscow. The trends started by Dionysios grew. The former anonymity of the iconographer began to disappear, and individual names became prominent. Painting became more complex; narrative elements and scenes from daily life found their way into pictures. Even didactic semipolitical ideas made their appearance, as in *Church Militant,* an allegory of Ivan IV's triumphant return to Moscow from the conquest of Kazan. Attention to detail grew at the expense of the picture as a whole. The trend found the clearest expression in the Stroganov school, named after a fabulously wealthy family of merchant princes, colonizers, and art patrons.

Unlike the earlier icons, the painting of the Stroganov masters is no longer a *Biblia pauperum* (Bible of the poor). It lacks the folk quality of Rublev. It is an art which expresses the taste of its wealthy patrons, an art of endless refinements. Although the artists try to stay within the Byzantine tradition, influences from Iran and India are evident. The tiny pictures have an enamel-like surface glittering with delicate tints and silver, which go well with the jewel-encrusted gold frames.

The middle of the seventeenth century witnessed a great extension of international trade, the introduction of foreign methods in manufacture, and the importation of foreign artists. In a special section of the czar's state armory about 60 foreign artists were employed—Dutch, German, Polish, and others, including an Arab and a Persian. Their task was to design coins and emblems, to make architectural drawings, to decorate palaces, and to paint *parsunas* (persons, in other words, portraits). They taught their trade to Russian artists and their far-reaching influence led to violent conflicts which were resolved in favor of *friaz* (western European methods).

Simon Ushakov (1626–1686) was the leading master of *friaz* painting. Varying a famous phrase by Shakespeare, Ushakov wrote that art must emulate the unique quality of the mirror to reflect nature faithfully. In his own practice, however, he did not go quite so far. His paintings combined abstract Byzantine conventions with western European realism of detail. Correctly drawn and correctly lighted parts of a picture are often combined in a manner utterly unrealistic. Ushakov's followers carried this tendency to fantastic lengths: buildings have no beginning or end; figures are related to each other by subject but lack a correct spatial relation to background. Detail crowds upon detail in a combination of great virtuosity. The colors have neither the monochrome quality of Kiev nor the brightness and purity of Novgorod; they are rather a blending of intermediate tints and shades. The *Annunciation,* which Ushakov painted jointly with Yakov Kondratiev and Gavrila Kazanets, typifies an entire trend of the time as well as the work of these individual artists.

Under Peter the Great (1672–1725) secular art rose to pre-eminence, but Byzantine painting did not disappear. It continued in a subordinate role throughout the eighteenth and nineteenth centuries. In the villages of Palekh, Mstera, and Kholui, where iconography had been practiced for centuries, the ancient technique continued up to the postrevolutionary period, when it was used with success in the portrayal of Soviet themes.

ART IN THE EIGHTEENTH CENTURY . . . Peter the Great completed with one drastic blow the disintegrating process in art and society that had begun half a century earlier. He continued to use the artists of the state armory; one of these was A. F. Zubov, a follower of Ushakov, who was the first to record the rise of the city of St. Petersburg in numerous views. Peter imported more artists from other countries and began to send Russian artists abroad to study. During Peter's reign and for years afterward, portraits retained the flatness and rigidity of the seventeenth-century *parsunas,* even when painted by artists like I. Adolski, I. P. Argunov (1727–1802), I. Y. Vyshnyakov (1699–1762), and A. P. Antropov (1716–1795). All these had received European training but divided their time and allegiance between the new secular subjects and the old iconography.

Peter, Elizabeth (1709–1761), and Catherine the Great (1729–1796) wanted to create in St. Petersburg a rival of other great European capitals. They built in rapid succession palaces, churches, forts, mansions, monasteries, where painters and sculptors were employed, under the supervision of the architects, to decorate walls, panels, and ceilings with allegories drawn from classical antiquity. For a time portraiture was relatively neglected, but it soon regained a status equal in importance with decoration. Where decoration was intended to surround court and nobility with pomp and splendor, portraiture emphasized the importance of the active commanding individual. The first stilted efforts of Vishnyakov and Argunov were succeeded by the accomplished classical portraiture of F. S. Rokotov (c.1730–1810), Dmitri G. Levitski (1735–1822), and V. L. Borovikovski (1757–1825).

The great period of Russian classicism received its most powerful inspiration from French revolutionary classicism as exemplified by Jacques L. David (1748–1825). The revolutionary perturbations that shook Europe were accompanied by peasant uprisings in Russia, which threw the monarchy and court into extreme terror. Yet some among the nobility and the intellectuals saw in those very events the need for popular reform. The Academy of Arts (organized in 1758 and officially established in 1764) was the creation of the court and a pillar of conservatism. Yet it was the carrier of the progressive classical ideal. A. P. Losenko (1737–1773) G. I. Ugryumov (1764–1823), and V. K. Shebuyev (1777–1855) chose themes from both classical antiquity and ancient Russia, which they interpreted to convey the ideas of civic duty, self-restraint, and sacrifice for the good of the nation. Popular heroes like Minin and Pozharski became favorite subjects. The most radical among all the artists was undoubtedly I. Yermenev. His peasants are drawn with a downright honesty and a vigor unique for the period, and Yer-

443

menev himself participated fittingly enough in storming the French Bastille. In portraiture the trend toward realism was particularly developed in paintings of untitled persons, as in Levitski's *Diderot* (in contrast to the idealized image of Catherine) and Borovikovski's *Madame de Stael.* This tendency was equally powerful in sculpture, in works by M. I. Kozlovski (1753–1802) and I. P. Prokofiev (1758–1828), and especially in the splendid portraits by F. I. Shubin (1740–1805)—*Lomonosov*—and the statuary of I. P. Martos (1752–1835)—*Minin and Pozharski.*

ART IN THE NINETEENTH CENTURY . . . In the first quarter of the nineteenth century, with reaction in the saddle both at home and abroad, classicism degenerated into mere formalism. The enormous pictures of K. P. Brulov (1799–1852) (*The Last Days of Pompeii*) and F. A. Bruni (1799–1875) (*The Brass Serpent*) adhered with great competence to all the academic canons of classical composition, but were cold and rhetorical in content. Hope of progress now lay in the field of realism. Alexander Ivanov (1806–1858), a forlorn figure, wandered between classicism and realism, between piety and enlightenment, and achieved an incompleted masterpiece in *Christ Appears to the People.*

In the meantime I. M. Tankov's eighteenth-century Italianate Russian peasants began to put on a more authentic Russian dress in A. G. Venetsianov (1780–1847) (*Reapers*) and V. A. Tropinin (1776–1857) (*Lace Makers*). It was Venetsianov who enunciated the admirable principle that an artist must paint not "à la Rembrandt" or "à la Rubens" but "à la nature." Though he did not quite live up to his own principle, some who followed him did. P. A. Fedotov (1815-1852), the satirist of middle-class society and impoverished nobility, was the link between Venetsianov and the next important school, called the Travellers, which was aggressively Russian, vigorously realistic, and frankly propagandistic.

The Travellers: V. V. Pukirev (1832–1890), V. G. Perov (1833–1882), V. E. Makovski (1846–1920), V. M. Vasnetzov (1848–1927), Ilya Repin (1844–1930), Vasili V. Vereshchagin (1842–1904), G. G. Myasoyedov (1835–1911), and K. A. Savitzki (1845–1905) strove for "contents worthy of a thinking mind." In content, their work dealt with every social injustice they observed in the surrounding world. They flayed religious superstition, marriage for money, the butchery of war; they pictured downtrodden suffering peasants, gluttonous priests, penurious students, corrupt *chinovniks* (bureaucrats), starving artists. They brought realism into historic painting (V. G. Shvartz, 1838–1869; Vasili I. Surikov, 1848–1916); into religious painting (N. N. Ge, 1831–1894; I. N. Kramskoi, 1837–1887); into landscape (I. I. Shishkin, 1831–1898; A. K. Savrasov, 1830–1898; I. I. Levitan, 1860–1900). Sculpture lost the pre-eminence it had held in the eighteenth century. Academic classicists like F. P. Tolstoy (1783–1873) and G. R. Zaleman (1859–1911); romanticists like Boris I. Orlovski (1787–1839); naturalists and psychological realists like N. S. Pimenov (1812–1864), Mark M. Antokolski (1843–1902), and V. A. Beklemishev (1861–1920); impressionists like P. P. Trubetskoi (1867–1938), and A. S. Golubkina (1864–1927); archaists like S. T. Konnenkov (1874–   ) and D. S. Stelletzki (1875–   ) typify and summarize every school of the nineteenth century.

The political and social movements of the 1860's and 1870's were followed by the reaction and hopelessness of the 1880's and 1890's. The young labor movement born of the country's industrial expansion found but a pale echo in art (N. A. Kasatkin, 1859–1930; A. Y. Arkhipov, 1862–1930). The Travellers were rebels of an earlier day, but in clinging to a peasant orientation they were now outdated, both for those who demanded a bolder social approach to art and for those who wanted no social message in art at all. The latter were in the majority. It was a period of mysticism, retrospectivism, individualism in every form. The social theme was in decline. In the ascendant were Levitan's landscapes of mood, M. V. Nesterov's (1862–1942) and Vasnetzov's revivals of religious and nationalist motifs, M. A. Vrubel's (1856–1910) imaginative symbolism, A. V. Riabushkin's (1861–1904) idealizations of Moscow's past, V. E. Borisov-Musatov's (1870–1905) elegiac nostalgia for the cherry orchards of his childhood.

All these soul searchings were brought into focus at the turn of the century by the World of Art, a group of artists who issued a publication of the same name. They were outspoken individualists, disillusioned with the people and with social idealism. They sneered at the sermonizing of the Travellers; they held that a preoccupation with moral, social, or other problems serves only to debase art, and that aesthetic pleasure is the beginning and end of creative activity. In preference to the Travellers' tragic themes done in gray and somber colors, they painted gay and frivolous themes in bright colors. They painted exotic subjects from the colorful East, from ancient Russia, from mythology and fairy tales, and themes from the high life of eighteenth-century France and Russia. They liked to picture with soft irony the perfumed robes and refined manners of the aristocratic idlers who passed their days gaily in rococo palaces or pursued amatory adventures in shady bowers, near spouting fountains. They excelled in theatrical decoration, especially in sets in which color is dominant, creating the mood of the play. The leading figures in this group were Vrubel, A. N. Benois (1870–   ), K. A. Korovin (1861–1939), A. Y. Golovin (1853–1930), L. S. Bakst (1866–1924), C. A. Somov (1869–   ), Nicholai K. Roerikh (1874–   ), V. A. Serov (1865–1911), Y. Y. Lancerai (1875–   ), M. V. Dobuzhinski (1875–   ); and later, S. Y. Sudeykin (1884–   ), B. D. Grigoryev (1886–1939), A. V. Yakovlev (1887–1938), B. M. Kustodyev (1878–1917), K. S. Petrov-Vodkin (1878–   ).

The artists P. P. Konchalovski (1876–   ), A. V. Letulov (1882–   ), V. V. Rozhdestvenski (1884–   ), I. I. Mashkov (1881–   ), and R. R. Falk (1886–   ) organized a group called the Jack of Diamonds (1909–1910) and translated the art of Cézanne into a more colorful Russian version. The futurists, led by David D. Burlyuk (1882–   ), gave an initial "slap in the face of public opinion," but their full development did not come until the October Revolution.

ART SINCE 1917 . . . During the revolution the Soviet government was busy fighting famine, intervention, and counterrevolution; the field of art awaited a resolute group to assume control and guidance. Which group or tendency could aspire to the role? The World of Art was patently antidemocratic and was tainted by the association with such enemies of the revolution as Hippius, Filosofov, Rozanov. Furthermore, two members of the group, C. A. Somov (1869–   ) and A. N. Benois (1870–   ), during the most critical years of the revolution, issued their two graphic series *Le Livre de la marquise* and *Versailles*. Anything more foreign to the spirit of the revolution would be hard to imagine. The Travellers had lost all their former fire of revolt. The futurists stepped into the breach and with the consent of the government took immediate direction of the art institutions and art policies of the country.

At first they went about their task with will and intelligence. It was obviously a period of change and transformation. The old was to be

446

thoroughly uprooted and the new installed in its place. The futurists set out to bring all this about. They abolished the hated Imperial Academy, founded the Free Workshops in its place, and reformed the entire art education of the country. They helped to reorganize the old museums and to open many new ones. They helped in transferring private art collections to the state and opening them to the public. They issued new publications, arranged lectures, and established art-study circles and clubs in the army, navy, and factories. They helped organize artists into a union, planned competitions for monuments to revolutionary heroes, established state commissions to purchase the work of artists. They staged revolutionary artistic festivals on a gigantic scale. They even performed one service that would appear alien to their profession. Several of the group, led by Vladimir V. Mayakovski (1894–1930), V. V. Lebedev (1891–   ), and A. M. Lavinski (1893–   ), despite their abstractionist theory turned out many hundreds of propaganda pictures for the Russian telegraph agency (*Rosta*). Simple, crude, but often strikingly effective, these pictures proved enormously helpful to the government in agitating against foreign intervention and domestic sabotage, in building discipline in the army, and in accomplishing industrial rehabilitation.

The futurists did not present a solid front. Among them were expressionists like V. Kandinski (1866–1944), P. N. Filonov (1883–   ), D. D. Burlyuk, and Marc Chagall (1887–   ); cubists like A. A. Morgunov (1884–   ), N. A. Udaltzova (1886–   ), L. S. Popova (1889–   ), and A. Pevsner (1886–   ); suprematists like K. S. Malevich (1878–1935), A. M. Rodchenko (1891–   ), and E. Lissitzki (1891–   ); and representatives of other trends akin to the modernism of western Europe. An active core, however, rechristened itself into comfuturism (communism-futurism) to denote their revolutionary orientation. These comfuturists saw in the collapse of the old social system the collapse also of the art which it had engendered, namely, realism in every form, whether literal or distorted. They sought a closer equivalent of the creative forces of the revolution. They found this in Lenin's constant demand for the development of industry and the training of specialists to run it. They called the new art constructivism. "Constructions" were neither paintings nor sculpture but both. They were made of materials which form the daily environment of workers

447

in industry, and which are the true product of modern science: steel, concrete, glass, paper, coal. The constructionists hoped to combine those materials in such a scientific manner that the worker's collective effort would be reflected in them, that the "constructions" would transmit to the spectator the constructive spirit of the age and make him thereby a convert to it.

Two examples of "construction" will be described: N. A. Altman's (1889–   ) *Russia* is a rectangular board near the lower narrow base of which the Russian *trud* (labor) is skilfully inlaid in such a way that the letter R, standing for both Russia and revolution, rises diagonally to the top. The spaces between the unevenly sized letters are filled by abstract patterns of metal, coal, ebony, and paper finished in a variety of surface textures. This piece of meticulous craftmanship was supposed to symbolize the powerful reality of the revolution and its glorification of labor.

V. A. Tatlin's (1885–   ) monument to the Third International was to be built in the form of a huge, iron spiral (*Symbol of Liberated Humanity*) 400 meters high, and leaning at an angle of 45°. Within this leaning tower of Moscow were stories to be encased in the form of a cylinder on top of a pyramid on top of a cube. These were to revolve, each on its axis at the velocity, respectively, of a day, a month, a year. This monument was designed to meet the formal demands of aesthetics and the concrete demands of utility. There were many other projects and constructions of similar design.

The futurists were uncompromising in their theoretical attacks on the older forms of art. One of their number, Arvatov, believed that easel painting was a product of capitalist market relations and said, "The problem of the Revolution in art is the problem of liquidating easel painting." Their exuberance, however, was restrained by government authority. Gradually, they and other modernist movements began to lose ground. The country was slowly settling down to a stable existence. The masses returned to normal occupations; youth sought education, soldiers returned from the front. People who sought in art a clear picture of the seething events, who wanted encouragement and guidance, found little in the futurist work to satisfy them. And these people, represented by their various organizations, clubs, and unions, were now the consumers of art. At the same time, the academicians, orientalists, impres-

448

sionists began to air their views publicly and loudly. They had never stopped working and exhibiting, though they had remained in the background while the futurists were busy with their reforms. They now came forward more boldly, and new organizations began to spring up, each with a special declaration of principles.

The most important organization in number of members, the ambition of its plans, and the public acclaim it received, was AKHRR (Association of Artists of Revolutionary Russia). It was formed during a discussion meeting at the forty-seventh annual exhibition of the Travellers. The young organization thus paid a tribute to the old but carried forward its heritage with this important difference: the Travellers had always taken a negative stand toward the society in which they were born; the stand of the AKHRR was one of affirmation. The declaration of principles proclaims:

"Our civic duty to mankind is to fix in artistic and documentary fashion the greatest moments of history in all their revolutionary upsurge.

"We shall depict our own day: the life of the Red Army, the life of the workers, the peasants, the revolutionaries, the heroes of labor.

"We consider content the sign of genuineness in a work of art."

To illustrate these principles a series of large exhibitions was circulated throughout the Soviet Union under such titles as "Life and Labor of the Red Army," and "Life and Customs of the Minor Nationalities." The membership of AKHRR, notably A. D. Drevin (1889–   ), Konchalovski, Kustodyev, K. F. Yuon (1875–   ), Kasatkin, and I. I. Brodski (1884–1939), included many schools ranging from cubism to naturalism. As the organization grew, its program broadened to include landscapes and still lifes as subject matter, along with "Life and Labor." The painting that caused perhaps the most heated debate in a decade was Brodski's *Second Congress of the Comintern* (1924). In an attempt at collective portraiture, the presidium, committees, orators on the platform, Lenin, Stalin, Molotov, and international delegates from all corners of the earth—about three hundred persons in all (including the artist in one corner, painting the picture)—were portrayed with the most scrupulous fidelity. The painting was widely exhibited and reproduced, and it was attacked and defended with equal vehemence.

Other artists' societies existed alongside AKHRR. The most notable were the Four Arts, a group of famous mature artists: Petrov-Vodkin,

P. V. Kuznetsov (1878–   ), M. S. Saryan (1880–   ), A. V. Shevchenko (1886–   ), and V. A. Favorski (1886–   ); and The Society
of Easel Painters including some of the most gifted young artists trained
after the revolution: A. A. Deyneka (1899–   ), A. A. Labas
(1900–   ), Y. I. Pimenov (1903–   ), P. V. Williams (1902–   ),
A. G. Tyshler (1898–   ), and D. P. Shterenberg (1881–   ).

During the decade of AKHRR's existence, when one artists' circle
after another declared its allegiance and offered its co-operation to the
Soviet government, a small militant group, more political than aesthetic,
the RAPKH (Russian Association of Proletarian Artists) raised a clamor
under the slogan "Ally versus Enemy"—"Enemy" including by implication some of the best Russian artists. As earlier in the case of comfuturism, the authorities quickly stopped the deliberate creation of a
cleavage among Soviet artists. After the famous decision of 1932, all
Soviet artists regardless of aesthetic persuasion were organized into one
Federation of Soviet Artists.

After that the range of themes grew wider. Artists cultivated whatever genre seemed most suited to their particular aptitudes. The younger
artists more readily turned to social themes, while others preferred landscape or portrait. Soviet art had come to embrace not only the heroic
Soviet theme of "Labor and Defense," but also Soviet fields and forests
and the products of Soviet soil. Government recognition and rewards,
including prizes and titles, were extended equally to Nesterov, famous
as a painter of religious subjects; to Saryan, a Fauve; to Konchalovski
and Tyshler; the Kukryniksi (from the names M. N. *Ku*priyanov,
1903–   , P. N. *Kry*lov, 1902–   , *Ni*kolai A. Sokolov, 1903–   , a
trio of satirists); and even to the Palekh artists, direct spiritual descendants of the ancient Russian iconographers.

Soviet art was fast becoming multinational; the Uzbeks, Turkomen,
Ukrainians, Bashkir, and others made substantial contributions to the
body of Soviet art. Amateur art grew phenomenally in factory, farm,
army, and navy. Sculpture followed parallel paths, though on a greatly
reduced scale. Among the well-known sculptors were I. M. Chaikov
(1888–   ); M. N. Manizer (1891–   ); S. D. Merkurov (1881–   ,
statues of Lenin and Stalin); N. A. Andreyev (1873–1932, portraits of
Lenin); V. A. Andreyev (1890–   , statue at top of Soviet Pavilion,

World's Fair, New York); P. V. Sabsai (1893–   ); I. S. Yefimov (1878–   , animals); A. T. Matveyev (1878–   ); G. I. Motovilov (1892–   ); I. G. Frikh-Khar (1893–   ); B. D. Korolev (1885–   ); S. Tavasyev (1894–   ); and the women sculptors N. V. Krandiyev-skaya (1892–   ), V. I. Mukhina (1891–   , *Soviet Youth* at Paris International Exposition), and S. D. Lebedeva (1906–   ). The list omits many names but suggests the most characteristic trends. The artist's economic security had been guaranteed by the constitution, and his audience was counted in millions.

Such was the state of Soviet art on the eve of the Second World War. The respect in which art was held and the artist's complete integration with the life and culture of the country, inevitably led artists to throw their efforts wholeheartedly into their nation's gigantic struggle for its very existence. The first war posters began to appear on the day after hostilities opened, and they continued in a never ending stream throughout the war; many artists went to the front as correspondents. Most artists, however, were not thus directly involved in the war, and they continued to work as formerly, though the war theme touched most of them. As the war continued many artists turned for subject matter to great historic events in Russia's past.

A brief mention of characteristic pictures and exhibitions will illustrate the state of Soviet art during the war. About a year after the war began, an all-national exhibition was held under the title "The Great Patriotic War." Typical exhibits were: *Driven into Slavery* by G. G. Ryazhski (1895–   ), *The Peoples' Avengers* by G. K. Savitski (1887–   ), *Blood Donors* by Konchalovski, *Artillery Attack* by Deyneka. Some historic themes were: *Alexander Nevsky* by Lancerai, *Stepan Razin* by V. S. Svarog (1883–   ), and *Ivan the Terrible* by P. P. Sokolov-Skalya (1899–   ). Many landscapes and sketches from the front were also shown. An exhibition held on the twenty-fifth anniversary of the Red Army was called "Red Army in the Fight Against the Fascist Aggressor." Very dramatic was the work done by Leningrad artists during the blockade of 1941–1942. Though every one, including the artists themselves, was half-starved and half-frozen, the artists bolstered public morale by posters, streamers, postal cards, wall decorations, easel pictures, drawings, and sculpture which showed how the

451

city was fighting the enemy, defending its children, preserving its cultural treasures.

On the twenty-fifth anniversary of the October Revolution, A. M. Gerasimov (1889–   ) was awarded the Stalin Prize for his painting *The Hymn to October*, which is significantly both like and unlike Brodski's *The Second Congress of the Comintern*, painted two decades earlier. *The Hymn to October* represents the plenary session of the Supreme Soviet held at the Bolshoy Theater to celebrate twenty-five years of Soviet power. Stalin, the commissar of defense, is speaking, and in the presidium along with Molotov and Kaganovich are the marshals of the Soviet Union in full regalia. The many nationalities of the sixteen republics are in the hall. In the loges can be recognized Moskvin, Mikhoels, Shostakovich, Mukhina, Grabar, and about two hundred other representatives of Soviet art and science.

Almost every nationality held its own wartime exhibition depicting its part in the war. The Tadzhik Republic, on the very border of India, held an exhibition, "The Tadzhik People in the Patriotic War." Some of the titles were *Evacuated Children in Tadzhikistan, Presents for the Red Army,* and *Muhamed Ibrahim, Hero of the Soviet Union, Son of the Tadzhik People.* There were also various special exhibitions. "In the Rear of the Enemy" showed work done by partisans behind enemy lines. "Exhibition in a Forest" showed pictures by Red Army men; the works were both created and exhibited near the fighting lines. Many exhibitions had no direct reference to war; said *Literature and Art,* March, 1943: "Excellent . . . painters of landscape and genre, in their eagerness to serve the country turn to themes of war. . . . This is a wrong conception of art's social significance. . . . It is not necessary to violate the nature of one's own gifts." "Veterans of Russian Art" gave full-sided retrospective showing of some of the oldest living artists: V. K. Byalynitski-Birulya (1872–   ), I. E. Grabar (1871–   ), B. N. Baksheyev (1862–   ), I. N. Pavlov (1872–   ), Lancerai, and Yuon. The exhibition was warmly received and all the artists were awarded the Order of the Red Banner.

As defeat of the hated enemy drew near, Russian artists were planning for the peace. For example, the Soviet press reported that immediately after the liberation of Kiev, Ukrainian artists and art students returned from temporary quarters in Tashkent, Alma-Ata, Ufa, and Samarkand.

They held a four-day conference with the participation of artists from Armenia and the RSFSR. Reports described the extent of the destruction of cultural monuments and plans were made for their restoration wherever possible. Among activities planned for the future were: the revival of Ukrainian folk art, the commemoration in painting and sculpture of heroic Ukrainian struggles against the Germans, and the reorganization of art schools and museums. Steps were taken to continue with renewed vigor and confidence in peacetime the evolution interrupted by the war. The same was also true of other Russian cities as their turn of liberation came. Within a week of Germany's capitulation, the Federation of Soviet Artists called a conference (May 17–24, 1945) where representatives from all the Soviet republics reviewed the state of art during the war and the prospects for the postwar period. One of the many results of the conference was the organization of a vast all-national exhibition dedicated to, and entitled, "Victory."

BIBLIOGRAPHY

Benois, A., *The Russian School of Painting* (New York, 1916).
Newmarch, Rosa, *The Russian Arts* (New York, 1916).
Réau, L., *L'Art Russe des Origines à Pierre le Grand* (Paris, 1921).
Réau, L., *L'Art Russe de Pierre le Grand à Nos Jours* (Paris, 1922).
Muratov, P., *Les Icones Russes* (Paris, 1927).
Kondakov, N., *The Russian Icon* (Oxford, 1927).
Farbman, M., ed., *Masterpieces of Russian Painting* (London, 1930).
Freeman, J., Kunitz, J., and Lozowick, L., *Voices of October* (New York, 1930).
Alpatov, M., and Brunov, N., *Geschichte der Alt-Russischen Kunst*, 2 vols. (Augsburg, 1932).
Wulf, O., *Die Neurussische Kunst Im Rahmen der Kulturentwicklung Russlands von Peter dem Grossen bis zur Revolution*, 2 vols. (Baden Bei Wien, 1932).
Ainalov, D., *Geschichte der Russischen Monumentalkunst*, 2 vols. (Berlin, 1932–33).
Rice, A. T., ed., *Russian Art* (London, 1935).
Holmes, G., ed., *Art in the U.S.S.R.* (London; New York, 1935).
London, Kurt, *The Seven Soviet Arts* (New Haven, 1938).
Milyukov, P. N., *Outlines of Russian Culture*, vol. III (Philadelphia, 1942).
Avinoff, A., *Russian Icons* (Pittsburgh, 1944).
Chen, Jack, *Soviet Art and Artists* (London, 1944).

CHAPTER XXVI

Architecture

By SIMON BREINES

EUROPEAN Russia, from the Gulf of Finland to the Caucasus, and from the Polish marshes to the Urals, is flat. This geographical fact has had a profound influence on Russia's history and on its architecture. Great plains and navigable rivers make natural trade routes. But where nature aids commerce it also encourages invasion.

Warriors from Scandinavia founded the Russian state in the ninth century, and wood architecture of strong national character developed in northern cities and in the southwestern Ukraine. This type of building was similar to the log cabins of America. From the south came other influences when the young empire was converted to Christianity. Byzantine culture brought with it the art of building in stone.

In the thirteenth century, these influences were for a time submerged under the conquering Mongol khans from the East. Evidences of Mongol culture survive in the Volga region. In the Crimea, the Tatars left the imprint of their 300 years' rule. During these Asiatic occupations, the wood architecture of Russia was largely destroyed, and the art of building virtually died. Except in the far north, in the Novgorod and Archangel districts, few important wooden structures escaped the torch and sword of the invaders. Fortunately, many stone churches, monasteries, and other religious buildings in various regions survived and even served occasionally as substantial fortresses.

By the fifteenth century the Tatars had been driven from the great plains, and Moscow became the political and religious center of Russia. An intensive period of court and ecclesiastical construction began in the reign of Ivan the Terrible in a style peculiarly Russian, though it embraced the original Byzantine motifs and newer influences from Italy. This trend continued until the eighteenth century when Peter the Great (1689–1725) built his new capital, St. Petersburg. Peter was determined to westernize his country including its architecture. He employed many foreign architects and engineers, most of them French and Italian. The classical style which they brought took strong root in Russia and is still highly regarded by Soviet architects.

FIRST PERIOD (TENTH-EIGHTEENTH CENTURY) . . . Russia, like the United States, is a country of vast forests. Even recently wood was the dominant building material. Except for the most important churches, entire cities were built of wood. But since wood is perishable (who will forget Tolstoy's description of burning Moscow in *War and Peace*), the recorded history of Russian architecture begins with the oldest stone churches.

The earliest important church is the Cathedral of St. Sophia in Kiev (1020), where Vladimir the Great established the first seat of a metropolitan of the Greek faith. This cathedral with its Syrian and Persian features stemmed almost directly from Byzantine prototypes. But, as the new faith swept northward, the Russian genius for adaptation made many stylistic modifications in architecture. In the Pokrov Church near Vladimir (1163) we see a lessening of Byzantine influence along with a happy blending of Romanesque details. With its wonderful setting on the Nerl River, its simplicity of form, its white stone and gay decorations, and its single golden, bulblike dome, this church is perhaps the loveliest historical monument in all Russia.

Another eleventh-century cathedral is St. Sophia in Novgorod. Here the great, austere walls show hardly a trace of the rich decorations of Byzantium. But crowning the Romanesque starkness of the exterior are six gilded domes, five of them forming the cluster which became typical of Russian churches.

In this first historical period, religion dominated Russian architecture. But since each church was a center for village life, a vigorous secular architecture of wood developed around the ecclesiastical buildings. During the Tatar invasion, these wood structures strongly influenced even the churches in northern cities. Some were built square, with great log walls. At some distance from the ground, the square was transformed into an octagonal tower by means of unique little arches called *kokozhniki*. The tower itself was topped by a steeply pitched, pointed roof. The Kolomenskoye Church near Moscow (1532), almost literally translating such wood architecture into stone, is a striking example of the power of native tradition.

Architectural historians of the past were wont to call old Russian architecture "semibarbaric" or "Asiatic." The nineteenth-century French architect, Viollet-le-Duc, though he never visited Russia, did much to acquaint western Europeans with Russian architecture. He discerned various Oriental influences: Russian churches reminded him chiefly of Chinese pagodas, Hindu temples, Arabian mausoleums, and Byzantine cathedrals. Without overlooking the influence of the East, modern scholars, particularly Russians, have found truer analogies in western European architecture.

In the far-away corners of Europe, particularly in the Russian north, a patriarchal pattern of life and an agricultural economy continued longer than elsewhere. The Romanesque foundation of folk art and building survived later here than in the West, and the influence of wood architecture and ornamentation on stone churches is in evidence everywhere. It is through considering the interplay of foreign culture with vigorous folk art and stubborn native traditions, rather than in observing a few externals, that we see the true Romanesque nature of old Russian architecture.

Moscow was the center of the later part of this period of Russian architecture. In the fourteenth and fifteenth centuries, master builders from Novgorod and Pskov built palaces and churches of incredible splendor to express the political and religious power of the czars. To rebuild the Moscow Kremlin, Ivan the Terrible imported Italian architects who brought the styles and construction techniques of Europe. For several centuries, this foreign influence was combined with the inevitable Russian flavoring to create many noteworthy structures, the most important of which is the Kremlin itself. The centers (kremlins) of most large Russian cities were enclosed by strong, battlemented walls, which protected the palace and government buildings, and the principal cathedrals, churches, and houses. The Kremlin wall in Moscow, built by Antonio Solario in 1490, is of great architectural interest. Although reminiscent in some details of Asiatic fortress walls, it has a native character of its own. Towers of many different styles and form are incorporated in the great wall; the most important of these is probably the Spasskaya Gate in Italian Renaissance style. Interesting old plans have been found in the archives showing the Kremlin redesigned along classic lines. Happily the plans were never realized.

Inside the Kremlin is an extraordinary grouping of secular and religious buildings designed by Russian as well as foreign architects. The Ivan Veliki (great) tower, which was finished in 1600 by Boris Godunov, is outstanding because of its dome-topped height and splendid design. Surrounding it are many churches with characteristic bulblike domes, convents, and secular buildings, including the Granovitaya or "lesser palace" designed by Italians. The fondness for grouping buildings, especially churches, is typically Russian. Similar free and almost spontaneous compositions are found in every corner of the land, and the same tendency is reflected in the multidomed churches found everywhere. A famous example is the cathedral of St. Basil, built in Moscow's Red Square in 1554 by Ivan the Terrible, with its numerous lanternlike domes and spires. It should be mentioned that the name Red Square did not originate, as many believe, with the revolution. In Russian, the words "red" and "beautiful" are synonymous. Red Square got its name centuries ago when it was Moscow's principal trading center or bazaar. This square had still other uses, however. Ivan the Terrible had his political enemies, the boyars, executed there, and Peter settled accounts in Red Square with the Streltsi (Imperial Guard) who rose against him.

In summary, we may say that medieval Russian architecture does not compare in some ways with the great architectures of the world. Many influences retarded its development. Geography encouraged destructive invasions of Russia. The long-lived feudal economy and the cleavage between the Greek and Roman church were constant barriers to the assimilation of Western civilization. The religious hierarchy restricted architectural innovations and even tried to establish a standard, five-domed church. The Russians relied too frequently on foreign talent, and yet their architecture was vigorous and individual.

SECOND PERIOD (EIGHTEENTH CENTURY TO 1917) ...
Peter the Great was a purposeful man. When he decided to change the backward empire into a modern Western nation he broke literally with

457

the past. He moved the capital to the marshy banks of the Neva where it joins the Gulf of Finland because here was the best "window on Europe" he could find. Both to symbolize and to help execute his purpose, he began to import outstanding architects; among them were Leblond from France, hired to make the city plan of St. Petersburg; Carlo B. Rastrelli, Quarenghi, and Rossi from Italy; Cameron from England. He also assembled the noted Russian architects of his day and forcibly gathered up the best masons, carpenters, and craftsmen in his realm. To create St. Petersburg as his paradise without rival, he issued a decree that henceforth no stone building could be constructed anywhere else in Russia.

Peter's methods brought results. The classic and baroque designs of the architects were soon translated into stone on a vast scale. After Peter's death in 1725, the momentum of his plan continued under Catherine the Great (1762–1796), aided by foreign court architects and the growing group of Russian masters. By the nineteenth century, the northern capital was one of the finest cities in Europe. Its systems of great boulevards and monumental open squares, frequently designed by a single architect, served as a worldwide example of city planning and established a deep tradition that is continued today by Russian architects.

According to contemporary accounts, Catherine was greatly interested in architecture; she took personal supervisory charge of many projects, examined buildings and plans, and offered original suggestions. Peter's stone decree was forgotten and the new architecture spread to Moscow and other cities.

As a result of Peter's ideas about commerce and industry, many secular buildings were completed during his reign and in the decades following his death. Important examples are the Admiralty (1806) by Sakharov, the Mining Institute (1806) by Voronikhin, the famous Winter Palace (1732) by the great architect, Rastrelli, the Tauride Palace (1783) by Starov, and the National Museum and Alexander Theater by Rossi (1819–1832). Many of these were built in a sort of Russianized version of Italian baroque. With the reaction in Europe against the excesses of baroque, Russian architecture also became more austere. The Corinthian order gave way to the Doric; the Roman style to early

Hellenic. The Hermitage, reconstructed as a museum in 1839 by Leo von Klenze, was in a restrained neo-Greek style. The most striking of St. Petersburg's religious buildings are the Kazan Cathedral (1801) by Voronikhin and the huge Cathedral of St. Isaac (1819) by de Montferrand, both in classic style.

Although St. Petersburg was the new capital, eighteenth-century Moscow continued to grow as a trading center. Architecturally, it tended to cling to the older Russian style, particularly in its churches. But since Moscow was the favorite abode of the nobility, many splendid town houses were built which aped the capital's neoclassic style. Examples are the residence of Prince V. N. Gagarin (1817) and the extraordinary façade of the stable on the estate of Prince Golitsyn (1823); the latter might well have served as the entrance to a railroad terminal or museum. Outside of Moscow and in other parts of the country, numerous elaborate mansions with pillared porticoes and classic details were built by the landed aristocracy who had an inexhaustible supply of serf labor. Many scenes of Leo Tolstoy's novels and Anton Chekhov's plays were laid in these grand houses so reminiscent of the mansions of our own Old South. All this architectural splendor was only a thin veneer on the poverty and illiteracy of the great mass of Russian peasants.

Under Nicholas I (1825–1855) the buildings constructed in St. Petersburg and Moscow were banks, hotels, post offices, and railroad stations. The architecture of these buildings was not very interesting and in general followed the neoclassical style of Andrea Palladio.

The two main features of this second period in Russian architectural history were the vigorous adoption of classicism and the extraordinary development of the architecture of great public squares, avenues, and river embankments. Both features, but especially the latter, continue in contemporary Soviet designs.

THIRD PERIOD (POST-1917) . . . The revolution changed many things. In architecture, it reduced for a time the role of the czarist architects. Those who replaced them had less practical experience with actual building, but they had a close relationship with the European extremists in art: the Dadaists, the surrealists, and the constructivists, whose roots went back to prerevolutionary days. To many young Soviet architects and artists, these radical schools symbolized a protest against the old order. In their work these architects broke completely with the accepted traditions.

The new designs were not only unprecedented but often incredibly naïve in their efforts at literal expression. The plans of the Monument to the Communist International by Tatlin (1918) included an ascending spiral form (never actually built), which was supposed to represent the aspirations of the socialist state. A workers' club by Golosov, had a roof in the form of a cogwheel, gears and all. Ladovski attempted to interpret current theories of psychoanalysis through architecture. Yet, some buildings of the time had architectural significance. Melnikov, for example, did outstanding work. In his Tram Workers' Club and in other buildings in Moscow, Melnikov strove to express the new social content with bold forms and with startling technical tricks, such as huge glass windows and great concrete cantilevers.

On the whole, these early architectural experiments failed. The excellent material and the precise construction techniques which would have been necessary to execute the designs were simply not available in Russia in those years. Thus, the effects intended failed to materialize, and when a building was completed the concrete edges chipped and the stucco deteriorated within a year or two. In those turbulent days there was no landscaping to set off the buildings, which did not help matters. Moreover, large glass areas were stressed in the designs, with the result that occupants froze in winter from inadequate heating and suffered in summer from the heat and glare of the sun.

Closely related to the extremist group, were the architects of the so-called "international" school. This style grew out of the worldwide technical advances in the science of building. Stimulated by the poverty economy of postwar Europe, the new architects rejected all nonessentials, such as applied ornament, and regarded themselves as functionalists. When the vast program of the First Five-Year Plan was set into motion, foreign architects were once more invited to Russia. Many of these—May, Meyer, Schmidt, Lurçat, and others—were adherents of the "international" school.

Since most of the Soviet planning and engineering offices were in Moscow, the architectural currents of the whole country flowed from there in those early years. Therefore, many important early examples of the new style are in the capital: a block of urban apartment houses by Ginsburg (1932), the Community Center in the Proletarian or auto works' district of Moscow by the Vesnin brothers (1934), the building for the Commissariat of Light Industry by Le Corbusier (1935), and the impressive home of the newspaper *Pravda* by Golosov (1936). Other examples are the dam and settlement at Zaporozhe (Dneprostroi) and some clubs at Baku.

These "international" style buildings were characterized by simple façades devoid of ornament and by continuous, horizontal windows and balconies expressive of the structural frame. They resemble buildings of the "international" school in the rest of Europe and of the world, though faulty materials and workmanship still plagued the early Russian experiments. The Russian worker, now that the driving tempo and the uncertainties of the First Five-Year Plan were over, finally had time to look about him. He was not impressed by the new architecture. It was not only often shabby, but to his taste seemed stark and unfamiliar.

History is continuous. Movements which seem to represent a sudden break or cleavage with the past usually prove, on examination, to have been developing for some time. While the International style was flourishing, from about 1925–1935, a third school was growing in influence. Most of its adherents were young Russian men and women who had grown up under Soviet institutions and who had had little direct contact with the outside world. They formed what may be called the neoclassic school; their designs are strongly linked to the classic tradition of the eighteenth- and nineteenth-century Russian cities, particularly Leningrad. During this same period, a number of academic architects of prerevolutionary days, for example, Zholtovski and Shusev, also continued to receive important commissions.

To the Russian people the splendid old buildings and the heroic squares and monuments of their large cities symbolized architecturally the good things of life. Now that the success of the industrialization and agricultural programs was assured, it became at last possible to think of better housing, schools, recreational facilities, and hospitals, not only for the few but for everyone. The popular interest in architecture grew more powerful and decisive daily. Public preference for the classical was expressed in the press, on the radio, and through popular participation in choosing the winners of numerous architectural competitions. More-

461

over, neoclassicism was linked directly with a tradition which was in evidence everywhere, and which had the advantage of being native rather than foreign. Noteworthy examples of this new classical trend are the stately, restful sanatorium at Sochi (Black Sea) by Kuznetsov, the Moscow Hotel by Shusev (1936), and, perhaps most outstanding, the star-shaped, porticoed Theater of the Red Army in Moscow by Karo Alabian (1938).

Parallel developments were occurring in many republics of the Soviet Union. Stalin encouraged the national minorities throughout the USSR to express their cultures in architecture as well as in the other arts. In Armenia and Georgia, the sheltering greatness of the Caucasus and the skill of the early Christian stone builders have helped preserve many architectural monuments. The church in Talin, Armenia, dates from the seventh century; ancient monuments like this still deeply influence the architecture of Transcaucasia. In 1942, A. Tamanyan was awarded a Stalin Prize for his Government House in Erivan. It is built of local, rosecolored tufa, in a style reminiscent of the old stone architecture. Curiously enough, Tamanyan, who was schooled in the classical traditions of the St. Petersburg Academy of Arts, returned with Soviet encouragement to carry on the proud native traditions of Armenia.

In the Central Asian republics there is an equally intense interest in the historical monuments of their again-great cities. Ancient Samarkand, with its magnificently colored tomb of Timur (fourteenth century) and the exquisite fifteenth-century street of tombs, Shah-i-Zind, is a model for contemporary Uzbek art. Many critics considered the Uzbek national pavilion the most beautiful building at the 1939 Agricultural Fair in Moscow.

The shift from the functional style was much criticized in certain foreign architectural circles. Some critics felt that the new architectural accent, with its emphasis on national forms, in the Russian and other republics, meant an abandonment of the international ideals of socialism. Others, identifying the classic styles of their own countries with conservatism in government and finance, felt that only the most advanced architectural forms could express the Soviet experiment. Similar controversies sprang up around parallel developments in Russian music, art, and literature.

Since most critics had no direct contact with the situation, they were unaware of the popular dissatisfaction in the Soviet Union with extremist, nondecorative styles. They were equally ignorant of the history of Russian art and architecture and of the intense popular pride in native traditions. They were also naïve in attributing political significance to so-called International or revolutionary art forms. A basic characteristic of Soviet architecture is variety in activities and trends. Its history shows it has been in a constant, vigorous state of flux, in which fixed rules never for long impeded natural creative forces. It cannot be adequately judged by isolated examples which reach the observer.

The state of Soviet architecture is well described in a quotation from a speech made in New York in 1939 by Karo Alabian, president of the Society of Soviet Architects and co-designer of the Soviet Pavilion at the New York World's Fair: "In our country, architects of *all* tendencies —classicists and constructivists—meet in creative competition. . . . In the reconstruction of Moscow and other cities, architects, representing widely divergent trends, such as Vesnin, Boris Iofan, Zholtovski, Ginsburg, Golosov, Melnikov, and Mordvinov—all have had a part."

Still another architectural school has appeared on the Soviet scene; it is a sort of modernized version of the classic styles. It has met great popular approval and during the postwar period it will probably develop more broadly than the more frankly classical school. The new trend is identified largely with one man, Boris Iofan, who achieved international renown by winning competitions for designs of the Palace of Soviets (1932), and of the pavilions at the Paris Fair (1937) and the New York Fair (1939). Iofan's works are characterized by simple, strong masses which, because of his early training in Rome, are never too far removed from the popular, classic tradition. Prominent sculptors, decorators, and mural painters have collaborated with him in his best buildings. The great stainless-steel figures surmounting the Paris and New York pavilions suggest significant future architectural development.

Two factors above all others are influencing Soviet architecture after the Second World War. First there is a need to commemorate the patriotism and heroism of the great struggle. Architects attempt to do this not only in pure monuments but in the architecture of everyday life: in houses, schools, hospitals, public squares, and even in whole blocks and neighborhoods. In all this, national tradition plays a large part,

463

but the most significant aspect of Russian tradition relates to the architectural composition of buildings, to the harmonious arrangements of structures, avenues, and squares. Developments in this field reflect the essence of the Russian architectural heritage.

Second, the industrialization of all building trades is being undertaken after the war, and this movement will greatly influence architecture. Before the war, the Soviets wisely devoted their best efforts and resources to branches of their economy which were related to national defense. The field of building lagged behind the more vital industries. In the period of peace, the Soviets emphasize civil construction. Factory-produced building materials and mechanized construction will influence architecture profoundly. Architects of the functional schools continue to play an important role together with their colleagues of the classical and related native traditions.

HOUSING AND CITY PLANNING . . . The young Soviet Union inherited very bad housing. Peasants and the urban workers were never adequately housed in czarist Russia. Conditions in the old rural villages were inferior enough, but most city workers did not even have privacy. Only in Petrograd (Leningrad) did some workers live in tenements and even here an average of 3½ workers lived in each room. Many buildings were destroyed during the First World War and in the years following, and there was no new construction. Under the Soviets the urban population had doubled by 1939. Moscow and Leningrad grew rapidly. The first step taken by the Soviet government was to redistribute the existing housing more equitably. In Moscow alone over 500,000 additional families were housed in the dwellings of the former middle and upper classes. By 1937 another million were provided with new housing in Moscow. But despite tremendous effort, conditions still remained unsatisfactory. The great postwar task was to double the nation's housing. Even under the stress of war the authorities were preparing to meet this problem; the establishment of the newest people's commissariat in the USSR, the Commissariat of Municipal and Housing Construction, was announced in May, 1944.

Before 1939, much housing was built in new industrial cities such as Magnitogorsk, Komsomolsk, Kirovsk, and Stalinogorsk. A number of foreign architects were used on these projects. Many radical experiments were tried and many mistakes were made in this early period. Then followed tendencies in both rural and urban housing toward individual homes and private apartments much in the English and American tradition. The new commissariat proposes that 75 per cent of the Russians made homeless by the war shall be rehoused in one-family dwellings and that "these should be cozy." Such a program needs years of peace.

Because of the extraordinary increase in new urban centers and because of the public ownership of land, the Russians had a great opportunity for city planning, of which they took full advantage. Between 1918 and 1939, the urban population doubled and the number of cities of 100,000 people or more increased from 14 to 74. In the older cities, the need was for reconstruction and expansion. Prominent foreign and native architects submitted planning proposals for Moscow and other cities. Some proposals suggested the wholesale demolition of Moscow; others suggested abandoning the old city and building a new Moscow elsewhere. Obviously, such proposals were rejected; but the redevelopment of great cities was begun according to an over-all master plan. The traditional principle accepted for work in this field was that buildings cannot be treated individually but only in relation to each other and to the neighborhood. In general, Moscow was divided for planning or redesign into sections, each of which was placed under the supervision of one architectural group. By 1937, comprehensive plans for the next 10 to 20 years had been prepared for industrial, residential, and other areas of most large Russian cities. Both Moscow and Leningrad will have wider streets, better rapid transit, and green belts of parks and forests in accord with Lenin's desire to eliminate too much difference between town and country.

It was possible to plan many new cities from the ground up. In these, industrial and residential planning was based on surveys of local natural resources, topography, and climate. Plans were constantly readjusted in the light of experience. About 1940 the Russians considered 50,000 persons a minimum urban nucleus, and half of all cities, existing and projected, fell in the population group of 50,000 to 1,000,000. The basic planning unit was a super-block of about 20 acres, housing 2,000 to 4,000 people. The typical super-block contained a 22-classroom school and social and shopping facilities.

No historical account of Russian architecture would be complete

465

without mentioning the havoc of the Second World War. The Germans followed a policy of systematic destruction of Russian art. No other nation suffered physical damage of such ferocity and extent. Many ancient cities like Pskov, Novgorod, and Kiev were almost completely destroyed; and many of Leningrad's monuments badly damaged. Yet even during the heaviest fighting Soviet architects and other citizens were working on plans for the restoration of their beloved monuments, and many reconstructions were under way before the end of the war.

Postwar city planning continued during the war. As towns were liberated from Nazi occupation, teams of architects, engineers, and builders moved in with these plans for reconstruction, so that even temporary and emergency building would fit into the master plan.

BIBLIOGRAPHY

Viollet-le-Duc, E., *L'Art russe* (Paris, 1877).

Kaganovich, L. M., *Reconstruction of Moscow and Other Cities in the USSR* (Moscow, 1931).

Simon, E. D., *Moscow in the Making* (New York, 1937).

Webb, Sidney and Beatrice, *Soviet Communism*, pp. 929–943 (New York, 1937).

Bunin, A. B., and Kruglova, M. G., *Architectural Composition of Cities*, Academy of Architecture of USSR, in Russian (Moscow, 1940).

Carter, Edward, "Soviet Architecture Today," *The Architectural Review* (London, 1942).

Blumenfeld, Hans, "Regional and City Planning in the Soviet Union," *Task* (Oct., 1942).

Meyer, Hannes, "The Soviet Architect," *Task* (Oct., 1942).

Zabello, S., Ivanov, V., Maximov, P., *Ancient Wooden Architecture*, Academy of Architecture of USSR, in Russian (Moscow, 1942).

CHAPTER XXVII

The History of Science

By WILLIAM M. MALISOFF

R USSIAN science is a tree with two roots—a deep root of tradition and the luxuriant root of the new system of economy.

EARLY HISTORIC BACKGROUND . . . The earliest scientific works in Russian were translations from the Greek which appeared in the Kiev principality during the tenth to thirteenth centuries. The ideas of Aristotle, Democritus, and Ptolemy became available, mixed with religious mysticism. A volume of Palestinian origin, the *Books of the Sacred Secrets of Enoch,* was typical of ancient astronomical knowledge served under the auspices of angels.

By 1500, however, religious architecture had advanced perceptibly in the Moscow principality, and the church structures erected there could not have been built without considerable knowledge of statics. In general, there are signs of an exit from the monasteries into the outside world under what was described even then as a "Jewish" influence by men who brought in the knowledge of Euclid, Hippocrates, Galen, and the Arabs. A manuscript on cosmography also circulated in Novgorod and in Lithuania in the fifteenth and sixteenth centuries, which influenced later works on land measurement and related subjects until well into the seventeenth century. These works, now mostly lost, were used in conjunction with the *Shestokril,* a set of astronomical tables prepared by the Italian Jew, Immanuel Bar Jacob. Calendrical interests were essentially practical and the performances were arithmetical.

THE ACADEMY OF SCIENCES IN THE EIGHTEENTH CEN-TURY . . . The remarkable world planner Gottfried Wilhelm von

Leibnitz must be credited with the idea of setting up a scientific academy and universities in Russia. About 1713, Peter the Great, who advocated Copernican ideas, gave a sympathetic ear to Leibnitz's plans. The activity of men like Blumentrost and Shumacher was enlisted. Blumentrost had studied at Halle, Oxford, and Leyden, and when the Academy of Sciences, founded by Peter the Great in 1724, was finally opened in 1726 he became its first president. Between 1725 and 1733 the academy consisted of 20 Germans, 5 Swiss, 2 French, and 1 Russian (Adadurov).

Invaluable assistance to the young academy was given by the great mathematician, Daniel Bernouilli, who spent several years in Russia and retained a lifelong interest in the academy. He invited the great mathematician, Leonard Euler, who arrived in 1727 at the age of 20 and with one interruption spent his life at the academy till his death in 1783, leaving about 800 works on scientific topics, including hydrodynamics, optics, astronomy, acoustics, and pure mathematics. Naturally, Euler founded a school and his enormous influence made the academy world famous. Some mathematicians have considered Euler in certain respects the greatest mathematician of all time.

The other eighteenth-century giant of the academy was M. V. Lomonosov (1711–1765), a universal genius like Leonardo da Vinci, Bruno, Galileo, and Descartes. Lomonosov was a great poet and a builder of the Russian language, as well as the most versatile of scientists. He wrote profusely on chemistry, physics, mineralogy, astronomy, practical metallurgy, glass making, naval construction, and other subjects. His achievements were epoch-making. Seventeen years ahead of Lavoisier, he discovered quantitative chemistry and the conservation principle of matter—by carrying on reactions in completely closed retorts. In conceiving of heat as internal motion and in formulating the principle of the conservation of energy, he founded thermodynamics. He had a clear idea of "elements and corpuscles," which were equivalent to atoms and molecules. His *Elements of Mathematical Chemistry* (1741) anticipated the ideas of John Dalton and Antoine L. Lavoisier. In 1743 his studies on the compression of gases were based on clear ideas of atomic motion. In 1756 he explained color as due to vibrations and motions of the ether, corroborating René Descartes and Euler. He was also the first scientist

468

to find an atmosphere around Venus; his experiments with atmospheric electricity immediately followed those of Benjamin Franklin; he postulated the idea of geological strata; and he even foresaw the potentialities of travel by Arctic routes. Unfortunately he died relatively young, and the fact that he wrote in Russian prevented the spread of his ideas to the rest of Europe.

THE NINETEENTH AND TWENTIETH CENTURIES UP TO THE REVOLUTION . . . The outstanding figure in mathematics of the first half of the nineteenth or "wonderful" century is N. I. Lobachevski (1793–1856), the Copernicus of geometry. He announced the discovery of non-Euclidean geometry on Feb. 24, 1826. His teacher, Bartels (1761–1836), was also the teacher of the German mathematician, Karl F. Gauss. A Russian worker, S. E. Guriev (1762–1813), influenced Lobachevski on the proof of the fifth postulate of Euclid, but Lobachevski's ideas were so much ahead of his time that even the great amongst his contemporaries failed to understand him. Thus, M. V. Ostrogradski (1801–1861) was unable to understand the *Universal Geometry* (Kazan University, 1835). Ostrogradski himself was a student of Pierre S. Laplace, Jean B. Furier, André M. Ampère, Siméon D. Poisson, and Augustin L. Cauchy, and a discoverer in the field of the calculus of variations, and the anticipator of the theorems of Green and Gauss. Another opponent was V. I. Bunyakovski (1804–1899), an original worker in statistical theory. A third contemporary, P. L. Chebyshev (1821–1894), was perhaps the greatest of the applied mathematicians; he made outstanding contributions to the theory of errors (1837–1841), made the first advances since Euclid on the theory of primes, and developed the theory of approximate solutions.

In the natural sciences many important thinkers appeared between Lomonosov and D. I. Mendeleyev (1834–1907). In mineralogy, Leman (1700–1767) made important contributions; in botany, E. Loxman (1738–1796) reflected the direct influence of Carolus Linnaeus; V. M. Severgin (1765–1826) edited the technical journal of the academy; T. Lovits discovered the absorption of various materials by carbon and developed the analysis of crystals by the use of the microscope; H. H. Hess (1802–1850), a student of Berzelius, was the founder of thermochemistry; A. A. Voskresenski (1809–1880) was an organic chemist and

469

the teacher of Dmitri I. Mendeleyev; Fritzsche (1808–1871) was an important figure in the development of organic chemistry. Another outstanding figure was N. N. Zinin (1812–1880) a student of Liebig, who discovered "benzide," which turned out to be aniline. Still another was A. M. Butlerov (1828–1886), who contributed greatly to "structural chemistry." He was also instrumental in introducing the work of Pierre E. Berthelot, Jean B. P. A. Dumas, Charles A. Wurtz, and Robert W. Bunsen to Russian scientists.

Dmitri I. Mendeleyev (1834–1907) worked with Bunsen for a short time. His ideas, however, were boldly original and he was clearly the discoverer of the periodic system of the elements, a discovery which summarized the classical age of chemistry and laid out a program of discovery for generations. There were other claimants to this honor, but none except Mendeleyev was able to predict and accurately describe new elements in advance of their actual discovery, sometimes many years later. Mendeleyev was versatile and he was interested in practical applications. He suggested setting a coal mine on fire and pumping water into the flames to generate water gas for power purposes; the Soviet government later put this idea into practice. His interest in the people led reactionary members of the academy to reject him as a member.

Physics and electrotechnics also went through an interesting development between Lomonosov and P. N. Lebedev (1866–1912). Following Franklin's work, G. Richman and Lomonosov performed experiments in 1752 and built an electrical lightning machine. Richman was killed by this machine during a storm—the first martyr to this kind of experiment. Lomonosov rejected the electric fluid theory, seeing electricity instead as a form of motion in the ether. The discovery of galvanic currents by Alessandro Volta (1745–1827) was followed by researches of V. V. Petrov (1761–1834?), who, in 1802–1803 constructed the largest battery of the time; it had 4,200 cells. Thus he discovered electrolysis and the voltaic arc seven years before Sir Humphrey Davy (1778–1829) did. Petrov's work was forgotten until the 1890's.

In 1836–1837, Academician Moritz Hermann Jacobi (1801–1874), a German who spent many years in Russia, discovered electroplating. In 1834, only three years after the discovery of electromagnetic induction, he constructed the first motor from a set of moving electromagnets and

470

another stationary set. Several years later this motor transported fourteen passengers along the Neva.

On March 30, 1853, Professor Savelev constructed an arc lamp able to illuminate the grounds of Kazan University. Satisfactory arc lamps, however, were first made in 1875–1876 by P. N. Yablochkov (1847–1894), who used parallel carbons. Yablochkov patented his invention in Paris on March 23, 1876, and commercial production began the next year. This inventor made some of the earliest studies in electrical transmission and in the design of dynamos and motors. In the 1880's he was aiming at the construction of flying machines. He devised the first direct chemo-electric generator to eliminate the combustion of fuel, and also the steam and electric generator, by the use of nitrates with coal. Another important inventor was A. N. Lodigin (1840–1923), who made a filament lamp used successfully in St. Petersburg in 1873. He discovered the necessity of a vacuum well before Thomas Edison did. (This fact was recognized in the patent suit between Edison and Swann.) In 1890 the General Electric Company acquired Lodigin's patent on molybdenum and tungsten filaments.

E. Lentz (1804–1865), who recognized the mechanical equivalent of electrical energy, contributed greatly to the theoretical aspects of electricity. Another worker in this field was A. G. Stoletov (1839–1896), who studied demagnetized iron. Hertzian waves were studied by A. C. Popov (1859–1905) in 1894, and in 1896 he spelled out the message "Heinrich Hertz," by wireless signals over a distance of 200 meters—the first radiogram. By 1900, twenty-seven fishermen in the Baltic had been saved by the radiogram system. Marconi obtained his patent a little after the first work of Popov.

The nature of electromagnetic waves was the subject of study of P. N. Lebedev (1866–1912). He is best known for his experimental demonstration and measurement of the pressure of light.

Important pioneer work was done in biology by P. S. Pallas (1741–1811), who made extensive geographical, geological, biological, and ethnographic studies. He stressed the significance of environment and believed in no final division between plant and animal life. K. E. Baer (1792–1876) studied ichthyology and developed revolutionary theories in embryology. Important work was done somewhat later by the brothers, A. O. Kovalevski (1840–1901) and B. O. Kovalevski (1842–

471

1883); the first was prominent in zoology, the second in paleontology. A. P. Karpinski (1847–1936) established many important generalizations.

Among biologists in a narrower sense, I. M. Sechenov (1829–1905) was a distinguished experimental physiologist. He performed brilliant experiments on brain reflexes and studied their integration into psychic action. Since the implications of his studies were materialistic he was rejected by the academy. Of equal fame was Élie Metchnikov (1845–1916). His classic discovery was of phagocytes, the white cells of the blood. He became head of the Pasteur Institute in Paris, through the efforts of Louis Pasteur and Pierre P. Roux. His labors on immunity led to a profound interest in the phenomena of aging and death. The phagocytes were found to destroy the weakening and aging cells; the weakening itself he attributed to toxins of intestinal bacteria.

The greatest Russian Darwinist was K. A. Timiryazev (1843–1920). In studying the effect of light on plants and the general physiology of plant growth and agronomy, he emphasized physicochemical procedures in biology. He was a most remarkable popularizer, especially of Darwinism, and joined in the revolutionary movement. He brought to public notice the name of the geneticist, I. V. Michurin (1860–1935), who produced many new plants of the greatest practical and theoretical significance.

A younger contemporary of Metchnikov and Timiryazev was the physiologist I. P. Pavlov (1849–1936), who became famous in the 1880's for his work on digestive juices; his work during the 1890's and later on conditioned reflexes, the physiological foundations of psychic phenomena, had great theoretical significance and was of great value to psychiatry.

SCIENCE AFTER THE REVOLUTION . . . The turn of the century brought many revolutionary changes in science. The Russian political revolution in 1917 brought still another qualitative change in the sociology and progress of science. Relativity, the quantum theory, the transmutation of elements, the radio, wonder drugs, plastics, medical and engineering feats—all these new discoveries challenged social utilization at the very time when Russian society was being reorganized. In accepting this challenge Soviet Russia has been planning its scientific progress as part of its planned economy.

472

Shortly after the revolution the Academy of Sciences was liberalized. In 1917 there were only 45 members and a staff of 212 workers. They worked in a few small laboratories, museums, commissions, and experiment stations. In 1941 there were 118 members, 5 honorary members, 182 corresponding members and a staff of 4,700 scientific associates, working in 76 institutes, 11 laboratories, 42 stations, 6 observatories, and 24 museums. Technologists were included in 1929, in recognition of the Marxist principle of "the unity of theory and practice," and in 1935 an entire department of technical sciences was established. The final step in liberalizing the academy was the election of Lina S. Stern, physiologist, who became its first woman member. Meanwhile the Soviet conception of the scope of the scientific method was broadened greatly, and in 1939 Joseph V. Stalin was elected an honorary member "for his outstanding services in the development of world science and for his extremely versatile development of Marxist-Leninist thought."

The academy consists of eight divisions devoted to (1) physico-mathematical sciences, (2) chemical sciences, (3) geologo-geographical sciences, (4) biological sciences, (5) technical sciences, (6) history and philosophy, (7) economics and law, (8) literature and language. The supreme authority is the General Session. The intervals between general sessions are administered by a representative Presidium and a president who is elected for a five-year term. The academy works closely with the Council of People's Commissars of the USSR in Moscow in connection with planning the country's economy in war and peace.

One of the major tasks of the academy since the revolution has been to explore the extensive resources of the country. Over 500 expeditions have been sent out and they have uncovered supplies of critical materials unknown in Russia before, such as nickel, aluminum, cobalt, and helium. Working toward practical ends, the Botanical Institute produced 11 volumes on *The Flora of the USSR*. The Institute of Soil Study has uncovered many new agricultural possibilities. A Council for the Study of the Productive Forces of the Country (S.O.P.S.), headed by the president of the academy, Vladimir L. Komarov (1869–1945), was set up to sift the vast accumulation of expeditionary data.

The various divisions of the academy control numerous institutes which carry on a very great variety of researches. For example, in the division of physico-mathematical sciences is the Astronomical Institute

473

which pursues activities as diverse as these: it carries on studies favoring a model of an infinite universe; it conducts detailed studies on the variation of gravity, directed toward the discovery of mineral resources; it conducts the studies useful in maritime and aerial navigation. Among the physicists there is the same variety of interests. Thus P. L. Kapitsa has made contributions to the theory of supraconductivity and has invented a machine which liquifies air or helium. The mathematicians of the V. A. Steklov Mathematical Institute have made outstanding contributions to the theory of numbers and to studies of the continuum.

The chemical sciences have had a separate division since 1938. This consists of seven institutes covering the following fields of knowledge: (1) general and inorganic chemistry under I. I. Chernyayev; (2) organic chemistry under A. N. Nesmeyanov; (3) colloido-electrochemistry under A. N. Frumkin; (4) chemical physics under N. N. Semenov; (5) radium under V. G. Khlopin; (6) biochemistry under V. N. Vernadski; and (7) hydrochemistry under P. A. Kashinski. These institutes have made important studies of equilibria in natural salt deposits, metallurgical equilibria and alloys, platinum complexes, the chemistry of glass and its surface layers, uranium radioactivity, rare gas analysis, radium concentration, cyclotron construction and its application to biochemistry, surface electrochemical reactions, absorptive reduction of hardness (P. A. Rebinder), flotation, the film theory of corrosion, catalysis and gaseous promoters, chain reactions and explosions (N. N. Semenov), combustion in motors, isoprene and rubber syntheses (A. E. Favorski), polymers, butadiene (S. V. Lebedev), aromatic syntheses (N. D. Zelinski), cellulose (P. P. Shorygin), alkaloids, terpenes, and camphor (S. S. Nametkin), dyeing and synthetic camphor.

The division of geological and geographical sciences was reorganized in 1938 to include the institutes of geography, geological sciences, theoretical geophysics, and study of frozen soil. These have carried on many explorations, volcanological studies, and so forth, and have prepared many volumes for publication. The new science called *Merzlotovedeniye,* or permafrost, studies soil which never thaws.

The division of biological sciences also became an organic entity in 1938. It includes the Komarov Botanic Institute, the Timiryazev Institute of Plant Physiology, the Institute of Biochemistry, the Dokuchayev Soil

474

Institute, the Institute of Microbiology, the Zoological Institute, the Institute of Genetics, the Severtsov Institute of Evolutionary Morphology, the Paleontological Institute, the Pavlov Physiological Institute, the Institute of Physiology, the Laboratories of Electrophysiology and Plant Physiology, and the Moscow Botanical Gardens. Numerous publications have appeared, and a herbarium of five million specimens has been built at the Botanical Institute. The Institute of Plant Physiology, headed by A. N. Bakh, has studied biosynthesis, hormonal control of growth, and the rotation of elements in plant nutrition. V. O. Tauson has proposed new theories of respiration. Through applied science, fruit ripening has been hastened, and improved processes have been developed for drying and storing grains. Among other achievements, the Institute of Biochemistry has discovered the enzymic character of myosin, the principal protein of muscle (V. A. Engelhardt and M. N. Lyubimova). Much attention is given to vitamin research. V. I. Isachenko of the Institute of Microbiology, has discovered purple sulphur bacteria. The Institute of Genetics, led by T. D. Lysenko, has doubled many crops through bold studies on chromosome structure and the origin of mutations. The Pavlov Institute continues the great work of I. P. Pavlov, and the Institute of Physiology under L. S. Stern has made pioneer studies on the treatment of shock involving the fluids of the brain. Soviet science first created blood banks, and it led the world in studies of artificial insemination, by which 50 million animals were produced in 1941.

The division of technical sciences includes the institutes and sections of metallurgy, mining, machinery mechanics, automatics, telemechanics, transport problems, water control, electrocommunications, electric welding, electrothermy, and technical terminology. Some of the problems studied deal with socialized power, high pressure steam, gasification of hard fuel including underground gasification, flameless burning, colloidal fuel, lightning protection, mechanical and electrical integrators, oil prospecting, petroleum chemistry, substitutes, automatic devices, wear resistance, dynamic stability, high speed planes, shell trajectories, elasticity, blast furnace operation, slag utilization, vanadium technology, and oxygen steel refining.

The division of economics and law (secretary, E. S. Varga) has made many studies and reports on the world economic crisis, on the theory of proof in Soviet law, and the like.

The division of literature and language (secretary, I. I. Meshchaninov) has carried on research projects on language structure and the theory of philology. It has also devised alphabets, orthographies, grammars, and dictionaries for many languages previously unrecorded.

In the division of history and philosophy (secretary, V. P. Volgin), the Institute of History (director, B. D. Grekov) has compiled textbooks, annals, etc., and has done much research toward an extensive world history. The Institute of Philosophy (director, P. F. Yudin) has translated the works of great philosophers of the past, done much research on the history of philosophy, and made numerous original studies on problems in dialectical materialism.

Many affiliated academies of science have grown up, notably in the Ukraine and White Russia, and other scientific groups have been formed in practically every republic. The Georgian Republic now has a full-fledged Academy of Sciences, formed in 1941.

Not all Russian science comes under the Academy of Science, though the work of the academy interpenetrates the scientific work of other branches of Soviet life. It maintains contact with a host of scientific laboratories and institutes administered by the commissariats of Education, Health, and Heavy Industry. These support thousands of science school research laboratories, medical research institutes, technical college laboratories, factory laboratories, about 1,000 industrial research institutes, and even pure science groups attached to industrial establishments. All these laboratories and institutes are well subsidized and they are the democratic source of many problems, and suggestions relating to over-all planning in which the Academy of Science participates with the State Planning Commission.

The tremendous popularization of science and technology under the Soviets should be especially noted. This popularization is reflected in many ways: for example, in the Stakhanov movement of rationalizing production; in the science laboratories of the children's clubs or "pioneer houses"; in the co-operation of newspapers; in the existence of numerous scientific and technical bookshops; in the organization at state expense of courses in technical schools for some 700,000 students of the Ph.D. level; and in scientific-technical classes in factories which are attended by millions.

BIBLIOGRAPHY

Sigerist, H. E., *Socialized Medicine in the U.S.S.R.* (New York, 1937).

Bernal, J. D., *The Social Function of Science*, appendix 7, note on "Science in the U.S.S.R.," by M. Ruheman (New York, 1939).

Tolpin J. G., "The Growth of Industry in U.S.S.R.," in *Chemical and Engineering News* (1943), XXI, 166.

Science in Soviet Russia, papers presented at Congress of American-Soviet Friendship, New York City, Nov. 7, 1943 (New York, 1944).

Joffe, A. F., *Development of the Exact Sciences in the U.S.S.R.* (New York, 1944).

Vinter, A. V., *Twenty-Five Years of Power Development in the U.S.S.R.* (New York, 1944).

Baikow, A. A., *Twenty-five Years of the Academy of Sciences of the U.S.S.R.* (New York, 1944).

Sovetskaya Nauka (*Russian Science*), monthly journal of the Academy of Sciences, Moscow, in Russian.

Index of Names

483

Index of Places

[AR, Autonomous Region; ASSR, Autonomous Soviet Socialist Republic; ND, National District; SSR, Soviet Socialist Republic.]

Abakan, 6
Abkhazian ASSR, 7
Adygei AR, 6
Adzhar ASSR, 7
Agin Buryat Mongol ND, 6
Aginskoe, 6
Alaska, 181, 182
Aldan River, 21, 29
Alma Ata, 7, 281, 452
Almalyk, 259
Altai Mts., 33
Amu Darya River, 20, 277
Amur River, 21, 59, 277
Anadyr, 6
Angrena, 258
Aral Sea, 21, 22
Archangel, 52, 94, 185, 256
Armenia (Armenian SSR), 7, 10, 29, 41, 79, 96, 159, 462
Ashkhabad, 7
Assyria, 33
Astrakhan, 46, 50, 58, 62, 94, 276, 282
Austerlitz, 75
Austria, 81, 189
Austria-Hungary, 87
Azerbaidzhan (Azerbaidzhan SSR), 7, 41, 77, 86, 96, 159, 308
Azov, 57, 61, 63

Baikal, Lake, 21, 22, 29
Bajgiran, 276
Baku, 7, 28, 461
Balkans, 37, 81, 107, 189
Balkhash, Lake, 21, 22, 259, 263
Baltic Sea, 35, 52, 55, 62, 70, 207
Baltic States or Provinces, 8, 77, 171, 271
Bashkir ASSR, 6
Batum (Batumi), 7, 96, 279
Belgorod, 201, 206
Belgrade, 207
Belomorsk, 279
Belorussia (Belorussian SSR), 7, 10, 29, 47, 57, 58, 70, 77-103 passim, 159, 203, 207; see also White Russia
Bering Straits, 63

Berlin, 69, 81, 107, 189, 204, 207, 348
Bessarabia, 77, 93, 97, 104, 171, 271
Bezhitsa, 272
Birobidzhan, 5, 6, 258
Black Sea, 23, 34-35, 63, 70, 79, 81, 278
Bokhara, 81, 96
Borodino, 75
Bosnia, 87, 189
Bosporus Kingdom, 34
Brest, 57
Brest-Litovsk, 92, 93, 154, 157, 184, 195
Bucharest, 207
Bucovina, 104
Budapest, 107, 207
Bulgar Kingdom, 35
Bureya, 258
Buryat-Mongolian ASSR, 6, 259
Byzantine Empire, see Byzantium
Byzantium, 35, 37, 38, 39, 422, 439

Carpathian Mts., 35, 191, 206
Caspian Sea, 21, 22, 27, 36, 63, 255
Caucasus, 5, 19-37 passim, 79, 94, 106, 172, 206, 243, 251-259 passim, 290, 300, 315, 439
Central Asia, Soviet, 5, 20-45 passim, 63, 79-104 passim, 243, 251-271 passim, 280, 300, 301
Chapayev, 279
Cheboksary, 6
Chechen-Ingush ASSR, 6
Chelyabinsk, 263
Cheremkhovo, 258
Cherkess AR, 6
Chernigov, 36, 47
Chesmé, 357
China, 41, 99, 103, 182-183
Chirchik, 264
Chirchik River, 260
Chu River, 260
Chukotsky ND, 6
Chuvash ASSR, 6
Chyaturi, 29, 259
Colchis, 27

4934

Date Due			
FEB 22 '54	FEB 26 '59	APR 20 '68	
8 54	MAR 5 59	FEB 18 '69	
8 0 '54	MAR 12 '59	MAR 4 69	
MAR 30	APR 8 '60	NOV 15 '69	
APR 13	MAY 13 '60	APR 16 '70	
APR 30 56	APR 18 '61	APR 27 70	
MAR 4 '57	MAR 26 '63	APR 27 '78	
APR 16 '57	MAY 14 '63	MAY 5 76	
MAY 7 '57	JAN 3 '64	F	
MAR 4 '58	MAY 5 64		
MAR 12 '58	MAR 30 '65		
MAR 19 '58	APR 2 '65		
APR 8 58	F MAR 2 67		
APR 22 '58	MAR 15 '67		
	APR 6 67		
JUL 9 58	APR 24 67		
JUL 29 58	APR 6 '68		